A Court in Exile

Court studies and Jacobitism have both received considerable attention from historians in recent years, yet so far no attempt has been made to provide a comprehensive examination of the Jacobite court in exile after the revolution of 1688–89. This book takes a completely fresh look at the Stuart court in France from 1689 to 1718, the years when the Jacobite movement posed its greatest threat to the post-revolution governments in London. What emerges is a major revision of an important aspect of late seventeenth- and early eighteenth-century British and European history.

The Stuart court at Saint-Germain-en-Laye is revealed not only as large and well financed, but also as magnificently located in a spectacular royal palace vacated only recently by Louis XIV, in very close contact with the French court at Versailles, yet maintaining the traditions, organisation and ceremonial of the English court at Whitehall. A special feature of the book is the attention given to the cultural patronage of the court, which employed the leading French portraitists and had a major influence on the development of French baroque music. The book also shows how the Stuart court in France came to an end, and explains why and how it has since been so badly misrepresented.

EDWARD CORP is Professor of British History, University of Toulouse. In addition to writing many articles on the Stuart court in exile, he has curated and written the catalogues of two major exhibitions, *La Cour des Stuarts à Saint-Germain-en-Laye au temps de Louis XIV* (Château de Saint-Germain, 1992) and *The King over the Water, 1688–1766* (Scottish National Portrait Gallery, 2001). Other publications include a biography of Sir Eyre Crowe, *Our Ablest Public Servant, 1864–1925* (1993) and four edited collections of essays.

A Court in Exile

The Stuarts in France, 1689–1718

EDWARD CORP

with contributions by

EDWARD GREGG
HOWARD ERSKINE-HILL
GEOFFREY SCOTT

CAMBRIDGE
UNIVERSITY PRESS

CAMBRIDGE UNIVERSITY PRESS
Cambridge, New York, Melbourne, Madrid, Cape Town, Singapore, São Paulo, Delhi

Cambridge University Press
The Edinburgh Building, Cambridge CB2 8RU, UK

Published in the United States of America by Cambridge University Press, New York

www.cambridge.org
Information on this title: www.cambridge.org/9780521108379

First published 2004
This digitally printed version 2009

A catalogue record for this publication is available from the British Library

Library of Congress Cataloguing in Publication data
Corp, Edward T.
A court in exile: the Stuarts in France, 1689–1718 / by Edward Carp; with contributions by
Edward Gregg, Howard Erskine-Hill, and Geoffrey Scott.
    p. cm.
Includes bibliographical references (p. 367) and index.
ISBN 0 521 58462 0
1. James II, King of England, 1633–1701 – Exile – France.   2. Mary, of Modena, Queen, consort of
James II, King of England, 1658–1718 – Homes and haunts – France – Saint-Germain-en-Laye.
3. James, Prince of Wales, 1688–1766 – Homes and haunts – France – Saint-Germain-en-Laye.
4. Great Britain – Court and courtiers – History – 18th century.   5. Great Britain – Court and
courtiers – History – 17th century.   6. Great Britain – Kings and rulers – Biography.   7. Great
Britain – History – Stuarts, 1603–1714.   8. British – France – History – 18th century.
9. British – France – History – 17th century.   10. Saint-Germain-en-Laye (France) – History.
11. Princes – Great Britain – Biography.   12. Stuart, House of.   I. Title.
DA452.C75   2003
944′.0042′008621 – dc21   2003043588

ISBN 978-0-521-58462-3 hardback
ISBN 978-0-521-10837-9 paperback

Contents

Illustrations

Photographic credits

Acknowledgements

The decision to write this book was taken in 1992, when I curated an exhibition entitled *La Cour des Stuarts à Saint-Germain-en-Laye au temps de Louis XIV* for the Bibliothèque Nationale de France, the Réunion des Musées Nationaux and the Ville de Saint-Germain-en-Laye. The positive reactions of the 30,000 people who visited the exhibition convinced me that a comprehensive study of the exiled Stuart court in France was badly needed.

During the following ten years, while carrying out the necessary archival research, I published many preliminary studies in academic journals and specialist collections of essays (all of which are listed on pp. xiv–xvi), partly to clarify my ideas and partly to invite criticisms from other historians with an interest in the subject. I also prepared a second and larger exhibition on the life of James III, in Italy as well as at Saint-Germain, which I curated with James Holloway, the Director of the Scottish National Portrait Gallery. That exhibition, entitled *The King over the Water, 1688–1766*, was put on in 2001 to mark the tercentenary of the death of James II and the accession in exile of his son James III. I am very happy to place on record here my gratitude to all those whose help and support enabled me to mount those two exhibitions, and especially to Bernard Cottret, Jacqueline Sanson and James Holloway. It is also a great pleasure to acknowledge the very generous help, during a period of well over ten years, of Alastair Laing.

In addition I have received invaluable assistance from many political and court historians, musicologists, historians of literature and art, museum curators and private collectors, and people descended from Jacobite families. I cannot mention them all here, but I should particularly like to thank the following for sharing with me their knowledge of certain subjects concerning the Stuart court: Andrew Ashbee (the musicians at Whitehall), Andrew Barclay (the household of James II and Mary of Modena at Whitehall), Jane Clark (the music of the exiled court, and Freemasonry), Peter Drummond-Murray (the families of the Dukes of Perth and Melfort), Nathalie Genet-Rouffiac (the Jacobites at Saint-Germain and Paris), Denis Herlin and Catherine Massip (the musical manuscripts of 'Copiste Z'), Kathryn King and Carol Shiner Wilson (the life and manuscripts of Jane Barker), the late Jean Lionnet (the life and music of

Innocenzo Fede), Robert Oresko (the European courts), Guy Rowlands (the Irish regiments of James II), Béatrix Saule (the court of Louis XIV at Saint-Germain), and Richard Sharp (the engraved Stuart portraits). More generally, I must acknowledge that my work on the Stuart court in exile would not have been written without the stimulus provided by other historians of Jacobitism, particularly Jeremy Black, Jonathan Clark, Eveline Cruickshanks, John Gibson, Paul Hopkins, Paul Monod, Murray Pittock, Daniel Szechi and the three contributors to the present book. This long list is of course by no means complete, and I hope I shall be forgiven by those whose names I have omitted.

When planning this book I realised at an early stage that there were some aspects of the exiled Stuart court which I ought to entrust to other people. I should like to pay tribute to Edward Gregg, Howard Erskine-Hill and Geoffrey Scott for generously agreeing to contribute those chapters which I did not feel sufficiently qualified to write myself. I hope they will not be displeased with the general context in which I have placed their contributions, but of course they cannot be held responsible for any of the opinions expressed in the chapters which I have written myself.

In pursuing my researches in Great Britain and France I invariably encountered a courteous and helpful reception from the archivists, librarians, curators and private collectors with whom I came into contact. I should particularly like to acknowledge the great kindness of Christine Johnson at the Scottish Catholic Archives in Edinburgh, and of Michelle Bimbenet-Privat at the Archives Nationales in Paris. I should also like to thank the staffs of the Royal Archives, the Royal Library and the Royal Collection, who have been extremely helpful to me on many occasions. The Stuart papers, books and portraits which they conserve are the property of Her Majesty Queen Elizabeth II, and I gratefully acknowledge her gracious permission to make use of them here.

My research and writing had to be squeezed into periods of free time from an otherwise busy university timetable. I am grateful to the Université de Paris VII for granting me paid sabbatical leave during the second semester of the academic year 2000–1, which gave me the necessary freedom to concentrate on planning and writing the book. I should also like to record my thanks to all those who elected me to Visiting Fellowships during my sabbatical. The Institute for Advanced Studies in the Humanities, of the University of Edinburgh, provided me with an ideal base from which to pursue my research and prepare the exhibition at the Scottish National Portrait Gallery. The Warden and Fellows of New College, Oxford (and particularly my sponsor

David Parrott) provided me with superb hospitality and an incomparable setting where I could finally start to write.

My greatest debt, of course, is to my wife and children. For their patience and understanding, as well as their loving and practical support, during the many years of research and writing, I can never adequately express my gratitude. This book is dedicated to them.

Contributors

Edward Corp is Professor of British History, University of Toulouse. In addition to writing many articles on the Stuart court in exile, he has curated and written the catalogues of two major exhibitions, *La Cour des Stuarts à Saint-Germain-en-Laye au temps de Louis XIV* (Château de Saint-Germain, 1992) and *The King over the Water, 1688–1766* (Scottish National Portrait Gallery, 2001). Other publications include a biography of Sir Eyre Crowe, *Our Ablest Public Servant, 1864–1925* (1993) and four edited collections of essays.

Edward Gregg is Professor of History, University of South Carolina.

Howard Erskine-Hill is Emeritus Professor of Literary History, University of Cambridge, and a Fellow of Pembroke College.

Geoffrey Scott OSB. is Abbot of Douai Abbey, Reading.

Abbreviations and note on sources

Archives

AAE   Archives du Ministère des Affaires Etrangères, Paris
CP   Correspondance Politique
AN   Archives Nationales, Paris
BL   British Library, London
BN   Bibliothèque Nationale de France, Paris
PRO   Public Record Office, London
SCA   Scottish Catholic Archives, Edinburgh
SP   Stuart Papers, Royal Archives, Windsor Castle

Publications

CSPD   *Calendar of State Papers, Domestic Series*
DNB   *Dictionary of National Biography*
HMC   Historical Manuscripts Commission

Secondary sources

Although there have been many biographies of the exiled Stuarts, and several important books about the Jacobite movement, there has been no previous analysis of the Stuart court in exile in France after 1689. The present book is the result of over ten years' research, during which the author has published numerous articles on different aspects of the exiled court. Where these are cited in the footnotes they are given short titles only, all of which are listed below with their full references. All other books and articles used in the preparation of this book can be found in the footnotes. There is no separate bibliography of all secondary sources but a list of further reading follows the 'Primary Sources' at the back of the book.

Books and articles by the author cited in the footnotes:

'Berwick'   'James FitzJames, 1st Duke of Berwick: A
                              New Identification for a Portrait by
                              Hyacinthe Rigaud', *Apollo* 141, no. 400
                              (June 1995), 53–60.

Burlington   *Lord Burlington – The Man and his Politics:
                              Questions of Loyalty* (edited) (Lampeter,
                              1998).

'Centre of Italian Music'   'The Exiled Court of James II and James III:
                              A Centre of Italian Music in France,
                              1689–1712', *Journal of the Royal Musical
                              Association* 120, part 2 (September 1995),
                              216–31.

'Clandestine Support'   'Lord Burlington's Clandestine Support for
                              the Stuart Court at Saint-Germain-en-Laye',
                              in Edward Corp (ed.), *Lord Burlington – The
                              Man and his Politics: Questions of Loyalty*
                              (Lampeter, 1998), 7–26.

'Copiste Z'   'The Musical Manuscripts of "Copiste Z":
                              David Nairne, François Couperin, and the
                              Stuart Court at Saint-Germain-en-Laye',
                              Revue de Musicologie 84, no. 1 (June 1998),
                              37–62.

'Couperin and the   'François Couperin and the Stuart Court at
    Stuart Court'   Saint-Germain-en-Laye, 1691–1712: A New
                              Interpretation', *Early Music* 28, no. 3
                              (August 2000), 445–53.

'Cour anglaise'   'Saint-Germain-en-Laye: la cour anglaise et
                              anglicane en France, 1689–1712', *Cahiers
                              Saint-Simon* 24 (Paris, 1996), 77–86.

Cour des Stuarts   *La Cour des Stuarts à Saint-Germain-en-Laye au
                              Temps de Louis XIV*, exhibition catalogue
                              (with Jacqueline Sanson, Réunion des
                              Musées Nationaux, Paris, 1992).

'Courtisans français'   'Les courtisans français à la cour
                              d'Angleterre à Saint-Germain', *Cahiers
                              Saint-Simon* 28 (Paris, 2000), 49–66.

'Crébillon'	'Crébillon fils et Marie-Henriette Stafford, histoire anglaise' (with Anne Feinsilber), *Revue d'Histoire Littéraire de la France* 96, no. 1 (January–February 1996), 21–44.
'English Royal Table'	'James II and James III in Exile: The English Royal Table in France and Italy, 1689–c.1730', in Léonor d'Orey (ed.), *Royal and Princely Tables of Europe: Commissions and Gifts* (Museu de Arte Antiga, Lisbon, 1999), 112–20.
'Etiquette and Use of Royal Apartments'	'The Jacobite Court at Saint-Germain-en-Laye: Etiquette and the Use of the Royal Apartments', in Eveline Cruickshanks (ed.), *The Stuart Courts* (Stroud, 2000), 240–55.
'Flight of Queen and Prince of Wales'	'New Evidence concerning the Flight of the Queen and the Prince of Wales to France in December 1688: A Recently Discovered Letter of James II', *Archives* 26, no. 104 (April 2001), 36–40.
'Inventory'	'An Inventory of the Archives of the Stuart Court at Saint-Germain-en-Laye, 1689–1718', *Archives* 23, no. 99 (October 1998), 118–46.
'Irish at Saint-Germain'	'The Irish at the Court of Saint-Germain', in Thomas O'Connor (ed.), *The Irish in Europe, 1580–1815* (Dublin, 2001), 143–56.
'Jacobite Chapel Royal'	'The Jacobite Chapel Royal at Saint-Germain-en-Laye', *Recusant History* 23, no. 4 (October 1997), 528–42.
'Jacques II lance maçonnerie'	'Jacques II en exil lance la maçonnerie en France', *Historia*, Paris, Numéro spécial 48: 'Les francs-maçons' (July–August 1997), 18–22.
'James II and Toleration'	'James II and Toleration: The Years in Exile at Saint-Germain-en-Laye', *Royal Stuart Paper LI* (London, 1997).
King over the Water	*The King over the Water: Portraits of the Stuarts in Exile, 1689–1766* (Edinburgh, 2001).

'Last Years of James II'	'The Last Years of James II, 1690–1701', *History Today* 51 (September 2001), 19–25.
'La Tour's Portrait'	'Maurice Quentin de La Tour's Portrait of Prince Charles Edward Stuart', *Burlington Magazine* 139, no. 1130 (May 1997), 322–5.
L'Autre Exil	*L'Autre Exil: les Jacobites en France au début du XVIIe siècle* (edited) (Montpellier, 1993).
'Maintaining Continuity'	'English Royalty in Exile: Maintaining Continuity in France and Italy after 1689', in François Laroque and Franck Lessay (ed.), *Figures de la royauté en Angleterre de Shakespeare à la Glorieuse Révolution* (Paris, 1999), 181–95.
'Maison du Roi'	'La Maison du Roi à Saint-Germain-en-Laye, 1689–1718', *Revue de la Bibliothèque Nationale* 46 (Winter 1992), 5–11.
'Melfort'	'Melfort: A Jacobite Connoisseur', *History Today* 45 (October 1995), 40–6.
'Music at Urbino'	'Music at the Stuart Court at Urbino, 1717–1718', *Music and Letters* 81, no. 3, (August 2000), 351–63.
'Prendcourt'	'Further Light on the Career of "Captain" François de Prendcourt', and '"Captain" Prendcourt Revisited', *Music and Letters* 78, no. 1, (February 1997), 15–23, and 79, no. 4 (November 1998), 645–6.
Stuart Court and Jacobites	*The Stuart Court in Exile and the Jacobites* (edited with Eveline Cruickshanks) (London, 1995).

Introduction

This book is a study of the second of the three periods of exile experienced by the Stuart kings of Great Britain. The first started with the execution of Charles I in 1649 and ended with the restoration of his son Charles II in 1660. The second lasted from the deposition of James II in 1689 until 1716, when the rising in favour of his son James III was defeated in Scotland. The third continued from 1716 until the death of James III in 1766. During each period the Stuart king established a court in exile and did what he could to maintain his royal status. As this book will show, the second of these courts, established in France at Saint-Germain-en-Laye in 1689–90, was by far the most important – socially, politically and culturally.

The Stuart court at Saint-Germain has nevertheless received the least attention. There are several reasons for this. In the first place Charles II was eventually restored, and returned to England with his courtiers, several of whom subsequently pursued important careers in both England and Scotland. Historians and biographers have naturally taken an interest in an exile which ended successfully, whereas the two others ended in defeat and failure. A second reason concerns the perceived interest of the leading characters involved. Charles II is one of the most popular figures in British history, whereas his brother James II has found few admirers. In addition, the exploits of the elder son of James III, known popularly as 'Bonnie Prince Charlie', have never ceased to attract the attention of a wide reading public. The early life of this charismatic figure has thus provoked an interest in the exiled court of his father in Rome, and drawn attention to the stormy relations between his parents. In comparison, the court of the elderly James II and of the young and still unmarried James III has seemed both much less significant and much less interesting.

The most important reason, however, is purely archival and concerns the accidental destruction of the relevant documentary evidence. The archives of the exiled court of Charles II were brought back to England in 1660. The archives of the court of James III from 1716 to 1766 were sent to the Royal Library at Windsor in the early nineteenth century. By contrast, those of the court of James II and James III in France were destroyed in Paris during the

French Revolution. Any study of that court therefore raises major problems of research and historical method. Writing the present book has involved identifying any documents which happen to have escaped the general destruction during the French Revolution, discovering alternative sources, particularly in the French archives, attempting to reassess the court by questioning received assumptions about it and posing those questions which have now become normal in recent studies of the other princely courts of early modern Europe.

The Whig tradition of British historiography, so dominant from the 1840s until recently, naturally dismissed an exiled court for which its leading exponents felt very little sympathy, and which seemed to them to have consisted of political and religious reactionaries, hopelessly standing in the way of an inevitable Progress. In the absence of its archives their writings naturally reflected the hostile attitudes of the anti-Jacobite propaganda pamphlets published after 1689.

The deposition and successful exclusion of James II and his son, on the grounds that they were Catholic, meant that the Stuart court at Saint-Germain had to be portrayed to Protestants as a centre of extreme, tyrannical Catholic bigotry, a seminary more than a court. The serious danger of a Stuart restoration meant that potential supporters had to be deterred by an active campaign to minimise the political importance of the court, by representing it as intolerant, financially bankrupt and infiltrated by spies. These attitudes have been accepted and perpetuated in numerous books published since the mid-nineteenth century.

This is hardly surprising, because few historians until recently were willing to take the Jacobite movement seriously, and even those few tended to accept these views about the court at Saint-Germain. The court itself has not until now been given a separate study, but it has been referred to in many books, including several biographies of James II, of Queen Mary of Modena, of their son James III and of their daughter Princess Louise-Marie. In the absence of any readily available evidence to the contrary, they have all reflected these views. The first to be published was a biography of Mary of Modena, which appeared in 1846–47 as part of Agnes Strickland's *Lives of the Queens of England*.[1] By then the archives of the court had been destroyed, the château in which it was based had been changed beyond recognition, and the families which had lived there had been dispersed. Strickland not only established the tradition for regarding the court as 'melancholy',[2] but was the first person to use the

---

[1] The biography was divided between volumes ix and x (London, 1846 and 1847).
[2] *Ibid.*, IX, 333, where the word is used twice.

correspondence of the queen with the Visitation nuns at Chaillot. Apart from some anecdotes which revealed nothing about the organisation of the court, the Chaillot papers concentrated exclusively on religious matters and were written in a style which was appropriate for a community of enclosed nuns.[3] By making very extensive use of them Strickland thus seemed to confirm the all-pervading atmosphere of pious if not bigoted Catholicism which Macaulay was to denounce with devastating effect in the fourth volume of his *History of England*.[4] The subsequent publication of James II's 'Papers of Devotion'[5] merely reinforced this impression, and encouraged several more generations of historians to accept uncritically this assumption.

No significant work was done on the Stuart court in France after the publication of the works by Strickland and Macaulay until the beginning of the twentieth century.[6] Then, in 1902, the Historical Manuscripts Commission began to publish the Stuart Papers preserved at Windsor Castle.[7] These were the archives of the Stuart court which had been assembled after 1716, although they also contained some earlier material which had escaped destruction, having been sent to Rome during the 1730s. The availability of this material, and the attention thus drawn to the Stuart Papers as a whole, resulted in the publication of a series of new books about the exiled Stuarts, including some very good biographies, in the years preceding the First World War.[8]

These books, however, gave additional support to another assumption of the Whig historians, namely that the Stuart court in France was impoverished.

---

[3] The Chaillot papers are AN κ/1301–3. Agnes Strickland's complete copy is Bodleian Library MSS French b.11–13. A second copy was made in 1842, sold to the Bodleian Library in 1867 (Add. c.106–7) and edited by Falconer Madan as *Stuart Papers Relating Chiefly to Queen Mary of Modena and the Exiled Court of King James II*, 2 vols. (London, 1889).

[4] T.B. Macaulay, *History of England* IV (London 1855), pp. 380–4.

[5] *The Papers of Devotion of James II*, ed. G. Davies (London, 1925), a facsimile edition taken from the original manuscript (now in Trinity College Library, Dublin), sent from Rome to Ireland in 1842. Extracts had already been published by the Historical Manuscripts Commission in 1887 (*10th Report*, appendix VI).

[6] The marquise Campana di Cavelli carried out research into the Stuart court at Saint-Germain between 1864 and her death in 1875, and published two large volumes of documents, covering the years 1672 to April 1689, in 1871 (*Les Dernières Stuarts à Saint-Germain-en-Laye*, Paris). Her planned third volume, to cover 1689 to 1719, was never published (Corp, *Cour des Stuarts*, 229).

[7] 7 vols. (London, 1902–23).

[8] The books included: Marquis de Ruvigny, *The Jacobite Peerage* (Edinburgh, 1904); M. Haile, *Queen Mary of Modena: Her Life and Letters* (London, 1905); A. Shield and A. Lang, *The King over the Water* (London, 1907); M. Haile, *James Francis Edward, the 'Old Chevalier'* (London, 1907); A. Fea, *James II and His Wives* (London, 1908); C.E. Lart, *The Parochial Registers of Saint-Germain-en-Laye: Jacobite Extracts*, 2 vols. (London, 1910, 1912); G. du Bosq de Beaumont and M. Bernos, *La Cour des Stuarts à Saint-Germain-en-Laye* (Paris, 1912).

The Stuart Papers referred generally to the financial problems experienced throughout France at the very end of the War of the Spanish Succession, and specifically to the difficulties of financing the Jacobite community at Saint-Germain *after* 1716. The new books used this information to argue *ex post facto* that the Stuart court in France had experienced the same financial difficulties during the previous twenty-five years. The present book will produce new evidence to show that that was not the case. Indeed, by contradicting both the religious and the financial assumptions about the court which were accepted throughout the twentieth century, it will offer a major revision of an important and neglected aspect of British and Anglo-French History. It will show that the court was large and well financed, not only able to maintain its courtiers but also to be an important centre of cultural patronage.

Some brief comparisons may be made here to indicate the fundamental difference of scale between the Stuart court in France after 1689 and those established by Charles II in 1649 and by James III after 1716. The court of Charles II was peripatetic, moving between France, the Spanish Netherlands, the Holy Roman Empire and the United Provinces. From 1690 until 1712 the court of James II and James III was permanently based at Saint-Germain. In the 1650s and after 1716 the Stuarts never enjoyed the consistent political support of France, the country best placed to help them, whereas Louis XIV remained committed to their cause for well over twenty years after 1689. The court of James III in Rome was established in the relatively modest buildings of the Palazzo Muti, whereas the Château-Vieux de Saint-Germain was a very large royal palace, previously used by Louis XIV as his principal residence, and with several additional royal buildings adjacent to it.

However, the most important comparison concerns the finances of the courts. James II and James III had a great deal more money at Saint-Germain than Charles II had previously had during the 1650s or than James III would himself have when he lived in Rome. The court at Saint-Germain was therefore maintained on a much larger and more lavish scale.

In 1652, for example, Charles II received an annual pension from Louis XIV of 192,000 *livres*.[9] At the same time the dowager Queen Henrietta Maria received a further 72,000 *livres*.[10] Even when the queen's pension was increased to 120,000 *livres*,[11] the combined total was still only a little more than half

[9] Arch. Dépt. du Val d'Oise, 68/H/8, *liasse* 3, Charles II's instructions to Richard Forster on how to manage the money received from the French Crown, 25 June 1652.

[10] *Ibid.*, 'copie de l'arret du conseil du 12 aout 1652 qui accordent à la reine d'Angleterre 72,000*l* . . . . pour l'Entretennement et Subsistence de sa Maison'.

[11] *Ibid.*, ordonnances of 1656, 1657 and 1658 'pour la Reyne d'Ang.re . . . pour l'entretennement de sa Maison'.

the 600,000 *livres* which Louis XIV gave every year to James II and James III. In 1652 the household of Charles II contained seventy-six people,[12] whereas that of James III in 1709 contained 140.[13] In 1653 Queen Henrietta Maria spent 7692 *livres* on her Bedchamber servants,[14] whereas in 1703 Queen Mary of Modena spent 30,629 *livres*,[15] approximately four times as much. At Rome in 1730 the court of James III contained 128 people (including several with pensions but no duties), who were paid a total of 96,456 *livres* per annum.[16] At Saint-Germain in 1696 the servants at the court of James II numbered approximately 225 people, and the combined total of salaries and pensions was 387,000 *livres*.[17]

In recent years the importance of Jacobitism has been significantly re-assessed, demonstrating that the Stuart kings in exile after 1689 enjoyed considerably more support in England than previously supposed and that the chances of a restoration, particularly in the years up to 1716, were proportionately much greater.[18] That, however, is not the main argument of this book. The fact is that the exiled Stuart court in France had considerably more money, was very much larger, and had a much more important permanent base than did the other two. Its interest for us today is directly related to this fact.

Comparison can also be usefully made with the exiled Bourbon court one hundred years later. In 1797 Louis XVIII was given a temporary residence by Tsar Paul I a thousand miles from France in the castle of Mitau.[19] The exiled king of France was expelled from Mitau in 1801, but allowed to return in 1804, only to be expelled a second time in 1807. He then went to England and lived in Gosfield Hall, a small country house in Essex. In 1809 he moved to Hartwell House in Buckinghamshire.[20] By that time the Emperor Napoleon I was at the height of his power, and a Bourbon restoration seemed completely out of the question. By contrast, at various times between 1702 and 1714 a Stuart restoration – to Scotland or England – seemed a distinct possibility. As

---

[12] Chiddingstone Castle, Bower MSS, the household of Charles II, *c*.1652.

[13] BL Egerton MS 2517, the household of James III, 1709.

[14] Arch. Dépt. du Val d'Oise, 68/H/8, *liasse* 3, Henrietta Maria's 'Bedchamber and Backstairs accounts', October 1652 to March 1653.

[15] SP 2/23, the household of Mary of Modena, 1703.

[16] SP 135/81, 'gages du Roy', March 1730; SP 137/39, pensions given by James III, May 1730.

[17] Sizergh Castle, Strickland Collection R.4, the households of James II and Mary of Modena, 1696.

[18] For convenient short summaries, see E. Cruickshanks, *The Glorious Revolution* (London, 2000), and D. Szechi, *The Jacobites* (Manchester, 1994).

[19] The castle, which had been the residence of the Dukes of Courland, had been vacant since the duchy had been annexed by Russia in 1795.

[20] From 1801 to 1804 Louis XVIII rented a house in Warsaw, in the recently expanded kingdom of Prussia. Gosfield Hall was lent to him by the Marquess of Buckingham, but he rented Hartwell House (E. Lever, *Louis XVIII* (Paris, 1988), 296–8).

it turned out, Louis XVIII was eventually restored and James III was not, but no one could have predicted either outcome at the time. 'Excluding courtiers' servants, and the households of other members of the royal family, there were 108 people in the *maison du roi* at Mitau in Courland in 1799–1801 and 45 at Hartwell in England in 1809.'[21] In 1709, as we have seen, the household of James III, excluding courtiers' servants, and the households of Queen Mary of Modena and Princess Louise-Marie, contained 140 people. These figures indicate the great difference in size between the second Stuart court in exile, at Saint-Germain, and the peripatetic Bourbon court in exile a hundred years later.

The Stuart and Bourbon courts were not the only ones to experience extended periods of exile during the seventeenth and eighteenth centuries, but they were the most important, because Charles II, James II, James III and Louis XVIII were kings whose dynastic claims to reign depended on the divine right of hereditary succession and could not therefore be renounced. They were thus able to draw upon enormous reserves of emotional loyalty among the peoples of their kingdoms. Hereditary monarchs such as Queen Christina of Sweden who abdicated (1654), and princes such as the Elector Maximilian Emmanuel of Bavaria who were forced to live abroad when their states were militarily occupied (1704–14), did of course maintain important households and retinues in exile, but they were not attempting to bring about a restoration by overthrowing a usurper. Even Stanislas Leszczynski, king of Poland from 1704 to 1709, who was deposed and who established an exiled court at Zweibrücken in 1714 and at Wissembourg in 1719,[22] was an elected, not an hereditary king. Having failed to regain the throne he had lost, he was eventually willing, and able, to renounce it.[23] This was not an option for the Stuarts and the Bourbons, even if they had wished to do so. Their exiled courts were consequently of a different nature. And among them the court of James II and James III merits special attention because of its size and importance.

In 1911 Edwin and Marion Grew published a book entitled *The English Court in Exile: James II at Saint-Germain*. As they explained in their preface,

---

[21] P. Mansel, *The Court of France, 1789–1830* (Cambridge, 1988), 42. Following this substantial reduction in the number of his servants Louis XVIII was still unable to live within his small income of £21,600. His annual expenditure while he was at Hartwell was £26,000 (Lever, *Louis XVIII*, 309–10).

[22] G. Doscot, *Stanislas Leszczynski et la cour de Lorraine* (Lausanne, 1969), 24–33. While he was at Wissembourg until 1725 King Stanislas was totally dependent on his small annual pension from the French government of 50,000 *livres*.

[23] He abdicated in 1709 and again (after an unsuccessful attempt to regain his throne) in 1733 (*ibid.*, 24, 105, 108).

'the authors . . . sought to reconstruct the life of James II and his family at the Château de Saint-Germain-en-Laye, and their relations with the French Court'.[24] The work was not therefore an analysis of the court, but rather a political biography, confined to the period before 1701. A single chapter, entitled 'The Household at Saint-Germain', attempted to identify the leading courtiers and to provide some biographical information about them. Nevertheless the Grews did consider an important question which has now become an essential aspect of court studies. They wondered what the royal apartments had looked like and how they had been furnished. By the time they were writing, the apartments had been completely destroyed. Indeed, parts of the château in which they had been located had even been pulled down. They therefore consulted 'M. Dunoyer, the authority for the period, at the *Archives Nationales*' in Paris, who informed them that: 'There does not exist any record among the *Archives de France* in Paris of the orders given by Louis XIV for the furnishing and setting in order of the Château de Saint-Germain for the reception of the King and Queen of England.'[25] This negative reply put a stop to any further research for nearly a century. But the French archives actually contain precise and very detailed information about the appearance of the Château de Saint-Germain throughout the Stuart period. They are used here for the first time, in chapter 2, to describe the royal apartments as they were when occupied by James II and his family.

Court studies, however, involve much more than physical description. The publication in 1967 of Hugh Murray-Baillie's seminal article 'Etiquette and the Planning of State Apartments in Baroque Palaces'[26] alerted people to the need to study the ways in which kings and other sovereign princes planned and made use of the available space within their residences. One of Murray-Baillie's most significant achievements was to demonstrate that the ceremonial of the French court differed from that adopted by most of the other European courts, and therefore that Versailles and the other French royal palaces had very little influence on the internal architecture of the palaces built elsewhere, notably in England. Given that the exiled Stuart kings of England were obliged to live for an extended period in one of the major French royal palaces, this raised the question of how they adapted their households and ceremonial to take account of the available space. It is surprising that no attention has previously been given to this, particularly by the biographers of James II.

---

[24] E. and M. Grew, *English Court in Exile* (London, 1911), v.   [25] *Ibid.*, 284.
[26] *Archaeologia* 101 (1967), 169–99.

In addition to the chapter describing the location of the court, and to several others which analyse the structure, ceremonial, organisation and servants of the royal household (chapters 3–5), the present book will break further new ground by considering the court as a centre of culture and patronage. Once again, it is surprising that this has not been done before. Art historians have given considerable attention to court portraiture at Whitehall, but have overlooked the painted portraits of the exiled Stuarts and their leading courtiers. They are to be found in major art galleries and are frequently used as illustrations, while the court portraitists who painted them have themselves been the subjects of several important exhibitions. Yet these canvases have only very recently been given a systematic study, by the present author.[27] A similar reticence has been shown by musicologists. Recent decades have witnessed an enormous increase in the performance and appreciation of baroque music, notably from the court of Louis XIV where it is known that musical tastes began to change during the 1690s. Yet not even anglophone musicologists, who have made a distinguished contribution to this musical revival, have shown interest in the exiled English court, established only a few miles from Versailles, in the years immediately before musical tastes there began to change. Both the portraits and the music of the court are examined in the present book (chapters 7, 8).

Some of the many aspects of the Stuart court in France are described here by a small team of collaborators. Chapter 1 sets the scene by providing a detailed and authoritative account of the policies pursued by the exiled Stuarts and their ministers from the Revolution of 1688–89 to the Treaty of Utrecht of 1713. This substantial chapter, contributed by Professor Edward Gregg, also gives the essential background against which the dynastic relations of the Stuarts and the Bourbons can be examined (chapter 5). An important contribution by Professor Howard Erskine-Hill enables us to consider poetry, in addition to painting and music, as part of the cultural legacy of the court (chapter 9). Finally there are two major contributions from Abbot Geoffrey Scott, who brings his specialist knowledge to examine the Catholicism of the exiled court, including the religious writings of James II and the education given to James III by his preceptor (chapter 10, 11).

Unlike the court of Charles II in 1660, or that of Louis XVIII in 1814, the court of James III was not able to return home. Instead of moving to London, James III was obliged by the terms of the Treaty of Utrecht to settle in Lorraine in 1713, and by the failure of the Jacobite rising of 1715–16 to go into a second

---

[27] Corp, *King over the Water*, 33–52, 102–3, 106–7.

exile in the Papal States. Chapters 12 and 13 describe the transformation of
the exiled court during these years, and explain how and why the court which
James III eventually established in Rome was fundamentally different from the
one he had had in France. Queen Mary of Modena, however, was allowed to
remain at Saint-Germain after the departure of her son, and she continued to
maintain there a large royal household. Chapters 14 and 15 examine both the
exiled court at Saint-Germain during its final years and the important Jacobite
community which remained there for several decades after the death of the
queen in 1718.

Strong feelings are often expressed concerning Jacobitism, particularly by
those who have little or no sympathy for it. This frequently results in disagreement and confusion concerning the name which should be given to the
legitimate son of James II. His enemies, perhaps understandably, attempted to
question his legitimacy and referred to him as the 'pretended Prince of Wales'.
When he succeeded his father they began to call him the 'pretender'. When,
much later, he married and had children, they distinguished between him and
his elder son by referring to him as the 'old pretender'. It was perfectly natural
that the Whigs and pro-Hanoverians of the late seventeenth and eighteenth
centuries should thus express their dynastic preference because they were politically committed and partisan. But it is the duty of the modern historian to
try not to be partisan, and to avoid using such obviously partisan terminology.
A king in exile might or might not be eventually restored, but such an outcome, depending on a combination of unpredictable political developments,
cannot retroactively confer legitimacy. Neither Charles II nor Louis XVIII,
nor even James II after 1689, is ever referred to as a 'pretender'. The word has
therefore been deliberately avoided in this book.

During the French Revolution Louis XVI was referred to by his enemies
as Louis Capet. Similarly James III was sometimes called James Stuart. More
recently, historians have adopted the practice of calling him James Francis
Edward Stuart, and of similarly loading his sons with more than one of their
Christian names. At one point James III briefly adopted an incognito as the
Knight of St George or, since he was in France at the time, the *Chevalier de
Saint-Georges*. These names have also been rejected in this book, either because
they unwittingly reflect partisan attitudes or because they attach permanent
significance to a transitory phase. James III was recognised by several contemporary European sovereign princes, notably the kings of France and Spain,
and the pope, as a legitimate king. Titles have traditionally been conferred
by superior or equal contemporaries, not by historians writing at a later time.
It is because no such recognition was afforded to the elder son of James III

(who might otherwise have become Charles III) that the third Stuart court in exile is considered here to have been terminated by James's death in 1766.

It must also be remembered that James III commanded considerable support in England, Scotland and Ireland, where for several decades he was regarded by many as the legitimate king. To study a royal court in exile, involving the examination of thousands of contemporary documents in English, French and Italian, all of which refer to James III by his royal title, and then to avoid using that title, would surely be particularly perverse. In thus deliberately calling the son of James II by the title always used at his exiled court, this book follows the precedent set by the Historical Manuscripts Commission in 1902–23, when it published its seven volumes of the Stuart Papers preserved at Windsor Castle.

Finally, the recent interest shown in Scotland's separate national identity has caused some people today to prefer to use the name James VIII, generally written as James VIII/III. While this is perfectly understandable as an expression of modern sentiment, it has little relevance to the political realities of the seventeenth and eighteenth centuries. James VI of Scotland, who became James I of England and Ireland (and *de jure* Jacques I of France), adopted the title James I of Great Britain. Charles I, Charles II and James II were similarly kings of Great Britain – just as the kings of Castile, who were also kings of Aragon and princes of Catalonia during the sixteenth and seventeenth centuries, called themselves kings of Spain. England and Scotland were united in 1707; the Iberian states (excluding Portugal) were united in 1716. The title James III used here refers to Great Britain (and Ireland); it does not refer exclusively to England. The name will be unwelcome to many people, and may even be unfamiliar to most. It might perhaps continue to be avoided by those who focus their attention on the courts and policies of Queen Anne and King George I in England. But it is important to explain and emphasise at the outset that it is the only correct name to be used when examining the exiled Stuart court in France. Without thereby implying any dynastic preference, the central figure of this book will be referred to as the Prince of Wales or James III, or simply as the king.

CHAPTER ONE

France, Rome and the exiled Stuarts, 1689–1713

EDWARD GREGG

Well before James, Duke of York became king in 1685, English suspicion of France in general, and of Louis XIV in particular, was universal, common to all classes and parties; 'His grand designe . . . is to make himself Master of all Europe', an Anglican bishop opined in 1676.[1] In 1691, when George Legge, first baron Dartmouth and James's favourite courtier, was being examined by the Privy Council, Dartmouth protested that he would defend England:

LORD DARTMOUTH: I am . . . not so weake as to fancy the King of France will conquer England only for King James. No, my Lords, if we should ever be so unfortunate, he will doe it for himselfe, or at least make us but trybutary.

LORD PRESIDENT [MARQUIS OF CARMARTHEN]: Nay, any man that can thincke at all can't surely immagine the King of France will doe it for King James, or any body but himself.[2]

After the Nine Years' War, Matthew Prior had no doubt that James's decision to flee to France had fatally injured his prospects in England: 'King James cast himself into the hands of the Enemyes of his Country, and justified in great measure the suspicions that were against him upon that account; a great many that were for him before, grew cold in his interest from the fear and hatred they had of his being restored by a French power.'[3]

Repeatedly throughout his career, James II displayed an incredible degree of self-delusion concerning the French and their intentions. What made James II's decision in 1688 to throw himself into the arms of Louis XIV even more fatal was the suspicion which that monarch had long borne of him. After the Anglo-French alliance of 1670, Louis had harboured thoughts of marrying his

---

[1] University of Glasgow, Hunterian Collection, MS 3708, f. 18: G[eorge Morley], bishop of Winchester, to Clarendon, 6 November 1676, Farnham Castle. All letters written in Great Britain are dated Old Style; those written from the Continent are dated New Style, unless otherwise indicated.

[2] HMC *Dartmouth* I, 289: Dartmouth's account of his examination by the Privy Council, 14 July 1691.

[3] BL Add. MSS 70,367, n.f.: Matthew Prior's private journal, 'a reflexion' for May 1699.

only legitimate son, the dauphin, to the elder daughter of the Duke of York.[4] Instead, in November 1677, James consented to the marriage of Lady Mary to her first cousin, William III of Orange, Stadhouder of the Dutch Republic and Louis XIV's most intransigent enemy. The French court took umbrage: 'it is certain the ministers and those of the council I converse with seem to consider that match as a thing done without any communication, counsel or consent asked or given from this side', the English chargé d'affaires in Paris notified Whitehall.[5] Louis XIV never entirely forgave James for this 'betrayal' and his discontent was well known in London: 'Heere is a fable about the towne', one newsy lady reported in April 1678, 'that the King of France should break a jesyt of the Prince of Orange and Lady Mary of two beggars well mett, which they say gave great offense to the Duke of Yorke.'[6] To compound Louis's anger, the Duke of York was prepared that spring to assume joint command of the allied armies in the Spanish Netherlands against the French.[7]

Between 1678 and 1681, in order to divide England internally and weaken the government of Charles II, Louis XIV supported the opposition Whig party financially throughout the Popish Plot, while the Whigs were working to exclude the Duke of York from the succession to the throne on the grounds that he was a Roman Catholic. Nevertheless, James continued to believe that Louis XIV was his firm friend. In 1679–81, fearing that the English Parliament would push him to extremities, James contemplated raising Scotland and Ireland on his behalf, a scheme in which Louis (who wished to stir up all possible trouble in the British Isles) encouraged him.[8] In 1683, Richard Graham, Lord Preston, Charles II's last envoy to France and a close friend of James, lamented that 'I am sorry that the Duke [of York] thinketh that France is firm to him. If I see anything, notwithstanding all promises, the old rancour against him

[4] HMC *Fitzherbert*, 51: letters of Sir William Throckmorton to [Edward Coleman?], 28 November, 1 December [1674], Paris, quoting the marquis de Pomponne.

[5] HMC *Fourteenth Report*, App. IX, 387–9: John Brisbane to Danby, 27 November 1677, Paris: this discontent was confirmed by Brisbane's further conversations with Honoré Courtin, newly returned from London where he had been French ambassador: *ibid.*, 394: Brisbane to Danby, 9 July 1678, Paris.

[6] HMC *Rutland* II, 50: Grace, Lady Chaworth, to Lord Roos, 23 April 1678, London.

[7] BL, Add. MSS 28,937, ff. 289–90: 'Memoire des points concernans la Réponse que M. Le Duc de Villa Hermosa a donné aux propositions que luy a fait le Chev. Churchill', 23 April 1678, Brussels; f. 291: 'Convention faite de la part de S.M. de la G.B. par le Col Churchill, avec S.A. Mr le Prince d'Orange', 3 May 1678, The Hague.

[8] Baron Charles van Grovestins, *Histoire des luttes et rivalités politiques entre les puissances maritimes et la France durant la seconde moitié du XVIIe siècle* (Paris, 1851–54), III, 340–5.

remaineth . . . I wonder that the practices about the bill of exclusion can so soon be forgotten, and other marks of kindness which he received from hence in his distress.'[9]

From the beginning of James II's reign, Louis XIV was suspicious of the new king's protestations of pro-French feelings.[10] Opinion at the French court was deeply divided as to whether James's pro-Catholic policies were wise or precipitate.[11] In April 1685, Louis XIV refused to continue to James the annual French subsidy which Charles II had received, and he later refused to provide financial aid during the Monmouth rebellion.[12] After a display of unexpected national unity on his behalf and his easy victory over the rebels, James II became even more difficult from the French point of view. Paul Barillon, Louis's resident in London, found James 'less docile than the late King, and more headstrong on what are called the true interests and honour of England'.[13] Not only was Louis suspicious of James's continuing relationship with William III, but he was also irritated by James's instructions to his envoys to act on behalf of the principality of Orange and of English Protestants residing in France, as well as James's financial support of French Huguenot refugees arriving in England. By 1688, there was not only no Anglo-French alliance, but Louis also had the deepest suspicions both of James's intentions and of his abilities.

Nothing happened during that year to change Louis's opinion. The inconstancy and willingness to reverse his policy completely which James displayed in domestic affairs was repeated in his foreign policy. Two weeks before the birth of a Prince of Wales on 10/20 June, Louis warned Barillon that William III was arming a fleet, possibly for an invasion of England; Louis offered to send sixteen French ships to join the English fleet, an offer which James initially accepted, but he then changed his mind, seeing no possibility of a Dutch invasion.[14] On 2/12 August, Louis again repeated his warning that James should prepare on land and sea for an invasion; at first, James seemed alarmed by the warning conveyed by Barillon, but by 20/30 August he had reverted and scarcely believed that his son-in-law would undertake such a

[9] HMC *Seventh Report*, 341: Preston to Halifax, 5 October 1683, Paris.

[10] Grovestins, *Histoire*, v, 141–2.

[11] Louis-François du Bouchet, marquis de Sourches, *Mémoires*, ed. comte de Cornac, 13 vols. (Paris, 1882–93), I, 190: entry for March 1685. Hereafter cited as Sourches.

[12] Paul de Noailles, duc de Noailles, *Histoire de Madame de Maintenon* (Paris, 1858), IV, 145, 154–5: Louis XIV to Paul Barillon, 6 April, 26 July 1685.

[13] Quoted in Noailles, *Maintenon*, IV, 161: Barillon to Louis XIV, 13/23 December 1685, London.

[14] Grovestins, *Histoire*, v, 440, citing Louis XIV to Barillon, 27 May/7 June 1688.

project.[15] Undeterred by the fact that James had twice rebuffed his offers of an alliance, on 2/12 September Louis XIV instructed his envoy at The Hague, the comte d'Avaux, to make a formal declaration to the States-General that Louis would regard an attack on England as an attack on France, and respond accordingly. To Louis's chagrin, James angrily and publicly disavowed the French declaration and (suspecting his envoy to Versailles of complicity in arranging it) recalled Bevil Skelton, and threw him into the Tower.[16] Even worse from the French point of view, after France began a siege of the imperial fortress at Phillipsburg on 17/27 September, James made a formal declaration at The Hague that this violated the Treaty of Ratisbon and that England, Spain and the Dutch Republic should unite in protest. In June and August, James had privately rejected offers of an Anglo-French alliance; in September he had publicly disavowed Louis's friendship and had effectively suspended diplomatic relations by recalling and imprisoning his envoy; now, in October, he had made something tantamount to a declaration of war.[17] Small wonder, then, that by 10/20 September Louis had abandoned all hope of saving James, speaking scathingly of his 'foiblesse'.[18] Nevertheless, on 7/17 October Louis sent 300,000 *livres* for James's use, but with instructions to Barillon to give James the money only if it appeared that he had a chance of winning.[19]

William III and a force of approximately 15,000 soldiers landed at Torbay on 5/15 November and rapidly proceeded to establish a base at Exeter. James dispatched his army towards the West Country and, on 17/27 November, left London to join them at Salisbury. There he was deserted by his son-in-law, Prince George of Denmark; his trusted servant and protégé, John Lord Churchill; his nephew, the Duke of Grafton; the young Duke of Ormonde, and a large number of less prominent officers. The French court was astonished by

[15] *Ibid.*, 441.

[16] *Ibid.*, 442. Skelton was released and on 27 November OS as a sop to Protestant opinion was appointed lieutenant of the Tower immediately after James II's return to London from Salisbury: HMC *Dartmouth* I, 261: Philip Musgrave to Dartmouth, 28 November 1688, London; cf. HMC *Hastings* II, 197: J. Smithsby to Earl of Huntingdon, 27 November 1688, London; Edward Irving Carlyle, 'Bevil Skelton', *Dictionary of National Biography*, XVIII, 325–6, gives 6 November 1688 as the date of appointment.

[17] Noailles, *Maintenon*, IV, 197, 208–11; Camille Rousset, *Histoire de Louvois et de son administration politique et militaire depuis la paix de Nimège* (Paris, 1862–63), IV, 103–4.

[18] Noailles, *Maintenon*, IV, 199: Louis XIV to Barillon, 20 September 1688; cf. Grovestins, *Histoire*, V, 444–5, quoting Louis to Barillon, 30 September 1688.

[19] Noailles, *Maintenon*, IV, 217.

the army desertions and the lack of support for James which they revealed.[20] During his return to London, James heard of the flight from Whitehall of his daughter, Princess Anne, news which seems to have 'disordered his understanding'.[21] From the moment of his return to the capital, the king's only view was to save first his wife and son, and then himself.

On 9/19 December, the queen, Mary of Modena, and the Prince of Wales left Whitehall under cover of darkness; their guide and protector was Antonin Nompar de Caumont, comte de Lauzun. They arrived at Calais on 14/24 December, but so little confidence did the French court have in James II that initially the queen and the Prince of Wales were treated as hostages. The minister of war, François Michel Le Tellier, marquis de Louvois, after consultations with Louis XIV, instructed de Béringhen, the *premier ecuyer* who had been sent to receive the queen, that despite any orders from James II to the contrary, the queen and the Prince of Wales were to be brought to Vincennes (which served as both a royal château and a prison). Louvois repeated these instructions to Lauzun the following day, urging that they be carried out 'sous tous les pretextes les plus honnêtes que vous pourrez vous imaginer'.[22] On the night of 11/22 December, the same day his son-in-law Henry, Lord Waldegrave had his first audience of Louis XIV as James's envoy extraordinary, James II fled the palace of Whitehall.[23] His first attempt to flee the country was foiled when he was apprehended by fishermen at Faversham in Kent, and he was eventually forced to return to London.

William III, who had advanced to Windsor, ordered James to retire to Rochester, accompanied by Dutch guards. William correctly anticipated that his father-in-law would make a second attempt to escape, which he did, landing near Gravelines on 25 December/5 January 1688/89.

From the time of James's arrival in France, Louis XIV was to treat the exiled Stuarts with the utmost courtesy, immediately making the château

---

[20] Marie Madeline de Motier, marquise de La Fayette, *Mémoires de la Cour de France pour les années 1688 et 1689*, ed. Gilbert Sageux (Paris, 1965), 132. This sense of astonishment is reflected in contemporary diary accounts, such as Sourches and Dangeau.

[21] Edward Gregg, *Queen Anne* (London, 1980), 66, quoting Bevil Higgons [a noted Jacobite], *A Short View of English History* (London, 1731), 429.

[22] Rousset, *Louvois*, IV, 151.

[23] Sourches, II, 312–13: entry for 22 December 1688; Waldegrave, who in 1683 married Henrietta FitzJames, the king's illegitimate daughter by Arabella Churchill, was appointed on 23 October 1688 OS and left London for Paris about 20 November, accompanied by Father Edward Petre, the king's Jesuit confessor: Gary M. Bell, *A Handlist of British Diplomatic Representatives, 1509–1688* (London, 1990), 125; HMC *Le Fleming*, 220: Newsletter of 20 November 1688, London.

of Saint-Germain-en-Laye (his own birthplace) available to them, furnishing it lavishly from the royal storehouses, and assigning the 'Jacobite' court an annual subsidy of 600,000 *livres* (approximately £50,000). Medals were struck depicting a beneficent Gallia receiving the British royal family, all depicting the magnanimous 'most Christian king'.[24] In reality, however, Louis XIV and his court regarded 'cette royauté vagabonde' with more disdain than pity.[25] On James II's arrival at Saint-Germain on 7 January 1689, the marquise de La Fayette commented: 'La figure du roi d'Angleterre n'avait pas imposé aux courtisans: ses discours firent moins d'egard que sa figure.'[26] Louis XIV had almost no choice but to support James II against William III, not so much from personal or professional sympathy with a dethroned king as in the interests of the French state. It was clear that William III would now lead a powerful international alliance, while France would not have a single important ally. Louis's best hope was that civil war in the British Isles not only would weaken William there, but might also ultimately undermine his position in the Dutch Republic.[27]

For his part, James II regarded himself as a martyr for his religion, and assumed that the Catholic princes of Europe would readily agree. He was quickly to be disabused of this idea. In early February 1689, he appointed the ubiquitous Bevil Skelton, who had joined him at Saint-Germain, as his envoy to Leopold I, the Holy Roman Emperor.[28] In his appeal, James portrayed himself as a martyr for the faith, who had fallen victim to the unnatural ambitions of his son-in-law. Leopold refused to receive Skelton; in his reply, which addressed James merely as 'serene highness' rather than as 'majesty', the emperor retorted that James had brought his troubles upon himself, and that as an ally of France, he could hope for no aid from the house of Habsburg.[29] Throughout the Spanish empire of Leopold's Habsburg cousin, Carlos II, the story was the same: 'the Spaniards in Messina', it was reported to

[24] At least seven variations were struck: Edward Hawkins, A.W. Franks and H.A. Grueber, *Medallic Illustrations of the History of Great Britain and Ireland* (London, 1885; reprint 1978), I, 652–5; Noel Woolf, *The Medallic Record of the Jacobite Movement* (London, 1988), 18–19.

[25] Grovestins, *Histoire*, VI, 119.

[26] La Fayette, *Mémoires*, 146.

[27] Rousset, *Louvois*, IV, 152–3.

[28] Philippe de Courcillon, marquis de Dangeau, *Journal*, ed. E. Soulié and L. Dussieux, 19 vols. (Paris, 1854–60), II, 322, 333: entries for 2, 18 February 1689. Hereafter cited as Dangeau.

[29] Marquise Campana de Cavelli, *Les Derniers Stuarts à Saint-Germain-en-Laye*, 2 vols. (London, 1871), II, 495–501: James II to Leopold I, 6 February 1689, Saint-Germain; Leopold I to James II, 9 April 1689, Vienna; for refusal to receive Skelton, *ibid.*, 506, fn. 2. Other German princes refused to receive Skelton, including the Elector of Bavaria: Archives des Affaires Etrangères, Paris (AAE), Correspondance Politique (CP) Angleterre 170, ff. 220–1: B[evil] Skelton to

Paris, 'sung the *te deum* for the prince of orang[e's] coronation with the greatest solmnitie Imaginable'.[30] The continuing hostility of the Habsburgs to Franco-Stuart pretensions was to prove crucial in influencing the attitudes of Catholic princes in both Germany and Italy.

Simultaneously, James II also turned to the pope, Innocent XI, despite his rocky relations with the Holy See.[31] Far from endorsing James II's policies as king, the pope had deplored them, fearing that they endangered the Roman Catholic community in Great Britain; James's ill-judged appointment of the most famous cuckold in Europe, Roger Palmer, Earl of Castlemaine, as his first ambassador to Rome did little to enhance the king's reputation there. Of overriding importance, however, was Innocent XI's hatred and fear of Louis XIV and France, stemming from a series of disputes over government of the Gallican church and fear of French expansionism in the Italian peninsula. Lewis Innes, principal of the Scots College in Paris and one of the exiled court's most important advisors, was warned from Rome: 'assure yourself wee would crucifie Christ agine to be revenged of the French'.[32] During his reign, James had largely ignored the advice ('slow, calm, and moderate courses') of the official cardinal-protector, Philip Howard (popularly known as Cardinal Norfolk), in preference for the counsels of his queen's uncle and contemporary, Rinaldo, Cardinal d'Este;[33] in November 1687, he had replaced Howard with d'Este as cardinal-protector.[34] In January 1689, Father William Leslie, resident in Rome for forty years, predicted that 'his Majestie may seeke help from this place, but sure will obteane none'.[35] In early February 1689, James selected his vice-chamberlain, Colonel James Porter, as his special envoy to plead his

Croissy, 2 July 1689, Turin. In January 1690, Melfort informed James II that 'the house of Austria . . . persecutes your Majesty's interest with all ye ill nature imaginable, even to that degree as to print that abominable letter the Emperor sent last to your Majesty, in which he reflects on your conduct as the cause of your own misfortunes and this war'. BL Add. MSS 37,360, f. 59v: Melfort to James II, 17 January 1690, Rome.

30   Scottish Catholic Archives (SCA), Edinburgh, BL 1/123/14: Lorenzo Leslie to Charles Whyteford, 26 July 1689, Rome.

31   Bruno Neveu, 'Jacques II, médiateur entre Louis XIV et Innocent XI', *Ecole Française de Rome: Mélanges d'Archéologie et d'Histoire* 79 (1967), 699–764.

32   SCA, BL 1/129/9: Lorenzo Leslie to [Lewis Innes], 26 April 1689, Rome.

33   Gilbert Burnet, *History of My Own Times* (Oxford, 1833), III, 78–9, quoting Cardinal Howard whom the future Anglican bishop met in Rome in the autumn of 1685.

34   Sir Henry Ellis, *Original Letters Illustrative of English History*, third series, IV (London, 1846), 313: Sunderland to [John Caryll], 4/14 November 1687, Whitehall; SCA, BL 1/115/5: James Lawrence Leslie to Charles Whyteford, 6 April 1688, Rome: The Jesuits 'stryves to do him [Cardinal Howard] all the mischief and is alleaged caused the King to take the title of protectour from him and give it to Cardinal d'Este which I asur you has mortified him'.

35   SCA, BL 1/123/17: William Leslie to Charles Whyteford, 18 January 1689, Rome.

case in Rome, where he arrived on 28 February. Porter resided and conferred with d'Este.[36] Despite a papal audience of three and a half hours, Porter came up against a stone wall: 'On Saturday last [16 April] . . . parted from hence Collonel Porter, but without any help at all from his Holynesse for either our King or Catholikes, his H. alledging that he hass to doe with his mony to defend this estat against the French.'[37] Porter left Rome leaving Cardinal d'Este as James II's unofficial representative, but with 4000 crowns sent by Cardinal Howard.[38]

While contending with the indifference or barely concealed hostility of his fellow Catholic princes abroad, James also had to contend with the scepticism of the French court. The powerful Louvois was convinced that James had little or no support in England;[39] his younger brother, Charles Maurice Le Tellier, archbishop of Rheims, openly ridiculed James 'avec un ton ironique: "Voila un fort bon homme; il a quitté trois royaumes pour une messe" '.[40] The foreign minister, Charles Colbert, marquis de Croissy, knew James from his earlier service as French ambassador to England, when he had predicted that the 'zeal inflexible et precipité' of the Duke of York would cause France great trouble.[41] Indeed, of those closest to Louis XIV, only Jean Talon, *secrétaire du cabinet* from 1670 until his death in November 1694,[42] and – much more importantly – Louis's morganatic wife, Françoise d'Aubigné, marquise de Maintenon, were sympathetic to James. From the moment of her arrival in France, Mary of Modena shrewdly set out to cultivate this powerful and intelligent woman, and

---

[36] Porter's instructions of 4 February 1689 are found in Bodleian, Carte 209, ff. 11–16, and are printed in Charles Gérin, 'Le Pape Innocent XI et la révolution anglaise de 1688', *Revue des Questions Historiques* 14 (1876), 477. Porter's mission is noted in a series of letters found in SCA, BL 1/123–6 *passim.*

[37] SCA, BL 1/123/19: William Leslie to Charles Whyteford, 19 April 1689, Rome; in the same letter, Leslie described Porter as 'a most reasonable, most capable, and most well enclined man'.

[38] AAE, CP Angleterre 168, ff. 166–7: Melfort to Croissy, 7 May 1689, Dublin; BL Add. MSS 37,360, ff. 21v–22v: Melfort to Lewis Innes, 21 December 1689, Rome: in this letter, Melfort labelled Porter 'a drunkend neglector of affaires'.

[39] HMC *Seventh Report*, 339: Letter from Paris [to Dykevelt], 20/30 December 1688: 'Le Marquis de Louvois auroit dit . . . hier qu'il y avoit trois partis en Angleterre sans qu'il en eust aucun pour le dit Roy [James]', apparently referring to Whigs, Tories, and a third party headed by the Earl of Halifax.

[40] La Fayette, *Mémoires*, 148.

[41] *Calendar of State Papers, Venice*, XXXVII (1671–72), 226, fn. quoting Croissy's letter to Louis XIV, 21 April 1672.

[42] Talon was a longtime friend of Lewis Innes and the Scots College, and a financial supporter of Catholic missions in Britain: in August 1688 a priest in London had spoken of Talon's 'incomparable charitie and bountie towards us': SCA, BL 1/111/4: Alexander Dunbar to Innes, 16 August 1688, London.

they were soon having private conferences.[43] Although Maintenon frequently referred to the queen as 'cette sainte Reine', she shared the irritation of her husband's ministers at what they regarded as the Jacobite court's total lack of secrecy.[44]

From the beginning, Versailles attempted to control Jacobite intrigue and diplomacy in so far as possible. Jacobite diplomats not only were subsidised by the French government, but were expected to confer with their French counterparts at their place of posting. In some cases, their primary energies were directed towards serving French rather than Stuart interests. Toby Bourke, who later served as James III's ambassador to Madrid from 1705 to 1712, also acted as a secret agent for the French war minister, the marquis de Chamillart, for 6000 *francs* per annum.[45] Rigorous censorship was imposed on any Jacobite publications printed in France.[46] Postal surveillance of Saint-Germain's correspondence was maintained, as was a strict rule that all aliens (including Jacobite agents) entering and leaving France had to have passes from Versailles. This requirement remained a continual problem: one Jacobite exile arriving at Calais on the Dover packet boat in May 1689 told the local commandant that 'I intended too make my Court at St Germans', an explanation which resulted in his confinement:[47] 'No English entering ye town without a pass from the King of France.'[48] Four months later, another agent reported to Lewis Innes from Calais that 'Our Governour sais he can't let me goe to England without a Passport, therefore I beg the continuance of your favour to Monsieur Tallon about it, that I may have it in readyness, tho' I never use it.'[49] The problem only worsened as French distrust of the Jacobites grew; in 1691, James Porter, acting as James's 'ambassador' to Versailles, complained that Croissy had given him only five passes 'that least concerned my Master's

[43] Martin Haile, *Queen Mary of Modena, Her Life and Letters* (London, 1905), 245, quoting Rizzini to the Duke of Modena, 2 March 1689.

[44] *Miscellanies of the Philobiblon Society* 13 (1871–72), 65: Mme de Maintenon to maréchal de Villeroy, 11 December 1716, Saint-Cyr; Emile Raunié (ed.), *Souvenirs et correspondance de Mme de Caylus* (Paris, 1889), 166–7; Mme de Caylus was Mme de Maintenon's niece.

[45] Valentine Emmanuel Patrick, Marquis MacSwiney of Mashanaglass, *Two Distinguished Irishmen in the Spanish Service: Sir Toby Bourke and Dr John Higgins* (Dublin, 1939), 5–6.

[46] AAE, CP Angleterre 170, ff. 6–7: de la Reynie to Croissy, 6 February 1689, Paris, refusing to print a French version of a letter from Melfort which raised 'une question odieuse': that the 'Pope can excommunicate or depose kings that are of another religion or contrary to the interests of his own religion.'

[47] SCA, BL 1/122/1: Andrew Hay to Lewis Innes, 30 May 1689, Calais.

[48] SCA, BL 1/128/1: J.B. to Lewis Innes, 17 June 1689, Calais.

[49] SCA, BL 1/120/9, 11: R. Clerke to Lewis Innes, 9 August, 1 September 1689, Calais.

service . . . All the rest . . . were all positively refused.'[50] The requirement to obtain French passes often hindered what the Jacobite court considered urgent business.[51]

The greatest point of contention, however, between Versailles and Saint-Germain concerned the quality of Jacobite intelligence, especially from England. The propensity of the exile community to gross exaggeration of the slightest favourable news alarmed the French court. In the spring of 1689, Charles Whyteford, assistant principal of the Scots College in Paris and a lifelong associate of Lewis Innes, assured his Roman correspondent that 'Sir John Fenwick, Sir Theophil Ogilthorp & several others are raising men in the North & declare for their true King . . . My Lord Preston, Lord Griffin, Collonel Graheme & many more are joyned to them . . . daily several, nay whole regiments flock to them . . . as for Scotland we heard that all unanimously are for the King.'[52] This Jacobite propensity for wishful thinking was to last throughout the Stuarts' residence in France, much to the irritation of the court of Versailles.[53] By the spring of 1689, Louis XIV was convinced that French intelligence from both England and Scotland was clearly superior to anything being received by the court of Saint-Germain.[54]

Most distressing to the French court, however, was the fact that very few men of ability – and even fewer Protestants – had joined James II in exile. The most prominent Protestant was Sir Edward Herbert, whose brother Arthur had commanded William III's fleet in 1688. Herbert, as lord chief justice of the king's bench, had endorsed the dispensing power in *Godden v. Hales* (1686) and had subsequently served on the illegal ecclesiastical commission. As a Protestant, however, he was never fully trusted by James and was never a member of the inner councils of Saint-Germain.[55] The outstanding figure

---

[50] Westminster Diocesan Archives (WDA), London, Browne MSS, f. 201: James Porter to [Henry Browne], 1 April [1691], Mons; cf. f. 75: Sir James Geraldine to Sir Edward Hales, 16 March 1691, Dunkirk.

[51] BL Add. MSS 37,611, f. 169: Melfort to James Scott, 15 December 1692, complaining that it sometimes took eight days to obtain passes.

[52] SCA, BL 1/126/15, 16: Charles Whyteford to William Leslie, 28 March, 4 April 1689, Paris. Whyteford displayed a blind faith that Louis XIV would restore James II against all odds and all enemies.

[53] Sourches, XI, 269–70, entry for 14 February 1709 with news at Saint-Germain that Queen Anne was dead 'mais souvent les nouvelles de cette cour-là n'étoient pas trop certaines'.

[54] *Négociations de M. Le Comte d'Avaux en Irlande, 1689–1690* (Dublin, 1934), 241: Louis XIV to d'Avaux, 24 May 1689, Versailles; hereafter referred to as D'Avaux.

[55] When Herbert (created titular Earl of Portland in 1692) died in November 1698, Matthew Prior, secretary of the British embassy, recorded: 'they [the Jacobite court] pretend to be sorry for his death, though they despised and neglected him when alive, for he remained a Protestant, so

at Saint-Germain-en-Laye was John Drummond, Earl of Melfort. With his elder brother, James Drummond, Earl of Perth, Melfort had converted to Roman Catholicism soon after James II's accession in 1685 and subsequently Perth and Melfort – as lord chancellor and secretary of state respectively – had established a virtual condominium over Scotland. Melfort, because of his office, was primarily resident in London and consequently participated in James's English councils as well. Eight days before James II first attempted to escape, Melfort fled London on 3/13 December ('and has they say abundance of money with him') and landed at Ambleteuse on 6/16 December.[56] Melfort immediately notified his friend, Father Lewis Innes (who had met Melfort both in London and in Scotland) of his arrival; Innes in turn promptly wrote to Jean Talon and, on the morning of 10/20 December, the *secrétaire du cabinet* personally informed Louis XIV (who was still in bed) of Melfort's arrival.[57]

Initially, the French welcomed Melfort: as the only obvious candidate they endorsed James II's decision to make him his principal minister in exile. As Louis XIV later recorded, even though the English, the Scots and the Irish seemed united in their hatred of Melfort, in the early spring of 1689 he seemed better suited than anyone else to give James II good advice.[58] Versailles's goodwill soon evaporated. Not only was Melfort insatiably ambitious, but he was also excessively suspicious and vindictive towards his enemies, real and supposed. Even James II admitted that Melfort 'avoit deux deffauts essentiels aux Escossois, qui sont d'estre fort colleres, et extremement jaloux de la moindre chose'.[59] Finally, Melfort zealously pursued those policies which he knew best appealed to his master, and was absolutely opposed to James II making any concessions whatsoever towards his rebellious subjects: 'God Almighty forbid that the King be restored by Composition with the People' was his motto[60] and it was his authorship of James II's uncompromising declaration to the Convention of the Estates of Scotland in April 1689 which

none of his services were held meritorious, and his good works went for nothing for want of faith'. HMC *Bath* III, 285: Prior to James Vernon, 8 November 1698, Paris.

[56] HMC *Hastings* II, 201–2: Elizabeth, Countess of Huntingdon, to Earl of Huntingdon, [3 December 1688, London]; cf. BL Add. MSS 72598, n.f.: Newsletter, 3/13 December [1688], London; for his arrival, Dangeau, II, 231: entry for 16 December 1688.

[57] SCA, BL 1/118/12: Talon to [Lewis Innes], 20 December 1688, Versailles.

[58] D'Avaux, 166–7: Louis XIV to d'Avaux, 16 March 1689, Versailles. Louis's favourable opinion of Melfort was undoubtedly influenced by the fact that Melfort had been virtually alone among James II's advisors in urging the king to flee to France: AAE, CP Angleterre 170, ff. 15–16: Lewis Innes to [Croissy], 13 March 1689, Paris.

[59] *Ibid.*, 437: d'Avaux to Croissy, 30 August 1689 NS, Dublin, quoting James II.

[60] BL Add. MSS 37,360, f. 74v–75: Melfort to Queen Mary, 24 January 1690, Rome.

destroyed what small hope there was for a peaceful restoration in the northern kingdom.[61]

To the French, the first logical move seemed to be an invasion of Ireland, where James's lord-lieutenant, Richard Talbot, Earl of Tyrconnell, had managed to maintain his government and his dominion over most of the island. Louis had earlier toyed with the idea of French intervention there with a view to making Ireland a satellite state;[62] if a Stuart restoration was impossible in Great Britain, as seemed probable, a permanent Franco-Jacobite presence in Ireland would hinder British participation in a continental war against France. James II, encouraged by Melfort, argued for an immediate invasion of either Scotland or England. Like the Stuarts before and after, James regarded the Celtic kingdoms as merely stepping stones to the great prize, the English throne. He was totally uninterested in Ireland. Louvois, with the rest of Louis XIV's ministers, was adamantly opposed to any attack on Scotland or England until Ireland had been completely secured, warning Melfort that a precipitate invasion could lose James all three kingdoms.[63] To demonstrate the importance he attached to the campaign, Louis XIV appointed one of his most accomplished diplomats, Jean-Antoine de Mesmes, comte d'Avaux (who had just completed nine years at The Hague, the diplomatic centre of Europe) as his ambassador-extraordinary to accompany James to Ireland, providing d'Avaux with 500,000 *livres* to finance the effort. Louvois, who was suspicious of James's abilities and was convinced that the expedition could be conducted on the cheap, sent only 'des plus mediocres officiers des troupes du Roi'.[64] James could barely conceal 'his disappointment of men, money, and arms from the French king'.[65] Madame de La Fayette concluded that the departure of James II for Ireland did not leave Louis XIV with any great hopes of seeing him restored to his throne. James had quickly been summed up by the French for what he had become: 'c'est a dire un homme enteté de sa religion, abandonné d'une maniere extraordinaire aux jesuites. Ce n'eut pas eté pourtant son plus grand défaut à l'égard de la Cour;

---

[61] Daniel Szechi, 'The Jacobite Revolution Settlement, 1689–1696', *English Historical Review* 108 (1993), 612–13.

[62] HMC *Seventh Report*, 337: Preston to Halifax, 20 September 1682, Paris: 'I believe this King [Louis XIV] would be very glad to possess himself of a country [Ireland] so advantageously situated for his designs, but whether or no he will endeavour to do it so hastily is what is to be considered.'

[63] Rousset, *Louvois*, IV, 192: Louvois to Melfort, 13 April 1689.

[64] La Fayette, *Mémoires*, 158.

[65] HMC *Eighth Report*, App. II, 399: Architel Gray to Sir Philip Gell, 28 February 1689, London, relaying intelligence reports from Brest.

mais il estoit faible, et supportut plutot ses malheurs par insensibilité que par courage.'[66]

The expedition began badly. Even before departing Brest on 7/17 March 1689, d'Avaux complained to Croissy of James's inability to keep secrets, and his propensity to speak of everything to everyone.[67] During the voyage, d'Avaux found James disorientated, plagued by irresolution and changing his mind constantly, not always for the better. 'Il s'arreste aussy beaucoup à des petites choses, ou il employe tout son temps et passe legerement sur les plus essentielles.'[68]

From the beginning, the Irish campaign proved a débâcle, not least because from the beginning James II was convinced the expedition was a folly.[69] D'Avaux's instructions were to do everything to promote religious reconciliation between Irish Protestants and Catholics;[70] instead, James presided over an overwhelmingly Catholic parliament in Dublin, whose anti-Protestant legislation was manna from heaven for Williamite propagandists in London. In England, it was claimed that 'All things in Ireland are governed by the French Ambassador, as if Ireland were the French King's, and King James under him.'[71] In reality, d'Avaux's position could hardly have been more difficult. He found himself refereeing continual struggles between the Irish nationalists, led by Richard Talbot, newly created Duke of Tyrconnell, and James II's English and Scottish advisors, headed by Melfort. Because French objectives were closer to those of the native Irish, d'Avaux naturally sympathised with Tyrconnell, while Melfort continually fed James II's 'strange jealousy' of the French, shamelessly flattering the king by assuring him that he was so well loved by his subjects that he needed only to appear somewhere in England or Scotland to make them lay down their arms.[72] In May 1689 Melfort presented

[66] La Fayette, *Mémoires*, 161.

[67] James Hogan (ed.), *Négociations de M. Le Comte d'Avaux en Irlande (1689–1690)*, supplementary volume (Dublin, 1958), 6: d'Avaux to Croissy, [14] March 1689, Brest; cf. 32: d'Avaux to Louvois, 30 October 1689, Ardee.

[68] D'Avaux, 23–5: d'Avaux to Louis XIV, 23 March 1689, Kinsale.

[69] *Ibid.*, 379: d'Avaux to Louis XIV, 14 August 1689, Dublin, quoting James II.

[70] *Ibid.*, 1–6: 'Memoire du Roy pour servir d'Instruction au Sr. Comte d'Avaux', 11 February 1689, Marly.

[71] HMC *Fifth Report*, 345: Charles Thompson [surgeon-general of Ireland] to Henry Gascoigne [secretary of the Duke of Ormonde], 9 April 1689, Chester; cf. HMC *Ormonde*, new series, VIII, 18–19: Thompson to Gascoigne, 13 April 1689, Chester: 'Ireland is put into French Government, and it is believed given to that King. Everything is ordered by the Count d'Avaux, and all the revenue in the possession of the French, and French officers expected daily to take possession of the army.'

[72] D'Avaux, 104–5, 109–13: d'Avaux to Louis XIV, 27 April, 6 May 1689.

d'Avaux with a memorandum urging an immediate invasion of Scotland or England, based not on particular assurances of support there, but on a general confidence that James's subjects loved him: 'I well believe there are many of them who have been duped by the Prince of Orange and are discontented with his conduct, but I do not know if that suffices to dare to count on them', d'Avaux sensibly commented.[73] By the end of June, even James was lamenting Melfort's lack of ability and had decided to replace him. In d'Avaux's opinion, the decision came none too soon: Melfort, he reported to Louvois on 10 July, was hated by everyone, especially by the despairing French commander, General Rosen, who complained 'qu'il ne lui étoit possible de pratiquer avec un homme qui n'avoit ni foi ni parole et qui ne dit pas un mot de vrai'.[74]

By this time, Louis XIV and his ministers had lost what little hopes they may have had for Jacobite success in Ireland. As early as 13 June, Louvois had noted darkly that if James II was driven from Ireland, 'il ne rentrera jamais en Angleterre'.[75] He was soon seconded by Louis XIV, who on 20 July informed d'Avaux that James II's irresolution on all important matters had ruined his chances of retaining Ireland.[76] As he had done in 1688, James II refused to believe Louis XIV's warning that the English were preparing for an invasion of Ireland, and in early August was thunderstruck by news from Chester that maréchal de Schomberg was there with an army of 20,000 men, preparing to embark.[77] On 22 August, the day James II left Dublin for Drogehda to head the army against Schomberg, Melfort left Dublin, having been assured by James II's confessor that a cabal of Tyrconnell and other Irish officers intended to assassinate him.[78]

Melfort, who sailed as James II's official envoy to the court of France,[79] returned to Saint-Germain in September 1689 to discover that Mary of Modena had assumed an importance which she had never had before the Revolution. In light of her husband's lethargy and his physical absence from France, the queen, with virtually no experience, had assumed the central political role in the court of Saint-Germain, one which she was to maintain for the

[73] *Ibid.*, 136: d'Avaux to Louis XIV, 16 May 1689, Dublin.

[74] Rousset, *Histoire de Louvois*, IV, 206–7: d'Avaux to Louvois, 10 July 1689.

[75] *Ibid.*, 203–4: Louvois to d'Avaux, 13 June 1689, Versailles.

[76] D'Avaux, 414–17: Louis XIV to d'Avaux, 20 July 1689, Versailles.

[77] *Ibid.*, 350–1: d'Avaux to Louis XIV, 9 August 1689, Dublin.

[78] For Melfort's departure, National Library of Scotland (NLS), Edinburgh, MSS 14,226: Journal of David Nairne, introduction; Nairne was Melfort's secretary. For the assassination plot, D'Avaux, 507–14: d'Avaux to Croissy, 21 October 1689, Ardee.

[79] George Hilton Jones, *The Mainstream of Jacobitism* (Cambridge, MA, 1954).

remainder of her husband's life and her son's regency. The queen exercised considerable influence with Louis XIV (always susceptible to feminine appeals) and Madame de Maintenon, but unfortunately she was vulnerable to political adventurers, particularly to Melfort and the comte de Lauzun to whom she attributed her safe escape from England. After James II's departure for Ireland, Lauzun had advised the queen to press Louis XIV to have control of the war taken out of Louvois's hands and placed in those of Jean-Baptiste Colbert, marquis de Seignelay, the naval minister.[80] Well aware of the tenor of d'Avaux's dispatches concerning her husband, she increasingly welcomed Lauzun's insinuations that his presence in Ireland, rather than that of d'Avaux, would soon rectify matters. Tyrconnell, among others, warned the queen that Lauzun's appointment would offend all career officers in Ireland, that Lauzun was a bitter enemy of Louvois, 'and Mons. De Louvois is soe too, which I fear will cost us dear, for if that man be against us, what can we expect from thence but delayes if not denayalls?'[81] Having consented to petition her husband for Melfort's recall,[82] Mary managed to extract Louis's reluctant agreement to reinforce James II. Against his better judgement, in September Louis promised that by December he would send an additional 6000 French infantry, and 7000 or 8000 arms and other supplies, for which he asked in return for 6000 Irish recruits. Louvois, in notifying d'Avaux that Lauzun would replace Rosen, spoke of 'la douleur avec laquelle le Roy voit les mauvaises mesures que l'on a prises au pays où vous estes, et l'apparence qu'il y a qu'on en va voir des fruits bien amers'.[83]

The French were furious with James II's reluctance to part with his Irish troops, but in November 1689 both d'Avaux and Rosen were formally recalled to France.[84] D'Avaux responded with a long letter of bitter complaints of James II's irresolution, his inability to administer, and – above all – his unwillingness to hear bad news.[85]

---

[80] Duke de La Force, *Lauzun* (Paris, 1919), 174.

[81] Latian Tate (ed.), 'Letter Book of Richard Talbot', *Analecta Hibernica* 4 (Dublin, 1932), 101: Tyrconnell to Queen Mary, 20 October 1689 NS, Camp at Ardes; for ministerial hatred of Lauzun, see La Fayette, *Mémoires*, 141.

[82] D'Avaux, 514–15: Louvois to d'Avaux, 17 September 1689, Marly.

[83] *Ibid.*, 516–22: d'Avaux to Louvois, 21 October 1689, Ardee; 585: Louvois to d'Avaux, 11 November 1689, Versailles. Louis's lack of confidence in James II's ultimate success was conveyed to his representatives in Rome: Gabriel Hanotaux and Jean Hanoteau (eds.), *Receuil des instructions données aux ambassadeurs et ministres de France: Rome II (1688–1723)* (Paris, 1911), 100: Louis XIV to Cardinal de Forbin, 15 May 1690, Versailles.

[84] D'Avaux, 585: Louvois to d'Avaux, 11 November 1689, Versailles.

[85] *Ibid.*, 543–57: d'Avaux to Louis XIV, 24 November 1689, Dublin.

By the end of the year, Schomberg's army had managed to occupy virtually all of Ulster and thus acquired a springboard for the next year's campaign. Incredibly, however, James II continued to press the French for an immediate invasion of England, making it the touchstone of French sincerity. From Ireland, Tyrconnell opined that if France did not immediately transport James II to England, where conditions appeared so favourable, 'I . . . must conclude we are only destined to serve a present turne, and att last be a sacrifice to our enemies.'[86] On 22 October, after his return from Ireland, Melfort had a long conference with Louvois to explain why the time was ripe for an invasion of England, but Louvois proved evasive. Seignelay was even more adverse to the prospect of hazarding the French fleet than Louvois. Louis XIV proved reluctant to risk the loss of his fleet against those of the combined Maritime Powers.[87] Louis repeatedly refused James's demands that an invasion be launched from Ireland, convinced that those who thus advised James were inspired by William III, who wished James to make a fatal mistake.[88] James II was equally convinced that the French ministers had been consistently wrong in their assessments of English affairs.[89]

By April 1690, Louvois was predicting privately to Louis XIV that if God did not perform a miracle in favour of James II, 'I fear the Prince of Orange will conquer Ireland much more easily than he imagines.'[90]

Lauzun, whose instructions were to avoid battle and to fatigue the enemy, arrived in Ireland in mid-May 1690 (a month before William III) with 7380 French troops. He promptly informed Louvois that James II's court 'is a chaos similar to that in Genesis before the creation of the world'.[91] Lauzun soon denounced James's principal advisors as anti-French, and even before the Franco-Jacobite army met that of William III, both he and Tyrconnell realised that defeat was inevitable.[92]

The battle of the Boyne, so crucial to Ireland's future, was fought on 1/11 July 1690; in reality, it was less a battle than a rout of an ill-trained, poorly supplied Franco-Jacobite force. James II, to the lasting disgust of the French, fled the field of battle, returning to Dublin where he only spent three hours,

---

[86] Tate, 'Letterbook', 104: Tyrconnnell to Queen Mary, 27 November 1689 NS, Dublin.

[87] Bodleian Library, Carte MSS 181, ff. 369–80: Melfort to James II, 25 October 1689, Saint-Germain.

[88] D'Avaux, 648–50: Louis XIV to d'Avaux, 4 January 1690, Versailles.

[89] BL Add. MSS 37,360, f. 78v: Melfort to Queen Mary, 24 January 1690, Rome, citing James II.

[90] Rousset, *Louvois*, IV, 381–2: Louvois to Louis XIV, 6 April 1690.

[91] Duc de La Force, *Lauzun* (Paris, 1919), 174–5.   [92] *Ibid.*, 177, 180–1.

and on 3/13 July sailed from Kinsale to Brest. To the local *intendant* who greeted him there, James did not appear at all concerned at the disastrous state of his affairs: 'le roi d'Angleterre paroit aussi insensible au mauvais etat de ses affaires, que si elles ne le regardaient point; il raconte ce qu'il sait en riant et sans aucune alteration'. James also assured him that the English people were entirely for him: 'Ce pauvre prince croit que ses sujets l'aiment encore!'[93] Maréchal de Luxembourg aptly summarised the attitude of the French king and court: 'Those who love the King of England should be very happy to see him in safety', he told Louvois, 'but those who love his *gloire* will much deplore the personage he made.'[94]

Incredibly, immediately after his return to Saint-Germain, while Lauzun and Tyrconnell were struggling to extricate themselves from the mess he had left behind in Ireland, James appealed to Louis to launch an immediate invasion of England with 10,000 infantry and 2000 horse and dragoons, claiming improbably that public opinion there was overwhelmingly in his favour.[95] Louis XIV's refusal was peremptory: he demanded that a Jacobite rebellion in England should be underway before France undertook any invasion.[96] 'On ne croit pas icy un mot de tout ce que nous disons', Queen Mary complained bitterly to Lauzun, 'et on n'a voulu escouter aucune de nos propositions pour faire une descente en Angleterre devant que le Prince d'Orange y retourne'.[97] For the next year, the Jacobite court was to find its proposals routinely rejected by Versailles.

Instead, Saint-Germain looked to Rome for aid, both financial and diplomatic. Innocent XI, so fiercely anti-French, had died on 12 August 1689, and the election of his successor, Alexander VIII, on 6 October served as a plausible excuse to send Melfort into another sort of political exile. Like subsequent representatives to Rome, Melfort was in French pay and subject to French

---

[93] Grovestins, *Histoire*, VI, 231: M. Foucault to [?Louvois?], 25 July 1690, Caen.

[94] Rousset, *Louvois*, IV, 423: Luxembourg to Louvois, 25 July 1690.

[95] A.W. Thibaudeau (ed.), *Catalogue of the Collection of Autograph Letters and Historical Documents formed . . . by Alfred Morrison*, first series, I (London, 1883), 332–3: James II to duc de Lauzun, 10 August 1690, Saint-Germain (hereafter cited as Thibaudeau, *Morrison Collection*). Thomas Bruce, Earl of Ailesbury and a leading English Jacobite, agreed that if a French army had been sent to England in the summer of 1690, it would have been successful (*Memoirs of Thomas, Earl of Ailesbury* (Roxburghe Club, London, 1890), 257–8); however, other evidence suggests that the overwhelming loyalty of the public lay with the government: HMC *Fitzherbert*, 27–8: Sir John Elwell to Sir George Treby, 21, 23, 28 July 1690 OS, Exeter.

[96] F.W. Head, *The Fallen Stuarts* (Cambridge, 1901), 71–7.

[97] Thibaudeau, *Morrison Collection*, first series, IV (London, 1890), 164: Mary of Modena to duc de Lauzun, 13 August 1690, Saint-Germain.

orders.[98] Melfort reported not only to Croissy, but also corresponded with Louvois, Seignelay and Talon and frequently consulted the French ambassador, the duc de Chaunes.[99] Melfort, who had no greater wish than to return to Saint-Germain at the first opportunity and realising the new-found political importance of Queen Mary, did everything in his power to cultivate her uncle, Cardinal d'Este. On his arrival in Rome in December 1689, Melfort absolutely refused to be accompanied to his papal audience by Cardinal Howard, and was later chagrined to discover that Alexander VIII (like Innocent XI before him) treated the latter as though he were still Protector of England rather than d'Este.[100] Melfort's hostility to Cardinal Howard may have stemmed in part from his instructions from Croissy, that while d'Este had been faithful to James II's interests, Howard had been lukewarm and, more importantly, had opposed French interests at Rome.[101]

Melfort quickly discovered that the Austrian interest in Rome was, if anything, stronger under the new pope than under the old. His instructions were to gain papal influence with Catholic princes on James II's behalf, as well as to secure financial assistance for the Irish campaign, which Alexander VIII had already refused to d'Este: 'if he should give it to ye King, the Emperor & family of Austria would look upon it as an indirect helping of France'.[102] Melfort was no more successful: in his first audience of the pope on 19 December, he was met with a flat refusal of money, and the assertion that peace was impossible at that time.[103] The pontiff ignored not only Stuart appeals on great matters, but their claims on small ones as well (Melfort was particularly disturbed when Alexander VIII made his nephew, Cardinal Ottoboni, Grand Prior of Ireland without consulting James II, who was still in that kingdom).[104] On the question of money, the pope later relented, giving a total of 30,000

[98] Gérin, 'Innocent XI et la révolution anglaise de 1688', 476. Melfort received 9000 *livres* annually in 'gratifications': AAE, CP Angleterre 171, f. 165: Order for payment, 11 October 1689; cf. 172, ff. 77, 188: similar orders of 4 January 1691, 2 April 1692.

[99] See Melfort's letter books for this embassy, BL Add. MSS 37,360 and BL, Lansdowne 1163 A, B & C *passim*. Even before his departure from Saint-Germain, Louvois predicted that Melfort's embassy would end in failure: BL Add. MSS 37,360, f. 96: Melfort to Louvois, 31 January 1690, Rome.

[100] BL Add. MSS 37,360, f. 14: Melfort to Cardinal d'Este, 17 December 1689, Rome; BL, Lansdowne 1163A, ff. 22v–24: Melfort to Queen Mary, 14 March 1690, Rome.

[101] Bodleian Library, Carte 181, ff. 353–8: Croissy's Mémoire for Melfort, September 1689.

[102] BL Add. MSS 37,360, f. 5: Melfort to Queen Mary, 13 December 1689, Rome.

[103] *Ibid.*, ff. 15–18: Melfort's speech to Alexander VIII, 19 December 1689; ff. 18v–21: Melfort to Queen Mary, 21 December 1689, Rome.

[104] BL, Lansdowne 1163A, ff. 29v–31: Melfort to Cardinal d'Este, 18 March 1690, Rome.

crowns (partly in March, partly in July 1690) for the relief of specific English, Scottish and Irish Catholics named by the papacy,[105] hardly the munificent papal bounty routinely described by Williamite propagandists. Melfort also noted that no cardinal, apart from Howard and d'Este, volunteered to give any money to James II.[106] 'I am doing all I can here, and that to no great purpose', Melfort informed James II's Jesuit confessor, 'the hearts here are harder than marble'.[107]

As early as February 1690, Melfort asked to be recalled,[108] but the continued hostility of the French ministers (especially Louvois) was such that the queen found it impossible. Melfort was bitterly disappointed when he was not summoned back upon James II's return to France, and in October 1690 appealed to both the king and the queen to secure his return,[109] again without result. In November, Melfort complained that France failed to pay him regularly because the ministers were convinced his stay in Rome was useless;[110] and one sympathetic observer noted of Melfort and his wife that 'as to their own table it is rather the table of a poor Religious man than of a King's minister'.[111] As Father William Leslie of the Scots College, Rome, noted: 'All the help that wee have gotten, is a number of faire and bonnie Words, well trimmed compliments, Wishes, protestations of earnest desyrs of our good and prosperitie . . . Which all in true and plaine language is to say, *Wee will not help you, and wee would willingly wish you should be so simple as to beelieve, that we cannot help you, and that wee doe well not to help you.*'[112]

French resistance to his recall and the death of Alexander VIII on 1 February 1691 served to keep Melfort in Rome.[113] The new pope, Innocent XII, was not elected until 12 July, and at the end of that month Melfort's *lettre de congé* was dispatched from Saint-Germain. When Melfort left Rome at the beginning

---

[105] BL, Lansdowne 1163B, ff. 96v–97: Melfort to Queen Mary, 22 July 1690; f. 126v: Melfort to Father Anthony Lucas, 12 August 1690, Rome.

[106] *Ibid.*, f. 11: Melfort to Father John Warner, 6 June 1690, Rome.

[107] Sir Henry Ellis, *Original Letters Illustrative of English History*, second series, IV (London, 1827), 190: Melfort to Father Maxwell, 23 April 1690, Rome.

[108] BL Add. MSS 37,360, f. 110: Melfort to Queen Mary, 14 February 1690, Rome.

[109] BL, Lansdowne 1163B, f. 132: Melfort to Innes, 26 August 1690; Lansdowne 1163C, ff. 84v–86: Melfort to Innes, 28 October 1690, Rome.

[110] BL, Lansdowne 1163C, ff. 105–7: Melfort to Innes, 11 November 1690, Rome.

[111] SCA, BL 1/131/13: Lorenzo Leslie to Charles Whyteford, 23 December 1690, Scots College, Rome.

[112] SCA, BL 1/131/116: William Leslie to [Lewis Innes], 18 November 1690, Rome.

[113] BL Add. MSS 37,662, f. 40: Melfort to Henry Browne, 3 March 1691, Rome.

of September 1691, the prospects for French support of a direct invasion of England appeared to have improved immensely.[114]

After James II's ignominious return from Ireland in July 1690 the French court – beneath the veneer of formal courtesy – had treated him with profound indifference, and began to drop hints abroad that they 'would be glad of a peace, and that the interests of the late King James should be no obstruction to it'.[115] Although James and Mary joined the French court in September for its annual excursion to Fontainebleau, an accompanying English courtier complained there was 'all this while not a word of England or anything that looked like thinking wee deserved ever to goe back'.[116] James II was particularly hurt by Louis XIV's refusal to allow him to accompany the French king to the siege of Mons in the spring of 1691.[117] In part, French disdain sprang from the universal conviction that the court of Saint-Germain was rife with spies, particularly when the English government was successful in apprehending a number of Jacobite agents: even Melfort reflected that it was 'most scandalous that no man goes from St Germains but is taken, this is such a misfortune that I am tempted freely to beleeve foul play'.[118] To compound matters, the Stuart court was notoriously indiscreet.[119] Furthermore, the French

[114] Bodleian, Carte 181, f. 426: James II to Innocent XII, 30 July 1691, Saint-Germain; BL Add. MSS 37,622, f. 263v: Melfort to Henry Browne, 4 September 1691, Rome.

[115] BL, Lansdowne 1163C, ff. 7v–8: Melfort to Lewis Innes, 2 September 1690, Rome: 'There are storys which show me that ye King has many unfriends [sic] at ye Court of France.' HMC Finch I, 438: Nottingham to Sir Robert Southwell, 30 August 1690 NS, Whitehall, citing a reported conversation between Croissy and the Venetian envoy in Paris; HMC Downshire I, 368: Nottingham to Sir William Trumbull, 13 February 1691, The Hague: 'It is certain that France has . . . insinuated its desire of a peace and to a degree as to hint also that (notwithstanding the pretended kindness to the late King) the interest of their Majesties should be no obstruction to it.'

[116] BL Add. MSS 37,622, f. 4v: Col. Robert Fielding to Henry Browne, 19 October 1690, Paris; cf. HMC Hastings II, 219: P. Barchman to Earl of Huntingdon, 8 August 1690 OS, London: 'King James diverts himself with hunting and good meat and drink, and leaves the King of France to study how he shall get his three Kingdoms again.'

[117] Lord Acton (ed.), 'Letters of James the Second to the Abbot of La Trappe', Miscellanies of the Philbiblon Society 14 (1872–76), 9: James II to abbé de la Trappe, 26 March 1691, Saint-Germain.

[118] BL, Lansdowne 1163B, f. 44v: Melfort to Lewis Innes, 1 July 1690, Rome. Even Madame de Maintenon believed that Mary of Modena was surrounded by spies: Raunié, Souvenirs . . . de Mme de Caylus, 166–7. Many English Jacobites were convinced that the court of Saint-Germain 'had many pensioners to England amongst them' and 'swarms of spies': Ailesbury Memoirs, 275, 316.

[119] In 1693, the assistant principal of the Scots College in Paris assured his Roman correspondent that 'Our court at St Germains imitat that at Versailles, that is, not a word of newes is spoken there, if this method had been kept from ye beginning, things would have been better.' SCA, BL 1/168/11: [Charles Whyteford] to Walter Lorenzo Leslie, 4 May 1693 [Scots College, Paris].

ministers were rapidly discovering that Jacobite intelligence from England and Scotland left a great deal to be desired; as late as January 1692, James II admitted to Louis XIV that 'je ne me flatte point sur mes Intelligences en Angleterre'.[120] Jacobite correspondence was routinely intercepted in the post by the British government and sent to Dr John Wallis, professor of mathematics at Oxford, who deciphered it; according to Wallis, the Jacobites 'were so little acquainted with the intricate methods of intelligence that their ciphers were easily discovered and their designs as easily prevented'.[121] In addition, there was James II's continued and patently unwise reliance on his priestly advisors, particularly those of the Society of Jesus: 'Plus les Français voyerient le roi d'Angleterre, moins on le plaignant de la perte de son royaume: ce prince n'était obsédé que des jesuites.'[122] In January 1691, Lord Preston was arrested in London while secretly embarking for France, carrying a paper described as 'the result of a Conference between some Lords and Gentlemen both Torries and Whigs' which, among other things, declared that Louis XIV 'must over-rule the Bigotry of St Germain . . . for there is one silly thing or other done daily there'.[123]

Nationalism also played its part in souring Franco-Jacobite relations. Courtiers at Saint-Germain had been less than discreet in publicly regretting English naval defeats at French hands in 1689 and 1690, something which had particularly galled Louvois.[124] As for the exiles, there was a widespread suspicion, as Henry Browne, secretary of state, informed James II in 1691, that 'ye King of France played ye Game he dos to ruin your Majesty's King-doms'.[125] In London, Jacobite refugees from the Irish war were outspoken in their anger: 'They all profess mighty duty to K. James and say they wou'd have spent their last drop of blood in his Cause', Lewis Innes was informed, 'but that they perceived the French King was playing his own game, and intended the ruine of that Country [i.e., Ireland] and not the Restoring of K. James. They say they have gone through wonderfull hardships, and yet will gladly

---

[120] BL, Lansdowne 1163c, ff. 66–9: Melfort to Lewis Innes, 14 October 1690: 'I pitty you for not having good intelligence from Scotland and England at a time when it is of such importance'; Bodleian Library, Carte 181, ff. 438–44: draft, James II to Louis XIV [January 1692].

[121] HMC *Downshire* I, 610: Dr Robert Gorge to Sir William Trumbull, 6 January 1696, St John's, Oxford, quoting Dr Wallis.

[122] La Fayette, *Mémoires*, 149.

[123] *The Arraignment, Trials, Conviction and Condemnation of Sir Richard Grahme, Bart . . . and John Ashton, Gent. for High Treason . . .* (Published by Her Majesty's Special Command, London, 1691).

[124] Rousset, *Louvois*, IV, 197; Ellis, *Original Letters*, second series, IV, 196: Melfort to Queen Mary, 12 August 1690, Rome.

[125] WDA, Browne MSS, f. 103: [Henry Browne] to James II, 29 September 1691, Saint-Germain.

serve K. James but they threaten nothing les than ruine to the falce [*sic*] French King.'[126]

Three events helped alter the intentions of the French court in James II's favour. First, on 3 November 1690, the naval minister, Seignelay, suddenly died; he was replaced by Louis Phélypeaux, comte de Pontchartrain, a more indolent and less influential minister who had little appreciation of the possibilities of naval power. Then on 16 July 1691, the great war minister Louvois suffered a fatal heart attack immediately after leaving Louis XIV's private study. Louvois had not only been the French king's most influential minister, but had also been the strongest opponent to further military aid to James II. (His successor, his ineffectual son Barbezieux, none the less 'was ever a bitter enemy to King James's interest'.[127]) Even after Louvois's removal from the scene, Louis XIV remained ambivalent about the prospects of a Stuart restoration.[128] In October 1691, the Treaty of Limerick was signed which brought the Irish war to an end. Under its lenient terms, the triumphant Williamite government allowed the French to evacuate not only their own troops but also those Irish troops which had supported them. As a result, between November 1691 and January 1692, some 19,059 Irish officers and soldiers (not counting their wives and children) sailed from Shannon, probably giving Louis XIV a total of 30,000 Irish soldiers in his service (who were quickly to become famous as the 'White Geese').[129] The sudden availability of these forces would make an invasion of England feasible without depleting France's armies on the Continent.

It was at this point that Melfort returned to the court of Saint-Germain. At Rome, by assiduously serving Cardinal d'Este, he had gained the queen's favour, and James II had never lost his fondness for him.[130] His return was ecstatically welcomed by the Catholic party at court. His friend Sir Edward Hales assured him that 'you will be necessary on many publick accounts & amongst others to clense ye Court of Protestants (the likelyest to be Spyes) who are dayly plotting & Caballing against Roman Catholicks, even in a Catholick Kingdom & in ye King's pallace'.[131] Melfort clearly recognised the

[126] SCA, BL 1/135/6: [Sir Robert Clerke] to [Lewis Innes], 22 December 1691 [OS, London].

[127] *Ailesbury Memoirs*, 285.

[128] Arsène Legrelle, *Notes et documents sur la paix de Ryswick* (Lille, 1894), 7: Louis XIV to Cardinal Janson, 6 August 1691.

[129] John Cornelius O'Callaghan, *History of the Irish Brigades in the Service of France from the Revolution in Great Britain and Ireland under James II to the Revolution in France under Louis XVI* (Glasgow, 1870), 29.

[130] SCA, BL 1/124/5: Father Maxwell to [Lewis Innes?], 27 November 1689 OS, Dublin.

[131] WDA, Browne MSS, f. 67: Sir Edward Hales to Melfort, 4 February 1691, Saint-Germain.

weakness of James II's party in Great Britain and the absolute necessity of securing French support if a Stuart restoration was to be achieved: 'Nothing is more against the King's interest', he wrote in March 1691, 'than to do anything without advice and participation of France, for its in vayne to flatter our selves, the King cannot be restored except by force so long as the Prince of Orange lives.'[132] In order to ensure that French participation, Melfort, now restored as secretary of state, was prepared to stop at nothing. Saint-Germain had already recognised the importance of controlling, or at least interpreting, news from England which reached Versailles. '[Take] a little care to consider what is strictly proper to give in to these [French] ministers', James Porter, who had accompanied Louis XIV to the siege of Mons in the spring of 1691, warned Henry Browne, 'for our Master's circumstances require such precaution'.[133] His first act was to order all Jacobites to correspond with Versailles only through him, 'et on n'eut que des extraits des lettres qu'on voyait auparavant en original'.[134] This was particularly important because during the autumn of 1691 a number of William III's most prominent advisors were surreptitiously establishing contact with the exiled court. Jacobite agents in London had interviews with, among others, Sidney, Lord Godolphin, first lord of the treasury; Charles Talbot, Earl of Shrewsbury, secretary of state; John Churchill, Earl of Marlborough and William's leading English general; and Edward Russell, admiral of the fleet. The protestations of these ministers were suspiciously similar: each man regretted his role in the events of 1688, reiterated his allegiance to James II, and promised to support a restoration 'when the time is right'.[135] The reports of these conversations were now forwarded to Versailles in translated excerpts, rather than in the original. Melfort, in his interpretations, stressed particularly the role of Admiral Russell, suggesting that he would desert along

---

[132] WDA, Old Brotherhood III (3), f. 239: Melfort to Sir Edward Hales, 24 March 1691, Rome; Melfort's sentiments were echoed in a slightly different way by a Jacobite speaking of English army officers: 'The English hate him [William III] & will certainly dis-serve him when occasion is offer'd, not that I would have you think these men have any Love for their true King (for they are all perjured Rogues) but they dos not love this man so that in effect K[ing] J[ames] must depend upon ye King of France's assistance & without it I am confident nothing will be done.' SCA, BL 1/140/13: 'Harrison' [Henry Morgan] to Lewis Innes, 20 October 1691 OS, London.

[133] BL Add. MSS 37,662, ff. 72v–73: James Porter to Henry Browne, 7 April 1691, camp before Mons. Porter had replaced Lord Waldegrave upon the latter's death in January 1690 as James II's envoy extraordinary to Louis XIV: AAE, CP Angleterre 172, f. 32: James II to Louis XIV, 18 February 1690, Dublin.

[134] Anthonine Villien, *L'Abbé Eusèbe Renaudot* (Paris, 1904), 52.

[135] J.S. Clarke (ed.), *The Life of James II . . . collected out of memoirs writ of his own hand* (London, 1816), II, 444–50; for the composition of these memoirs, see Edward Gregg, 'New Light on the Authorship of the *Life of James II*', *English Historical Review* 108 (1993), 947–65.

with his fleet to the French rather than oppose an invasion attempt on behalf of James II. There can be little doubt that this consideration, above all
others, finally prompted Louis XIV to agree to an invasion proposal, detailed
work for which began immediately. On 15 December, James II left Saint-
Germain for Brittany to review the Irish troops arriving there, returning on
11 January 1692.[136]

In a memorial written by Melfort and submitted to Louis XIV soon after his
return, James II painted the rosiest possible picture of the degree of Jacobite
support in England, claiming that 'there are ten who would not take oaths
of fidelity to the Usurper, to one who has taken them'.[137] Preparations began
almost immediately for the transportation to England of a French army of
30,000 men, including 13,000 Irish troops. The army was to be commanded
by maréchal de Bellefonds and the fleet by the comte de Tourville.[138] On
20 April 1692, Louis XIV paid a visit to Saint-Germain to bid farewell to
James, and the next day the exiled king went to La Trappe and from there
to Normandy under the strictest secrecy. At the same time a proclamation
was drawn up for publication and distribution in England before the French
fleet sailed: the proclamation, which excluded twenty-five leading Whigs and
Tories (as well as the Faversham fishermen who had foiled James's first escape
attempt in 1688) from any hope of a royal pardon, was uncompromising and
unconciliatory, concluding that 'if any of our Subjects shall after all this remain
so obstinate as to apear in arms against us . . . they must need fall unpitied under
the Severity of our justice'. James himself regarded this declaration as 'much
more indulgent than could reasonably have been expected, considering the
provocations the King had received from all ranks of people'.[139] News of the
intended invasion reached London on 22 April/2 May, when distribution of
the disastrous proclamation began, and public opinion immediately began to
rally behind the government. The Dutch resident, L'Hermitage, believed that
if James succeeded in landing, it was doubtful that he would be supported
by more than 2000 people throughout the kingdom, especially if he was

---

[136] Dangeau, III, 442; V, 8; O'Callaghan, *History of the Irish Brigades*, 30.

[137] James Macpherson (ed.), *Original Papers containing the secret history of Great Britain from the
Restoration to the accession of the House of Hanover* (London, 1775), I, 399; for the general reliability
of Macpherson's transcriptions, see Gregg, 'New Light', 956–7.

[138] The most complete account of the invasion attempt is that of Philip Aubrey, *The Defeat of James
Stuart's Armada 1692* (Leicester, 1979).

[139] The proclamation, dated 20 April 1692, Saint-Germain, is printed in Clarke, *Life of James II*, II,
479–88, along with James's comments.

accompanied by French and Irish soldiers, the two nations most hated by the English.[140]

James, accompanied by Melfort, proceeded to Cherbourg, where they discovered that Tourville's fleet had been badly damaged by storms. Nevertheless, James and Melfort confidently asserted that half of the English ships would desert to the French. Not believing this information, Tourville twice appealed to Versailles, but on 13 May Louis XIV dispatched positive orders to Tourville to engage the combined Anglo-Dutch fleet, commanded by Russell, on the strength of James's repeated assurances.[141] The result was the battle of Cape La Hogue (19–24 May), in which Tourville was out-numbered two to one. France's Atlantic fleet was virtually destroyed in what was, until then, the greatest military disaster of Louis XIV's long and glorious reign. James (who resignedly attributed the catastrophe to the hand of God)[142] sent Melfort in person to Louis XIV, who was besieging Namur, to explain what had happened and to secure Louis's permission for James to join him for the land campaign.[143]

It was with some trepidation that Melfort approached the French king with news of 'this misfortune': although permission for James to join the French army was denied, Melfort claimed that 'the King of France took the whole matter infinitely better than he would have expected' and promised that 'the matter was only retarded by this accident, he being resolved never to abandon him [James II] or his cause, & that he hop'd to be yet in a condition to furnish him with Ships & men sufficient to restore him &c.'.[144] Some credulous Jacobites believed that Louis XIV had ordered 'all the Carpenters

[140] Grovestins, *Histoire*, VI, 316–18, 323: L'Hermitage's dispatches of 22 April/2 May, 26 April/6 May, 3/13 May 1692, London; Bodleian Library, Carte 76, ff. 197–8: Newsletter to Earl of Huntingdon, 23 April 1692 OS, London: 'Last night some seditious Papers in the nature of a Declaration were scatter'd about the streets.'

[141] Thibaudeau, *Morrison Collection*, first series, III (London, 1888), 238: Louis XIV to James II, 13 May 1692, Compiègne; cf. the comments of the duc de Saint-Simon in Dangeau, IV, 98.

[142] Lord Acton (ed.), 'Letters of James the Second to the Abbot of La Trappe', *Miscellanies of the Philobiblon Society* 14 (1872–76), 15: James II to abbé de la Trappe, 9 July 1692.

[143] John Agnus Skeet (ed.), *Stuart Papers, Pictures, Relics, Medals, and Books in the Collection of Miss Maria Widdrington* (Leeds, 1930), 13: Queen Mary to [duc de Lauzun], 6 June [1692], Saint-Germain: 'I tremble for fear least he should not be permitted to do what his reputation and the welfare of his affairs demand of him [i.e., join Louis XIV in the French army].'

[144] WDA, Browne MSS, f. 119: Lewis Innes to Sir Edward Hales, 15 June 1692, Saint-Germain, quoting Melfort; Mary of Modena accepted Melfort's account of Louis XIV's obliging reception at Namur: Falconer Madan (ed.), *Stuart Papers Relating Chiefly to Queen Mary of Modena* (London, 1889), I, 15: Mary of Modena to Sister Priolo, 14 June [1692], Saint-Germain.

of the Kingdome to fall at working and to have 30 great Ships ready for the
next Spring, for he is resolv'd to revange this afront in spite of all the world
to reestablish our gratious King'.[145] As L'Hermitage remarked of the Jacobites,
'La passion les aveugle.'[146]

The reality was that, beneath the condescending graciousness natural to
Louis XIV, the French king was furious: he believed that, inadvertently or
deliberately, he had been duped by fallacious Jacobite information. His resolution was absolute that henceforward nothing would be undertaken for the
Stuarts until a rebellion was actually underway in England or Scotland. Louis
adopted the policy which France would continue to pursue and which was
defined by the marquis d'Argenson fifty years later: France would favour the
Stuarts 'without spending too much or making too many sacrifices'.[147]

Shortly before his own departure from Saint-Germain for the coast, James
II had dispatched Sir John Lidcott on a diplomatic mission to Rome: Lidcott's
instructions were to obtain financial support for the invasion, as well as papal
diplomatic support with the Catholic princes of Europe. Lidcott left Saint-
Germain on 18 April and arrived in Rome on 3 May, having his initial audience
with Innocent XII (accompanied by Cardinal Howard) on 6 May.[148] The pope
pleaded financial exhaustion, but agreed to send a meagre 20,000 crowns for
the expedition: 'He has bin so teas'd by *ye House of Austria* that he is in a manner
forc'd to Trim, even contre cœur. Nay, so far, that even the *mony* mentioned
to me is, he said, to pass as *subsistence* for the poor *Catholicks* and Church
men.'[149] The political climate in Rome was patently unfavourable for French,
and consequently for Stuart, interests. 'Our rotten oranges in Rome', noted
one disgruntled Scottish priest, ruled the roost.[150] When news was received
of James II's arrival on the coast, 'A Jes[uit] the other day said in a cardinal's
anticamera, that the King of France had sent the K. of England to the butchery
come un'agnello innocete.'[151] While the blessed sacrament was exposed in the

[145] NLS, Advocates MSS 13.1.8., f. 5: Alexander Robertson to his mother, Lady Robertson, 5 July
1692, Dunkirk.
[146] Grovestins, *Histoire*, VI, 340: L'Hermitage's dispatch of 7/17 June 1692, London.
[147] E.J.B. Rathery (ed.), *Journal et mémoires du marquis d'Argenson* (Paris, 1859–67), II, 262: journal
entry for 3 September 1739.
[148] SCA, BL 1/150/7: Walter Lorenzo Leslie to Charles Whyteford, 6 May 1692, Rome. Abstracts
of Lidcott's correspondence with Melfort are printed in Macpherson, *Original Papers*, I, 416–20.
[149] Bodleian Library, Carte MSS 208, ff. 5–6: Sir John Lidcott to [Melfort], n.d. [6 May 1692,
Rome]; italicised words in cypher in original. Printed with slight variations, Macpherson,
Original Papers, I, 417.
[150] SCA, BL 1/150/17: Walter Lorenzo Leslie to Charles Whyteford, 19 August 1692, Rome.
[151] SCA, BL 1/150/10: Walter Lorenzo Leslie to Charles Whyteford, 27 May 1692, Rome.

national churches of France, England, Scotland, Ireland (SS Louis, Thomas, Andrew and Isidore), it was noted that 'no Roman cardinals came ever to any of them because they knew it was for the King of England. Let your court of St Germans reflect upon this, and then draw their consequences', Lewis Innes was warned.[152] After the disaster at La Hogue, Lidcott reported that Innocent XII had given up any prospect of ever seeing James II successfully restored,[153] and he left Rome in August to return to Saint-Germain, his mission largely fruitless.[154]

Jacobite representation at Rome henceforward was to remain in the hands of Cardinals Howard and d'Este, although there was little they could do when the reigning pontiff regarded James II as 'a weak man who lets himself be guyded by men [the Jesuits] who are the cause of his being turned out of kingdomes'.[155] Cardinal Howard was openly defeatist: having received orders from James II to solicit a papal pension of 30,000 *livres* quarterly, 'his Eminence said to one after reading his letters that he knew the Pope neither would or could give the said mony, & that it would be in vain to ask it'.[156] Howard died on 17 June 1694. Cardinal d'Este, who increasingly had devolved his English responsibilities on his associate, Monseigneur Alexandro Caprara, was regarded by the French as increasingly Austrian in sympathy, as was Caprara. When d'Este became England's sole official representative upon Cardinal Howard's death, Father William Leslie warned Lewis Innes that 'its perfectly known that he is a great Imperialist: and the French takes it very ill, as also that Mgr. Caprara should treat our affairs'.[157] 'To make Caprara the man to compeir with such commissions', complained another Scottish priest in Rome, 'will give the French a great jealousie, for they hold him for an Imperialist.'[158] Cardinal d'Este's position was transformed, however,

---

[152] SCA, BL 1/150/13: Walter Lorenzo Leslie to [Lewis Innes], 8 July 1692, Rome. Sir John Lidcott informed Melfort: 'Many here pretend at least great inward zeal in their prayers for *the King*. But if they do pray, they indeed do it so as not to be seen of men, either in their closets or, perhaps, the primitive grottoes and catacombs.' Macpherson, *Original Papers*, I, 419.

[153] Bodleian Library, Carte MSS 208, ff. 21–2: Sir John Lidcott to Melfort, 22 July 1692, Rome.

[154] AAE, CP Angleterre 172, ff. 440–1: James II to Cardinal Janson, 16 August 1694, Saint-Germain: writing of Lidcott's 1692 mission, James said 'mais quand nous vismes que ses sollicitations ne faisoient aucun effect auprez du Pape, nous creumes devoir le rappeller pour sauver une depense inutile'.

[155] SCA, BL 1/175/10: Walter Lorenzo Leslie to Charles Whyteford, 23 March 1694, Rome.

[156] SCA, BL 1/173/4: Walter Innes to Lewis Innes, 9 March 1694, Rome.

[157] SCA, BL 1/178/9: William Leslie to [Lewis Innes], 10 August 1694, Rome.

[158] SCA, BL 1/176/1: [Walter Lorenzo Leslie] to Charles Whyteford, 1 June 1694, Rome. In August 1694, Cardinal Janson, the French ambassador, told Father William Leslie 'that our King & his interest was actually betrayed at this Court . . . & for example specified Mr Caprara, & his

when on 6 September 1694 Francesco II, Duke of Modena (Queen Mary's only brother) died without children, and was accordingly succeeded by his uncle, the cardinal. Duke Rinaldo, as he now became, quickly resigned the cardinal's hat which had been procured for him by James II (Rinaldo had never taken holy orders), married a daughter of John Frederick, Duke of Brunswick-Lunebourg-Hannover (who was closely allied to the house of Habsburg)[159] and himself became increasingly anti-French and detached from Stuart interests. As the court of Saint-Germain was warned in 1694, 'All our Italians still conclude that seeing the obstinate rage of the English nation against France, and the witt of the Prince of Orange to make them still continue the war notwithstanding all their losses, its folly to think that the said English will ever call home our Sovereign.'[160] By 1696, even the court of Saint-Germain realised that no significant Roman aid would be forthcoming during Innocent XII's reign, and David Nairne, *premier commis* of the secretary of state, sadly noted that 'I have orders now to reduce ye Roman corespondence to as small expenses as possible.'[161]

Melfort, eager to distance himself from the disaster of La Hogue, flatly denied having had a hand in James II's April 1692 declaration: 'it was not of my making & I never gave my Consent to ye publishing of it nor was it done by authority'. He later asserted (as did the author of the latter part of the *Life of James II*) that the declaration had been drawn up by Sir Edward Herbert to please Protestants.[162] Such protestations did little to fool anyone, including the French. From the moment of his return to Saint-Germain, Melfort had seized control of virtually all business. There is no evidence that Herbert was ever consulted on any point of significance, much less composing a political manifesto. The declaration is remarkably similar in wording to memoranda Melfort wrote earlier, and an eye-witness, Thomas Sheridan, later recorded that 'The declaration then published in England was his sole contrivance, without the privity of the King's confessor.'[163]

Eminence added that when & how long the Court of Saint-Germains took such measures, or made use of such Methods, the Court of Versailles could neither confyd or communicate their Secrets or intentions therunto unless they would have their ennemies as well as their friends know their desyns': SCA, BL 1/174/6: Walter Innes to Lewis Innes, 17 August 1694, Rome, quoting Father Leslie.

[159] In 1699, his daughter Amalia would marry the emperor's eldest son and heir, the king of the Romans, who in 1705 would be elected as Emperor Joseph I.

[160] SCA, BL 1/177/14: William Leslie to [Lewis Innes], 13 April 1694, Rome.

[161] SCA, BL 2/17/16: David Nairne to William Leslie, 20 February 1696 [Saint-Germain].

[162] BL Add. MSS 37,661, ff. 2v–3v: Melfort to Sir Robert Clerk, 4 July 1692; f. 13: Melfort to Earl of Ailesbury, 1 August 1692; Clarke, *Life of James II*, II, 488.

[163] HMC *Stuart* VI, 64: Thomas Sheridan's 'An Historical Account' [1702].

It was clear to Louis XIV that the court of Saint-Germain (and especially Melfort) had to be taken into hand, and the task fell to the foreign secretary, Croissy, who in turn relied on his principal authority on English affairs, the abbé Eusèbe Renaudot, editor of the *Gazette de France* from 1679. Renaudot had a considerable command of the English language, and had numerous personal contacts in England. He believed early on that the principal reason for the lack of Jacobite success was the complete isolation from reality of the court of Saint-Germain. In Renaudot's opinion, most of James II's councillors were devoted, but ill prepared to take on their roles.[164] As early as September 1692, Renaudot had suspicions of Melfort's ultimate loyalties.[165]

The first test came in November, when the French proposed that James try to undo the pernicious effects of the April declaration by issuing a conciliatory one along the lines of Charles II's 1660 Declaration of Breda. On 1 November, Melfort submitted a proposed draft to Versailles, in which James promised that, on his restoration, he would leave to a 'free' Parliament the 'security of the Church of England by law established' and 'the case of Dissenters and the settlement of liberty of conscience'; in other words, proposing that James promise what England had already secured under William III.[166] Both Croissy and Renaudot realised that such a document was inadequate, and on 23 November Croissy presented Melfort with his own draft, which had James promising 'to agree to any laws, that shall be desired at our hands to secure the Protestant religion, as now established by law in the Church of England'; even more objectionable to a guarantee of a religion in which James did not believe was the further promise 'to secure liberty and property, not only from any mal-administrations that may fall in during our reign, but likewise against any invasion [that] may be designed by our posterity'.[167] Melfort immediately drew up a counter-proposal which omitted the offending language and again vaguely promised 'a free Parliament, to which we will leave the settlement of the Protestant religion'.[168] The upshot was that James II declined to

---

[164] Anthonine Villien, *L'Abbé Eusèbe Renaudot* (Paris, 1904), 49; cf. François Duffo, *Correspondance inédite d'Eusèbe Renaudot avec le Cardinal François-Marie de Médicis (années 1705, 1706, 1707)* (Paris, 1915), xi.

[165] *Archives de la Bastille, documents inédits*, ed. François Ravaisson, ix (Paris, 1887), 362, 387: Renaudot to Pontchartrain, 14 September, 8 November 1692.

[166] Macpherson, *Original Papers*, i, 425–30: 'E. Melfort's project of a letter from his Majesty to the parliament, 2 November 1692'.

[167] *Ibid.*, 430–1: 'Project of a letter to be sent to England, 23 November 1692, proposed by Mr. de Croissy'.

[168] *Ibid.*, 431–2: 'Project of a letter to be sent to England, thought more proper than the other, proposed by the most Christian King, 23 November 1692, St Germain'.

send any declaration whatsoever, alleging that his English supporters advised against it.[169]

This refusal angered Renaudot, who a few days later produced for Croissy a complete indictment of the mismanagements of Saint-Germain, alleging that James II's advisors had lost the trust of all the best people in England, who would now rather trust Louis XIV and the French ministers.[170] On 28 November, Renaudot informed Croissy of his suspicion that Melfort was transmitting French and Jacobite secrets to William III.[171] In early December 1692, Melfort admitted to a sceptical Renaudot that he had been remiss in not sending Croissy and Pontchartrain all the intelligence he had received from Great Britain.[172] (What Melfort did not add was that he had used his control over what Jacobite reports were sent to Versailles to make them more palatable, a practice the French had long suspected.[173])

Croissy was as unimpressed by Melfort as was his subordinate, informing Renaudot on 15 December that Melfort 'm'a fait confidence de beaucoup de bagatelles que je ne crois pas'.[174] Among other tools at Renaudot's disposal was the careful postal surveillance which had been maintained over the court of Saint-Germain ever since James II's arrival in the kingdom. In January 1693, he discovered that Melfort's letters to England urged Jacobites there to be prepared for an invasion in March, and that the English government had made use of this to secure parliamentary financing for the forthcoming campaign.[175] In light of this, Croissy and Renaudot pinned their hopes on James II's agreement to send a special envoy to his Protestant supporters in England, particularly to Charles, Earl of Middleton. Middleton was a Scot,

---

[169] Ibid., 433–40: (draft) [James II to Louis XIV], November 1692.

[170] Archives de la Bastille, ed. Ravaisson, IX, 369–77: Renaudot to Croissy, n.d. [c. 26 November 1692].

[171] Ibid., 377–9: Renaudot to Croissy, 28 November 1692. Each Jacobite principal minister in turn was accused of being in the employ of the British government: Edward Gregg, 'The Politics of Paranoia', in Eveline Cruickshanks and Jeremy Black (eds.), The Jacobite Challenge (Edinburgh, 1988), 42–56. No evidence has been found that Melfort was acting as a double agent.

[172] Ibid., 384–5: Renaudot to Croissy, 6 December 1692, Paris.

[173] Bodleian Library, Carte 209, ff. 105–6, an undated, unaddressed letter in Melfort's hand: 'As to the Magnifieing or dimmishing [sic] your accounts of our friends, you must doe in that as you shall think best for our Service.' Endorsed by David Nairne: 'Instructions to Pouel (I believe) after ye La Hogue busines'. For another example of Melfort's editing to change the tenor or hide the sources of his correspondence, see Carte 181, ff. 566–7: 'Propositions faits par Messrs. Le Comtes de Montgomery, Ailesbury, Yarmouth, Le Chev. Fenwick, le Sieur Jenkins, et autres', 21 February/3 March 1694.

[174] Archives de la Bastille, ed. Ravaisson, IX, 386: Croissy to Renaudot, 15 December 1692, Versailles.

[175] Ibid., 392: Renaudot to Croissy, extract of a letter from London of 30 December/9 January 1692/3, London.

but there his resemblance to Melfort ended. Middleton was a man of honour and integrity, had extensive political experience as secretary of state both in Scotland and in England (from August 1684 to December 1688), 'and his affection and firmness to Protestancy was never once suspected'.[176] Middleton, who accompanied James II to Rochester before he fled the country, advised the king to retire to the Spanish Netherlands 'but by no means would not have him go into France'.[177] Middleton subsequently refused to swear the oaths to William and Mary and had embarked on Jacobite intrigue, becoming the leader of the 'compounders', those Jacobites who realised that only the most far-reaching concessions could make James II's restoration possible. During the invasion scare in May 1692, Middleton was arrested and imprisoned in the Tower, where he remained until August.

The agent selected by Saint-Germain to contact Middleton was a Roman Catholic priest, Father Edward Cary.[178] Cary returned to France with a list of eight demands (including an unambiguous promise to 'protect and defend the Church of England', to recommend establishment of liberty of conscience to Parliament, and to submit the dispensing power to parliamentary limitation). Middleton agreed that if James II accepted these demands and incorporated them into a new declaration, he would leave England and take up residence at Saint-Germain. James baulked at promising to 'protect and defend the Church of England' and was backed up by his confessors:[179] they unanimously advised the king that he risked his immortal soul in promising to maintain a heresy and its institutions. They insisted that the words 'members of' should be inserted into any such guarantee, thereby diluting its effectiveness as far as the compounders in England were concerned. Despite this, Louis XIV insisted that James accept the proposed declaration, the implicit threat being that France would withdraw its support if he did not.[180] (After the event, Melfort solicited the opinion of five French clerics, including the famous Bossuet, bishop of Meaux; unfamiliar with the issues involved and perhaps influenced

---

[176] Charlwood Lawton, *A French Conquest Neither Desirable nor Practicable, dedicated to the King of England* (London, 1693).

[177] WDA, Old Brotherhood III (3), f. 259: Conversation between Sir Edward Hales and James II, 13 October 1694, Saint-Germain.

[178] Clarke, *Life of James II*, II, 498, 501, mentions only his surname; he is identified in Joseph Gillow, *Bibliographical Dictionary of the English Catholics* (London, 1885), I, 415–16.

[179] Those consulted included Father Lewis Innes, almoner to the queen and principal of the Scots College, Paris; Francis Sanders, SJ, confessor to the king and later one of his biographers; Father Francis Fenwick, chaplain to the queen; and Dr John Betham, later preceptor to the Prince of Wales.

[180] Noailles, *Maintenon*, IV, 518.

by their own government, they all accepted the declaration without demur.[181])
As James later explained his acceptance, France had been so devastated by the
war that 'should the King have refused those proposals how hard soever they
apear'd, the clamor of the whole Country would have been so great his Most
Christian Majesty could not have been able to have resisted it, and probably
the King would have been sent out of the Kingdom as an opiniatre bigot'.[182]
His demands accepted, Middleton surreptitiously left England in disguise in
March 1693, then proceeded to Saint-Germain. He first appeared publicly at
Versailles on 16 April, when Louis XIV granted him a long audience. On 17
April, the Declaration was formally signed and subsequently published, and
on 23 April Middleton was named joint secretary of state with precedence
over Melfort.[183] Not only the Compounders but also the French had scored a
victory over the Catholic party at Saint-Germain.[184]

None the less, it quickly became clear that James II, in agreeing to the 1693
declaration, had made only a tactical surrender. At Saint-Germain, Melfort
continued to rule the roost, in part because the great majority of Jacobites there
were his Catholic co-religionists, in part because he continued to monopolise
the ears of both the king and the queen. Within three months of Middleton's
appointment, Renaudot was again complaining to Croissy about the lack of
business being given to him.[185] In June 1693, Louis XIV and his ministers
reached a crucial decision: France was prepared to enter into a peace based
on a *de facto* recognition of William III, although Louis expressly refused to
repudiate James II's claims or to expel him from France, either to Avignon or to
Rome.[186] One sign of Louis's new policy was an apparent drop in the number
of encounters between the French and Jacobite courts after 1693.[187] Peace

---

[181] François Gaquère (ed.), *Vers l'unité chrétienne: James Drummond et Bossuet, leur correspondance
(1685–1704)* (Paris, 1963), 116–17: Bossuet to Cardinal de Janson, 23 May 1693; cf. 118–22:
Bossuet's 'Preuves du sentiment de M. L'évêque de Meaux sur la Déclaration du roi
d'Angleterre', 22 May 1693; Clarke, *Life of James II*, II, 508–10.

[182] Clarke, *Life of James II*, II, 505.

[183] Dangeau, IV, 266, 271: entries for 16, 23 April 1693.

[184] Szechi, 'Jacobite Revolution Settlement', 620–2; Jones, *Mainstream of Jacobitism*, 31–5; George
Hilton Jones, *Charles Middleton: The Life and Times of a Restoration Politician* (Chicago, 1967),
246–54.

[185] *Archives de la Bastille*, ed. Ravaisson, IX, 417–21: Renaudot to Croissy, 13 July 1693.

[186] Mark A. Thomson, 'Louis XIV and William III, 1689–1697', in Ragnhild Hatton and J.S.
Bromley (eds.), *William III and Louis XIV: Essays 1680–1720 by and for Mark A. Thomson*
(Liverpool, 1968), 24–48; cf. Claude Nordmann, 'Louis XIV and the Jacobites', in R.M. Hatton
(ed.), *Louis XIV and Europe* (London, 1976), 86–7; Head, *Fallen Stuarts*, 76.

[187] Bruno Blasselle, 'Les relations entre les cours de Saint-Germain-en-Laye et Versailles', in Edward
Corp (ed.), *La Cour des Stuarts à Saint-Germain-en-Laye au temps de Louis XIV* (Paris, 1992), 72.

feelers began to be put out through neutral courts, and by the end of the year the English government was in no doubt that France was prepared to recognise William as king, provided other matters could be adjusted satisfactorily.[188]

Although no formal announcement was made of this momentous policy decision, the courtiers at Saint-Germain soon became conscious of an increasing *froideur* on the part of Versailles, and they became correspondingly desperate, sending Croissy and Renaudot extracts of reports from England which became progressively more unrealistic.[189] On 1 October, Croissy (who increasingly appreciated the antipathy of the English towards the Jacobite cause) rejected Melfort's request for an invasion force of 30,000 men, citing the formidable logistical difficulties in transporting them to England and maintaining them in the field against the army of William III, 'suivy de toutte la nation'.[190] Melfort had justified the proposal by claiming that, among others, Danby, Godolphin, Marlborough, Shrewsbury, Admiral Russell, three dukes, four marquesses, twenty earls, three viscounts and eleven barons (approximately 25 per cent of the lay membership of the House of Lords), six Anglican bishops and four out of five Anglican clergymen were for James II, although Melfort admitted 'Il est vray que de tout cecy il n'y a point de preuves convaincantes.'[191] None the less, in his reply to Croissy's refusal, Melfort relied on the hope that Admiral Russell would be placed in command of the English fleet, the victor of La Hogue 'ayant promis absolument de servir le Roy si jamais le Commandement luy tomboit entre ses mains'.[192] It is difficult to conceive of an argument less calculated to succeed, when the French had been led to the ruin of their Atlantic fleet only a year earlier on the basis of the same claim. James II was more realistic, confiding in the abbé de la Trappe that there had never been less chance of his restoration, because Louis XIV could not send him across the Channel.[193]

---

[188] Grovestins, *Histoire*, vi, 418: Heinsius to William III, 21 December 1693, The Hague; Dorset Record Office (Dorchester), d/blx/x 40: Sir John Trenchard to John Robinson, 9 January 1693[4], Whitehall. News of Louis XIV's decision was reported in London newsletters in June 1693: Bodleian Library, Carte 76, ff. 229–30, 235–6: Newsletters to Earl of Huntingdon, 8, 13 June 1693 OS, London.

[189] For an example of this, see Bodleian Library, Carte MSS 181, ff. 529–34: Summary of reports from Sir George Barclay and Capt. Williamson, 28 December 1693, written in French to be forwarded to the French ministers.

[190] AAE, CP Angleterre 172, ff. 318–20: 'Memoire sur les difficultez qui se peuvent rencontrer dans l'Execution du projet du Roy d'Angleterre, remis à Mylord Melfort', 1 October 1693.

[191] *Ibid.*, ff. 343–63: Melfort to Croissy, n.d. [October 1693].

[192] *Ibid.*, ff. 329–37: Melfort to Croissy, 4 October 1693, Fontainebleau.

[193] Lord Acton, 'Letters of James II', 24–5: James II to abbé de la Trappe, 19 February 1694.

In England, those Compounders who had encouraged Middleton to go to Saint-Germain had lost all patience with the exiled court, and centred their discontent upon Melfort. The 1693 Declaration had done little to bolster Jacobite support, as its promises had already largely become reality under William III. Nor had Middleton's presence at court significantly altered the policies being pursued there. A resolution was taken to risk sending several envoys to France, even though such trips in wartime constituted high treason, in order to procure Melfort's dismissal. On 11/21 January 1694, while preparing to leave London, Sir James Montgomery, one of Melfort's leading critics, was arrested and placed in a messenger's custody. He managed to escape one week later and, accompanied by Sir Theophilus Oglethorpe, arrived at Saint-Germain by 31 January/10 February. Renaudot, for one, suspected that Melfort had been responsible for Montgomery's arrest.[194] Oglethorpe, in particular, set out to James II the complaints of his English and Scottish supporters concerning Melfort and their demands for his dismissal; the king demurred, saying that it was impossible because of the high regard in which Melfort was held by the French court![195] Yet the gossip at Saint-Germain held that Melfort's days were numbered. Charles Whyteford of the Scots College, Paris (who had obtained his information from Lewis Innes) assured his Rome correspondent that 'Midleton is generally beloved by all; sure is not Melfort . . . I fear ye last will fall, he hath noe friends but K[ing] &c.'[196]

James's intransigence concerning Melfort could not have come at a worse time. The financial strains imposed on France by the war, combined with a series of disastrous harvests, had created widespread public discontent, and much of it was focused on James II: 'It is inexpressible', it was reported from Rouen, 'how the people cry against him, openly cursing him, that his being there is the cause of their miseries.'[197] It was to be one of the few times that the general French population was not warmly supportive of the Stuarts, regarding them (as they did themselves) as martyrs for the faith.

In early April, Edward, Lord Griffin, a lifelong servant of James II, arrived at Saint-Germain to reside permanently, carrying anti-Melfort messages from the

[194] *Archives de la Bastille*, ed. Ravaisson, IX, 443–4, 446: Renaudot to Croissy, 5, 6, 10 February 1694.

[195] *Ibid.*, 452–3: Renaudot to Croissy, 5 March 1694.

[196] SCA, BL 1/172/6: Charles Whyteford to William Leslie, 22 March 1694, Scots College, Paris, quoting Innes.

[197] *Calendar of State Papers, Domestic* (hereafter *CSPD*), *1694–1695*, 173: extract of a letter from a French Huguenot to his wife, 15 May 1694, Rouen; cf. *CSPD 1695 & Addenda*, 253: Newsletter to the Earl of Derwentwater, 5 May 1694, London, quoting letters from Paris of 27 April/7 May: 'The people clamour at King James, and say he is the cause of the war and their starving.' An identical newsletter was sent on the same date to another Jacobite supporter, the Earl of Huntingdon: Bodleian Library, Carte 76, ff. 400–1: Newsletter, 5 May 1694, London.

king's friends in England.[198] Simultaneously, Thomas Bruce, Earl of Ailesbury, one of the leading Jacobite noblemen and an outspoken critic of Melfort, secretly visited France under the strictest incognito. In 1696, Sir John Fenwick confessed that Ailesbury 'told me at his coming back that he had been with the King of France in his Closett, and was a good while with him'. He told Louis XIV that the party in England hoped for an invasion of no fewer than 30,000 French troops: 'he told me the King heard him, but I do not find he brought back any encouragement'.[199] Although Ailesbury failed to obtain Louis's promise for an invasion, he was undoubtedly successful in tipping the balance against Melfort. Before the end of April, Croissy informally made it clear to the exiled court that Melfort had to go as he was 'repugnant to his Britannic Majesty's subjects'.[200]

The result was a month-long crisis at Saint-Germain during which Melfort, supported by the king and queen, dug in his heels. On 17 May, Melfort drew up a twenty-two-page 'memoir justificatif' in which he blamed his problems principally on Sir James Montgomery, who Melfort claimed had been encouraged to come to France by Abbé Renaudot, who had succeeded in turning Croissy against him.[201] The upshot was that on 26 May, through Croissy, Louis XIV publicly asked James II to withdraw Melfort as his envoy to Versailles, saying he could no longer accommodate himself to Melfort. James had difficulty in accepting this final humiliation, but Mary of Modena argued that if their first minister no longer pleased Louis, that was sufficient reason to dismiss him.[202] The following day, James reluctantly agreed to Melfort's dismissal,[203] although the French court was not satisfied until Melfort was exiled completely from Saint-Germain as well as Paris in the following month. Even then, James II retained his kindness for Melfort, but was forced to surrender further direct contact with him.[204] Through forcing the

---

[198] *Archives de la Bastille*, ed. Ravaisson, IX, 453–4: Renaudot to Croissy, 9 April 1694.

[199] BL, Lansdowne 488, ff. 10–16: Sir John Fenwick's Information taken by James Vernon, 23 September 1696. Griffin and Ailesbury may have travelled together: Griffin arrived at Saint-Germain on 7 April and Fenwick later placed Ailesbury's trip at 'Easter 1694' (11 April).

[200] Villien, *Renaudot*, 51; François Duffo, *Lettres inédites de l'abbé Eusèbe Renaudot au ministre J.B. Colbert, 1692–1706* (Paris, 1931), 13.

[201] Bodleian Library, Carte 209, ff. 150–61: 'Memoir justificatif du Comte de Melfort', 17 May 1694, Saint-Germain.

[202] Sourches, IV, 332: entry for 26 May 1694.   [203] Dangeau, V, 17: entry for 27 May 1694.

[204] Melfort apparently left Saint-Germain on 20 June and subsequently visited Moulin and Bourbon; on 13 September, he informed his successor as secretary, John Caryll, 'I am sensibly obliged to His Majesty for honoring me with his advice not to reside at Paris instead of sending me his Commands'; Melfort and his family established themselves in November at Orléans,

1693 Declaration and the dismissal of Melfort in 1694, Louis XIV had fully established his authority over both the policies and the personnel of the exiled court.

James II had few illusions about where he stood. He informed Cardinal Howard 'that he perceived underhand the King of France would leave him in the Lurch with excluding him in the Peace &c.'.[205] In Rome, Cardinal Albani (the future Clement XI) told William Leslie, in speaking of a possible peace settlement, that 'he was much affraid that our King & his interest would be sacrificed therin'.[206] Croissy adopted a high hand in dealing with Jacobite ministers, and took offence when Middleton called upon him at Versailles without being summoned. Through the intercession of Renaudot, the matter was smoothed over, Renaudot reporting that the king and queen were full of Croissy's praises and promised to have entire confidence in him in the future.[207] The French may well have discovered that, like Melfort, Middleton was not above editing Jacobite intelligence to make it more palatable to Versailles. The *premier commis* of Saint-Germain, David Nairne, noted in his private journal: 'I writt over fair E[arl] Arrans letter to ye K[ing] in french, taking out of it what was not fitt to be showen to ye K[ing] of F[rance] in which I was directed by E[arl] Mid[dleton].'[208]

The hopes of both Versailles and Saint-Germain were temporarily lifted at the end of 1694 when James II's elder daughter, Queen Mary II, died of smallpox in December. Her death left William III as sole monarch, with an heir apparent, Princess Anne of Denmark, who had a better hereditary claim to the crown than he did. In addition, Princess Anne had been publicly and bitterly estranged from her sister and brother-in-law for nearly three years. However, in the interests of the Protestant cause, William and Anne were coaxed by their advisors into a public reconciliation, although beneath the public façade the mutual antipathy between the two continued,[209] a fact which the French ministers quickly conveyed to Saint-Germain. Nicholas Dempster, an under-clerk in the secretary's office, sourly noted that 'Je ne suis point fasché que

---

where they remained for the duration of the war: Bodleian Library, Carte 209, ff. 200–2: Melfort to David Nairne, 20 June 1694, Paris; f. 238: Melfort to [John Caryll], 13 September 1694 [Bourbon]; f. 274: Melfort to Nairne, 23 November [1694], Orléans. Dangeau, VI, 228–9: entry for 17 November 1697.

[205] SCA, BL 1/173/16: Walter Innes to Lewis Innes, 29 June 1694, Rome; cf. *ibid.*, 1/174/1: Walter Innes to Lewis Innes, 6 July 1694, Rome.

[206] SCA, BL 1/174/5: Walter Innes to Lewis Innes, 10 August 1694, Rome, quoting William Leslie.

[207] Duffo, *Renaudot et Colbert*, 45: Renaudot to Croissy, 18 February 1695.

[208] NLS, MSS 14,266: Nairne journal, entry for 10 June 1695.

[209] Gregg, *Queen Anne*, 102–4.

cette nouvelle vienne de Versailles, où on n'est pas naturellement d'humeur à rien croire d'Angleterre qui nous soit avantageux.'[210]

The campaign of 1695, which militarily was William III's most successful during the Nine Years' War, saw France hard pressed to keep its armies in the field, let alone create new ones. Louis's ministers were more eager than ever to obtain peace. In the autumn, John Caryll complained to the Duke of Perth in Rome: 'Your Lordship has sometimes taken notice . . . how violently ye Italians are bent for a peace upon any terms without any consideration of us . . . ye ministers here are not one jott behind them in that point, they long & labour under hand incessantly for it, nor will our concerns be any *remora* [i.e., restraint] to ye Conclusion of it when ever a formall treaty is sett on foot.'[211]

During the summer of 1695, a promising conspiracy was formed in London and presented to James II by Robert Charnock on 17 June: the English Jacobites promised to furnish 2000 horse to assist a French army, which should consist of 10,000 men. An agent reported to the English government, that during the Stuart court's annual visit to Fontainebleau, 'King James begins to be a charge. He is ever talking of a revolution in England, the power of the Jacobites, and of what the new Parliament is going to do. But he finds no credit.'[212] Louis XIV, however, apparently reacted more positively than the report suggested, for Middleton wrote into England, 'I assure you wee have earnestly press'd the performance of the match [i.e., invasion], to which we found him as well dispos'd as wee could wish.'[213] Louis insisted, however, that French armed support would be forthcoming *only after* an armed rebellion was on foot in England. The English Jacobites either were not told this, or did not appreciate its significance, as they never had any intention of rising until French arms were at hand: Sir John Fenwick, for one, insisted 'he would not meddle with raising his Regiment 'till he heard King James was landed'.[214] The risks were too obvious: stormy weather, inept planning, or bad faith on the part of the French might delay the arrival of an invading force, giving the government

---

[210] SCA, BL 2/1/12: Nicholas Dempster to William Leslie, 14 February 1695 [Saint-Germain].

[211] Bodleian, Carte MSS 181, f. 627: Caryll to Perth, 3 October 1695, Saint-Germain; cf. BL, Add. MSS 79598, n.f.: Newsletter from Paris, 22 August 1695: 'Il est certain que les intérets du Roy Jacques ne seroit point un obstacle à la paix parcequ'il n'y a point de traitté qui engage notre Roy à faire pour luy plus que ce qu'il fait.'

[212] HMC *Downshire* I, 584–5: Intelligence from France, 9 November 1695 NS, enclosed in de Chenailles to Trumbull, 22 November 1695, The Hague.

[213] Jones, *Mainstream of Jacobitism*, 45.

[214] Sir Richard Blackmore, *A true and impartial History of the Conspiracy against the Person and Government of King William III . . . 1695* [*sic*] (London, 1723), 114.

and its army time to crush a rebellion completely. For the French, the proposed invasion was widely regarded as the last chance for the Jacobites: 'c'est une coup de désespoir, après lequel il n'y aura plus d'esperance pour le Roy Jacques à l'égard de la France'.[215]

By early February 1696, an invasion force of 16,000 men had been assembled in the Channel ports of Normandy and Brittany, to be commanded by the marquis d'Harcourt.[216] On 6/16 February, James FitzJames, Duke of Berwick (James II's eldest bastard by Arabella Churchill) left Saint-Germain for Calais, from there to travel incognito to England via the Romney marshes. His mission was to organise and command the rebellion which was to precede the invasion. When Berwick reached London, however, he found that the leading conspirators were adamant that they would undertake nothing until a French army had landed. He also discovered that the conspiracy for a rebellion had become inextricably entwined with one for the assassination of William III, which was originally scheduled to take place on 15/25 February.[217] Berwick, who was disappointed to discover during his week in London that public support for a rebellion was neither so general nor so enthusiastic as he had hoped, left England before the appointed date, realising that his mission had failed in leading the English into rising before the French had landed. The intended capture and murder of William III had been postponed one week, to 22 February/3 March. Before that day, however, one of the conspirators had got cold feet and had revealed the conspiracy to the government; instead of the intended ambush of the king, a large wave of arrests began that day which caught up most of the principal plotters, and the government was handed a propaganda weapon which William III and his ministers knew how to exploit to the full.

Meanwhile, on 18/28 February, James II left Saint-Germain for Calais and the invasion fleet. One of his ministers, John Caryll, was convinced that his trip would prove fruitless: 'I confesse it is my opinion that nothing at all will be done, and that those encouragements which are expected from England, *without any actuall appearance wherof his Majesty will not nor can not cross ye Sea*, will fall short of what is promised & expected, so that ye worst that can happen

---

[215] BL Add. MSS 79598, n.f.: [Unknown] to Mr. de Marmande in London, 6 March [1696], The Hague.

[216] Noailles, *Maintenon*, IV, 520. Dempster put the total at 14,000 – eighteen battalions of infantry, two regiments of dragoons and four of cavalry: SCA, BL 2/162/1: Nicholas Dempster to William Leslie, 5 March 1696, Saint-Germain.

[217] The most complete account is that of Jane Garrett, *The Triumphs of Providence: The Assassination Plot 1696* (Cambridge, 1980).

is but a journy to Calais taken in vaine.'[218] Berwick met his father on the road, and then proceeded to Versailles where he and Louis XIV had two long conferences in the apartment of Madame de Maintenon on 29 February and 1 March, before Berwick left to rejoin James at Calais.[219] By the time he arrived there, the Assassination Plot had been discovered in London, where alone some 330 people were arrested. Almost immediately an 'Association' (based on the Elizabethan model directed against Mary, Queen of Scots) was drawn up and circulated, pledging the signatories to avenge any violence offered to William III and to prevent the succession of anyone who hoped to profit by it. 'There is not a prison in town that is not full', noted one observer, 'I ne'er see to [sic] town so pleasant in all my life, for now they are all of a side, for it is the hardest matter in the world to find a Jacobite.'[220] In England, the reaction to the Assassination Plot was so adverse that it not only immeasurably strengthened William III's position, but even men who had served as active Jacobite agents abjured their former loyalties: 'Harry Bacely [i.e., Henry Bulkeley], I hear has taken the oaths, and so has Ned Sheldon, even that of supremacy', James Vernon notified the secretary of state.[221] Williamite propagandists proclaimed that both James II and Louis XIV had been complicit in the proposed regicide.

In France, where the aborted invasion became the subject of mockery for those who dared speak of it,[222] Louis XIV was humiliated and enraged by his involuntary involvement in the scandal; nothing in his long reign had so impugned his *gloire*. There is no evidence that the French had foreknowledge of the Plot, although James II may have known. What is certain is that Berwick, who learned of it in London, did nothing to stop it and told both his father and Louis XIV about it. Both monarchs seem to have been willing to profit from a favourable result, and later James II was to receive and reward those conspirators who managed to escape England, while Louis allowed them to reside in France despite protests from the English government.[223]

---

[218] Bodleian Library, Carte MSS 181, f. 635v: Caryll to Duke of Perth, 27 February 1696, Saint-Germain. My italics.

[219] Dangeau, v, 373: entries for 29 February and 1 March 1696.

[220] HMC *Various* VIII, 81: T. Tash to Viscount Irwin, 21 March 1696, London.

[221] G.P.R. James (ed.), *Letters Illustrative of the Reign of William III, from 1696 to 1708* (London, 1841), I, 61: James Vernon to Duke of Shrewsbury, 12 November 1696 OS, Whitehall. Bulkeley committed suicide two years later; in his will, he recommended that his son renounce his Roman Catholic faith and return to England: Basil Duke Henning, *The House of Commons, 1660–1690* (Landon, History of Parliament Trust, 1983), I, 742–3.

[222] BL Add. MSS 79598, n.f.: Newsletter from Paris, 23 March [1696]. These papers were examined before they were rearranged and reclassified as BL Add. MSS.

[223] Jones, *Mainstream of Jacobitism*, 50–1.

James remained on the coast throughout March and April 1696, a forlorn object of pity to some, returning to Saint-Germain only on 5 May.[224] By July he was well aware, as he informed the abbé de la Trappe, that Louis XIV might be forced to recognise the Prince of Orange as king.[225] 'On a beaucoup parlé d'un paix générale de maniere à donner beaucoup d'inquietude à nostre Cour', Dempster noted, 'mais je crois leurs Majestez en assurance et que cette craint n'a point esté jusqu'à elles.'[226] The Stuart court's annual visit to Fontainebleau was uncomfortable, and it was reported that 'King James and his Queen came very heavy-hearted from Fontainebleau to St Germains before their time.'[227] Louis XIV remained courteous and gracious, but aloof: 'this king', Queen Mary reported to Caryll, 'is very civil & kynd to us, as he used to be, but dos not care to enter into busenesse with us'.[228] The harsh speeches were left to Louis's ministers, who informed James Porter, the Jacobite envoy extraordinary, that although Louis XIV would serve James II on all occasions,

the accounts King James gave their Master of the English Navy was half and half less than they really are or can make upon occasion, which their Master was very well informed of; that a great many King James looked upon to be his friends are his foes in misrepresenting things and giving him a false account of matters to please him; that their Master could not believe any such thing as his having a great party for him in England till he saw some convincing reason for it.

Unless several towns declared for James and there was a considerable party in arms for him, 'what reason could anybody have to believe that King James had that interest in England?'.[229] Madame de Maintenon, although characterised as 'the onely staunch freind St Germains has in France', none the less reportedly spoke her mind to Queen Mary:

Mme de Maintenon has likewise told the Queene that the King of France would never depend upon any intelligence that St Germain could give him out of England. He would employ some people himselfe for that purpose upon whom he could reley,

---

[224] NLS, MSS 14,266: Nairne journal, entry for 5 May 1696.

[225] Lord Acton, 'Letters of James II', 53–5: James II to abbé de la Trappe, 20 July 1696.

[226] SCA, BL 2/16/6: Nicholas Dempster to William Leslie, 9 July 1696, Saint-Germain.

[227] HMC *Downshire* I, 698–9: Col. Maurice Hussey to Sir William Trumbull, 29 October 1696 [OS, London]. In the same letter, Hussey reminded the secretary of state: 'You know I told you all that passed at Fontainebleau this time 12 months very early, and you found every tittle of my news true.'

[228] BL Add. MSS 28224, f. 23: Mary of Modena to John Caryll, 15 October 1696, Fontainebleau.

[229] HMC *Downshire* I, 702: Col. H. [Maurice Hussey] to Sir William Trumbull, Thursday [5 November 1696 OS, London].

& no other, which King James seems to be very much troubled att, because he believes he has a vast partie in this kingdome & the King of France does not att all believe it.[230]

The response of the Jacobite court was to deny reality: in November 1696, Shrewsbury (now a secretary of state) noted that 'Mr Caryl has lately writt to a Correspondent here, to give no credit to the Peace, but be assured he should see him soon',[231] and in January 1697 James II publicly announced to the court at Saint-Germain that it was not true, as the Prince of Orange claimed, that Louis XIV had agreed to recognise him as king of England.[232] Many Jacobites in England accepted these assurances at face value,[233] although the more politically astute realised that 'the French King will not deny any thing to King William to make him consent to peace'.[234]

In fact, Louis XIV was suspicious of William III's willingness to reach a peace agreement and was willing to drive a hard bargain for the benefit of the Stuarts, but his hands were tied by the actions of James II. When the death of King John Sobieski in 1696 created a vacancy on the throne of Poland, Louis XIV – anxious to elect a French nominee – was willing to spend money to advance the candidacy of James II, but the English king rejected the proposal out of hand: acceptance of the Polish crown would imply a renunciation of his English rights.[235] In early 1697, when a peace conference opened at Ryswick, James issued an ill-written and ill-considered manifesto to the Catholic princes of Europe urging them to unite in defence of the True Faith and the monarchical principle. He repudiated any suggestion of compromise with William III, specifically that William should rule for the remainder of his life, to be succeeded by the Prince of Wales. A similar manifesto to the Protestant princes followed. Both documents were poorly

---

[230] BL Add. MSS 72570, n.f.: [Col. Maurice Hussey] to Sir William Trumbull, Tuesday, 12 January [1697 OS, London]; printed in HMC *Downshire* I, 729–33.

[231] Nottingham University Library, Portland Collection (PWA) 1385: Shrewsbury to Earl of Portland, 10 November 1696 OS, Eyeford.

[232] Sourches, V, 235: entry for 21 January 1697; BL, Add. MSS 72599, n.f.: Newsletters from Paris, 1, 8 March 1697.

[233] Grovestins, *Histoire*, VI, 590: William III to Heinsius, 13/23 November 1696, London; HMC *Downshire* I 715: W[illiam] C[ourtenay] to Sir William Trumbull, 11 December 1696 OS. Some ardent believers, such as Dr Nathaniel Johnstone, who lived in the household of the second Earl of Peterborough, could not bring themselves to believe that Louis XIV would ever desert James II to recognise William III, even as the Treaty of Ryswick was being signed: see his letters to the Earl of Huntingdon in 1696 and 1697, HMC *Hastings* II, pp. 279–96 *passim*.

[234] Levens Hall Papers, on loan to Cumberland Record Office, Kendal, File w.3, n.f.: Viscount Weymouth to James Grahme, 10 September 1696 OS, Longleat.

[235] Clarke, *Life of James II*, II, 561.

received, especially by the French plenipotentiaries: one of them, Harlay, 'upon speaking of King James's Manifesto, observed there was nothing more contradictory than this two papers, and that he was mighty ill served and advised in the publication of them'.[236] Finally, in June 1697, James issued a proclamation announcing that he would regard as null and void any settlement prejudicial to his interests.[237]

The real negotiations for peace took place not at Ryswick, but in a series of conferences between Hans Bentinck, Earl of Portland (William III's closest friend and confidant) and Louis François, marquis de Boufflers and maréchal of France during June and July 1697. It was clear that France would, at the successful conclusion of negotiations, recognise William III as king of England, Scotland and Ireland (although typically the French quibbled endlessly about the form of such recognition, in order to squeeze every possible advantage out of their 'sacrifice'). The central questions were where the exiled Stuarts were to reside and how they were to be provided for financially. For the English government, the first question was vital, and for the French the second was equally important.

The English goal was to send James II 'beyond the Alps', to Italy, where only the Papal States would be likely, albeit reluctant, to receive him. Not only would the exiled court be removed from close proximity to the British Isles, but also the fact that the Stuarts were the guests of the papacy would underline their devotion to the Roman faith and be another nail in their political coffins. As Shrewsbury pointed out to Portland in August,

> it would be of very dangerous consequence to the King's affairs here, that King James should be permitted to live in any place so near these kingdomes, that letters and messages might frequently pass, and that Persons of Consideration might have pretence of going, where they would have opportunitys of discoursing with him without its being visible that that was their Errand. To be convinced of the consequence of this, one need but reflect on the advantage the Present King, when Prince of Orange, made of such a free Intercourse, as was then between London and The Hague.[238]

If and when the Stuarts left France for Italy, the English indicated that they were willing either to pay James II a pension (a possibility which James had already foreclosed as tantamount to a recognition of William's rights) or, more

---

[236] HMC *Bath* III, 114: Matthew Prior to Sir William Trumbull, 3 May 1697, The Hague.

[237] The first two manifestos are found in *Actes et mémoires de la paix de Ryswick* (2nd edn, The Hague, 1707), I, 452–537; the final protestation is in *ibid.*, II, 410 ff.

[238] Nottingham University Library, PWA 1390: Shrewsbury to Portland, 27 July/6 August 1697, Whitehall.

probably, to honour Mary of Modena's rights to her marital jointure of some £50,000 (which in any event could not be denied her under law). The English also demanded that Louis promise to expel from France any Jacobites named by William III.

For his part, Louis XIV refused to expel James II from France under any conditions (although he may have nourished the secret hope that James might choose to leave voluntarily):[239] James was his first cousin and his fellow monarch, whose just rights Louis could never renounce in his own conscience, no matter what political exigencies might dictate. In addition, James had come voluntarily into France, and it would demean Louis to expel him by force. While flatly rejecting the expulsion of James from France to Italy during the course of his negotiations with Portland, Boufflers suggested that James might choose to retire to Avignon, a papal enclave in the south of France. Although no French promises of any kind were made (and the final treaty was to ignore entirely the question of James's future residence), Portland seized upon Bouffler's casual suggestion and regarded it as a tacit agreement that James would at least be removed to a more remote part of the kingdom. In return for such a removal, the English would pay Mary of Modena's jointure (although this, too, was not mentioned in the final treaty).[240] The upshot was a misunderstanding: Louis XIV had no intention of removing the Stuarts from Saint-Germain involuntarily, and William III had no intention of paying them anything so long as they remained in France.

In August 1697 it was reported from Paris that Louis had finally explained personally to James the necessity of making a peace,[241] which France signed at Ryswick with the Maritime Powers and Spain on 20 September and with the Emperor on 30 October. 'C'étoit abandonner entièrement le véritable roi d'Angleterre', the marquis de Sourches noted in his diary, reflecting the general view of courtiers at Versailles.[242] For Louis XIV, French recognition of William III 'and his heirs and successors' was a blow to his pride; the attitude of Madame de Maintenon may be inferred from her invariable continued references to William as 'le prince d'Orange'. Having tasted the bitter

[239] The English government had some reason to believe this was the case: *CSPD, 1690–1691*, 511: 'Extract of a letter from the Spanish Ambassador', 6/16 September 1691, Rome: 'King James already begins to be looked upon with disfavour in France, and knowing that he causes embarrassment and that they could expel him from that kingdom, it has been insinuated to the Pope [Innocent XII] on his behalf that he wishes to come to Rome.'

[240] Mark A. Thomson, 'Louis XIV and William III, 1689–1697', in Hatton and Bromley, *William III and Louis XIV*, 41–6 for the Boufflers–Portland negotiations.

[241] BL Add. MSS 72599, n.f.: Newsletter to M. De Marmande, 12 August 1697, Paris.

[242] Cited by Mark Thomson, 'Louis XIV and William III', 47.

potion, however, Louis was resolved to make the best of it. He renewed, indeed increased, his public courtesies to James and Mary while simultaneously preparing for the reception of the Earl of Portland as William III's first ambassador to Versailles.

Whatever resignation James II showed in accepting Louis's decision was not shared by his courtiers at Saint-Germain, whose denunciation of the French monarch was outspoken and dangerously public: one 'was imprisoned for talking too loosely of His Most Christian Majesty for having deserted his ally King James and made the Peace'.[243] So bad did the situation become that in November James summoned his entire court to explain the peace and to forbid absolutely any public discussion of it on pain of his highest displeasure.[244]

Jacobite courtiers were further mortified in February 1698, when Portland and his suite arrived in Paris. On 17 February, Portland had his first private audience of Louis XIV; there was an exceptionally large number of Jacobites present at Versailles for the occasion, and Louis XIV sent word to Middleton that, in future, they should avoid court when it was known the English ambassador would be present.[245] It quickly became apparent that Louis XIV had no intention of expelling James II from France, nor would William III pay Queen Mary's jointure unless he did. Yet there soon evolved a tacit understanding between the two monarchs to shelve questions concerning the exiled Stuarts in favour of settling a more pressing and important problem: the rapidly approaching death of the last Spanish Habsburg, Carlos II, and the disposition of his vast empire. From 1698 onwards, Louis and William were consumed in negotiations of the First (1698) and the Second (1700) Partition Treaties; it was in their mutual interest to ignore the Stuart question, in so far as possible.

During the years between 1697 and 1700, the Jacobite party was to discover (if it had not realised before) that it had become a war party. With French recognition of William III 'and his heirs and successors', it became clear that any slender hopes which James II or his son might have for an eventual restoration depended upon the renewal of international hostilities. Peace made it possible for Catholic envoys to France to visit the exiled court, but such visits did not lead to formal recognition of James II's title by any prince in Europe. English diplomats in Paris (who carefully avoided the French court at

[243] HMC *Bath* III, 194: Matthew Prior to James Vernon, 28 February 1698, Paris. The Jacobite in question was the famous actor Cardell Goodman, who was one of the Assassination Plot conspirators and fled to France, where he died in 1699.

[244] BL Add. MSS 72599, n.f. Newsletter from Paris, 4 November 1697.

[245] Dangeau, VI, 297: entry for 17 February 1698.

Fontainebleau when James and Mary were in residence) noted sourly that 'King James and his Queen were never better received or more courted than they are at present' in October 1698. 'Our friends of St Germains shine extremely', reported Matthew Prior,

all the court is made to Queen Mary; everybody is at her toilette in the morning, from whence the King of France leads her to chapel: the two Kings and the Queen in the midst sit at the head of the table at dinner with equal marks of distinction and sovereignty, and '*à boire pour le Roi d'Angleterre!*' *ou* '*Pour la reine*' is spoke as loud and with the same ceremony as '*pour le Roi*' when they mean their own King.[246]

The reality was quite different: referring to the same visit, Queen Mary told Caryll 'wee have seen this king *in private* but once & I sayd nothing of my concerns'.[247] The same story was repeated during the visits in 1699 and 1700: 'You know that wee make our Court [with Louis XIV] by not meddling with any busenesse . . . This King has been but once in privat with us . . . he is as civil and kynd to us, as he uses [*sic*] to be, & wee as modest & as silent as to any thing of busenesse .'[248]

In part, the political dormancy of the court of Saint-Germain was due to the fact that James II was slowly but clearly dying. In December 1699 a courtier noted: 'I saw ye K[ing] at dinner, he was caryd to ye table in a rouling Chaire.'[249] The continuing Jacobite tendency to exaggerate and distort English political news to their own advantage did little to add to their credibility: 'the storys they [the French ministers] have of our affairs are so monstrously ridiculous that I perceive they will believe them no longer', Matthew Prior noted with satisfaction.[250] In November 1698, he reported that '*King James* has less credit with *Louis XIV* than ever. *Queen Mary* recommended an officer for a vacancy the other day without success, and *Louis XIV* told *King James* that he must retrench the pensions, upon which *Queen Mary* was in tears for a day or two.'[251] Prior regarded the French as equally ill disposed towards the two English factions: 'they are civil to us and hate us, and they are civil to King James and despise him'.[252]

---

[246] HMC *Bath* III, 276–7: Matthew Prior to Portland, to James Vernon, 17, 18 October 1698, Paris.

[247] BL Add. MSS 28,224, f. 29: Queen Mary to John Caryll, 19 October [1698], Fontainebleau.

[248] *Ibid.*, f. 34: Queen Mary to Caryll, 3 October [1700], Fontainebleau: on this occasion, however, Madame de Maintenon 'entered also with me to speake of other affaires which is mor[e] than she had don a long time befor'.

[249] NLS, MSS 14,266: Nairne journal, entry for 13 December 1699.

[250] HMC *Bath* III, 278: Prior to Portland, 20 October 1698, Paris.

[251] *Ibid.*, 296–7: Prior to Portland, 29 November 1698; italicised names are in cypher in the original.

[252] *Ibid.*, 278: Prior to Portland, 20 October 1698, Paris.

On 1 November 1700, Carlos II died, leaving his entire empire to the second grandson of Louis XIV, Philippe, duc d'Anjou; on 16 November, Louis accepted the will on behalf of his grandson, who henceforward became Philip V of Spain. Louis XIV's acceptance of the will not only guaranteed war with Leopold I, who had advanced his second son, the Archduke Charles, as the Habsburg candidate, but also contravened the Second Partition Treaty, which France had signed in March 1700 with the Maritime Powers. Initially, however, Louis's acceptance of the will was popular in both England and the Dutch Republic, because under the Second Partition Treaty Naples and Sicily (and, it was feared, naval domination of the Mediterranean) would be given to France. However, in December 1700, Louis XIV filed an edict in the Parlement de Paris specifying that Philip V, in becoming king of Spain, had not sacrificed his right to succeed to the French crown, unnecessarily raising the spectre that the two crowns might one day be united.

Then in February 1701, the Earl of Melfort suddenly reappeared on the international scene. Melfort had been allowed to return to Paris in 1697, where he resided, although he also acquired a secondary residence in Saint-Germain.[253] His elder brother, James Drummond, Earl of Perth, had been summoned to Saint-Germain in 1696 when he had been made governor of the Prince of Wales; the Drummond interest was still represented in James II's inner councils. In February 1701, Melfort wrote a long letter from Paris, directed to his brother at nearby Saint-Germain, discussing the prospects of a Franco-Jacobite invasion of England said to be in the planning stages, the re-establishment of the Roman Catholic church there, recent treasonable correspondence with the Duke of Hamilton, and reasons for dismissing Middleton. (In the eyes of the French ministers, however, Melfort's worst crime was to have cited Madame de Maintenon as the source of much of his information.) Because of the carelessness of a French postal clerk, the letter addressed to Perth 'à la cour d'Angleterre' was placed in the London post bag and was duly intercepted by the English government. On 17/28 February 1701, it was laid before the House of Commons, which soon petitioned William III to begin negotiations with other powers for a defensive alliance against France and Spain. In April, William III appointed John Churchill, Earl of Marlborough, as his ambassador and plenipotentiary to the Dutch Republic, with instructions to begin negotiations for a new Grand Alliance with the Dutch, the emperor, and other European powers. This Marlborough did throughout the spring and summer of 1701, acting under the personal supervision of William III.

[253] Jones, *Mainstream of Jacobitism*, 59.

The French reaction to the Melfort letter was apoplectic: Melfort was immediately interviewed by Jean Baptiste Colbert, marquis de Torcy, who had become secretary of state for foreign affairs in succession to his father Croissy (who died in 1696) and his father-in-law, the marquis de Pomponne (who died in 1699). Melfort initially denied that the letter was his, but when Torcy had established the truth to his and Louis XIV's satisfaction, Torcy after a pro forma consultation with James II sent Melfort into a second internal exile, this time at Angers.[254]

When James II first heard the news, on 4 March, he and the queen were about to attend a Lenten service in the Chapel Royal of Saint-Germain: when the words from Lamentations, *Remember, O Lord, what is come upon us: consider and behold our reproach. Our inheritance is turned to strangers, our houses to aliens*, were chanted, James II suffered a major stroke. It was quickly decided by physicians from both the English and the French courts that he would profit by taking the waters at Bourbon: consequently, the king and queen left Saint-Germain on 6 April for a prolonged stay there. During their absence, the Prince of Wales 'went to Ver[sailles] & visited all that Court & ye King of Fr[ance] was very kind to him & told take [*sic*] ye same care of him he did of his own children'.[255] When James and Mary returned home on 9 June, it was clear to all that little improvement in the king's health had taken place.[256]

While Marlborough was negotiating the Grand Alliance and James was seeking a cure, the English Parliament was establishing the future succession of the English crown. William and Mary had been childless; only one of Princess Anne's eighteen children had survived beyond infancy. William Henry, named after his triumphant uncle, was born in July 1689 and had been created Duke of Gloucester. During his short life he was depicted in propaganda as the great hope of the Protestant cause, in contrast to his uncle, the Prince of Wales. Gloucester, however, had died in July 1700 of smallpox, immediately after his eleventh birthday. Since it seemed impossible that either William or Anne would ever produce heirs of their bodies, the necessity of further delineating a Protestant Succession was apparent. Consequently, in June 1701, Parliament passed the Act of Settlement, which vested the succession to the crowns of England and Ireland in the dowager Electress Sophia of Hanover 'and the heirs of her body being Protestant'. The legislation, which

[254] *Ibid.*, 59–60; 'All the people at St Germain, Papists as well as Protestants, do believe the whole letter to be genuine . . . King James is mighty angry at my Lord Melfort': HMC *Cowper* II, 422–3: John Coke to Thomas Coke, 10 March 1701, Paris.

[255] NLS, MSS 14,266: Nairne journal, entry for 24 April 1701.

[256] Haile, *Mary of Modena*, 349–51.

met with little opposition in either house, was designed to consolidate the Revolution settlement and to exclude permanently James, Prince of Wales, even if he should choose to convert to Protestantism at some point in the future.

Surprisingly, there seems to be no evidence that the French government seriously considered what action, if any, it would take should James II die, despite the fact that James suffered a second stroke in July. However, on 2 September, James suffered a third massive stroke and it quickly became apparent that his end was at hand. On 11 September, Louis XIV visited his dying cousin at Saint-Germain, where Mary of Modena appealed to Louis to recognise her son as king on his father's death, arguing that without such recognition he would be only 'un simple', without identity or rank in the world.[257] Louis replied 'that the matter required some reflection . . . he looked upon her husband as a saint . . . and had a great inclination towards the Prince of Wales, but he could not recognise him without assembling his Council'. The *conseil d'en haut* was duly assembled the next day, with most of the ministers arguing that a recognition would violate the Treaty of Ryswick. Louis XIV, the dauphin and the other princes of the blood, however, argued that William III was merely a *de facto* king, whereas James III would be a *de jure* monarch possessed by God of hereditary rights of which no one could deprive him. Louis argued that 'moreover he had no intention of assisting him to regain his dominions, as that would be contrary to the treaty' of Ryswick.[258]

While it is probable that the combined influence of Mary of Modena and Madame de Maintenon convinced Louis XIV to overrule his council, it is also clear that Louis realised that war with England was inevitable: on 7 September, Marlborough had signed the Treaty of Grand Alliance at The Hague between England, the Dutch Republic and the emperor. Undoubtedly Louis hoped to extract some future political and diplomatic advantage from recognising the Stuart heir. In addition, Louis had never forgotten what he regarded as one of the greatest of Cardinal Mazarin's mistakes: in 1654, Mazarin had allied France with republican England and at Cromwell's behest had expelled Charles II from the kingdom. Six years later, against all expectation, Charles had been restored to the English crown. If one Stuart restoration had taken place against all the odds, a second was not beyond the realm of possibility.[259]

[257] Ragnhild Hatton, 'Louis XIV and His Fellow Monarchs', in John C. Rule (ed.), *Louis XIV and the Craft of Kingship* (Columbus, OH, 1969), pp. 162, 187 n. 48.

[258] Haile, *Mary of Modena*, 352; for ministerial opposition, see Edward Gregg, *The Protestant Succession in International Politics, 1710–1716* (New York, 1986), 91.

[259] Hatton, 'Louis XIV and His Fellow Monarchs'.

On the afternoon of 13 September, Louis XIV, accompanied by Madame de Maintenon, again visited Saint-Germain. After conferring privately with Queen Mary and the thirteen-year-old Prince of Wales, he proceeded to visit his dying cousin, who earlier in the day had forgiven his 'three greatest enemies', the Prince of Orange, the Princess of Denmark and the emperor. There he publicly assured James II that, upon his death, he would recognise his son as king of England, Scotland and Ireland. The attendant courtiers, who had been on tenterhooks, were overcome: as a French account put it, 'the officers in the room, forgetting where they were, all cried "God save the King!" which was perhaps the first time the cry was ever raised in the chamber of a dying monarch'.[260] Three days later, on 16 September, James II died at Saint-Germain, where French heralds proclaimed his son as 'James III'. The English ambassador, the Earl of Manchester, immediately withdrew from the country without formal notification to the government, effectively breaking diplomatic relations.

What Louis XIV did not perhaps fully anticipate was the firestorm of indignation which swept throughout England, and many courts of Europe. Having given a king to Spain, Louis now appeared to be giving a king to England as well: 'The French King never pretended before, and has not a right no more than formerly to name us a king', the Earl of Derby commented indignantly, 'for whatever gloss may be put, this is the true state of the case.'[261] French recognition of James III was hard to square with Louis's promise in the Treaty of Ryswick that he would give no assistance whatsoever to anyone who challenged William III's title; no French legalistic arguments could obscure the fact that Louis was in breach of international treaties. In short, as one English Catholic cleric shrewdly noted, 'the King of France, by declaring the Prince of Wales, had done service to King William'.[262]

William did not live long to profit by Louis's error. On 8 March 1702, the king died at St James's Palace of complications following a broken collar bone, and was succeeded to the English crown by his sister-in-law, the Princess of Denmark, who became Queen Anne. The accession of Anne virtually ensured that Jacobitism would remain quiescent for the greater part of her reign. Those non-jurors who had refused to swear oaths of allegiance to William

---

[260] NLS, MSS 14,266: Nairne journal, entries for 11, 12, 13 September 1701; Sourches, VII, 116, 117: entries for 11, 13 September 1701; Dangeau, VIII, 193: entry for 14 September 1701, comments that James II 'speaks better sense than he did before his illness'.

[261] HMC *Third Report*, 270: Earl of Derby to Peter Legh, 28 October 1701, Knowsley.

[262] HMC *Buccleuch* II, 758: Shrewsbury's Roman journal entry for 26 November 1701, quoting Bishop Philip Ellis.

and Mary during James II's lifetime now felt perfectly free after his death to swear the same oaths to his daughter Anne. The new queen and her principal advisors, John Churchill, Earl (and soon to be Duke) of Marlborough, and Sidney, Lord Godolphin, had assiduously cultivated the spurious notion that Anne secretly sympathised with her exiled half-brother and would someday do something which would ensure his succession after her. At times, even the court of Saint-Germain seemed half-possessed by this idea.[263]

Alone among European princes, Philip V of Spain followed his grandfather in recognising James III, as did the new pope, Clement XI. As early as 1690, Melfort had identified the then Cardinal Albani as 'one of ye most favourable of ye Cardinals for ye King's cause'.[264] However, in 1694, Bishop Philip Ellis, resident in Rome, had referred to 'C. Albano, the chief abbettor of ye Austrian interest'.[265] In truth, Clement XI was prepared to bend to the prevailing breeze, and at the moment of his election on 23 November 1700 that breeze came from Versailles rather than Vienna. Louis XIV had just accepted the Spanish throne for his grandson, which included control of the duchy of Milan and the kingdoms of Naples and Sicily. The house of Bourbon, rather than that of Habsburg, was now predominant in Italy and Clement XI was prepared to adapt to the change. In early 1701, James III's half-brother, the Duke of Berwick, was sent on a special congratulatory mission to the new pope in Rome.[266] The papal nuncio in Paris, Philip Antonio Gualterio (later created a cardinal), became one of the closest friends and most faithful supporters of the young king and his mother. But little was forthcoming from Rome other than kind words and modest grants for the relief of endemic poverty among Jacobite exiles.

After the death of James II, the Catholic predominance at the exiled court seems to have become more pronounced. The queen mother spent long periods of time in prayerful retreat at the convent of Chaillot; the Duke of Perth, the king's governor, was a prominent *dévot*; Gualterio served as a trusted advisor. It was against this background that in August 1702 the Earl of Middleton, the most prominent Protestant in the Jacobite court, informed Queen Mary that he wished to abjure his religion and moved into the English College in Paris to receive instruction. The queen was overjoyed: 'She confessed that she had not had any consolation but this one since the death of the king', Gualterio

[263] Edward Gregg, 'Was Queen Anne a Jacobite?', *History* 57 (1972), 358–75.

[264] BL, Lansdowne 1163B, f. 76: Melfort to Queen Mary, 18 July 1690, Rome.

[265] Bodleian Library, Carte 209, ff. 126–9: Bishop Philip Ellis to Caryll, 17 August 1694, Rome.

[266] NLS, MSS 14,266: Nairne journal: Berwick left Saint-Germain for Rome on 17 January 1701 and returned there on 2 April.

reported, 'and it is so much the greater that she remembers that the event was predicted by him a little before passing to a higher life.' Middleton, having converted to Roman Catholicism, returned to Saint-Germain in January 1703 'in greater favour than ever'.[267] Middleton's conversion may well have resulted from motives of conscience, as he claimed and as Mary and James III always believed. But in England and Scotland, it proved yet another disaster for the Stuarts, seeming to prove beyond doubt that the only means of securing oneself in their eyes was to enter the church of Rome. Middleton's conversion did little to appease his Catholic critics such as Melfort and Perth, and infuriated virtually all Protestants, both at home and abroad.

At the beginning of the war in 1702, France – now allied with the Spanish empire – seemed to be in a stronger position than ever before in Louis XIV's reign. Yet the international coalition arrayed against France proved much more formidable than during the previous conflict. William III's role as political and military head of the alliance had been filled by Marlborough, who at the age of fifty-two had finally found an opportunity to display fully his military genius. In 1704, with Marlborough's stunning victory at Blenheim on the Danube, the French were driven out of Germany; in May 1706, in the aftermath of Marlborough's second great victory at Ramilles, the French evacuated most of the Spanish Netherlands; and in September 1706, the defeat of the Franco-Spanish army by the imperial commander, Prince Eugene, in the battle of Turin ended France's presence in Italy and would, by 1708, allow the Habsburgs to regain control of all Spanish possessions in the peninsula. Only in Spain were the Allies held at bay. In April 1707, a Franco-Spanish army under the command of the Duke of Berwick decisively defeated them in the battle of Almanza. By the end of 1707, not only had the war been brought to the borders of France, but economic dislocation caused by the war and a series of poor harvests confronted Louis XIV with a financial crisis. In 1706, after Ramilles, he had extended peace feelers via the Dutch, but had discovered that the Allies were inflexible in their demands that the entire Spanish empire should be given to the Allied candidate, the Archduke Charles, styled 'Carlos III': Philip V would lose not only his crowns, but his title and rank as king. In desperation to break the alliance, or at least weaken its engine, Louis now turned his eye to Great Britain.

A major defect of the Act of Settlement of 1701 was that it applied only to the crowns of England and Ireland, not to that of Scotland for which the Parliament at Westminster had no right to legislate. William III, in his

---

[267] Jones, *Middleton*, 270–2.

last speech to Parliament, had urged consideration of a Union of the two kingdoms, and it was to become one of the great glories of his successor's reign. The Scottish Parliament, realising that it held the ace of trumps, in 1704 had passed the Act of Security, which provided that Queen Anne's successor in Scotland should be a Protestant, but not the same person who came to the English crown. This effectively forced the English into negotiations on terms highly favourable to the northern kingdom. By the autumn of 1706, an agreement had been signed to be submitted to both Parliaments. In Scotland, despite the promised benefits, there was considerable nationalist opposition to the Union based on fear that England, which was larger, wealthier and more populous, would erase Scottish national identity. Through a mixture of reason, bribery and political coercion, the Union was ratified by the Scottish Parliament, followed shortly by the English: the United Kingdom of Great Britain became a reality on 1/12 May 1707. Henceforward, Jacobitism in Scotland was to become inextricably linked with – indeed, dominated by – a desire to dissolve the Union.

The French had long kept an eye on developments in Scotland, although they relied exclusively on their own agents, rather than the news that Saint-Germain provided. In 1705, a naturalised Irish Jacobite (and a Protestant), Colonel Nathaniel Hooke, was sent to Scotland to make contact there with leading dissidents.[268] Hooke discovered what the French ministers had long suspected: Scottish Jacobites wished to have no contact with the court of Saint-Germain. The fear of spies there was pervasive. Even the Scottish nephews of Middleton and Perth, Lords Erroll and Strathmore respectively, demanded that their contacts with the French remain secret to Saint-Germain. After his conversion, there was a widespread suspicion, particularly in Scotland, that Middleton was in treacherous communication with the British government, a charge which the marquis de Torcy did not reject in his private journal.[269] Unlike the previous invasion attempts, anything which France would undertake for James III would this time be revealed to the Stuart court only at the last minute.

James III had attained his majority at the age of eighteen in 1706, when the regency of his mother officially had ended, although she continued to enjoy great influence in Jacobite councils. The young king himself was eager to make a name for himself in the world, the traditional means of which was to participate in a military campaign. In March 1706, Mary of

---

[268] For Hooke's missions, see W.D. Macray (ed.), *Correspondence of Colonel Nathaniel Hooke, Agent from the Court of France to the Scottish Jacobites, 1703–1707*, 2 vols. (Roxburghe Club, London, 1870–71).
[269] Gregg, *Protestant Succession*, 101.

Modena asked Louis XIV's permission for her son to participate in the campaign in the Spanish Netherlands, as it would 'be much to his honour & reputation',[270] but Louis refused, ostensibly from a desire not to hazard the young king's life. The real reason was because Louis realised that the Stuarts would finally have to be jettisoned as part of any peace package. Indeed, in his informal peace proposals to the Allies in August 1706 following Marlborough's victory at Ramilles, Louis promised to recognise Anne as queen and 'to take no further interest' in the English succession.[271] Although the peace proposals remained secret, Louis's refusal to allow James III to campaign in 1706 and 1707 did little to alleviate fears in the exiled court: 'The inferior part of the family at St Germain believe they are shortly to remove from thence', it was reported in England, 'but they do not know where.'[272]

The attempted Franco-Jacobite invasion of Scotland in 1708 sprang from despair and desperation. From the beginning, according to Madame de Maintenon's later account, Louis XIV had personally had a poor opinion of the project and its prospects of success, doubts which she shared.[273] At most, the French may have hoped that James would secure the Scottish throne and be able to succeed to the English crown eventually. More probably, the hope was that a successful invasion would spark a domestic rebellion, forcing the British government to withdraw troops from the Netherlands and be more forthcoming in a peace settlement. Significantly, both Madame de Maintenon and the king's grandson and heir presumptive, the duc de Bourgogne, referred to the invasion as 'une diversion'.[274] By comparison to the fleet prepared in 1692, the 1708 effort was a flotilla of some thirty ships of all sizes, including

[270] Bodleian Library, Rawlinson D.21, f. 32: Father Francis Sanders to Father Edward Meredith, 20 March 1706, Saint-Germain.

[271] Gregg, *Protestant Succession*, 92.

[272] HMC *Portland* IV, 177: Erasmus Lewis to Robert Harley, 5/16 May 1705, Whitehall. Lewis, who entered the secretary's office as a chief clerk under the Earl of Manchester in January 1702 and served as under-secretary from May 1704 to September 1714, appears to have served under Manchester during his embassy to France from 1699 to 1701 and to have handled Jacobite intelligence in Paris: 'I know you understand it [i.e., intelligence] better having managed it so well at Paris': *ibid.*, 96–7: John Macky to Erasmus Lewis, 13 July 1704, Florence; J.C. Sainty, *Officials of the Secretaries of State, 1660–1782* (London, 1973), 87.

[273] A. Geoffroy, *Madame de Maintenon, d'après sa correspondance authentique* (Paris, 1887), II, 159–63: Mme de Maintenon to Princesse des Ursins, 22 April 1708, Saint-Cyr.

[274] *Ibid.*,155–8: Mme de Maintenon to Ursins, 4 March 1708, Versailles; marquis de Vogüé (ed.), *Le Duc de Bourgogne et le duc de Beauvilliers, lettres inédites, 1700–1708* (Paris, 1900), 251–2: Bourgogne to Mme de Maintenon, 7 August [1708]; cf. Alfred Baudrillart and Léon Lecestre (eds.), *Lettres du duc de Bourgogne au roi d'Espagne Philippe V et à la Reine* (Paris, 1916), II, 236–7: Bourgogne to Philip V, 8 March 1708, Versailles.

transport ships for 6000 troops.[275] The duc de Saint-Simon later claimed that
the naval minister, Jérome Phélypeaux, comte de Pontchartrain, delayed the
preparations for the invasion in so far as he could, allegedly from hatred of
its planner, the war minister Michel de Chamillart.[276] The plan called for the
French fleet to sail along the eastern coast of Scotland to the Firth of Forth:
local Jacobites would light bonfires in the hillsides to show where it would
be safe to land and disembark troops. A naval hero, Claude, comte de Forbin,
was named to command the expedition. Considering the apparent public tranquillity in Scotland and the lack of any safe Scottish port to serve as a place
of refuge, Forbin was dubious about the project from the beginning: 'Quel
est donc l'ignorant qui a formé ce projet?', he demanded of Pontchartrain.[277]
James III, under cover of secrecy, left Saint-Germain early on 7 March and
arrived at Dunkirk on the evening of 9 March, where the fleet was lying in
preparation. The next morning the king awoke with measles, and thirty-eight
English ships under the command of Sir George Byng appeared off Gravelines. When James's physicians refused to allow him to embark immediately,
Forbin sought and obtained from Versailles a cancellation of the invasion;
however, after Mary of Modena personally visited Versailles and appealed to
Louis XIV, the cancellation was immediately revoked.[278] 'The K[ing]'s sick-
ness & ye English fleet appearing, made us lose a whole week at Dunquerque',
David Nairne recorded, and boarding began only on 17 March, with the fleet
sailing on the evening of the same day. The delay proved fatal. The British
government had ample time to arrest and imprison suspected Jacobites in
Scotland. After Forbin had successfully eluded Admiral Byng's fleet and had
reached the Scottish coast, the promised bonfires were nowhere to be found.
Ignoring the reiterated pleas of the young king, Forbin refused to risk landing
his troops and turned back to France, reaching Dunkirk on 7 April. The fleet
had been at sea for three weeks: James III had not touched foot on British
soil.[279] Forbin, who had spent 40,000 *livres* to maintain a table for James III
fit for a king ('de douze couverts magnifiquement servie'), complained bitterly
when Louis XIV gave him only a gratification of 1000 *livres* and an annual
pension of 1000 *écus*.[280]

---

[275] The most complete account of the 1708 attempt is by John S. Gibson, *Playing the Scottish Card:
The Franco-Jacobite Invasion of 1708* (Edinburgh, 1988).

[276] Dangeau, XII, 97: entry for 13 March 1708 and Saint-Simon's note.

[277] Jacques Boulenger (ed.), *Mémoires du comte de Forbin, chef d'escadre, 1656–1710* (Paris, 1934),
215–17.

[278] *Ibid.*, 218.

[279] The dates of James III's movements are taken from NLS, MSS 14,266: Nairne journal.

[280] *Mémoires de Forbin*, 226–7.

James III, dejected by this humiliating débâcle, remained secluded at Dunkirk for ten days before leaving on 17 April, returning to Saint-Germain on the 20th where he was formally received by Louis XIV with the news that he would be allowed to serve in the forthcoming campaign with the king's own grandsons, the ducs de Bourgogne and Berri under the incognito of 'the *Chevalier de Saint-Georges*'. James's presence in the French army was used to sustain English apprehensions that France might mount another invasion attempt by quickly diverting him and accompanying French troops to the Channel coast.[281] Indeed, in both 1709 and 1710,[282] Saint-Germain proposed such action as a last, desperate attempt to save France by removing Marlborough and British troops from Flanders to fight a civil war at home. These proposals were seriously considered by Louis's council but – apart from the king's personal appreciation of the superiority of Anglo-Dutch naval power[283] – France's plight was too desperate to stake all on a weapon which had previously proven a dismal failure. Neither the finance nor the naval ministers, Voysin and Pontchartrain, could promise adequate support for any invasion attempt[284] and on both occasions Torcy supported the king's decision to renew peace negotiations.[285]

It was no secret that James III would be forced to leave France when peace came. As early as March 1706, a joint resolution of both houses of the English Parliament had urged Queen Anne not to make peace until France had recognised her title, recognised the Protestant succession in the House of Hanover, expelled 'the Pretender' from France, and demolished the port of Dunkirk. 'Nobody offer'd to speake a word against any thing in it in our H[ouse]', one MP noted.[286] In March 1709, when Louis XIV sent a leading diplomat, Pierre

---

[281] Martin Haile, *James Francis Edward, the Old Chevalier* (London, 1907), 94, fn. 1; Macpherson, *Original Papers*, II, 101: James's instructions to Charles Farquharson, 25 April 1708; BL Add. MSS 61,556, 61,657 *passim:* Letters of Marlborough's 'Paris spy', 16, 23, 27 April, 21, 28 May, 11, 15 June 1708.

[282] For the 1709 proposal, AAE, CP Angleterre, supplément 4, ff. 42–4: mémoire by Lewis Innes, 7 January 1709; for French consideration of a Jacobite invasion in 1709–10, see John Rule, 'France and the Preliminaries to the Gertruydenberg Conference, September 1709 to March 1710', in R.M. Hatton and M.S. Anderson (eds.), *Studies in Diplomatic History: Essays in Memory of David Bayne Horn* (London, 1970), 97–115; Macpherson, *Original Papers*, II, 163–70: Middleton to Torcy, 29 August 1710; Winston S. Churchill, *Marlborough: His Life and Times* (London, 1933–39), IV, 227, fn. 23.

[283] Head, *Fallen Stuarts*, 108–9; Frédéric Masson (ed.), *Journal inédit de Jean-Baptiste Colbert, Marquis de Torcy* (Paris, 1884), 55–6; P. Coquelle, 'Les projets de descente en Angleterre', *Revue d'Histoire Diplomatique* 15 (1901), 451–2.

[284] Torcy, *Journal inédit*, 66–8, 119–22, 126–30, 253–4.

[285] Rule, 'Gertruydenberg Conference', 110–14.

[286] HMC *Eleventh Report*, App. III, 115: Thomas de Grey to Sir Christopher Calthorp, 5/16 March 1706, London.

Rouillé, to The Hague to open negotiations with the Allies, Whig majorities in both houses renewed this motion as official British government policy. The French accepted the expulsion of James III without demur; the question was not whether, but where he would go. Both Switzerland and the Papal States were suggested as being suitable, but were rejected out of hand by James.[287] As early as 1694, Saint-Germain had been warned that the idea of supporting the Stuart court financially was 'a dreadfull thought to ye Romans, who are ye most interested and covetous of all men'.[288] The unhappy memory of the long and costly residence of the exiled Queen Christina of Sweden, who died in 1689, was still very much alive in the Roman Curia. For his part, James III was keenly aware that residence in the Papal States (or remote Switzerland) would hinder his communication with his 'subjects' in Great Britain; actually living cheek-by-jowl to the pope would only exacerbate British anti-Catholicism, which he realised was the greatest bar to his restoration. Yet he also recognised the desirability of leaving France. As his confessor put it in July 1709, when peace came 'then Our Master will certainly leave this Kingdom. 'Tis the advice of his friends as well as the request of his Enemyes.'[289] He realised the anomaly of his position, saying 'qu'il regardoit un roy sans royaume, comme un appotiquaire sans sucre'.[290] Secretly disgusted with the French and disillusioned with the increasing irresolution of Louis XIV, James believed that the conduct of French affairs, in the words of a modern critic, 'smacked of paradox, of uncertainty, and of drift'.[291] Well aware of Louis's disinclination to support another invasion attempt and conscious that many Englishmen opposed him because of his close association with France, James confided to his chief minister, the Earl of Middleton, that he was 'quite weary' of his residence in France 'on all accounts'.[292]

If James was dissatisfied with France, he was even more so with the papacy. In 1709, after imperial troops had crossed the Papal States to occupy Naples

---

[287] Bodleian Library, Carte MSS 180, ff. 235–6: Middleton to Torcy, 30 April 1709, Saint-Germain.

[288] Bodleian Library, Carte MSS 209, ff. 106–8: Bishop Philip Ellis to James II, 21 March 1694, Rome.

[289] WDA, Epistolae Variorum (henceforward EV) II, f. 89: Dr John Ingleton to Lawrence Mayes [at Rome], 29 July 1709, Saint-Germain.

[290] Emile Bourgeois (ed.), *Lettres intimes du cardinal Alberoni au comte Rocca, ministre du duc de Parme, d'après le manuscrit du collège S. Lazare* (Paris, 1892), 68: Alberoni to Rocca, 16 March 1708, Versailles, quoting James III.

[291] Rule, 'Gertruydenberg Conference', 109; cf. Macpherson, *Original Papers*, II, 153: James to Middleton, 2 June 1710.

[292] Torcy, *Journal intime*, 55–6; Macpherson, *Original Papers*, II, 160: James to Middleton, 25 July 1710.

and Sicily, Clement XI had signed an alliance with Joseph I, once again making the papacy a Habsburg ally, as were most of the other Italian princes. 'We . . . are all unanimous for the House of Austria', one English observer noted of them.[293] There was to be no further papal encouragement for James III.[294] In April 1711, James nominated Cardinal Gualterio as Protector of England and his ambassador at Rome, but Clement XI made difficulties about the protectorship and delayed two years in accepting Gualterio because of his connections to France.[295] James was particularly sensitive to papal slights involving his rights as a 'reigning' king. One bone of contention was the nomination of vicars apostolic for England; another, of even older origin, was the appointment of Irish bishops. After great pressure, Clement XI only recognised James III's right to nominate the latter in February 1714, although he continued none the less to appoint them without consulting the king.[296] 'I think it very disedifying to see how little regard is had for him [James III] at Rome', Dr John Ingleton, his confessor wrote, 'where he ought to expect his chief support and countenance. Nothing keeps him out of his Kingdoms but his religion, and adhesion to the Apostolick see.'[297] The king, as one courtier put it, 'ne s'attend pas à des grands égards de la Cour de Rome sous ce Pontificiat'.[298]

On one point concerning religion, James III hoped to please both Rome and his subjects in England: his decision to remove Jesuits quietly from the exiled court. To do so with too much *éclat* would seem an open disavowal of his father's legacy. In June 1711, Ingleton noted with pleasure that the king was 'of late very much weaned from the Fathers', and by the time he was attacked by smallpox in April 1712, he had dispensed with their services altogether.[299]

In London, the 'Great Changes' of 1710 had resulted in the fall of the Marlborough–Godolphin coalition, which was predominantly Whig, and its replacement by a largely Tory administration led by Robert Harley.[300] Even before Harley had re-entered office in August 1710, he had established contact

[293] HMC *Portland* IV, 672: Alexander Cunningham to Robert Harley, 17 April 1711, Rome.

[294] Head, *Fallen Stuarts*, 149.

[295] For the nomination, marquis de Ruvigny and Raineval, *The Jacobite Peerage* (London, 1974), 226, 232; BL Add. MSS 31,256, ff. 28–31: Perth to Gualterio, 18 October 1711, Saint-Germain; Head, *Fallen Stuarts*, 149–50.

[296] Head, *Fallen Stuarts*, 150–1; BL Add. MSS 31,259, ff. 22–4, 29–31: Nairne to Gualterio, 15 March, 5 April 1714, Bar-le-Duc.

[297] WDA, EV IV, 86: Dr John Ingleton to Lawrence Mayes, 17 July 1712 [Saint-Germain].

[298] BL Add. MSS 31,259, ff. 14–15: Nairne to Gualterio, 15 February 1714, Bar.

[299] WDA, EV IV, ff. 30, 76: Ingleton to Mayes, 17 June 1711, 18 April 1712 [Saint-Germain].

[300] For a detailed account of the 'Great Changes', see Gregg, *Queen Anne*, 297–329.

with Torcy, the French foreign minister, through Edward Villiers, Earl of Jersey, and a London agent of Torcy's, the abbé François Gaultier. Peace, Harley told Gaultier through Jersey, was to be negotiated on the basis of a secret under-standing with France, at the expense of the Allies. Philip V would be allowed to retain Spain and the Indies; in return, Great Britain would receive exclu-sive and extensive commercial advantages in Europe and the Americas. In so doing, the new government would take the first step in undoing the life-work of William III: the dissolution of the union of the Maritime Powers.[301] To secure themselves after Queen Anne's death against retribution for such a gross betrayal of the Allies (including the Elector of Hanover), Jersey in-formed Gaultier in 1710 that the new ministers' third proposal was to restore James after the queen's death, 's'il pensoit comme Eux', principally on reli-gion.[302] In January 1711, Gaultier was dispatched from London to Versailles. Acting on verbal instructions from Harley (soon to be appointed lord trea-surer and created Earl of Oxford), Shrewsbury and Jersey, Gaultier carried peace proposals to Versailles, arriving there on 21 January. If France accepted these conditions, the abbé assured Torcy, the British government could in-sert an article in the final peace treaty providing for James's restoration upon Anne's death. The English considered it mandatory, Gaultier reported sepa-rately to both Torcy and Berwick, that Queen Mary and Middleton should not know of the secret negotiations. Gaultier also presented Berwick with two further conditions. First, James must provide adequate assurances for the preservation of the established church and the liberties of England; Saint-Germain had routinely offered such promises since 1702. The second de-mand reflected the fact that Jacobite strength was greater in the Commons elected in 1710 than it had ever been since Anne's accession.[303] The Jacobite party was to be instructed to support the ministry. At Berwick's instigation, James immediately dispatched such orders to his friends in England[304] and undoubtedly helped contribute to Oxford's success in subduing his more rad-ical supporters. With only slight exaggeration, James III later informed Torcy

[301] Head, *Fallen Stuarts*, 158–9.

[302] G.M. Trevelyan, 'The "Jersey Period" of the Negotiations Leading to the Peace of Utrecht', *English Historical Review* 49 (1934), 102: Gaultier to Torcy, 7 October 1710 NS, London.

[303] Geoffrey Holmes, *British Politics in the Age of Anne* (London, 1967), 93; Onno Klopp, *Der Fall des Hauses Stuart und die Succession des Hauses Hannover in Groß-Britannien und Irland*, 14 vols. (Vienna, 1875–88), XIV, 673.

[304] Macpherson, *Original Papers*, II, 222; Felix Salomon, *Geschichte des letzten Ministeriums Königin Annas von England und der englischen Thronfolgefrage* (Gotha, 1894), 68–9; *Mémoires du Maréchal de Berwick*, vol. LXIV in *Collection des mémoires relatifs à l'histoire de France*, 219–20.

that Oxford could never have achieved peace without Jacobite support in Parliament.[305]

With peace as their first priority, both the British and the French governments had a mutual interest in keeping the Jacobite movement quiescent during their negotiations.[306] Yet the proposals conveyed by Gaultier placed Torcy in a quandary. Here were English minsters whose interest seemingly made it probable that they would undertake a restoration, yet Torcy knew full well that their fundamental condition – James's conversion – was precluded by his Stuart obstinacy. Even if Torcy's personal religious convictions had allowed him – which they did not – to urge James's conversion, he was in no position to do so as a minister of His Most Christian Majesty.[307] In order to secure peace for France, Torcy, using Gaultier as his London agent and Berwick as his spokesman at Saint-Germain, was happy to establish himself as the exclusive channel for the British government's negotiations with James. He intended to keep the Jacobites quiet while encouraging the hopes of the Tories that James would not prove difficult on the religious issue, and to ensure thereby that the Jacobite question would prove no hindrance to the peace. If the negotiations ultimately led to James's restoration, Torcy could claim major credit; if a Stuart restoration proved to be a mirage, James's refusal to convert would provide an excellent cover for Torcy's 'failure'.[308]

Torcy had forbidden Gaultier to obey Jersey's orders that he inform James of the negotiations on the pretext that the Chevalier would not accept the condition that his mother should be kept in ignorance.[309] James's initiation into the secret became urgent in May, when he dispatched a letter to English Jacobites announcing that he was 'resolved never to dissemble in religion'.[310] From the initial enthusiasm with which James received this news, it is virtually certain that the question of James's religion was not broached by Torcy.[311] James immediately agreed that all communications with Queen Anne and her

---

[305] AAE, CP Angleterre 242, f. 139: James to Torcy, 12 October 1712, Châlons; cf. Macpherson, *Original Papers*, II, 417: Thomas Carte's memorandum of 3 March 1724.

[306] Salomon, *Geschichte des Letzten Ministeriums Königin Annas*, 68.

[307] John B. Rule, 'King and Minister: Louis XIV and Colbert de Torcy', in R.M Hatton and J.S. Bromley (eds.), *William III and Louis XIV: Essays 1680–1720 by and for Mark A. Thomson* (Liverpool, 1968), 218.

[308] Gregg, *Protestant Succession*, 114.

[309] Salomon, *Geschichte des Letzten Ministeriums Königin Annas*, 68; Ottocar Weber, *Der Friede von Utrecht* (Gotha, 1891), 74; AAE, CP Angleterre 232, ff. 169, 170, 175, 177, 183, 192: Gaultier to Torcy, 12, 15, 19, 22, 26 May, 2 June NS, 1711, London.

[310] Macpherson, *Original Papers*, II, 225.

[311] AAE, CP Angleterre 235, ff. 265–7: Torcy to Berwick, 17 June 1711; partly printed, [John Allen], 'Cooke's *Memoirs of Lord Bolingbroke*', *Edinburgh Review* 125 (1835), 17.

ministers should pass through Torcy's hands. Although James was willing to exclude his mother from the negotiations, he adamantly refused to accept another English demand: that he should dismiss the Earl of Middleton. It was a point which Torcy apparently pressed with some vehemence, for Gaultier's subsequent letters repeatedly warned of the strong ministerial aversion to Middleton.[312] This was to become a major sticking point in the negotiations between James III and Oxford over the next two years.

In July 1711, Gaultier returned again to Versailles, this time accompanied by the British diplomat Matthew Prior. Torcy later informed Berwick that he had learned 'par rapport' with Prior that 'les dispositions pour luy [James] sont tres bonnes, mais qu'elles ne pourront paroistre qu'après la paix'. Oxford, unlike the Whigs in 1709, had no intention of insisting upon James's expulsion from France as a condition of peace.[313]

During his visit to France, Prior also had one or more meetings with Lieutenant-General Richard Hamilton, who had served James II in Ireland in 1689–90 and who, during James III's three campaigns with the French army, had been charged by Queen Mary with responsibility for her son's safety.[314] Hamilton was, nevertheless, a discreet leader of the anti-Mary, anti-Middleton faction at Saint-Germain. Although a Catholic himself, he was conscious of the fatal impact of the Franco-Catholic connection for James's cause in England.[315] He obviously suited the new 'moderate' image which Oxford was determined to impose on Saint-Germain, and Gaultier had apparently suggested to Torcy in April that Hamilton was a fit successor for Middleton as James's prime minister.[316] James III subsequently claimed with some plausibility that Oxford could not know Hamilton, who had not been in England since 1689, and suggested that the nomination was really the result of an unholy alliance between Gaultier, Prior and Hamilton. Oxford's determination that 'he would never be concerned in any affair with Lord Middleton' was genuine and permanent,

---

[312] AAE, CP Angleterre 232, ff. 169, 192, 263: Gaultier to Torcy, 12 May, 2, 12 June 1711 NS, London; cf. Salomon, *Geschichte des Letzten Ministeriums Königin Annas*, 68, fn. 3.

[313] Gregg, *Protestant Succession*, 121.

[314] Ruth Clark, *Anthony Hamilton, His Life, His Works, and His Family* (London, 1921), 296–8: Queen Mary to Richard Hamilton, 1 September 1709, 12 August 1710. For Richard Hamilton, see Richard Hayes, *Biographical Dictionary of Irishmen in France* (Dublin, 1949), 113.

[315] BL Add. MSS 61, 559, ff. 133–8: Marlborough's 'Paris spy', 25 November 1709, Paris, quoting Richard Hamilton.

[316] L.G. Wickham Legg (ed.), 'Extracts from Jacobite Correspondence, 1712–1714', *English Historical Review* 30 (1915), 502; cf. AAE, CP Angleterre 248, f. 34: James to Torcy, 5 January 1713, Châlons. Gaultier's letter to Torcy of 12 May 1711 (*Ibid.*, 232, f. 169) indicates that he had suggested someone (undoubtedly Richard Hamilton) as a successor to Middleton during his April visit to France.

being repeated as late as 1718. James was disingenuous in raising the personal question to the exclusion of the political issue which he consistently refused to recognise: the English ministers would have nothing to do with Middleton.[317]

By October 1711, the French and British governments had signed both public and secret preliminary articles and had called for an international peace conference, which was scheduled to open in Utrecht in January 1712. The Allies, and especially George Ludwig, Elector of Hanover, protested vociferously against the content of the articles and the fact that they had been negotiated behind the Allies' backs, in direct contravention of the treaty of Grand Alliance. As the breach between the Tory ministry and Hanover continued to widen during the Utrecht negotiations, the Jacobites had little doubt that Oxford and his colleagues could not survive Queen Anne's death without a Stuart restoration: the Tory 'lawsuit', one Jacobite reported to Saint-Germain in allegorical code, 'is now so linked with yours that one cannot subsist without the other'.[318] James readily accepted the fundamental conditions laid down by Oxford through Gaultier: first, that no substantive negotiations concerning a restoration could begin until after the formal Anglo-French peace treaty was concluded; secondly, that Anne should reign peacefully during her lifetime.[319] James's conduct would be, in Berwick's words, 'tout comme si par le present traité il se trouvoit abandonné et sans esperance; cela cacheroit encore mieux le Secret [of Oxford's favourable intentions]'.[320]

The two issues to be resolved concerning the Jacobites – James's place of residence and the payment of Queen Mary's dowry – were secretly negotiated by Oxford and Torcy, using Gaultier as their intermediary. The dowry was seemingly the easier matter. In January 1712, Oxford promised Gaultier that Mary's pension would be paid (albeit without arrears, which Saint-Germain never seriously expected to obtain) from the time James withdrew from France. Although in this informal agreement the method of payment was never specified, the French and the Jacobites assumed that an accredited French diplomat (in the first instance, Gaultier) would be empowered to accept payment as

---

[317] AAE, CP Angleterre 248, f. 69: James to Torcy, 19 January 1713, Châlons; for Oxford's anti-Middleton position, see HMC *Stuart* vi, 491–2: John Ogilvie to Mar, 30 May 1718, Dunkirk.

[318] Macpherson, *Original Papers*, ii, 278: Letters from 'John Scringer', undated.

[319] For James's acceptance, AAE, CP Angleterre 237, ff. 123–4: 'Memoire pour le Sieur Gaultier' [by James], 28 March 1712; cf. 241, f. 60: Torcy to Gaultier, 28 February 1712. For the conditions, H.N. Fieldhouse, 'Bolingbroke's Share in the Jacobite Intrigue of 1710–1714', *English Historical Review* 52 (1937), 444–5; cf. AAE, CP Angleterre 240, f. 242: [Gaultier to Torcy, (?) December 1712]; 248, ff. 186–7: Gaultier to Torcy [8 February 1713 NS].

[320] AAE, CP Angleterre 241, ff. 74–6: Berwick to Torcy, 23 March 1712.

Mary's agent, thereby relieving her of the necessity of directly recognising the Revolution settlement and Anne's title as queen. (In the event, when Oxford did arrange the payment in January 1714, instead of paying an intermediary like Gaultier, as had been expected, he self-protectively paid it under royal sign manual directly to Queen Mary, who could hardly be expected to accept such payment without directly recognising the legitimacy of the Revolution settlement and, indirectly, the illegality of her son's claims. The Stuarts never saw a penny of her jointure.[321])

The issue of where James should reside was much thornier. In January 1712, Oxford suggested that James should withdraw to Rome, pretending that 'ce Prince estant à Rome sera plus prest de Londres qu'à St Germain'.[322] This was a sharp reminder that James would eventually be forced to choose between Rome and London. Oxford, however, did not attempt to follow William III's policy of pushing the Stuarts into the pope's arms: he never again suggested that James should retire to the Papal States. In May 1712, Oxford suggested that James should settle in Lorraine, again promising to pay Mary's jointure.[323] When Oxford's rival and secretary of state Henry St John, Viscount Bolingbroke, accompanied by Gaultier and Prior, visited Paris in August 1712, however, Bolingbroke initially held out against the suggestion of Lorraine in discussing the matter with Torcy, proposing instead that James should retire to a more remote place – Rome, Germany, Switzerland or Spain. Finally, after Torcy rejected these possibilities, he secured Bolingbroke's agreement to Lorraine: 'Il convînt mesme avec moy', Torcy noted, 'qu'il pouvoit arriver des cas, ou les bien intentionés en Angleterre seroient faschés que ce Prince vecust dans un pays eloigné des Isles Britanniques.' Bolingbroke also promised that Mary's jointure would be paid from the time James left France.[324]

The French attitude regarding James III was much more equivocal than Torcy's negotiations with the British revealed. Louis XIV's first goal was peace: neither Philip V nor James III would be allowed to prevent the completion of the treaty nor thereafter to imperil the peace. Louis and Torcy had little hope for a Stuart restoration, for they knew (as James still did not) that his conversion was the fundamental basis of Oxford's negotiations. For this reason, France was willing to divorce herself publicly from the Jacobites, even at the risk of offending James. Louis XIV, in the Treaty of Utrecht (1713), formally recognised the Hanoverian succession and gave an all-encompassing promise

---

[321] Gregg, *Protestant Succession*, 173, 203.
[322] AAE, CP Angleterre 241, f. 9: Gaultier to Torcy, 27 January 1712 NS, London.
[323] *Ibid.*, 238, f. 47: Gaultier to Torcy, 12 May 1712 NS, London.
[324] *Ibid.*, 239, ff. 193–207: Torcy's memorandum of his meeting with Bolingbroke, 19 August 1712.

to provide no support whatsoever to the 'pretended king of England'. Yet, given the utter unpredictability of British politics, hope – however small – remained that Louis's investment in the Stuarts might yet pay the most handsome of dividends.

While strictly subordinating Stuart interests to those of France, Louis nevertheless asked James to leave France 'avec tous les mesnagements possibles'.[325] He promised to divide the annual Stuart pension of 600,000 *livres* equally between James, who would be accompanied only by a small entourage, and his mother, who was to remain at Saint-Germain with most of the Jacobite community.[326] Furthermore, Louis attempted to satisfy one of James's principal demands, by obtaining an Allied safeconduct for him under his incognito, the *Chevalier de Saint-Georges*. This was all the more important after April 1712, when smallpox swept the château of Saint-Germain: both the king and his twenty-year-old sister, Louise-Marie, fell victim to it. He lived, but she died. James III was now the only living Stuart claimant, without heirs of his body. If his life ended at this point, Jacobitism would cease to exist. Throughout the autumn of 1712, British demands for James's removal from France became shriller, because the Tory ministers, faced with domestic and Allied opposition to the peace, wished to avoid any appearance of secretly favouring him. Louis XIV, however, genuinely feared that imperial or Hanoverian raiding parties might kidnap James from his intended – and unfortified – residence, Bar-le-Duc, and refused to expel him until he received the safeconduct. In September 1712, to placate the British, James withdrew from the Paris region, settling at Châlons – 'where he will be more private than at Reims and at less expence', Prior reported to Oxford. 'He went with absolute resignation.'[327]

Torcy believed that Bolingbroke had promised during their August meeting to use British influence to obtain safeconducts from the Dutch and the emperor, but Bolingbroke's report of their conversation threw the entire burden of procuring such guarantees upon the French.[328] For several months, responsibility was tossed back and forth between Versailles and Whitehall, but it quickly became clear that the British government had no intention of

[325] Arsène Legrelle, *La Diplomatie française et la Succession d'Espagne* (second edition, Braine-le-Comte, 1899), VI, 730.

[326] AAE, CP Angleterre 241, f. 83: Torcy to James, 31 March 1712, Versailles.

[327] BL Add. MSS 70,253, n.f.: Prior to Oxford, 9 September 1712, Fontainebleau.

[328] AAE, CP Angleterre 239, ff. 193–207: Torcy's memorandum of his meeting with Bolingbroke, 19 August 1712; *Letters and Correspondence of Henry St John, Lord Viscount Bolingbroke* (London, 1798), III, 21: Bolingbroke to Dartmouth, 21 August 1712.

committing itself to James in so public a manner. At Utrecht, the British envoys refused even to discuss the question with their French counterparts.[329]

In December, through the intercession of the Duke of Lorraine with Vienna, an imperial passport was procured, conditionally allowing James to reside in Lorraine, a neutral fief of the empire, provided that he did nothing prejudicial to either the Allied cause, the emperor, the empire or any of the several Allies.[330] Versailles regarded these conditions as worse than no safeconduct whatsoever, but the British were now desperately anxious to conclude the treaty and announced at Utrecht, and to Gaultier in London, that they would never sign while James remained in France.[331] Louis claimed that James's forced withdrawal without adequate protection against his enemies 'seroit contre le droit des gens et en quelque façon contre l'humanité'.[332] And he offered James an escort of French troops to conduct him to Nancy and to remain there as his guard until the treaty was concluded and a full safeconduct could be obtained.[333] James, however, decided to hasten the Anglo-French peace;[334] on 20 February 1713, twenty-four years after his family had fled England, James III left France to settle at Bar-le-Duc without any further Allied guarantees for his safety.

Despite France's public divorce from the Jacobite movement, Torcy and Berwick secretly continued to manage James III's affairs in cooperation with Oxford and Gaultier for, according to the latter, all Tory ministerial negotiations with James would still pass through Torcy's capable hands.[335] This was advantageous for each government: Oxford could confide in Torcy without

---

[329] AAE, CP Angleterre 240, ff. 288–91: Gaultier to Torcy, 25 December 1712 NS, London; Public Record Office, London, SP 103/102: French Plenipotentiaries to Louis XIV, 29 March 1713, Utrecht; AAE, CP Lorraine 85, ff. 173–9: d'Audiffret to Louis XIV, 13 April 1713. The British representatives were Dr John Robinson, bishop of Bristol, and Thomas Wentworth, Earl of Strafford.

[330] *Bolingbroke Correspondence*, III, 252–4: Leopold of Lorraine to Torcy, 16 December 1712.

[331] PRO, SP 100/100, 102: French Plenipotentiaries to Louis XIV, 8 August 1712, 23 January 1713, Utrecht; AAE, CP Angleterre 243, ff. 123–7: Gaultier to Torcy, 31 January 1713 NS, London; f. 144: d'Aumont to Louis XIV, 2 February 1713 NS, London; H.N. Fieldhouse, 'Oxford, Bolingbroke, and the Pretender's Place of Residence, 1711–1714', *English Historical Review* 52 (1937), 291.

[332] AAE, CP Angleterre 242, ff. 243–5: Louis to d'Aumont (additional instructions), 28 December 1712; cf. ff. 240–2: Torcy to Gaultier, 28 December 1712.

[333] Fieldhouse, 'Pretender's Residence', 291, fn. 5: Torcy to James, 28 January 1713.

[334] AAE, CP Angleterre 248, ff. 197–9: James to Torcy, 13 February 1713; 243, f. 162: Torcy to Gaultier, 15 February 1713.

[335] *Ibid.*, 248, ff. 305–9: Gaultier to Torcy, 20 March 1713 NS, London; cf. HMC *Stuart* I, 256, 279–80, 300, 319: Berwick to James, 24 February, 17 October 1713, 21 February, 27 April 1714.

fear of the leaks for which the Jacobite court was notorious,[336] while Torcy could retain his control over James.

Ironically, the Treaty of Utrecht made a Stuart restoration less necessary to France than to the Tory ministry, which had completely alienated Hanover.[337] The Utrecht settlement left the house of France, in Torcy's words, 'superior to the state in which it had been in the time of Charlemagne'.[338] Following James's withdrawal to Lorraine, Torcy played a very deep game. While assuring James and Berwick that he was doing everything possible to encourage Oxford to proceed with a Stuart restoration, Torcy really attempted to prevent further negotiations on this issue. A Franco-imperial peace, the negotiation and ratification of an Anglo-French commercial treaty, and a final settlement on the destruction of the Dunkirk naval fortifications might all be imperilled if Oxford's negotiations with James, based on the premise that James might be brought to enter the Church of England, collapsed prematurely. Torcy therefore suggested to Oxford on the one hand that James would prove compliant with his wishes while, on the other, he advised James that he should avoid giving any answer whatsoever to requests that he should change his religion. Furthermore, Torcy imposed absolute silence about James's interests upon his London representatives. In short, he continued to avoid *éclat*.

The story of James III's future relations with the Tory ministers is dealt with elsewhere. While they were resident at Saint-Germain, who got the best of the bargain, the Stuarts or the French? 'The French King only minded our King', the Scottish Jacobite George Lockhart lamented in 1714, 'in so far as his own Interest led him, and made use of him as a Tool to promote and to be subservient to his own private Designs.'[339]

[336] AAE, CP Angleterre 244, f. 70: [Gaultier to Torcy], [August 1713].

[337] Berwick, *Mémoires*, 224.   [338] Head, *Fallen Stuarts*, 158–9.

[339] [George Lockhart], *Memoirs concerning the Affairs of Scotland from Queen Anne's Accession to the Throne, to the Comencement of the Union of the Two Kingdoms of Scotland and England in May 1707* (London, 1714), 359–60.

CHAPTER TWO

The Château-Vieux de Saint-Germain

The news that Mary of Modena had arrived in France with the infant Prince of Wales in December 1688 took Louis XIV completely by surprise. When the queen wrote to him from Calais on 21 December (NS),[1] asking to be allowed to live under his protection, his immediate reaction was to lend her the Château de Vincennes, to the east of Paris. Within days, however, he changed his mind and decided that the Château-Vieux de Saint-Germain-en-Laye would be more suitable.[2] It was conveniently close to Versailles and had a very much more attractive location. Louis received the queen at Chatou on 6 January 1689, and escorted her for the last few miles of her journey. He then returned to Saint-Germain to greet James II when he arrived there the following day.[3]

The royal estate at Saint-Germain-en-Laye was situated 16 kilometres to the west of Paris at the south end of a plateau which commanded spectacular views east over the river Seine towards the city. It had been an important royal residence since the middle ages, but had been progressively expanded and improved during the sixteenth and seventeenth centuries, particularly since 1661. By 1689 it consisted of two châteaux, some impressive gardens and various dependent buildings. To the north was an extensive hunting forest, well stocked with game. To the west was a small town which provided additional accommodation for courtiers and services for the court. It was an ideal location and had been Louis XIV's principal residence from 1666 to 1682.[4]

James II was given the larger of the two royal châteaux, known as the château-vieux. The other one, the château-neuf, was retained by Louis as the official residence of the governor of the town, the marquis de Montchevreuil, but the exiled Jacobites were able to use all the gardens surrounding both buildings.

[1] SP 1/23, Mary of Modena to Louis XIV, 11/21 December 1688, a copy made in 1701, quoted in full in Corp, *Cour des Stuarts*, 60.

[2] Sourches, III, 4, 3 January 1689.

[3] Dangeau, II, 289–92, 6–7 January 1689; Sourches, III, 6–7, 6–7 January 1689.

[4] *Louis XIV à Saint-Germain, 1638–82: de la naissance à la gloire*, exhibition catalogue, ed. B. Saule (Saint-Germain-en-Laye, 1988).

FIG. 1. *La Réception faite au Roy d'Angleterre par le Roy à St. Germain en Laye le VIIe Janvier 1689*, anonymous engraving from the Almanach Royal of 1689 (BN Est. Qb¹ 1689). Louis XIV and his courtiers are shown greeting James II in the Queen's Guard Chamber, with the Earl of Melfort on the extreme left. The engraving also shows Mary of Modena and her ladies waiting for James II in the Queen's Bedchamber. (For the Guard Chamber, cf. Fig. 10; for the true position of the Bedchamber, see Fig. 6.)

Detailed maps and plans of the period show us exactly how the châteaux and gardens were arranged when the Stuarts resided there.[5] The approach to the royal estate was by a road which rose up steeply from the river around the southern end of the plateau, and then continued north past a series of royal buildings until the south-west corner of the château-vieux came into view. These buildings included the royal stables, *manège* and kennels, a *Jeu de Paume*

[5] The plans of the château-vieux are preserved in AN O/1/1721; BN Est. Va. 78c, t. 2, B.8550–57; and BN Est. Va. 448e, H.188573–92. For the surrounding area, see BN Est. C.79045, 'Plan général des châteaux et ville de St. Germain-en-Laye', 1705; and BN Cartes et Plans, Ge DD 2987, no. 843, 'Plan général de Saint-Germain-en-Laye et ses environs', 1709. For the plans of the water supplies of both the château and the town, see AN O/1/1719, nos .23, 39.

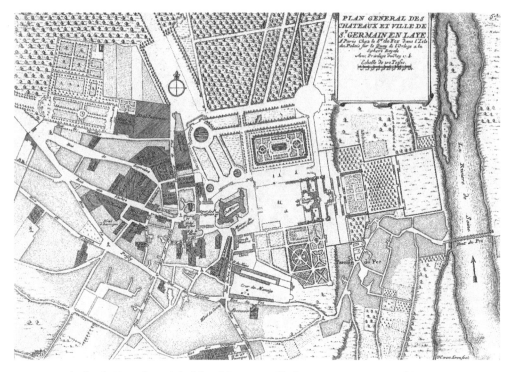

FIG. 2. Nicolas de Fer, *Plan Général des Châteaux et Ville de St. Germain en Laye*. This engraving was first published in 1702 and republished in 1705.

(specially restored for James II in 1691 and looked after by Monsieur Basin), and the house of the *Contrôleur des Bâtiments* (Monsieur Ruzé), responsible to the *Surintendant des Bâtiments du Roi* (Jules Hardouin-Mansart) for the maintenance of all the royal buildings.[6] To enter either of the châteaux one turned sharp right after the *Maison du Contrôleur* into a large area which lay between the two buildings, covered in grass and divided into sections by gravel paths. The main entrance to the château-vieux, via a drawbridge, was on one's left, with the château-neuf straight in front to the east.

The château-vieux was situated approximately 100 metres from the edge of the plateau. The château-neuf, a much smaller and lighter building, was perched on the very edge, above an 800 metre drop. To approach it, one had to take a central path through the large grassed area and then enter a square

6 For the *Jeu de Paume*, see Corp, *Cour des Stuarts*, 97–8. For Basin and Ruzé, see *L'Etat de la France* (Paris, 1708), 345, and Sourches, VI, 192, 196, 10 and 28 October 1699. For the personal involvement of Hardouin-Mansart, see Nairne, 20 November 1699. For the maintenance of the château and gardens throughout the Stuart period, see *Comptes des Bâtiments du Roi sous le Règne de Louis XIV*, ed. Jules Guiffrey, III–V (Paris, 1891, 1894, 1901).

FIG. 3. *Le Château Neuf de St. Germain en Laye du côté de la Cour . . . Jacques II Roi d'Angletterre . . . y tient sa Cour,* anonymous engraving published by J. Mariette. This engraving dates from the 1670s, before the five pavilions were added to the corners of the château-vieux (seen on the left). It shows what by 1689 was the view of the château-neuf looking eastwards towards the river Seine and Paris from the queen's Guard Chamber in the south-east pavilion.

courtyard with apsed bays in the four sides of its enclosing wall. The château itself was not large and consisted of a central hall (used by the Assembly of the French Clergy), with a pavilion at each of its four corners. To the north and south there were galleries containing apartments for the marquis and marquise de Montchevreuil, together with small chapels overlooking the river, and service wings running parallel to the courtyard.

The gardens and terraces of Saint-Germain were internationally famous. In front of the north wing of the château-vieux there was a magnificent *grand parterre*, recently laid out by André Le Nôtre. It consisted of two sections of box broderie, separated by a wide central alley which led to a large basin and fountain. There were two smaller fountains placed at either side, in front of the château, and the axis of the central alley was extended for several miles into the forest beyond.

The gardens of the château-neuf consisted of a large rectangular parterre to the north called the *Jardin de la Dauphine*, linked to the *grand parterre* by a triangle containing three basins of different shapes, and an ensemble to the south known as the *Boulingrin* (Bowling Green). These two gardens were

FIG. 4. Jacques Rigaud, *Vüe du Vieux Château de St. Germain en Laye*, 1725. This engraving shows the north façade, viewed from the *grand parterre*. The king's staircase can be seen in the centre, separating the *Appartement du Roi* (occupied by James II) on the left from the *Appartement du Dauphin* (occupied by James III) on the right. The royal apartments are on the second floor with the balcony.

supported on the east by two gigantic retaining walls attractively decorated in brick and stone. At the north-east corner of the *Jardin de la Dauphine* was a *rond-point*, from which extended a huge promenade known as the *grande terrasse*. This was about 300 metres wide and about 2.5 kilometres long, and ran along the forest above the escarpment of the plateau, supported by another massive retaining wall. Near the far end was a hunting lodge, the Château du Val.

Immediately below the château-neuf itself, dropping steeply down towards the Seine, were the famous hanging gardens of Saint-Germain, connected by a series of terraces and ramps. At the heart of these gardens was the *Jardin des Dentelles*, flanked to north and south by arms extending from the terrace and culminating in two small pavilions. Below it were two walled enclosures which led gently down to the river; above it, within the arms of four double ramps leading up to the château-neuf, were some of the most celebrated and elaborate grottoes in Europe.

The main château was known as the château-vieux because it was built on medieval foundations, and incorporated within its overall design both a *donjon* and a Gothic chapel. These traces of the château's medieval past, however, had largely been hidden behind more modern façades. Its shape was an irregular pentagon built around a central courtyard, with pavilions projecting from the five corners. Running around the entire building, half way up the façades, was a terrace with an attractive gilded wrought-iron grill. Below the terrace there were two storeys overlooking a dry moat faced with a light-coloured stone,

F I G . 5. David Duvivier, *Veüe de L'eglise Royale de Saint Germain en Laye, Rebatie . . . en l'année 1682* (BN Est. Va. 421, t.1). The west façade of the château-vieux can be seen in the background, showing the entrance from the *cour des cuisines*.

and incorporating some of the old machicolations. Above the terrace there were two, and in the corners and pavilions three, more storeys in an elegant Italianate style combining stone and red brick. Finally, there was a flat roof to provide panoramic views, and a campanile on top to mark the position of the original *donjon*.

Louis XIV's decision to transfer the French court from the Château-Vieux de Saint-Germain to his new château at Versailles had been taken for two main reasons, the shape of the building and its relative shortage of accommodation for courtiers.[7] With narrow wings built around a central courtyard, there were serious problems of circulation, with the need to go up and down stairs, and even out of doors, to get from one apartment to another. This inconvenience remained with the Stuarts when they established their court in the château. The shortage of accommodation, however, was less of a problem, partly because

[7] Saint-Simon, XXVIII, 131; XLI, 245.

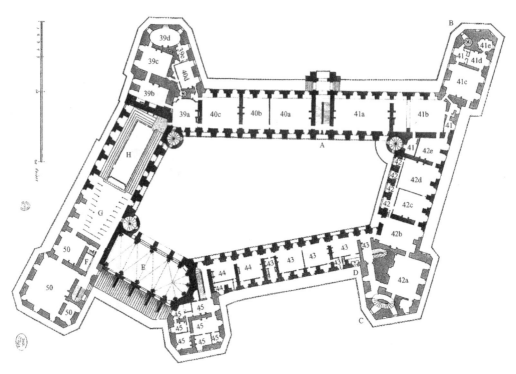

FIG. 6. The Château-Vieux de Saint-Germain: second floor (BN Est. Va. 78c, t.2, B.8553).

The second floor of the château, showing the distribution of the apartments, and their allocation in April 1692

39 *Appartement de la Dauphine:* vacant
40 *Appartement du Dauphin:* vacant
41 *Appartement du Roi:* James II
42 *Grand Appartement du Roi:* Mary of Modena
43 *Appartement des Enfants de France:* Prince of Wales
44 The prince's under-governess (Lady Strickland)
45 The prince's governess (Countess of Erroll)
50 *Pour habiller les danseurs:* vacant

The second floor entresols

above 41: The king's necessary woman (Elinor Skelton)
              The king's confessor (Father John Warner)
              Page of the queen's Bedchamber (Arthur Lavery)
above 43: 46 Marquis d'Albeville (former secretary of state)
above 44: 47 Gentleman waiter to the prince (Lawrence Du Puy)
              The servants of the under-governess
above 45: 48 The servants of the governess
           49 Page of the prince's Bedchamber (Baltassare Artema)
above 50: 51 Page of the prince's Bedchamber (William Lonning)
           52 Rocker to the Prince (Mary Waldegrave)

The other parts of the château

A King's staircase
B King's backstairs
C Queen's staircase
D Little Chapel (2nd floor)

the exiled court was smaller than the court of France, and partly because during the 1680s Louis XIV had ordered Hardouin-Mansart to add a pavilion to each of the five corners of the château. He had thus increased the size of the royal apartments and added over twenty-five new apartments for his courtiers — in addition to considerably improving the external appearance of the rather oddly shaped building.[8] Even though most of the Jacobites had to find lodgings in the town, a much higher proportion of courtiers could be accommodated in the château than had been the case when Louis XIV lived there.

The royal apartments were situated on the second floor of the château, with the terraces outside, and occupied the north, east and south wings. The north

---

[8] *Louis XIV à Saint-Germain*, 114–24; and the plans of the château cited in note 5 above.

←————————————————————

E   Chapel
F   *Petite cour des cuisines*
G   Stage of the theatre (2nd floor)
H   Theatre (2nd floor)

The use of the royal apartments

James II, 1690–1701
41a   Guard Chamber
41b   Antechamber
41c   Bedchamber
41d   Closet
41e   Oratory

Prince of Wales, 1695–99; James III, 1702–12
40a   Guard Chamber
40b   Presence Chamber
40c   Privy Chamber
39a   Withdrawing Room
40d   Bedchamber
39c   Closet
39b   Private Cabinet
39d   Private Cabinet
39e   Chapel

Mary of Modena, 1689–99
42a   Guard Chamber
42b   Presence Chamber
42c   Privy Chamber
42d   Bedchamber
42e   Little Bedchamber

Prince of Wales, 1699–1701; James III, 1701–2
41a   Guard Chamber
41b   Antechamber/Presence Chamber?
42e   Privy Chamber?
42d   Bedchamber?
42c   Closet?
42b   Private Cabinet?
42a   Guard Chamber?

Mary of Modena, 1699–1702
40a   Guard Chamber
40b   Presence Bedchamber
40c   Bedchamber for receiving visits
40d   Bedchamber

Princess Louise-Marie, 1699–1702
39a   Guard Chamber
39b   Antechamber
39c   Bedchamber
39d   Closet
39e   Chapel

Mary of Modena, 1702–18
42a   Guard Chamber
42b   Presence Chamber
42c   Privy Chamber
42d   Bedchamber for receiving visits
42e   Bedchamber

Princess Louise-Marie, 1702–12
41a   Guard Chamber
41b   Antechamber
41c   Bedchamber
41d   Closet
41e   Oratory

wing was the longest and was divided in the middle by a large stone staircase, thus providing an apartment on its west side (originally for the dauphin) as well as one on its east side for the king. The east wing was occupied by the queen, whose apartment was thus linked with that of the king in the north-east corner. The south wing was intended for the royal children, and shared a staircase with the queen's apartment in the south-east corner. Finally, the west wing contained a magnificent theatre, while the chapel connected the south and west wings and completed the irregular pentagon.

The central courtyard was entered from the south and gave access both to the king's staircase in the middle of the north wing and to a newly built queen's staircase, which was oval, in the south-east pavilion. Additional staircases were placed in each of the five corners of the courtyard, three of them small spiral ones outside the north and west wings, entered from the courtyard itself, while the other two were within the building, at either end of the south wing. There was thus a constant traffic of people walking across the courtyard from one staircase to another.

When the Stuarts arrived at the beginning of 1689 the interiors of the five pavilions had not all been completed, and it took some time before all the new apartments could be inhabited.[9] But the most important work needed to be carried out in the apartments of the king and queen themselves. This was partly because the rooms, particularly the new ones in the pavilions, contained no furniture and were not even properly decorated, partly also because the queen's apartment in the east wing had recently been redesigned by Louis XIV as a second apartment for the king.[10]

After the death of the queen of France in 1683, Louis XIV had reproduced at Saint-Germain the new arrangement introduced at Versailles in 1684, whereby there was a *Grand Appartement du Roi*, without a Bedchamber, to be used for receptions and entertainments, as well as the normal *Appartement du Roi* where he actually lived and had his formal Bedchamber. When the Stuarts arrived this meant that the new *Grand Appartement du Roi* had to be transformed into an apartment for the queen at the same time as being decorated and furnished. Life for the Stuarts must therefore have been uncomfortable when they first arrived at Saint-Germain. James II was spared further inconvenience when he left for Ireland in February 1689, but Mary of Modena had to wait until June 1689 before the first phase of work on her apartment could be completed.

[9] G. Lacour-Gayet, *Le Château de Saint-Germain-en-Laye* (Paris, 1935), 119–22.

[10] Sourches, III, 6, 6 January, 1689: 'l'appartement . . . qui étoit l'appartement de la défunte Reine, sa femme, mais augmenté de beaucoup par les bâtiments neufs qu'il y avoit faits'.

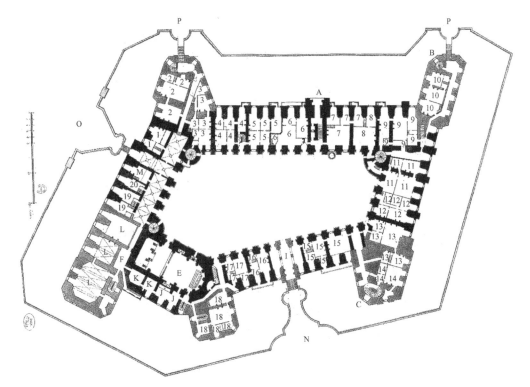

FIG. 7. The Château-Vieux de Saint-Germain: ground floor (BN Est. Va. 78c, t.2, B.8550).

The ground floor of the château, showing the distribution of the apartments, and their allocation in April 1692

  1 *Chapelain* (Monsieur des Viviers, abbé de Beaumont)
  2 Yeoman of the Larder (John Martinash)
  3 *Concierge* (Henri Soulaigre) and the king's master cook, in a room lent him by the *Concierge* (Thomas Atkins)
  4 Groom of the king's Bedchamber (Richard Trevanion)
  5 The queen's apothecary (Matthew Harrison)
  6 Groom of the king's Bedchamber (Francis Stafford)
  7 Gentleman Usher in the king's Antechamber (Walter Innes)
  8 Chaplain to the queen (Father La Croix)
  9 Clerk of the kitchens (Nathaniel Gautherne)
 10 King's Wardrobe
 11 The king's vice-chamberlain (James Porter)
 12 Groom of the king's Bedchamber (Sir Randall MacDonnell)
 13 Closet keeper and page of the king's Bedchamber (Jacques Delabadie); and dry nurse to the prince (Mary Anne Delabadie)
 14 Master of the queen's robes (Francesco Riva)
 15 Gentleman of the queen's Privy Chamber (William Crane)
 16 *Lieutenant des Gardes en quartier*
 17 Admiral Sir Roger Strickland
 18 Sir Daniel Arthur (the king's banker)
 19 Gentleman usher of the queen's Privy Chamber (Thomas Neville)
 20 The prince's nurse, formerly wet nurse (Frances Smith); and page of the queen's Presence Chamber (Matthew Smith)

The other parts of the château

  A King's staircase
  B King's backstairs
  C Queen's staircase
  E Chapel
  F *Petite cour des cuisines*
  I Vestibule; *gardes de la porte*
  J Sacristy

  K Visiting preachers
  L Pastry, bakehouse, kitchens and larder
  M *Gardes de la porte*
  N Main entrance
  O Entrance from the *cour des cuisines*
  P Entrances from the *grand parterre*

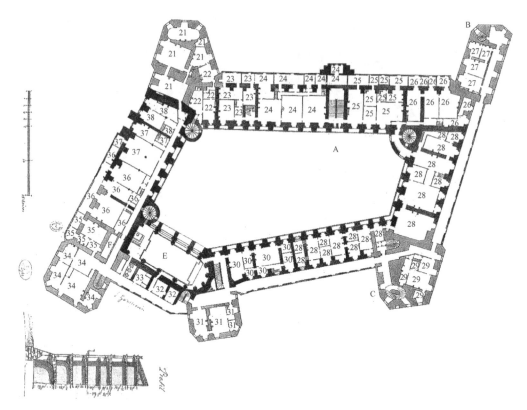

FIG. 8. The Château-Vieux de Saint-Germain: first floor (BN Est. Va. 78c, t.2, B.8552).

The First Floor of the Château, showing the distribution of the apartments, and their allocation in April 1692

21 Comptroller of the household (Bevil Skelton)
22 Lady of the Bedchamber (Duchess of Tyrconnel)
23 Groom of the queen's Privy Chamber (William Hyde)
24 Lord Chamberlain (Duke of Powis)
25 Duke of Berwick
26 Lord Henry FitzJames
27 Lady of the Bedchamber (Countess of Almond)
28 East: secretary of state (Earl of Melfort)
   South: the queen's private secretary (John Caryll)
29 Bedchamber woman (Contessa Veronica Molza)
30 Gentleman daily waiter of the queen (Matteo-Maria Turrini)
31 Bedchamber woman (Pellegrina Turrini)
32 Officers of the *Gardes du Corps*
33 Officers of the *Gardes du Corps*
34 Lady of the Bedchamber (Lady Sophia Bulkeley)
35 Henrietta, Lady Waldegrave
36 Clerk controller of the Greencloth (Henry Conquest)
37 Clerk controller of the Greencloth (Sir John Sparrow)
38 2nd Earl of Dumbarton (son of the 1st Earl, gentleman of the king's Bedchamber, died March 1692)

FIG. 8. (*cont.*)

The other parts of the château

A King's Staircase

B King's Backstairs

C Queen's Staircase

E Chapel

F *Petite cour des cuisines*

The allocation of the apartments on the third floor of the château in April 1692

53 Henry Browne (former secretary of state)

54 Keeper of the King's Privy Purse (Fergus Grahme)

55 John Stafford (former Ambassador)

56 Officers of the Guard

57 Chaplain to the king (Father Dominic White)

58 The king's barber (Michael Bedingfield)

59 The queen's physician (Sir William Waldegrave) and Bedchamber woman (Isabella, Lady Waldegrave)

60 Comte de Lauzun (created duc de Lauzun in May 1692)

61 Groom of the king's Bedchamber (Richard Biddulph)

62 The queen's vice-chamberlain (Robert Strickland) and Bedchamber woman (Bridget Strickland)

63 The queen's equerry (Charles Leyburne)

64 Junior almoner to the queen (Father Lewis Innes)

65 The queen's confessor (Father Marco Antonio Galli)

66 Rocker to the prince (Elizabeth Delattre)

67 Rocker to the prince (Jane Chappell)

68 Rocker to the prince (Elizabeth Rogé)

69 Lady Lucy Herbert

70 *Garde meuble au dessus de la chapelle*

71 Chaplain to the queen (Father Bartolemeo Ruga)

72 Chaplain to the prince (Father Lewis Sabran)

73 Sir Edward Hales (created Earl of Tenterden in May 1692)

The allocation of the apartments on the fourth floor of the château (in the five corner pavilions only) in April 1692

North-west:

74 Yeoman rider to the queen (Robert Buckenham)

75 Yeoman of the confectionary (Michael Noble)

76 The prince's under-preceptor (Thomas Codrington)

The prince's necessary woman (Anne Clarke)

North-east:

58 The king's barber (Michael Bedingfield)

59 The queen's physician (Sir William Waldegrave) and Bedchamber woman (Isabella, Lady Waldegrave)

South-east:

61 Groom of the king's Bedchamber (Richard Biddulph)

77 The king's surgeon (François de Gassis de Beaulieu)

South:

78 Rocker to the prince (Elizabeth Simms) and gentleman waiter to the prince (James Simms)

79 Page of the queen's Bedchamber (Dominique Dufour)

80 Senior and junior almoner to the queen (Father Giacomo and Father Peregrino Ronchi)

South-west:

81 *Garde meuble*

82 Gentleman usher in the king's Antechamber (Joseph Ronchi)

(The lists in Figs. 6–9 are based on Bodleian Library, Carte MSS 208, ff. 287–8, 'A Liste of such as Lodge in ye Castle', April 1692, with additional information from: BN Est. Va. 78c, t.2 b.8725ff., 'Logement du Chasteau de St. Germain, ce qui est fait de neuf y estant compris', 25 February to 4 March 1685; Arch. Dépt. des Yvelines, a.369/2 and 3, 'Etat des Appartements du Vieux Château Royal de Saint-Germain-en-Laye' and 'Le nom des habitants, étage par étage, le nombre de pièces qu'ils occupent, cheminées comprises, ainsi que les sous-sols, au Château-Vieux de Saint-Germain-en-Laye', 1737–38.)

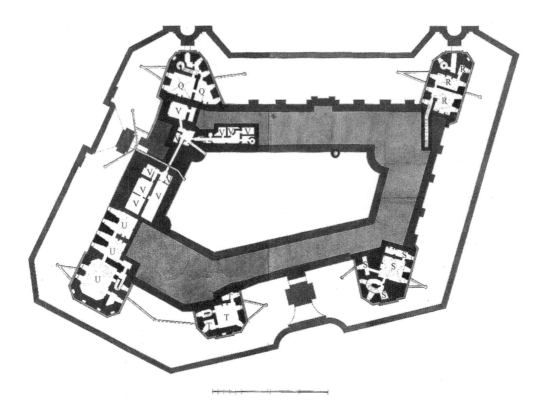

FIG. 9. The Château-Vieux de Saint-Germain: below stairs (BN Est. Va. 448e, H.188585).

The distribution of the basements of the Château below stairs
Q Butteries and chaundry
R Woodyard
S Confectionary
T Cellars
U Pantry and ewry
V Additional cellars

When James II returned from Ireland in 1690 he was confronted with another problem, because his apartment, originally planned for French not English court ceremonial, was not large enough. Even by contemporary French standards the Château-Vieux de Saint-Germain was considered too small. It was the only major French royal residence which still had one antechamber and not two between the king's Guard Chamber and his Bedchamber. But a king of England was accustomed to having not only two antechambers (a Presence Chamber and a Privy Chamber) but also a Withdrawing Room, a Privy Gallery, a separate Eating Room and (in his secret lodgings) a separate Council Chamber. Instead of all these, James II had to make do with the single antechamber and a little closet beyond his Bedchamber.[11] It inevitably influenced his daily life and the way that he organised his household.

The *Grand Appartement du Roi*, however, was much larger and contained five rooms, which meant that the new queen's apartment could have both a Presence Chamber and a Privy Chamber. There was also room for a Little Bedchamber, where the king and queen could sleep together, beyond the queen's formal Bedchamber. This was accessible to the king through a small corridor behind the east wall of his antechamber.

The contents of the apartments of James II and Mary of Modena during the 1690s are described in detail in the *Journal du Garde Meuble*.[12] Some though not all of the rooms are also described in the *Inventaire Général du Mobilier de la Couronne*.[13] It is therefore possible to give at least an idea of what the royal apartments at Saint-Germain looked like when they were occupied by the Stuarts after 1689.[14]

Some of the contents of the apartments were the same as they had been when occupied by Louis XIV. In particular the king's Guard Chamber was not redecorated for the Stuarts and still had the decorations specially made for it in 1672. It contained 'une tenture de tapisserie de brocatelle aurore et vert, avec des bordures et montants aurore et rouge'. Beyond that the antechamber

---

[11] Corp, 'Etiquette and Use of Royal Apartments', 242.

[12] AN o/1/3306, 3307, 3308. These volumes of the 'Journal du Garde Meuble' cover the years 1689 to 1711. The most important descriptions are in o/1/3306, particularly 'Etat de plusieurs meubles de broderie anciennes faits et livrez cy devant pour les App.ts du Chau. de St. Germain en Laye non encore enregistrez', June 1689, and various entries for January 1689. The entries concerning Saint-Germain continue at regular intervals throughout the period.

[13] *Inventaire Général du Mobilier de la Couronne sous Louis XIV*, ed. Jules Guiffrey, 2 vols. (Paris, 1885–86) prints most but not all of the information relevant to the Stuart court in AN o/1/3330–3. The most important descriptions are in vol. II, 383 and 386–9.

[14] The sequence of rooms (with their French descriptions) was as follows. In the *Appartement du Roi*: Guard Chamber (*Salle des Gardes*); the Antechamber (*Antichambre*); and the Bedchamber (*Grande Chambre*). In the *Appartement de la Reine*: Guard Chamber (*Salle des Gardes du Grand Appartement*); Presence Chamber (*Antichambre du Grand Appartement*); Privy Chamber (*Grand Cabinet du Grand Appartement*); and the Bedchamber (*Grande Chambre du Grande Appartement*). The room in the angle, probably intended as a *Salle du Conseil*, was the Little Bedchamber of both the king and the queen and is, exceptionally, referred to as *la Petite Chambre du Roy*. The two apartments also each had a small staircase which led, via a small cabinet, directly to the *Antichambre*, thus bypassing the *Salle des Gardes* ('un cabinet attenant la d. antichambre et servant de passage'). In the case of the *Grand Appartement* there was also an extra *Antichambre* between the small staircase and the cabinet. The existence of these additional rooms, the confusingly similar names given to them and the illogical sequence in which they are presented in both the *Journal du Garde Meuble* and the *Inventaire Général* partly explain why these valuable documentary sources have never been used before to describe the appearance of the royal apartments of the English court at Saint-Germain.

was decorated with a *tapisserie* 'représentant des emblèmes et des fleurons enfermez par des bandes en compartimens de large passement vieux, de soye rouge cramoisy à fleurs veloutées fonds de satin, ayant au milieu un grand rond . . . représentant une salamandre au pied d'un laurier, entre deux escussons, avec ces mots "Extinguo Nutrisco"'. It was in this room that Mignard's large portrait of *The Family of James II* was placed in 1695. The king's Bedchamber was more fully furnished and contained 'un riche emmeublement de velours rouge cramoisy . . . consistant en un lit, deux fauteuils, deux carreaux, huit sièges plians et une tapisserie'. The bed was decorated 'de plusieurs tableaux de broderie à personnages or, argent et soye, repésentant l'histoire de Joseph . . . garny de crespine, frange et molet d'or de Milan à la milanoise, supportez de soye rouge cramoisy'. The *fauteuils, carreaux* and *sièges pliants* were 'de velours plain garnis de frange molet et galon d'or suportez de soye cramoisy avec leurs fausses housses de serge de Londres rouge et les bois peints de rouge avec un filet d'or'. Finally the *tapisserie* consisted of five separate pieces, two behind the bed and one on each of the other three walls, 'dans chacune desquelles est un grand lion enparqué, tenant dans sa gueule une branche de grenadier'.

The queen's Guard Chamber contained 'une tapisserie de broderie d'or et soye . . . dont partie représentent les armes de Navarre, partie remplie de compartimens de retaille fonds d'argent et partie représent des histoires de l'Ancien Testament'. The Presence and the Privy Chambers were the last to be decorated and had not been finished when the *Journal du Garde Meuble* was brought up to date in June 1689. The plans, however, were recorded. The Presence Chamber was to have a 'tapisserie des devizes de Pau . . . représent divers sujets de metamorphozes rehaussez d'or, d'argent et soye . . . et aux 4 coins . . . les armes de Bourbon et de Navarre'.[15] The *tapisserie* of the Privy Chamber was to be 'de velours rouge cramoisy en broderie' with 'des grandes figures . . . représentant diverses histoires de l'Ancien Testament'. The queen's Bedchamber, like that of the king, was more fully furnished and also contained 'un emmeublement de velours rouge cramoisy . . . consistant en un grand lit, deux fauteuils, douze sièges ployans, deux carreaux et une tapisserie'. The bed was decorated 'de plusieurs tableaux . . . représentant des oyseaux, animaux, fleurs et fruits, et d'autres tableaux de broderie or, argent et soye, représentant des salamandres; le reste remply de compartimens de taillure de toile d'or filé et des enclos de toile d'argent', and 'garny de crespine, frange et mollet d'or

---

[15] The antechamber which gave access to the cabinet leading directly to the queen's Presence Chamber was decorated with a 'tapisserie . . . représentant . . . Charles le Grand . . . Judas Macabée et . . . Hector de Troyes . . . à cheval'.

FIG. 10. The Château-Vieux de Saint-Germain: 'Profille et Coupe du pavillon ou est l'appartement de la Reine" (AN o/1/1721/2, no. 16). This drawing shows the south-east pavilion (though without the top floor), seen from the queen's staircase. Apart from the queen's Guard Chamber on the second floor, with the balcony, the rooms shown are (below stairs) part of the confectionary and (above stairs) the apartments of the master of the queen's robes (Francesco Riva, ground floor), one of the queen's Bedchamber women (Contessa Veronica Molza, first floor), and the queen's vice-chamberlain (Robert Strickland, third floor, with an *entresol*). The apartment on the top floor (not shown) was occupied by the king's 'chirurgeon' (François de Gassis de Beaulieu).

de Milan à la milanoise, supporté de soye rouge cramoisy'. Around the bed was a 'balustrade de bois . . . de 3 pieds de hault . . . garny de fil de laton jaune et ferrure dorée'. The *fauteuils, carreaux* and *sièges pliants* were de 'velours remplis de compartimens et feuillages de taillure de toile d'or et des petites roses . . . garnis de franges molet et galon d'or avec leurs fausses housses de taffetas cramoisy, les bois peints de rouge avec un filet d'or'. Finally the *tapisserie* was of 'velours rouge cramoisy, enrichie de tableaux . . . représentant des Fables, des Métamorphoses et d'autres tableaux ronds . . . représentant la devise de la salemandre avec ces mots "Et Extinguo Nutrisco"'. The queen's Bedchamber also contained 'une magnifique toilette' which was 'sur un pied de bois de sculpture . . . avec une dentelle de guipure de soye, rebordé d'or et d'argent, doublée de taffetas incardin'.[16]

The Little Bedchamber was not furnished until after the return of James II from Ireland in 1690. According to the plans, it also had an 'emmeublement de velours rouge cramoisy en broderie'. On the outside of the bed there were '4 tableaux carrez . . . représentant l'Enlevement de la belle Hélène', and on the inside four *tableaux* showing 'un mouton de broderie d'argent ancienne emparqueté dans son parc de broderie d'or et aux cotez deux arbres de troux ausquels sont attachez un ecusson des armes de Bourbon'. Among the 'pieces de broderie . . . a raporter sur le velours du dossier et de la courtepointe du lit' were 'un grand tableau representant la vente de Joseph' and 'un tableau rond' showing 'l'embrazement de Sodome et Gomorre'. On the walls there was a *tapisserie* 'représentant l'histoire de Judée et autres sujets de l'Ancien Testament avec les armes de Bourbon, des Ecriteaux et une terrace'.

From this description we can see that the *boiseries* of the royal apartments at the English court were mainly covered by tapestries which had been hastily assembled and adapted for the purpose, with no obvious thematic consistency. The salamander with the words 'Et Extinguo Nutrisco' was visible in both the king's Antechamber and the queen's Bedchamber. The story of Joseph was shown in both the king's Bedchamber and the Little Bedchamber. The stories from the Old Testament were in the queen's Guard Chamber, her Privy Chamber and the Little Bedchamber. There was a balustrade in the queen's Bedchamber only and not in either the king's Bedchamber or the Little Bedchamber, to which the courtiers were not normally granted access. There is no reference in the French sources to either a throne or a canopy in the king's Antechamber, the queen's Presence or her Privy Chamber. As they

---

[16] According to Sourches (III, 7), this toilette was given to the queen on 6 January 1689, 'accompagnée de six mille louis d'or'.

would have required the English coat of arms, it is not surprising that they are absent from a list of items lent by Louis XIV, but we cannot state that they were definitely there. In any event they would have had to be specially commissioned.

The *Journal du Garde Meuble* also refers to 'chandeliers de cristal a couronne dessus et des branches de cuivre doré', to various tables (both 'a tiroirs de bois de traitre les piliez tournez' and 'de bois de noyer aplacages') and to '15 miroirs noeufs' of different sizes and shapes. It is not stated, however, where all these objects were placed. Although the king's and the queen's Bedchambers contained only two armchairs in 1689, it seems clear that each was provided with a third after the return of James II from Ireland. The French sources do not mention the paintings in the royal apartments, as they belonged to the Stuarts themselves. Apart from the Mignard already mentioned, these included Benedetto Gennari's portrait of the Prince of Wales (1689) and Nicholas de Largillière's double portrait of the prince and his sister (1695), both of which were in the queen's apartment. There was also a portrait of the queen by François de Troy and a copy by Van Dyck himself of his second portrait of the *Three Children of Charles I*.[17]

The two children of the king and queen (the Prince of Wales, born in London in 1688, and Princess Louise-Marie, born at Saint-Germain in 1692) were brought up in the south wing of the château, in the apartment previously used by the *Enfants de France*. In 1695 the seven-year-old Prince was 'put into men's hands' and given his own apartment.[18] This was the former apartment of the dauphin, in the north wing, entered from the other side of the king's staircase. This apartment contained two antechambers, in addition to the Guard Chamber and the Bedchamber, and thus permitted its occupant to have both a Presence Chamber and a Privy Chamber. Beyond the apartment of the dauphin was a much smaller one in the north-west pavilion intended for the dauphine, where the prince probably had lessons with his tutors.

In the autumn of 1699 the royal apartments at Saint-Germain were rearranged and redecorated. The queen and the Prince of Wales changed places, and the young Princess Louise-Marie, now seven years old, was moved to the former apartment of the dauphine in the north-west pavilion. In effect, father and son now lived on one side of the grand staircase, and mother and

---

[17] These pictures, which are now in England, are listed in the inventory of the possessions of James II, 22 July 1703, Brotherton Library, University of Leeds, MS Dep. 1984/2/5. The triple portrait by Van Dyck had previously belonged to the duc d'Orléans: see chapter 7.

[18] Nairne, 4 June 1695; *Comptes des Bâtiments*, III, cols. 1158–61, 1195; AN 0/1/3306, 'Journal du Garde Meuble', 20 July 1695.

daughter on the other side. The sequence of rooms in the apartment of the prince, previously the apartment of the queen, was reversed: the oval staircase became the backstairs, and the apartment was now entered from the king's Antechamber.[19]

The fact that the king and queen now occupied apartments which started at the same place, and then progressively separated, meant that there could no longer be any direct contact between their Bedchambers, which were now situated in the north-east and north-west corners of the château respectively. The Little Bedchamber, which had previously been at the meeting point between the king's and queen's apartments, was therefore abolished and replaced in January 1700 by a new arrangement whereby the queen had only one antechamber but two Bedchambers. The first, immediately beyond the Privy Chamber, was described as 'la Chambre ou la Reine recoit ses visittes' and contained three armchairs. The second, which was beyond, was described as 'la Chambre' and contained only two armchairs.[20] This means that Mary of Modena compromised with French court etiquette by receiving visitors in what appeared to be her Bedchamber rather than her Privy Chamber, while her real Bedchamber remained private, with strictly limited access.

When the period of mourning at the English court was over at the end of 1702, James III decided not to occupy his father's old apartment and instead returned to the *Appartement du Dauphin*. He now also used the dauphine's apartment to add a Withdrawing Room and a Closet. Mary of Modena returned to her former apartment in the east wing, where she continued to have two Bedchambers, and the princess (still only ten years old) maintained direct access to her mother by occupying the former apartment of James II. The young king was given new armchairs and *tabourets* 'couverts d'ouvrage de la Savonnerie' in bright and attractive colours: 'fond jaune representant au milieu une rose sur fond bleu, et aux coins des cignes, garnis de frange de soye de plusieurs couleurs, les bois peints convenable à l'etoffe'. The portraits by Gennari, Largillière and Mignard were withdrawn into the king's Closet and replaced by new ones by François de Troy and Alexis-Simon

---

[19] AN o/1/1716, 'estat de ce qu'il est proposé . . . de payer aux ouvriers qui ont travaillé au chateau . . . de Saint-Germain en Laye, suivant l'ouvrage qu'ils ont fait pendant les 2 semaines finies le samedy 17 jour octobre 1699', *Comptes des Bâtiments*, IV, cols. 502–5, 562–4, 18 October to 15 November 1699. (There is no reference in Nairne because he was away from Saint-Germain at the time.)

[20] AN o/1/3307, 'estat des meubles de Deuil faire pour la Cour d'Angleterre pour le Deuil du Roy d'Angleterre deffunt Jacques 2ᵉ decedé a St Germain en Laye le 16ᵉ septembre 1701, et livré . . . pendant le moi d'octobre dernier'.

Belle.[21] For his eighteenth birthday in June 1706 James III's Privy Chamber was totally redecorated by Louis XIV in 'damas rouge cramoisy'.

James III's apartment gave him direct access to the theatre in the west wing. This had originally been designed by Vigarani and was equipped with the *machines* required for the most elaborate baroque productions. It was also the largest theatre in any of the French royal châteaux. The amphitheatre was entirely made of wood and was in the shape of a square U, with four tiers of seats on the north, east and west sides capable of seating approximately 550 people. These surrounded the central area, reserved for the royal family and its immediate entourage, where about sixty people could be comfortably accommodated. There was no proscenium arch, but an orchestra pit of 5.50 × 1.65 metres separated the auditorium from the exceptionally deep stage, capable of comfortably holding sixty performers at a time and containing fifteen flats on each side with the back wall beyond.[22] The auditorium had been decorated by Jacques Rousseau with scenes from Lully's operas.[23]

Beyond the theatre, in the south-west of the château, lay the chapel, dedicated to St John the Baptist. Although originally a free-standing medieval building, erected by St Louis in the thirteenth century, it had subsequently been incorporated into the château itself, to form just one of the five wings surrounding the interior courtyard. The rose window in the west facing the altar, the windows behind the altar, and the windows on the south, or exterior, of the chapel, had in the process been covered over, leaving the north side, facing the château's interior courtyard, as the only remaining source of natural light. The chapel was therefore relatively dark for most of the time. Moreover the ceiling of the chapel had recently been lowered, to create a furniture store above.[24] This meant that the original vaults were no longer visible, and that even the light coming in on the north side had been reduced.

We know more about the appearance of the chapel than about that of the royal apartments.[25] Its main entrance was from the interior courtyard, on the

---

[21] The fact that the pictures were withdrawn to the king's closet is stated in a note on James II's inventory (see note 17).

[22] T. Boucher, 'Un haut lieu de l'Opéra de Lully: la salle de spectacles du château de Saint-Germain-en-Laye', in J. de La Gorce and L. Sawkins (eds.), *Jean-Baptiste Lully: Actes du Colloque, 1987* (Laaber, 1990), 457–67.

[23] J.O. Hedley, 'Charles de La Fosse's "Rinaldo et Armida" and "Rape of Europa" at Basildon Park', *The Burlington Magazine* 144, 1189, (April 2002), 205–6.

[24] BN Est. Va. 78c, t.2, 'Logement du Chasteau de St. Germain, ce qui est fait neuf y estant compris', 25 February to 14 March 1685.

[25] *Louis XIV à Saint-Germain*, 42–51; Corp, 'Jacobite Chapel Royal'.

FIG. 11. The painting which faced the Jacobite courtiers whenever they entered the Chapel Royal from the courtyard: *Le Triomphe de David* by Matteo Rosselli, 1630 (225 × 295 cm, Musée du Louvre).

side of the chapel near the back of the nave. As one entered, the body of the chapel was on one's left, with a smaller space on one's right. This space contained some pillars supporting the royal tribune, which connected directly with the first floor of the château. On the ground floor, the chapel was divided into two areas of roughly equal size, separated by a step and a gilded iron balustrade. There was the nave, and beyond that the choir. Above the choir was a separate tribune, projecting into the chapel like a gallery or balcony around the walls.

When a Jacobite entered the large chapel from the interior courtyard the first things he saw were two paintings, illustrating famous stories from the Old Testament, in which the weak vanquished the strong. Both included a severed head, and thus served as a constant reminder of the fate of Charles I. Directly in front was *Le Triomphe de David* by Matteo Rosselli.[26] It showed the young David carrying in his right hand the head of Goliath, whom he had just killed,

[26] Musée du Louvre, Paris, inv. 592, 225 × 295 cm (reproduced in *Louis XIV à Saint-Germain*, 48).

with his sword in his other hand over his left shoulder. He was surrounded by young women singing, and playing various musical instruments. The other picture, on the right under the tribune, was *Le Triomphe de Judith*, also attributed at the time to Matteo Rosselli, but probably by Francesco Curradi.[27] It showed Judith standing before the priest Ozias, after having killed the Assyrian general Holofernes. Judith was accompanied by servants, one of whom carried the head, and another the sword, of Holofernes. Apart from these pictures, the nave was undecorated, the walls being made of carved stone. The nave contained only one confessional, something which was felt at the time to be rather inconvenient.[28]

Turning left towards the altar at the east end, the walls of the choir were covered with sculpted and varnished boiseries. There were two side altars immediately beyond the balustrade, each one with a painting by Jacques Stella. The one on the left showed *St Anne Taking the Virgin Mary, When Still a Child, to the Temple*.[29] Directly opposite, the one on the right showed *St Louis Distributing Alms*.[30] The king, who was a direct ancestor of James II, wore a crown, and an ermine-lined cloak covered in *fleurs de lys*. Beyond these two side altars, but still in front of the high altar, were two doors. The one on the left led to a small staircase which gave access to the tribune above. The one on the right led into the sacristy.

On either side of the high altar there were two columns. The bases and capitals were made of white marble, but the columns themselves were of black marble. Above the altar was a very large painting by Nicolas Poussin showing the *Last Supper*.[31] It was this painting of Christ and the twelve disciples, now in the Louvre, which the members of the Jacobite court faced each time they attended a service in the large chapel. Above it was another painting, this time by Simon Vouet, which showed the *Holy Trinity and the Virgin Mary*.[32] On either side of it, to complete the decoration of the east end, were stucco angels holding the arms of France, sculpted by Jacques Sarazin.

The ceiling above both the nave and the choir was made of wood, and had been installed between 1681 and 1685, when the five corners of the château

---

[27] Musée des Augustins, Toulouse, inv. Ro. 375, 234 × 295 cm (reproduced in *Louis XIV à Saint-Germain*, 48).

[28] AN o/1/1714, abbé de Broüains to Angiviller, 22 February 1781.

[29] Musée des Beaux-Arts, Rouen, inv. 803–27, 136 × 102 cm (reproduced in *Louis XIV à Saint-Germain*, 47).

[30] Eglise Saint-Jean, Bazas (Gironde), 140 × 104 cm (reproduced in *Louis XIV à Saint-Germain*, 47).

[31] Musée du Louvre, Paris, inv. 7283, 325 × 250 cm (reproduced in *Louis XIV à Saint-Germain*, 40).

[32] The painting is now lost.

had been expanded and given an extra storey.[33] It seems to have been left undecorated, probably painted white.

The Stuart royal family normally saw the chapel from the tribune at the west end, facing the high altar. This, like the gallery around the choir, had a wooden parquet floor, and a gilded wooden balustrade. At the back of the tribune was an organ, with a buffet decorated with fluted composite columns. Although the tribune connected directly with the first floor of the château, the royal apartments were on the second floor. This meant that, in order to reach the tribune, the Stuarts had to go down a small circular staircase, which was entered from the theatre in the west wing of the château. The daily procession of the royal family to the tribune of the chapel involved leaving the apartments of the king and the queen, and walking through the north and west wings of the château to reach the chapel in the south. The route took them through the entire length of the *Appartement du Dauphin*, and then the length of the theatre. The far end of the theatre, at the edge of the stage, gave access to the small spiral staircase which led directly down to the tribune. This meant that the daily visit to the chapel also involved a twice daily journey through the theatre.[34]

When Louis XIII ordered the redecoration of the chapel in 1639, he also endowed it with enough money to pay for a permanent staff of four people, each of whom was to have food and lodging in the château. There were a chaplain and two priests, all of whom were Lazaristes, secular priests of the 'Congregation of the Mission', founded by St Vincent de Paul. They were supported by a sacristan. These four people remained attached to the chapel after the French court was transferred to Versailles in 1682. Even though James II and Mary of Modena had their own staff of royal chaplains, almoners and confessors, the French clergy remained attached to the *Chapelle Royale* at Saint-Germain-en-Laye after the arrival of the Jacobite court.[35] They continued to say three masses every morning, and Vespers and Compline every evening, the chaplain and the two priests doing this in rotation. Their services were in addition to those performed by the royal priests, whether employed by Louis XIV before 1682, or by the Stuarts after 1689. Most of their services were

---

[33] For the expansion of the château, see Pierre A. Constant-Clement, 'Les Châteaux de Saint-Germain: aménagements et transformations (1663–1685)', in *Louis XIV à Saint-Germain*, 118–24.

[34] The plan of the royal apartments on the second floor is shown in Fig. 6.

[35] The foundation was confirmed by Louis XIV on 1 March 1684. Full details, including the names of the priests and their duties, are in AN O/1/608. From 1689 until at least 1708 the chaplain was the abbé de Beaumont (Monsieur des Viviers). New priests were nominated in December 1691 and May 1696.

said in the absence of the king, just as though the chapel was an ordinary parish church.[36] This establishment of three Lazaristes remained in the *Chapelle Royale* throughout the Jacobite period, and even after it, until the end of the eighteenth century.[37]

The *Chapelle Royale* had a particularly rich collection of plate. None of it has survived, as it was melted down either in 1709 or during the French Revolution, but we do have some general descriptions. We are particularly told of the great beauty of the chandeliers, and the gold and gilt vases. There were two very fine large crosses for the high altar, one of gold and one of silver, and a lamp suspended in front of the altar.[38] The plate not actually being used in the chapel was kept in the sacristy. This room was to the right of the choir, and contained another altar on which was placed an ivory crucifix. There were also two further paintings in the sacristy by Jacques Stella, either side of the crucifix. One showed the *Virgin Mary with the Infant Jesus*;[39] the other showed the *Virgin Mary with the Crucified Jesus*, after he had been brought down from the Cross.[40]

The chapel plate remained permanently at Saint-Germain, but most of the vestments and other fabrics had been removed after Louis XIV had transferred the French court to Versailles in 1682. When the Stuarts arrived in 1689 the chapel therefore needed to be re-equipped. In January 1689 various items were delivered to Saint-Germain from the *garde meuble* at Versailles. The most important were thirty-six large silver candlestands, two silver fonts and a large crimson mohair carpet.[41] In March 1689 there was a further delivery of rich

---

[36] In this respect the *Chapelle Royale* at Saint-Germain was the same as the *Chapelle Royale* at Versailles. See Alexandre Maral, 'La Chapelle Royale de Versailles sous Louis XIV: Architecture, Institutions, Liturgie', 5 vols., Université de Paris IV doctoral thesis, 1997, III, 60–87.

[37] The Lazaristes are listed as still serving in the chapel in AN O/1/1716, 'Etat des Reparations . . . dans les Chateaux de St Germain en Laye' of 1737; and AN O/1/1717, 'les details des objets qui ont été supprimés depuis 1737', 26 September 1784.

[38] Monique Chabaud, 'La Chapelle du Château-Vieux', in *Louis XIV à Saint-Germain*, 41–51. The principal source is *Inventaire Général*, taken from AN O/1/3330–6. The 'ornemens et linge de chapelle' were not reproduced by Guiffrey, but are listed in AN O/1/3333.

[39] The painting is now lost.

[40] Musée Municipal de Limoges (on deposit from the Musée du Louvre, inv. 7966), 65 × 54 cm (reproduced in *Louis XIV à Saint-Germain*, 49).

[41] These items were delivered on 12, 13 and 15 January 1689 (AN O/1/3306, 'Journal du Garde Meuble'). The details of the silver are given in *Inventaire Général*, I: 'Deux petits bénitiers et un goupillon d'argent blanc pour le service de Leurs Majestez Britanniques, à St. Germain-en-Laye, pesons ensemble 2 m[arcs], 5 o[nces], o g[ros]' (21, no. 121); 'Trente six flambeaux pareils pour servir au Roy et à la Reine d'Angleterre à St. Germain-en-Laye, pesons ensemble 75m., 6o., 3g.' (100, no. 1181). Two of the 'flambeaux' were melted down in September 1708, the rest in 1709 (*ibid.*, II, xi; and a marginal note not reproduced by Guiffrey in AN O/1/3330, 'Argent blanc', no. 1181).

vestments, altar cloths, curtains and linen of various kinds.[42] These items, delivered in 1689, were used for sixteen years.[43] Then, between January and April 1705, the entire chapel was re-equipped with rich vestments and other materials transferred from the chapels at Versailles and Marly.[44]

The great value of the plate belonging to the large chapel inevitably posed problems of security. Already, before the arrival of the Stuarts, part of the plate had been stolen on two separate occasions.[45] The security problem was now made worse as a result of the shortage of accommodation. Although the chaplain continued to live in the château, and enjoy free food,[46] the two priests were deprived of both food and lodging, and ordered to live in the town, so that their apartments could be given to Jacobites.[47] Even more serious was the fact that the sacristan, who was directly responsible for the security of the chapel plate, was dismissed and not replaced.[48] Presumably it was felt that the security of the plate could be entrusted to the servants employed by James II and James III. For twenty years there was apparently no problem, but around 1710 there occurred another theft of part of the plate. The man was found, and hanged, but the incident resulted in the appointment

---

[42] AN O/1/3306, 'Journal du Garde Meuble', 13 and 15 March 1689. Very detailed descriptions of all these 'ornemens et linges de chapelle', including all dimensions, are given in AN O/1/3333, ff. 165v–166r, nos. 109–29.

[43] Further items were transferred from the chapel at Versailles in May 1698 (AN O/1/3306, 'Journal du Garde Meuble'; and AN O/1/3333, f. 170v, nos. 193–5). In December 1690 the abbé de Beaumont presented to the chapel 'un vaze d'argent vermeil d'oré à mettre les saintes huilles, hault de 4 pouces, compris le croix qui est dessus le couvercle, gravé des armes du Roy . . . pesant 2m., 40., 0g.' (AN O/1/3306, 'Journal du Garde Meuble'; *Inventaire Général*, I, 21, no. 122).

[44] AN O/1/3308, 'Journal du Garde Meuble', January to April 1705; AN O/1/3333, ff. 171r–172v, nos. 208–30, 232–5, 241–2. The items transferred to Saint-Germain were all relatively new. Those from Versailles had only been in the chapel there since 1697, those from Marly since 1699.

[45] AN O/1/1710, 'Mémoire pour les Reparations du Logement du Chapelain du Roy dans le Chateau Vieux de St Germain en Laye', 3 May 1751. (The robberies had taken place in 1648 and 1674.)

[46] AN O/1/1711, Pointeau to Marigny, 1 August 1757.

[47] AN O/1/608, 'Requête des deux prêtres clercs de la Chapelle du Chateau de St Germain en Laye a Son Altesse Royale, Monseigneur le Régent', February 1722 (or 1723). A similar petition, asking for the return of their food and lodging, was sent to Cardinal Fleury in 1728 (no month given). It is clear from a later document that the second petition was successful: AN O/1/1710, Perrain to Vandière, 17 January 1754.

[48] AN O/1/1714, Broüains to Angiviller, 27 October 1780. This letter also specifies that 'lors de l'etablissement de la Cour d'Angleterre, dans le chateau de St. Germain, on ordonna le logement du sacristan au Lord Bulkeley [sic]; depuis ce tems, il a été occupé par le fils de ce seigneur'. (Henry Bulkeley had been master of the household to both Charles II and James II at Whitehall. After his death in 1698 the apartment was used by his widow, Lady Sophia Bulkeley, and then by his son, Lt. General Francis Bulkeley.)

of a new sacristan, with a room which connected directly with the royal Tribune.[49]

Two other chapels, or oratories, were built inside the château-vieux while the Stuarts lived there. The first, known as the little chapel, was created in the south wing of the château in the spring and early summer of 1689, in the first room of the apartment of the *Enfants de France*, then used by the baby Prince of Wales. To reach it the queen had to walk from her Bedchamber, through her Privy and Presence Chambers, but not through her Guard Chamber, and then across a corridor at the top of the queen's staircase. The apartment of the prince was entered from the other side of this vestibule. The little chapel was created by dividing the first room in two with a plaster wall, and by blocking off the window.[50] The room thus divided served as a corridor to the apartment of the Prince of Wales, with the entrance to the little chapel on the left.

The painting and decoration of the chapel, in white and gold, were finished by the beginning of July 1689.[51] Its most significant item was perhaps a rich *prie-dieu* which was presented to Mary of Modena by Louis XIV at Marly in May 1689. The present was very magnificent and very beautifully made. It was described as 'a cabinet which, on being opened, becomes a *prie-Dieu*, and then one can make an altar out of it; everything that one uses in a chapel is contained in it on a small scale'. When the queen first saw it she was apparently 'astonished to see so many beautiful objects enclosed in such a small space'.[52] Apart from the *prie-dieu*, we have no details of the contents of the chapel. There is, for example, no indication as to whether or not it contained a painting. If there was one it would probably have been painted by Benedetto Gennari, who had decorated the Catholic chapels at St James's Palace and Whitehall, and who had followed the queen to France. He worked at Saint-Germain from 1689 until early 1692, but produced only four religious works, three of which were given to people outside the Jacobite court. The fourth painting, dated 1690, showed the *Virgin Mary with the Child Jesus*. Its subject matter and small dimensions would have made it an ideal painting for the little chapel.[53]

---

[49] AN O/1/1714, Broüains to Angiviller, 30 August and 11 October 1780.

[50] AN O/1/1713, Galant to Marigny, 26 July 1770. The little chapel was also used by James II: Nairne, 1 January 1697 ('to Mass wth ye King in the little chappell'), and 25 December 1700 ('I heard Mass wth ye King in ye little chappell').

[51] *Comptes des Bâtiments*, III, cols. 321–6.

[52] Dangeau, II, 387, 14 May 1689. See also the inventory drawn up for James III in Italy in November 1725, which includes 'the rich prie dieu wch came from France': SP Box 4, Folder 2/12. The little chapel was being built at the time that the present was given.

[53] The painting is in a private collection in Paris, 91 × 71 cm. (It is reproduced in Corp, *Cour des Stuarts*, 137.)

The plate of the little chapel was made of silver, and is all listed in the inventory of the possessions of James II.[54] In addition to the objects one would expect, there were six great candlesticks to be placed on the altar, either side of the cross. The vestments were the ones made for the Catholic chapel at Whitehall, and were very rich. When Mary of Modena died in 1718 there were still two trunks of them which had not yet been used, and which were regarded as of great value. Finally, the little chapel also contained 'fine manuscript old church books'.[55]

The other new chapel was created in the north-west pavilion in the first half of 1701, in what had originally been the *Appartement de la Dauphine*, and named the *Chapelle de la Princesse*, after Princess Louise-Marie. As a child she lived in the south wing of the château, so both she and the queen enjoyed easy access to the little chapel. But when the queen exchanged her apartment with that of the Prince of Wales in 1699, the little chapel, which had been made for her, was no longer easily accessible. Thus a third chapel was built. It was in the *Appartement de la Dauphine*, occupied by the princess, but was intended to be used by both the princess and the queen. It was painted and decorated between January and June 1701, though we have no details of its contents.[56]

When James II died in September 1701, the new king, James III, took over both the *Appartement du Dauphin* and the *Appartement de la Dauphine*, with the effect that the *Chapelle de la Princesse* became the private chapel of the king. This arrangement then continued for the rest of the period that the Jacobite court remained in the château-vieux. The large chapel was used by the members of the royal household, and the court as a whole. The little chapel was used by the queen and the princess and their closest servants. The *Chapelle de la Princesse* was for James III's private use, and was situated in his *cabinets intérieurs*, immediately beyond his Bedchamber.

Throughout the period that the Stuarts lived at Saint-Germain the château-vieux and the gardens were maintained at considerable expense by the servants of the *Surintendance des Bâtiments du Roi*.[57] The royal apartments were constantly

---

54 Brotherton Library, MS Dep. 1984/2/5. The inventory is dated 22 July 1703.

55 HMC *Stuart* VI, 486, James III to Middleton, Sheldon, Dillon and Dicconson, 28 May 1718; HMC *Stuart* VII, 194, Innes to James III, 23 August 1718.

56 *Comptes des Bâtiments*, IV, cols. 754–9. We do know, however, that it contained a carpet which measured two and a half 'lez' by three and a half 'aunes', and four hassocks (one for each member of the royal family): AN O/1/3307, 'Journal du Garde Meuble', November 1701.

57 The servants are all listed in *Comptes des Bâtiments*, III, cols. 365–6 and 377–8; IV, cols. 641, 695; and V, col. 444; as well as *L'Etat de la France*.

cleaned, and their decorations and furnishings regularly repaired or replaced. The moat was thoroughly cleared of all rubbish on three occasions during the 1690s,[58] while a team of gardeners (headed by the Delalande family[59]) maintained the *grand parterre*, the *Jardin de la Dauphine*, the *Boulingrin*, and both the *Jardin des Dentelles* and the grottoes of the hanging gardens. It was in these spectacular surroundings that the Stuart court in exile was established and maintained between the arrival of Mary of Modena in 1689 and her death in 1718.

[58] The moat was cleaned in August 1691, February 1693 and March 1697 (*Comptes des Bâtiments*, III, cols. 600–5, 881–5; IV, cols. 226–8). It was not cleaned again until 1739 (AN O/1/1710, Soulaigre to Tournehem, undated, 1739; O/1/1714, Galant to Angiviller, 27 January 1776).

[59] The Delalande family had been gardeners at Saint-Germain since 1625 (AN O/1/1715, Delalande to Angiviller, 9 September 1787). See chapter 8 for the composer Michel-Richard Delalande.

CHAPTER THREE

The royal household under James II, 1690–1701

When Mary of Modena and James II left England in December 1688 each was accompanied by no more than a few servants.[1] Some others had already crossed over to France with the Earl of Melfort, and were in attendance on Louis XIV when the Stuarts first arrived at Saint-Germain,[2] but for several weeks it was impossible for James II to create even a skeleton household. As a result he was totally dependent on the servants hastily assembled by Louis XIV and seconded from Versailles.

Day by day during January 1689, and particularly at the end of the month, James's and Mary's own servants began to arrive. By 1 February there were enough of them to prepare the food and to wait upon the king and queen at table, and thereafter the French were steadily withdrawn and a provisional English household was established. It was agreed, however, that the château itself would continue to be protected by French guards. One reason for this was that James II left Saint-Germain for Ireland on 28 February, taking with him all the English and Irish soldiers who had joined him.[3]

No information has survived concerning the household at Saint-Germain from 1689 to 1692. James took with him to Ireland his own servants, and was

[1] The queen was escorted by the comte de Lauzun, the Marquess of Powis and Count Raimondo Montecuccoli. They were accompanied by three servants from her Bedchamber (Montecuccoli's sister Vittoria Davia, lady; Pellegrina Turrini, woman; and Dominique Dufour, page), and three from her Chamber (Francesco Riva, master of the robes; Father Marco Antonio Galli, confessor; and Sir William Waldegrave, physician). The prince was accompanied by four servants (the Marchioness of Powis, governess; Lady Strickland, under-governess; Mary Anne Delabadie, dry nurse; and Frances Smith, wet nurse). The king's equerry (Ralph Sheldon) crossed the Channel three times with messages, and eventually joined the queen at Beauvais. The king was escorted by the Duke of Berwick, Richard Trevanion (captain of the royal yacht *Henrietta*), and Randall MacDonnell (captain of the royal yacht *Assurance*). They were accompanied by two servants from his Bedchamber (Richard Biddulph, groom; Jacques Delabadie, page).

[2] Melfort had landed at Ambleteuse on 6/16 December 1688 (*DNB*), and is shown in the engraving for the *Almanach Royal de 1689* entitled 'La réception faite au Roy d'Angleterre par le Roy à Saint-Germain-en-Laye le 7 janvier 1689' (BN Est. Qb¹. 1689). See Fig. 1.

[3] Campana di Cavelli, *Les Derniers Stuarts*, II, 465–503; J.S. Clarke (ed.), *The Life of James II*, 2 vols. (London, 1816), II, 248, 283; Sourches, III, 28 and 31, 27 January and 1 February 1689; Dangeau, II, 323 and 326, 4 and 9 February 1689; BL Add. MSS 51320, f. 113, the equipage, horses, officers and servants ordered to be sent to France for James II, January 1689.

not expected to return to France, but the queen maintained a small household during his absence. When he was unexpectedly defeated at the Boyne in the summer of 1690, and returned immediately afterwards, he was soon followed by his servants, so that a much larger and more permanent household was then established. But James still expected to be restored in the near future. His hopes were dashed by the battle of Cap La Hogue in the summer of 1692, when his planned invasion of England had to be cancelled. It was at that point that the households of the king and queen were finally established on a permanent basis.[4]

The departments

The royal household at Saint-Germain was much smaller than it had been at Whitehall for several reasons, of which the most important was financial. But this should not be overemphasised, because Louis XIV offered James II a larger pension than the one he accepted.[5] Those Jacobites who followed the Stuarts into exile needed to be given permanent employment, rather than to serve for limited periods on rotation, because they could not return to their estates. This reduced the numbers of people in many of the posts. Moreover the household in England had included many yeoman of the guard, and others attached to specific royal palaces. Thus they were not needed in France, where James II had only one residence, maintained for him by a full-time French concierge (Henri Soulaigre) and a staff of over twenty people.[6]

In 1696 the household of James II contained eighty-eight people (less than one-sixth of the total before 1689).[7] The queen's contained seventy people, with an additional thirty-five servants employed to take care of the prince and princess, thus making a combined total for the king and queen of 193. This was approximately the same as when they had been Duke and Duchess

---

[4] *Life of James II*, II, 472–3.

[5] According to Sourches, Louis XIV offered James II a pension of 200,000 *livres* each month (= 2,400,000 *livres per annum*), but James refused to accept so much (III, 7, 7 January 1689). He agreed to accept no more than 50,000 *livres* each month (= 600,000 *livres per annum*). Madame de Sévigné, *Correspondance, vol. 3 (1680–96)*, ed. R. Duchêne (Paris, 1978), 474, no. 1057, to Mme de Grignan, 17 January 1689.

[6] The Soulaigre family held the post of concierge of the Château-Vieux de Saint-Germain *en survivance* from father to son from 1633 until the French Revolution. While the Stuarts and Jacobites were there the concierges were Henri (1676–1701), Henri-Louis (1701–33) and Jacques–Louis (1733–84). For the staff of twenty people, see above pp. 78 and 102, notes 6 and 57.

[7] Sizergh Castle, Strickland Collection R.4, list of salaries and pensions for 1696.

of York.[8] This figure, however, needs to be qualified. Many people, such as the secretaries of state, the musicians and various messengers, were given pensions, along with others waiting for vacancies in the household to occur. The true figure was more like 225. Many of these servants employed their own under-servants,[9] most of them were accompanied by their families, and a large number of pensioners also lived at Saint-Germain. The size of the Jacobite court at Saint-Germain during the 1690s, before the Irish regiments in the French army were disbanded and reformed in 1698,[10] was probably about 1000 people.

Although the household of James II at Saint-Germain was a smaller version of the one he had had at Whitehall, the architecture of the château meant that it could not be the same. In particular, the shortage of space in the king's apartment obliged James to merge the Bedchamber department into the Chamber, under the control of the lord chamberlain, and thus to revert to the departmental structure which had existed before 1603, when there had been no separate Bedchamber and no groom of the stole. Because he had only one antechamber he also had to employ his gentlemen ushers without specifying those serving in the Presence or Privy Chambers.

Until his death in 1696 the lord chamberlain was the Duke of Powis, who controlled a staff of forty people. These included the yeomen and groom of the robes, a confessor, an almoner and three chaplains, a physician, a surgeon, an apothecary, two barbers, an armourer and some others in more humble positions. The king's Guard Chamber and Antechamber were staffed by six gentlemen, one groom and one page, his Bedchamber by two gentlemen, seven grooms and four pages. The lord chamberlain was assisted by a vice-chamberlain, James Porter. Powis was the only official at Saint-Germain to hold one of the most senior household posts. James II never appointed a lord steward or a master of the horse.[11] When Powis died he was not replaced,

---

[8] A.P. Barclay, 'The Impact of James II on the Departments of the Royal Household', unpublished PhD thesis, University of Cambridge, 1993, 212.

[9] This is clear from the parish registers (Archives Municipales de Saint-Germain-en-Laye), in which the under-servants identified the people by whom they were employed. Sir Adam Blair, brother-in-law of the Duchess of Melfort, stated that he had '7 or 8' servants at Saint-Germain (SP 85/16, Blair to Inverness, 6 August 1725).

[10] For the Irish regiments, see Guy Rowlands, 'An Army in Exile: Louis XIV and the Irish Forces of James II in France, 1691–1698', *Royal Stuart Paper* LX (London, 2001).

[11] This was partly because some of the most senior officials in England had remained loyal, whereas the lord chamberlain (Lord Mulgrave) had supported William and Mary. In 1688–89 James II's groom of the stole had been Lord Peterborough and his master of the horse had been Lord Dartmouth. The position of lord steward had been vacant since the death of the Duke of Ormonde in July 1688.

FIG. 12. The lord chamberlain, shown in his robes as a Knight of the Garter: *The Duke of Powis* by François de Troy, 1692 (127 × 101.5 cm, Powis Castle).

and the vice-chamberlain remained the officer responsible for the Chamber, though one of the gentlemen of the Bedchamber, Richard Hamilton, was then appointed master of the robes and given independent responsibility. Only eighteen of the forty had served in the king's Chamber and Bedchamber in England,[12] the others being recruited in France from among the Jacobites who had followed their king into exile. For example, two of the grooms of the Bedchamber, Randall MacDonnell and Richard Trevanion, were naval captains who had previously commanded royal yachts.[13] Apart from the new appointments to replace people who had left the court, the king's Chamber remained the same until his death in 1701, except that a second gentleman of the Bedchamber (Lord Melfort) was appointed in 1698 when the only other one (the Earl of Clancarty) went to London and was imprisoned.

The organisation of the household below stairs was also influenced by the architecture of the château de Saint-Germain. The building contained no basements, except in the five new corner pavilions, and these had been designed for the requirements of the smaller French *Maison du Roi*. The latter contained only seven sub-departments (the *sept offices*) whereas the household at Whitehall under the lord steward had been divided into fifteen sub-departments.[14]

Two of the seven French sub-departments, the *gobelets* and the *cuisines*, which together formed the *bouches du Roi et de la Reine*, had been situated in the basements of the château, while the other five, which together formed the *offices communs*, had been situated in an adjacent building outside the west wing of the château, surrounding three sides of a rectangular area known as the *cour des cuisines*. Four of the five basements had been occupied by the *gobelets*, while the south-west pavilion had been dedicated to the *cuisines* – the queen's in the basement and the king's on the ground floor above. The *bouches du Roi et de la Reine* in the château provided food, wine and plate for the royal tables, and thus contained the equivalent of the privy kitchens at Whitehall. The *offices communs* outside provided similarly for the household, and thus contained the equivalent of the household kitchen at Whitehall. The latter had been abolished by James II in 1685, but had previously provided food for the few servants at Whitehall entitled to communal dining at the king's expense (known as diet). James II had transferred this responsibility at Whitehall to the privy kitchen which had thus had to provide more food during his reign than previously.

[12] I am grateful to Andrew Barclay (see above, note 8) for exchanging information about the servants employed at Whitehall and Saint-Germain.

[13] See note 1; and Corp, 'Flight of Queen and Prince of Wales', 36–41.

[14] Corp, 'Etiquette and Use of Royal Apartments', 246–8.

FIG. 13. One of the secretaries of state, later a gentleman of the
Bedchamber, with the star of the Order of the Garter: *The Duke of
Melfort*, anonymous miniature, *c.*1692 (Belton House).

The pressure on the privy kitchen was increased at Saint-Germain. The
building around the *cour des cuisines* was not made available to the English
court, perhaps because it was retained by Louis XIV for the French guards,
so all the other sub-departments of the household below stairs had to be
accommodated, with the privy kitchen, in the château (i.e. in the south-west
pavilion and the four other basements). Wishing to help his exiled courtiers,

James II increased the number of people entitled to diet, by reintroducing a gentlemen's table,[15] but in so doing he increased the amount of food to be provided by the privy kitchen in more difficult circumstances.

Faced with this shortage of space, some of the sub-departments of the household (the accatry, scaldinghouse and spicery) were abolished, while others (the chaundry and buttery; the ewry and pantry; the kitchen and pastry) were merged and then fitted with the surviving ones (the woodyard, confectionary, cellars, larder, bakehouse and silver scullery) into the areas previously occupied by the French *cuisines* and *gobelets*.[16]

James II's privy kitchen shared the ground floor of the south-west pavilion with the larder and bakehouse, while that of the queen was in the basement below with the combined ewry and pantry. They were not very conveniently situated. Despite their being within the château, food could not easily be transported from them to the royal apartments without going out of doors and across the interior courtyard, an obvious inconvenience in bad weather. By contrast the former apartment of the dauphin, used by the Prince of Wales after 1695 and then by the queen from 1699 to 1701, could be reached directly via the staircase in the south-west pavilion, followed by a procession through the theatre.

James II and Mary of Modena dined together privately in the queen's Bechamber and publicly in the queen's Privy Chamber, but when James ate alone he used his own Bedchamber and Antechamber respectively. They adopted English ceremonial and made a point of dining in the same way as they had at Whitehall.[17] In order to achieve this, James II placed large orders with goldsmiths in Paris to provide the royal tables with all the objects which they needed. These included three sets of gold *couverts* and many items in gilt, such as two cadinets, four other *couverts*, thirty-five plates, two salts, a mustard pot, a cup and two salvers. Other items commissioned by James in Paris were made of silver, some of them for the household servants who had diet.[18] The Stuarts also had a large supply of damask and diaper tablecloths and napkins, sent to them from Whitehall at the beginning of 1689.[19]

James II entrusted the management of the household below stairs to a comptroller. This was Bevil Skelton, previously the English ambassador in

[15] See *ibid.*, 253, notes 27 and 29, for the details.

[16] For the locations of the sub-departments, see the plan of the château in Fig. 9.

[17] Corp, 'Etiquette and Use of Royal Apartments', 248.

[18] They included seventy-two plates, forty dishes, six salts, twelve couverts, a gravy pot, a basin, a ewer and a salver.

[19] Corp, 'English Royal Table', 114–15, 118.

Paris, who replaced Lord Waldegrave in 1690. After Skelton's death in 1696 the post was given to John Stafford, and then in 1700 to Francis Plowden.[20]

The comptroller was responsible for a staff of twenty-eight servants, and was assisted in his work by a clerk controller of the Greencloth and by a yeoman and messenger of the accounting house (thus making thirty-one in all). Only seven of these people had previously served the king at Whitehall, the rest having been recruited while he was in Ireland or after his return to Saint-Germain. The combined kitchen and pastry, which was the largest of the sub-departments, was headed by two clerks, a master cook and three yeomen. Of the others, two were headed by a gentleman (cellars, butteries), the rest only by a yeoman.

The guards at Saint-Germain continued to be French, even after the return of James II from Ireland in 1690. There were obviously enough exiled Jacobites, particularly those serving in the Irish regiments of the French army, to have provided an effective military presence at the English court, so the decision to retain the French guards must have been taken by Louis XIV. The two main entrances to the château, the principal one in the middle of the south wing and the other in the west, approached from the *cour des cuisines*, were controlled by the *gardes de la porte*, while a group of *gardes du corps* manned the Guard Chambers of the royal apartments on the second floor. These guards were commanded for three months at a time, in rotation, by a lieutenant (one of whom was a nephew of James II's friend Abbé Rancé de La Trappe), but the available documents do not state how many guards there were.[21] Outside the château, the gardens and royal estate were protected by a detachment of Swiss Guards, referred to as the *cent Suisses*.

The royal stables were situated to the south of the château and employed a further twenty-five servants, headed by two equerries and a riding purveyor. Once again most of the servants had been recruited in Ireland or in France, as only seven of them had previously served the king at Whitehall. Apart from two pages of honour, four footmen, eight grooms, three saddlers, two

[20] Sir Henry Waldegrave, Bart., had married James II's illegitimate daughter Henrietta FitzJames and been created Lord Waldegrave of Chewton in Somerset. Skelton was from Ravely in Huntingdonshire; Stafford (a younger brother of the 1st Earl of Stafford) was from Shiffnal in Shropshire and Stafford, Staffordshire; and Plowden was from Plowden Hall in Shropshire.

[21] The number of guards serving the Prince of Wales was increased from six to fourteen in 1700 (Sourches, VI, 147, 19 April 1699; C. Cole, *Memoirs of Affairs of State* (London, 1733), 260, Manchester to Vernon, 11 December 1700). See also *Life of James II*, II, 599: in September 1701 Louis XIV ordered the 'Officer of the Guard who waited upon the King . . . to follow and attend the Prince of Wales, as soon as the King was dead, and to show him the same respect and honours he had done to the King his Father when he was alive'.

coachmen and one farrier, James also employed a harbourer of the deer. At the end of the 1690s, when his health began to fail, James increased the number of grooms and began to employ a chairman.

The household of Mary of Modena was smaller than that of the king, but her apartment was larger, so she was able to separate her Bedchamber, which was mainly staffed by females, from her Chamber, staffed by men. The Bedchamber employed fourteen people: three ladies (who took it in turns to serve her for one week at a time),[22] four women and four pages, with a laundress, a sempstress and starcher, and a 'necessary woman'. The ladies (the Duchess of Tyrconnell, the Countess of Almond and Lady Sophia Bulkeley, joined in 1700 by the Countess of Perth) were the wives and daughters of peers, whereas the women (Pellegrina Turrini, Isabella Waldegrave, Bridget Strickland and Veronica Molza) were the wives of gentlemen. The pages, whose number had increased to seven by 1701, included musicians such as John Abell (counter-tenor), Thomas Heywood (counter-tenor) and Gian-Battista Casale (organist).[23]

The queen's Chamber was headed by her vice-chamberlain, Robert Strickland, until 1700. He was then given a new post as her treasurer and replaced by John Stafford (previously the comptroller of the king's household). These officials supervised a staff of twenty-four men and one woman. (The latter was the assistant to the master of the queen's robes.) The queen employed three grooms in her Guard Chamber, one gentleman in her Presence Chamber, and two gentlemen and one groom in her Privy Chamber, as well as two gentleman waiters. In addition to her confessor and three almoners, she also employed four chaplains and two other servants in her private chapel or oratory. The remaining members of her Chamber were her secretary (John Caryll), her physician (Sir William Waldegrave) and her apothecary.[24]

Unlike the king's servants, most of those employed in the Chamber of the queen had previously worked for her at Whitehall. In 1693 only ten of them seem to have been recruited in France: they included Lewis Innes, the principal of the Scots College in Paris, who was one of the queen's almoners. At that time all the members of the Bedchamber had previously served the queen at Whitehall.

---

[22] Dangeau, v, 291, 10 October 1695; and vi, 221, 3 November 1697.

[23] See the household lists for 1693 and 1696 (SP 1/79; note 7); and the warrants published in Melville Henry Massue, marquis de Ruvigny et de Raineval, *The Jacobite Peerage* (Edinburgh, 1904), 216–18.

[24] Robert Strickland was from Catterick in Yorkshire; Caryll was from Ladyholt and West Grinstead in Sussex; and Waldegrave (a cousin of Lord Waldegrave) was from Borley in Essex.

FIG. 14. The master of the queen's robes (Francesco Riva) with his English wife
Anne and their two sons: *The Riva Family*, by Benedetto Gennari, 1689 (95.5 ×
126.5 cm, Pinacoteca Nazionale, Bologna).

The queen's household below stairs was much smaller than that of the
king, and mainly consisted of her privy kitchen and pantry, situated in the
basement of the south-west pavilion. In addition to her three cooks (two of
them French) and the yeoman of her pantry, she employed two clerks of the
Greencloth and a yeoman of her own separate cellar. Three of these seven had
previously served her at Whitehall.

In contrast to her household below stairs, the queen's stables employed
almost as many people as the king's. Her equerry (Charles Leyburne, replaced
in 1698 by Arthur Magennis) supervised a staff of twenty-one people, similar to
that of the king but organised to serve a lady. Thus there were more coachmen,
chairmen and footmen, fewer grooms and no saddler or harbourer of the deer.
Although the queen received her coaches and horses from England,[25] only
four people (including Leyburne himself) had served the queen there.[26]

---

[25] M. Haile, *Queen Mary of Modena, Her Life and Letters* (London, 1905), 239.
[26] Leyburne was from Nateby in Westmorland; and Magennis was from County Kerry in
Munster.

These figures show that there was considerable continuity from the royal household at Whitehall to that at Saint-Germain, particularly in the household of the queen where thirty-seven people out of fifty-nine had previously served her in England. But because only thirty-two out of the King's ninety-eight servants had followed him from Whitehall, the majority of the servants at Saint-Germain (eighty-eight out of 159) was recruited after the Stuarts went into exile. This was particularly the case in the stables (thirty-six out of forty-seven) and below stairs (twenty-nine out of thirty-nine). Nevertheless, continuity was maintained where it most mattered, and was most visible, in the Chamber.

The household of the Prince of Wales had been established by James II in September 1688 and contained eleven people under a governess (the Marchioness of Powis) and an under-governess (Lady Strickland), as well as a small number of others below stairs and two footmen in the stables.[27] Twenty-one out of the total of twenty-seven followed the Stuarts to France, including all the servants attached to the Chamber, so the people who surrounded the baby prince were not changed by the fact of his going into exile. Lady Powis, who became a duchess in 1689, died in 1691 and was replaced by the Countess of Erroll. Lady Strickland, the under-governess, left Saint-Germain in 1692 and was replaced by Mary Stafford (wife of John Stafford). The birth of Princess Louise-Marie in 1692, followed by the death of Lady Erroll in 1693, then resulted in a further change. Mary Stafford was appointed governess of the baby princess and Lady Strickland returned to Saint-Germain at the beginning of 1694 to become the prince's governess for the remaining one and a half years before his seventh birthday in June 1695. He was then given his own apartment in the north wing and handed over to be cared for and served by men.[28]

The Prince of Wales already had two pages of the Bedchamber, and in 1692 had been given a preceptor and a team of other teachers. In 1695, when he was given his own apartment, he was entrusted to two under-governors and various other male servants, notably three grooms of the Bedchamber and two gentleman waiters.[29] By 1696, when the Earl of Perth was appointed

---

[27] BL Add. MSS 51320, the establishment of the household of the Prince of Wales, 18 September 1688. Lady Powis was a sister of the Duke of Beaufort and of the Duchess of Norfolk; Lady Strickland was married to Sir Thomas Strickland, from Sizergh in Westmorland (a first cousin of Robert Strickland).

[28] See chapter 2, note 18.

[29] See below, pp. 257–8; and Bodleian Library, Rawlinson MSS D.21, f. 3, unidentified to Meredith, 27 June 1695.

FIG. 15. The governor of the Prince of Wales, later a gentleman of the
Bedchamber, with the star of the Order of the Garter: *The Duke of Perth*, by Nicolas
de Largillière, 1706 (79 × 66 cm, Drummond Castle).

governor and additional teachers were also employed, the prince's household contained twenty-two people. It then continued to expand. By 1701, when he had exchanged his apartment for that of the queen, the prince had seven grooms of the Bedchamber and three gentleman waiters.[30] The death of James II in September 1701 left the prince, now James III, with the delicate problem of combining his own household with that of his father.

The household of the princess followed a similar pattern. By 1693 Mary Stafford was in charge of a team of ten women and two pages of the Bedchamber. When the princess was seven years old her mother exchanged apartments with the prince and moved into the apartment formerly occupied by the dauphin. This meant the princess could be given the adjacent apartment of the dauphine. In 1700 a team of five Bedchamber women was appointed and Mary Stafford, who had died, was replaced as governess by the Countess of Middleton.[31]

This large group of people, living at the exiled English court with their families and in many cases with their own servants, needed to be regulated and disciplined, if only to avoid embarrassing problems with the French authorities. This was the task of the Board of Greencloth, which at Whitehall had been chaired by the lord steward, and had contained the four most senior members of the household below stairs, supported by four clerks. At Saint-Germain the board was normally chaired by the comptroller of the household (Skelton; Stafford; Plowden), and contained the commissioners of the household, supported by three clerk controllers (Sir John Sparrow, Christopher Chilton and Henry Conquest).[32] When new servants were employed they were required to take an oath of loyalty and obedience,[33] and it was the Board of Greencloth which arbitrated in disputes and punished any offenders.[34] In February 1697 David Nairne noted that the king 'sent for me and gave me a paper to copie containing new orders for regulating ye family and preventing disorders'.[35] Disputes between the most senior officials could not be handled by the Board of Greencloth. When Henry Bulkeley (the husband of one of the ladies of the Bedchamber) picked a quarrel with Lord Clancarty (a gentleman of the Bedchamber) he was ordered by the king to 'beg pardon before ye D. of Powis'.[36]

---

[30] See note 23.   [31] Nairne, 5 May and 10 July 1700.

[32] Sparrow was from Havering in Essex; and both Chilton and Conquest possibly from London.

[33] SP Box 3/70/1.   [34] Nairne, 17 September 1696, provides an example.

[35] Nairne, 26 February 1697.

[36] Nairne, 4 and 15 March 1695. James II was advised on how to handle this quarrel by Innes: Nairne, 12 March 1695.

The secretariat

Although they were not all members of the household, James II's ministers and secretaries were increasingly regarded as part of it, and should therefore be examined here.

In the autumn of 1688 the king's leading officers of state in England had been the first lord of the treasury, Baron Belasyse; the two secretaries of state, the Earls of Middleton and Preston; the lord chancellor, Baron Jeffreys; and the Scottish secretary, the Earl of Melfort.

Once he had established himself at Saint-Germain in 1690, James II did what he could to re-establish a similar group of leading ministers, and through them maintain a continuity with his government in England. Both Lord Belasyse and Lord Jeffreys had died in 1689, but the other three men had remained loyal, and James hoped to employ them in a new ministry at Saint-Germain. As it happened Lord Preston was captured while attempting to cross the Channel in January 1691, and then imprisoned in the Tower, but Lord Melfort fled to France in December 1688, and Lord Middleton succeeded in reaching Saint-Germain in April 1693.

The exiled ministry of James II consisted of two secretaries of state to deal jointly with both England and Scotland, and a lord chancellor of England. There was no need for a first lord of the treasury in exile, but James added a secretary of state and war for Ireland, who was responsible for the king's army of Irish regiments in France. The secretaries of state were Lord Melfort and Lord Middleton, who thus provided an obvious link with the ministry at Whitehall. The new lord chancellor was Sir Edward Herbert, who had previously been lord chief justice of common pleas. James II seems to have regretted appointing him, because he advised his son in 1692 that he should never appoint a lawyer to be lord chancellor, but only a nobleman or a bishop.[37] The Irish secretary, Sir Richard Nagle, was also a lawyer, who had previously been attorney general in Ireland.[38]

These ministers formed the nucleus of a new Privy Council to conduct the king's business at Saint-Germain. There were other councillors, of whom the most important was probably the Earl of Perth, who arrived in 1696, and who had previously been lord chancellor of Scotland. But as the years went by it became impossible for James II to maintain such an impressive ministry. The first problem came in 1694, when James was requested by the French government (as well as by Jacobites in England) to dismiss Lord Melfort. He was quickly replaced, but his successor, the queen's private secretary John

---

[37] *Life of James II*, ii, 642.   [38] Corp, 'Maintaining Continuity', 186–8.

Caryll, had not held high office in England. It then became clear that there was virtually nothing for the lord chancellor of England to do. He assisted in the drafting of two important Declarations in 1692 and 1693, but thereafter became redundant. He was not replaced when he died in 1698. The same happened when the Irish secretary died in 1699. Sir Richard Nagle had originally been fully occupied with the management of James II's Irish army. The troops were paid by Louis XIV's 'trésoriers généraux de l'extraordinaire des guerres', but they were otherwise totally independent, commissioned and commanded by officers whose loyalty was solely to their own king.[39] When the Treaty of Ryswick brought to an end the War of the League of Augsburg, and Louis XIV was obliged to recognise William of Orange as the 'de facto' king of England, the regiments were reorganised and fully integrated into the French army. James II thus lost the possession of his own independent force. By 1699 James's ministry had been reduced to no more than the two secretaries of state, one to deal with France and the English correspondence, the other to deal with the Roman correspondence.

The three secretaries of state each had an under-secretary or chief clerk. These were David Nairne (Melfort, then Caryll), David Lindsay (Middleton) and John Kearney (Nagle). It was normal practice for secretaries of state to appoint their own chief clerks, and thus to dismiss the clerks of their predecessors, but James II insisted at Saint-Germain that the clerks should be employed by him and not by the secretaries of state: 'Each of their cheif clerks to be named by the King, to have Warrants to be so, and Salarys, and to remain in their places tho' the Secretary shall chance to dy or be removed, that books of entrys remaine in the Office.'[40] The new system came into operation in 1694, when Lord Melfort resigned and his chief clerk, David Nairne, remained in office and began to work for John Caryll. When the post of secretary for Ireland lapsed in 1699 John Kearney also remained in his post and continued to do what was left of the work previously done by Nagle.

The salaries and pensions

The royal household at Saint-Germain was financed by Louis XIV, who gave James II an annual pension of 600,000 *livres*. The Stuarts kept one third of this for themselves, and used the other two thirds to pay the salaries of their household servants and the pensions of various Jacobites in exile, many of

---

[39] Rowlands, 'An Army in Exile'. For Nagle, see particularly 6–8.   [40] *Life of James II*, II, 641.

whom lived in Saint-Germain or in Paris.[41] Mary of Modena paid monthly pensions to various people attached to the court, such as the master of the music (Innocenzo Fede) and her surgeon, and after 1695 to the women who had previously served in the household of the prince and had not joined that of the princess. Other monthly pensions were given as additional payments to favoured servants who were already receiving salaries, such as her secretary (John Caryll) and her master of the robes (Francesco Riva). Mary also paid various quarterly pensions. Apart from one to Lady Melfort, these were mainly given to support widowed ladies in convents or wives whose husbands had no incomes in exile. James II's pensions were also paid to various people attached to the court, such as his Anglican chaplain (Denis Granville), his messengers and his ceremonial musicians, as well as widows and orphans. The largest pensions were given to the king's two illegitimate sons, the Dukes of Berwick and Albemarle, and to the members of the ministry, their under-secretaries and clerks.

As the 1690s went on, the money spent on pensions steadily increased, because people continued to arrive from England, such as the Earl of Middleton, and because servants died leaving their widows and families to be supported, such as Bevil Skelton. The household also began to expand after the birth of Princess Louise-Marie and because the prince was growing up and needed to be educated. A crisis was reached in 1695 when preparations were being made to give the prince his own apartment with a new household of male servants. James II decided that priority had to be given to maintaining the household salaries and that any necessary cuts must come from the list of pensions. In March 1695 all pensions were temporarily suspended.[42] Then in May it was announced that some would be cut off and the others retrenched.[43] The one concession the king was able to make was in not giving the prince his own servants below stairs because of the shortage of space in the basements. His meals continued to be prepared in the king's privy kitchen.[44]

The household itself continued to be well paid, but it was the reduction of the pensions in 1695 that laid the foundations for the later belief that the English court in exile was short of money. Some pensioners returned dissatisfied to England and Scotland, others had to depend on charity. The French clergy responded by giving the queen 6000 *livres* in July[45] and Louis

[41] See the various lists of salaries and pensions, included in Corp, 'Inventory', 134.

[42] Nairne, 7 March 1695.

[43] Nairne, 11 May 1695; Bibliothèque de l'Arsenal MS 10533, Stafford to Bromfield, 10 August 1695.

[44] Bodleian Library, Rawlinson MSS D.21, f. 3, unidentified to Meredith, 27 June 1695.

[45] Nairne, 18 July 1695.

XIV arranged for her to win 1200 *livres* at Marly in November,[46] followed by another 1560 in August 1697.[47] Additional money was received from the Duke of Modena.[48]

James II's pension was received in monthly instalments of 50,000 *livres* from the French Treasury. This was collected by Bevil Skelton, the comptroller of the household, whose job it was to pay all the salaries and pensions.[49] When Skelton died in 1696 he was succeeded by Robert Strickland, the queen's vice-chamberlain, but the latter paid a short visit to England at the beginning of 1698 so the responsibility was shared with the new comptroller, John Stafford, either of them being allowed to collect the money.[50] In 1700 when Francis Plowden succeeded Stafford as comptroller, and Stafford succeeded Strickland as the queen's vice-chamberlain, the latter was given the title of treasurer and receiver-general. These men delegated the actual payment of the salaries and pensions to their subordinates, the king's clerk controller of the Greencloth (Sir John Sparrow) and the queen's clerk of the Greencloth (Henry Conquest).[51]

All financial matters were overseen by the commissioners of the household. From 1691 until 1696 there were three: the Duke of Powis (in charge of the king's Chamber), Robert Strickland (in charge of the queen's Chamber) and Bevil Skelton (in charge of the household below stairs). Skelton and Powis both died in 1696 and were replaced, respectively, by John Stafford and Henry Conquest. Faced with the increased size of the household and the arrival of growing numbers of demobilised Irish soldiers, James II appointed two additional commissioners in 1698: Sir William Ellis (previously secretary to the Duke of Tyrconnell, Viceroy of Ireland), and Sir Richard Nagle. When the latter died in 1699 he was replaced by another Irishman, Thomas Sheridan (previously married to one of James II's illegitimate daughters). In the reshuffle of posts in 1700, Strickland was succeeded by Sir Richard Bulstrode, formerly ambassador at Brussels and then an old man of eighty-three years of age.

The arrival of many poor and starving Jacobites at Saint-Germain-en-Laye increased the contrast between the well-paid members of the royal household and the rest of the exiled community.[52] Confronted with this situation the

---

[46] Nairne, 9 November 1695.

[47] Nairne, 8 August 1697.   [48] Haile, *Mary of Modena*, 326.

[49] HMC *Stuart* I, 97, James II to Skelton, 28 February 1695.

[50] HMC *Stuart* I, 128 and 130, James II to Stafford, 25 January and 17 April 1698.

[51] HMC *Stuart* VII, 578, Charles Chilton to Mar, 28 November 1718.

[52] With the return of peace Louis XIV reduced the size of the French army and made it clear that he was no longer willing to pay for all the Irish regiments in the Jacobite army. They too had to be reduced. As a result they were all disbanded in February 1698 and reconstituted to form five foot regiments instead of ten and one cavalry regiment instead of two regiments and two troops

Stuarts began to sell their jewels to save their Irish subjects. A large diamond belonging to the Prince of Wales was sold in January 1698 and further sales of diamonds, pearls and gold plate followed throughout the rest of the year. By the end of 1698 James II had thereby raised 31,328 *livres* 'for the reliefe of such distressed Families, and other faithful subjects who having follow'd the . . . King in his misfortuns, must have perish'd . . . had not this extraordinary means of selling our owne jewells and plate been made use of, for their support'.[53]

But it was not enough. To help James II deal with the situation, Pope Innocent XII sent him 37,500 *livres* in August 1699,[54] and the French clergy voted him 49,414 *livres* in December,[55] but by the summer of 1700 the money was running out. In April 1700 Mary of Modena won 600 *livres* in a lottery organised by Louis XIV.[56] In May 1700 she received 400,000 crowns from the Duke of Modena.[57] But it was clear that more jewels would have to be sold sooner or later. In August Mary of Modena determined to speak to Madame de Maintenon and ask her to intervene with Louis XIV. The result, as she explained in a private letter of 29 August, was a humiliating failure:

Vous allés donc estre surprise et peut estre troublée de ce que je m'en vai vous dire . . . la personne à qui j'ouvris mon cœur là dessus ne jugea pas à propos de seulement m'ouvrir sa bouche l'autre jour quoi que je fusse une bonne demi heure seule avec elle. Je vous avoue que je suis estonnée et humiliée, cependant je ne crois pas estre assés humble pour lui en reparler une seconds fois quelque incomodité que je souffre.

of horse guards. Over 8000 officers and men were dismissed the service (J.C. O'Callaghan, *History of the Irish Brigades in the Service of France* (Glasgow, 1870 and Shannon, 1968), 141–2, 157, 188–91). At the end of 1699 Louis XIV decided that the French army would have to be reduced a second time. James II wrote to Louis in his own handwriting to ask that the Irish might be excepted from this second reform (Nairne, 18 and 20 December 1699), but in January 1700 Louis decided he could make no exceptions. More Irish soldiers (and their families) were then reduced to unemployment and poverty.

[53] Brotherton Library, University of Leeds, MS Dep. 1984/2/5, inventory of the possessions of James II, 22 July 1703. This includes a 'List of Jewels sold'.

[54] Nairne, 16 August 1699. There is a certificate in the papers of the papal nuncio dated January 1700 which shows that of this sum 35,305 *livres* 13 *sols* was given to 'poor Catholics', and that the money was distributed as follows: 'Irish 27818 *livres* 12 *sols*; English 5314 *livres* 4 *sols*; Scottish 2172 *livres* 17 *sols*' (BL Add. MSS 31245, f. 114, a certificate signed by Peregrine Ronchi and Lewis Innes of money given to poor Catholics by James II, 19 January 1700). Of the remaining 2194 *livres* 7 *sols*, James II gave 2000 *livres* to the convent of English Benedictine nuns at Pontoise, which had been struck off the list of establishments receiving alms from the king of France (Archives Dépt. du Val d'Oise, 68/H/5, the account book of the English Benedictine nuns at Pontoise, 1652–1703). The rest of the money was presumably kept to be given, wrapped in small pieces of paper, to the poor Jacobites who visited him in his cabinet. The pope also sent money separately for the banished Irish clergy (Nairne, 6 January and 5 August 1698; 12 and 24 February, 17 March, 14 April and 7 June 1699).

[55] Nairne, 18 December 1699.   [56] Nairne, 2 April 1700.   [57] Nairne, 24 May 1700.

Il n'y a non plus aucun ordre de Rome à l'esgard de nos pauvres. Au contraire le Pape a esté très mal et je crois qu'il mourra avant que d'en doner, si bien que hier nous prisme la résolution de vendre quelque pierrerie pour payer les pensions du moi de septembre et en suitte il faudra faire le mesme chose touts les mois, à moins qi'il ne vienne du secours d'ailleurs et ce de quoi je ne vois nulle apparence . . . Pour moi je vous assure que j'en suis plus estonnée qu'affligée, et à l'esgard de nos pauvres, je ne croirai jamais avoir fait mon devoir que je n'aye donc tout ce que j'ay, car je ne sera qu'alors que je pourrai dire avec vérité qu'il ne me reste rien et qu'il m'est impossible de doner davantage.[58]

As a result the sale of Stuart jewels was resumed in September and by the end of 1700 a further 50,000 *livres* had been raised for the Irish.[59] In 1701 the newly elected Pope Clement XI sent a further 37,492 *livres*,[60] so no more jewels were sold until after the death of James II.

Although the household was not financially affected by the presence of the impoverished Irish soldiers, the sale of so many jewels considerably weakened the finances of the Stuarts themselves, and encouraged people to believe (both then and now) that the exiled court was poverty stricken. In fact the Stuarts had other sources of income and had been investing in jewels since their arrival in France. Some of their money came from England, such as when Henry Slingsby (groom of the king's Bedchamber) brought James II £1300 (approximately 17,355 *livres*) from London in September 1700,[61] and some came from Mary of Modena's investments in France and Italy. These had been inherited from her mother, and brought her an annual income from the salts of Brouage[62] and the *Monts de Piété* in Rome.[63]

Just as the Stuarts had sources of income in addition to their pension from Louis XIV, so many members of their household were not totally dependent on the salaries they received from James II and Mary of Modena. At first the English all continued to have their rents sent to them in France.[64] In 1692 the Duke of Powis and some of the wealthiest Jacobites had their estates

---

[58] *Stuart Papers Relating Chiefly to Queen Mary of Modena and the Exiled Court of King James II*, 2 vols., ed. F. Madan (London, 1889), I, 41, no. 37, Mary of Modena to Mother Priolo, 29 August 1700.

[59] See note 53.

[60] Nairne, 24 January and 2 May 1701.

[61] Cole, *Affairs of State*, 213, Manchester to Vernon, 2 October 1700.

[62] Nairne, 6 May 1698; SP 46/57, 112, 139; SP 48/38, 82. Details are given in HMC *Stuart* IV, 1.

[63] SP 44/38, Nairne to James III, 12 August 1719; BL Add. MSS 20311, f. 130, Caprara to Caryll, 19 June 1709.

[64] *CSPD: William and Mary, 1689–1690* (London, 1895), 375–6, an account of Englishmen in France with King James, giving the value of their estates.

sequestered,[65] but it was not until 1696 that the government in London confiscated the property of everyone actually in service at Saint-Germain.[66] Most
members of the household thereby lost their additional sources of income,
but some had already placed their estates in trust and were protected from this
loss of property, while others received money from their families in England.
Children who already owned property in their own right were not affected.[67]
Some Catholics, like the Carylls, already had investments in the Hôtel de Ville
in Paris, while others, like David Nairne, had additional pensions from the
king of France. There was also a group of thirty officers, many of whom lived
at Saint-Germain, who were nominated by James II and given a pension from
Louis XIV, the so-called Colonels' List.[68]

Worst hit were the Irish, whose estates had already been confiscated after
the Treaty of Limerick in 1691,[69] while the least affected were the Italians in
the household of Mary of Modena who continued to receive their rents in
France as they had in England. The position of the leading Jacobites at Saint-
Germain thus varied a great deal. Lord Melfort's property was all confiscated
in 1691,[70] but Lord Middleton disponed his estates in 1695 to a friend who
was able to take sasine of them the following year and thereafter send him his
annual rents.[71] Lord Perth had disponed his entire estate to his eldest son in
1687, and also enjoyed an additional income from Scotland.[72]

The members of the household at Saint-Germain lived in a large ex-patriot
community in close proximity to their king and queen and with easy access
to both Paris and Versailles. The community was large enough to be self-
contained, so that many of the exiles never learned to speak French. For their
entertainment there was music in the chapel, the theatre and the apartments.
There were regular court balls during the carnival season and on the anniver-
saries of royal birthdays. Outside the château the members of the household
could participate in the festivals observed by both the parish church and the

---

[65] *Calendar of Treasury Papers, 1556–1696* (London, 1868), 240, inquisitions taken and returned to
the Exchequer of the goods of various Jacobites in France with King James, 3 June 1692; Haile,
Mary of Modena, 319.

[66] Haile, *Mary of Modena*, 323.

[67] For example, the three daughters of Jane Chappel (rocker) owned a house in Brownlow Street,
London (E.E. Estcourt and J.O. Payne, *The English Catholic Nonjurors of 1715; being a Summary of a
Register of their Estates* (London and New York, no date), 179).

[68] For the establishment of the Colonels' List, see Rowlands, 'An Army in Exile', 11.

[69] J.G. Simms, *Williamite Confiscations in Ireland, 1690–1703* (London, 1958), 177–92.

[70] *Calendar of Treasury Papers, 1556–1696*, 160; *Calendar of Treasury Books, ix 1689–92, part iv*
(London, 1931), 1678.

[71] G.H. Jones, *Charles Middleton: The Life and Times of a Restoration Politician* (Chicago, 1967), 258.

[72] *House of Lords Sessional Papers, 1852–53*, xxvi, 105.

religious foundations of the town. For their recreation there were billiards,[73] the *Jeu de Paume* and walks to be enjoyed in the gardens and along the *grande terrasse*. Finally there was the forest stretching to the north and west, well stocked with game. The members of the royal household no doubt yearned to return home to Whitehall and to their estates, but as a place of exile Saint-Germain had many compensations.

[73] Nairne, 3 June 1696.

CHAPTER FOUR

The royal household under James III, 1701–1712

The departments and the secretariat

When James III succeeded his father in September 1701 he also inherited his household. Given the relatively small size of his own, and the fact that old servants could not conveniently be laid off, this meant that he merely added his own servants to the household of his father.

James III needed this larger household because he returned to the apartment of the dauphin, which he had occupied from 1695 to 1699, rather than moving into the apartment of the king. The impact of this on the Chamber was immediate, because he had two antechambers whereas his father had only had one, and both a Withdrawing Room and a set of private cabinets (formerly occupied by his sister) beside and beyond his Bedchamber.

At first James III's Bedchamber remained part of his Chamber. Neither of his father's two gentlemen (Lord Clancarty and Lord Melfort) was given a new warrant, but all his grooms were renewed, so that the new king had thirteen in all (soon increased to fourteen). A dispute about precedence, which predictably broke out between the grooms of James II and those of the former Prince of Wales, was then settled by the queen in favour of the latter.[1] It was not until February 1703 that the Bedchamber was finally re-established as a separate department, independent of the Chamber. There was no groom of the stole, but the king's governor, recently created Duke of Perth, and the Earl of Newcastle, were both appointed gentlemen. A little later the Earl of Clancarty was given a new warrant, though he was actually living in Hamburg. James stated that when he had returned to England he would employ eight gentlemen of the Bedchamber, and that all the vacant posts would be reserved for those who had most contributed to his restoration. Thus when Perth's son, Lord Edward Drummond, was appointed in 1711, Perth was obliged to resign his post to make way for him, so as not to reduce the number of vacancies.[2]

James III appointed six additional grooms of the Bedchamber who were living in England, and perhaps for this reason he reduced the number at

---

[1] Nairne, 30 September and 7 October 1701.
[2] BL Add. MSS 31256, f. 34, Perth to Gualterio, 14 December 1711.

Saint-Germain from fourteen to ten. Excluding his former under-governors and preceptors, the king's Bedchamber staff at Saint-Germain numbered twenty-two people by 1709.

The king's Chamber continued to be directed by the vice-chamberlain (James Porter, succeeded in 1711 by Dominic Sheldon)[3] but it was now larger than it had been. There were two grooms of the Guard Chamber, five gentlemen of the Presence Chamber, and six gentlemen and three grooms of the Privy Chamber. Another reason for the expansion of the Chamber under James III was that the Anglican chaplain and the ceremonial musicians were brought into the household, with salaries rather than pensions. By 1709 the staff of the Chamber numbered forty-five.

James III also brought the secretaries into the household and gave them salaries, and added a Latin secretary to their number. When David Lindsay, who had served Lord Middleton as his under-secretary, decided in 1703 to return to Edinburgh (where he was arrested and sent to London for an extended interrogation),[4] he was not replaced. Instead David Nairne, who was underemployed as under-secretary to John, now Lord Caryll, became the chief assistant to both of the secretaries of state.[5] Similarly, when Caryll died in 1711 his work was taken over by Lord Middleton.

The only change in the king's household below stairs was the decision to merge the privy kitchens of the king and the queen into a single unit, because James III and his mother took their meals together in the apartment that Mary had vacated for her son. The queen's cooks moved upstairs from the basement to the ground floor of the south-west pavilion, thereby liberating space for the ewry and pantry,[6] and allowing a small reduction in the number of servants. The household below stairs remained under Francis Plowden, as comptroller of the household, but when he died in 1712 he was not replaced. Instead James III left the management in the hands of the clerk controllers of the Greencloth (Sir John Sparrow and Sir William Ellis).[7]

There were also minor modifications in the organisation of the stables under James III. His father had employed two equerries and a riding purveyor, but the new king added a third equerry with specific responsibility for the great stables, meaning, as at Versailles, the horses for riding rather than for drawing the royal carriages. This was a natural addition for a young king who enjoyed

---

[3] Porter was from Aston-sub-Edge in Gloucestershire; and Sheldon was from Beoley in Worcestershire.

[4] *CSPD: Queen Anne, 1703–1704* (London, 1924), 60, 204, 219, 472, 478–9. Lindsay was probably a relation of Lord Balcarres.

[5] Nairne, 1–11 June 1703.   [6] Corp, 'Etiquette and Use of Royal Apartments', 247.

[7] Ellis was a son of the rector of Waddesdon, Buckinghamshire.

riding. Less obvious, perhaps, was James III's decision to increase the number of his footmen.

No changes are known to have taken place in the provision of the French guards, though it is likely that their numbers were increased after the resumption of war in 1702. In 1706 Louis XIV reorganised their officers so that there were always five *chefs de brigade*, one of whom would serve for a week at a time with James III, leaving the other four with Louis himself. Each *chef de brigade* was assisted by two other officers, who also served at Saint-Germain for one week at a time.[8]

After the death of her husband, Mary of Modena increased the size of both her Bedchamber and her Chamber, still directed by her vice-chamberlain, John Stafford. She already had four ladies of the Bedchamber. When one of them (Lady Almond) died in 1703 she was replaced by the daughter of the Duke of Tyrconnell (Lady Charlotte Talbot). When the Duchess of Tyrconnell (the duke's second wife and not the mother of Lady Charlotte) left the court because she had recovered her husband's estates in Ireland, she was replaced in 1706 by the widowed Viscountess Clare. The numbers therefore remained the same, but as the queen continued to pay the duchess her full salary,[9] there were now five ladies from a financial point of view. The queen also increased the number of her Bedchamber women from four to six, though a little later, when two of the older women died, she briefly replaced them with three maids of honour. One of the maids (a daughter of Bridget Strickland) married John Stafford and was promoted to be a Bedchamber woman.

Because Mary of Modena became the Regent for her son, she also changed the balance of her Chamber servants. She reduced the number of grooms in her Guard Chamber from three to two, but increased the numbers of gentlemen in both her Presence and her Privy Chambers from two to four. Taking her meals with her son in his apartment meant that she no longer employed any gentleman waiters. The rest of the queen's household remained approximately the same size. By merging her privy kitchen with that of the king she reduced her staff by two. In the stables she reduced by one the number of coachmen and footmen, but she employed an extra equerry. Overall, then, the queen's household, like that of the king, expanded in the years following the death of James II.

The household of the princess, by contrast, did not increase, and even had a slight reduction because two of her Bedchamber women were transferred to become servants of the queen. In November 1711, shortly before her death,

---

[8] Sourches, x, 1, 1 January 1706.
[9] SP Box 3/89, a list of the royal household and pensions, July 1717.

FIG. 16. One of the ladies of the Bedchamber: *Charlotte (née Bulkeley) Viscountess Clare*, by François de Troy, c.1697 (145 × 111 cm, Château de Breteuil).

the princess created a stir by replacing two of her Bedchamber women. (One of the new ones had previously been a maid of honour to the queen.[10]) When the princess died in April 1712 she had a household of fourteen women and

[10] *Œuvres du comte Hamilton*, ed. J.-B.J. Champagnac, 2 vols. (Paris, 1829), I, 336, 'Supplément aux relations véritables de différens endroits d'Europe', 14 November 1711: 'Ce fut par son [i.e. the Earl of Newcastle's] arrivée [at FitzJames] que l'on sut les nouvelles promotions faites à la cour

two pages of the Bedchamber. Some of them, notably Lady Middleton and the two pages, were transferred to join the household of the queen, which expanded yet again, but the others had to be pensioned off.

The Board of Greencloth, now chaired by Francis Plowden, continued to be responsible for maintaining discipline, but from 1701 to 1706 it was the queen-regent, rather than the king, to whom it reported. When James III was absent from the court during the summer months of 1708 and the following three years, the queen resumed her position as the final arbiter of disputes. A record has survived of her intervention in a quarrel between Thomas Sheridan, a member of the Board, and Henry Parry, one of the clerks of the kitchen. An undated note by Francis Plowden records that

upon due consideration of what happened between Mr Sheridan and Mr Parry at the board on Satterday last was sennet, her Maiestie has ordered mee, to tell you first Mr Parry tis her pleasure that you aske the Board in generall, pardon for the disrespect you shewd to it in that dispute. Secondly that you aske Mr Sheridan pardon in particular for the affront you gave him, and for you Mr Sheridan her ma.tie requires it from you that you say to Mr Parry you heartily forgive him and are sorry for the abusive words you lett fall.[11]

Mary of Modena was particularly keen to prevent disorderly behaviour among the royal household which might offend Louis XIV. On one occasion two of the young men at the court, David Floyd (whose father was a groom of the Bedchamber) and Henry Lavery (son of a page of the queen's Bedchamber) went out of the château at night, deliberately leaving the gate open so that they could return later on. Returning to find that it had been locked by Soulaigre, the concierge, Floyd then tried to break it open. Soulaigre reported the incident to James Porter, the king's vice-chamberlain, recommending that the two men should be confined, but Porter apparently did nothing. Soulaigre then complained to the queen. Furious, she ordered that both men be arrested and summoned Porter to give an explanation. She commented to Caryll that 'if it were not in consideration of Lloyd's [sic] father, the punishment should have been mor proportionable to the crime, which certainly was a very great one, and the less the K. of France meddles in these matters, the mor I think

de Saint-Germain, au sujet des dames de son altesse royale madame la princesse d'Angleterre. On raisonna fort sur cet événement. Les prétensions de celles qui avaient été exclues furent balancées. Il y eut du pour et du contre dans les raisonnemens; mais on tomba d'accord à la fin, que, comme il fallait des sujets robustes pour suppléer à la délicatesse du tempérament de celles qui étaient déjà en place, on ne pouvait guère mieux choisir.'
[11] Bodleian Library, Carte MSS 209, f. 475. See also Nairne, 11 April 1703.

myself bound to shew displaisur to those that offend him, and I hope you will make Mr Lloyd sensible of all this'.[12]

Another dispute which the queen had to settle concerned the arrest and trial in London of David Lindsay, on a charge of high treason.[13] The Duke of Perth had a public disagreement with Lord Middleton when he read the reports of Lindsay's defence, because they seemed to imply that Middleton was half-hearted in working for a restoration.[14] A few days later, according to David Nairne, 'the Q made a short speech after dinner by way of reprimande upon ye occasion of the dispute and heat that happend upon ye occasion of Mr Lindsay's words'.[15]

The relations between the impetuous Perth and the moderate Middleton steadily deteriorated in the next few years, when Perth did nothing to discourage the idea that Middleton and Caryll were both traitors. He found an ally in Colonel Nathaniel Hooke, who was used by the French government as an intermediary with the nobles in Scotland and who wanted to increase his own importance at Versailles by discrediting the two Jacobite secretaries of state. When Hooke had the affrontery to suggest to the queen that they were both traitors and were giving away her secrets she rebuffed him, saying that she was well aware of Perth's jealousy and had no intention of being drawn into his quarrels.[16] But Hooke's insinuations were believed at Versailles where the French ministers, faced with continued military defeats, began to suspect that the English court could not be trusted. In 1708, at the time of the Franco-Jacobite attempt to invade Scotland, the secretary of state for the French navy even convinced himself that the queen herself could not be trusted.[17]

The idea that the household at Saint-Germain could not keep its own secrets (like the notion that it was poverty stricken) has been widely believed,[18] but there is no evidence to support it. Very few people at Saint-Germain had

[12] BL Add. MSS 28224, 40, Mary of Modena to Caryll, 31 May 1711(?); Bodleian Library, Carte MSS 210, f. 372, Floyd to Middleton, undated.

[13] *CSPD: Queen Anne, 1703–1704*, 511 515, 603; BL Add. MSS 20311, f. 6, Lindsay to Nottingham, 8 December 1703.

[14] BL Add. MSS 20311, ff. 32 and 34, Lindsay to Nottingham, 23 December 1703, with a report of the examination of Lindsay; Nairne, 25 July 1704.

[15] Nairne, 3 August 1704.

[16] N. Hooke, *Correspondence, 1703–1707*, ed. W.D. Macray, 2 vols. (London, 1870–71), I, 194, Hooke to Torcy, 10 June 1705.

[17] AN CHAN 257, AP 2d.5, Pontchartrain to Louis XIV, 2 and 7 March 1708.

[18] Haile, *Mary of Modena*, 262: 'St. Germains . . . was a safe and easy hunting-ground for spies, and during the thirty years of its occupation by the Stuarts there was *never* a time when the English Court [in London] was not *immediately* and *fully* informed of *all* that was going on, in spite of the elaborate systems of secrecy always in use there' (my emphases).

access to political secrets,[19] and none of them has ever been shown to have been a traitor or even indiscreet. All that the English archives show is that a small number of homesick servants approached the government in London, or the English embassy in Paris during the period 1697–1701, in the hope of obtaining permission to return to England. Thomas Woolhouse, the groom of the king's Privy Chamber, did so in 1698,[20] as did John Bayly, the purveyor of the poultry, in 1703.[21] The most that any potentially disloyal servant could do was give away the names of secret visitors to the court, but they had no access to sensitive political secrets.[22]

Disloyal servants were also tempted to steal from the royal apartments, just as they did at the French court. The worst incident took place in July 1703 when 15,000 *livres* of diamonds were stolen from the cabinet of Princess Louise-Marie.[23]

The salaries and pensions

The increase in the size of the household after the death of James II had important financial implications, and within eighteen months it was clear that something had to be done. The last time that a crisis had been reached, in 1695, it had been the pensions which had been reduced. In January 1703 Mary of Modena decided that she would have to reduce the amount of money spent on salaries as well as pensions, because 'our disbursements exceed our receipts near 4000 *livres* per month'.[24]

There were no further reductions, but the War of the Spanish Succession placed an enormous strain on the French Treasury, and by 1709 all of France, not just the Stuart court, was suffering from the shortage of money. The pension from Louis XIV fell into arrears so that the queen could no longer pay the salaries of the household servants on time. They had to subsist on

[19] A.C. Biscoe, *The Earls of Middleton* (London, 1876), 204, Middleton to Bruce, 23 December 1695.

[20] HMC *Bath* III, 290, Woolhouse to Prior, 16 November 1698.

[21] *CSPD: Queen Anne, 1703–1704*, 222, Bayly to Nottingham, 6 December 1703.

[22] Corp, *Stuart Court and Jacobites*, xx–xxiii.

[23] Nairne, 2, 3 and 5 July 1703. For Middleton's report to Pontchartrain, the secretary of state for the *Maison du Roi* at Versailles, see Bodleian Library, Carte MSS 238, f. 19, 'vol fait au cabinet de la Princesse'.

[24] HMC *Stuart* I, 180. The retrenchment took effect in February 1703, at the same time as the re-establishment of the king's separate Bedchamber department (Nairne, 3 February 1703. See also SP 112/86, Ellis to James III, 2 December 1727). Two months later, Louis XIV increased Berwick's annual pension from 12,000 to 20,000 *livres* (Dangeau, IX, 168, 13 April 1703), and held a lottery at Marly which was deliberately organised so that the prizes were won by the English (Dangeau, IX, 177–8, 16–27 April 1703; Haile, *Mary of Modena*, 372, Rizzini to the Duke of Modena, May 1703).

their other sources of income or live on credit, and those who could not obtain credit elsewhere had to borrow money from the king and queen.[25] By June 1710 the salaries were seven months in arrears.[26] Lord Caryll, who had important investments in the Hôtel de Ville, agreed to waive his salary altogether.[27] One of the Italian Bedchamber women (Veronica Molza) later agreed to have her salary paid in Rome from the queen's *luoghi di monte*.[28] Meanwhile the pensions for the thirty officers on the Colonels' List also fell into arrears, and Mary of Modena ordered the Duke of Perth to intercede directly with the French secretary of state for war.[29]

The shortage of money obliged the queen to cut back her own expenses from the one third of the French pension which the Stuarts kept for themselves. But this coincided with a substantial increase in the expenses incurred by James III. The pope was asked to help finance the attempted invasion of Scotland in 1708,[30] but after his return the king joined the French army as a volunteer for the three campaigns in Flanders of 1708, 1709 and 1710. He adopted an incognito, as the *Chevalier de Saint-Georges*, but he had to take some household servants with him and these campaigns inevitably involved considerable expense. They were followed by the king's tour of the French provinces in the summer and autumn of 1711. The queen found herself expected to provide him with sufficient money, while at the same time giving charity to the poor (generally Irish) Jacobites at Saint-Germain and lending money to the household servants who could not obtain credit. By November 1708 she commented that 'I believe I shall be forced to sell the rest of the jewels, but I will not tell him [James III] so.'[31]

The following year placed the queen in the same financial predicament. In September 1709 she decided she would have to make serious cut-backs in

---

[25] SP Box 3/87 and 86, money owed to James III and Mary of Modena by members of their households after 1709 and 1711.

[26] BL Add. MSS 31256, f. 5, Perth to Gualterio, 7 June 1710.

[27] Nairne, 5 October 1706. Other courtiers with annual incomes from *rentes* on the Hôtel de Ville included: Jean Delattre (gentleman armourer, 150 *livres* in 1708); Lewis Innes (almoner, 100 *livres* in 1708); Randall MacDonnell (groom of the Bedchamber, 584 *livres* in 1707); Melfort (1257 *livres* in 1706); Perth (300 *livres* in 1709); and the widow of Richard Waldegrave (gentleman of the Privy Chamber, 315 *livres* in 1704). (I am grateful to Nathalie Genet-Rouffiac for these details, taken from the papers of Delanges, a *notaire*, in a private collection at Saint-Germain-en-Laye, and from BL Add. Ch. 12511–621.)

[28] BL Add. MSS 20311, f. 130, Caprara to Caryll, 16 September 1709; BL Add. MSS 31254, f. 23, Mary of Modena to Gualterio, 24 October 1712.

[29] Archives de la Guerre, A.2140, no. 234, Perth to Voysin, 8 October 1709.

[30] Haile, *Mary of Modena*, 404, Mary of Modena to Clement XI, 8 March 1708.

[31] HMC *Stuart* I, 228, Mary of Modena to Dicconson, 1 November 1708.

her pensions and charities.[32] She was so successful that James III wrote back from the army one month later that he had been able to maintain himself there without either 'retrenching or selling'.[33] But Mary of Modena also had to draw on her own investments, particularly her *luoghi di monte*, for additional income. She transferred substantial sums from Rome to Saint-Germain in June 1709 and April 1710,[34] and sold one of her pearl necklaces in May 1712.[35]

However unpleasant this was at the time, it did not imply that the members of the royal household were badly paid. Their problem was shared by the court of Versailles[36] and the rest of France, and came to an end with the return of peace. Even during the most difficult times they continued to enjoy the various perks provided by their employment. A substantial number were given grace and favour apartments in the château. Approximately ten more received lodging allowances on top of their salaries because they could not be accommodated. Approximately fifty-five people received diet, prepared for them by the privy kitchen,[37] or board wages of 2 *livres*, 10 *sols* each day if they had to accompany the king when he was away from Saint-Germain. Special daily rates, of roughly the same amounts, were given to anyone else who accompanied the king.[38] The French guards were each given one 'bottle of ordinary wine and a small loaf of bread' each day, and there was a generous allowance of candles for the royal apartments (white wax and yellow wax), for the French guards (tallow) and for all the sub-departments of the household below stairs (tallow). The guards and sub-departments also received generous wood allowances, while fires were constantly maintained in the Presence Chambers to provide warmth for anyone admitted beyond the Guard Chambers, an important benefit during the long cold winters at the end of the War of the Spanish Succession. Finally, the footmen, grooms, chairmen, coachmen and postillions employed in the stables all received money to pay for their liveries.[39]

After the death of James II the French pension continued to be collected each month by Francis Plowden (the comptroller) and Robert Strickland (the

---

[32] HMC *Stuart* I, 232, Mary of Modena to Dicconson, 4 September 1709.

[33] HMC *Stuart* I, 233, James III to Dicconson, 11 October 1709.

[34] BL Add. MSS 20311, f. 130, Caprara to Caryll, 19 June 1709; Haile, *Mary of Modena*, 426, quoting BL Add. MSS 20294, f. 120 of April 1710.

[35] BL Add. MSS 20311, f. 218, memorandum by Gualterio, 2 May 1712.

[36] See Sourches, x, 216, 18 November 1706 for retrenchments in the French *Maison du Roi* at Versailles.

[37] See Corp, 'Etiquette and Use of Royal Apartments', 253, notes 27 and 29 for the details.

[38] SP 39/117, 'Travelling Charges per Diem'.

[39] SP 39/117, 'Wax lights candles and flambeaus for ye 5 winter months', and a list of various other allowances.

queen's treasurer and receiver-general). The latter died in March 1708 and was succeeded by William Dicconson,[40] who had been one of James III's two under-governors until 1706. Dicconson had already become involved in the queen's finances, because Mary of Modena had been secretly buying *rentes* on the Hôtel de Ville in Paris in his name since November 1703.[41] The task of paying the salaries, pensions and bills remained the responsibility of Sir John Sparrow (clerk controller of the Greencloth) for the household of the king, and of Henry Conquest (clerk of the Greencloth) for that of the queen until 1708 when the latter, following the death of Robert Strickland, was given the sole responsibility, with the new title of paymaster. When he died in 1709 the task was entrusted to Dicconson, who thus became jointly responsible for receiving the money from the French Treasury and solely responsible for all payments. One other servant was given financial responsibility. When James III achieved his majority in the summer of 1706 he appointed one of the grooms of his Bedchamber (Thomas Neville) to be the keeper of his privy purse, though at first this was kept secret.[42]

The five commissioners of the household (Plowden, Conquest, Ellis, Sheridan and Bulstrode),[43] who had to authorise all payments, remained the same until 1708, when Conquest, appointed paymaster, relinquished his place to Dicconson. The death of Bulstrode in 1711, followed by those of both Plowden and Sheridan in 1712, left Ellis and Dicconson as the only remaining commissioners.

Despite the long war and the arrears in the payment of the French pension after 1708, the exiled court of Saint-Germain was a most agreeable place, particularly for the young. James III and his sister Louise-Marie attracted around them the generation of Jacobites born at Whitehall during the 1680s and at Saint-Germain during the early 1690s, who were confident of an eventual restoration. They attended regular balls, concerts and theatrical entertainments during the winter months, and went for promenades and picnics in the forest when the weather was good.[44] The Duke of Perth noted disapprovingly at the beginning of 1711 that 'il n'y a icy en vogue que les dames et les divertissements du carnavalle',[45] but the poet Anthony Hamilton, who had an eye

[40] Nairne, 2 March 1708. Dicconson was from Wrightington Hall, Lancashire.

[41] HMC *Stuart* I, 190; Nairne, 11 January 1704.

[42] Nairne, 2 July 1706. Neville was from Holt in Leicestershire.

[43] Sheridan was from County Meath in Leinster; and Bulstrode was from Horton in Buckinghamshire and Astley in Warwickshire.

[44] *Œuvres de Hamilton*, I, 389, Hamilton to Berwick, 30 May 1703; 500, 'Bouquet pour Madame la Princesse d'Angleterre', 24 August 1710(?); 410, Hamilton to Berwick, autumn 1710 (or 1711).

[45] BL Add. MSS 31256, f. 24, Perth to Gualterio, 28 January 1711.

for the ladies, referred with approval to 'la troupe adorable de nos nymphes de Saint-Germain'. He admired 'Nos rimailleurs de Saint-Germain / Qui vont faisant des chansonnettes / Depuis le soir jusqu'au matin'.[46]

It was because the courtiers enjoyed themselves so much at Saint-Germain that people like the Duke of Perth became uneasy. The agreeable life at the exiled court seemed to him to be reducing people's enthusiasm to strive for a restoration. There were also suspicions, completely unfounded, that some would actually prefer to have no restoration at all because they would be worse off. One Scot who visited Saint-Germain in 1704 explained this point of view, even going so far as to accuse Perth himself of sharing it:

la plupart sont beaucoup mieux icy qu'ils ne seroient chez eux; car au fait le Duc de Barwick n'a rien en Engleterre, et est tres bien icy. My Lord Middleton n'a rien en Engleterre et encore moins en Ecosse. My Lord Perth a du bien en Ecosse, mais à la Revolution il devoit plusqu'il n'avoit, et depuis qu'il vit icy de ses pensions, il a payé ses debtes et achepter du bien. Une infinité d'autres qui ont icy des pensions parcequ'ils sont sortis de leurs payis, les perdroient s'ils y rentroient; ce qui fait qi'ils n'ont aucun empressement pour le retablissement de leur Roy.[47]

The accusation was absurd, even for the younger generation which had only known a life of exile. It presupposed that the Jacobites would not have recovered their confiscated estates, that James III would not have rewarded those who had supported him in exile, and that he would have stopped employing the members of his household who had served him at Saint-Germain. But the accusation is nevertheless useful. It contradicts the commonly held view that the Jacobites at Saint-Germain were bored and desperately short of money.

[46] *Œuvres de Hamilton*, I, 389, Hamilton to Berwick, 30 May 1703; 528, 'Les Sœurs de Saint-Dominique de Poissy aux Filles de Sainte-Marie de Chaillot, Salut'.

[47] Hooke, *Correspondence*, I, 62–3, 'memoir de M. Leviston', February 1704.

FIG. 17. One of the younger generation of 'nymphes de Saint-Germain': the
Duke of Melfort's daughter, *Lady Mary Drummond*, by Jean-Baptiste Oudry, *c*.1714
(137 × 105 cm, Museu Nacional del Prado). In 1713 Lady Mary married the Count
of Castelblanco, who was created Duke of St Andrews in 1717.

CHAPTER FIVE

The household servants

The national groups

The majority of the household servants at the court of Saint-Germain were English, but there were also Irish, French, Italians and Scots. In 1696, for which we have Robert Strickland's complete list of both the king's and the queen's servants,[1] there were approximately thirty Irish, twenty French, fourteen Italians and eight Scots. In later years the number of Irish increased to over fifty, the number of French remained approximately the same, and the number of Italians went down to about ten. The Scots increased to about twelve. The very small number of Scots needs to be emphasised, because so many historians, and notably the French, have assumed that the Jacobite court was essentially a Scottish court.

The Irish served in all the departments of the household and occupied posts at all levels, but were numerically predominant in the stables. Most of the higher-ranking Irish came from Munster, but Connacht, Leinster and Ulster were all represented. While James II was alive there were no Irish in the households of his children, but James III made a point of changing this and appointed a significant number to both his own and his sister's households.[2] The French servants had already worked for the Stuarts at Whitehall, and do not seem to have been locally recruited.[3] They were only employed in the Bedchamber, the Chamber and below stairs, and mainly occupied specific, perhaps predictable posts. Two of them were wine merchants who acted as purveyors to the king, but were formally employed as the gentleman of the butteries and a page of the Bedchamber. Another was the yeoman of the queen's wine cellar, while three others worked in the kitchens. Of these six, two had wives who were employed as sempstresses. James II also had a French tailor, armourer, barber and surgeon. There were no Italians either in the stables or below stairs. Most of them were from Modena and occupied important positions in the queen's Bedchamber and chapel. James II employed an Italian

[1] Sizergh Castle, Strickland Collection R.4.   [2] Corp, 'Irish at Saint-Germain', 147–8, 150.
[3] Pierre Dotroe, a French cook recommended by Lauzun, provides an exception (SP Box 3/1/89).

gentleman usher, who was the brother of two of the queen's almoners, and James III also had an Italian page of the Bedchamber.[4]

There were so few Scots that it is impossible to make useful generalisations, except that they were extremely influential and were divided into two groups. Lord Melfort, from Perthshire like his brother Lord Perth, patronised Lewis Innes, from Drumgask, south-east of Loch Ness, and had him appointed one of the queen's almoners. (One of his brothers became a gentleman usher to the queen.) Innes, in his turn, patronised David Nairne from Fife, who already lived in Paris and was appointed to be Lord Melfort's under-secretary. When Lord Perth joined the court in 1696 he naturally joined this group. The other consisted of Lord Middleton, who had lived most of his life in England but owned estates at Montrose and, a little further north, at Fettercairn, and his under-secretary David Lindsay from Lanarkshire. When Nairne succeeded Lindsay in 1703 he tried to create a united Scottish front, but it was left to the younger generation to bring the two factions together. In 1709 Lord Middleton's English wife helped arrange the marriage of one of their two daughters to Perth's son, Lord Edward Drummond.[5]

Most of the Jacobites at Saint-Germain married within their own national groups, but with such a large population there were some exceptions. Sir William Waldegrave already had an Italian wife, the sister of the two almoners of the queen already mentioned. Francesco Riva, the master of the queen's robes, had an English wife. Joseph Ronchi (gentleman usher of the king's Presence Chamber), brother of the two almoners and brother-in-law of Sir William Waldegrave, married an Irish girl in 1702, while John Nugent (equerry to the King), an Irishman who later became 5th Earl of Westmeath, married one of the daughters of Veronica Molza (Bedchamber woman) in 1711. Relatively few Jacobites married French people, though the French servants who had previously worked at Whitehall already had English wives. Close links were developed between the servants employed in the household below stairs at Saint-Germain and those employed at Versailles, and these links were strengthened by several marriages.[6]

The English at Saint-Germain came from most areas of the country, particularly the midlands. There were no important servants from East Anglia,

---

[4] See the various household lists shown in Corp, 'Inventory', 134; and the parish registers of Saint-Germain (Archives Municipales de Saint-Germain-en-Laye).

[5] BL Add. MSS 31256, f. 34, Perth to Gualterio, 14 December 1711.

[6] Several examples may be found in Corp, 'Courtisans français', 58, note 32. Further details are given in the index to the papers of the *Secrétariat de la Maison du Roi*, 1610–1786 (AN 0/1/27–49, salle des usuels).

Lincolnshire and the extreme north-east, but elsewhere the majority of counties was represented. Loyalty, family circumstances and previous service at Whitehall were more importmant than geographical origins.

The northerners included Sir Thomas and Lady Strickland and Charles Leyburne from Westmorland,[7] Fergus Grahme and William Dicconson from Lancashire,[8] and Robert and Bridget Strickland, Admiral Sir Roger Strickland, John Ingleton and Henry Slingsby from Yorkshire.[9] From the west country there were Denis Granville and Richard Trevanion from Cornwall,[10] Charles Wyndham from Devonshire,[11] Lord Waldegrave and Sir Charles Carteret from Somerset,[12] and Thomas Codrington and Lord Portland from Wiltshire.[13] From the south-east there were John Copley and Thomas Wyvill from London,[14] Sir Richard Bulstrode and Lord Castlemaine from Buckinghamshire,[15] William Hyde from Oxfordshire,[16] Ralph and Dominic Sheldon from Hampshire,[17] Edmund Perkins from Berkshire,[18] Henry Browne and Lord Caryll from Sussex,[19] and Sir John Sparrow and Sir William Waldegrave from Essex.[20] The midlands were represented by Bernard Howard from Derbyshire,[21] Joseph Bryerly, Sir John Gifford and Thomas Neville from Leicestershire,[22] Bevil Skelton from Huntingdonshire,[23] Lord Griffin and James Simms from

[7] Strickland of Sizergh (under-governess, then governess, then Bedchamber woman); Leyburne of Nateby (equerry, then groom of the Bedchamber).

[8] Grahme of Netherby (keeper of the privy purse); Dicconson of Wrightington Hall (under-governor, then commissioner of the household, and treasurer and receiver-general).

[9] Strickland of Catterick (vice-chamberlain, then treasurer and receiver-general; Bedchamber woman); Ingleton of — (under-preceptor); Slingsby of Scriven (groom of the Bedchamber).

[10] Granville of Kilkhampton (Anglican chaplain); Trevanion of Carkey (groom of the Bedchamber).

[11] Wyndham of Tale (page).

[12] Waldegrave of Chewton (comptroller of the household); Carteret of Toomer (and Jersey) (gentleman usher of the Presence Chamber).

[13] Codrington of Sutton Mandeville (under-preceptor); Portland (Herbert) of Wilton (lord chancellor).

[14] Copley of Southwark (gentleman usher of the Presence Chamber); Wyvill of Soho (gentleman usher of the Presence Chamber).

[15] Bulstrode of Horton (commissioner of the household); Castlemaine (Palmer) of Dorney Court (no post).

[16] Hyde of Stanlake (groom of the Privy Chamber).

[17] Sheldon of Winchester (equerry; under-governor, then vice-chamberlain).

[18] Perkins of Ufton (under-governor).

[19] Browne of Midhurst (secretary of state); Caryll of Ladyholt and West Grinstead (secretary of state).

[20] Sparrow of Havering (clerk controller of the household); Waldegrave of Borley (physician).

[21] Howard of Glossop (equerry, then groom of the Bedchamber).

[22] Bryerly of Belgrave (equerry to the Duke of Berwick); Gifford of Frisby and Burstall (groom of the Bedchamber); Neville of Holt (groom of the Bedchamber).

[23] Skelton of Ravely (comptroller of the household).

Northamptonshire,[24] John Betham from Warwickshire,[25] James Porter from Gloucestershire,[26] Charles Booth from Herefordshire,[27] Francis Plowden from Shropshire[28] and Richard Biddulph from Staffordshire.[29] The family of John Stafford and his brother Francis had important estates in Shropshire, Staffordshire and Gloucestershire.[30] The Duke of Powis came from over the Welsh border in Montgomeryshire,[31] while Henry Bulkeley, the only other important Welshman, was from Anglesea.[32]

Despite their widespread geographical origins, many of the Catholic English at Saint-Germain were already related by marriage. Sir Thomas Strickland of Sizergh was a first cousin of Robert Strickland of Catterick and his brother Admiral Sir Roger. Lady Strickland was a first cousin of Richard Biddulph. The latter's brother-in-law was married to a sister of Francis Plowden, whose brother Edmund was brother-in-law of both John Caryll's wife and Richard Trevanion's mother.[33] The Duke of Powis was first cousin of the Earl of Castlemaine, while his daughter Mary was sister-in-law of Henry Browne (later 5th Viscount Montagu). The Duchess of Powis's sister was the Duchess of Norfolk, who was the aunt of Bernard Howard. Thomas Codrington was the nephew of Edmund Perkins. Sir John Gifford was a cousin of William Dicconson's wife. Lord Waldegrave was a cousin of Sir William Waldegrave. Given the many links which existed between the English Catholic families, this list could no doubt be extended. There were also many family connections between the lower servants, particularly those who had already been working together in the household at Whitehall.

Living in exile at Saint-Germain inevitably increased these links. For example, the daughter of Thomas Neville's sister, the latter married to James Simms, married Charles Booth in 1701. Some of the senior officials married the daughters of their colleagues. Francis Plowden married the daughter of John Stafford in 1699. John Stafford married a daughter of Robert Strickland in 1708. The three daughters of Jane Chappel married Thomas Wyvill, Charles

---

[24] Griffin of Dingley (no post); Simms of Daventry (gentleman usher of the Privy Chamber).

[25] Betham of Rowington (?) (preceptor).   [26] Porter of Aston-sub-Edge (vice-chamberlain).

[27] Booth of Brampton (groom of the Bedchamber).

[28] Plowden of Plowden Hall (under-governor, then comptroller of the household).

[29] Biddulph of Biddulph Grange (groom of the Bedchamber).

[30] Stafford of Shiffnal, Stafford and Thornbury (comptroller of the household, then vice-chamberlain; groom of the Bedchamber).

[31] Powis (Herbert) of Powis Castle (lord chamberlain).

[32] Bulkeley of Baron Hill (master of the household at Whitehall; lady of the Bedchamber).

[33] The three daughters of Sir Maurice Drummond married John Caryll, Edmund Plowden and John Trevanion.

Wyndham and Nicholas Dempster, in 1694, 1705 and 1713 respectively. The latter marriage was one of the few between the English and the Scots, but Lord Middleton's elder daughter provides another example. In 1702 she married Sir John Gifford. Three years after her husband's death in 1707, and against the wishes of her father, she married an Irishman, Michael Rothe, later a lieutenant-general.[34]

Their accommodation

The Château de Saint-Germain contained sixty-eight apartments for courtiers on the ground, first, third and fourth floors, distributed on each one as follows: twenty, eighteen, twenty-one and nine. The second floor, which was primarily taken up by the royal apartments, contained some additional apartments for courtiers in the south wing and three of the pavilions. Most of them, seven in number, were *entresols* above the apartment known as that of the *Enfants de France* and used as a nursery by both the prince and the princess. There were also three more on the second floor itself, intended for the governesses. In total, therefore, there were seventy-eight apartments in the château to be allocated by the king and queen, and an additional one when the nursery was no longer needed in 1699 (see Figs. 6–8).

The apartments were all numbered in a clockwise sequence around each floor of the building, and detailed ground plans have survived for all of them, including the *entresols*.[35] There is also a list which shows the occupants of all the apartments in the spring of 1692.[36] When an occupant was asked to move out in order to make way for a newly arrived Jacobite regarded as more deserving, he was compensated by being given lodging money of 12 *livres* each month to find alternative accommodation in the town. The lists of household salaries thus enable us to identify those servants who were obliged to give up their apartments, both before and after the 1692 list was drawn up. No further lists of the occupants of the château have survived but we have enough information to draw general conclusions.

As one might expect, most of the apartments were allocated to the servants working in the Bedchamber and Chamber.[37] All the female servants attached

---

[34] Chappel of Holborn (rocker); Dempster of Muresk (clerk in the secretariat); Jones, *Middleton*, 285.

[35] BN Est. Va. 448e, H.188573–92; and Va. 78c, t.2, B.8550–7.

[36] Bodleian Library, Carte MSS 208, f. 287.

[37] The two senior members of the queen's stables were given apartments, but none of the servants attached to the king's stables lived in the château. None of the queen's below stairs servants had an apartment, though one of her cooks had lodging money. The comptroller of the household

to the queen's Bedchamber lived in the château, as did two of her pages who were married. James II reserved apartments for his gentlemen of the Bedchamber and for four of his six grooms of the Bedchamber. One of his four pages (who was French) also had one, probably because his wife was sempstress to the queen. The masters of the robes both lived in the château, though the king's assistants did not. The queen's confessor, almoners and two (out of four) chaplains were accommodated, but of the king's priests only his confessor and one chaplain had an apartment. The lord chamberlain, both vice-chamberlains and some of the gentleman ushers had apartments. Other servants who were given priority were the queen's secretary and physician, and the king's armourer, barber and surgeon. The women who looked after the little prince and princess lived in the château, and so did the governor and under-governors, and the grooms and pages of the prince's Bedchamber, when he was given male attendants. Finally one apartment was reserved for the concierge and another for the comte (after 1692 duc) de Lauzun, in recognition of the part he had played in escorting the queen to France in December 1688. With very few exceptions, all the important members of the household were thus given apartments in the château.

Much, however, depended on their locations, as the best ones were on the first floor, immediately below the royal apartments, followed by those on the third floor immediately above them. The apartments below those of the king and queen enjoyed immediate access to a small circular staircase which led up to the king's Antechamber, thus bypassing his Guard Chamber. In 1692 these were occupied by the Duke of Berwick and the Earl of Melfort. The queen's Italian servants were well provided for and were situated closer to her than her English ones. When the apartment of the *Enfants de France* was vacated by the princess in 1699 it was given to Lord and Lady Middleton. The staircases which led to the royal apartments were all supervised by the officers responsible. The lord chamberlain lived on the first floor beside the king's staircase, while the queen's vice-chamberlain lived on the third floor beside hers. The king's vice-chamberlain had a ground-floor apartment which guarded both the circular staircase leading up to his Antechamber and the entrance to a small corridor which led to his backstairs.[38] The French guards who served in the Guard Chambers and who manned the

---

and the clerk controller of the Greencloth both had apartments, as did the heads of three sub-departments: the confectionary, the larder and the king's privy kitchen.

[38] For Lord Ailesbury's description of his visit to James II in 1693, when he had to go past the vice-chamberlain's apartment in order to go up the backstairs, see his *Memoirs*, ed. W. Buckley (London, 1890), 323ff.

two gates of the château had an apartment on the third floor beside the king's staircase.

Some Jacobites were accommodated in the stables and the other buildings belonging to the château, such as the *chancellerie* and the *surintendance*. In the Hôtel de Religion (between the rue de Pontoise and the rue de Lorraine), the queen's equerry (Arthur Magennis) and the king's dancing master (Jean Faure) lived alongside an unspecified *anglais*, a tailor and three servants of the duchesse d'Orléans.[39] Those who lived in the town were mainly accommodated in a small number of streets beyond the *cour des cuisines*, of which the closest and most convenient were the rue de la Salle and the rue au Pain. The former contained an English inn and the latter an English bookshop. Beyond these roads there were several others where the Jacobites congregated, in an arc stretching from the rue de Pontoise in the north to the rue de Versailles in the south.[40] Very little is known about the addresses of individual Jacobites, as the tax returns tend to say no more than that a house was occupied by *des anglais*.[41] The gentleman of the king's cellars (Charles Macarty) and one of his cooks (Jeremiah Broomer) both lived in the rue de Pontoise, as did one of the queen's gentleman waiters (Matteo Maria Turrini) and Lady Albeville, whose husband had been secretary of state. Sir Richard Bulstrode lived in the rue de Lorraine, where one of his neighbours was the portrait painter Alexis-Simon Belle. The Duchess of Tyrconnell, who occupied a relatively small apartment on the first floor of the château, bought a house in the rue de Versailles which she eventually rented out to some of the *cent Suisses* who guarded the gardens and the royal estate. The king's barber (Michael Bedingfield), who originally had an apartment in the château, bought a house in the town and helped finance it by taking in Thomas Sheridan (commissioner of the household) and his wife as lodgers,[42] but the rent of 15 *livres* a month was paid on Sheridan's behalf by the French *Bâtiments du Roi*.[43]

---

[39] The detailed plans of the stables and the other buildings are in AN O/1/920, 1720B and 1721. The occupants of the Hôtel de Religion are shown with the plan in O/1/1721.

[40] The main ones occupied by the Jacobites were, moving anti-clockwise from north-west to south-west, the rues de Lorraine, aux Vaches, Saint-Pierre, de Mareil and des Recollets, all of which still exist today, and the rue Sansonnet (called the rue Ducastel since the 1890s).

[41] For the tax returns, see Arch. Dépt. des Yvelines, B.451–70 Saint-Germain. The parish registers specify that Abraham Baumeister (musician) lived in the Hôtel de Soubise, beside the *cour des cuisines*; Etienne du Mirail de Monnot (clerk) in the Hôtel de Duras in the rue des Ecuyers; and Charles Langhorne (chaplain) in the rue Sansonnet.

[42] SP 196/31, Elizabeth Bedingfield to Thomas Sheridan (junior), 5 May 1737.

[43] AN O/1/1716, 'loyer de la maison dans la ville qu'occupe le Sr Cheridon, officier du Roy d'Angleterre', 1702–12.

Their standard of living: a case study

The standard of living of the Jacobites obviously depended on their incomes, both from the court itself and from their own private resources. No generalisations can be made, beyond the fact that even the lowest servants received salaries which enabled them to live decently according to their status.[44] But we do possess the private diary of one Jacobite courtier, David Nairne, which gives us an interesting insight into the relative prosperity and way of life of an average exile.

Nairne's employment and income placed him in the middle level of the exiled court, with a monthly pension from James II of 89 *livres*, 7 *sols* and 6 *deniers*. Taking salaries and pensions together, there were sixty-eight people at Saint-Germain who received more money than he did in 1696. The highest monthly pensions were 750 *livres* each for the Dukes of Berwick and Albemarle, 714 for Lord Melfort, 514 for Lord Middleton and 500 for Sir Edward Herbert (created Earl of Portland).[45] The highest monthly salaries were 500 *livres* for the governor of the Prince of Wales (Lord Perth), 385 for the gentlemen of the Bedchamber, 350 for the comptroller of the household, 343 for the ladies of the Bedchamber, 342 for the king's vice-chamberlain and master of the robes, and 325 for the queen's physician.[46] Compared with these, Nairne's income was very modest indeed, and many of these better-paid servants also had apartments in the château to supplement their incomes in kind. Nairne received approximately the same amount of money each month as the pages of the Bedchambers, the laundress and starcher to the prince, the rockers of the princess, and the master cook and barbers of the king. His private diary, which contains the details of his domestic circumstances, thus gives us an

---

[44] In 1696 only fourteen servants were paid less than 20 *livres* each month. They included the two farriers, the assistants in the kitchens and the other sub-departments, a musician, a man employed to clean the candle holders, another who looked after the plate on the gentlemen's table, and the purveyor of the poultry.

[45] To continue: 250 Mary Skelton; 201 Lady Melfort; 200 Lady Strickland; 175 Lady Elizabeth Hatcher; 166 Sir Richard Bulstrode, Lord Dundee, Lady Albeville and Anthony Hamilton; 162 Sir Richard Nagle; 150 Lord Dumbarton; 117 Mr Cannetta (the king's engineer); 103 Lady Kingston; 100 Denis Granville.

[46] To continue: 283 the queen's vice-chamberlain; 257 the under-governors of the prince and the governess of the princess; 222 the grooms of the king's Bedchamber; 197 the Bedchamber women and John Caryll; 188 the queen's equerry; 171 the king's first physician; 166 the prince's preceptor; 150 the grooms of the prince's Bedchamber; 128 the king's equerries and riding purveyor, the clerks of the Greencloth and the nurses of the princess; 115 the queen's yeoman rider; 107 the clerks of the kitchen; 102 the king's surgeon; 100 the prince's under-preceptor; 97 the queen's coachmen.

FIG. 18. The secretary of the closet for the king's private letters and despatches previously an under-secretary: *David Nairne*, by Alexis-Simon Belle, 1714 (76.2 × 63.5 cm, private collection).

opportunity to examine the standard of living enjoyed by an average Jacobite at the exiled court.

Unlike many Jacobites at Saint-Germain, Nairne received no money from his family in Great Britain. He was the heir to a small estate in Fife, but by the time he inherited it from his elder brother in 1706 it had already been confiscated by the government in Edinburgh.[47] He did, however, have a small monthly pension of 33 *livres* from Louis XIV, which he had obtained while living in Paris during the 1680s.[48] He also invested his spare money in supporting the Jacobite privateers operating in the Channel, and on two occasions received a share of prize money.[49]

Nairne felt that his post as under-secretary to Lord Melfort, then John Caryll, should entitle him to an apartment in the château, but each time he asked for one he was disappointed.[50] He therefore lived in a rented apartment in the rue de la Salle, to the south-west of the *cour des cuisines*, which was conveniently close.[51] On one occasion he asked to be given lodging money to supplement his income,[52] but his request was not granted. He also asked that his wife should be given a position in the household of the prince, but that too was refused, probably because she was French and there were more deserving exiles.[53] Nairne's diary tells us very little about his domestic life during the 1690s,[54] though in February 1698 he was sufficiently prosperous to invite his friends to 'a great supper' at his home, which he ordered from Henry Parry, the clerk of the king's privy kitchen.[55] In 1698, however, his financial circumstances improved and his diary contains details of how he spent his money.

In March James II agreed to give him an additional pension of 41 *livres*, 13 *sols* and 3 *deniers* (i.e. three *louis d'ors*), thus bringing his combined income from the court up to 131*l*. 0*s*. 9*d*.[56] In June his French father-in-law died, leaving his wife one third of a small estate at Compigny (near Sens), though legal difficulties delayed the settlement of the inheritance until January 1699.[57]

Nairne's income from the court was now similar to that of the king's equerries, but still very modest compared with those of the more senior officers. He began by investing money in cutlery. Between June and September 1698 he spent 186*l*. 10*s*. on five sets of silver knives, forks and spoons, a silver cup and

---

[47] *CSPD: William III, 1700–1702* (London, 1937), 379; *CSPD: Queen Anne, 1703–1704* (London, 1924), 433.

[48] Nairne, 8 September 1694 and 8 September 1695.

[49] He received 149 *livres* in 1696 (15 March) and 70 *livres* in 1698 (29 January).

[50] 28 January 1692; 6 November 1698; 8 March 1700.   [51] 12 November 1691.

[52] 29 October 1695.   [53] 2, 19 and 21 February 1692.

[54] There is a reference to the purchase of 'a plain cloth suite couleur de prince, with a damas veste' (15 August 1696) and to 'a supper and a bal at our house' (18 February 1697).

[55] 1 February 1698.

[56] The augmentation was to be paid in cash, so it was not shown in the lists of salaries and pensions. Just before he died the king arranged for the additional money to be entered on the list of pensions in Caryll's name: 27 June, 2 and 11 July, and 2 September 1701.

[57] This inheritance obliged his wife to pay the *capitation* (15 June 1697).

a silver salt,[58] which he subsequently had engraved with his coat of arms.[59] In November he spent a further 100*l.* on his kitchen. He purchased a table, a dresser and some shelves, but also a 'marmite, chaudron, visselle d'etain, faillance, vers, tournebroche etc'.[60] In December he paid a stone mason 2*l.* 2*s.* to raise the balustrade on his staircase,[61] and then went to Paris to buy a new desk. He paid 52*l.* 13*s.* for a 'bureau bois de grenoble' which he found on the pont Notre Dame, but he also visited a goldsmith and ordered two more sets of knives, forks and spoons.[62] Shortly after returning to Saint-Germain he bought a *tapisserie* for his *salle.*[63]

For most of 1699 Nairne seems to have made no further changes to his home, but his diary continues to give us details of his standard of living. He made his own cherry jam at the end of July, having kept the pots from the previous year,[64] and spent 12*l.* 3*s.* at the beginning of August to make his own cherry brandy.[65] In September he bottled his own ratafia.[66] He also laid down three cords of wood for the winter,[67] and in October brought his own corn from Compigny which he sent to be milled in Poissy.[68]

Between November 1699 and January 1700 Nairne spent 686 *livres* having his bedchamber, which he described as 'my wife's chamber', redecorated and furnished. This involved hanging new tapestries on the walls and recolouring the wooden floor boards, lowering the chimney, and buying new chairs and a new four-poster bed with an imperial and serge hangings.[69] He employed people to do all the work for him, but economised by hanging the 'bed with green curtains in the little bedchamber' himself.[70] Nevertheless he celebrated by giving a large dinner party to his friends which cost him 20 *livres.*[71] Nairne bought his wine from the nearby vineyards at Triel and Conflans, though he also had some barrels transported down river from his wife's estate at Compigny.[72] He noted, however, that John Caryll's wine came from Beaune

[58] 4, 17, 23 and 26 June, and 24 September 1698. He saved 48 *livres* by offering some old silver spoons and forks in exchange.
[59] 17 February, and 14 and 21 March 1699.   [60] 19, 25 and 28 November 1698.
[61] 13 December 1698.   [62] 18 December 1698. Transporting the desk cost a further 17 *sous.*
[63] 24 December 1698.
[64] 24 July 1699. The previous year he had spent 9*l.* 15*s.* on twenty pots of cherry jam (30 July 1698).
[65] 1 and 11 August 1699.   [66] 9 September 1699.
[67] 11 August 1699. The previous year he had spent 23 *livres* on two cords, and 28 *livres* on two others of 'bois d'actiere' (23 August and 1 September 1698).
[68] 18 and 27 October 1699.
[69] 17 November, and 4 and 9 December 1699; 12, 14, 15 and 16 January, and 15 February 1700.
[70] 16 February 1700.   [71] 17 February 1700.
[72] 18 and 26 October 1700; 15 and 16 December 1701; and 20 November 1702.

and Champagne, and cost 383 *livres*.[73] Caryll was one of the many Jacobites who were much better off than Nairne, and at the end of 1699 he gave Nairne a present of a silver sugar box engraved with the arms of Lord Dumbarton.[74]

Having equipped his table, his kitchen, his *salle* and his bedchamber, Nairne then set about purchasing some new clothes. At the end of 1699 he bought a new gown for his wife costing 42 *livres*[75] and a new black coat and breeches for himself.[76] Other suits and coats were acquired in the next few years, including one with brass buttons.[77] Nairne also considered other aspects of his personal appearance. In January 1700 he bought a new wig for 52 *livres*,[78] and in October 1702 he bought a new suit and sword for 58*l*. 14*s*. As part of the deal he traded in his old sword,[79] but he still bought a second sword for 20 *livres* three and a half years later.[80] His recreation was also catered for. In October 1702 he bought himself a new bass viol, for 26 *livres* and the return of his old one.[81]

These details are not important in themselves, but they provide conclusive evidence of the relative prosperity of a middle-ranking Jacobite at the English court in exile and should help lay to rest the old legends, originally spread by the government in London but given official circulation by the Whig historians of the nineteenth and early twentieth centuries, that the members of the court lived in relative penury.

After the death of James II, the queen increased Nairne's monthly pension from 41*l*. 13*s*. 3*d*. to 83*l*. 13*s*. 3*d*., thus bringing his income from the court to a total of 173*l*. 0*s*. 9*d*.[82] He now received a little more than the queen's equerry. In 1703, however, the expansion of the household obliged the queen to retrench all the salaries and pensions, so Nairne's combined income from both sources went down by over 12 *livres* a month to 159*l*. 19*s*. 7*d*. Three years later, however, the queen informed him that she would compensate him for this retrenchment by giving him lodging money of 26 *livres* a month. This he received in cash every quarter.[83] In 1708 James III increased Nairne's salary from 81*l*. 18*s*. 7*d*. to 104*l*. 17*s*. 6*d*., so that within a few years he was receiving much more than before the retrenchment of 1703. The arrears in the payment of the French pension in the closing years of the War of the Spanish Succession then affected him like everyone else, but this is yet more evidence

[73] 26 November 1700.   [74] 13 November 1699.   [75] 21 October 1699.

[76] 6 November 1699.   [77] 19 and 24 October 1702.

[78] 6 January 1700. His previous one had cost 39 *livres* in January 1697 (25 January 1697).

[79] 29 October 1702.   [80] 29 April 1706.   [81] 14 October 1702.

[82] 12 March, and 6 and 7 October 1702.

[83] 17 June, 15 July, and 9 August 1706.

that the household, as distinct from the rest of the Jacobite community, was well provided for.

The education of their children

The members of the household at Saint-Germain needed to pay for the education of their children. English Catholics already had a long tradition of sending their children abroad to be educated, so there were plenty of schools available, but the ones in and around Paris only catered for girls. The choice was between the convent of English Augustinian nuns in Paris, known as Notre Dame de Sion (rue des Fossés Saint-Victor),[84] the English convent of the Immaculate Conception also in Paris, known as the Blue Nuns (rue de Charenton),[85] and the convent of English Benedictine nuns in Pontoise.[86] The two latter were the more prestigious and very generously subsidised by the queen and her ladies. For those wishing to send their daughters further away, there were the convent of English Poor Clares in Rouen[87] and several in the Low Countries, most notably that of the English Augustinian canonesses at Bruges.[88] The most popular school for boys was the one run by the English Jesuits at Saint-Omer, near Calais,[89] but some parents wanted a French education and sent their sons to the Jesuit *Collège de Navarre* in Paris[90] or the Jesuit

---

[84] Abbé F.M.T. Cédoz, *Un Couvent de religieuses anglaises à Paris de 1634 à 1884* (Paris, 1891). The families at Saint-Germain which patronised the convent included Biddulph, Conquest, Hales, Howard, Leyburne, Martinash, Molyneux, Perkins, Stafford and Waldegrave.

[85] *The Diary of the Blue Nuns, 1658–1810*, ed. J. Gillow and R. Trappes-Lomax, (London, 1910). The families included Biddulph, Crane, Howard, Plowden, Stafford, Strickland and Waldegrave, and also the Duchess of Tyrconnell.

[86] Arch. Dépt. du Val d'Oise, 68/H/3, 4, 5, 10; Catholic Record Society, *Miscellanea 10* (London, 1915), 'The Registers of the English Benedictine Nuns at Pontoise'. The families included Booth, Browne, Carteret, Connock, Conquest, Constable, Crane, Dillon, FitzJames, Fitzroy, Gifford, Herbert of Powis, Hyde, Macarty, Magennis, Mildmay, Molza, Nagle, Nugent, Plowden, Sackville, Simms, Stafford, Trevanion, Waldegrave, Watkins and Wyvill.

[87] A.M.C. Forster, 'The Chronicles of the English Poor Clares of Rouen', Parts 1 and 2, *Recusant History* 18, no. 1 (1986), 59–102, and 19, no. 2 (1988), 149–91. The families included Leyburne, Plowden, Skelton, Stafford and Strickland.

[88] HMC *Portland* IV, 470, memorandum on the English Catholic seminaries in the Low Countries, 1707; P. Guilday, *The English Catholic Refugees on the Continent, 1558–1795* (London, 1914). Concerning the Augustinain convent at Bruges, where Lady Lucy Herbert (daughter of the Duke of Powis) was prioress, Guilday notes: 'All the leading Catholic noble families of England are represented on the school register' (388).

[89] *The Letter Book of Lewis Sabran, Rector of St. Omers College*, ed. G. Holt, (London, 1971). The families included Baggot, Blair, Carney, Carteret, Copley, Crane, Macleane, Martinash, Meagher, Nairne, Porter, Slingsby, Stafford, Strickland, Trevanion and Watkins.

[90] The two youngest sons of the Duke of Perth were educated there.

college at La Flèche (north-east of Angers).[91] For those of more modest means, like David Nairne, there was a school run by a certain Monsieur Hennemont, on a hill just outside Saint-Germain-en-Laye.[92]

James II and Mary of Modena were determined that the Irish, particularly the poor ones, should be given some education. In 1697 James visited Paris to discuss the question with the curé of Saint-Sulpice (Joachim de la Chétardie). The result was the establishment in Paris later that year of a school for fifty Irish boys under the direction of Jean-Baptiste de la Salle and run by the Frères des Ecoles Chrétiennes.[93] Three years later James arranged for a school for Irish girls to be opened in Saint-Germain, run by the Sœurs de Saint-Thomas de Villeneuve.[94] The mother superior, Jacquette de Quervers, established a formidable reputation and attracted numerous benefactors to provide dowries for the girls. In addition to these schools founded by the king, Mary of Modena appointed a school master named John Walsh to provide education for the sons of her servants at Saint-Germain,[95] and a 'Communauté Royalle de demoiselles angloises, ecossoises et irlandoises de St Germain en Laye' to educate forty poor girls, many of whom were orphans and boarded at the school.[96]

These were all Catholic schools, maintained without difficulty in a Catholic country. By contrast, the upbringing of the children of Protestant Jacobites must have been particularly difficult. They were presumably educated by their own parents and by family friends, but no information has survived.

The Protestant minority

When the English Protestants began to arrive at Saint-Germain in January 1689,[97] it was still only three years and three months since the revocation of the Edict of Nantes. Louis XIV at first stated that he was not prepared to allow any Protestant Jacobites to come to France, but he later gave his agreement on the specific condition that they must make no request to be

---

[91] The Duke of Berwick and the 2nd Duke of Powis were educated there.

[92] Nairne, 3 February, 11 May and 10 November 1706.

[93] S. de Doncourt, *Remarques historiques sur l'église et la paroisse de Saint-Sulpice* (Paris, 1773), 59, 153.

[94] Arch. Dépt. des Yvelines, 3/Q/84; G. Bernoville, *Les Religieuses de Saint-Thomas de Villeneuve* (Paris, 1953), 146–7.

[95] There are references to him in the parish registers of Saint-Germain, including the entry describing his death on 18 September 1717.

[96] SP Box 11/307. In her will Mary of Modena left 6000 *livres* to the *Communauté des Demoiselles Irlandoises* (SP 44/30, Debenoist to Dicconson, 5 August 1719).

[97] Campana di Cavelli, *Les Derniers Stuarts*, II, 478, Lady Almond to the Duke of Modena, 27 January 1689.

allowed to hold Protestant services, either inside or outside the Château de Saint-Germain.[98] James II and Mary of Modena were embarrassed by this, but the Jacobite exile was not expected to be permanent, and they were obliged to accept the King of France's decision. When it became clear that the hopes of an immediate restoration had been dashed, they found themselves unable to change this original condition. All they could do was to make it clear to their courtiers that they personally favoured toleration, and would protect their Protestant subjects, both inside and outside the château. But that was all. They could not secure from Louis XIV permission to hold Protestant services. Mary of Modena herself said on one occasion, when regretting this fact, that she assumed her Protestant subjects said their prayers privately in their own rooms.[99]

In England, before 1689, the king's household had contained about 600 people, of whom approximately forty had been Catholic.[100] In France, by 1693, it contained about 100 people, of whom sixteen were Protestant.[101] The percentage of Protestants at Saint-Germain was therefore more than double what the percentage of Catholics had been at Whitehall. When the king established his household at Saint-Germain he gave priority to those people who had already served him in England, the forty Catholics, and nine of the sixteen Protestants already mentioned, who had followed him into exile. The remaining posts, fewer than fifty, were mainly given to Catholics in order to satisfy Louis XIV,[102] though seven were also given to Protestants.

The household of the queen was smaller than that of the king, but the same situation applied. As only one of her Protestant servants had followed her into exile, her household was in effect totally Catholic, but she also recruited a new Protestant servant, making a total of two.[103]

The Protestants were employed in all the departments of the king's household, the servants retaining the same posts they had had in England. On the whole the Protestants had important positions, but there were also some

---

[98] National Library of Wales (NLW) Celynog 24 Add. MSS 550B, 'An account of what passed in relation to ye obtaining ye libertie from ye King of France to use ye Liturgie of ye Church of England at St. Germains en Leye, in Publick, for ye King of Englands subjects', by Dr Ralph Taylor, September 1694; HMC *Stuart* IV, 466, Dicconson to Mary of Modena, 26 July 1717.

[99] NLW, Celynog 24 Add. MSS 550B.

[100] Barclay, 'The Impact of James II', 130.

[101] *Ibid.*, 211–12; Corp, 'Etiquette and Use of Royal Apartments', 240–1. See above, pp. 105–6, which refers to the servants of the king who received pensions.

[102] Many posts were filled when James II was in Ireland, so the number of vacancies at Saint-Germain-en-Laye was actually very much less than fifty.

[103] The Protestant who had served in England was William Macdonnell, a groom of the Great Chamber; the new recruit was James Bayly, a bottleman.

who had humble jobs. When, during the 1690s, other Protestants who had served the king in England began to arrive, they were where possible given their former posts, and by 1696 the number of Protestants had risen to nineteen.[104]

In addition to the members of the household, who received salaries, many other Jacobites came to Saint-Germain hoping to obtain employment. They were given pensions by both the king and the queen, but few of them obtained the employment they were seeking, as so few posts were available.[105] These pensioners were both Catholic and Protestant. It is impossible to say how many Protestants there were, outside the household, because we have no registers of baptisms, marriages and burials. But when James II lay dying in September 1701, the Anglican chaplain was wrongly accused of holding a service with a congregation of as many as 150.[106] For the accusation to have been credible, there must have been at least as many as that.

We know the names of six Anglican clergymen who served at the court of Saint-Germain, and we have engraved portraits of four of them: Dean Denis Granville, Dr Ralph Taylor, Dr George Hickes and Dr Charles Leslie.[107] Granville and Taylor lived permanently at Saint-Germain during the 1690s, but Hickes and Leslie only visited, during 1693.[108] There was also John Gordon, the Scottish bishop of Galloway, who was eventually converted by Bossuet, and who moved on to Rome,[109] and there was an Anglican clergyman named Thorp, who had arrived by 1697, and was still at Saint-Germain over twenty

---

[104] These figures are based on a minute study of the household lists, the parish registers and contemporary correspondence, supported by Andrew Barclay's study of the court of James II in England before 1689. The names of all the Protestants in the royal household, together with the positions they held, are given in Corp, 'Cour anglaise', 83–4.

[105] This was referred to by Jane Barker, who lived at Saint-Germain in the 1690s. In her novel *The Lining of the Patch Work Screen* (London, 1726), 33, one of her characters comments: 'I found, I cou'd do his Majesty no Service, there being more Officers come out of Ireland than cou'd be imploy'd; so that many remain'd chargeable Pentioners.' (The novel has been reprinted in Jane Barker, *The Galesia Trilogy and Selected Manuscript Poems*, ed. Carol Shiner Wilson (Oxford, 1997), where this passage is on p. 194.)

[106] 'The Remains of Denis Granville', *Journal of the Surtees Society* 47 (1865), 200, Granville to Proud, 1 October 1701.

[107] The engravings of Granville, Taylor, Hickes and Leslie are reproduced in Richard Sharp, *The Engraved Record of the Jacobite Movement* (Aldershot, 1996), 13, 63, 157, 160 and 172.

[108] Granville moved away to Tremblay (near Corbeil) in 1698, ('Remains of Denis Granville', 195, Granville to Proud, 4 August 1701), but kept in contact with the Anglicans at Saint-Germain by correspondence, and returned during part of 1701. Taylor eventually moved to Rotterdam (HMC *Portland* IV, 692, Drummond to Oxford, 29 May 1711).

[109] See my article on John Gordon (1644–1726) in the *Oxford DNB*.

years later.[110] When Granville made his will he lamented the 'want of publick worship and Christian burial',[111] and it seems clear that Protestants at Saint-Germain were buried at night, 'in gardens and fields',[112] a situation which continued until a Protestant cemetery was finally opened at the Porte Saint-Martin in 1720.[113]

Although the Anglicans were protected and well treated at the court of Saint-Germain, they had problems when dealing with French people outside the court. The experience of Sir Edward Herbert is well documented. Although not a member of the king's household, he lived at Saint-Germain on a large pension given him by James II,[114] with an apartment in the château, and his own house outside the town. James II rewarded his loyalty in exile by creating him Earl of Portland, and appointing him lord chancellor of England.[115] Unfortunately his brother (Lord Torrington) served William III and defeated the French fleet at the battle of Cap La Hogue in 1692. When therefore Portland accompanied James II to Fontainebleau in the autumn of that year he was very badly treated by the French courtiers, so badly indeed that he refused to go there again.[116] In the autumn of 1693 he was accused, apparently with the support of the governor of the Ville de Saint-Germain, of killing too many animals when hunting in the forest of Saint-Germain, and also of holding illegal Protestant services in his house.[117] The accusations were unfounded, but typical of the attitude of some French Catholics to the Protestant Jacobites who had arrived in their town. Portland was defended by Mary of Modena and by one of the vicars of the parish of Saint-Germain-en-Laye,[118] but his position was damaged. He seems to have withdrawn from

[110] HMC *Stuart* IV, 466 and 479, Dicconson to Mary of Modena, 26 and 29 July 1717. I owe the date of Thorp's arrival to Nathalie Genet-Rouffiac.

[111] 'Remains of Denis Granville', 211, the preamble to Granville's will, 1 June 1695.

[112] *Ibid.* 210, memorandum (by Proud?) written on the back of Granville to Proud, 26 February 1703. Many Protestants were perhaps buried in 'le trou Huguenot' in the forest of Saint-Germain (*La Vie religieuse à Saint-Germain-en-Laye*, exhibition catalogue, Saint-Germain-en-Laye, 1986, 57, D.401).

[113] Jacques Michel, *Du Paris de Louis XV à la Marine de Louis XVI: l'œuvre de Monsieur de Sartine* (Paris, 1983), I, 137. 'La situation des protestants français s'améliora à partir de 1763' when Sartine, whose mother was a Jacobite, was *Lieutenant de Police* at Paris.

[114] The only people at the court of Saint-Germain who received more money than Herbert (Portland) were Melfort and Middleton, and the king's two illegitimate sons, the Dukes of Berwick and Albemarle (see above, p. 144).

[115] Ruvigny, *Jacobite Peerage*, 150.

[116] *Archives de la Bastille*, Ravaisson, IX, 423, Renaudot to Croissy, 20 September 1693.

[117] *Ibid.*, 432, Renaudot to Pontchartrain, 28 November 1693.

[118] *Ibid.*, 433, Renaudot to Pontchartrain, 7 December 1693; *Stuart Papers*, ed. Falconer Madan, no. 220, p. 374, 'Mémoires historiques relatifs à SM. la Reine d'Angleterre. 1711, 1712, 1713'.

public life, particularly in 1698 when Louis XIV received as English ambassador the Dutchman Hans Willem Bentinck, to whom William III had given the very same title. Portland died in his apartment in the Château de Saint-Germain in November 1698. His body was taken to his country house, and buried privately in the cellar. One of Portland's Protestant servants recorded that when James II heard of it 'he wept, and said he had lost the very best of his subjects'.[119]

The Protestants at Saint-Germain were mainly Anglicans, but there were also Dissenters. This posed problems at the court because the Anglicans, while wanting toleration for themselves in France, had not been willing to give it to Dissenters in England. An interesting case concerned Edward Nosworthy, a former Whig who was a Baptist. He visited Saint-Germain in the summer of 1695, and then returned to live there permanently the following year.[120] But he only remained for four years, because he was not popular with some of the Anglicans: he was an old political rival of Dean Granville's brother (the Earl of Bath), and was opposed by the Earl of Middleton, the secretary of state. Nosworthy, a Baptist, was known to be a supporter of Middleton's Catholic rival, the Earl of Melfort.[121] But Nosworthy was not the only Baptist at Saint-Germain. There were two others (named John Jones and Edward Roberts), who visited Saint-Germain in the second half of 1690, before the arrival of either Lord Middleton or Lord Melfort. They were said to have spent almost every evening of their visit in private conversation with James II himself.[122]

The majority of Dissenters at Saint-Germain were Quakers. William Penn himself visited more than once during the early 1690s,[123] but the most prominent was William Bromfield, a doctor of medicine, who had become a

---

[119] Nairne, 5 November 1698. The details of his burial are contained in the testimony of a former servant of Portland called Sefton: 'The Ld Ch. Justice Herbert . . . was buried in a Cellar at St. Germains very privately' (Thomas Hearne, *Remarks and Collections*, 6 vols., ed. C.E. Doble and D.W. Rannie, (Oxford, 1885–1918), v, 124). For James II's concern during Portland's last illness, see BL Add. MSS 28224, f. 27, James II to Caryll, 15 October 1698: 'should he miscarry it would be a very great losse to me'.

[120] Nosworthy was sent to Saint-Germain by a group of peers, including Lords Worcester, Peterborough and Clarendon, in June 1695 (Bodleian Library, Carte MSS 181, f. 592). His return in February 1696 is noted in Nairne's diary. He was not given his former post as gentleman of the Privy Chamber.

[121] HMC *Bath* III, 398, Macky to Jersey, 12 March 1700.

[122] Carstares State Papers, 149, 'Information for my Lord Sidney, secretary of state for the Kingdom of England'. I am very grateful to Paul Hopkins for this reference.

[123] Paul Monod, *Jacobitism and the English People, 1688–1788* (Cambridge, 1989), 155; *Archives de la Bastille*, ed. Ravaisson, IX, 328–9.

merchant.[124] Bromfield's papers[125] contain many letters from his Quaker friend Captain Henry Griffith, who was James II's yeoman saddler. Bromfield was well treated at the court of Saint-Germain,[126] and even taken by James II on one of his visits to the Abbaye de La Trappe.[127] But it was nevertheless Bromfield who alleged to the French court that Granville had held an illegal service for 150 Anglicans in his room in the château, when James II lay dying in September 1701.[128]

What then was the attitude of the Stuarts themselves to their Protestant subjects? James II, Mary of Modena and then James III consistently tolerated and protected both the Anglicans and the Dissenters. James II, as we have seen, employed them in every department of the king's household, particularly the Chamber, where there were Protestant gentlemen, grooms and pages.[129] In 1701, when James II died, two of the five commissioners of the household were Anglicans. In addition, the clerk controller of the Greencloth and the clerk of the kitchen were both Anglicans, as was the purveyor of the stables. When he went riding, James II's horse was saddled by a Quaker. When he went by coach to Marly or Versailles his body coachman was an Anglican. In 1692, when he was about to invade England, James II left written instructions to be given to his son in the event of his death or capture. He specified which posts in the government and the royal household should be given to Anglicans, Dissenters and Catholics.[130] In 1693 he appointed an Anglican, Lord Middleton, to be secretary of state at Saint-Germain, and kept him as his chief minister for the rest of his life.

[124] HMC *Portland* III, 529, Robert Harley to Edward Harley, 17 June 1693. For Bromfield, see Monod, *Jacobitism and the English People*, 156; and Pierre Burger, 'Spymaster to Louis XIV: A Study of the Papers of the Abbé Eusèbe Renaudot', in Eveline Cruickshanks (ed.), *Ideology and Conspiracy: Aspects of Jacobitism, 1689–1759* (Edinburgh, 1982), 114.

[125] Bibliothèque de l'Arsenal, Paris (BA) MS 10533. The dossiers concerning Bromfield's imprisonment are in BA MS 10492 and 10522, published in *Archives de la Bastille*, ed. Ravaisson, IX.

[126] Bromfield was arrested on the orders of Louis XIV, and imprisoned in the Bastille from June 1691 to August 1692. James II asked that special care should be taken of him because his health was not good (*Archives de la Bastille*, ed. Ravaisson, IX, 327, Torcy to Besmans, 7 June 1691).

[127] Burger, 'Spymaster to Louis XIV', 115. The visit was in June 1696.

[128] 'Remains of Denis Granville', 200, Granville to Proud, October 1700. When Mary of Modena discovered this she had Bromfield put in one of the prisons at Saint-Germain-en-Laye. In October 1701 he was transferred to the Bastille, but the queen was anxious that he should be properly treated (*Archives de la Bastille*, ed. Ravaisson, IX, 330, Pontchartrain to Saint-Mars, 16 November 1701).

[129] See note 104.

[130] *The Life of James II*, II, 641–2; Corp, 'Maison du Roi', in *L'Autre Exil*, 61, 75. He repeated this in his last will in September 1701 (Corp, *Cour des Stuarts*, 144–5).

In September 1694 James informed his courtiers publicly that he was in favour of Protestant services being held at the court and gave them permission to ask Louis XIV to allow them to be introduced. Lord Middleton persuaded him that this would be politically unwise, but the King never changed his opinion.[131] As the duchesse d'Orléans wrote in 1700, 'King James is always saying that he does not approve of religious freedom being withheld, and he maintains that that has always been his maxim.'[132] Two years before he died he added a codicil to his will appointing two Anglicans (Middleton and Granville) to be members of the Council of Regency for his son.[133] In his last will, written just before he died, James II advised his son to employ people 'without distinction of Religion'.[134] Although James II died a Catholic, Granville was allowed to be at his bedside until two hours before his death.[135]

Mary of Modena, despite being a very devout Catholic, followed the example of her husband. Her household remained Catholic, but when she needed a new singer, to replace a Catholic who had left the court in 1697, she arranged for an Anglican to be transferred from the king's household to her own.[136] She insisted that she was not influenced by questions of religion when making appointments,[137] and she protected Granville from various attacks he received from both the Quakers and the French Catholics. Granville apparently had no problems with the English Catholics at Saint-Germain. He felt that the queen was a saint, and said she showed 'great moderation to those who differ in opinion from her, when they are vertuous'.[138] The Queen was not willing to offend Louis XIV, on whose generosity the Jacobites depended, so she would not protect any Protestants who mixed with Huguenots,[139] or held illegal services.[140] But she gave Granville a formal appointment as Anglican chaplain to the royal household in 1702,[141] and when he died the following year she

---

[131] Corp, 'James II and Toleration', 9.

[132] *The Letters of Madame: The Correspondance of Elizabeth-Charlotte of Bavaria, Princess Palatine, Duchess of Orléans*, ed. G.S. Stevenson (London, 1924), 197, to the Duchess of Hanover, 18 July 1700.

[133] Corp, *Cour des Stuarts*, 144.   [134] *ibid.*, 145.

[135] 'Remains of Denis Granville', 199, Granville to Proud, September 1701.

[136] Corp, 'Centre of Italian Music', 220. The singer was Thomas Heywood. Although he and his wife were both Anglicans, they allowed their daughter, born in 1699, to be baptised a Catholic. She died aged four months (C.E. Lart, *The Parochial Registers of Saint-Germain-en-Laye: Jacobite Extracts* (London, 1910), i, 81–2). Heywood remained an Anglican, and served the queen until her death in 1718 (HMC *Stuart* iv, 466, Dicconson to Mary of Modena, 26 July 1717). He then lived in Barbados, where his brother was governor (SP Box 3/1/89).

[137] HMC *Stuart* iii, 373, Mary of Modena to Mar, 30 December 1716.

[138] 'Remains of Denis Granville', 201, Granville to Proud, 1 October 1701.

[139] HMC *Stuart* i, 180, Mary of Modena to duc Mazarin, 22 January 1703.

[140] HMC *Stuart* iv, 466 and 479, Dicconson to Mary of Modena, 26 and 29 July 1717.

[141] Ruvigny, *Jacobite Peerage*, 222.

obtained permission from Louis XIV for him to be buried at the cemetery of the Saints-Innocents in Paris.[142] This was done at her own expense, attended by Dr Ralph Taylor the other Anglican chaplain, and various Anglican Jacobites, including Granville's nephew Thomas Higgons. A few years later the queen received the Quaker Bromfield at the convent of the Visitation at Chaillot, and explained to the nuns that the Quakers were 'not wicked' and 'loved the late King very much'.[143]

James III pursued the same policy as his parents.[144] As Charles Leslie wrote in 1713, 'there is no sort of Bigotry about him':

He . . . knows well the difference betwixt the Office of a King and a Missionary . . . about six Months after the King, his Father's Death, he . . . endeavour'd to secure for his Protestant Servants the free Exercise of their Religion . . . the Queen, his Mother . . . not only concurred in this, but did herself solicit it to my knowledge. But the maxims of that Court [i.e. the French] would not admit it. Ten years after this, in the year 1711, being then of Age, he did attempt it again, but could not prevail.[145]

This failure by both James II and James III to persuade Louis XIV to allow Protestant services to be held at Saint-Germain was not only inconvenient but also politically unfortunate, as the governments in London were able to use it to allege that the Stuarts were bigoted and intolerant Catholics, and that Protestants were not welcome at the exiled court.[146] As Louis was obviously aware of this danger, we need to re-examine his relations with the Stuarts in more detail.

[142] See note 112; 'Remains of Denis Granville', 254, Doughty to Hope, 21 February 1712.

[143] Agnes Strickland, *The Lives of the Queens of England*, x (London, 1847), 146. Bromfield had been imprisoned in the Bastille for speaking against the queen. He was eventually transferred to Charenton and not released until January 1711 (*Archives de la Bastille*, ed. Ravaisson, IX, 330–3). In 1714 the queen received him again, and this time even introduced him to the former papal nuncio, Cardinal Gualterio (Strickland, *The Lives of The Queens of England*, x, 172). At the very end of her life, she recruited two more Anglicans to join her household. They are shown in the list of the queen's household when she died in May 1718, as is Charles Leslie, who lived at Saint-Germain-en-Laye from 1717 to 1718 (SP 281/166).

[144] The attitude of James III and his advisors was well summed up several years later by Lewis Innes: 'can any man of sense that knowes anything of England think that your Majesty can ever be King of a Protestant people without employing Protestants in your affairs, and in your family? Or can there be a more binding argument to persuade Protestants that your Majesty is resolved to entrust and employ them when you are at home, than by letting them see you employ them whilst you are abroad?' (SP 141/110, Innes to James III, 1 January 1731).

[145] M. Haile, *James Francis Edward, 'the Old Chevalier'* (London, 1907), 460. James III's letter to Charles Leslie of 2 May 1711, emphasising his belief in religious toleration (for himself as well as others), is among the Bower Manuscripts at Chiddingstone Castle.

[146] As the duchesse d'Orléans explained, James II 'is unhappy because his true sentiments are not known' (*Letters of Madame*, 197, to the Duchess of Hanover, 18 July 1700).

CHAPTER SIX

The Stuarts and the court of France

In the first chapter of this book, which contains a classic account of the political relations between France and the exiled Stuarts, Edward Gregg has drawn attention to the divisions which existed within the French government, between Louis XIV and his ministers, in their attitudes to the Stuarts. The nature of these divisions, and their practical effects on the formulation of French foreign policy, need to be recalled when examining Louis's relations with his exiled cousins.

The king of France and his ministers were in complete agreement over many things regarding James II. Before 1689 they had 'the deepest suspicions both of James's intentions and his abilities',[1] considering him to be anti-French and incompetent. When he took refuge in France they regarded him with 'more disdain than pity'.[2] They supported him by giving him an army and a fleet to take it to Ireland, but they were disillusioned with James's lack of resolution, and 'lost what little hopes they may have had for Jacobite success' there.[3] Thereafter they seem to have agreed that there was relatively little support for James in England, and considered the prospects of a Jacobite restoration to be small. Louvois was opposed to giving any further military aid to James, and even after the minister's death 'Louis XIV remained ambivalent about the prospects of a Stuart restoration.'[4]

The differences between the king and his ministers emerged during the early 1690s, when the latter became increasingly anti-Jacobite. Barbezieux was even described as 'a bitter enemy to King James's interest'.[5] Louis XIV, on the other hand, made it clear that he was not willing to desert his exiled English cousin.

Edward Gregg's chapter contains several examples of these growing differences. In 1692, after the defeat of the French fleet at Cap La Hogue, and when he was 'furious' at having 'been duped by fallacious Jacobite information',[6] Louis said that he was 'resolved never to abandon him [James II] or his cause'.[7] The following year, 'in June 1693, Louis XIV and his ministers reached a crucial

---

[1] See above, p. 13.   [2] *Ibid.*, p. 16.   [3] *Ibid.*, p. 24.   [4] *Ibid.*, p. 32.
[5] *Ibid.*, p. 32.   [6] *Ibid.*, p. 36.   [7] *Ibid.*, p. 35.

decision: France was prepared to enter into a peace based on a *de facto* recognition of William III'. Nevertheless Louis 'expressly refused to repudiate James
II's claims or to expel him from France'.[8] In 1695 John Caryll wrote that 'ye
ministers here . . . long and labour under hand incessantly for . . . a peace
upon any terms without any consideration for us'.[9] Nevertheless Louis XIV
'reacted more positively . . . Middleton wrote into England . . . "we found
him as well dispos'd as wee could wish".'[10] In 1696, when Louis was very
pessimistic about support for James in England, he nevertheless said that he
'would serve James II on all occasions'.[11]

Louis XIV was no doubt well aware that 'the general French population
was . . . warmly supportive of the Stuarts, regarding them . . . as martyrs for
the faith'.[12] But that was not the only reason why he consistently overruled
the almost unanimous advice of his ministers. As Edward Gregg has clearly
explained, 'for his part, Louis XIV refused to expel James II from France under
any conditions' because 'James was his first cousin and his fellow monarch,
whose just rights Louis could never renounce in his own conscience, no matter
what political exigencies might dictate'.[13] In other words, he supported James
because he was a fellow Catholic monarch, whose claim to be king of England
was by the divine right of hereditary succession.

Louis's independence from his ministers and his willingness to ignore their
advice over a long period of twenty-five years need to be emphasised, because
they contradict the received notion that in France 'the period 1661–1715 saw
greater "control, centralization and bureaucratization"'.[14] In a recent article
on Louis XIV, Guy Rowlands has challenged 'the current orthodoxy . . . that
ministerial power, under the King's direction, exercised an ever-tightening
grip'.[15] His arguments may be extended from the French army to Louis XIV's
management of foreign or dynastic policy. 'Historians must be wary of at-
tributing too many modern notions of governmental and military efficiency
to Louis XIV's management of his armies, for if efficiency were the principal criterion for administration then some of Louis's actions were clearly
counter-productive. In fact, Louis was always principally concerned with the
future of the dynasty.'[16] Those French historians of the later years of the
reign of Louis XIV, apparently unaware that the old Whig assumptions about
the unimportance of Jacobitism have now been discarded in Great Britain,

[8] *Ibid.*, p. 42.   [9] *Ibid.*, p. 47.   [10] *Ibid.*, p. 47.
[11] *Ibid.*, p. 50.   [12] *Ibid.*, p. 44.   [13] *Ibid.*, p. 53.
[14] Guy Rowlands, 'Louis XIV, Aristocratic Power and the Elite Units of the French Army', *French
History* 13, no. 3 (1999), 303–31, at 303.
[15] *Ibid.*, 305.   [16] *Ibid.*, 330.

are still content to take at face value the opinions of the French ministers as being truly representative of French government policy. In fact, Louis XIV formulated his own policy regarding the Stuarts and was prepared to overrule his ministers whenever they disagreed with him. As Guy Rowlands has aptly put it, 'Louis's overriding general dynastic concerns . . . were the dominant factors behind royal policy towards the state machinery.'[17] It was the Catholic religion which provided the bond between Louis XIV and James II, and later between Louis XIV and James III, and the story of Franco-Jacobite relations cannot be properly understood unless this fact is constantly kept in mind. In this sense Louis's policy was not even intended to be efficient, but it *was* totally consistent. It was a Catholic dynastic policy, not a secular foreign policy. The decision to support the Stuarts and yet to forbid Protestant services at Saint-Germain, like James III's later refusal to convert, had nothing to do with modern notions of efficiency. Louis was irritated by the fact that the Catholic Stuarts wished to tolerate Protestantism, but if they had ever converted to Protestantism he would immediately have withdrawn his support from them. James II and James III knew that their Catholicism carried more weight with the king of France than did the 'efficient' advice of the French ministers.

Another factor which has often been overlooked is that there was a close emotional bond between Louis XIV and James III, which was much stronger than that between Louis and the latter's father. French support for the Stuarts therefore increased after 1701. James III was only six months old when his parents took refuge in France. Louis informed him in 1708 that 'I promised God, seeing you still in your cradle, if my life was prolonged, to restore you to your Kingdom.'[18] Even when he had accepted that James II would never be restored, Louis maintained his determination to support his son. Indeed Louis, who loved children, came to regard James III as though he were his own son. This feeling was shared by the dauphin, who already had three sons, born in 1682, 1683 and 1686. The Prince of Wales, born in 1688, was treated as a younger brother to the Dukes of Bourgogne, Anjou and Berri. And as he grew to manhood the Bourbon princes felt an affection and respect for him which were far stronger than their feelings had been for his father.

Louis's total commitment to James III was made possible because he always differentiated between kings whose claims were *de jure* and those who ruled *de facto*. While not accepting the traditional claims of the kings of England to

[17] *Ibid.*, 330.
[18] SCA, SN 3/24/8, Louis XIV to James III, [6 or 7?] March 1708, translated into English from an Italian copy, in Bruce P. Lenman and John S. Gibson, *The Jacobite Threat* (Edinburgh, 1990), 101–2.

be *de jure* kings of France, he understood and respected them as part of a well-understood code of European dynastic practice. Thus he accepted that James II and later his son would adopt violet rather than black when they were in mourning, because that was the colour reserved for the kings of France,[19] and he allowed them to be admitted as canons of Saint-Martin-de-Tours because that was a privilege enjoyed by the *de jure* Counts of Anjou.[20]

This distinction was of major importance when Louis was obliged to accept William III as *de facto* king of England, as a condition of the Treaty of Ryswick in 1697. James II remained the *de jure* king of England and his son remained the *de jure* Prince of Wales. William III claimed to be more than a ruler *de facto*, describing himself as king of France as well as England *de jure*.[21] The practice was clearly understood on both sides, and meant that when James II eventually died his son would unquestionably be recognised by Louis XIV as James III *de jure*. This was obvious to the diplomats who negotiated the Treaty of Ryswick and would in no sense be a breach of it.[22]

The only person who seems to have had doubts about this was James II himself, who was tormented by the prospect of his son's becoming 'un simple', without identity or rank in the world.[23] Early in 1699 he therefore concluded a formal agreement with Louis. The latter would become the guardian of both of James's children, and would recognise his son as James III *de jure*, so long as the latter remained a Catholic. James II recorded Louis's side of the agreement in a codicil to his will, dated 5 March 1699:

Ayant par mon Testament signé le vingt neuvième de Janvier dernier entre autres choses constitué et declaré la Reyne ma tres chere Epouse Gardienne et Tutrice de Mon Tres Cher Fils le Prince de Galles pendant le tems de sa minorité, et jusqu'a ce qu'il aura achevé la quatorzième année de son age; Et tant que je n'ay rien tant a cœur que la sureté de sa Personne et son etablissement dans ses droits, Je me sens obligé comme Père d'y pourvoir par tous les moyens les plus convenables et les plus efficaces: Et sachant bien qu'on ne peut trouver pour luy un plus ferme appuy, que celuy de la protection du Roy tres Chretien mon tres cher Frere, laquelle Il a accordé pour le passé avec tant de generosité a Moy et a ma Famille pendant nos malheurs, J'ay pris la resolution de faire ce codicille escrit de ma main, par lequel après avoir confirmé en toutes les autres choses mon dit Testament, je nomme et constitue le dit Roy tres Chretien mon tres cher Frere Gardien et Tuteur de mon dit Fils le Prince de Galles

[19] BL Add. MSS 10118, Benet Weldon, 'History of . . . James II', 336; Corp, 'Inventory', 130.
[20] Dangeau, II, 338, 25 February 1689; VII, 153, 19 September 1699; VII, 426, 19 November, 1700.
[21] 13 William III, c. 2, *The Act of Settlement*, clause 1.
[22] Dangeau, VIII, 198, 20 September 1701, with a note by the duc de Luynes.
[23] See above, p. 58.

pendant sa Minorité conjointement avec la Reyne ma tres chere Epouse; et je le prie tres instamment, qu'en regardant cette nomination comme la plus grande preuve que je puis donner de ma confiance en Son Amitié, de vouloir par sa bonté accoutumée se charger de cette tutelle de Mon Fils conjointement avec la Reyne ma tres chere Epouse, et de prendre en main effectivement sa cause et ses interets; ce qui sera sans doute et devant Dieu, et devant les hommes une des actions les plus dignes de son Regne.[24]

Two years later, when James II fainted in March 1701 and it seemed that he could not live much longer, Louis XIV told the Prince of Wales in public at Versailles that he would 'take ye same care of him as he did of his own children'.[25]

In reaching this agreement Louis XIV ignored his ministers completely. As Edward Gregg has observed, 'surprisingly, there seems to be no evidence that the French government seriously considered what action, if any, it would take should James II die'.[26] As a statement of archival fact, regarding a complete absence of documentation, this observation is extremely important. But of course the French government did seriously consider how it should react when James II was dead. It was unavoidably one of the most important issues of French foreign policy once the Treaty of Ryswick had been signed in 1697, as everyone could see at the time. The absence of documentation thus clearly demonstrates that Louis XIV was not prepared to discuss it with his ministers or the bureaucracy, and preferred to make his own decision on such an important dynastic question. When the time finally came to put his decision into practice, he knew that the constitution obliged him to consult the *conseil d'en haut*. He did so in September 1701. But that was a formality and merely confirmed that most of the ministers disagreed with him. He recognised James III anyway.[27] The decision to do so had already been taken in March 1699.

James II knew that Louis would only stick by his decision to recognise his son so long as the latter remained a Catholic,[28] and on his death bed

---

[24] SP Add. 1/45. The codicil, which recorded James II's secret agreement with Louis XIV, was written in French.

[25] Nairne, 24 April 1701.   [26] See above, p. 58.

[27] Dangeau, VIII, 197 footnote, duc de Bourgogne to Philip V, 4 October 1701: 'je suis persuadé que vous aurez été de même sentiment que moi sur la reconnoissance du prince de Galles, et je ne crois pas qu'un honnête homme pût penser autrement . . . J'avoue que je fus fort soulagé quand j'appris que le roi avoit déclaré qu'il reconnoissoit le prince de Galles, et quoique je n'en doutasse pas, j'en témoignai ma joie à tout le monde. Je suis persuadé que vous n'en aurez pas été fâché non plus.'

[28] In 1692 he warned his son that 'the Church of Rome . . . is the only true Catholick and Apostolick Church, and let no human consideration of any kind prevaile upon you to depart from her' (*Life of James II*, II, 619).

he repeatedly reminded his son of the fact. According to the Duke of Perth, he said: 'My son, I only have four things to say to you, in giving you my blessing . . . Be a good Catholic; fear God; obey the Queen your mother; and, after God, put all your trust in the King of France.' According to Perth he then repeated: 'Never separate yourself from the Catholic religion.'[29] Louis XIV himself then 'spoke . . . to the young King, and promised him that he would always defend him so long as he remained faithful to the [Catholic] religion, but that he would become his declared enemy if he failed to do so'.[30] Just as Louis had ignored his ministers when he recognised James III, so the latter would ignore both the French ministers and English Tories when they later urged him to convert to Anglicanism and thus turn Louis into his declared enemy.

In March 1708, at the time of the Franco-Jacobite attempt to invade Scotland, when James III was about to leave Saint-Germain, Louis XIV sent him the following letter, which confirms the nature of their relationship both before and after the king of France agreed to become his 'Gardien et Tuteur':

I received you from the hands of a King who was such a good Christian that he preferred to abandon his own Kingdom rather than that of Jesus Christ. God now calls you back to your own country. I am the instrument he deigns to use so that you may return. I have already prepared everything that lies within my power, and I hope that Providence itself will lead you. I have prudently kept completely secret and impenetrable my designs on those who are your enemies and mine. I know that Europe will be stirred and that your embarkation begins to make heresy tremble . . .

I can claim that I have never relented in matters of Religion, nor have my enemies been able to prevail. The God who has protected my arms will also bless yours. It matters little or nothing to be a King, unless one is a Christian King. I speak to your Majesty as a father. King James, whose memory will be eternal, commended you when dying to me warmly, and my heart has always loved you; indeed I promised God, seeing you still in your cradle, if my life was prolonged, to restore you to your Kingdom. I give voice for the last time, Sire, to all my tenderness for you. Remember

[29] The Duke of Perth wrote a detailed account of James II's death in two long letters to the abbé de La Trappe, dated 17 September and 9 October 1701 (AN κ. 1717/26/4). A much briefer account was published in London in 1701 entitled *The Last Dying Words of the Late King James to his Son and Daughter, and the French King,* reprinted in 1704 as *King James the Second His Last Expressions and Dying Words.* See also Perth to Wallace, 5 September 1701, cited by Bruno Neveu in 'A Contribution to an Inventory of Jacobite Sources', in Eveline Cruickshanks (ed.), *Ideology and Conspiracy: Aspects of Jacobitism, 1689–1759* (Edinburgh, 1982), 157: 'He did now exhort the P. to obey God and the Q., to depend upon the K. of F., to live and dye a good Catholic, cost what it wold and to be a good man.'

[30] Neveu, 'A Contribution to an Inventory of Jacobite Sources,' 143 (my translation).

this: I have always loved you as my own son. I can say to your Majesty that you could never have caused me the least displeasure. – All is ready at Dunkirk for your departure, nor can you not be astounded at the efforts which I have made.

Love me and also love the Princes my Sons, with whom you have been brought up. I know well how great is their tenderness towards your Majesty . . .

Remember me, Sire, after my death in the persons of my Sons. Maintain peace between our two crowns. You will read from time to time the memorials regarding the good order of your Monarchy, all written in my hand, but share them only with your most intimate subjects. Go now. I wish never to see you again.[31]

Although the attempt to invade Scotland did not succeed, in part because of the deliberate obstruction of the minister in charge of the French navy (Jérome Phélyppeaux, comte de Pontchartrain),[32] Louis immediately informed him that this failure had in no way changed his attitude: 'Vous devez compter que de ma part je seray toujours . . . porté à . . . soutenir [votre rang] . . . Je ne . . . separe [mes interets] des votres.'[33] This commitment needs to be kept in mind when considering Franco-Jacobite relations in the years that followed, because Louis's later letters to James have not survived and historians have had to rely on the ministerial correspondence.

In the winter of 1709–10 Louis began to make preparations for another expedition to Scotland, despite the objections of his ministers. These preparations came to nothing because Louis was worried about James's safety, but as late as September 1710 Torcy noted that the king was still thinking

[31] See note 18.

[32] The French ministers constantly tried to turn Louis XIV against the Stuarts by insinuating that they could not keep any secrets and would therefore give away any planned invasion to restore them to the thrones of Great Britain. If a leak ever took place from somewhere, they hurried to blame the court of Saint-Germain, partly in order to exculpate themselves. The 1708 invasion attempt provides a good example. The British government discovered what the French were planning by the beginning of March, so on the 2nd of that month Pontchartrain informed Louis that 'le secret . . . depuis quatre jours est divulgé à Paris. Je puis assurer V.M. que cela vient de St. Germain. J'en ay des preuves.' Five days later he added that the secret 'dans cette ocasion a esté gardé par la marine plus qu'il n'est permis de l'esperer'. Louis brushed the matter aside (AN CHAN. 257, AP 2d.5), but the accusation seems to be convincing. However, the British archives, thoroughly examined by John Gibson for his study entitled *Playing the Scottish Card: The Franco-Jacobite Invasion of 1708* (Edinburgh, 1988), reveal that the secret was actually divulged by the French navy at Dunkirk and then transmitted to London by the British Minister at The Hague (pp. 115–16). Dangeau, who was not privy to political and military secrets, referred to the expedition for the first time in his diary on 3 March (xII, 90). Two days later (therefore three days after Pontchartrain's accusation), David Nairne, who was one of the very few people at Saint-Germain with access to such secrets, noted in his diary: 'I writt to my wife and told her for the first time yt I was going on a journy wher my duty calld me, and wch the Curet would explaine to her to whom I gave my letter to be sent to her after my departure.'

[33] AAE, mem. et doc. Angleterre 226, f. 38, Louis XIV to James III, 11 April 1708.

'sérieusement à faire passer le Roy d'Angleterre en Ecosse'.[34] In the following month the Tories won a large majority in the British general election, and (as Edward Gregg has shown) Louis then began to negotiate a peaceful restoration with the ministers of the new government in London.

James was to be forced to leave Saint-Germain and expelled from France. Thus the negotiations were intended to separate him from the French in the minds of the English people, and thereby facilitate a peaceful restoration as in 1660, by giving the impression that Louis had finally stopped supporting him. It is remarkable that certain French historians still accept this at face value. In fact, as Lord Oxford said in January 1712, James 'estant . . . [en Lorraine] sera plus prest de Londres qu'à St. Germain'.[35] This was the 'Secret'. James III was actually glad to leave Saint-Germain,[36] but he agreed to cooperate by appearing dejected. As Berwick put it in March 1712, James would act 'tout comme si par le present traité il se trouvoit abandonné et sans esperance; cela cacheroit encore mieux le Secret'.[37] Lord Middleton, who was party to the 'Secret', denied privately that there was anything in the proposed Anglo-French treaty expelling James from France which was 'contraire et prejudiciable à la Religion et au retablissement de S.M. Brit.'.[38]

But Louis's support for James had always depended on his remaining a Catholic, and this condition had not changed. Louis explained to the pope on one occasion, when discussing 'le retablissement du roy d'Angleterre': 'ce mesme intérest y avoit plus de part que la simple considération des estroittes liaisons de sang'.[39] Torcy was well aware of this, yet he allowed a disastrous misunderstanding to arise which effectively sabotaged the hoped for restoration: 'here were English ministers whose interest seemingly made it probable that they would undertake a restoration, yet Torcy knew full well that their fundamental condition – James's conversion – was precluded'.[40] This was the result not of Stuart obstinacy, but rather of Louis's inflexible religious position (whether regarding Protestant services at Saint-Germain or a tactical

---

[34] Torcy, *Journal inédit*, 253, 1 September 1710.

[35] AAE, CP Angleterre 241, f. 9, Gaultier to Torcy, 27 January 1712, quoted above, p. 72.

[36] Bibliothèque Municipale de Versailles, MSS P.67, 420, Mary of Modena to Madame de Maintenon, 16 August 1712.

[37] AAE, CP Angleterre 241, ff. 74–6, Berwick to Torcy, 23 March 1712, quoted above, p. 71.

[38] BL Add. MSS 31257, f. 127, Middleton to Gualterio, 28 August 1712; BL Add. MSS 31258, f. 154, Stafford to Gualterio, 28 August 1712.

[39] *Catalogue of the Renowned Collection of Autograph Letters and Historical Manuscripts formed by the Late Alfred Morrison Esq. of Fonthill* (London, 1917), 93, no. 653, Louis XIV to Clement XI, 28 August 1701.

[40] See above, p. 69.

conversion by James), combined with James's warm feelings of filial gratitude[41] and genuine fear of provoking his hostility. The duchesse d'Orléans speculated in October 1712 that 'if anyone were to ask our King and the Queen of England whether the young King should turn Protestant, they would reply no. But if he were to do so without their knowledge, they would have to accept the accomplished fact'.[42] James III knew that she was wrong.

The intimate relations between the English and the French royal families were reflected in the frequency with which they visited each other. Saint-Simon once commented that 'il ne se passoit guères quinze jours que le Roi n'allât à Saint-Germain'.[43] He was exaggerating, but if we qualify his comment to include the other Bourbon princes and princesses, then it is an accurate summary of the frequency with which the French royal family visited the Stuarts during most of the period from 1689 to 1712. As the Stuarts also regularly visited their French cousins at Versailles, Marly, Trianon, Fontainebleau, Saint-Cyr, Saint-Cloud, Meudon and elsewhere, and arranged to meet them while hunting in the royal forests or at troop reviews, it is probably safe to say that there was contact between the two families at least once a week.

Most of the meetings between Louis XIV and the Stuarts were recorded at the time, but there is much less information available concerning the visits of the other Bourbons. Our most comprehensive source of information is undoubtedly the diary of David Nairne, who recorded not only these family visits but also the other ones paid by the Stuarts to Paris, Chaillot and elsewhere. Nairne's diary, however, only includes the visits from August 1694 to March 1708, so we have to look elsewhere for the earlier and the later years.[44] Fortunately they are all covered in the diary of the marquis de Dangeau. A comparison of the two diaries for the intervening period demonstrates that Nairne's is very much fuller, but it is also clear that Dangeau's diary is itself much more complete for the years before than after 1694. The diaries therefore complement each other very effectively.

The availability of other sources shows that neither Nairne nor Dangeau recorded all the visits, partly because they were sometimes absent from court, and partly because many others can be discovered in the diary of the marquis de Sourches and the private correspondence of both Mary of Modena and

[41] Bibliothèque Municipale de Versailles, MSS P.67, p. 552, James III to Louis XIV, 18 February 1713.

[42] *Letters of Madame*, II, 64, to the Raugravine Louisa, 9 October 1712. See also Bibliothèque Municipale de Versailles MSS P.67, 505, Mary of Modena to Madame de Maintenon, 10 September 1712.

[43] Saint-Simon, XXVIII, 373.

[44] The diary also includes some of the visits of January and February 1692, and of April and May 1693.

Table of meetings between the Stuarts and Louis XIV

	Visits by Louis XIV to the Stuarts at Saint-Germain	Visits by the Stuarts to Louis XIV at Versailles, Marly, Trianon and Fontainebleau	Other meetings	Total
1689	36	19	10	65
1690	9	15	5	29
1691	11	16	10	37
1692	14	15	6	35
1693	9	15	13	37
1694	6	14	6	26
1695	8	14	13	35
1696	10	14	5	29
1697	10	17	7	34
1698	7	16	10	33
1699	8	10	8	26
1700	7	13	3	23
1701	9	11	2	22
1702	6	12	0	18
1703	7	13	2	22
1704	5	15	1	21
1705	4	13	1	18
1706	1	16	2	19
1707	1	10	6	17
1708	3	16	0	19
1709	2	8	0	10
1710	0	11	0	11
1711	2	13	1	16
1712	1	6	0	7
1713	1	3	0	4

Each of these meetings took place on a single day, except those at Fontainebleau, most of which lasted approximately two weeks. The visits to Fontainebleau have nevertheless been counted here as single ones, regardless of length.

the duchesse d'Orléans. We cannot therefore pretend that our information is complete. However, putting all these sources together, it is unlikely that many visits between Louis XIV and the Stuarts have remained unrecorded, and we can therefore regard the available statistics as approximately accurate. Any inaccuracies they contain would be in minimising the number of visits after 1708 (see table).

The frequency of visits was obviously influenced by various extraneous factors, including illness and bad weather. When the Stuarts first arrived in January 1689 the two kings clearly felt the need to confer together more frequently than they did later on. While James II was in Ireland from 1689 to

FIG. 19. *Le Roy déclare Monseigneur le Duc d'Anjou Roy d'Espagne le 16 novembre 1700*, anonymous engraving from the *Almanach Royal* of 1701 (BN Est. Qb. 1700). This engraving shows the Stuarts with the Bourbons in the *grande galérie des glaces*, during one of their visits to the Château de Versailles (though they were not in fact present on the occasion represented). The kings of Great Britain, Spain and France are the only gentlemen wearing hats. James II stands on the left, beside Philip V of Spain. The Prince of Wales can be seen on the right with the duc de Berri, the duc de Bourgogne and the duchesse de Bourgogne.

1690 Louis XIV made a point of paying courtesy calls on Mary of Modena with a regularity which was less necessary when her husband returned. The Stuarts, who had less money and more free time, tended to visit Louis XIV rather more than he visited them. Particular events, such as the marriage of the duc de Bourgogne in 1697 or the death of James II in 1701, increased the number of visits. James III's long absences from Saint-Germain after 1708, like his mother's lengthening residences at Chaillot, had the opposite effect. The departure of the duc d'Anjou to be king of Spain in 1700 was offset by the growing intimacy between the Stuarts and the duchesse de Bourgogne, but the death of the dauphin in 1711, followed by those of Princess Louise-Marie and both the duc and duchesse de Bourgogne in 1712, dramatically reduced the contact between the two families. The visits virtually stopped in 1712. None was recorded after 1713.

During the first half of the 1690s the Stuarts mainly visited Louis at Versailles rather than Marly or Trianon. In the years that followed, which coincided with the Treaty of Ryswick, the balance changed. The total number of visits remained approximately the same, but there were fewer to Versailles, more to Marly (which was closer), and hardly any to Trianon. The accession of James III in 1701, when he was still only thirteen years old, increased this trend, but as James and his sister grew up the number of visits began to increase. During these years more visits were recorded in 1704, 1706, 1708 and 1711 than in the other years. Louis meanwhile visited Saint-Germain steadily less as he grew older, and went there very infrequently after 1705. Unfortunately the visits of the dauphin, his sons, the duchesse de Bourgogne and the other members of the French royal family (notably the princesse de Conti), which seem to have increased, generally went unrecorded.

In addition to all these visits there was for many years an annual one by the Stuarts to Fontainebleau. The first took place in October 1690 and lasted for one week, the second from October to November 1691 and lasted nearly three weeks. Thereafter the Stuarts always went to Fontainebleau at the end of September or the beginning of October for approximately two weeks. James II's last visit was in 1700. After a period of mourning for the death of his father, James III paid his first visit in 1703. The kings were always accompanied by Queen Mary, but when she was ill in 1705 James III went by himself. The French court did not go to Fontainebleau in 1706, so there was no visit that year. The last took place in 1707, when Princess Louise-Marie accompanied her brother and mother.[45]

These annual holidays at Fontainebleau brought the Bourbons and the Stuarts even closer together and increased the sense of family solidarity between them. The simple fact was that they liked each other, and Louis said that he regarded the Stuarts as 'des gens véritablement ses amis'.[46] The letters of the

[45] In 1708 the French court was at Fontainebleau from June to August, while James III was with the French army, and thereafter there were no visits because of James's campaigning and his travelling in 1709–11.

[46] Dangeau, VI, 197, 26 September 1697.

duchesse d'Orléans are probably representative of opinion within the French royal family. She did not have a high opinion of the intelligence of James II,[47] but after his first visit to Fontainebleau in October 1690 she commented: 'Now that I have come to know more of this good King, I like him better. He is the best fellow in the world.'[48] Her letters normally refer to him as 'good King James'.[49] Writing in 1692 she states that 'our dear King James is good and honest'.[50] As the exiled king turned increasingly to religion as a consolation for his misfortunes, so he earned the respect and sympathy of his Bourbon cousins, notably Louis XIV who began to regard him as a saint.

Mary of Modena was even more popular, because of her beauty and her natural dignity. Louis's comment was 'Voilà comme il faut que soit une reine et de corps et d'esprit, tenant sa cour avec dignité.'[51] The letters of the duchesse d'Orléans are also full of her praises. She is described as 'generous and a true Christian',[52] 'the best princess in the world',[53] 'courteous and pleasant and . . . always cheerful'.[54] And after her death: 'she should be regarded as a saint . . . She was very generous, courteous and tactful . . . She never complained of her misfortune.'[55]

James III was also very much appreciated. The duchesse wrote in September 1696: 'The Prince of Wales is the most charming child you could wish to see . . . He is lively, gay and not at all shy, and will talk as much as you like.'[56] The following year she added: 'I am extremely fond of this Prince, and it is impossible to see him without falling in love with him. He has such a charming disposition.'[57] Her later letters reveal the same warm feelings after he had grown up. She writes that 'he is an amiable and well-brought-up Prince',[58] 'gentle and courteous',[59] 'the best and most charming fellow in the world':[60] 'I don't know how the English can hate him; he is one of the best and most honourable men that the Lord God ever made.'[61] There is no reason

---

[47] *Letters of Madame*, I, 96 and 106, to the Duchess of Hanover, 30 July 1690 and 6 June 1692.

[48] *Ibid.*, I, 99, to the same, 20 October 1690.

[49] E.g. *ibid.*, I, 142, to the same, 20 September 1696.

[50] *Ibid.*, I, 106, to the same, 6 June 1692.

[51] Sévigné, *Correspondance*, III, no. 1057, p. 475, to Madame de Grignan, 17 January 1689.

[52] *Letters of Madame*, I, 224, to the Raugravine Amelia-Elisabeth, 22 April 1702.

[53] *Ibid.*, II, 61, to the Raugravine Louisa, 10 September 1712.

[54] *Ibid.*, II, 170, to the same, 8 May 1718.   [55] *Ibid.*, II, 170, to the same, 29 May 1718.

[56] *Ibid.*, I, 142, to the Duchess of Hanover, 20 September 1696.

[57] *Ibid.*, I, 154, to the same, 15 September 1697.   [58] *Ibid.*, II, 56, to the same, 24 March 1712.

[59] *Ibid.*, II, 235, to the Raugravine Louisa, 17 December 1719.

[60] *Ibid.*, II, 101, to Harling, 3 December 1715.

[61] *Ibid.*, II, 91, to the Raugravine Louisa, 8 August 1715.

to doubt that these sentiments were shared by Louis XIV, the dauphin, the latter's three sons, and most members of the French royal family. If they were not, it is hard to believe that they would have wished to visit and be visited by the Stuarts so frequently over such a long period of time.

The ceremonial during these visits was settled in 1689, when the Stuarts first arrived. James II and Mary of Modena were given precedence over the dauphin, and the Prince of Wales was given precedence over the dauphin's three sons. As there was neither a queen of France nor, after 1690, a dauphine, Mary of Modena was always treated as the first lady of the French court. When James II died in 1701 James III was given exactly the same honours: equality with Louis XIV and precedence over the dauphin. When Princess Louise-Marie came of age, and began to visit Versailles and Marly without her mother, she became the first lady of the French court. As the daughter of a king, she outranked Marie-Adelaïde de Savoie, the duchesse de Bourgogne, who was only the granddaughter of a king. This changed in 1711, after the death of the dauphin, when the duchesse became the new dauphine and was given precedence over Louise-Marie.[62]

At first the two kings organised their visits formally, greeting each other beyond their Guard Chambers at the tops of their staircases and escorting each other back there, but they quickly abandoned these ceremonies and agreed to meet and separate in their Antechambers.[63] When James III succeeded his father in September 1701, Louis XIV greeted him at the top of his staircase on the occasion of his first visit to Versailles, but then reverted to the previous arrangement.[64]

No one but the queen was allowed to have an armchair in the presence of either of the kings, so the other members of the royal families sat on *tabourets*, a privilege shared with all princesses and duchesses. James II showed his respect for the dauphin by always receiving him standing up, to avoid making this distinction. But Mary of Modena discovered that Queen Henrietta Maria, in

[62] Bibliothèque de l'Arsenal MS 3862, 155–6, and MS 3863, 239, 'Mémoires du baron de Breteuil'; BN MS Fd. Fr. 6679, ff. 1–6, 667–72, 'Journal du marquis de Sainctot'; Dangeau, II, 293–4, 297, 314 (8, 12 and 30 January 1689), 327 (10 February 1689), 383 (29 April 1689); VIII, 196–8 (20 and 21 September 1701); X, p. 227 (8 January 1705), 263 (23 February 1705); XI, 468 (23 September 1707); XIII, 384 (16 April 1711), 440 (12 July 1711); Sourches, VIII, 70 (26 April 1703); IX, p. 158 (8 January 1705); X, 268 (6 March 1707); Saint-Simon, XXI, 97 and 397; XXII, 11–13.

[63] Dangeau, II, 293–4, 299, 301–2, 311, 313–14 (8, 13, 15, 16, 27 and 30 January 1689); Sourches, III, 9, 17, 20, 22 (8, 13, 15 and 16 January 1689); Bibliothèque de l'Arsenal MS 3860, 409–10 (17 November 1700).

[64] Dangeau, VIII, 198 (21 September 1701), Saint-Simon, IX, 296–7.

exile during the 1640s and 1650s, had given an armchair to both Gaston, duc d'Orléans and Louis XIV's brother Philippe, so she used this precedent to give one to the dauphin, to Philippe, now duc d'Orléans, to their wives, and even to the dauphin's three sons, whenever they visited her and neither of the kings was present. When James II was in the queen's apartment at Saint-Germain, and she could not do this, the Stuarts both sat on *tabourets*. James III adopted the same tactful approach when he succeeded his father.

It is worth observing, however, that the exceptional privilege enjoyed by Louis's brother Philippe, duc d'Orléans was not extended to his son, the duc de Chartres, who was thus treated in the same way as the other princes of the blood and made to sit on a *tabouret*. Chartres resented this, and suggested a compromise whereby he be allowed to sit on a chair with a back but with no arms. Louis XIV expressly forbade this,[65] and when the duc de Chartres succeeded his father as the new duc d'Orléans in 1700 he was not allowed to inherit the privilege of having an armchair in the presence of the queen. In the short term Chartres-Orléans avoided going to Saint-Germain, and only went there with Louis XIV or the dauphin, in whose presence he would not have had an armchair at the French court either. He seems to have been the only member of the French royal family who disliked the Stuarts. When James III later complimented his Bourbon cousins by permitting the dauphin and his sons, and the dowager duchesse d'Orléans, to have armchairs in his presence, so long as Louis XIV was not also present, he thus inadvertently increased the resentment already felt by the new duc d'Orléans at this discrimination.[66] The greatest tragedy that ever befell James III – and there would be many in his long life – was that the dauphin and his three sons, who loved him as a son and a brother, never inherited the French throne, whereas the duc d'Orléans became Regent of France after the death of Louis XIV during the most critical phase of James's attempts to achieve a restoration.

There was another difficulty to be settled, as the practices at the English and the French courts were not the same. In January 1689, when the ceremonial between the two royal families was regulated, Mary of Modena discussed with Louis XIV how she should receive French courtiers when they visited her at Saint-Germain.

[65] Sourches, III, 9, 17 (8 and 13 January 1689); Dangeau, II, 294, 299, 301, 313 (9, 13, 15 and 29 January 1689), 339 (26 February 1689), 372 (13 April 1689); III, 118 (7 May 1690); VI, 27, 30 (10 and 16 November 1696); XIII, 391 (21 April 1711); Saint-Simon, XIV, 404–6; XXI, 127; Bibliothèque de l'Arsenal MS 3862, 156; *Letters of Madame*, I, 190, to the Raugravine Louisa, 1 November 1699.
[66] Bibliothèque de l'Arsenal MS 3862, 157–8; BN MS Fd. Fr. 6679, ff. 667–72.

La reine d'Angleterre dit qu'elle traitera les dames ou comme les reines les traitent en Angleterre ou comme les reines les traitent en France; elle en laisse le choix au roi, et ne veut rien faire que ce qui lui sera le plus agréable. Les reines en Angleterre baisent les princesses et les duchesses et ne les font point asseoir, et ici les reines font asseoir les princesses et les duchesses et ne baisent point.[67]

Louis XIV left the choice to the ladies, 'qui s'assemblèrent pour délibérer sur ce choix, et, comme elles optèrent d'être traitées à la françoise, le Roi régla qu'elles ne baiseroient pas la reine d'Angleterre et qu'elles seroient assises devant elle'.[68] It was then 'réglé que la reine d'Angleterre se lèvera de dessus sa chaise quand les officiers de la couronne ou leurs femmes iront lui faire la cour'.[69]

The decision to allow the French princesses and duchesses to sit down in the presence of the queen was inconvenient because none of the English ladies, not even the duchesses, were allowed to do so. A personal exception had been made by Mary of Modena for her childhood friend, Donna Vittoria Davia, one of her ladies of the Bedchamber. The discrepancy was all the greater because the title of princess was not given in England to anyone who was not royal. Moreover the title of duchess was much rarer in England than it was in France and there were none at the court of Saint-Germain in January 1689. As a result, the decision meant that several or even many French ladies would be permitted to sit in the presence of the queen while her own ladies would be obliged to remain standing. To emphasise the point, when the Marquis of Powis was sent by the queen to speak to the dauphine, the latter refused even to see him because he was not a duke.[70] The French also resented the fact that Vittoria Davia (née Montecuccoli) was allowed to sit down: 'il y eut une chose qui scandalisa un peu les princesses, qui fait que la reine d'Angleterre fit asseoir auprès elle Mme de Montecucolli, sa dame d'honneur'.[71] As a consequence the Marquis of Powis was made a duke:

Le roi d'Angleterre fit milord Powits duc, afin que sa femme . . . pût être assise devant Mme la Dauphine; car, pour devant la reine d'Angleterre les duchesses angloises ne s'y asseyoient jamais; et ceci est une nouveauté, parce que, les duchesses françoises s'asseyant devant la reine d'Angleterre, elle vouloit que Mme Powits eût aussi le droit de s'y asseoir, seulement quand les princesses et duchesses françoises s'y trouveroient.[72]

---

[67] Dangeau, II, 294 (9 January 1689). See also Sourches, III, 11 (10 January 1689). Cf. Sévigné, *Correspondance*, III, no. 1055, p. 471, to Madame de Grignan, 12 January 1689, which is unreliable in this as in her other comments on James II and Mary of Modena.

[68] Sourches, III, 11 (10 January 1689). See also Dangeau, II, 295 (10 January 1689).

[69] Dangeau, II, 298 (13 January 1689).   [70] Dangeau, II, 292 (7 January 1689).

[71] Sourches, III, 11 (10 January 1689).   [72] Sourches, III, 15 (12 January 1689).

The English court at Saint-Germain was soon joined by one of the illegitimate daughters of Charles II (the Countess of Sussex) and three of the illegitimate children of James II, two sons and one daughter (Lady Waldegrave). It was then decided to treat the two ladies as though they were princesses, in order to increase the number of English ladies entitled to sit down, and by May 1689 it was noted that

il y a quatre dames de la reine d'Angleterre qu'elle fait asseoir quand il y a quelques princesse ou duchesse françoise: madame Powits, comme duchesse d'angloise, madame de Montecuculli qu'on fait comtesse d'Almont, comme sa dame d'honneur, et mesdames de Sussex et de Waldegrave comme fille du roi. C'est le roi notre maître qui leur a donné ce rang-là, car elles n'en ont aucun en Angleterre.[73]

The number of English ladies permitted to sit down when French courtiers were visiting the queen remained very small, was never more than five at any one time and was sometimes as few as three. Both the illegitimate sons of James II were dukes (of Berwick and of Albemarle), so their wives became entitled to *tabourets* as duchesses – though the Duchess of Albemarle insisted (successfully) on being treated as a princess.[74] The other three ladies at Saint-Germain who were entitled to sit down with the French duchesses were the wives of the newly created Jacobite Dukes of Tyrconnell (1690), Perth (1701) and Melfort (1705), whose titles were all recognised in France.[75] By 1701 the queen had eighteen *sièges pliants* in the *Chambre* where she received her visits. If we take into account those English courtiers who had the right to sit, that means that she could receive up to about fourteen French princesses and duchesses at any one time. In June 1701 the duc d'Orléans visited her and (according to his wife) 'told us how many important people he had seen on his visit to the Queen of England'.[76]

Many of the visits between Louis XIV and the Stuarts involved long and secret political discussions, about which we know nothing. When they received each other in public Mary of Modena always sat between the two kings, with

---

[73] Dangeau, II, 390 (9 May 1689).

[74] Dangeau, VII, 383 (28 September 1700); Saint-Simon, VII, 397.

[75] The Earl of Perth was publicly created a duke after the death of James II in 1701. According to Saint-Simon, 'Louis XIV le lui confirma en 1701, lors de la mort de Jacques, comme aux autres ducs créés de même, Berwick, Albemarle, Melfort' (VIII, 98). See also, 'Melfort . . . et sa femme eurent en France le rang et les honneurs de duc et de duchesse comme tous ceux qui l'avoient été faits à Saint-Germain, ou qui y étoient arrivés tels' (XII, 451); Berwick 'étoit duc d'Angleterre, et, quoiqu'ils n'aient point de rang en France, le Roi l'avoit accordé à ceux qui avoient suivi le roi Jacques' (XIX, 376).

[76] *Letters of Madame*, I, 210, to the Duchess of Hanover, 12 June 1701.

her husband or son on her right and Louis on her left. When the queen was not present, Louis always gave the position of honour on the right side to the king of England. Evening entertainments involved suppers, generally preceded by games such as portique and lansquenet, with a great deal of music, sometimes in the background, sometimes performed in formal concerts. Mary of Modena was accompanied to the French court only by those who were entitled to a *tabouret* and by the other ladies of the Bedchamber, though both the Duchess of Tyrconnell and the Countess of Sussex took their daughters with them on at least one occasion.[77] There were regular balls and, in the summer months, visits to the gardens at Marly and Versailles. As James III and Louise-Marie grew up, the number of balls increased. It became normal for James and his sister to open the first dances on these occasions, and whenever James danced Louis stood up to show his respect for a fellow monarch.[78] Until 1706 James III was accompanied by his governor, the Duke of Perth. Louise-Marie was accompanied by the Countess of Middleton and, later, by the latter's daughter Lady Elizabeth, who married Lord Edward Drummond in 1709.

The most important visits were the extended ones to Fontainebleau, each of which apparently cost Louis XIV 60,000 *livres*,[79] a sum which indicates the high priority he gave to entertaining and enjoying the company of his Stuart cousins. The pattern was established on the occasion of James II's first visit in October 1690. Louis XIV and all the French royal family met him and the queen at the northern edge of the forest and then escorted them to the château, where they were lodged in the superb apartment, called *de la reine-mère*, situated between the *Cour du Cheval Blanc* and the *Cour de la Fontaine*. There they were 'attendus par une foule incroyable de dames et de gens de qualité'. That evening they had supper with all the Bourbon princes and princesses. The following morning all the ladies of the court attended 'la toilette de la reine d'Angleterre', but Louis asked James not to attend his lever, preferring to fetch the king and queen of England from their apartment and escort them across the vestibule into the adjacent chapel royal for mass. Louis always made a point of walking a little behind James. The rest of the day was spent looking at the château, walking in the gardens and watching some matches of *jeu de paume*. There were then games in the evening, with music by Delalande, followed by supper. The following days were passed with hunting, visits to parts of the forest and walks in the gardens and around the canal, with

---

[77] Dangeau, v, 285 (29 September 1695); v, 370 (23 February 1696).

[78] Dangeau, x, 263 (23 February 1705); xII, 80 (19 February 1708); Sourches, IX, 181 (23 February 1705); Saint-Simon, XII, 439.

[79] Dangeau, vII, 383 (28 September 1700).

games and music in the evenings. When the Stuarts left they were escorted by Louis back to Chailly at the northern edge of the forest.[80]

The visit the following year was the same, except that the evening entertainments included the performance of plays.[81] In 1692 these arrangements were continued, and Dangeau noted that James II and Mary 'ont amené plus de dames et une plus grosse cour que l'année passée . . . Le roi mange toujours en public avec eux, et toutes les princesses y mangent aussi . . . On jouera au lansquenet le jour d'appartement, parce que la reine aime ce jeu-là.'[82] Before the visit in 1693 the Stuarts let Louis know that they preferred to have concerts than plays, and Dangeau noted that whenever there was music they always remained until the very end.[83]

James and Mary were unhappy that their visits obliged Louis to travel to the edge of the forest to greet them and to say goodbye, and they tried to persuade him to drop this ceremony. He finally gave way in 1695,[84] but insisted on again going to the edge of the forest the following year.[85] It was not until 1697 that a new practice was established of meeting and parting in the salon at the top of the horseshoe staircase of the *Cour du Cheval Blanc*.[86] At the end of the 1699 visit Dangeau noted that James and Mary were 'plus contents que jamais de la bonne réception qu'on leur a faite ici et de tous les honneurs qu'on leur a rendus'. More signficantly, perhaps, he added: 'On a été fort content d'eux aussi; rien n'est égal à la vertu, à la politesse et à l'honnêté de la reine.'[87] The effect of these family holidays, during which the two kings spent every day together, and knelt at mass either side of Mary of Modena in the chapel royal, should not be underestimated.

James III's first visit to Fontainebleau took place in 1703 and was equally successful. The *Appartement de la Reine-Mère*, which had been occupied by the queen and her husband, could not be shared by the queen and her son, so Louis gave them two separate apartments at the far end of the *Galérie de Diane*, which served as their joint Guard Chamber. This meant that they could only reach the chapel royal by walking through two rooms which overlooked the *Jardin de la Reine* (now the *Jardin de Diane*) and then the sequence of rooms

[80] Dangeau, III, 233–6 (11 to 18 October 1690). Also Sourches, III, 311–17.
[81] Dangeau, III, 405–15 (22 September to 11 October 1691).
[82] Dangeau, IV, 179–84 (7 to 18 October 1692).
[83] Dangeau, IV, 364–72 (23 September to 7 October 1693).
[84] Dangeau, V, 285 (28 September 1695). Also Sourches, V, 59.
[85] Sourches, V, 204 (10 October 1696); Dangeau, VI, 435 (8 October 1698).
[86] Dangeau, VI, 195 (24 September 1697); VI, 435 (8 October 1698); VII, 150 (15 September 1699); VII, 383 (28 September 1700). Also Sourches, V, 342; VI, 76; VI, 186.
[87] Dangeau, VII, 161 (1 October 1699).

overlooking the *Cour de l'Ovale*. This increased the contact between the two royal families, because these rooms formed part of the apartments of the duc and duchesse de Bourgogne and that of Louis himself. Beyond them lay the frescoed *Galérie François I*, which led to the salon outside the chapel royal.

On later occasions Louis met them at the top of the staircase in the *Cour de l'Ovale*, but on this first visit he greeted them at the foot of the staircase. He then conducted them to their apartments, after which they all had supper together. The days were passed with similar activities to those offered to James II, though the queen had stopped playing lansquenet in the evenings since the death of her husband. Louis also arranged a series of theatrical performances for the young king. These included plays by Racine (*Phèdre, Alexandre*) and operas by Lully (*Atys*) and Destouches (*Le Mariage du Carnaval et de la Folie*), among others. There was also a concert of Italian music, sung by two castrati from Rome, acompanied by two violins and harpsichord.[88] When the visit was over Dangeau noted that 'c'est un très-joli prince et qui se fait fort aimer'.[89]

James III's later visits were equally successful, particularly the one in 1707 when he was accompanied by Louise-Marie as well as his mother. All three of them had adjacent apartments at the end of the *Galérie de Diane*. The plays included works by Corneille (*Cinna, Horace*), Racine (*Mithridate*) and Molière (*Monsieur de Pourceaugnac, Le Bourgeois Gentilhomme*), and the music was mainly by Lully (*Phaëton*, and the complete ballets to accompany the *comédies* of Molière). Louis also arranged that there should be a concert of Italian music. Because Louis XIV and Queen Mary did not attend the plays, operas and ballets, James III was able to insist that the dauphin, the duc and duchesse de Bourgogne, the duc de Berri and the dowager duchesse d'Orléans (but not her son the duc d'Orléans) all had armchairs.[90]

The absence of Louis XIV and Mary of Modena from these theatrical performances was not simply motivated by a matter of taste. It was part of a deliberate plan to foster intimate relations between the younger members of their two families. James and his sister, the duc and duchesse de Bourgogne and the duc de Berri had known and liked each other since childhood, and both Louis and Queen Mary were determined that they should become and remain firm friends. The queen even hoped that the duc de Berri would marry Louise-Marie, though Louis sensibly realised that good Stuart–Bourbon

---

[88] For the visit, Dangeau, IX, 309–22 (3 to 16 October 1703). Also Sourches, VIII, 189–97. For the queen's stopping playing lansquenet after the death of James II, Dangeau, IX, 425 (4 February 1704).

[89] Dangeau, IX, 321 (15 October 1703).

[90] Dangeau, XI, 468–81 (23 September to 7 October 1707). Also Sourches, X, 403–13.

relations were already guaranteed and that the princess might more usefully be married to a prince from another dynasty after the restoration of her brother.

Three examples may be given to demonstrate the way Louis and Mary encouraged these good relations between their families. In August 1704 Louis arranged 'une collation magnifique' for them in the gardens at Marly. Once they had all sat down to eat, Louis and Mary left them to be by themselves: 'le roi la mena au pavillon des globes'.[91] In June 1705 James III, his mother and his sister arrived at the Château de Trianon at 6 o'clock in the evening and walked in the gardens with Louis XIV and the French royal family. Then James and Louise-Marie embarked in a *chaloupe* on the canal with the duchesse de Bourgogne, the duc de Berri and various English and French ladies. They sailed to the *Ménagerie* at the far end of the cross of the grand canal, where they had a 'magnifique collation'. 'Il n'y eut à ce souper ni fauteuils, ni cadenas, ni soucoupe; ils étaient dix-huit à table. Après le souper ils dansèrent aux chansons, et jouèrent à de petits jeux dans le salon.' While they were away Louis and Queen Mary had a quiet supper at Trianon with the older members of the royal family.[92] In August 1707 Louis arranged for a large party to go down from the Château de Versailles to the *Ménagerie*. After they had been there a little while, Louis and the queen returned to the château, leaving James and Louise-Marie behind with their Bourbon cousins, 'avec beaucoup de dames, tant angloises que françoises'.[93]

Their intention on these as on many other occasions was perfectly clear. They were not in love. The duchesse d'Orléans commented in 1717 that Mary of Modena 'was too friendly with Madame de Maintenon for it to be credible that the late King [Louis XIV] was in love with her'.[94] They were attempting to pave the way for an extended period of Anglo-French peace, when James III would be restored, and the dauphin and then the duc de Bourgogne would be kings of France. They were trying to provide France and England (as well as Spain) with kings who had known and even loved each other throughout childhood, adolescence and early manhood, something which would have been unique in European history. It was a legacy worth struggling for and took priority over ministerial objections. Louis concentrated his efforts, his time and his money on achieving it, and never wavered in his support for the young

[91] Dangeau, x, 94 (12 August 1704).
[92] Dangeau, x, 375 (23 July 1705). Also Sourches, ix, 302. On this occasion the duc de Bourgogne remained with Louis XIV and Mary of Modena.
[93] Dangeau, xi, 432 (10 August 1707). Also Sourches, x, 374.
[94] *Letters of Madame*, ii, 149, to an unnamed person, 8 October 1717.

Stuart king whom he respected, loved as a son and regarded as a good Catholic. If the dauphin, the duc de Bourgogne and the duc de Berri had not all died before Louis XIV himself, leaving the duc d'Orléans to become Regent for his five-year-old great-grandson, then his aim might have been achieved. Those historians who have claimed that Louis never seriously supported James II and James III, or that he abandoned James III after 1712, do not seem to have taken account of the reality of the relations between the Stuarts and the court of France during these years.

CHAPTER SEVEN

The portraits of the Stuarts and their courtiers

The close relationship between James III and the sons of the dauphin was emphasised as early as 1694 in a celebrated set of six engravings entitled *Appartemens ou amusemens de la Famille Roiale a Versailles*. Each engraving shows the members of the French royal family, and some of their household servants, during an evening reception in the rooms of the *grand appartement* at Versailles. In the first the six-year-old Prince of Wales is shown playing *portique* with the duc d'Anjou and the duc de Berri.[1]

In fact the prince had not yet visited Versailles. His first recorded visit to the French court was in June 1694, when he spent the day with his three cousins at Trianon.[2] At that time he could only speak English and Italian, and it was not for another two years that he could converse with them in French. In September 1696, having recently paid 'une visite sérieuse dans les formes' to Louis XIV at Versailles, he was shown the fountains there with his cousins.[3] Thereafter he met them with increasing frequency.

In 1696, when the duc d'Anjou was thirteen years old, he and his two brothers were painted by François de Troy.[4] The portrait of Anjou was important because five years later in 1701, when James also reached the age of thirteen, he was painted by Troy in a composition which immediately recalls the one of his older cousin.[5] By then the duc d'Anjou had become King Philip V of Spain and the close relationship between the cousins had become even more important. It was emphasised again in the engraving published with the *Almanach Royal* of 1701, which showed the ceremony when Louis XIV announced at Versailles that his grandson had inherited the Spanish throne.

---

[1] BN Est. Ed. 95 Fol. The set was published by Antoine Trouvain between 1694 and 1698. Mary of Modena is shown sitting in an armchair in the 'Cinquième Chambre des Apartemens'.

[2] Dangeau, v, 31, 21 June 1694.

[3] Sources, v, 187, 5 September 1696; Dangeau, v, 476, 26 September 1696; Nairne, 26 September 1696.

[4] D. Brême, *François de Troy* (Paris and Toulouse, 1997), 48–9.

[5] *Ibid.*, 51; Scottish National Portrait Gallery no. 909.

FIG. 20. Antoine Trouvain, *Premier Appartement*, 1694 (34 × 43 cm, BN Est. Ed. Fol.). This engraving shows the Prince of Wales playing a game of *portique* in the Château de Versailles with the duc d'Anjou (later Philip V of Spain) and the duc de Berri.

Although the Stuarts were not present at that ceremony, James II is shown standing beside the new king of Spain, while the Prince of Wales stands with the duc de Berri and the duc de Bourgogne.[6]

François de Troy was the third of the four principal painters employed by the Stuarts and their courtiers between 1689 and 1712. The others were Benedetto Gennari, Nicolas de Largillière (one of whose portraits was copied for the engraving of the *Premier Appartement*) and Alexis-Simon Belle. In addition to these artists, an important commission was placed with Pierre Mignard and two with Hyacinthe Rigaud. The portraits of the Stuarts themselves have been the subject of a separate study[7] and do not need to be re-examined here in the

---

[6] BN Est. Qb 1700 (72c 55978), reproduced as Fig. 19.
[7] Corp, *The King over the Water*.

same detail. Those of the Jacobites at Saint-Germain remain largely unknown, often wrongly attributed, and in some cases unidentified.

Gennari and Largillière had both worked in England before 1689, but the former had lived there permanently since 1674, whereas the latter had only visited from 1676 to 1679 and then twice in 1685.[8] It was therefore Gennari – who followed the king and queen to Saint-Germain at the beginning of 1689 and who was much better known by their courtiers – who was mainly employed by the Jacobite court when it first arrived.

Between 1689 and 1692 Gennari painted a double portrait of the queen and the prince of Wales, one portrait of the prince, and two of the queen. In addition to these four portraits, three of which were produced with replicas, Gennari also painted nine of the Jacobites at Saint-Germain: Francesco Riva (master of the queen's robes), Robert Strickland (vice-chamberlain to the queen), Bishop Philip Ellis, Captain Randall MacDonnell (groom of the Bedchamber), James Porter (vice-chamberlain to the king), Joseph Ronchi (gentleman usher of the Presence Chamber), the Countess of Almond (lady of the Bedchamber), the Duke of Berwick and his brother Lord Henry FitzJames (later Duke of Albemarle).[9]

In the spring of 1692, when James II was preparing to invade England, Gennari returned to Italy. It is possible that he had grown homesick, or that he had no desire to go back to England in the event of a Jacobite restoration. It is more likely, however, that his work had been overshadowed by that of Largillière, who had received two important commissions from James II and Mary of Modena in 1691. Gennari's decision to leave also coincided with the return to Saint-Germain of Lord Melfort. The latter was an established connoisseur who had accumulated a very large collection of paintings in England, but who had never patronised Gennari.[10] It was probably the return of Melfort, the king's secretary of state and principal minister, which prompted Gennari to leave. On his departure he was rewarded with a warrant naming him James II's 'First Painter'. He never returned, but the warrant was renewed in December 1701, after the accession of James III.[11]

---

[8] D. Brême in *La Cour des Stuarts*, 108; M.N. Rosenfeld, 'La Culture de Largillière', *Revue de l'Art* 98 (1992), 44–53.

[9] Corp, *King over the Water*, 33–4, 102, 106; P. Bagni, *Benedetto Gennari e la Bottega del Guercino* (Bologna, 1986), 163–5. Of the Stuart portraits, only the double one and the one of the Prince of Wales have survived. Of the Jacobite portraits, only the one of Riva (with his family) has survived (Fig. 14), though the one of Berwick is known from an engraving.

[10] Melfort's collection is listed in *Calendar of Treasury Books, 1689–92*, IX, part IV, 1679–81. For the list of Gennari's paintings and patrons in England, see Bagni, *Benedetto Gennari*, 147–61.

[11] Ruvigny, *Jacobite Peerage*, 216, 221.

Before 1689 Largillière had already produced two portraits of James II, one of Mary of Modena and one of the Duke of Berwick. His first portrait of James II showed him when he was still Duke of York. It is three-quarter length and has always been described as by an 'unknown artist, c.1690'.[12] One reason for this failure to attribute and date the portrait is that it was never engraved.[13] The same is true of the portrait of the Duke of Berwick, who is shown with his tutor: this was wrongly identified until very recently.[14] Largillière's other two portraits, of James II and Mary of Modena, provide an interesting contrast because they were not only engraved but also frequently copied and very widely circulated before 1689.[15] Largillière's image of James II was the more successful of the two. It was already greatly admired by the time the king went into exile at Saint-Germain and, given its use for propaganda purposes, even better known by the time he returned from Ireland in 1690.[16] It is not surprising, therefore, that Largillière was commissioned in 1691 to paint a portrait of the Prince of Wales, to be engraved and sent to England and Scotland.[17]

Between 1691 and 1695 Largillière painted three other separate portraits of the Prince of Wales, a large family group in which the prince was shown with the king and queen, and a large double portrait in which he was shown with his sister, Princess Louise-Marie.[18] These portraits were displayed in the Château de Saint-Germain, but copies were also given away as diplomatic presents[19] and sent to Jacobites in England.[20] In addition, the images of the prince and

[12] National Portrait Gallery no. 366.

[13] It did, however, probably influence the engraving of James II in the anonymous family group of c.1695, reproduced in Sharp, *Engraved Record*, 8, no. 684.

[14] Corp, 'Berwick', 53. The sitter was previously identified as either the duc du Maine or the dauphin.

[15] They were engraved in reverse by both Smith and Beckett. The portrait of James II is in the National Maritime Museum, Greenwich. The one of Mary of Modena is lost.

[16] The engravings of the king were copied in reverse from those by Smith and Beckett, thus reproducing Largillière's original image. For an example of the use of this portrait in anti-Jacobite propaganda, see BN Est. Qb¹, 1689–90 (M.93726).

[17] Corp, *King over the Water*, 34–5; Sharp, *Engraved Record*, no. 91. Lord Ailesbury recorded that when William III heard that a copy had been acquired by the Earl of Essex, he asked to be shown it: *Memoirs*, 283.

[18] Corp, *King over the Water*, 35, 37–8.

[19] The family group was placed in the king's antechamber and has not survived. Copies of two of the portraits of the prince were sent to the pope (SCA, BL 1/181/11, Nairne to Lesly, 2 August 1694; James Drummond, Earl of Perth, *Letters to His Sister, the Countess of Erroll*, ed. W. Jerdan (London, 1845), 104, 10 March 1696).

[20] For example, Lord Peterborough was given a portrait of the prince in 1692 and Lady Peterborough was given one of the princess in 1695 (*The Diary of John Evelyn*, ed. W. Bray, 2 vols. (London, 1907 edition, revised 1952), II, 321, 20 March 1692; Nairne, 26 November 1695). See

princess were all engraved and sent over to England and Scotland in multiple copies.[21] Largillière's portraits thus served an important political purpose in introducing the prince to the people who could not see him for themselves. John Evelyn's reaction was perhaps typical: 'I visited the Earl of Peterborough, who showed me the picture of the Prince of Wales, newly brought out of France, seeming in my opinion very much to resemble the Queen his mother, and of a most vivacious countenance.'[22] Given the 'warming-pan myth', by which the Whigs pretended that the prince was a surrogate baby smuggled into the queen's bed during her labour, this was exactly the reaction which the portraits were intended to provoke.[23]

Unlike Gennari, who had had no other patrons in France, Largillière did not accept any commissions from the Jacobite courtiers at Saint-Germain until much later. All the known portraits from the exiled court during the 1690s were painted by François de Troy, who lived six doors away from the *Collège des Ecossais* in the rue des Fossés-Saint-Victor in Paris[24] and was probably recommended by Lewis Innes.

Troy's earliest known Jacobite portrait shows the Duke of Tyrconnell, who visited France between September 1690 and January 1691. It was presumably commissioned to commemorate his creation as a Knight of the Garter in November, and it shows him with the blue sash and star of the order – though the star is actually shown upside down.[25]

The next surviving portraits by Troy probably date from 1692 and were commissioned by the Duke of Powis (lord chamberlain). There are two different portraits of the latter's daughter Mary, Viscountess Montague, and one

also Nairne, 26 June 1695, 7 July 1695 and 12 July 1695 for the sending of other portraits of the prince to England.

[21] Sharp, *Engraved Record*, nos. 89, 92, 116, 115, 114; Nairne, 23 June 1694, 8 July 1694, 12 January 1696. (Sharp no. 92 is wrongly said to be missing in Corp, *King over the Water*, 37.)

[22] Evelyn, 20 March 1692.

[23] These engravings inspired Sir Godfrey Kneller's famous comment at Corpus Christi College, Oxford on 28 September 1697: '[Even though I am] not of his party, [it is] a lye [that the Prince of Wales is not the true heir]: I must tell you wat I am sure of, and in wat I cannot be mistaken: His Fader and Moder have sat to me about 36 times a piece; and I know every line and bit in their Faces. Be Got I could paint King James just now by memory. I say the child is so like both, that there is not a feature in his Face but wat belongs to Fader or Moder; this I am sure of, and be Got I cannot be mistaken. Nay te Nails of his Fingers are his Moder's te Queen that was . . . I can't be out in my Lines. Signed: Dr. Charlett, Dr. Gregory, Mr. George Harbin present, at Dr. Wallis's' (Bodleian Library, Carte MSS 198, f. 9).

[24] Corp, 'Couperin and the Stuart Court', 452, note 7.

[25] It presumably belonged to the Duchess of Tyrconnell and was taken back with her to Ireland when she left the court. For the locations of all these portraits by Troy, see Corp, *King over the Water*, 102, unless otherwise stated.

of her sister Lady Lucy Herbert, who left the court to become a nun at Bruges in 1692. Powis himself is shown in his robes as a Knight of the Garter, an honour he received from James II in April of the same year (Fig. 12). These portraits were probably sent back to the members of his family who had remained in England, as is indicated by the existence of two additional copies of the portrait of Lady Lucy.[26]

Apart from the portraits themselves, no documents have survived linking Troy with the Jacobite courtiers, so we are dependent on the chance survival of individual pictures. Troy's patrons included Lord Drummond (later 2nd Duke of Perth), whom he painted in 1694, and particularly the Duke of Berwick. There are three copies of a portrait of the duke's first wife, painted c.1695–97, and one of the duke himself, presumably painted at about the same time. A portrait of Anthony Hamilton can be dated to about 1700, while another portrait of an unidentified Jacobite lady, of which there are two versions, is inscribed on the reverse 'Peint à Paris par François de Troy en 1700'.[27] Two other unidentified Jacobite portraits can be dated to the same period,[28] while a portrait of Charlotte, daughter of Lady Sophia Bulkeley (lady of the Bedchamber) was presumably painted some time after her marriage to the 5th Viscount Clare in 1697 (Fig. 16).

In that year the Treaty of Ryswick, by which Louis XIV was obliged to recognise William III as *de facto* king of England, Scotland and Ireland, provoked a strong reaction from James II. Even before the treaty was signed, he sent a manifesto to all the rulers of Europe, both Protestant and Catholic, protesting against anything which might prejudice his interests in the forthcoming peace.[29] Once it had been signed he commissioned an important series of medals and paintings bearing the image of his son.

The medals were all produced by Norbert Roettiers, whose father (John) had been engraver-general to Charles II and James II in England, and whose

[26] There are copies at Everingham and Brahan Castle.

[27] The inscribed version is at Meiklour, where it is wrongly identified as a portrait of Grisel Mercer. The other is reproduced in F. Camus, 'Alexis-Simon Belle, portraitiste de cour', *Bulletin de la Société de l'Histoire de l'Art Français* (1990), 58, fig. 64, where it is wrongly attributed to Belle.

[28] *Gazette de l'Hôtel Drouot*, 10 June 1994, 55, an unidentified lady, wrongly attributed to Largillière; Christie's, 18 December 1931, lot no. 123, an unknown gentleman, wrongly identified as the Duke of Berwick.

[29] BN Fd. Fr. 6557, f. 319; 12159, f. 145; 12160, ff. 133–49; AN K. 1301, no. 17. The manifesto was dated 8 June 1697. Arch. Dépt. des Yvelines, B.537 Saint-Germain, contains an interesting document, dated 9 May 1697, which records a bet of 8 *louis d'ors* placed by John Stafford with Matteo Maria Turrini (gentleman usher of the queen's Presence Chamber) that William III would be recognised by Louis XIV. Turrini, who lost the bet, should have paid the 8 *louis d'ors* to Stafford in September.

uncle (Joseph) worked for Louis XIV at the royal mint in Paris. Roettiers had recently left England and, with ready access to the facilities of the mint in Paris, been appointed engraver-general of the mint at Saint-Germain-en-Laye in November 1695.[30] In 1697 he produced his first group of medallic portraits of the Prince of Wales. As a protest against the Treaty of Ryswick, the reverse of one of the 1697 medals shows a dove bearing an olive branch, and states that there will be no permanent peace until the Stuarts are restored. Two years later Roettiers produced another group of medals. One carried the message 'Pax vobis', Peace be with you; but another showed the bust of the Prince of Wales conjoined with that of James II, thereby reminding people that one day the exiled king would inevitably be succeeded by his son as James III.[31] Roettiers himself smuggled several thousand of these medals to England between 1697 and 1700.[32]

The paintings of the Prince of Wales were all commissioned from François de Troy, who thus replaced Largillière as the principal painter to the Stuart court. His first royal portraits were actually of James II and Mary of Modena, probably exchanged as mutual presents to mark their twenty-fifth wedding anniversary in 1698. Then, from 1699 to 1701, Troy painted seven separate portraits of the prince, some of them supplied in multiple copies which were no doubt partly the work of his assistant Alexis-Simon Belle, and perhaps also of Jacob van Schuppen. Troy also painted two portraits of Princess Louise-Marie, to be used as pairs with those of the Prince.[33] As before, these portraits were given away as diplomatic gifts[34] and sent to England and Scotland, while two of the portraits of the prince and one of the princess were also engraved. It was one of the portraits of the prince which was not engraved, probably painted to mark his thirteenth birthday in June 1701, which deliberately recalled Troy's earlier portrait of the duc d'Anjou.

It is difficult to assess the impact of the widespread distribution of all these medals, paintings and engravings during the period 1697–1702, when England and France were at peace. Much depends on one's opinion as to

[30] Ruvigny, *Jacobite Peerage*, 247.

[31] N. Woolf, *The Medallic Record of the Jacobite Movement* (London, 1988), 46–8. The medals all show the Prince of Wales/James III facing left, but on coins Roettiers showed him facing right because those of James II had faced left.

[32] Nairne, 19 January 1698; HMC *Bath* III, 400, Macky to Jersey, 9/20 April 1700; Cole, *Memoirs*, 146, 195, 270, Manchester to Jersey, 19 June 1700, 18 August 1700, 22 December 1700; *CSPD: William III, 1700–02* (London, 1937), 136, Head to Vernon, 27 October 1700.

[33] Corp, *King over the Water*, 37, 40–4, 106.

[34] HMC *Stuart* I, p. 135, Mary of Modena to Count Alessandro Caprara, February 1699; BL Add. MSS 28224, f. 33, Mary of Modena to Caryll, 21 September 1699; *Inventario dos bens da Rainha da Gra-Bretanha, D. Catarina de Bragança*, ed. Virginia Rau (Coimbra, 1947), 83.

FIG. 21. François de Troy, *James II*, 1698 (137 × 106 cm, Barrett-Lennard Collection).

the strength of the Jacobite movement within England and Scotland. There seems little doubt, however, that by the time James III succeeded his father in September 1701 his image had become familiar to a very large number of people within Great Britain.

The death of James II resulted in the production of many copies of a posthumous portrait of the late king. Since going into exile James II had not wished to be painted very often, preferring to maintain the public image created for him in England by Largillière and other artists before his nervous

FIG. 22. François de Troy, *Mary of Modena*, 1698 (137 × 106 cm? later reduced to 99 × 79 cm, Sizergh Castle).

breakdown in November 1688. In order to provide a permanent royal presence in the antechamber of his apartment at Saint-Germain he had commissioned Largillière in 1691 to paint a family group showing him with the queen and the prince. This had been replaced in 1694 by a second family group, including Princess Louise-Marie, painted by Pierre Mignard.[35] Other than these, the

[35] Corp, *King over the Water*, 35–7. (See the cover.)

only portrait showing James II in exile was the one painted by Troy in 1698. After his death, however, a new engraved portrait was badly needed, and none of these was considered to be appropriate.

Between 1701 and 1703 a series of miraculous cures took place throughout much of France which were attributed to the intercession of the late king,[36] and in June 1702 Archbishop Noailles of Paris instituted proceedings towards his canonisation.[37] The king's confessor, meanwhile, had written a 'Short Relation of the Life and Death of James the Second King of England'. The book was unlikely to appeal to Protestant readers in Great Britain, even after it had been amended by Caryll, Nairne and Innes, but Mary of Modena felt it would make a useful contribution to the canonisation of her husband and to the maintenance of the Jacobite cause in Catholic Europe. She therefore ordered that it should be translated into French and submitted to the well-known Jesuit François Bretonneau.[38] When it was finally published in 1703, it was attributed to Bretonneau, but entitled *Abrégé de la Vie de Jacques II, roy de la Grande-Bretagne . . . tiré d'un écris anglois du R.P. François Sanders . . . Confesseur de S.M. . . . avec un recueil des sentiments du mesme roy sur divers sujets de piété.*[39] It was for the frontispiece of this book that a new engraved portrait was needed.

The queen selected the full-length portrait which had been painted by Sir Godfrey Kneller in 1684–85, at the time of James II's accession to the throne.[40] The original portrait was not available, but it had been engraved by John Smith, and Mary decided that that engraving should provide the image for the frontispiece. The task was entrusted to Gérard Edelinck, whose engravings of the Stuart portraits by Largillière and Troy were the best which had been published. Edelinck's new engraving showed a bust of James II wearing the Garter sash over armour and looking to his left, thus reversing Kneller's portrait in which he looks to his right. This posthumous image, inspired by the first portrait to show James II as king, was copied in oils during the years which followed, in most cases being reversed again to show

[36] B. and M. Cottret, 'La Sainteté de Jacques II, ou les Miracles d'un roi defunt (vers 1702)', in Corp, *L'Autre Exil*, 79–106.

[37] G. Scott, ' "Sacredness of Majesty": the English Benedictines and the Cult of James II', *Royal Stuart Papers* XXIII (Huntingdon, 1994).

[38] Corp, 'Inventory', 129.

[39] Mary of Modena's letter of 20 March 1703 to Mère Gobert announced that 'l'abrégé de la vie du Roy est enfin achevé': *Stuart Papers*, ed. F. Madan, 106, no. 91 See also 112, no. 95, Mary of Modena to Mère Priolo, 9 April 1703 (wrongly dated as November), sending her six copies of the book.

[40] National Portrait Gallery no. 666.

the king as originally represented by Kneller.[41] In all these copies James II is shown wearing armour.

Several years later, in 1712–13, a new set of copies was produced by Alexis-Simon Belle, in which the king is shown instead wearing a breastplate which, although anachronistic, is identical to the one worn in the portraits of James III painted at the same time.[42] The similarity of these portraits had the same purpose as in the 1690s: to refute the 'warming-pan myth' in both England and Scotland. At the French court, however, no such refutation was necessary. The duchesse d'Orléans asked in May 1706: 'Can you possibly believe that our King of England is a suppostious child and not his mother's son? . . . he is as like his mother as two drops of water.'[43] In January 1713, when Belle was painting his posthumous portraits of James II wearing a breastplate, the duchesse commented that 'the young King is too like all his race for his legitimacy to be doubted'.[44]

Of all the painters who worked for the Stuarts at Saint-Germain, Belle was the one who was most closely associated with the court. Born in 1674, he came from a family of Huguenots but had converted to Catholicism.[45] After initial training from his father, a minor portraitist, he had become a pupil of François de Troy and worked as the latter's principal assistant at Saint-Germain between 1699 and 1701.

Belle's first independent work for the Stuart court, a double portrait of the Prince of Wales and his sister, was painted in 1699. His second, a portrait of the prince, dates from 1700.[46] Painting these portraits of his own composition, as well as copying those of Troy, kept Belle so busy at Saint-Germain that when he won the *Prix de Rome* in August 1700 he preferred to continue his Jacobite commissions than travel to Italy. Troy painted some more Stuart portraits in 1704 and 1711, but he seems to have handed over to Belle this lucrative source of patronage at Saint-Germain in order to concentrate on working

---

[41] Examples are at Sizergh Castle (National Trust); Douai Abbey; and Campion Hall, Oxford. There is a miniature in the National Portrait Gallery, L. 152(15). Two other miniatures which were not reversed are at Drummond Castle and in the Victoria and Albert Museum, M146–1962.

[42] Corp, *King over the Water*, 50–1.

[43] *Letters of Madame*, I, 261, to the Raugravine Amelia-Elisabeth, 20 May 1706.

[44] *Ibid.*, II, 65, to Sophia, Dowager Electress of Hanover, 12 January 1713. This provides an interesting comparison with her earlier opinion, expressed in a letter of 20 September 1696, also sent to the mother of the future George I: 'He is well-built and has beautiful little legs, pretty feet and a grand air. He is not at all like his father or mother, but resembles very much the pictures of his uncle the late King of England, and I am sure that if the English people could see the child they could no longer doubt that he was of Royal birth' (*ibid.*, I, 142).

[45] Biographical details concerning Belle are all taken from Camus, 'Alexis-Simon Belle'.

[46] Corp, *King over the Water*, 44–5.

for the French court at Versailles. In November 1701, when Belle married the miniaturist Anne Chéron, he described himself as 'peintre ordinaire du Roy d'Angleterre'. In 1702 he acquired a house at Saint-Germain and quickly became integrated into the Jacobite community.

The renewal of war in 1702 made it more difficult to smuggle Stuart portraits across the Channel, and resulted both in an increased production of miniatures, supplied by Jacques-Antoine Arlaud, Anne Chéron and Jacqueline de La Boissière,[47] and in three more medallic portraits by Roettiers. The latter were produced in 1704, 1708 and 1712 and all showed James III as a Roman emperor. The reverse of the 1704 medal confidently predicted that Virtue would soon dispel the clouds,[48] whereas the later ones adopted the simple formula of a portrait on the obverse with the inscription 'Cuius est', Whose is this, and a map of the British Isles on the reverse with the single word 'Reddite', Render (unto Caesar that which is Caesar's).[49]

Despite this emphasis on miniatures and medals, new paintings of both James III and his sister were needed as they grew older, and were in fact commissioned nearly every year from 1702 to 1712.[50] Although they attempted to provide the exiled Stuarts with a distinctive image of their own, some of these portraits were clearly intended to invite comparison with a recent one of the duc de Bourgogne, painted by Rigaud in 1702,[51] and with recent ones of the Bourbon princesses.[52]

In both 1702 and 1703 the new portraits of James III were painted by Belle.[53] The second of these two was a particularly significant work, because it showed James full length wearing armour, accompanied by a page, standing beside the Channel. He points with his right hand across the sea, where several warships can be seen, to the cliffs and castle of Dover.[54] The following year Troy was commissioned to provide two new portraits, one of which is a variant of the full-length one by Belle. In Troy's version, James is shown

[47] *Ibid.*, 45–6, 107.   [48] Woolf, *Medallic Record*, 53.

[49] *Ibid.*, 55, 64–5. Roettiers issued several versions of these medals, and one of the 1712 ones had a portrait of Princess Louise-Marie on the reverse. He also produced two sets of coinage, for both England and Scotland, in 1708, with the king's head facing right (*ibid.*, 59).

[50] Corp, *King over the Water*, 45–9.

[51] Iveagh Bequest, Kenwood House, no. 58; Château de Versailles MV.2101.

[52] For example, the portraits by François de Troy of Mademoiselle de Blois (*c.*1690–91) and the princesse de Conti (*c.*1690–91 and *c.*1697), reproduced in Brême, *François de Troy*, 47, 126 and 128.

[53] The first is in Rome and was probably sent there at the time: Corp, *King over the Water*, 45, 106.

[54] The painting was commissioned for the Scots College in Paris, where it still hangs. Nairne's diary entry for 26 December 1703 records the payment: 'I writt to Bel ye painter and to Mr Whytef[ord] and sent them mony.'

three-quarter length without the page. He is still pointing with his right hand to warships in the Channel, but Dover Castle is not visible.[55]

New portraits of James were painted in both 1706 to mark the achievement of his majority at the age of eighteen, and 1708 just before he embarked on the unsuccessful invasion of Scotland. The former was by Belle.[56] The latter, which unfortunately has not survived, was the only Stuart portrait commissioned from Hyacinthe Rigaud.[57] It was not engraved, but copies of a miniature by Arlaud and of the 1706 portrait by Belle were both published in 1708.[58]

Meanwhile three new portraits were painted of Princess Louise-Marie.[59] In 1704, when she was twelve years old, she was painted by Belle. The portrait was exhibited at the Paris *Salon* of that year and was copied several times in the years which followed.[60] In 1710, when she was eighteen years old, she was painted again by Belle. She was shown wearing a crimson cloak over her white satin dress and picking orange blossom from a tree in a large decorated gilt urn on her right-hand side. Finally, in 1711 she was painted by both Troy and Belle. By then she was of marriageable age and a very regular visitor to Versailles and Marly, where she enjoyed taking part in the various balls and other entertainments. The portrait by Belle is interesting because it shows her dressed for one of those balls in masquerade costume.[61]

During these years Belle, who was elected to the *Académie Royale de Peinture et Sculpture* in August 1703, also painted many of the members of the exiled court. His earliest known portraits are of Roger and Thomas, two of the sons of Lady Strickland (Bedchamber woman), and date from 1703.[62] This suggests

[55] Nairne's diary for 9 May 1705 records sending one of Troy's portraits to Scotland.

[56] For the copies sent to Scotland, see Nairne, 11 September 1706: 'I gave H.S. a picture of ye King from him for my Ld Strathmore, and orderd 3 more at Mr Bels to be sent to Scotld.' For other references, see Nairne, 20 September 1706; Hooke, *Correspondence*, II, 177–8, Fleming to Lady Erroll and to Marischal, 16 March 1707; Nairne, 11 September 1707.

[57] It is listed in Rigaud's *Livre de Raison*, ed. J. Roman (Paris, 1919), 137 as a 'buste en armure, tout original'.

[58] Corp, *King over the Water*, 46–7.   [59] *Ibid.*

[60] Copies were made in 1706 (Nairne, 28 May 1706); and some were sent to Scotland in 1707 (Hooke, *Correspondence*, II, 177, Fleming to Lady Erroll, 16 March 1707).

[61] SP 44/131, James III to Contessa Molza, 18 September 1719, 'Per il ritratto della mia povera sorella, di una maniera o altra, glie sara inviato'; SP 46/57, James III to Dicconson, 14 April 1720, 'I would have you send here, without frames, the little round picture of my sister in mascarade, and one of the busts which De Troyes made of her, I think not long before she dyd'; SP 46/112, Dicconson to James III, 6 May 1720, 'I shall as soon as possible send the two pictures of ye late Princess.'

[62] For the locations of the portraits by Belle, see Corp, *King over the Water*, 103, unless otherwise stated.

FIG. 23. Alexis-Simon Belle, *Princess Louise-Marie*, 1710 (135 × 103 cm, Sizergh Castle).

that whereas Troy had painted the Jacobites for several years before he received a commission from the Stuarts, Belle's experience was the reverse.

Once again we are mainly dependent on the chance survival of individual portraits, but there are a few documents which provide additional information about Belle's life and work at Saint-Germain. In particular it is clear from the

FIG. 24. Alexis-Simon Belle, *James III*, 1712 (136 × 107 cm, Government Art Collection).

diary of David Nairne that he and Belle became friends and gave each other reciprocal hospitality.[63] In January 1704 Nairne noted that 'I went to see Mr Bel

---

[63] Nairne, 7 February 1706, 'I gave a supper to Mr Bel and Du Mont'; 11 February 1706, 'I supd at M le Bels'; 16 February 1706, 'I gave a dinner to Dr Wood, Mr bel and his wife, ye Vicaire and Mr Geoghahan'; 8 March 1707, 'I dind with my wife and daughter at Mr bel's'; 7 June 1707, 'I gave a dinner to Mr Gerald Knightly and bell.'

draw Mr Carylls picture.'[64] In 1704 Belle exhibited nine portraits at the *Salon*. In addition to his full-length portrait of James III with a page, and his portrait of Louise-Marie, both already referred to, there were three connected with the Jacobite court. They showed Sir John Gifford (groom of the Bedchamber, and son-in-law of Lord Middleton), Sir Andrew Lee (an Irish officer whose wife, Rose, was a Bedchamber woman to the princess) and the abbé des Viviers (chaplain of the Chapel Royal). These portraits are all lost, as also is one of Henrietta, daughter of Lady Sophia Bulkeley (lady of the Bedchamber), which is referred to in one of the letters of Anthony Hamilton.[65]

Apart from these we only know about the portraits which happen to have survived. There is an attractive one of an unidentified lady,[66] another of Bernard Howard of Glossop (equerry) and two versions of a portrait of the Duke of Berwick. The fact that there are also three portraits of English Augustinian nuns[67] suggests that Belle was employed by the exiled Jacobites to paint their relations beyond the court itself. Belle was kept so busy by the Jacobite community that from 1705 he was able to invest annually in the government *rentes*. By 1706 he seems to have been employing a small *atelier* to help him meet the steady demand for portraits.[68]

Belle's most famous work, another portrait of James III, was painted in 1712 during the negotiations for the Treaty of Utrecht.[69] It showed James standing three-quarter length inside a tent, and quickly became the standard image of the exiled King. It was copied several times by Belle himself and engraved by François Chéreau (whose plate described Belle as 'peintre de S.M. Brit'). It was also frequently copied by other artists in the years which followed, in both paintings and engravings. James is shown wearing a breastplate over his coat and resting his outstretched left hand on a helmet. His right arm is placed on his hip, beside the blue sash and Lesser George of the Garter. As with all his other portraits, no crown or other indications of royalty are to be seen anywhere. James thus made it clear that he was prepared to await the eventual

---

[64] Nairne, 4 January 1704. This refers to a lost portrait of John Caryll (gentleman usher of the Privy Chamber), a nephew of Lord Caryll.

[65] *Œuvres de Hamilton*, I, 454–5, Hamilton to Henrietta Bulkeley, 17 November 1705, 'le portrait que Le Bel fit de vous pendant que vous fricassiez de la fleur d'orange.'

[66] Camus, 'Alexis-Simon Belle', 59, fig. 66 (National Gallery of Ireland).

[67] *Ibid.*, 32 (The Vyne, National Trust); 59, fig. 67 (private collection); Sotheby's, 1995 (private collection).

[68] See note 56.

[69] Corp, *King over the Water*, 49–51. The portrait was apparently painted, and subsequently engraved, at the suggestion of Lewis Innes. See B. M. Halloran, *The Scots College Paris, 1603–1792* (Edinburgh, 1997), 83, L. Innes to W. Stuart, 13 February 1713.

death of Queen Anne, but that a military solution would be necessary if no peaceful Jacobite restoration could be achieved thereafter.

It is unfortunate that so little documentary evidence has survived to explain in more detail either the circumstances in which the portraits were produced or, more particularly, to whom they were given or sent. The survival of pictures in private collections can give us some clues, but all too often the surviving portraits have changed hands since they were originally painted. However, the failure to attribute and identify Stuart portraits, which is normally such a disadvantage, has in one case proved particularly instructive. The debate which for a long time has divided historians as to the extent, if any, of Marlborough's commitment to a Jacobite restoration after the death of Queen Anne has over-looked the existence at Blenheim Palace of a particularly revealing miniature. It shows the 1st Duke of Marlborough standing beside James III and pointing to a document which the king is holding in his left hand. The portrait of James is clearly based on the 1712 portrait by Belle, but it has been wrongly identified as showing the 3rd Earl of Sunderland[70] – the reason, presumably, why this incriminating miniature was not destroyed long ago!

It may be assumed that most of the portraits of the Jacobites at Saint-Germain were destroyed through choice, accident or neglect long ago. As a result we have no portraits of many of the leading courtiers at Saint-Germain, though in some cases we do have pictures painted before they went into ex-ile.[71] It is particularly unfortunate that we have nothing of Lord and Lady Middleton, Lord Caryll, John Stafford, the Duchess of Melfort or the Duchess of Perth (to name only a few), all of whom played a major role at the exiled court. Even the image of the Duke of Melfort, who is known to have commis-sioned several portraits of himself, has only survived in a small miniature.[72] On the other hand there are unattributed portraits of both John Betham (precep-tor) and John Ingleton (under-preceptor),[73] an unattributed portrait of the 5th Viscount Clare,[74] and a family group which may show Sir William Waldegrave (physician) and his wife Isabella (sister of Giacomo Ronchi, senior almoner to the queen).[75] There is also a portrait of Count Carlo Molza (gentleman usher of the queen's Privy Chamber), painted after his return to

---

[70] Reproduced in S. Reid, *John and Sarah* (London, 1914), opposite 406.

[71] See Corp, *Cour des Stuarts*, 165 for the portrait of Lord Middleton (Kneller), 173 for that of Lady Sophia Bulkeley (after Lely), 177 for that of Lady Strickland (Wissing), and the list on 237 for those of Lord Caryll and Lord Griffin. See also A. Laing, *In Trust for the Nation: Paintings from National Trust Houses* (London, 1995), 24, for the portrait of the Marchioness (later Duchess) of Powis (Huysmans: 'the *ne plus ultra* of Baroque portraiture in Britain'); and *Revue de la Bibliothèque Nationale* 46 (hiver 1992), 47 for the portrait of Francis Plowden.

[72] Belton House (National Trust). See Fig. 13.   [73] Corp, *Cour des Stuarts*, 140–1.

[74] *Ibid.*, 189.   [75] Corp, *King over the Water*, 102–3.

Modena in 1718 by Giuseppe Maria Crespi,[76] one of David Nairne, painted by Belle in 1714 when the court was in Bar-le-Duc,[77] and another of Anthony Hamilton, painted by Belle later the same year at Saint-Germain.[78] Finally there are two particularly fine portraits of the Duke of Berwick and the Duke of Perth. In the former, painted in 1708 by Rigaud, Berwick is shown as a *Maréchal de France*, wearing the blue sash of the *Saint-Esprit* and red ribbon of the *Toison d'Or*, with the citadel of Nice in the background, in a composition originally created for the dauphin.[79] In the latter, painted by Largillière in 1706, Perth is shown wearing the blue sash and star of the Garter.[80] Another portrait shows Perth wearing the robes of the Order of the Garter in 1714.[81]

It would be a mistake, however, to assume that painting at the court of Saint-Germain only involved portraits, even though it is very difficult to know what other pictures were displayed there. In this context the collection of the Duke of Perth is worth mentioning. In 1689 he had entrusted his seventy-two paintings to his sister (Lady Erroll) at Slains Castle,[82] but in May 1707 he had them all sent to him at Saint-Germain.[83] We do not know what they were, but the arrival of so many pictures must have considerably altered the appearance of Perth's apartment. His brother, the Duke of Melfort, had had an even larger collection in England, which was confiscated and auctioned in 1693,[84] but since coming into exile had assembled a second one. He began it while he was in Rome in 1689–91 and added to it after his return to Saint-Germain.

---

[76] Corp, *Cour des Stuarts*, 237.

[77] For the identification of this portrait as David Nairne, previously believed to show Lord Nairne, see Corp, 'Berwick', 59. See also David Nairne's letter of 1 December 1717, written nearly three years later, when he gave away a copy to Cardinal Gualterio: 'Je suis honteux du petit portrait que Milord Edward [Drummond] vous aura donné de ma part. C'est une copie de la dernière qui a été faite de cette sorte, et je n'en ay point d'autre, car du reste ce n'est plus en effet mon portrait' (BL Add. MSS 31260, f. 233). (See Fig. 18.)

[78] Corp, *King over the Water*, 103.   [79] Corp, 'Berwick'.

[80] Corp, *King over the Water*, 103. Traditionally dated 1714, but for no apparent reason, the portrait was almost certainly painted in 1706 when Perth was given the Garter (see Fig. 15). It inspired Largillière's portrait of Jean Pupil de Craponne in 1708, reproduced in *Visages du grand siècle*, exhibition catalogue (Nantes and Toulouse, 1997), 66.

[81] Corp, *King over the Water*, 103. It is a copy after Belle, previously on loan to the Scottish National Portrait Gallery, but sold by Christie's, Edinburgh, 1 November 2001, lot no. 5.

[82] BL Add. MSS 19254, ff. 79–81. The paintings are listed, but only the portraits (of Charles I, Charles II, Lord Balcarres, Lord Dunfermline, John Dryden and Perth's own family) can be identified.

[83] Hooke, *Correspondence*, II, 282, Lady Erroll to Perth, undated (May 1707).

[84] See note 10; and *Calendar of Treasury Books, 1693–96*, x, part 1 (London, 1935), 54, 60, 246, 248, 273, 297, 303.

The detailed narrative of Melfort's embassy to Rome[85] records the acquisition of two paintings by Francesco Albano and one by Guido Reni, both
Bolognese artists, three by Pietro da Cortona and one by Pier Francesco
Mola, both based in Rome, and one by the itinerant Caravaggio. This eclec-
ticism suggests that Melfort's aim was to collect canvases by the great Italian
painters of the early and mid-seventeenth century. But he also commissioned
portraits of both himself and his wife from Carlo Maratta, the leading portraitist in Rome at that time, from Henri Gascars, who had previously worked
in England, and from Francesco Trevisani, the latter still relatively unknown.
Melfort frequently visited Trevisani's studio and purchased from him a *Blind
Belisarius Receiving Alms*, believed to have been painted by Van Dyck, though
now recognised as the work of the Genoese painter Luciano Borzone.[86]

Melfort's pictures were all brought back to the Château de Saint-Germain
in the autumn of 1691 and installed in his apartment.[87] However he left behind
him a considerable amount of money which he entrusted to two agents for
the purpose of acquiring further pictures, sending out more money as and
when it was needed.[88] In November 1693 he decided to stop, saying that he
was not satisfied with the recent ones he had received,[89] but it may be that
by then he had started purchasing pictures by French artists or merely that
there was no more space in his apartment.

The Melforts occupied the large apartment in the east wing of the château,
on the first floor immediately below that of the queen. It had been created in
the 1670s by Louis XIV for the marquise de Montespan, and contained carved
wall decorations by Philippe Caffieri and Matthieu Lespagnandelle beneath
richly painted ceilings by Nicolas Loir.[90] It was in this setting that Melfort
hung his collection of Italian paintings and provided the exiled court with a
display and magnificence that attracted and impressed visitors from Versailles
and Paris.

After his fall from power in 1694 Melfort had to remove all his pictures from
the château, but he eventually took an apartment in the Hôtel de Soissons,
near Saint-Eustache, described as 'la plus noble [maison] dans le royaume'

[85] Nairne, various dates between 10 January and 1 September 1691.
[86] It was sold by the Duchess of Melfort to Lord Burlington in April 1714 and is now at
Chatsworth (Corp, 'Clandestine Support', 11).
[87] Nairne recorded that one picture was stolen on 14 January 1692.
[88] SCA, BL 1/140/9, Melfort to Lesly, 17 December 1691; 1/153/1, Melfort to Lesly, 7 January
1692; 1/166/17, Nairne to Lesly, 15 June 1693.
[89] SCA, BL 1/166/21, Nairne to Lesly, 16 November 1693.
[90] *Louis XIV à Saint-Germain*, 116, 132–3.

after the Louvre,[91] and for a long time an important centre of Italian influence in Paris. While he was there Melfort himself took up painting as a pastime. None of his works is known to have survived, but he thought sufficiently highly of them to send several to his sister in Scotland as a present.[92]

In December 1712 Melfort was obliged to give up his apartment when the Hôtel de Soissons was allocated to be the new British embassy in Paris.[93] He therefore moved to occupy 'la plus belle maison de la rue des Petits Augustins' (now the rue Bonaparte), where he opened to the public his large collection, described as 'un des plus beaux et des plus riches qui se puissent souhaiter'.[94] Although not strictly part of the Stuart court in exile, Melfort's home in Paris was a place to which many members of the court frequently went, and where they were able to appreciate his pictures. It is probable that smaller collections were meanwhile assembled by the Jacobites who lived at Saint-Germain itself,[95] but the only paintings other than portraits for which we have documentary evidence are the ones belonging to Louis XIV in the Chapel Royal.[96]

[91] Germain Brice, *Description de la ville de Paris*, 9th edition (Paris, 1752), I, 478.

[92] Hooke, *Correspondence*, II, 283, Lady Erroll to Melfort, 29 May 1707.

[93] Sourches, XIII, 549, 15 December 1712; Dangeau, XIV, 282 and 323, 21 December 1712 and 13 January 1713. (The ambassador was Lord Middleton's nephew, the Duke of Shrewsbury.) Melfort had originally rented his apartment from the prince de Carignan, but the latter had forfeited the Hôtel de Soissons in September 1711 as a punishment for serving against France in the army of the Duke of Savoy (Dangeau, xiii, 488, 29 September 1711).

[94] Brice, *Description de la ville de Paris*, 6th edition (Paris, 1713), III, 168–70, 385. It contained Borzone's *Blind Belasarius* and Luca Giordano's *Acis and Galatea*, both of them now at Chatsworth; a *Deposition of Christ* by Caravaggio and *King Priam at the Fall of Troy* by Pietro da Cortona, both of them probably brought back from Rome; a copy of the *Aldobrandini Marriage*, and paintings by or after Michelangelo and Pinturicchio. There were also drawings by Polidoro, and portraits by both Rembrandt and Van Dyck. In addition there were a 'quantité d'autres excellentes pièces des maîtres les plus illustres', among which there must have been several portraits of the Stuart royal family in exile and no doubt of the Duke and Duchess of Melfort themselves.

[95] Lord Caryll had portraits 'of the late King, the Princess and his present Majesty's in round gilt frames with a small one of his Ma.ties when young' (BL Add. MSS 28250, f. 229); Mary Anne Delabadie (sempstress to the queen) possessed one portrait of Charles II, two of James II, one of Mary of Modena, one 'roi equestre', and two ovals of James III and Princess Louise-Marie (AN Etude XVII, liasse 549). Lady Strickland had one portrait of Charles II (probably copied by Belle), one of James II (Belle after Edelinck), one of Mary of Modena (Troy), two of James III (Belle or Van Schuppen; Belle), one of the princess (Belle); one of Queen Margaret of Scotland (Largillière), one each of her sons Roger and Thomas (Belle), and one of the abbé Gaultier (Belle) (*Sizergh Castle Guidebook*, National Trust (London, 2001)).

[96] See above, pp. 96–7, 99.

It is not known if Louis XIV acquired any portraits of the Stuarts. None is mentioned in his inventories of 1706–10,[97] but he was probably given a portrait of James III when the latter moved to Bar-le-Duc in 1713, at the same time as Mary of Modena commissioned for her son a copy of the famous 1700 state portrait of Louis XIV by Rigaud.[98] Portraits may well have been exchanged with other members of the French royal family, notably with Philip V after he had gone to Spain, but no evidence of this has survived, and the Stuart portraits which are still in the Spanish royal collection all date from a later period.[99] All that is known for sure is that the duc d'Orléans, whose first wife had been James II's youngest sister Henriette-Anne, owned the version of the triple portrait of the first three children of Charles I by Van Dyck, which had originally belonged to Queen Henrietta Maria. During the 1690s he either sold or gave it to James II.[100]

Like the other royal and princely courts of the late seventeenth and early eighteenth centuries, the Stuart court at Saint-Germain was a major centre of artistic patronage. The acquisition of prestigious canvases and the commissioning of new portraits were not in themselves surprising. What is interesting about the exiled court is the extent to which it chose to patronise the leading portrait painters of the time. The Stuarts themselves needed an unusually large number of portraits for political reasons – to refute the 'warming pan myth', to stimulate loyalty, to circulate the image of James III to the people of England and Scotland who could not otherwise see him, and to indicate that the real English court was not at Whitehall, or St James's Palace, or elsewhere in and around London, but at Saint-Germain. The Jacobite courtiers needed portraits for domestic reasons – as a means of remaining in touch with the members of their families from whom they found themselves separated for an unexpectedly long period of time. These two factors ensured that for over twenty

---

[97] AN o/1/1971, 1972, 1974. According to these inventories, Louis possessed no paintings by either Largillière or Belle, only one by Troy (a portrait of the dauphine), two by Rigaud (the 1700 portraits of Louis himself and Philip V), one by Gennari (a *Sainte Famille avec Sainte-Anne*, given him by the painter in 1691), and two by Lely (a *Mary Magdalene* and a portrait of the Duchess of Portsmouth). But the inventories may not be reliable. The 1706–8 inventory lists twenty-six pictures by Trevisani, whereas that of 1709–10 lists only one.

[98] *Stuart Papers*, ed. Madan, 462, 'memoirs historiques relatifs à S.M. la Reine d'Angleterre: suite', 17 July 1713.

[99] Corp, *King over the Water*, 59, 61. In 1713 Mary of Modena was brought portraits of the Duke and Duchess of Lorraine by Gobert (*Stuart Papers*, ed. Madan, 440, 'memoirs historiques relatifs à S.M. la Reine d'Angleterre: suite', 12 August 1713).

[100] PRO 78/128, inventory of the possessions of Queen Henrietta Maria at Colombes, 31 October/ 5 November 1669; Brotherton Library, University of Leeds, MS Dep. 1984/2/5, inventory of the possessions of James II at Saint-Germain-en-Laye, 22 July 1703.

years the court at Saint-Germain remained of considerable artistic importance. The Stuart and Jacobite portraits conformed to the ideals and standards
which were prevalent in France at the time, most noticeably those showing
the royal family, which were deliberately intended to invite comparison with
the contemporary portraits of their Bourbon cousins. Thus the Stuart court
did not influence the style of French portraiture, a fact which was emphasised
by the early departure of Gennari. The court's influence, if anything, was the
reverse, bringing the French portraits of Largillière, Troy and Belle to the
attention of large numbers of British people, who were encouraged to employ
the same or similar artists when the return of peace enabled them once more
to travel abroad to Paris.

CHAPTER EIGHT

The court as a centre of Italian music

The cultural importance of the Stuart court at Saint-Germain was not restricted to the patronage of portrait painters. The exiled English court was also an important centre of Italian music in France, where it had a decisive influence on the development of musical taste by helping to introduce and popularise Italian styles during the 1690s.[1]

When James II came to the throne in 1685, the king's musicians at Whitehall were divided into three departments: the Anglican Chapel Royal; a group of singers and instrumentalists known as 'His Majesty's Private Musick'; and a group of trumpeters and drummers who provided the music for ceremonial occasions. In addition to these three bodies, all inherited from Charles II, there were several musicians and priests who served in the Catholic chapel of the queen at St James's Palace.

Because James II did not wish to attend the Anglican Chapel Royal, he commissioned the construction of a new Catholic chapel at Whitehall, to be staffed by an additional group of musicians, specially employed for the purpose, under the direction of a new master of the music. This was Innocenzo Fede, recruited in Rome during the embassy of John Caryll from 1685 to 1686. Fede had a tenor voice, was an experienced organist and had already served as *maestro di cappella* in one of the churches in Rome. When he arrived in London in the summer of 1686 he was about twenty-five years old. At Whitehall, where he worked for two years, he built up a large group of seventeen instrumentalists, one organist and over twenty singers, including eight boy sopranos under their own master. He probably also collaborated with the musicians of the queen's chapel, as both groups contained a significant number of Italians.

In addition to his duties in the Catholic chapel, Fede performed in secular court concerts, most notably in June 1688 when he composed the music for the public concert on the River Thames to celebrate the birth of the Prince of Wales. In February 1689 Fede left England, accompanied by the Italian

---

[1] Corp, 'Centre of Italian Music', 216–31. The following paragraphs are based on that article, except where shown.

organist and one of the Italian instrumentalists from the king's Catholic chapel, and joined the court at Saint-Germain-en-Laye.

By the time Fede arrived there, James II had already left for Ireland. He therefore entered the service of Mary of Modena, who gave him a monthly pension, and began to employ him as her master of the music. At first all arrangements were regarded as temporary. It was not until James II returned in the summer of 1690 that the musical establishment, like the rest of the royal household, was organised on a more permanent basis.

There was a small but significant group of other musicians who had followed the king and queen into exile. They included several members of the king's Catholic chapel, the entire establishment of the queen's chapel and some of the ceremonial musicians. There was only one person from the 'Private Musick', and no one from the Anglican Chapel Royal, the departments which had contained Henry Purcell and his circle.

It is impossible to say how many musicians were at the court of Saint-Germain, because most of them seem to have been employed as and when they were needed, and are not therefore shown in the surviving lists of the members of the royal household. Moreover, the series of lists is incomplete, so a musician might have come and gone without his presence being recorded. But the lists contain enough names to make it clear that the Chapel Royal was particularly well served. In addition to the ten members who had previously worked in the queen's chapel at St James's Palace,[2] there was Fede himself and Gian-Battista Casale, the organist from the king's Catholic chapel at Whitehall. Another member was the French composer and oboe player Jacques Paisible, who had also worked in the new Catholic chapel, and was married to the singer Mary Davis, one of Charles II's ex-mistresses. Paisible and his wife came to Saint-Germain in 1689, and remained there until 1693.[3]

Of the ceremonial musicians employed in England, four of the sixteen trumpeters, and the only kettledrummer, had all come to Saint-Germain and now received permanent salaries.[4] Four other musicians are shown in the household lists. The Bavarian Abraham Baumeister had worked at Whitehall

[2] They were Marco Antonio Galli, Nicolas La Croix, Claude Mansuet, Anthony Naish, Giacomo Ronchi, Peregrino Ronchi, Bartolomeo Ruga, Bernardino Sachelli, Francesco Sachelli and Dominic White. They are all included in Andrew Ashbee and David Lasocki, *A Biographical Dictionary of English Court Musicians, 1485–1714*, 2 vols (Aldershot, 1998).

[3] Michel Antoine, 'De quelques musiciens nommés Paisible', *Recherches sur la Musique Française Classique* 15 (1975), 96.

[4] They were Michael Meyer, Nicholas Meyer, Louis du Monninx and Peter Monsett (trumpeters), and Joseph Nosetto Dumont (kettledrummer). They are also included in Ashbee and Lasocki, *Biographical Dictionary*.

as both a Gregorian and an instrumentalist. The French dancing master Jean Faure,[5] first employed in 1693 to teach the Prince of Wales, was a violinist. John Abel, a versatile Scot who was not only a counter-tenor but also a composer, lutenist and violinist, worked at the court until 1695. Finally Thomas Heywood, who had been a member of the 'Private Musick', was a tenor. Heywood was an Anglican and presumably never performed in the Chapel Royal, but he was appointed page of the Bedchamber to James II and then to Mary of Modena, for whom he could perform privately.

Of the forty-five members of the king's Catholic chapel at Whitehall, only those mentioned above are shown in the Saint-Germain household lists. But as only six took service with William III, it is possible that many more may have gone into exile. It is known, for example, that three of the eight boy sopranos were at Saint-Germain with their parents, and that François de Prendcourt, who had been master of the children at Whitehall, applied unsuccessfully to be given a post at Saint-Germain in 1697.[6]

In addition to these professional musicians, there were also several gifted amateurs, all of them capable of performing in public concerts. These included Sir William Waldegrave (the King's physician), who was a skilful player of the lute, John Caryll (the former ambassador at Rome and now joint secretary of state), who played the viol, and David Nairne (his under-secretary), who played the bass viol, the violin and the flute.

As was normal at other royal courts, there was a great deal of music to be heard at Saint-Germain. In the first place there were frequent and probably daily performances of motets and *sonate da chiesa* in the chapel. Secondly there was the music provided by the trumpeters and kettledrummer for formal ceremonial occasions, perhaps mainly out of doors.[7] There was also dance music to accompany the regular court balls, some of which celebrated the birthdays of the king, the queen, the prince and the princess, and table music for the royal family's formal dinners and suppers.[8] Finally there were court

---

[5] Jean Faure had been one of the most celebrated dancers at the *Académie Royale de Musique* during the 1670s and 1680s (Madame de Sévigné's letter of 6 May 1676, quoted in Jérome de La Gorce, *L'Opéra à Paris au temps de Louis XIV* (Paris, 1992), 56; Dangeau, 1, 70, 13 November 1684).

[6] Corp, 'Prendcourt'. His request was rejected, partly because he had previously criticised the Italian music which Fede performed, though mainly because he had spent over seven years in the Bastille on a charge of spying for William III.

[7] The trumpeters and kettledrummer perhaps took part in the ceremony proclaiming James III as king in September 1701: 'What was done in the town was in a tumultuous manner, by crying, Long Live James the Third, etc.' (Cole, *Memoirs*, 419, Manchester to Vernon, 17 September 1701).

[8] David Nairne recorded on one occasion that he heard 'a Welsh harper' at the prince's supper (3 August 1698).

concerts. In addition to those in the royal apartments, we know that some were organised by John Caryll and that a weekly series was given by Francesco Riva (master of the queen's robes).

As James II grew older he seems gradually to have withdrawn himself from the social life of the court, and perhaps even to have discouraged musical performances, but things changed after his death in September 1701. From the spring of 1702 onwards there was a sudden and marked increase in the musical life of the court.

Our only source of information is the diary of David Nairne, which does not consistently refer to musical matters. Nairne did not live in the château and was much too busy to participate in all the concerts. But his diary does provide us with some information about the numbers of performances. For example, he refers to seven concerts in an eight-week period in the spring of 1702. The following winter he mentions thirty concerts in a twenty-week period, ending in March 1703. Details are sparse. But comments that 'we had a fine voice', 'there was a great assembly' or 'there was a great consort with trumpets, and hautbois and basseson' confirm that these were sometimes large-scale concerts and that the court therefore employed numerous local French musicians.

There was also a great increase in the number of court balls after 1702: every June to celebrate the birthdays of the young king and his sister; and others throughout the carnival season. Nairne mentions seven during an eleven-week period at the beginning of 1707, and six during the seven weeks at the beginning of 1708 which immediately preceded the attempted invasion of Scotland.

This increased musical activity enhanced the status and reputation of Innocenzo Fede. He and Baumeister were both given an increase to their pensions before 1703. That year also saw the publication in Amsterdam of some of Fede's flute sonatas, useful testimony to his growing reputation.

In addition to all these musical activities, the Château de Saint-Germain contained the finest court theatre in France, used by Louis XIV to put on Lully's *comédies-ballets* in the 1660s and his *tragédies-lyriques* in the 1670s. James II had disapproved of theatrical performances, so it was probably not used very much during the 1690s. In one of the old king's 'Papers of Devotion' appears the following comment: 'as for Balls, Operas, [and] plays, the best are dangerous, and not very proper, for such as have a mind to live well, and therefore ought to be avoided by such'.[9] James III, however, enjoyed them, and had begun to attend them at the court of Louis XIV. The new king and his sister were

---

[9] Godfrey Davies (ed.), *The Papers of Devotion of James II* (London, 1925), 73.

therefore keen to use the theatre. Mary of Modena was troubled by this, and in 1702–3 consulted the Jesuit Père Bourdaloue, who advised her that her children should be allowed to attend operatic performances, so long as they did not do so too frequently, and so long as care was taken over the selection of the scenes. From then on the theatre seems to have been used regularly. The performances were on a reduced scale, as was often the case at Marly and Versailles. One work which was probably performed was Charpentier's sacred opera *David et Jonathas*, the libretto of which had been written by Père Bretonneau, the author of the *Abrégé de la vie de Jacques II*.[10] After a few years, when the theatre needed to be restored in 1709, it was Alexis-Simon Belle who was employed to redecorate it.

Numerous musical manuscripts have recently been identified which can be associated with the Jacobite court, thus giving us a good idea of the repertory performed there. Most of the music is Italian, or composed in the Italian style by French composers. The theatrical and dance music, on the other hand, is all French.[11] The manuscripts, which have been discussed elsewhere,[12] fall into five groups of unequal size and importance. The first is a large group in the handwriting of a single unidentified copyist, referred to for convenience by French musicologists as 'copiste Z'. The second is a collecton of seven volumes of cantatas and sonatas assembled by Fede in 1703–5, to which can be added a related manuscript of sonatas and suites. The third is a volume of vocal *canzoni*[13] and the fourth consists of three large collections of trio sonatas. Finally there is a small collection of English viol music. With so many available manuscripts it is possible not only to draw conclusions about the musical life of the court but also to show that the court influenced the history of baroque music in France.

[10] This is an inference from the presence of Charpentier's overture in the 'Recueil de pièces choisies pour le clavessin', assembled by Charles Babel in 1702. Peter Holman has argued that it was probably copied by Babel in France from an arrangement for short score already there, and brought to England during the period of peace between England and France from 1697 to 1702. See his article 'An English Manuscript of Music by Marc-Antoine Charpentier', *Bulletin de la Société Marc-Antoine Charpentier* 16 (1999), 13–15.

[11] During the 1690s the exiled courtiers introduced the English country dance to the French court, where it was quickly adopted as the *contredanse* (Corp, 'Courtisans français', 55). Delalande composed a *contredanse* as early as 1698, in the *Ballet des fées*, first performed during the visit of James II and Mary of Modena to Fontainebleau in September of that year. Raoul Feuillet published thirty-two *contredanses* in Paris in 1706.

[12] Jean Lionnet, 'Innocenzo Fede et la musique à la cour des Jacobites à Saint-Germain-en-Laye', *Revue de la Bibliothèque Nationale* 46 (hiver 1992), 14–18; and Corp, 'Copiste Z', 37–62. The paragraphs which follow are based on these two articles, except where shown.

[13] University of California at Berkeley MS 118, a collection of forty-five arias and cantatas, discovered since these two articles were published.

The works contained within these manuscript volumes fall into three main categories: vocal and instrumental music for the Chapel Royal, vocal and instrumental music for secular concerts, and operas and ballets for the theatre. This repertory, but particularly the theatrical works, would also have provided the table music for the royal dinners and the dance music for the court balls – though English country dances were also performed at the latter. Most of the sonatas, like the collection of viol music, were brought to Saint-Germain from Whitehall. The rest of the Italian music, with the exception of works composed by Fede himself, was mainly brought from Whitehall or sent to Fede in manuscript from Rome. The music by French composers, on the other hand, whether in the Italian or the French style, was obviously acquired locally, but some of it seems to have been composed especially for the Stuart court.

The music for the chapel includes a substantial number of motets and elevations by Giacomo Carissimi, Giovanni Paolo Colonna and Giovanni Legrenzi, all of whom were established Italian composers of the previous generation. In addition there are all the known *petits motets* of both Jean-Baptiste de Lully and François Couperin. Those by Lully, who died in 1687, had been composed before the arrival of the Stuart court, but the motets of Couperin were written during the 1690s and probably first performed at Saint-Germain. There are also settings of all the 150 psalms by the abbé Abeille, who is known to have been in correspondence with the Jacobite court.[14]

In addition to all these motets, there are about a hundred trio sonatas, many of them specifically *sonate da chiesa* rather than *da camera*. These include the published sonatas of Archangelo Corelli, Giovanni Battista Bassani and Gottfried Finger, as well as a few works by Henry Purcell. The only sonatas not brought from Whitehall are the six early ones by François Couperin, all composed in the early and mid-1690s.

Taken together, these motets and sonatas provide us with a good indication of the music performed in the Chapel Royal at Saint-Germain-en-Laye. We also have two oratorios by Carissimi and one by Marc-Antoine Charpentier, as well as the two organ masses by Couperin. If there are too few of these works to allow us to draw any additional conclusions, they do at least confirm that the repertory was Italian and Italian influenced, and they provide evidence linking Couperin with the Stuart court.

There is an equally large repertory of music which has survived from the secular concerts at Saint-Germain, notably nearly a hundred cantatas, approximately 150 arias and *duetti*, and the *sonate da camera* already referred to. Apart from Fede himself, the composer most frequently represented in these vocal

[14] *Œuvres de Hamilton*, 1, 466, Hamilton to Abeille, undated.

works is Alessandro Scarlatti. The discovery of these cantatas and sonatas is of the greatest significance, because they demonstrate the important influence which the Stuart court had on French musical history. Before 1689 no French composer had written any works in these two forms. The Stuart court then arrived, bringing with it a very large number of sonatas and cantatas, and creating an important centre of Italian music in France. The first Frenchman to write trio sonatas was François Couperin, in the winter of 1691–92. He was followed in the next few years by Sébastien de Brossard, Elisabeth Jacquet de La Guerre and Jean-Ferry Rebel, after which the composition of sonatas by French composers became commonplace. The first ones to be published (by François Duval) appeared in 1704. Meanwhile other French composers, notably Nicolas Bernier, Jean-Baptiste Stück and André Campra, as well as Jacquet de La Guerre, began writing cantatas, of which the first to be published (by Jean-Baptiste Morin) appeared in 1703.[15] During the first decade of the eighteenth century, sonatas and cantatas became extremely fashionable throughout the Paris area, and indeed became the most popular forms for small-scale secular domestic music making. They would no doubt sooner or later have been adopted by the French anyway, but nevertheless the English court at Saint-Germain has the distinction of being the place where they were introduced and where they were popularised amongst French musicians.

There is no evidence, however, that the court exercised any such influence as regards theatrical music. On the contrary, the surviving manuscripts suggest that the ballets and operas performed at Saint-Germain were all French. They include all the ballets of Lully, which had been commercially available in six-volume sets since 1682, four *tragédies-lyriques* (*Thésée* of 1675 and *Atys* of 1676 by Lully; *La Naisance de Vénus* of 1696 by Pascal Collasse and *Hésione* of 1700 by André Campra) and one *opéra-ballet* (*Les Fêtes galantes* of 1698 by Henri Desmarets). Although there must have been other works performed at the court, such as *David et Jonathas*, these manuscripts, which provide a representative sample of the operatic works being performed in France at the time, are sufficient to show that the Stuart court at Saint-Germain enjoyed a varied programme of French theatrical music.

If most of this Italian and French music is already perfectly well known, and some of it regularly performed and recorded, it is important to remember that none of it has ever before been linked with the exiled Stuart court at

---

[15] James Anthony, *French Baroque Music from Beaujoyeulx to Rameau* (London, revised edition, 1978), chapters 21 and 23.

Saint-Germain. Moreover the works composed by Innocenzo Fede himself have remained totally unknown until now. They include twelve arias, three cantatas, three flute sonatas, one violin sonata, one suite for three flutes and two motets,[16] some of them of very good quality.[17] The discovery of these manuscripts has thus enabled us to hear some of the music composed by the man who served as master of the music throughout the period that the English court was in France, and whose compositions presumably reflected the taste of the queen, who was his patron and employer. Indeed, this large collection of Stuart court music casts an interesting light on the different tastes of Mary of Modena and James III. It was the queen who particularly liked Italian music and who employed Fede. Her son, by contrast, increasingly favoured the French *tragédie-lyrique*, *comédie-ballet* and *opéra-ballet*.

Because Mary of Modena did not approve of the French works that she saw at Trianon and Fontainebleau with Louis XIV,[18] it is unlikely that her children became familiar with any of them before the death of James II. The prince was taught the Italian language by Innocenzo Fede himself[19] and from an early age must have heard the Italian music favoured by his mother. But after 1702, when he began to hear and see scenes from the dramatic works of Lully and his successors, he developed his own taste to supplement that of his mother. It is most likely that James III appreciated both French and Italian music and was thus a supporter of 'les goûts réunis'.

---

[16] The surviving works of Innocenzo Fede include: twelve arias: 'Amor fiori un di coglica' for soprano, 'Annodami abbracciami' for bass, 'Ardo sospire e peno' for soprano and bass, 'A torte bella bocca' for two sopranos (or tenors), 'Bellezze voi siete tiranne' for soprano, 'Bell'onde tranquille' for bass, 'La mia vita' for two sopranos, 'Langue geme sospira' for soprano, 'Moriro poichè volete' for soprano, 'Mio contento mio tesoro' for two sopranos, 'Sei pur dolce ò liberta' for two sopranos, 'Vieni ò caro' for soprano. Three cantatas: 'Ardo sospiro e peno' [*sic*] for soprano, 'Presso un fiume tranquillo' for two sopranos (dated 1 May 1699), 'Se ci potesso l'oro' for soprano. Three sonatas for flute, in G minor, D minor and D minor. One sonata for violin, in F minor. One suite for three flutes, in C. Two motets: 'Exurgat Deus' in D major for soprano, contralto, tenor and bass, 'Laudate pueri Dominum' in A minor for four choirs.

[17] Some of these works were performed by Charles Medlam and his ensemble 'London Baroque' in a programme broadcast by Radio 3 on 18 July 1992. The only commercially available recordings (of 'Bellezze voi siete tiranne' for soprano, 'Sei pur dolce ò liberta' for two sopranos, and the sonata for violin in F minor) are included in the CD *Kings over the Water: In the Steps of the Exiled Stuarts* by the ensemble 'Janiculum', released in 2001 (JAN D205).

[18] Mary of Modena saw *Atys* (1690), *Roland* (1691) and *Acis et Galatée* (1695) by Lully; *Enée et Lavinie* (1690) by Collasse; and *Issé* (twice in 1697) and *Amadis de Grèce* (1698) by Destouches. She also saw *Didon* (1693) by Desmarest at the *Académie Royale de Musique* in Paris with the dauphin. These details are given in Dangeau, III, 246, 249, 274; IV, 385; V, 224; VI, 204, 248, 443.

[19] Versailles, Arch. Dépt. des Yvelines, B.537 Saint-Germain, 'liste des officiers de la Reine qui, par suite de son décès, demeurent sans emploi', 1718.

Although no evidence has survived of specific performances at Saint-Germain, we do know that from 1703 James III attended numerous concerts at Marly and Fontainebleau, which must have included extracts from French operas.[20] On one occasion Louis XIV even arranged for him to be greeted in the salon at Marly with 'la symphonie jouant une belle ouverture d'opéra de la façon du fameux Lulli'.[21] James also heard works by Lully and Destouches at Fontainebleau,[22] and attended the *Académie Royale de Musique* in Paris on at least seven occasions between 1706 and 1712, to hear works by Lully, Marais and Collasse.[23] It is significant that when he set off to invade Scotland in March 1708, the composer who accompanied him to Boulogne-sur-Mer, and provided the cantata to celebrate his final departure from French soil, was one who also composed French operas with Italianate touches. This was Jean-Baptiste Stück, whose first opera (*Méléagre*), composed at around the same time, contained a prologue entitled 'l'union de la musique italienne et française'. The cantata he composed for James III was 'Les Festes bolonnoises', scored for violins and trumpet, in which the concluding air ('Que de la Seine à la Tamise, Tout reconnoisse ce héros') expressed the hope that James would soon return from Saint-Germain-en-Laye to the palaces of his father and uncle.[24]

---

[20] Dangeau refers to seven concerts at Marly (19 May 1706; 21 July and 8 November 1707; 3 May and 13 June 1709; 16 October and 12 November 1710) and four at Fontainebleau (15 October 1703; 2, 4 and 10 October 1707). Other concerts at Marly are mentioned by Sourches (12 August 1704; 6 March 1707; 19 December 1709), who also refers to two of the ones mentioned by Dangeau. The relevant volumes of Dangeau are IX, 321; XI, 107, 419, 478, 480; XII, 5, 405, 443; XIII, 262, 280. The references in Sourches are IX, 45; X, 83, 268, 424; XII, 128.

[21] Sourches, X, 268, 6 March 1707.

[22] *Atys* by Lully (5 October 1703); *Le Mariage du Carnaval et de la Folie* by Destouches (14 October 1703); and *Phaëton* by Lully (30 September 1707). In addition to these operas, James III also attended performances of Lully's *comédie-ballets*: *Le Bourgeois Gentilhomme* twice (27 September and 3 October 1707); and *Monsieur de Pourceaugnac* (1 October 1707). The information is given by Dangeau: IX, 312, 320; XI, 472, 476, 478, 479.

[23] Dangeau refers to five visits with the dauphin, to see *Bellérophon* by Lully (14 January 1706), *Roland* by Lully (27 April 1706 and 31 January 1709), *Sémélé* by Marais (30 April 1709) and *Persée* by Lully (4 December 1710). Another visit, to see *Le Ballet des saisons* by Collasse (26 August 1712) is mentioned by Dangeau and others because Lord Bolingbroke was present at the same performance. (Dangeau, XI, 10, 86; XII, 320, 399; XIII, 292; XIV, 215; BL Add. MSS 31258, f. 154, Stafford to Gualterio, 28 August 1712). David Nairne also mentions a visit to see *Alceste* by Lully (11 January 1707). There were probably several other visits. The list of works performed at the *Académie Royale de Musique* during these years is shown in Jérome de La Gorce, *L'Opéra à Paris*, 201–2.

[24] I am grateful to the late Jean Lionnet for this reference. The cantata was included in Stück's fourth *Livre*, published in 1714. It was probably first performed on 8 March 1708, when James III

Works such as this necessitated the employment of outside French musicians, most of whom cannot be identified. Jacques Arnould, a Frenchman who
had worked as a Gregorian at Whitehall, described himself in April 1701 as
'ordinaire de la musique du Roy d'Angleterre',[25] while one François Charvil-
hat, who had lived in Saint-Germain for many years, signed the parish register
in May 1692 as 'Trompete de la Chambre du Roi d'Angleterre'.[26] The lack
of surviving evidence makes it difficult to know how much contact there was
with the musicians at the French court, but it seems to have been considerable. Marin Marais had published his first book of *Pièces de Viol* in 1686
without the continuo parts. In 1689 he issued a supplement containing those
parts, explaining that 'toutes ont été composées pour satisfaire à la demande
de quelques étrangers'.[27] At least three of the French musicians employed at
Versailles continued to own property at Saint-Germain during the Jacobite
period.[28] The organist of the parish church of Saint-Germain was the son
of one of the counter-tenors in the Chapel Royal at Versailles.[29] Fede was
a personal friend of Jacques Le Roy, a member of the *Petits Violons du Roi*
who became the father-in-law of Louis XIV's music librarian, André-Danican
Philidor.[30] Le Roy's close friend Antoine Hardelay (another member of the
Petits Violons)[31] lived in the same street at Saint-Germain as David Nairne and

reached Boulogne-sur-Mer (Dangeau, XII, 93). For Stück's career, and musical style, see the
articles by Jean Duron in *Dictionnaire de la musique en France aux XVIIe et XVIIIe siècles*, ed.
Marcelle Benoit (Paris, 1992), 448; and *The New Grove Dictionary of Opera*, ed. Stanley Sadie, 4
vols. (London, 1992), IV, 589.

[25] BL Add MSS 12592, *quittance de rente*.   [26] Lart, *Parochial Registers*, I, 126.

[27] Corp, 'Couperin and the Stuart Court', 452, note 7. Many of the early *pièces de viol* of Marin
Marais had been acquired during the early 1680s by Nairne's cousin, Lord Panmure, in
manuscript copies also without the continuo parts.

[28] The three musicians were all violinists: Pierre Huguenet, Jacques Delaquièze and Jean-Noel
Marchand (Marcelle Benoit, *Versailles et les musiciens du roi, 1661–1733* (Paris, 1971), 317).

[29] The organist was Pierre Jonquet the younger (died 1727). He was the son of Pierre Jonquet the
elder (died 1735), who was appointed *haute-contre de la chapelle* at Versailles in 1691, but who also
lived at Saint-Germain by 1718 and died there (Benoit, *Versailles*, 276). For Jonquet's original
connections with English Jacobites in 1700–1, see the diary of Thomas Marwood in Catholic
Record Society, *Miscellanea VI, Bedingfield Papers* (London, 1909), 87, 90, 96. The exceptionally
fine organ which he played in the parish church of Saint-Germain, and which is still there, was
built in 1698 by Alexandre Thierry. Jonquet's elder brother was a merchant in Lyons who later
supplied James III in Rome with wine from the Côte-Rôtie (SP 130/184, 131/109, 153/30).

[30] Fede and his wife both became godparents to his son, Innocent Le Roy, on 8 January 1698
(Archives Municipales de Saint-Germain-en-Laye). See also Jean-François and Nicolas
Dupont-Danican Philidor, *Les Philidor, une dynastie de musiciens* (Paris, 1995), 35–6.

[31] Catherine Massip, 'Musique et musiciens à Saint-Germain-en-Laye, 1651–1683', *Recherches sur la
Musique Classique Française* 22 (1984), 136–7.

taught music to the latter's daughter.[32] Nairne was acquainted with both the daughter of the composer Jean-Ferry Rebel and the celebrated soprano Marie Chappe, who sang at the Jacobite court.[33] These facts all suggest that there were important musical links between the two courts. But the most important French musicians with connections at Saint-Germain were Delalande and Couperin.

Michel-Richard Delalande was appointed *Surintendant de la Musique* by Louis XIV in January 1689. His parents both came from Saint-Germain-en-Laye, and both sides of his family continued to live there.[34] The Delalandes were a family of gardeners, responsible for the maintenance of the gardens of the Châteaux de Saint-Germain.[35] On his mother's side, one of the composer's close relations was married to the daughter of Henri Soulaigre, the concierge of the château,[36] responsible for the maintenance of the building itself, both inside and out. Delalande, although born in Paris, was thus closely related to those who had responsibility for maintaining the fabric of the Jacobite court, both château and gardens. He remained in close personal contact with his Saint-Germain relations, and continued to visit them during the Jacobite period.[37] Delalande knew François Couperin and probably introduced him to the Stuart court in 1689 or 1690. But the younger composer was almost certainly already acquainted with David Nairne, and thus may have been introduced by the latter after his return from Rome in 1691.

[32] Nairne, 12 November 1691, 10 June 1702, 22 February 1704; Massip, 'Musique et musiciens' 136, 138, 147–8.

[33] Nairne, 29 July 1706; 29 and 30 August 1707.

[34] The parish registers of the various churches in Paris were destroyed in the Hôtel de Ville during the Commune in 1871. Delalande's father (Michel) was a master-tailor in Paris. His mother was born Claude Dumoutier. They both died in 1684. Both families appear frequently in the parish registers of Saint-Germain-en-Laye throughout the seventeenth century.

[35] The division of the gardens between various members of the family is shown in the *Etat de la France*, and in the volumes of *Comptes des Bâtiments du Roi*.

[36] Louis Dumoutier (brother of Delalande's mother) was a *Huissier de la Chambre* of Louis XIV. His son, also called Louis (Delalande's first cousin), married in 1685 Antoinette Soulaigre. Antoinette's father, Henri Soulaigre, was concierge of the Château-Vieux de Saint-Germain until his death in December 1701. He was succeeded by his son (Antoinette's brother), Henri-Louis.

[37] In the spring of 1691 Delalande lent 5000 *livres* to Louis Dumoutier and his wife Antoinette. The money had been repaid by the end of 1692. The notarial documents providing security for the loan and recording the repayments were signed at Saint-Germain-en-Laye on 4 March 1691, 5 September 1692 and 11 November 1692. They are quoted in *Notes et références pour servir à une histoire de Michel-Richard Delalande*, ed. Norbert Dufourcq (Paris, 1957), 132. Louis Dumoutier is described as *Ordinaire de la Chambre du Roy, fourier des logis de SM*. Given these close personal links, it is surprising to find in the *Revised New Grove Dictionary* (London, 2000), XIV, 139, that 'no firm evidence has yet been adduced to support the assertion of a particular musical connection between Lalande [*sic*] and the exiled Jacobean [*sic!*] Court at Saint-Germain-en-Laye at this time'.

Unlike the other Jacobites at Saint-Germain, Nairne had lived in France since 1676, long before the exile of James II. It is possible that he had partly earned his living during the 1680s by copying music, and that he had frequented the musical circle of the duchesse de Guise, where he would have met Marais, Charpentier and Delalande.[38] Nairne was in Ireland for much of 1689 and then in Rome for the next two years with Lord Melfort, but when he returned in November 1691 he brought back to Saint-Germain a quantity of new Italian music, some of which he had copied in the papal city on the instructions of Lord Melfort.[39] It was shortly afterwards that Couperin, fired with enthusiasm for Italian music, composed his first trio sonatas, and had them performed (anonymously) at the Jacobite court.[40]

This is significant because it seems likely that Couperin, one of the greatest of French composers, was then regularly employed by the Jacobite court from 1692 until 1712.[41] Although he served as the organist in the Chapel Royal at Versailles from January to March each year, he spent most of the rest of his time at Saint-Germain, thus maintaining a permanent link between the musical establishments of the two courts. As with the other musicians hired by the English court, Couperin's activities at Saint-Germain-en-Laye must have been paid for out of the privy purse of the king or the queen, because they have left no trace: he was never made a member of the Stuart household. But Couperin's prominence seems to have posed a threat to Innocenzo Fede, which would explain why in October 1699, over ten years after his arrival in France, Fede obtained from the king a warrant confirming that he was both master of the music of the chapel, and master of the king's private music.[42]

Couperin's employment at Saint-Germain would have included giving harpsichord lessons to James III and his sister, and playing the organ in the Chapel Royal, particularly after the death of Gian-Battista Casale in 1706. But he would also have performed in small chamber concerts for James III, which raises the possibility that some of them may have been similar to the celebrated *concerts royaux* organised for Louis XIV at Versailles in the apartment of Madame de Maintenon after 1712.[43] In September 1713, shortly after James III

---

[38] Corp, 'Centre of Italian Music', 228–9; Corp, 'Copiste Z', 50–1.

[39] Corp, 'Centre of Italian Music', 224–5.   [40] *Ibid.*, 229–30.

[41] Corp, 'Couperin and the Stuart Court', 445–53.

[42] The warrant is in SP Misc. 18. Dated 18 October 1699, it was not copied into the book of warrants by Nairne until 26 November 1699.

[43] Couperin referred to these concerts in the preface to his *Concerts royaux* (1722): 'Je les avois faites pour les petits Concerts de chambre où Louis quatorze me faisoit venir presque tous les dimanches de l'année . . . Je les ay . . . conservé pour titre celuy sous lequel elle étoient connues à la Cour en 1714 et 1715' (cited in Philippe Beaussant, *François Couperin* (Paris, 1980), 250).

had left Saint-Germain, and when Couperin's services there would no longer have been required, we find Mary of Modena writing to Madame de Maintenon that 'je suis bien aise qu'il [Louis XIV] s'ocupe à la musique chés vous, cela lui est necessaire'.[44]

The shortage of documentary evidence makes it very difficult to draw firm conclusions about the musical life of the court at Saint-Germain. We shall never be able to know how frequently Couperin and the other French musicians performed there, or the detailed programmes of sacred and profane music that Fede prepared for the chapel, the royal apartments and the theatre. But of two things there can be no doubt. Music played a very important role in the daily life of the exiled court; and the court itself played an important part in the development of musical taste at Versailles and in Paris.

[44] Bibliothèque Municipale de Versailles, MS 1461, P.67, 505, Mary of Modena to Maintenon, 10 September 1713. (The copy at Versailles is dated 1712, but the rest of the letter shows that it was really written in 1713.)

CHAPTER NINE

Poetry at the exiled court

HOWARD ERSKINE-HILL

Introduction

by Edward Corp

It is not surprising that the Stuart court at Saint-Germain produced a great deal of literature. The need to argue the Jacobite case within the British Isles and to advance it at the other courts of Europe necessitated the publication of a substantial body of political pamphlets (declarations, protestations, manifestos) which were important at the time and which have been given considerable attention by historians.[1] But alongside these overtly political works there were many other writings for which political persuasion was not the main or the only motive. The present chapter will consider the poetry of the court, leaving various works of a religious and educational nature to be discussed later on.

Four poets are known to have followed James II into exile and to have lived at Saint-Germain-en-Laye: Lord Maitland, Anthony Hamilton, Jane Barker and John (later Lord) Caryll. All four were Catholic, and are referred to in this chapter, contributed by Howard Erskine-Hill.[2]

Richard, Lord Maitland was the eldest son of the 3rd Earl of Lauderdale. After serving with James II in Ireland, Maitland followed the king to Saint-Germain in 1690, where he was joined by four of his brothers. He succeeded as 4th Earl of Lauderdale after the death of his father in June 1691. It was while he was still Lord Maitland that he wrote the poetry discussed below.

The Maitland brothers were enemies of the Earl of Melfort, who returned from Rome in November 1691. There were two reasons for this. In the first place their father, the 3rd Earl of Lauderdale, had in 1682 been accused of corruption by Melfort and his brother Perth. He had been found guilty and forced to resign as treasurer-depute of Scotland, his post being given to Melfort. The second reason was that their cousin Sophia Maitland had been Melfort's first

---

[1] See particularly Daniel Szechi, 'The Jacobite Revolution Settlement, 1689–1696', *English Historical Review* 108 (1993), 610–28.

[2] There is evidence that Marco Antonio Galli (1623–1703, confessor to the queen) was also a poet. David Nairne, who made a copy of one of Caryll's poems (see below), recorded that he copied one of the Italian poems of Galli on 3 and 4 November 1699.

wife. After her death he had remarried, and subsequently arranged that all his peerages and estates should pass to the children of his second wife, thereby effectively disinheriting Sophia's children. Melfort's return from Rome, and his emergence as James II's chief minister, was therefore unwelcome to Maitland and his brothers.

Maitland's position was difficult because his Protestant wife, Anne (née Campbell), was the sister of the 10th Earl of Argyll and left Saint-Germain to rejoin her anti-Jacobite family in Scotland. This did not stop James II appointing Maitland to be treasurer-depute of Scotland and creating him a Knight of the Thistle in April 1692, but it was awkward and his position was made more uncomfortable when Lord Middleton, another enemy of his family, arrived at Saint-Germain the following year. Maitland withdrew from the court and settled in Paris, where he began to be suspected by the French authorities of being a spy for William III. Investigations carried out by the police in Paris showed that he was spending a great deal more money than his pension from James II should have allowed. As he claimed to have no other source of income, he was clearly in receipt of a secret income from England or Scotland. Before the matter could be cleared up, he died in June 1695. His brothers, who were equally under suspicion, returned to Scotland two months later.[3]

Anthony Hamilton, by contrast, remained at Saint-Germain, where he seems to have been popular and where he enjoyed the friendship of the Duke of Berwick. He had fought in Ireland before joining the exiled court.[4] He never had a post in the royal household, but his younger brother Richard was a gentleman of the Bedchamber and (after 1696) master of the king's robes. His sister Elizabeth was married to the comte de Gramont, and was a particular favourite of Louis XIV. Unlike many Jacobites, Hamilton spoke and wrote French fluently, having as a young man served in the French army with his

---

[3] Corp, 'James II and Toleration', 12–13; Corp, *Cour des Stuarts*, 201; and the articles by the present author on the 1st Duke of Perth, the 1st Duke of Melfort and the 2nd Earl of Middleton in the forthcoming *Oxford Dictionary of National Biography*. The patent creating Melfort a duke on 17 April 1692 was counter-signed by the 4th Earl of Lauderdale as treasurer-depute (*House of Lords Sessional Papers, 1852–53*, XXVI, 114).

[4] The following paragraphs about Hamilton are based on the introduction to *Stuart Court and Jacobites*, xviii–xix; and the articles by the present author on Anthony Hamilton and Elizabeth, comtesse de Gramont in the forthcoming *Oxford Dictionary of National Biography*. Hamilton was given a pension of 2000 *livres* per annum, later reduced to 1320 *livres* in 1703, but increased to 2200 *livres* by 1717. The *Memoirs* of Sir Richard Bulstrode, 'one of the minor authorities for the history of the great civil war', were also written at Saint-Germain after 1704, but not published (by Nathaniel Mist) until 1721. See C.H. Firth, 'The *Memoirs* of Sir Richard Bulstrode', *English Historical Review* 10, no. 38 (April 1895), 266–75 (the citation is at p. 266).

elder brother George, who had been made a French *comte*. Anthony Hamilton had inherited his brother's title in 1678, whereas his widowed sister-in-law, having remarried, had become the Duchess of Tyrconnell.

At the exiled court Hamilton was on particularly good terms with the Duke of Berwick's second wife Anne (née Bulkeley) and her three sisters Charlotte (Viscountess Clare), Henrietta and Laura (both unmarried), and many of his letters to them have survived. In 1701 he accompanied Berwick on his mission to Rome to obtain the support of the new Pope Clement XI for the Jacobite cause. At the French court Hamilton frequented the circle of the duc and duchesse du Maine, particularly after 1700 when the latter first occupied the Château de Sceaux.

In May 1703 Louis XIV gave Hamilton's sister the use during her life-time of a house near Meudon called 'Les Moulineaux'. In the five years until her death in June 1708 it was much frequented and became the centre of Hamilton's social world. The comtesse de Gramont wished to rename her house 'Pontalie', and this was the inspiration for the first of Hamilton's *contes*, entitled *Le Bélier*. Its aim was to furnish a romantic etymology for the new name, the principal incident being a contest between a prince and a giant for the daughter of a druid. Hamilton produced several other *contes*, including *L'Histoire de fleur d'épine*, satirising the popular imitations of the 'Arabian Nights' Entertainments', which Hamilton described as 'plus Arabe qu'en Arabie', and two which were unfinished, *Les Quatre Facardins* and *Zénéyde*. The first three were published in Paris in 1730, the fourth the following year in a collection entitled *Œuvres mêlées en prose et en vers*. Most of the poems, which seem to have been written during the years 1699 to 1709, are addressed to various 'nymphes de Saint-Germain'. These nymphs included Princess Louise-Marie, Berwick's sister-in-law the Duchess of Albemarle, and the daughters of some of Hamilton's Jacobite friends (Bevil Skelton, Robert Strickland, John Stafford, Lord Melfort and Lord Middleton). Hamilton also included passages of verse in his prose letters, some of which were later published in *Œuvres mêlées en prose et en vers*. They include some charming descriptions of life at the court of Saint-Germain during the years 1702–10.

Hamilton's decision to write the *Mémoires de la vie du comte de Grammont* (*sic*), his brother-in-law, was originally taken in 1704, while the two men were at Séméac in Gascogne, two years before Gramont's death in January 1707. The work was planned in three parts, but only the first two were published. It is not known if the third part was written, although it is promised in all five extant manuscript copies. The first two parts were circulating in manuscript by May 1712, when the duchesse d'Orléans sent a copy to the dowager-electress of Hanover, and they were published anonymously and without authorisation the following year, allegedly at 'Cologne' though probably in reality at Rouen.

The first part of the memoirs contains an entertaining account of Gramont's early life in France, but the work's fame largely rests on the second part. This is concerned with Gramont's life at the court of Charles II between 1662 and 1664, and is based on Hamilton's own experiences as well as the recollections of his friend. It provides a detailed and invaluable description both of the Restoration court and of its leading courtiers, concentrating on their various intrigues and love affairs. It ends when 'the Chevalier de Grammont, as the reward of a constancy he had never before known and which he never afterwards practised . . . was at last blessed with the possession' of Hamilton's sister Elizabeth, whom he married and took back with him to France.

The book was greeted with considerable critical acclaim on account of its brilliance and vivacity. An English translation was published in London in 1714. But it was resented by many at Saint-Germain. Among other things it described in some detail the amorous adventures of James II while Duke of York with the future Countess of Erroll (governess of the Prince of Wales), with Hamilton's sister-in-law the future Duchess of Tyrconnell (lady of the Bedchamber), and with Arabella Churchill (mother of the Duke of Berwick). Berwick himself commented to James III in May 1713 that 'I wonder M. Anthony Hamilton will still be rambling, his age and infirmitys should induce him to be quiet some where with his friends.'[5]

In his last years Hamilton continued to live in the Château de Saint-Germain, where he had an apartment, and where he was looked after by Mrs Lockhart, the widow of a fellow Jacobite. He died unmarried at the age of seventy-four at Saint-Germain on 21 April 1719 and was buried in the parish church.

Hamilton's four *contes* had a considerable influence in eighteenth-century France, particularly on Claude Crébillon (*fils*), who regarded himself as Hamilton's literary heir. His manuscripts, which included the continuation of *Les Quatres Facardins* and possibly also the third part of the *Mémoires de la vie du comte de Grammont*, remained in the Château de Saint-Germain, where they were all burned at the end of 1754. Some works, however, had been copied. Two more *contes* were included in the collected edition of 1776, and two other short works in the collected edition of 1812.

Compared with Hamilton, Jane Barker was then and until recently an obscure figure, who lived on the periphery of the court, with neither a salary nor a pension from the Stuarts. She came from a family of minor gentry, which

---

[5] HMC *Stuart* I, 267, Berwick to James III, 23 May 1713.

had suffered financially from supporting the royalist cause in the English Civil War. Her father held the lease on the manor house and land of Wilsthorpe, near Stamford in Lincolnshire. At some point during the 1680s, when she was in her thirties, Barker moved to London, converted to Catholicism, and was received into her new faith by the Benedictine monks attached to the queen's chapel at St James's Palace. In 1689, after the fall of James II, she fled to France and joined the Jacobite community at Saint-Germain-en-Laye. She remained in exile until 1704, when she finally returned to England.[6]

During these fifteen and a half years Barker divided her time between the Stuart court at Saint-Germain-en-Laye and the convent of English Benedictine nuns at nearby Pontoise. She wrote a considerable amount of poetry, much of which refers to specific and easily dated incidents. In a poem of 1696 she recorded that cataracts in her eyes had recently had to be removed, and that she had become virtually blind. The last of the many poems which can be dated was inspired by her visit to the body of James II in September 1701, 'as it lys at the English Monks', in the monastery of the English Benedictines in Paris. Jane Barker was one of many Jacobites who were given a small piece of rag dipped in the blood of the king immediately after his death. She took it with her when she returned to manage her family estate at Wilsthorpe in 1704.

Back in England, Jane Barker developed a 'cancer' in her breast, which was eventually cured in 1713 after being touched by the king's blood.[7] The same year saw the publication of her first novel, entitled *The Amours of Bosvil and Galesia, as related to Lucasia in St. Germain's Garden*. The name 'Galesia' was adopted by Barker as her semi-autobiographical literary persona, and this was the first of the trilogy of Galesia novels. (It was republished in 1719 with a new title, *Love Intrigues*.) The other two, entitled *A Patch-Work Screen for the Ladies; or, Love and Virtue* and *The Lining of the Patch Work Screen: Design'd for the Further Entertainment of the Ladies*, were published in 1723 and 1726 respectively.

Apart from these novels, all of which are interspersed with poems, Barker also found the time to publish two other books, both inspired by Fénelon: a novel entitled *Exilius; or the Banish'd Roman*, written after the manner of *Télémache*

---

[6] The following paragraphs about Barker are based on the introduction by Carol Shiner Wilson to Jane Barker, *The Galesia Trilogy and Selected Manuscript Poems*, and the review of that book by the present author published in the *Royal Stuart Review 1998*, 9–11. The fullest account of Jane Barker's life and work is now Kathryn R. King, *Jane Barker, Exile: A Literary Career, 1675–1725* (Oxford, 2000).

[7] SP 208/129, Jane Barker to Lady Lucy Herbert, 14 August 1713. The date on the letter in which Barker describes this incident is difficult to decipher, and Wilson and King (like the archivists at Windsor Castle) have assumed that it was written in 1730. I am convinced from internal evidence that it was really written in 1713. (See King, *Barker*, 104.)

(1715); and a translation of some of the archbishop's Lenten meditations, entitled *The Christian Pilgrimage* (1718). She remained an active Jacobite, and eventually in 1727, at the age of seventy-five, returned to live at Saint-Germain-en-Laye, where she died five years later. For an unmarried woman, who had been almost blind since 1696, it was a remarkable career.

The fourth poet at Saint-Germain was John Caryll, who has been referred to frequently in previous chapters and who needs no further introduction here. As secretary to Mary of Modena, and joint secretary of state from 1694 until his death in 1711, he occupied a central position at the court and, as we shall see in chapter 10, was involved in several literary pursuits other than the writing of poetry discussed here.

The Poetic Character of James II

by Howard Erskine-Hill

The poetry at the court of the exiled Stuarts at Saint-Germain-en-Laye is a complex and relatively little known body of work. New investigation is certainly required, in the light of which the present chapter will appear no more than a sketch. This phase of Jacobite poetry may fairly be divided, however, into verse of an epic strain, closely connected with new translations of Virgil; verse that is largely courtly and complimentary; verse that is largely panegyrical in intent but which may be better described as occasional and reflective; and verse that is sceptical and satirical. A dominant theme emerges from most of this work: the character of James II, a man feared, scorned, derided, respected, loved, idealised and, in the third decade of the eighteenth century, the person on whose behalf there was a prolonged attempt to secure beatification from the papacy. Just as in the last major Jacobite rebellion it is the contested character of Prince Charles Stuart that is stamped on that surprising endeavour, so the contested character of James II is stamped upon England's troubles of 1685–88 and before, on the renewed exile of the Stuart dynasty, and on the prolonged civil wars in Scotland and Ireland, which, after his expulsion, *profugus*, to France, asserted his right under the ancient constitution to the throne of his ancestors.

Never himself an exile, John Dryden, Poet Laureate to Charles II and James II, had nevertheless, as will become clear, links enough with the exiled court to be the right starting-point of this chapter. In the new scholarly edition of Dryden[8] one page gives us the close of *Britannia Rediviva*, Dryden's

---

[8] *The Poems of John Dryden*, ed. Paul Hammond and David Hopkins (London, 1995, 2000), hereafter cited as *Poems*.

1688 poem on the birth of the Prince of Wales, the next Dryden's versions of Dr Archibald Pitcairne's heroic epitaph in Latin on the death of Viscount Dundee, killed on the very field of his Jacobite victory at Killiecrankie, the first major military engagement in the forthcoming long Jacobite wars.[9] Practised already in the imitation of Virgilian epic, Dryden had no difficulty in following Pitcairne's epic tone, incited by an undeniably epic occasion:[10]

O last and best of Scots, who didst maintain
Thy country's freedom from a foreign reign!
New people fill the land now thou art gone,
New gods the temples, and new kings the throne.[11]

Dryden was not the only poet to respond to the times in epic mode. Richard, Lord Maitland (1653–95, later 4th Earl of Lauderdale) states in his manuscript dedication to Queen Mary of Modena, dated 1 January 1691, that he began to translate Virgil's *Aeneid* Book VI, in 1689 'when I durst not appear for the Usurpers' and had continued with Books IV and VIII. He hopes that his translation may be 'useful one day' to 'ye Prince our rising hope', that is James Prince of Wales, and makes it clear that he thinks Virgil's text, faithfully translated, speaks to 'ye affairs of England': 'Stafford's murder; Dr Oates his testimony; the unnatural Usurper and some of his chiefe Agents'. It is no surprise that Maitland translated *Aeneid* Book VI first, where we read of the punishment of the wicked, but it is equally clear that, in Maitland's mind, the text of Virgil is something which helps him understand his times rather than merely affording him an opportunity for attacking what has happened.[12]

Dryden, who had the manuscript translations of Maitland by him as he worked on his own version, and who acknowledges him in his own Dedication, also had in mind the possibility of dedicating his own *Virgil* to the Stuarts, on the occasion of their hoped-for restoration.[13] It is thus clear that in the case of these two notable versions of Virgil in the 1690s we are not just dealing with two poets casting around for ways of exerting their talents (profitably in the case of Dryden): rather the sufferers in the political crisis of 1688–89 sought to understand their situation and if possible vindicate their

---

[9] *Poems*, III, 218–19.

[10] Attested also by the Latin epic, *The Graemeid* (1691) by James Philp of Almerieclose, on Dundee's expedition (*Poems*, III, 218).

[11] *Poems*, III, 219, lines 1–4.

[12] Howard Erskine-Hill, *Poetry and the Realm of Politics: Shakespeare to Dryden* (Oxford, 1996), 202–3.

[13] John Dryden, Dedication to the *Aeneid*, in *Works*, ed. E.N. Hooker and H.D. Swedenberg, Jr. *et al.*, 20 vols. (Berkeley and Los Angeles, 1961–), VI, 872; Dryden, *Letters*, ed. C.E. Ward (Durham, NC, 1942), 85–6.

cause intellectually through renewed and detailed attention to Virgil. Maitland, in his Dedication to Mary of Modena, recalls the two other complete English translations of the *Aeneid*: that by the royalist Scot, John Ogilby in 1649, and the much earlier one by Gavin Douglas, bishop of Dunkeld, another Scot, some of whose work was preserved in the literary collections of Maitland's own family. That the two next translations of the *Aeneid* – with the *Eclogues* and *Georgics* – should both appear in the 1690s, and both be the work of Jacobites, makes clear the special bond in their eyes between the works of Virgil and the Jacobite cause.[14]

The quality of Maitland's translation is generally high, though in more traditional verse-mode than that of Dryden. First printed, probably, in 1708, eleven years after Dryden's *Virgil*, it could hardly have made way against the version of the famous Dryden, indebted to Maitland though Dryden had been. To illustrate Maitland we may turn, not to the punishment of the wicked in *Aeneid* Book vi, but to the pledging of the alliance between the followers of Aeneas and the kingdom of Evander in Book viii. In the history of the two peoples there had first, perhaps, been enmity, in so far as Evander had descended from the Greeks, Aeneas from the Trojans; yet more recently there had been friendship between the Trojans and the subjects of Evander. Here, in Maitland's version, Aeneas makes a case for common ancestry:

Trusting to this, I scorn'd, like other kings,
To send before to sound and try my Fate;
My self I bring, thus lowly I entreat.
The fierce *Rutulians* you and us pursue
With cruel Wars, if to their Arms we bow,
They think all let's remov'd which stop their way
To stretch their Empire out from Sea to Sea.
Give yours, receive our Faith, long us'd to War
Our Courage try'd, our Hearts are void of fear:
Aeneas thus, Evander (whilst he said)
With piercing Eyes from Head to Foot survey'd;
Then briefly spoke. Best of the *Trojan* Race,
Whom I most willing in these Walls embrace,
And in your Voice and Air your Father find,

---

14 Maitland's Dedication of his *Aeneid*, Books iv, vi and viii is in the National Library of Scotland MS 221/62, and was included as item 265 in Corp, *Cour des Stuarts*, 201. Maitland's complete Virgil was published as *The Works of Virgil, Translated into English Verse. By the Right Honourable Richard late Earl of Lauderdale* (London, ?1708).

Though long ago, I freshly call to mind
King *Priam*'s Visit to his Sister's Court,
(Who than at *Salamina* had resort)
Who in his Progress view'd th'*Arcadian* Shore,
A youthful Down my Chin then cover'd o'er.
I saw the *Trojan* Chiefs with wond'ring Eyes;
Priam himself I saw, yet my surprize
Was more to see *Anchises* top the rest;
I knew the Man . . .
The League you ask'd, by this Right Hand I plight,
When Phoebus next displays his chearing Light
My Wealth shall ease, my Troops shall force your way.[15]

Dryden, by far the more experienced versifier, is more swift, more smooth, more elegant, more stylishly patterned: Maitland is sometimes more clumsy, but sometimes more dramatic and direct. This is the case with the opening, where Dryden has:

I sent no news before,
Nor asked your leave, nor did your faith implore;
But came without a pledge, my own ambassador.

Maitland's 'send before to sound', 'My self I bring' and later 'I knew the Man'[16] are more plain and performative than Dryden, and closer to the original. The same may be said of the line 'The League you ask'd . . .' when compared with Dryden's more courteous and politically aware: 'The League you ask, I offer as your right.' Once we have understood that Dryden is not in all respects better than Maitland, there is no need to pursue a running comparison between the two Jacobite translations. More important is to imagine what this meeting of Evander and Aeneas must have meant to followers of James II, recently fugitive from England to France without prior embassy, and now proposing to Louis XIV a league against a common foe. No exact parallel between Evander and *le grand monarque*, or between Evander's lowly kingdom and Louis XIV's mighty France is necessary, to recognise the emotional charge this scene must have had for Jacobites in the early 1690s. As in Dryden's Jacobite dramas, James II is not *portrayed*, but, in the figures of Don Sebastian, Arthur, Cleomenes and Ramirez, is certainly *recalled* through common issues in their situations, so

---

[15] *The Works of Virgil, Aeneid*, VIII, 261–2, lines 161–92.
[16] In the first two instances compare 'meme ipse meumque/ Objeci caput, & supplex ad limina veni', Book VIII, lines 144–5 in the Ruaeus Edition of Virgil used by Dryden.

here Aeneas (no king though Maitland has him so) recalls without portraying the exiled Stuart prince. This is how political allusion usually works at this time in literature: not through systematic parallel or totalising allegory, but through comparative reminder which explores crucial issues in common.[17]

It is also with Dryden that the courtly poetry of Saint-Germain begins. Quite different from the heroic epitaph on Dundee, Dryden's 'Lady's Song' is a masque-like lyric in which the players perform as they sing. Like the epitaph on Dundee this poem circulated widely in manuscript before being posthumously printed. It is included in *A Collection of Loyal Poems, Satyrs and Lampoons*, bearing the royal cipher 'J.R.', which has been plausibly dated to the period 1689–93 and might possibly, as Anne Barbeau Gardiner has suggested, have actually been presented to the exiled monarch.[18]

'The Lady's Song' constitutes an interrupted ceremony:

A choir of bright beauties in spring did appear,
To choose a May Lady to govern the year;
All the nymphs were in white, and the shepherds in green,
A garland was given, and Phyllis was queen;
But Phyllis refused it, and sighing did say:
'I'll not wear a garland while Pan is away.

'While Pan and fair Syrinx are fled from our shore,
The Graces are banished, and Love is no more;

[17] The general case for such unsystematic political allusion is made in Erskine-Hill, *Poetry and the Realm of Politics*, 1–4 and chapters 6 and 7.

[18] *Poems*, III, 245 (headnote). The suggestion that this poem has a special connection with the court of Saint-Germain rests on the fact that a version of it (with an extra stanza) appears in 'A Collection of Loyal Poems, Satyrs and Lampoons', evidently bearing the royal cypher 'J.R.', and plausibly dated to the period 1689–93 (Yale University, Beinecke Library, Osborn b 111). Anne Barbeau Gardiner has suggested that the volume may have been presented to James II at the court of Saint-Germain. I have read the volume on microfilm, but not seen the royal cipher, presumably on the outer binding. Knowledge of the cipher in itself cannot tell when the volume was presented to the exiled king, or to which exiled king, though the apparent termination of the volume at *c.* 1693 might suggest that James II were the more likely of the two. The collection suggests that it is a body of strongly Jacobite poetry written in England and Scotland. Numerous lines suggest this location, of which one must serve as an example: 'For when Royale James was banish'd from hence' (83–4, 'Bonny Dundee'). In addition, the poems seem to follow English events after 1689 more closely than it would have been easy to do from Saint-Germain. Some of the poems are courtly in intention, for example, 'On the Birth of the Princess. A Pindarique' (dated in another hand 15 July 1692), one of several Pindaric odes in the collection. With the exception of recognisable works of Dryden, for example the Prologue to *The Prophetess* and, of course, 'The Lady's Song' itself, the standard of the work is very low. In the case of the songs there seems to be so little metre, or of the match of the words to a stated air, that one wonders whether one is not dealing with the work of a bored and casual scribe.

The soft god of pleasure that warmed our desires
Has broken his bow and extinguished his fires;
And vows that himself and his mother will mourne
Till Pan and fair Syrinx in triumph return.

'Forbear your addresses, and court us no more,
For we will perform what the deity swore;
But if you dare think of deserving our charms,
Away with your sheephooks and take to your arms.
Then laurel and myrtles your brows shall adorn,
When Pan and his son and fair Syrinx return.'[19]

One of those pastorals which own the inadequacy of the pastoral mode, this is likewise a courtly poem in the act of repudiating courtliness: 'Forbear your addresses, and court us no more' – the buoyant dactylic couplets and graceful artifice hardly can masque the political and military implications of the text bespoken by words such as 'in triumph return' and 'take to your arms'. It is no surprise that the poem provoked Williamite replies marking out the violence beneath the pastoral:

'Cause Syrinx and Pan are both out of the way?
Why when they were here they were bloodily so.'[20]

Dryden's lyric, however, enjoins noble action: the faithful heart of the poem, no doubt, is the declaration 'we will perform what the deity swore' where the word 'perform' reaches from 'acting' to action: the deeds now required of the shepherds. Likewise the 'deity' is more serious here than 'the soft god of pleasure'. The demands of the love god are starting to transcend masque, and the pleasures of the pastoral must be postponed until after the hoped-for triumph.

Where courtly verse was concerned, Saint-Germain had no need to rely on the loyal poets who remained in England. In Anthony Hamilton (1644–1719), author of the *Mémoires de la vie du comte de Grammont* (1713), it possessed a poet who could celebrate with ease the exiled royal family, especially Princess Louise-Marie, and all the beauties in her train. An early posthumous edition of some of his poems showed a close connection with the court[21] but a larger body of Jacobite court poetry is to be found in the various mixed collections in verse and prose published in the 1762 edition of his *Œuvres*. Hamilton's *métier* is one deriving from a cavalier tradition of verse compliment though

---

[19] *Poems*, III, 244–8.   [20] *Ibid.*, 246.
[21] Comte Antoine Hamilton, *Œuvres mêlées en prose et en vers* (Paris, 1731); *Cour des Stuarts*, 168, no. 225.

now in more neo-classical form. His grace and lightness can be seen in his *Chanson*, 'Les Nymphes de Saint-Germain se baignant. Sur l'air: De Joconde':

L'astre du jour sur son déclin
Descendoit vers l'Espagne,
Quand nos Astres de Saint-Germain
    Le mirent en campagne.
Les Graces marchoient sur leurs pas,
    Zéphire étoit leur guide;
La Seine reçut leur appas
    Dans son empire humide.[22]

Another touching piece is Hamilton's 'Impromptu' in which he and Bevil Skelton, with permission, toast the monarch:

Tu boiras comme je bois,
Au plus aimable des Rois.[23]

Some of Hamilton's more sustained efforts are in honour of the princess, as here in 'Portrait pour Madame la Princesse d'Angleterre':

Ce n'est point sur notre Terrasse;
Ni dans le fond de nos forêts:
Mais c'est à plus haut de Parnasse
Qu'il faut tracer de tels portraits.

Célébrons sa gloire éclatante
Par des accents tendres et doux;
D'un air le plus commun qu'on chante,
D'un air qui soit connu de tous.

Commençont ce divin ouvrage
En mêlant ses vives couleurs,
Dont l'éclat sur un beau visage
Efface le brillant des fleurs.[24]

This is a complimentary poet-as-painter poem, untouched by the satirical use to which in the later seventeenth century Marvell had turned the mode, but retaining the convention which, thirty years later, Pope would develop with a beautiful blend of compliment and mockery in his Epistle *To a Lady* (1735).

---

[22] Comte Antoine Hamilton, *Œuvres*, 4 vols. (Paris, 1762), II, 263.
[23] *Ibid.*, II, 302.   [24] *Ibid.*, II, 303.

Hamilton (who sought to translate Pope's *An Essay on Criticism* into French, c.1713[25]) is nothing if not fluent in his courtly mode: all is ease and elegance, *l'éclat* on every face.

Hamilton, however, had been a soldier, though now a courtier. He had obviously seen death and did not turn away when Saint-Germain confronted him with a death of exceptional significance, a very different subject for poetic painting. The outcome was his poem, 'Sur l'Agonie du feu Roi d'Angleterre':

> Dans cette triste conjoncture,
> Ou tout mortel subit les loix
> Que nous a prescrit la Nature;
> Dieu! quelle touchante peinture,
> De voir a ses derniers abois
> Un de plus saints, jadis des plus grands Rois,
> N'emporter dans la sepulture
> Que son innocence et ses droits!

Deeply moved by the spectacle and the reflections to which it gives rise, the poet addresses both God, that He may save those who remain of the English blood royal, and also the king of France, that Heaven may reward him for his protection of the English king:

> Grand Roi, dont la puissante main
> Fait regner ton sang en Espagne,
> Et qui, de la grande Bretagne
> Protege ici le Souverain,
> Daigne le Ciel, pour récompense
> De tant de précieux bienfaits,
> Egaler partout les succès
> A ta sagesse, à ta puissance![26]

Hamilton's *peinture* of King James on the point of death draws us close to the extraordinary figure who was the *raison d'être* of the exiled court. What Hamilton wrote from a courtier's angle is, from a distance, also written by the poet Jane Barker (1652–1732) who lived, not at court, but in the town of Saint-Germain. Barker's manuscript volume, 'Referring to the times; since the King's Accession to the Crown. Occasionally writ according to the circumstances of

---

[25] *The Poems of Alexander Pope*, ed. John Butt *et al.* (London, 1939–69), I, 208; *The Correspondence of Alexander Pope*, ed. George Sherburn (Oxford, 1956), I, 192, Pope to Hamilton, 10 October 1713.
[26] Hamilton, *Œuvres*, III, 261–3.

time and place',[27] constitutes a poetic commentary extending from an English viewpoint to that of an exile in France. Her whole volume is of great interest, opening as it does with an optimistic dedication to the Prince of Wales in 1701 (occasioned by the death of the young Duke of Gloucester in England, and the recognition in France of the Bourbon claim to the crown of Spain) and ending with a ferocious satire on the Williamites on the same occasion, so promising for Jacobite hopes. Whether the volume was actually presented to the prince may be uncertain, but the intention could not be more clear, and it must have a much stronger claim to embody the poetry of Saint-Germain than does 'Loyal Poems, Satyrs and Lampoons'.[28] Many of Barker's poems are dialogues in a dramatic setting, in which she figures as Fidelia. In 'Fidelia in a convent garden the Abbess comes to her',[29] the Abbess asks her gently whether James II had not attempted to abridge the liberties of his people. Fidelia in reply gives a fighting defence of the short English reign of James II:

No Madam, no, for he allow'd 'em more
Than all his predecessors did before,
None was abridg'd in person or estate
Or any party illegitimate,
A general liberty to all he gave,
More large, than they in modesty cou'd crave,
This goodnes, mallaice made misunderstood,
Their EYE was evil, because his was good,
The King say they will arbitrary be,

---

[27] In quoting from Jane Barker, many of whose most interesting poems have not yet been published, I have drawn first on BL Add. MSS 21621, her collection 'Referring to the times; since the King's Accession to the Crown. Occasionally writ according to the circumstances of time and place.' It is explicitly dedicated to the Prince of Wales, on 1 January 1701, and, whether actually handed to him or no, presents itself as a volume in which many poems are written from a Saint-Germain viewpoint. It has been pointed out that this manuscript is closely duplicated by Part 1 of Magdalen College MS 343, which is overall more extensive and later, and may contain more revised versions of poems in BL Add. MSS 21621. The latter, indeed, shows some marks of incompleteness and of revision still in process. However, I have chosen to use it, for material I wished to quote not yet in print, on the grounds that it probably embodies texts nearer to Barker's Saint-Germain experience than those more retrospectively revised, perhaps from the time of her return to England. (I appreciate the force of different editorial policy either way.) For material in print, I have drawn on, first, *The Galesia Trilogy and Selected Manuscript Poems* and, second, Jane Barker, *The Magdalen College Manuscript*, ed. Kathryn R. King (Oxford, 1998), particularly 2 and 14. This is in fact a selection from the Magdalen College manuscript, though it helpfully highlights Barker's 1701 dedication to the Prince of Wales.

[28] Beinecke Library, Osborn b 111.   [29] BL Add. MSS 21621, f. 43r.

Becaus he gives his people liberty,
Tis surely so the thing itself declares,
He gives his people leave to say their prayer's.[30]

Barker shows an intelligent understanding of the positive intentions behind
James's religious policy, and does so in mordantly ironic couplets. Having
mounted to more conventional panegyric (James as a 'mighty Monarch, gracious Patriot'),[31] Fidelia reserves her most searing irony for the end when,
'Whether set on by Sunderland, or Hell, / By Orange, or our mad Phanatick
zeal', the disaffected 'got the Non resisters to rebell'.[32] The Abbess assures
Fidelia that the Almighty will support the king's cause, and departs to her
chapel.

Barker's positive assessment, or idealisation, of James is seen in her later
poem, 'At the sight of the body of Our Late gracious sovereign Lord King
James 2d As it lys at the English Monks'. It anticipates the case that would
be made for the beatification of James, and it is no accident that Barker was
one who would testify to miracles wrought by the dead king.[33] The opening
of her poem strikes an effectively familiar note:

Hic jacet, oft hic jacet poets sing,
Of such who acted many a glorious thing,
But ne'er Hic Jacet Hero, saint and King.
But here lys one, whom all the world must grant,
Was prince, and Hero, King and glorious saint.[34]

Barker's position as a townswoman is apparent from the viewpoint of these
Saint-Germain poems. She is responsive to hearsay and is aware of what is
outside the palace as well as within. This is how, five years earlier, she had
reported James's departure from Saint-Germain to Calais for the 1696 invasion
attempt:

My eys bound down, I heard the people say
The King, the King's for England gone away.[35]

More close to reality than Barker, more close perhaps than the king himself,
was John Caryll: 'I confess 'tis my opinion yt nothing at all will be done, and
yt these encouragments . . . will fall short of what is promised and expected,
so yt ye worst yt can happen is but a journy to Calais taken in vain.'[36]

---

[30] *Ibid.*, f. 44v.   [31] *Ibid.*, f. 46r.   [32] *Ibid.*, f. 46v.   [33] *Galesia Trilogy*, xxxi.
[34] *Ibid.*, 310.   [35] *Ibid.*, 295.   [36] Bodleian Library, Carte MSS 181, f. 627.

This is a case where the strong prose record of Saint-Germain experience, in letter and memoir, counterpoints the idealising texts of the poets. In one of her most memorable poems, however, 'The Miseries of St. Germains, writ at the time of the pestilence and famin, which reign'd in the years, 1694 et 95', Jane Barker gives us so far as I know a unique account of a politically active court in exile, the *point de retour* for numerous military and civilian supporters after the Scottish and Irish campaigns on behalf of the Stuart king. Well organised and well financed as the court was, it found it well nigh impossible to support an army of refugees in a period of pestilence. Barker seems faithfully to record 'The Miseries of St. Germains' but her experience does not, we notice, shake her admiration for the royal family:

But to return with King and Queen up stairs,
We find no miserie can equal theirs,
They run the gantlet, 'twixt the pittious noyse,
Of ladys sighs, and wretched colonell's crys . . .
Then what compassion must our Royal Pair,
Have for the suffering oth' brave and fair,
Whose very souls compos'd of pitty are.[37]

It has recently been suggested that Barker is a different kind of Jacobite because she does not share the general Jacobite confidence.[38] Her Jacobite poems, however, do not show that she doubted her loyal principles. Principles may be held in times of affliction. As to practical hopes of political success, they are another matter: that such hopes were not always shared by the best judges can be seen from the correspondence of Caryll. As to the quality of her poetry, Barker is a less skilful versifier than Hamilton and by higher standards not really accomplished. With the exception of Hamilton's poem on the dying king, however, Barker's poetry is more humanly interesting. Hamilton's *chansons* must have been delightful as court compliment set to music, but 'The Miseries of St. Germains' is a far more interesting poetical survival.

---

[37] *Galesia Trilogy*, 305, lines 68–71, 77–9.

[38] See Toni Bowers, 'Jacobite Difference and the Poetry of Jane Barker', *English Literary History* 64, no. 4 (1997), 857–69. Jane Barker is probably a feminist rather than a Jacobite discovery, and Toni Bowers follows Carol Barash, *English Women's Poetry, 1649–1714* (Oxford, 1996), 195–208, in seeking to make a link between her independent female consciousness, on the one hand, and her Roman Catholicism (hence devotion to the Virgin Mary) and her Jacobitism (hence devotion to Mary of Modena) on the other hand. However, without in the least dispraising Queen Mary, Barker has a good deal more to say in praise of James II, and indeed has a warm sympathy for the sufferings of men of all conditions. See King, *Barker*.

Towards the end of Hamilton's 'Portrait pour Madame la Princesse d'Angleterre', tribute is paid to another poet of Saint-Germain:

Carill, sans dout la Muse Insigne,
Deployant jadis ses tresors,
Du bon Naboth chanta la vigne
Pour elle animez vos accords.[39]

In his religious satire *Naboth's Vineyard* (1679) John Caryll (1625–1711) had protested against the injustices of the Popish Plot, the beginning of the serious troubles of James, Duke of York, despite his eventual accession to the throne. Though a skilful small-scale translator from Virgil and Ovid, Caryll the politician and diplomat is what comes through his chief works. Apart from his new English translation of the *Psalms* from the Vulgate, published in 1700 and evidently intended, like Maitland's *Aeneid*, for the edification of the Prince of Wales, Caryll was one of the best letter-writers of the exiled court, his correspondence with the Earl of Perth during the latter's mission to Rome on behalf of James II being especially impressive in its political scepticism, intelligence, religious faith and plain English. His more routine political correspondence went doggedly on, reciting the coded names of Godolphin and Marlborough, lord treasurer and general. In the new decade, when James II was dead and 'le jeune Roy d'Angleterre', James III, in his place, Caryll's political assessment of England found expression in a new poem, *The Duumvirate* (?1705), in which Godolphin and Marlborough, both men Caryll must have known, and with whom he was now sparring in dissimulative correspondence, are the focus of his satirical attack.[40]

---

[39] Hamilton, *Œuvres*, ii, 309.

[40] For Caryll's motivation in translating the Psalms, see the two *approbationes*, by the *Praeceptor* (John Betham) and the *Subpraeceptor* (John Ingleton) of the Prince of Wales, printed in the prefatory matter of the book. It is probable that Caryll's reputation as a writer and poet gained more recognition in the exiled court than in his pre-exile decades in London. We have seen Hamilton's tribute to *Naboth's Vineyard*. A footnote to one of Barker's poems which makes use of the same Old Testament episode states that 'The author had never seen the poem calld Naboth's vinyard, else she wou'd not have put her cicle in another's harvest' (BL Add. MSS 21621, f. 31). Caryll's The *Duumvirate* is in the Bodleian Library, Carte MSS 208, ff. 397r–398v. It is noted in David Foxon (ed.), *English Verse, 1701–1750*, 2 vols. (Cambridge, 1975), i, 210, item D564, where it is designated 'Jacobite propaganda, particularly directed against Godolphin and Marlborough' and provisionally assigned to the year 1705. Nairne's diary establishes Caryll's authorship of the poem (18 December 1705 to 19 December 1706). Though in a manuscript collection, it is actually printed and, so far as I know, the unique surviving copy. Probably printed at Saint-Germain, it is written as if by an Englishman and was no doubt designed to be distributed in England.

The *Duumvirate* is as hard-hitting as the most powerful passages of *Naboth's Vineyard* (itself the clear precursor of Dryden's *Absalom and Achitophel*). It is strong, plain and with a magisterial sarcasm:

Our floating Isle allmost an Age has spent
In wandring through all Forms of Government,
Still fond of Change, lesse constant than the Winds,
Or Wives, or Women in their Modes and Minds!
Without the least regarding Wrong or Right,
To cast their Riders is their great delight,
Tho' still the weight more willingly they bear
Of an Usurping Power, than of a Lawful Heire.[41]

In the vein of this opening paragraph Caryll narrates the history of seventeenth-century England, the Rump Parliament, the execution of Charles I and the hegemony of Cromwell, all monstrous deviations from kingly rule.

But storms their Period have; Heaven has decreed,
Monsters should be short lived, and leave no seed;
So when the hand of Fate, propitious grown,
These several sprung up monsters had mow'd down,
England once more beheld a serene sky,
A Lucid interval of Loyalty.[42]

This was the Restoration, after which again the English choose kings of 'their own making', 'And of old England a new Poland make'. Providence and Nature, however, 'have denyd / Offspring to Wombs guilty of Paricide': neither Mary II nor Queen Anne had surviving children, and thus the constitution is usurped by a Duumvirate:

They who refuse their Lawful Kings t'obey
Of two usurping Upstarts tamely bear the sway,
And they our lives and fortunes now command,
Who scarce would claim by birth one foot of land.
With *Maires de Palais* England now is curst,
Which is of all *French Governments* the worst . . .
Their Easy Queen without controle they rule
And guide, even as a workman guides his Tool . . .
None but by them must hope for any favour,

---

[41] Bodleian Library, Carte MSS 208, f. 397v.   [42] *Ibid.*

She speaks, she thinks, only as they will have her.
To bind her to themselves all Natures tyes
They make her break, and her own blood despise.
Thus is the Nation governd to this houre,
She has the Name, and they have all the Power.[43]

Monsters have no seed, paricides no posterity. Even of 'profuse Fortune', writes Caryll with powerful Jacobite implication, 'None of her Gifts are from Redemption free.' Fortune, indeed, in the longer run, turns out to be Providence which 'Can conquer with the Jaw-bone of an Ass':[44] this adroit allusion to the Old Testament story of Samson brilliantly merges divine purpose with the idiom of the contemptuous satirist.

The reputation of James II, incredibly to those brought up in the still influential traditions of Whig History, is seen in a positive light in the literature of Saint-Germain. He emerges in Maitland's Aeneas who brings himself to Evander, in social setting in Hamilton's 'le plus aimable des rois', grieving and compassionate with his queen in 'The Miseries of St. Germains'. He is there in his last hours in Hamilton's poem on his death, and there lying in state in that of Jane Barker's. He epitomises the providential and legal kingship which is the positive value of Caryll's *Duumvirate*. In this light he is the king who did not abdicate but who withdrew to fight again and did fight again, who lost his throne for his religious faith and who was even likened to Abraham offering to sacrifice Isaac in being ready to jeopardise his son's succession to the crown.[45]

During the long effort to obtain the beatification of James II in the 1730s, Lewis Innes wrote to James III in Rome on the character of his father. In a long and well-written letter he divided the life into three periods:

The first part of the B[lessed] Kings life represents a Prince perfectly accomplished in all respects, universally esteemed, and beloved by all who knew him.

The 2d part represents a Christian Hero, envied and persecuted merely and only for his Religion, exposed to the greatest temptations, – three Crowns being at stake, and yet so steddily fixt to his principle that he had not the least regard either to the persecution of his most implacable enemies, or to the entiseing arguments of his friends to move him to comply, but God Allmighty (who certainly had in his mercy

---

[43] *Ibid.*, ff. 397v–398r.   [44] *Ibid.*, f. 398v.

[45] BL Add. MSS 28252, f. 28v. The treatise from which this view and this detail are drawn is 'Reflections Upon the League of Ausburg', in the Caryll Papers in the British Library. It is briefly discussed by Howard Erskine-Hill, 'John, First Lord Caryll of Durford, and the Caryll Papers', in Corp, *Stuart Court and Jacobites*, 81–2.

determind to make him one day a greater saint than he was a Hero) inspired him with that Christian courage and greatness of Soull that firm like a rock he persisted steddily in his Religion without ever disembling or complying with the Protestants in the least, and that for about 20 yeares that the persecution lasted more or lesse. Ther is no exaggeration in what I say, his enemies who were witnesses at the time could not deny it, only they gave it other names, calling his courage and Zeall for Religion, obstinacy, and bigotry. I have not place to say what might be said of the 3d part of the B. Kings life that represents him as a Penitent penetrated with the deepest sence of his past failings etc.[46]

In so far as the character of James II is a major theme in the poetry of the exiled court – and there are of course other themes – that theme is well summed up here in prose. Indeed verse and prose do not here counterpoint one another, but, for once, form a single verdict.

[46] SP 197/96, Innes to James III, 20 May 1737.

CHAPTER TEN

The court as a centre of Catholicism

GEOFFREY SCOTT

Introduction

by Edward Corp

The evidence for what Lewis Innes described as the third part of James II's life, during which the exiled king was 'a Penitent penetrated with the deepest sence of his past failings', is mainly to be found in fourteen 'Pious Sentiments' which he wrote during the 1690s on loose sheets. They were collected after his death by Innes and bound up into a quarto volume of 173 pages in September 1701.[1] Further evidence is to be found in the letters which James II sent to the abbé de La Trappe, which were temporarily returned to Saint-Germain and copied in January 1702 by David Nairne.[2] These papers were used by Father Sanders when he wrote his 'Short Relation of the Life and Death of James the Second King of England etc.'. Corrected by Caryll, Nairne and Innes between October 1701 and July 1702, the 'Relation' was sent to Père François Bretonneau and published in 1703 as *Abrégé de la vie de Jacques II . . . tiré d'un écris anglois du R.P. François Sanders.*[3] These writings, for which Innes had 'not place to say what might be said', will be examined in this chapter by Abbot Geoffrey Scott.

James II's fourteen papers of devotion were published in London in 1704 under the title *The Pious Sentiments of the Late King James II of Blessed Memory upon Divers Subjects of Piety.*[4] In an additional, fifteenth paper, known only from its French translation as 'Avis à un Protestant, ou reflexions sur la religion anglicane', James argued that it was reasonable that the Dissenters should feel entitled to break away from the Anglican church, since that was precisely

---

[1] Corp, 'Inventory', 130. A copy in 174 octavo pages, including a table of contents, was made by David Nairne in October and November 1701, and certified by Mary of Modena on 27 January 1702. A French translation was made by Nairne and Monnot in November and December 1701, sent to Cardinal Caprara in Rome in July 1702, and given to James III in 1743 (SP 248/150).

[2] Corp, 'Inventory', 130. The original letters were in 'a volume stitchd together but not bound up'. The copy made by Nairne was in 240 quarto pages, and attested by the abbé's successor.

[3] *Ibid.*, 129.

[4] A facsimile of the original manuscript was published by the Roxburghe Club (London) in 1925 as *The Papers of Devotion of James II*, edited by Godfrey Davies.

what the Anglicans had themselves done when they challenged the universal Catholic church and created their own schism.[5]

The King's thirteenth 'Pious Sentiment', entitled 'A Letter to —— concerning frequent Communion', was originally a private letter written to Louis XIV in October 1694. In the previous month James II had informed his courtiers that he was in favour of both Anglican and Dissenter services being held at his court, and that he had no objection to their asking Louis for permission to do this.[6] When Lord Middleton objected that such a sensitive subject ought only to be broached by James himself, the latter resolved to speak to Louis during his annual visit to Fontainebleau a few weeks later. Just as he was about to do so, news arrived that Mary of Modena's brother had died, necessitating a premature return to Saint-Germain. James expressed his disappointment in a private note: 'I am even more annoyed [about leaving early] because I had intended to speak to the King as a real brother and friend on a subject of great importance to him, and which I think it is my duty to do, confident that he would take it in good part.'[7] It is not clear when or if James finally broached the subject of toleration for the Protestant Jacobites with Louis, but these were the circumstances in which he wrote the letter. It did not refer specifically to the question of toleration, but it urged Louis to serve God 'in Liberty of Spirit out of the Motive of Filial Love, and not under the Restraints of a Servile Fear', as well as encouraging him to take communion more frequently.[8]

James II's devotional writings were not the only religious literature produced at the exiled court. John Caryll made a translation of a book published in 1683 by the Jesuit Jean Croiset, *Considérations Chrétiennes pour toute l'année*.[9] His translation is not dated but it must have been finished by December 1696, when Caryll and Nairne began to translate all the Psalms into English. Their translation was finished by March 1697 and eventually published under Caryll's name in October 1700, with an anonymous preface by Nairne, and with approbations by John Betham and John Ingleton (preceptor and under-preceptor

---

[5] SP 248/150/p.13.   [6] See above, p. 156.

[7] *Papers of Devotion*, 152 (translated from the original French).   [8] *Pious Sentiments*, 44–5.

[9] Bibliothèque Mazarine, Paris, MS 1272, 'Christian considerations for every day in the month by way of Orall meditation, chiefly designed for these of such as either have not the leisure or the facility to make mentall prayer, translated from the French by Crasset, by John Caryll Esqr of Ladyholt', on parchment, 6 + 178 pp. The following comment appears at the end of the preface: 'What the Translator has to add from himself is . . . He owns himself much affected with the Thoughts of this Pious Author (who was F. le Clerc of the Society of Jesus) and hopes it may have the same Effect on the well disposed Reader, to whose Remembrance and Good Prayers he recommends himself.'

of the Prince of Wales).[10] Caryll and Nairne also made a translation of the entire New Testament between August 1697 and June 1700.[11] After extensive revisions and the addition of cross-references, the work was then examined by John Betham and taken in August 1702 by the Duchess of Tyrconnell to England 'to be left there for ye [Catholic] B[isho]ps to be examind, and printed with their approbation'.[12] Although Nairne added a preface at the end of November,[13] the book was never published and it is not clear what became of it. Nairne's diary contains no further references to these translations and, as will be seen, Betham's religious orthodoxy began to be called into question during 1703.

The piety of James II

by Geoffrey Scott

English historians have generally treated James II's piety with scant regard. As far as the post-revolutionary period is concerned, the evidence of his piety has merely strengthened the view of his critics that here was a guilt-ridden depressive who became increasingly introverted as he approached his end. The preface to the only recent published edition of the scraps of devotional manuscript which the king left suggests that these pious jottings unravel 'the psychological enigma' presented by a king who revealed 'a curious blend of childish folly, petty revengefulness, and moral cowardice' in his attempts to recover his throne. A suffocating piety, it continues, blinded him to the true causes for his downfall which he blamed not on political insensitivity and pig-headedness, but on divine retribution for his moral lapses. Critics from Gilbert Burnet onwards have taken the religious outpourings of the king as symptoms revealing the degeneration of a once brave and active leader into a tortured and broken man.[14]

Even by the time he had succeeded to the throne, James's remorse for his incontinence had become 'a habit of mind, and in the secret places of his heart,

---

[10] *The Psalmes of David, Translated from the Vulgat* (Saint-Germain, 1700). Full details of the progress made by Caryll and Nairne in translating the 150 Psalms are given in Nairne's diary. Copies were given to James II and Mary of Modena on 14 October, and some were sent to England on 6 November.

[11] Details of the progress translating each book of the New Testament are similarly given in Nairne's diary. The two men started with the 'Epistles', continued with the 'Acts of the Apostles', then the 'Revelation', and finished with the 'Gospels'.

[12] Nairne gives full details and adds that the translation was examined by Betham in May 1702, and bound in two volumes and given to the duchess on 31 July 1702.

[13] Nairne, 29 November 1702.   [14] *Papers of Devotion*, xxiv–xxv.

he was a very unhappy man', and during the decade of exile, which began in his fifty-fifth year, this had brought about an 'extreme senility . . . very rare in a man so young and so physically fit' and which manifested itself in 'a complete apathy' to his misfortunes and to the possibility of a restoration, 'perfect contentment with his present surroundings . . . and a distressing proneness to fits of garrulity'. We are told that from 1696 the rest of his life was dominated by his devotions. 'If God had decided that he would no longer be king, he would try to be a saint, and failing that, he would at least do all he could to earn his salvation. James's preoccupation with his own salvation was a totally selfish activity, and it is not surprising that, despite his reputation for piety, he never did become a saint.' Contemporary comments on his abstracted imperturbability have been seized upon to demonstrate James's turning away from worldly concerns and seeking instead an unreal refuge in prayer. Thus, Rizzini, the Modenese envoy at St James's, reported that the king 'lives always surrounded by friars and talks of his misfortunes with indifference'. Madame de La Fayette regretted seeing him sinking into a *sottise*, which led to an infatuation with religion and a domination by Jesuits. The duchesse d'Orléans concluded in October 1690 that, by playing the saint, James's piety made him look very stupid – sentiments which led a modern historian to comment that it was 'only the useless fag-end of his life that he in any real sense dedicated to God', in the melancholy court of Saint-Germain where, as the visitor Anthony Hamilton put it, 'there is no mercy here for those who do not spend half the day at their prayers or at any rate make a show of doing so'.[15]

Traditional Whig Protestant propaganda could not believe James's conversion to a life of prayer was genuine. Mrs Schimmelpenninck could not see any change of heart in the old man who as king had 'authorised the decisions of a Jefferies, or the executions of a Kirk', and would have been happier to join in the abbot of La Trappe, Armand de Rancé's eulogy of James if there had been more solid proofs of his conversion than merely a friendship with the monks of La Trappe. By contrast, some modern commentators have taken a less cynical line, arguing that there was no clear conversion to things of the spirit, but simply a recrudescence of that puritan streak which had long been part of his character, and which by the 1690s led him to an overwhelming desire for death.[16] Few English historians have attempted to develop a revisionist hermeneutic, thereby setting the king's devotional life within the

---

[15] P. Earle, *The Life and Times of James II* (London, 1972); F.C. Turner, *James II* (London, 1948), 302, 456–9, 497.

[16] M.A. Schimmelpenninck, *Select Memoirs of Port-Royal*, III (London, 1829), 320–2; and for a summary of hostile views, see M.V. Hay, *The Enigma of James II* (London, 1938), xii, xvi, 1, 33, 37; J. Miller, *James II: A Study in Kingship* (Hove, 1978), 235.

context of contemporary trends in European Catholicism. To do so, however, helps to make more sense of the king's obsessive interest in the practice of his Christian faith and to invigorate that barren coda of his last ten years.

Like Tutankhamen, James II shares a historical legacy disproportionate to the length of his reign. James's inheritance to posterity lies in the survival of his memoirs, some edited, some directly autobiographical. We are told the king 'had an aptitude for putting down remarkable events on paper . . . often in haste on loose sheets'. This wealth of autobiographical material is both impressive and unusual for an English king and has been the subject of much debate, especially since the destruction of the volumes of the royal autobiographical memoirs during the French Revolution.[17] However, to my knowledge, no scholar has asked why the king felt compelled to write such detailed memoirs in the first place. The diary of his military campaigns as Duke of York between 1652 and 1660 suggests that he was naturally predisposed to writing out his reminiscences, but the full memoirs, left mostly to us in edited versions, reveal that there may have been other motives at work. Sections of the *Life*, edited by J.S. Clarke in 1816, which remain in the first-person singular seem to portray a royal spiritual odyssey which under divine providence led first to the king's conversion and then to the surrender of his dominions in order that he might come to know and love God better. He resolved to praise God throughout his life for five mercies: for deliverance from rebels, preservation in battles, sufficient patience to endure injury, conversion to Catholicism and the gift of true repentance. One cannot but be struck by his frequent assertion that Providence guided his destiny during the last ten years of his life which he himself preferred to be judged as blessed rather than cursed. If this is the case, then the memoirs are in the genre of the *Confessions* of St Augustine, and drafted when Augustinianism was a profound influence in theological and spiritual circles of the time. It also means that the so-called Writings of Devotion of James II should not be treated separately from the king's memoirs, whose style and content they resemble.

This theme of providential conversion to Catholicism is more stridently proclaimed, however, in the controversial tract on Charles II's conversion, purported to have been written by Charles and published in 1694 by James, who announced that he had discovered the papers in a strong box and inside a cupboard. Modelled on the famous devotional work relating to the martyr-king, Charles I, this latest 'pourtraicture', based on numerous editions of the conversion published at the beginning of James's reign, sought to establish a

---

[17] See especially E. Gregg, 'New Light on the Authorship of the *Life of James II*', *English Historical Review* 108, no. 429 (October 1993), 947–65; and Corp, 'Inventory', 127–9.

common martyrological tradition in the three Stuart kings, the father dying for his faith, the sons suffering for theirs. It convinced English Catholics that Charles II had been a closet and devout Catholic for many years, probably since around 1659, and James admitted that he supervised its publication and personally distributed it to Protestants at the court of Saint-Germain, hoping it might convert them to Catholicism. James sent the account to the abbot of La Trappe in 1691, and the Earl of Perth recollected that after the king had handed the original manuscript to him in London in March 1685, he was driven to study Bossuet's writings and convert to Catholicism that autumn.[18]

The narrative of Charles's conversion, to which James coupled that of the Duchess of York, infuriated leading Anglicans, notably Edward Stillingfleet, dean of St Paul's and notorious anti-Roman apologist, and precipitated a pamphlet war between Stillingfleet and English Catholics.[19] In the 1694 account, Charles is depicted in language redolent of Catholic sentimentalism as having all the qualities we later associate with James in exile. He is represented as a devotee of Our Lady, many chapters concluding with verses in her honour; his escape to White Ladies, 'a quondam nunnery', is seen as providential, as is his refuge with recusants, 'where the Holy Fathers did use to retire from the fury of Protestant Persecution . . . so that my first and last Retreat must be to the Catholicks'. In a style which evokes the Reproaches in the Liturgy of the Passion on Good Friday, the persecuted Charles contrasts his sufferings with the smug and prosperous of this world. Charles admits that his brother James, while still 'catched in the same snare' of unchastity, is able, unlike himself, to 'resist the Charms of Love'. By the 1690s, James doubtless identified himself

---

[18] [James II], *EIKON BASILIKE DEUTERA [Greek Characters]. The Pourtraicture of his Sacred Majesty King Charles II. With his Reasons for turning Roman Catholick: published by K. James. Found in the strong box. Printed in the year 1694.* For Charles I and the original *EIKON BASILIKE*, see Bernard and Monique Cottret, 'La sainteté de Jacques II, ou les miracles d'un roi défunt [vers 1702]', in Corp, *L'Autre Exil*, 81–2. For editions of Charles II, *Copies of two papers*, publ. 1685–86, see D. Wing, *Short-Title Catalogue of Books Printed in England &c. 1641–1700*, I (New York, 1972), E2942–1946A. For the 1694 tract, see *The Memoirs of King James II. Containing an Account of the Transactions of the last twelve years of his life; with the circumstances of his death* (London, 1702), 18, *Abrégé*, Avertissement, 96–7, 216–20, 277–9; *Pious Sentiments*, 30–2; *Papers of Devotion*, xvii, 58. (The *Abrégé* incorporates much of James's own writings found in *Papers of Devotion*.) See also *Life of James II*, II, 8–9; Turner, *James II*, 370; M. Ashley, *James II* (London, 1977), 72, 188; A.J. Krailsheimer, (ed.), *Abbé de Rancé: Correspondance* (Paris, 1993), IV, 82–3; Benet Weldon, 'Memorials', I, 172; II, 535–48 (Douai Abbey Archives, Woolhampton, Berks.).

[19] E. Stillingfleet, *Answer to some papers lately printed* (London and Dublin, 1686), *A Vindication of the answer to some late papers* (London, 1687); John Dryden, *A Defence of the Papers* (London, 1686); R. Huddleston, *A Short and Plain Way to the Faith and the Church* (London, 1688); J. Leyburn, *A Reply to the Answer Made upon Three Royal Papers* (London, 1686).

with Charles who earlier had found himself 'in Paris, safe from the fury of my
rebellious subjects . . . a king without people . . . The Sword of an Usurper
did serve me with Ejection.' At Saint-Germain, James retained clear memories
of his brother's providential conversion to a Catholicism visible, authoritative
and apostolic in contrast to Protestantism, as well as of Charles's identification
with Christ in his suffering.[20]

Despite exhaustive research on James's own conversion to Catholicism,
which came 'after much mature consideration', we are still no closer to pin-
pointing its date with any accuracy. It seems to have taken place sometime
between 1669 and 1672, in which year he refused to attend any further Anglican services. His acknowledgement of Providence in his conversion appears
early: a nun he met in Flanders counselled him to pray daily that if 'he was not
in the right way, [God] would bring him to it'. The Anglican James initially
argued the case against the Puritans for breaking up church unity, employing Richard Hooker's *Treatise on the Laws of Ecclesiastical Polity*, and the high
churchman Peter Heylyn's, *Aerius Redivivus: or, The History of Presbyterianism*,
the latter published only in 1670 and which he gave the Duchess of York
to read. The duchess herself admitted that she owed her own conversion in
1669–71 to reading Heylyn's *Ecclesia Restaurata; or the History of the Reformation*
[1661]. James then persuaded himself that the Anglican church itself lacked the
convincing authority of the church of Rome, which derived from its apostolic
succession, and was guilty of the same divisiveness as the Puritan sects.[21]

Many late Stuart converts to Catholicism spurned rationalist apologetic,
being attracted rather more by Catholic devotional life, to which they added
convincing arguments based on the workings of divine providence in history.
The conversions of James and his wife followed a similar pattern. We know
that James was attracted to Catholic devotions and eagerly read 'Histories'. He
was impressed by the church's moral teaching, which encouraged its members
to lead exemplary lives and converts to abandon 'their vicious habits'. More
lay behind James's turning to Catholicism than the commonly expressed view
of later commentators that James, as a pragmatic soldier, felt easier with the
authority and security found with Catholicism, and that he believed that the
Church of England was born from rebellion. For James had a pervading sense

---

[20] *Pourtraicture*, I, 14, 28, 30, 48, 51, 60, 309ff; *Abrégé*, 97, 277–80; *Papers of Devotion*, 23–7, 140;
Krailsheimer, *Correspondance*, IV, 82.

[21] *Abrégé*, 10–12, 17, 274–7; *Papers of Devotion*, xvii–xxi, 23–7, appendix I; *Life of James II*, I, 440,
452, 537, 540, 629–31; Turner, *James II*, 34, 43, 45, 87, 95, 98, 107–8, 125; Earle, *James II*, 84, 87,
93, 97–8; Miller, *James II*, 49–50, 57–8; Krailsheimer, *Correspondance*, IV, 83; Wing, *Catalogue*, III
(New York, 1988), Y46 and 47 for the Duchess of York's accounts of her conversion.

of divine Providence guiding his life. In a famous prayer, possibly composed as early as 1667–68 following an attack of smallpox, which he returned to in 1696, he spoke of the 'mercies of God' protecting him through exile, mortification, rebellion, 'all battles, sieges & fights at sea and land', his recovery from smallpox, his good health, his preservation from plots, and 'for giving me a true sense of past sins, for opening my eyes to being a true convert to his true Church'. This Augustinian sensitivity to the workings of Providence in his reign and exile saturates his memoirs.

Since the time of Elizabeth, Catholic apologists had compared favourably the unity and continuous infallible tradition of Catholicism with the fissiparous Babel of Protestant sectarianism, and James in his years as a Catholic constantly returned to this theme as his chief argument for persuading Protestants to popery. An interest in such Augustinian providentialist history attracted James to the writings of Bossuet, bishop of Meaux in 1681, royal preacher and preceptor, who was known as 'the theologian of Providence'. As king, James had encouraged English translations of Bossuet. He must also have been aware of the impact of Bossuet's *Histoire des variations des eglises protestantes* (1688), whose central theme was the continuing adherence of Catholicism to the apostolic tradition in the midst of Protestant divisions and 'equivocations'. Bossuet's apologetics converted James's close friend James Drummond, Earl of Perth, to Catholicism, but he had been first led to Bossuet through having read James's account of his brother's conversion referred to earlier. It was probably Drummond who first introduced James to La Trappe, where the abbot corresponded with Bossuet.[22] Bossuet's favourite quotation from St Augustine, 'he who doesn't groan like a pilgrim, cannot rejoice as a citizen', eminently defines the theological explanation James II gave of his afflictions. The seventeenth century generated an immense devotional literature, mostly by Jesuits, relating to life's journey as a pilgrimage of the Cross, and much of it, thanks partly to its use of emblems, achieved in translation an unusual popularity in England. Bunyan therefore had his Catholic counterparts. Translations of such

---

[22] P. Talbot, *A Treatise of the Nature of Catholick Faith and Heresie. By N. N.* (Rouen, 1657) (T. H. Clancy, *English Catholic Books 1641–1700: A Bibliography. Revised Edition* (Aldershot, 1996), no. 939 notes that this work, which ends with a dialogue between a learned Protestant and a Catholic clown, was supposed to have been instrumental in James's conversion); *Papers of Devotion*, 107–9; Earle, *James II*, 87; Turner, *James II*, 370; A.J. Krailsheimer, 'La Trappe et Jacques II', in Corp, *Cour des Stuarts*, 133; A.J. Krailsheimer, *Rancé and the Trappist Legacy* (Kalamazoo, MI, 1985), 81; A.J. Krailsheimer, *Armand-Jean de Rancé: Abbot of La Trappe* (Oxford, 1974), 265; J.-B. Bossuet, *Œuvres* (Paris, 1841), XVII, 172, 244–5, 349; J. Le Brun, *La Spiritualité de Bossuet* (Paris, 1972). For Bossuet and the Jacobites, see G. Scott, 'A Benedictine Conspirator: Henry Joseph Johnston (c. 1656–1723)', *Recusant History* 20, no. 1, (May 1990), 58–75.

pilgrim books by Lorenzo Scupoli, Hermann Hugo and Henri-Marie Boudon were produced for Catholics and their sympathisers at the Stuart court, and once the Jacobite court had been established at Saint-Germain, it would have itself become exposed to innumerable French editions of such devotional works.

This, then, is the context for James's own theology of the Cross and suffering, which matured through the bitter years of exile, and bore fruit in the king's deathbed agony. Students of Christian spirituality have noted that misery and mysticism are often related phenomena, and the king's downfall and his deepening appreciation of salvation through the meritorious suffering of Christ have been interpreted, with some originality, in the light of a contemporary resurgent Arianism which rejected the divinity of Christ at the same time as the Revolution 'laicised' the king. There is no doubt, however, that the doctrine of Redemption through the Cross was fundamental to James's Christian faith. His resignation allowed him to conduct himself with a 'habitual grandeur of soul', which to the ignorant made his patience and 'seeming easiness' appear 'an insensibility'. He discoursed on the happiness coming from suffering for God, and the Christian obligation to take up the Cross and follow Christ; Thomas a Kempis's *Imitation of Christ* was well known to him. For James, love of suffering was a certain proof of love for God, and like many seventeenth-century Catholics, James saw his own sufferings as a providential expiation. His 'particular devotion' to the Feast of the Exaltation of the Cross (14 September) gave him the opportunity 'to offer up himself as a sacrifice to God'. Found on his person at his capture at Faversham was King Edward the Confessor's gold crucifix which contained a relic of the True Cross, and which had been discovered during James's brief reign. It was from the Confessor that James derived the grace of the Royal Touch. As we shall see later, the spiritual works of the Spanish Jesuit Jean-Eusebe Nieremberg (1595–1658) exercised a profound influence on James. For this Jesuit, mortification was an essential way to reach the truth, and the Christian needed to conform his or her liberty to the divine will to the point of total renunciation in order to consummate the supreme sacrifice and thus acquire an anticipated joy of future heavenly felicity. Nieremberg was a teacher of that revived Christian Platonism so powerful in seventeenth-century *dévot* circles, among whom one must include James II. For such Platonists, the eternal and invisible might only be glimpsed through a meditation on earthly symbols, like the Cross, and to contrast the temporal and the eternal, Nieremberg employed that artifice so common in contemporary baroque religious art, the *clair-obscur*, or *chiaroscuro*. It was a device frequently resorted to by James II in his own writings to reveal the constancies and contraries of the visitations of divine providence.[23]

Observers were struck by the dominance of the Cross in the king's understanding of his faith and his destiny. As 'the most Abus'd of all mankind', he presented an effigy of 'a suffering Prince', whose great love for penance 'changed all his afflictions in consolations'. His coronation on the Feast of the Finding of the Cross (3 May) was seen as a happy coincidence, determining that he would be 'comformable to the Image of Jesus Christ Crucified, whose kingdom was not of this world'. He is shown wearing a crown of thorns in a book of 1692 describing his solitude and sufferings. On his deathbed, his aversion to Peruvian bark and other medicines disappeared when he recollected how Christ had willingly taken gall and vinegar on the cross. James died on a Friday, at the same hour his Master had died, and the panegyric at his funeral and his epitaph spoke of him as 'a victim for his Church and his Religion'. It is not surprising that, thanks to his perceived sanctity, his *cultus* soon developed, encouraged by English Jacobites and by Rancé (died 1700), the influential abbot of La Trappe who had been impressed by his resignation and told him he was treading the same road as his Master.[24]

James's devotional life, with its emphasis on mortification and Christian sacrifice which consecrated his afflictions, was nourished by the liturgy. For the royal chapels in London, Henry Hills, the king's publisher, had printed the service books and the texts of sermons delivered to the royal family. Here liturgy was celebrated openly and magnificently, as 'in a cathedral', especially the services held in the new chapel at Whitehall, which was opened at Christmas 1686. At Saint-Germain, the rites were the same, with allowances made for Gallican customs, and the liturgy was celebrated in the three chapels of the château by the chaplains who were among the sixteen or so resident

---

[23] [Henry Keepe], *Edovardus Confessor Redivivus. The Piety and Vertues of Holy Edward the Confessor, Reviv'd in the Sacred Majesty of King James the II. Being a Relation of the Admirable and Unexpected finding of a Sacred Relique . . . since worn sometimes by his present Majesty* (London, 1688); Cottret, 'La sainteté', 81; *Memoirs of King James II*, 9–20. For the high value given to resignation to providence in the King's exile, see Esprit Fléchier, 'Sermon des Afflictions preché devant le Roi et la Reine d'Angleterre, à S. Germain en Laye', in his *Sermons sur differens sujets*, II (Brussels, 1696), 77–102.

[24] *Memoirs of King James II*, preface, 8, 9, 17, 26; B. Weldon, *Chronological Notes . . . of the English Congregation of the Order of St. Benedict* (Worcester, 1881), 242, 243, 245, 248; Weldon, 'Memorials', v, 516; *Abrégé*, 148, 160, 161; *Royal Tracts. In Two Parts . . . The II Containing Imago Regis: Or, the True Portraicture of His Sacred Majesty, in his Solitude and Sufferings* (Paris, 1692), frontispiece, 82–4. Sylvester Jenks, *A Contrite and Humble Heart* (Paris, 1692), lists the acts of treachery towards James. Krailsheimer, *Trappist Legacy*, 114; Krailsheimer, *Rancé: Correspondance*, IV, 92, 400; A.J. Krailsheimer, *The Letters of Armand-Jean de Rancé: Abbot and Reformer of La Trappe* (Kalamazoo, MI, 1984), letters 890105, 901129.

priests. The celebration of the liturgy remained central to James's religious life. He heard two or three masses daily, communicated twice weekly, and 'nothing stopped him from assisting at public prayers each day in the Chapel, and at Vespers [*Salut*] in the parish church or in neighbouring churches'. During High Mass and the Divine Office, onlookers noted that he prayed 'totally fixed on God without interruption and without the slightest distraction', refusing the offer of a hassock and kneeling on the bottom step of the altar.[25]

It is important to realise, therefore, that James behaved as an orthodox Catholic in the sense that his private devotions derived essentially from the Church's liturgy. The celebration of Mass and the sacraments, as well as the Divine Office, inspired his membership of confraternities, his devotion to relics of the saints, his praying of the rosary and his attendance at Benediction and Quarant' Ore, as well as that other famous sacramental rite, the imparting of the Royal Touch. The derivation of his, and others', private prayer-life from liturgical forms explains the reason behind John Caryll's translation in 1700 of *The Psalmes of David* from the Vulgate, 'intended only for the privat devotions of Lay persons' at the Jacobite court. The work was published at Saint-Germain by William Weston, the successor to Henry Hills as royal publisher.[26]

While the Confraternity of the Rosary in London throughout James's reign had been the preserve of an aristocratic elite, and was responsible for the publishing of some devotional works which inspired the king, James seems himself to have been more attached to the Confraternity for a Happy Death (the Confraternity of 'the Agony of Christ' or 'Bona Mors', as it was commonly known), a Jesuit-inspired confraternity which had a phenomenal popularity. Seventeenth-century interest in the deathbed bordered on the obsessive,

[25] Of the liturgical books, the binding and rarity of *Short Prayers for the Use of All Good Catholics in the Hearing of the Holy Mass* (London, 1688) suggests it was printed for use in the king's chapel. For one of the royal preachers, see G. Holt, 'Edward Scarisbrick, 1639–1709: A Royal Preacher', *Recusant History*, 23, no. 2 (October 1996), 159–65. See also *Life of James II*, ii, 6; Turner, *James II*, 246; Ashley, *James II*, 158. Printed sermons will be found in Clancy, *English Catholic Books*, and include nos. 95, 235, 235.3, 347.3, 348.47, 359, 416, 417, 481.2, 514, 516, 519, 549, 683, 764, 857, 858, 864, 1912.7. For Saint-Germain, Corp, *Cour des Stuarts*, 32, 136, and Corp, 'Jacobite Chapel Royal', 528–42. *Abrégé*, 84; Krailsheimer, *Letters of Rancé*, no. 901129.

[26] *Catholic Record Society* 25 (London, 1925), 106–7 for relics; *Abrégé*, 82; *Papers of Devotion*, 79 for Vespers from the Manual, and daily evening Rosary in chapel, Benediction on Fridays, Benediction, fasting and prayers for the conversion of England on third Wednesday of each month; Turner, *James II*, 427 for Quarant' Ore; G. Scott, 'Sacredness of Majesty: The English Benedictines and the Cult of King James II', *Royal Stuart Society Papers* XXIII (Huntingdon, 1984), for the Touch. Weston also published for Princess Marie-Louise, *A manual of devout prayers and other Christian devotions fitted for all persons &c occasions* (Saint-Germain, n.d.).

especially among religious persons, and it was the common belief that a
sudden and unprovided death led to hell. Charles II's deathbed conversion
remained imprinted on James's mind and he advised the Duke of Berwick
to reflect how, as a soldier, he was constantly exposed to the danger of a
sudden death. James often spoke of being profoundly affected by the calm
and casual sacrifice which the edifying monks of La Trappe made of their
lives, and within months of being introduced to the community, he became
a confrater on the understanding that 'those who belong to God . . . are
able to help those afflicted and in difficulty'. It was to La Trappe that the
king sent a *relation* of the edifying death in 1695 of his close companion
Sir Edward Hales. In exile, James, and his chief advisors, like David Nairne,
continued to perform the exercises demanded of the confraternity's members,
which formed a meditation on the human suffering of Christ and which urged
them to proselytise. The Confraternity of the Bona Mors thus further deep-
ened the king's understanding of Christ's passion as well as familiarising him
with the traditional English Catholic translations of the hymns in the Manual. His holy desire of death was further enlivened by the popular books on
the subject by Pierre Lallement (1622–73), whose *The Holy Desires of Death* he
specifically encouraged his disciples to read. The English translation of this
book appeared in 1678, the work of the chaplain to the Confraternity of the
Rosary, the Benedictine Dom Vincent Sadler, 'at the instance of a Person of
Honour'. In this patristic *florilegium*, whose titlepage quotes Augustine, 'The
Perfect Man Lives Patiently and Dies Pleasantly', Lallement urged his readers
'to be attentive to the agitations of human passions, the shortness of life, and
the uncertainty of death' so as never to engage themselves in the tumults of
the world 'and be evermore prepared to die'. James's writings of devotion are
impregnated by Lallement's sentiments.

James stood firm in his belief that a frail sinner should often pray to die
well, and was inclined to give moral anecdotes about easy-going aristocrats
who thought they had covered all contingencies, including a chaplain at hand,
and had gambled on a conversion *in extremis*, but were fated to die suddenly
without Extreme Unction. It was James's graphic illustration of Nieremberg's
counsel: 'With what art men keep their temporal things, even when they run
no hazard . . . But as we are in a continual danger from death, we ought to be
continually prepared. It is good ever to have our Accompts made with God.
It is good to play a sure game.' When James's own 'happy hour' came, his joy
was evident, and onlookers noted that his lips seemed to become glued to the
crucifix which he kissed on his deathbed, while the prayers for a Happy Death
were being recited. For her part, Queen Mary Beatrice expressed her unease

at the king's morbid desire for death, but it was in vain, and he continued to look death joyfully in the face, confessing that 'what hinders us from desiring to die is want of love of God'.[27]

It is clear that the guiding spirit in James's conversion and devotional life was the Society of Jesus. Indeed, he had been mistaken as a Jesuit when captured at Faversham, and Voltaire later started the malicious rumour that he had been a covert member of the Society. Characteristic of late seventeenth-century Jesuit spirituality was its emphasis on the mastery of the will, the relation of free will to grace, its humane approach to penitents and its inculcation of a spirit of prayer which was practical rather than contemplative and which enlivened an active and involved Christian life. Jesuit influence can be traced in the structured daily round of the king's religious duties, which involved discursive and pictorial meditation as well as intensive self-examination. In his devotions centred on Christ's Passion, for instance, the king prayed and meditated on each of the Five Wounds in turn and was instructed to keep 'a Picture or Image of our Saviour crucified [and his Mother] in her agony of Grief' to represent in his mind the mystery of the Redemption. His Jesuit confessor directed him to read Jesuit authors like Rodriguez, and in his monthly retreat he read the Jesuit Jean Croiset's *Retraite spirituelle* (1694), 'whose method he followed exactly', and extracts from which he gave to close friends like David Nairne. Jesuit involvement can also be discerned in his enthusiasm for hagiography, his own spiritual odyssey being written by his confessor, Francis Sanders S.J. The influence of the Society also lay behind his continual struggle to conform his own will to that of God, by disengaging himself from a world that was

---

[27] *Life of James II*, I, 748–9; II, 589–91; *A Pious Exercise of Devotion to the Sacred Passion of Our Saviour, For obtaining a happy Death, to be Performed every Fryday in Her Majesties Chapel* (London, H. Hills, ?1686); J.M. Blom, *The Post-Tridentine English Primer*, Catholic Record Society Monograph 3 (London, 1982), 226, for the Stabat Mater ['Under the world-redeeming rood']; *Memoirs of King James II*, II, 21, 23, 31, 49, 50; Krailsheimer, 'La Trappe et Jacques II', 133; Krailsheimer, *Correspondance*, IV, 136, 401; *Abrégé*, 132–4, 137–8, 150–1, 159; *Pious Sentiments*, 33–44; *Papers of Devotion*, xxvii–xxviii, 9–10; Henri Brémond, *Histoire littéraire du sentiment religieux en France depuis la fin des guerres de religion jusqu'à nos jours*, IX (Paris, 1932), 351; P. Lallement, *The Holy Desires of Death. Or a Collection of some Thoughts of the Fathers of the Church to shew how Christians ought to despise Life, and to desire Death. Englished by T. V. at the Insistance of a Person of Honour* (1678), London, 216; Francis de Sales, *Introduction to the Devout Life*, ed. M. Day (London, 1956); Eusebius Nieremberg, *A Treatise of the Difference Betwixt the Temporal and Eternal* (London, 1672), dedicated to Catherine of Braganza by the Jesuit John Warner-Clare (original Spanish edition, 1640), 128; Krailsheimer, *Armand-Jean de Rancé*, 268; Nairne's diary for latter's membership of Bona Mors; BL Add. MSS 10118, 416b, 417b; Phillip's Sale Catalogue of the contents of Corby Castle, Carlisle, 18 May 1994, item 38, Jacobite memorial panel, with text, of last hours of James II, 1712; *Papers of Devotion*, 87–8, 96–9.

but 'vanity and affliction of spirit'. This was to be 'his first study', and his determined zeal impressed the abbot of La Trappe.

Above all, James's perspective which sharply divided the temporal from the eternal derived from contemporary Jesuit ascetical theology. Not only did he frequently read *The Holy Desires of Death* of Lallement (a Genovefain, not a Jesuit) and Nieremberg's *Time and Eternity*, but he recommended the latter book to courtiers whose nights were disturbed by nightmares caused by 'the Revolutions in England'. It had, he said, allowed him to sleep quietly 'in the midst of my misfortunes'. Nieremberg, who was popular among both Anglicans and Catholics, proposed a model of a Christian knight who would reach the truth through mortification and the use of the human will assisted by divine grace. Adversity would be overcome through the will fixing its attention on the eternal world, and by a lively desire for death. This use of the human will achieving a liberty by conforming itself to the divine will lay at the heart of Ignatian spirituality, and was behind James's vow to accomplish God's will by detachment, mortification and humility.

It was Nieremberg's lively contrast between the temporal and eternal, developed from his synthesis of Renaissance Neoplatonism and Augustinianism, which particularly appealed to James, whose 'calm originated from a disengagement of all the things of this world and a high esteem for eternal wealth'. Man's vain, tangled and toilsome life was, according to the Jesuit, like a spider forming 'his Pavilion' from the excrements of its own entrails, consuming and disembowelling itself to weave its web. Time and the visible world were only a reflected and ambiguous shadow of eternity and its invisible world. The world was 'like a house filled with smoke, wherein nothing could be seen either within or without'. 'Having framed a lively conception of Eternity, it is necessary to retain it in continual memory'; that was the principal object to which the king's prayer was directed. James was struck by the Jesuit's central idea that our life in the world was essentially an anamorphosis, and by sharpening of our focus away from the temporal world and the *visibilia* through a devout life, we are granted the means to reach eternity. Death and suffering are proof that the prison of the flesh is not eternal, and they are borne in the knowledge that the soul's true home is elsewhere. Our temporal prison provides us with signs which allow us to glimpse and decipher the real, though invisible, world. According to Nieremberg, God conducts himself as a *Magister comoediae*, leaving the visible world, stuffed with illusion, unreality and deception, to transform and alter itself by means of angelic and human will. James thus imbibed the central Jesuit doctrine that by conforming and utterly renouncing his own will to the divine will, he would consummate the supreme sacrifice and thus experience here on earth something of heavenly felicity. This was, furthermore, an ideal which he shared with the Trappists, who strove to subjugate the individual to the divine will and to discard any attachment to transitory values in their appreciation of the immediacy of the eternal.[28]

If Nieremberg encouraged James to look beyond the confines of this lower world towards eternity, the king's daily living out of his Christian vocation found sustenance in the teachings of St Francis de Sales, the early seventeenth-century bishop of Geneva whose books have enjoyed enduring popularity, and who had himself been educated by the Jesuits. The king and the queen were frequent visitors to the monastery of the Visitation at Chaillot, in Paris, whose community had been founded by St Francis, and which was to be responsible for preserving memories of the king's life. De Sales wrote to help lay-folk leading 'an ordinary life', which partly explains why James found his doctrine attractive, and he took to heart the saint's advice to find a sound spiritual director. Whilst admiring the eremitical and Trappist life, James insisted that he had to work out his salvation in the world and not hide himself in the desert or in the enclosure of the cloister: 'we must all have the same Christian spirit and to save ourselves each according to the situation'. St Francis taught that self-control, attention to prayer, perseverance in virtue and a sense of dedication were as essential to the laity's vocation as they were to professional religious. Some of St Francis's sunny optimism must have rubbed off on James and its mark on the king's thought helps to soften any extreme characterisation we might be tempted to make of him as a depressive introvert in the last decade of his life. It was, for instance, wholesome Salesian teaching for James to affirm that 'God showed his love by giving us his Son, and if we consider and reflect on this, we shall see he continues the same love towards us by bringing us into this world, to capacitate us to be members of his heavenly kingdom.'

We are told that it was from de Sales's two most famous books, *Treatise on the Love of God* and *Introduction to a Devout Life*, that James 'drew the Rules

---

[28] Miller, *James II*, 206; Ushaw College, Durham, Lingard Letters 411, 412; H. Outram Evennett, *The Spirit of the Counter-Reformation* (Cambridge, 1968), 43–4; *A Pious Exercise*, 20–1, 42–3; Nairne, 18 February, 19–20 October and 18 November 1701, 11 January, 16–18 March and 11, 13–15 July 1702, and 2 May 1703; Nieremberg, *Treatise*, 2, 3–12; *Papers of Devotion*, xx, 18, 80; *Cour des Stuarts*, 132; *Abrégé*, 57, 59–63, 66–9, 82, 85, 93–5, 111–12, 114, 127–30, 221–35; *Life of James II*, 1, 440–1; [James II], *EIKON BASILIKE DEUTERA*, 259; *Memoirs of King James II*, 10, 13–15, 18, 21–3, 27; M. Viller *et al.*, (ed.), *Dictionnaire de Spiritualité*, xi (Paris, 1982), cols. 328–35; H. Thurston, 'A Curious Literary Imposture', *The Month* (May 1885), 1–14; Krailsheimer, *Trappist Legacy*, 75.

of his Conduct', and that 'he never passed a day without reading a chapter out of one or other of them, that there was no purer Doctrine, nor more conformable to the Gospel, than that of this great Saint'. From *The Love of God,* published in 1616, the king learned that God was to be loved above all else, and derived that sense of resignation and patient submission to the will of God which marked his last years. St Francis also provided the framework for his faith. St Francis had taught that all were bound to follow the evangelical counsels suitable to their circumstances, that the will might repulse the sensual appetite, that the desire of paradise was praiseworthy, that the just man might die suddenly but never unprovidedly, that afflictions and anguish of which life is full are 'ladders to ascend to heaven', and that 'love is at its height' when we embrace afflictions 'for the sake of the Divine good-pleasure'. Indifference was, furthermore, superior to resignation, 'for it loves nothing except for the love of God's will'. These were, as we have seen, among the principal concerns of James during his exile at Saint-Germain, where, following St Francis's exhortation to frequent reception of communion – 'weak people should communicate often' – he communicated twice weekly from 1696, and kept rigorously to his daily exercises of devotion. In his letter to an unknown correspondent, he explained 'that those who have lots of worldly business should also frequently communicate because they need it. For the man who works hard has to eat solid meat and nourish himself with good food. You have only to read the 20th and 21st Chapter of the *Introduction to the Devout Life* to convince yourself that there is nothing so necessary as frequent communion for those persons who wish to live Christian lives.'

Critics of James have been quick to seize upon his avoidance of balls, the theatre and opera, and his disdain of gambling, as killjoy symptoms of his depression, but his practice here followed Salesian teaching. St Francis had cautioned that while harmless in themselves, dances encouraged vanity, over-familiarity and moral laxity. They were spongy, like pumpkins and mushrooms, and absorbed vices. The saint counselled prudence and discretion for those who took part in such amusements out of charity, and James followed his advice, avoiding as far as possible attendance 'at the ball, opera and Comedie', but not shunning such diversions when invited so as 'not to appear singular or affected'. Instead of wasting time entertaining oneself, he thought it preferable to visit prisons and hospitals. In James's opinion gambling games excited greed, oaths and anger; they wasted time and made the losers depressed. This 'vicious habit' was 'a great form of slavery' which dominated even very sensible people, for as St Francis had himself noticed, 'There is no concentration so morose, gloomy and depressing as that of gamblers; no one may speak or laugh, or even cough, while they are playing for fear of annoying them.'[29]

Jesuit books of devotion and the works of Francis de Sales were familiar to the English court in London. Exile introduced the king to the religious life as a setting and support for his personal piety. In his first exile, he had occasionally met monks and nuns. In 1649 he had lodged some weeks in the Flemish monastery of St Armand, his 'first serious contact with Roman Catholic discipline and practice', and in 1651 he had attended masses in Brussels 'upon pretence of hearing good music'. In 1698, he looked back on these events as the means of kindling his Catholic faith and as encounters granted him by Providence to 'acquire a greater degree of perfection'. In his second exile, James had begun making a regular retreat at Chaillot, near Paris, where the heart of his mother was enshrined, as early as Lent 1689, and had prayed there before the exposed Sacrament. Frequent visits followed which turned into annual visits, and these the king used to come to a deeper understanding of conformity to God's will, especially after the failure of the Irish expedition. In addition, he spent one day each month in retreat, reading the Jesuit, Jean Croisset's, *Spiritual Retreat* (English editions, 1698 and 1700). Holy Week was usually spent on retreat in Paris where the king celebrated the offices of the church. He and his retinue, for instance, lodged with the English Benedictines in the rue Saint-Jacques in 1694 and 1696, staying in solitude in the monastic infirmary from where a squint looked out onto the high altar of the monks' church. His faith, however, attained a new level of maturity in his second exile, through his journey to the reformed Cistercian house of La Trappe, whose guiding light, Abbot Armand-Jean de Rancé, exercised a profound influence over the *dévot* party in late seventeenth-century France.[30]

La Trappe, with its extreme austerity, seems to have been the king's preferred place of retreat. He began his visits there in November 1690, out of curiosity, having read about the monastery before the Revolution, and was taken there by his friend, the maréchal de Bellefonds. Even at La Trappe, the Jesuit influence

---

[29] Evennett, *Spirit*, 32; *The Memoirs of King James II* contain 'A Circular Letter from the Religious Convent of Chaillot', which is found in numerous other editions, see especially 4–6, 8, 14, 25; Francis de Sales, *Treatise on the Love of God*, ed. B. Mackey (London, 1884), 22, 114, 307, 346, 366, 372; F. de Sales, *Devout Life*, 172–7; *Abrégé*, 74, 77, 83, 95–6, 100, 144, 152, 175–85, 189–92, 235–42, 254; *Pious Sentiments*, 1–5, 8–14; *Papers of Devotion*, 10–11, 16, 31–5, 42–9, 56, 112, 117–24, 154–60, 169; *Life of James II*, II, 497, 583, 587; Brémond, *Histoire*, IX, 48.

[30] *Papers of Devotion*, xvii–xix; *Life of James II* I, 540; II, 582–3; Turner, *James II*, 22; Ashley, *James II*, 72; Krailsheimer, *Armand-Jean de Rancé*, 269; *Memoirs of King James II*, 2–3, 23–4, 28; Weldon, 'Memorials', IV, 266–7, and *Chronological Notes*, 235; *Orthodox Journal*, 31 January 1835, no. 58; *Cour des Stuarts*, 132, 134, 138.

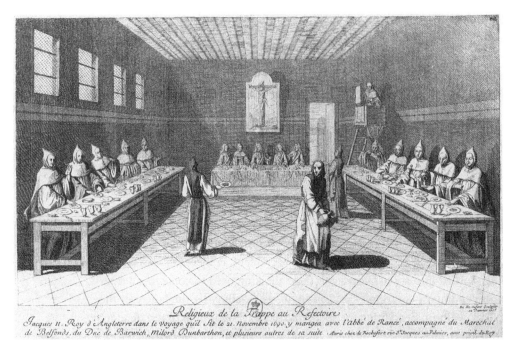

FIG. 25. De Rochefort, *Religieux de la Trappe au Refectoire. Jacques II Roy d'Angleterre dans le voyage qu'il fit le 21 novembre 1690. Y mangea avec l'abbé de Rancé, accompagné du Maréchal de Belfonds, du Duc de Barwick, Milord Dunbarthon, et plusieurs autres de sa suite* (BN Est. Qb¹ M.93848). This engraving, published in 1708, shows James II in the middle, below the painting of the crucifixion. The others at the same table are, from left to right, the Duke of Berwick, Rancé, the marquis de Bellefonds, and the gentleman of the Bedchamber in attendance (the Earl of Dumbarton).

on James was pervasive, for during his visits he was accompanied by his Jesuit confessor, and James's interest in the moralistic maxims he found painted on the walls of the refectory perhaps indicate his fondness for Jesuit mnemonics. Annual visits followed, in which he made a retreat of three or four days, living and praying with the community, grateful that Providence had brought him to this place, 'a proper School of Christian patience'. The Trappist 'spirit of penance' profoundly affected him, and taught him that through mortification one was able to be touched by 'the Divine goodness'. He was especially edified by the happy death of certain of the monks, some of whom were Jacobites, and by the community's 'fervent devotions'.

James's virtues made an immediate impression on Rancé, and he accorded him the status of ancient saints and heroes, raised to sanctity by their patient endurance of misfortunes. He spoke constantly of the sweetness of the king's conduct and his 'tranquillity and evenness of mind', his 'disengagement from worldly things and a resignation to the will of God'. It is clear that king and abbot shared the same religious outlook, for both acknowledged the absolute sovereignty of God, and accepted that love of God must replace self-love through penance and mortification in a world which was only a stormy sea of glittering delusion. James, in Rancé's opinion, enjoyed a peace and holy repose, possessed also by those in monasteries, which was a proof of divine protection; in him 'nature has given way to peace'. The monastic life at La Trappe, formed according to the spirituality of Rancé, with its intense antithesis between life and death, love of self and love of God, worldly bondage and heavenly freedom, provided a living example of what James held to be the epitome of the Christian life. Since Rancé had insisted that all could imbibe the spirit of La Trappe without necessarily becoming professed religious, it also provided a working framework for James to put his cherished Jesuit and Salesian ascetical lessons into practice.[31]

From what has already been said, James II emerges as an example of that dynamic Christian humanism which the Catholic Reformation sought to inculcate especially among the aristocratic laity who, by following its disciplines, might aspire to a high level of perfection 'even in the middle of this world'. He was acknowledged as such by Pope Clement XI in the papal panegyric following his death in 1702. We are told that what James jotted down after his arrival in France was 'of a different nature to that which he wrote at other times', for here, he was preoccupied with his salvation and his Christian duties, and he took care 'to make note of the reflections which he made for his own education and for the education of those persons whose conversion and advancement was dear to his heart'. In countries affected by the Catholic Reformation, education in its humanism took place pre-eminently within the family, and the biographies of James clearly emphasise the devotion he had to his wife and family. He took great care to train his sons and daughter in the virtues he strove for himself, and was critical of parents who indulged their children. As a father, he advised the young James FitzJames, Duke of Berwick to beware of being led away by 'deceitful pleasure'. Blessing his heir,

[31] Ashley, *James II*, 280, and Earle, *James II*, 213–15, for Protestant feelings about La Trappe; *Memoirs of King James II*, 11–12, 41; Miller, *James II*, 233ff; *Life of James II*, II, 495–6, 528–9, 582, 589, 614–16; Corp, *Cour des Stuarts*, 133–8; *Abrégé*, 112–25; *Papers of Devotion*, xxviii, 63–8, 111; Krailsheimer, *Trappist Legacy*, 53, 75–6, 80 98, 113–15; *Relations de la Vie et de la Mort de quelques religieux de l'Abbaye de La Trappe* (Paris, 1716), 1–84; Lallement, *Holy Desires*, 288, 294; Krailsheimer, *Correspondance*, I, 35–40; IV, 62–4, 69–71, 92–3, 368–9, 387–8, 400–1, 445–6, 453, 458, 460; Krailsheimer, *Letters of Rancé*, nos. 881229a, 890105, 890117, 890414, 9001129, 901221, 910120, 920609a, 920619a, 960700, 970314; Krailsheimer, *Armand-Jean de Rancé*, 51, 86, 95, 98, 265, 329–30; Schimmelpenninck, *Memoirs*, III, 312–20.

James Edward, with the Sign of the Cross, the king's last recorded words to him were: 'We can never lose too much for God.' The king's 'Instructions to the Prince of Wales' are a recapitulation of the ideals of a Christian humanist ruler with obligations to God and to his subjects achieved through faith and personal moral integrity.

The doctrines of the post-Reformation Catholic church, which were dispersed rapidly throughout seventeenth-century France, demanded an educated and reinvigorated laity as an active instrument in a missionary endeavour which had the Society of Jesus in the forefront. The church's aim here was nothing less than the sacralisation of society, and it was aware that 'a publick person instructs well, who lives well'. This was the vocation adopted by James II, who made fervent efforts to bring converts to Catholicism from among Protestants. He was persuaded that they might be prompted to tread the same providential path as he had himself, from 'a libertine life' to one lived 'according to the rules of evangelical perfection'. He was harsh on those who had lapsed from their original calling; as his eyes traversed the 60,000 French soldiers encamped at Compiègne in 1698, he had the 'melancholy reflection' that 'few of them think of their duty to the king of kings', preferring instead the fond amusements of the world.[32]

James followed a daily pattern of life with great exactness: morning prayer was followed by meditation or *lectio divina* in private, the hearing of two masses daily, and the day rounded off with vespers and the recital of the rosary. Determined to mortify himself and to make satisfaction for his past life, he secretly wore on his body an iron chain with sharp points on certain days and took the Discipline. In ascetical theology, this, the lowest stage of the spiritual life, is traditionally termed *praxis*. Such examples of physical austerity were common in the penitential culture of seventeenth-century Catholicism where Augustinianism was so prevalent. Nieremberg remarked on similar heroic austerities practised by St Ignatius, and counselled that 'the peccant humours of our soul are not purged by living pleasantly', and that 'voluntary austerities make man have a more frequent recourse to God, and being void of

[32] *Abrégé*, 4; *Memoirs of King James II*, 31, 40; *Cour des Stuarts*, 140 and no. 147; *Abrégé*, Avertissement, 105–11, 141, 164–71, 177, 190, 196, 242–72, 281–301; *Pious Sentiments*, 16–18; *Papers of Devotion*, 4–9, 16–19, 53–4, 59, 65–6, 126–9, 135–9; *Life of James II*, II, 588, 593, 619–31; Nieremberg, *Treatise*, Epistle Dedicatory; Krailsheimer, *Correspondance*, IV, 63; *Pious Exercise*, 20; H. Brémond, *A Literary History of Religious Thought in France* (London, 1928), I, 405. *The works of . . . Armand de Bourbon, Prince de Conti, with a discourse on Christian Perfection by the Archbishop of Cambray* (London, 1711) contains typical teachings on conduct given by aristocratic fathers to their sons, similar to that given by James II to his son.

sensible gust they dispose him better for divine illustrations . . . Make thyself formidable to thyself.' It appears that the king had some doubts about the full efficacy of such practices, questioning whether the performance of works of mercy might be preferable. He was, indeed, discouraged from extreme austerity by his confessor, while Rancé taught that the main purpose of such penitential exercises was to foster the love of God by eradicating all trace of self-love. These were also the sentiments of Francis de Sales, who believed such 'macerations of the flesh' were less meritorious than resignation with sweetness and patience to afflictions sent by the Divine will. Why beat the poor ass, your body, he asked, which cannot help you and is not the cause of God's sword being drawn against you? Such distinguished masters of the spiritual craft placed love of God before hatred of the body and King James adopted from them his own powerful sense of self-abandonment to divine providence.[33]

The nature of James's devotional life is most clearly reflected in the spiritual works which informed his piety and in his own autobiographical writings. Henri Brémond, in his magisterial work on the history of seventeenth-century religious thought, argued that devotional literature is 'never platonic, it addresses itself to the imagination and the intellect solely to influence the will . . . A devotional book . . . starts a vibration . . . while biography colours their [the readers'] mind and imagination . . . These two branches of devotional literature [should be placed] side by side . . . Spiritual masters lived their books and have told their own life-stories in writing them . . . [The devout are] an incarnation of some particular aspect of the religious genius of the epoch.' With King James II we have already seen how his biographical writings were a remembrance of past graces and provided an impulse towards mastery of the will in the future, helped by a regular pattern of life which was calculated to bring him to that elevated state which he also determined to inculcate in his son and heir.

In his exile, the king's humility was proverbial and afforded an example of a human warmth and humour which starkly contrasted with the usual serious intensity and earnestness of his lifestyle. On a wet afternoon, he turned up, for

[33] *Memoirs of King James II*, 12, 16; *Abrégé*, 70–6, 79–83; *Papers of Devotion*, 63, 79, 162; *Life of James II*, II, 585–6. For mortification, see Ann W. Ramsey, 'Flagellation and the French Counter-Reformation: Asceticism, Social Discipline, and the Evolution of a Penitential Culture', in Vincent L. Wimbush and Richard Valantasis (eds.) *Asceticism*, (New York and Oxford, 1995); Krailsheimer, *Trappist Legacy*, 40–1, 95. James's Discipline afterwards became a notable relic at Chaillot, Earle, *James II*, 282 footnote; Nieremberg, *Of Adoration in Spirit and Truth* (London, 1673, edition of 1871), 78–80; F. de Sales, *Treatise*, 371; *Devout Life*, 153.

instance, at the English Benedictine priory in Paris, wrapped up and disguised by his cloak, begging shelter. The short-sighted porter, 'taking him only for a Gentleman [and] not aware of his Star . . . trudged to acquaint [the] worthy superior . . . The King followed him into the Cloister . . . where H.M's. great Piety took great delight in the pleasantness of the mistake.' In this case, the notion of 'hiding the king', noted by Paul Monod as a metaphor for Stuart propaganda, whereby his identity was hidden from all except those who loved him, exemplified the royal virtue of humility. James never ceased to emphasise the *noblesse oblige* incumbent on kings and their need to balance their superiority of status by cultivating the virtue of humility. As early as 1686, he had heard the secular priest Thomas Codrington relate how the confessor of the Emperor Charles V had refused to allow the emperor to excuse his political negligences by concentrating solely on his personal failings: '*And is this all* [he said], *O Emperor? Sure it cannot be; Dixisti peccata* Caroli, *dic nunc peccata* Caesaris: *You have confess'd the Sins of* Charles *only; now confess the Sins of* Caesar!'[34]

It seems, then, that King James II's piety exhibited a greater spiritual maturity than perhaps has generally been admitted. In his low devout melancholy and zeal to lead a Christian life through submission of self to the divine will, he is representative of that remarkable lay seventeenth-century Christian spirit which was nourished by the Catholic Reformation, and more specifically by members of the Society of Jesus. More than anyone else, he was responsible for introducing into Protestant England the energy and enthusiasm of that reforming tide. It was to remain a permanent possession of English Catholicism. His later exile provided him with the opportunity to enter more deeply into the currents of the Catholic revival within a more sympathetic context and in the eyes of many contemporaries he was recognised as a saint after his death.

[34] Brémond, *Literary History*, I, xiv–xv; *Cour des Stuarts*, 140. G. Scott, 'John Betham et l'éducation du Prince de Galles', *Revue de la Bibliothèque Nationale*, 46, (hiver 1992), 32–9; Miller, *James II*, 203, 207, 220; *Abrégé*, 90–2; Weldon, 'Memorials', I, 266–7; P.K. Monod, *Jacobitism and the English People* (Cambridge, 1989), 72; T. Codrington, *A Sermon Preach'd before their Majesties, in St. James's on Advent-Sunday, November 28, 1686* (London, 1741), 48–9.

CHAPTER ELEVEN

The education of James III

Given the circumstances of his exile and the fact of his growing piety, it was natural that James II should attach the greatest importance to providing his son with a carefully planned education. This was no simple matter, because English Catholics were divided at the time between the secular and the regular clergy (notably the Jesuits), and James II had to choose a preceptor from one or other of these opposing groups.

According to an account written by Thomas Sheridan, the king originally intended to appoint a Jesuit,[1] but in 1691 the Catholic bishops in England sent a letter urging him to commit the education of his son 'to some of the secular clergy'. Louis XIV apparently supported them and in March 1692, when the Prince of Wales was still only three years old, James II appointed two secular priests to the posts of preceptor and under-preceptor. The former was Dr John Betham, who had been educated at the English College in Douai, and whose career will be discussed in detail below by Abbot Geoffrey Scott. The latter was Thomas Codrington, previously one of the preachers in the Catholic chapel at Whitehall, who died in February 1694 and was not immediately replaced.

Following normal practice, James II intended to entrust the Prince of Wales to a governor, and to give him his own household, when he reached the age of seven in June 1695. However, the unexpected death in October 1693 of his governess, the Countess of Erroll, upset these plans. The king recalled Lady Strickland, a former under-governess, to take temporary charge, and determined to appoint a permanent governor and a separate household as soon as suitable people could be found.

During 1694 the secular and regular clergy each put forward candidates for the post of governor. The Jesuits apparently suggested Lord Castlemaine,

[1] SP Misc. 7, Thomas Sheridan, 'Political Reflexions on the history and Government of England, the late Revolution and other State affairs, written by an impartial hand in the year 1709', a manuscript of 199 pages, of which the relevant ones are 91–3. Sheridan's account is far from impartial, as he wanted to be one of the prince's under-governors and blamed Betham for allegedly blocking his appointment. His account is full of pejorative comments about Betham, Plowden, Perkins, Sheldon and Dicconson, and is used here with considerable caution.

but his appointment was very strongly opposed by Betham, and no one else already at Saint-Germain was considered suitable for this important position. Betham is said to have recommended either George Holman (a brother-in-law of John Stafford) or Lord Dunbar (a brother-in-law of Lady Middleton),[2] both of whom were in England, but they in turn were opposed by the Jesuits. In the end James II compromised by appointing two under-governors, 'to officiat by turns, and supply the place of Governor.'[3] One was Francis Plowden, allegedly recommended by Lord Melfort; the other was Edmund Perkins, an uncle of Thomas Codrington, with property near Lord Middleton's at Winchester. Plowden was already at Saint-Germain with no household employment, but Perkins, who had been educated at Douai and was the candidate of Betham, was living in England. Middleton explained in a letter of May 1695 that 'Young Master here . . . had been removed from women alreadie if our Hampshire neighbor had come sooner, who after long expectation is at last arriv'd.'[4] Meanwhile Betham secured the appointment of Dr John Ingleton, a young secular priest who had been teaching at Douai,[5] to be the new under-preceptor.

These three appointments were dated 2 June 1695,[6] two days before Nairne noted that 'the Prince was put into mens hands'.[7] But Plowden and Perkins were deliberately given little independence and obliged to follow a set of detailed 'Rules for the family of our dearest son, the Prince of Wales', already prepared for them by Nairne and Caryll, and approved by the king on 31 May.[8] Nairne, who was chiefly responsible for drawing up these rules, which paid particular attention to the prince's security, noted with some satisfaction over a year later, when they were renewed, that the king 'spoke very kindly of

---

[2] George Holman of Warkworth Castle, Northants, was married to Anastasia Stafford. Robert Constable, 3rd Viscount Dunbar married Dorothy (née Brudenell), Countess of Westmorland after she became a widow in September 1691.

[3] SP Misc. 7, 92.

[4] Bodleian Library, Carte MSS 208, f. 78, Middleton to Lady Middleton, May 1695.

[5] Catholic Record Society, *Miscellanea XI* (London, 1917), 'The Register Book of St Gregory's College, Paris', 112.

[6] Ruvigny, *Jacobite Peerage*, 217. The warrant appointing Ingleton (overlooked by Ruvigny) is in Bodleian Library, Carte MSS 208, f. 259.

[7] Nairne, 4 June 1695. See also Bodleian Library, Rawlinson MSS D.21, f. 3, unidentified to Meredith, 27 June 1695: 'Our young Prince of Wales is newly put amongst the men who are very vertuous persons. I think Mr Perkins one of his (Under-)Governors is a very good ingenious honest man and pleases now he is here more than a little. Mr Plowden you know is ye other Dep.y Govern.r; Mr Nevil, Mr Bellasis, and young Strickland (Sr Thomas's son) are Grooms of the bed Chamber; Mr Syms and young Du Puy, waiters: he has no more addition of servants at present.'

[8] Nairne, 10, 12, 14, 18, 20 May 1695; 1 June 1695.

them'.[9] They specified that 'the office of Preceptor' was 'independent' of the under-governors, and that the latter should serve alternate weeks, sleeping in the prince's Bedchamber and waiting upon him during his meals.

It seems clear that James II regarded this arrangement as no more than temporary and still hoped to appoint an important aristocrat to the post of governor. An opportunity arose at the beginning of the following year. The Earl of Perth, previously lord chancellor of Scotland and recently released from captivity in Stirling Castle, had been travelling in Italy, where he had been recruited as the Jacobite ambassador to the Holy See. The king decided that he might more usefully be employed at Saint-Germain, and in February 1696 instructed Caryll to invite him to accept the post.[10] Perth arrived in May, gave his approval to the rules and was declared governor on 28 July.[11] Given the rivalry between the secular and regular English clergy, and the importance of preparing the Catholic prince for his Protestant inheritance, it was no easy task.[12] But as a Scottish nobleman Perth was not closely aligned with either English faction, and moreover he enjoyed the friendship of Jacques Bossuet, the Gallican bishop of Meaux, who had previously served as preceptor to the dauphin.

Perth remained governor, before and after the prince succeeded as James III, until 1706, when he sent a long letter to Pope Clement XI explaining how he had carried out his responsibilities.[13] For most of this period he was assisted

---

[9] Nairne, 18 July 1696. The copy which has survived is the revised version, slightly amended to include the duties of the governor, dated 19 July 1696 (reproduced in HMC *Stuart* I, 114–17).

[10] *Letters from James, Earl of Perth to his sister*, 103–4, 10 March and 26 March 1696, in the second of which he stated: 'If you do not hear from me very soon again, do not impute it to unkindness. You will soon know the reason.'

[11] Nairne, 13, 15, 24 May 1696; 18, 19, 28 July 1696. According to the revised Rules, the preceptor remained independent, and it was the governor who normally slept in the prince's Bedchamber and waited upon him during his meals. The duties of all the prince's other household servants are specified in detail.

[12] Bodleian Library, Rawlinson MSS D.21, f. 4, Perth to Meredith, 17 September 1696: 'altho' the office of Governour to the prince of Wales caries with it more honour than I had Ambition to pretend to, yet the Dangers that are hanging over my head are so many, and of such consequence both as to this life, and that wch is to come, that I must be fond beyond measure of worldly honour to embrace it at this rate if I had no better motive: but being called without my pursuing of the matter: commanded by the best of Masters and Mistresses: supported by their Divertion: and having no end but to serve God, the Church, Their Ma.tys, His Ma.tys Dominions, The Prince, and to follow what I believe to be the Will of God, my hope is placed in His Divine Goodness.'

[13] BL Add. MSS 19254, f. 138, Perth to Clement XI, July? 1706. Perth explained that he preferred to use 'sweetness and perswasion' rather than 'authority and severity', that the curriculum emphasised 'History, and knowledge of the Laws of his Dominions', and that he taught the young king that he must be worthy of being restored by trying to make his subjects happy rather than himself great.

by the under-governors and the preceptors. Perkins died in August 1697, and Betham recommended that he should be replaced by William Dicconson, another former pupil of Douai. 'The King consented, but he [Dicconson] stayd so long in settling his privat affairs [in Lancashire], that, before he came Major General [Dominic] Sheldon, on account of his . . . skil in martial affairs, was put into the place.'[14] This happened in June 1700, when Nairne noted that James II promised Louis XIV that 'his waiting on the P.ce as Under Governor should not hinder his attendance to his Regt when it was necessary'.[15] Dicconson finally arrived at Saint-Germain in August 1700 and replaced Plowden, who was appointed comptroller of the household. Betham, meanwhile, remained preceptor until January 1705 when, as we shall see, he left the court. Ingleton continued as under-preceptor until James III achieved his majority in June 1706, and was then appointed almoner to the queen.[16]

The education of the prince was thus primarily the responsibility of Betham, assisted after 1695 by Ingleton, and they seem to have taught him history, chronology, geography, civil law, natural history and morality. But the prince also studied other subjects and had other teachers. By 1693 he was being taught writing by Christopher Williams (later yeoman of the accounting house), and mathematics (consisting of arithmetic, geometry and the physical sciences) by Michael Constable.[17] The latter, who had been headmaster of the English Jesuit College at Saint-Omer (1688–93), was also the prince's confessor, in charge of his religious instruction, and his appointment was clearly intended to balance the secular influence of Betham. In 1694, when the prince began to learn Latin,[18] he also started French with Etienne du Mirail de Monnot (a clerk employed by Melfort since 1689),[19] and dancing with Jean Faure (an experienced member of the *Académie Royale de Danse*), with whom he also had to speak French.[20] In 1695 Monnot replaced Williams as writing master,[21] and the prince began to study Italian with Innocenzo Fede, and music with both Fede and Abraham Baumeister.[22] Finally, in May 1696 he began to ride with Robert Buckenham (yeoman rider to the queen and later equerry of the

---

[14] SP Misc. 7, 93.   [15] Nairne, 3 June 1700.

[16] BL Add. MSS 31255, f. 29, James III to Gualterio, 3 February 1715.

[17] SP 1/79; G. Holt, 'Some Chaplains at the Stuart Court, Saint-Germain-en-Laye', *Recusant History* 25, no. 1 (May 2000), 47.

[18] Bodleian Library, Carte MSS 208, f. 78, Middleton to Lady Middleton, May 1695.

[19] Dangeau, v, 31, 21 June 1694; SP 54/96, Monnot to Inverness, 11 August 1721.

[20] Ruvigny, *Jacobite Peerage*, 223.   [21] Nairne, 21 September 1695.

[22] Sizergh Castle, Strickland Collection R.4; Arch. Dépt. des Yvelines, B.537 Saint-Germain-en-Laye.

great stables),[23] and to play billiards with Caryll.[24] At some point he was also taught drawing.[25]

With such a wide curriculum, James III was given a very thorough education. It turned him into a highly polished courtier, and prepared him for the responsibilities which it was hoped he would eventually assume. He quickly became fluent at speaking and writing both French and Italian, and although his handwriting soon became very difficult to read, this was because he wrote too quickly and had to deal with too much correspondence. He was a more than competent dancer, and had a strong appreciation of music. Except when thrown off balance by adversity after 1716, he remained moderate and tolerant throughout his life. Indeed he became and remained a cultivated and thoroughly agreeable English gentleman. He was also a particularly good rider. In May 1698, when not yet ten years old, the Modenese envoy reported that 'he is always pleasant to look upon, but on horseback he is seen to wonderful advantage for the grace, lightness and gallant daring which at his tender age give him a special dignity and charm'.[26] In January 1706, when he was seventeen years old, he was allowed to begin riding what Nairne described as 'ye great horses'.[27]

The prince's political and constitutional instruction came from his father. In April 1692, immediately after Betham's arrival at Saint-Germain, James II was preparing to invade England, and was conscious that he might be killed or captured. In case he should never see his son again, he wrote a quarto volume, containing fifty-four manuscript pages, with the title 'For my Son, the Prince of Wales', which he left behind in the Château de Saint-Germain. This book was full of advice and considered how England, Scotland and Ireland should be governed.[28]

After the failure of the invasion attempt James II returned safely to Saint-Germain-en-Laye. His book was then put on one side, to be eventually used by his son. But during the remaining years of his life he added to it several other documents. These included some advice within his 'Pious Sentiments', some detailed advice in his last will and its codicil,[29] and certain specific

---

[23] Nairne, 30 May 1696.   [24] Nairne, 3 June 1696.   [25] Corp, 'Inventory', 132.

[26] Haile, *Mary of Modena*, 334, Rizzini to the Duke of Modena, 14 May 1698.

[27] Nairne, 12 January 1706. See also 19 January 1706 and 10 April 1706.

[28] The original volume has not survived, but a copy in 138 octavo pages is in the Royal Library at Windsor Castle. It was published in *The Life of James II*, II, 619–42. See Corp, 'Inventory', 129; and Corp, *Cour des Stuarts*, 140.

[29] Windsor Castle, Royal Archives, Add. Stuart MSS 1/45 and 46; Corp, 'Inventory', 133; Corp, *Cour des Stuarts*, 144–5.

instructions which he gave his son on his deathbed, and which were carefully written down at the time by Lord Perth.[30]

Shortly before he died, James II also instructed Caryll and Nairne to revise and correct his memoirs, and to add to them his private correspondence, in order to produce a single and uniform account of his life, a sort of official biography. This work, started in 1699, was not finished until after his death, but James II read and approved everything that the two men wrote covering the years from his birth until 1677, and the rest of this 'Life of James II' was written in the same style and also based on his original memoirs, journal and correspondence.[31] These documents of James II (his advice, his 'Pious Sentiments', his will, his last words and his 'Life') together record the political advice that he gave to his son.

At the beginning of the book, in order to explain his aim, James II referred to the doctrine of the divine right of hereditary succession:

Kings being accountable for none of their actions but to God and themselves, ought to be more cautious and circumspect, than those who are in lower stations, and as tis the duty of Subjects to pay true allegiance to him, and to observe his Laws, so a King is bound by his office to have a fatherly love and care of them; of which number you being the first, I look on myself as obliged to give you these following Advices, which I am more enduced to do, considering your age, my own, and the present posture of my affairs.[32]

James II then continued with his most important piece of advice, fundamental to all that he had to say:

In the first place serve God in all things as becomes a good Christian and zealous Catholick of the Church of Rome, which is the only true Catholick and Apostolick Church, and let no human consideration of any kind prevaile with you to depart from her; remember always that Kings, Princes and all the great ones of the world, must one day give an account of all their actions before the great tribunal.[33]

---

[30] The Duke of Perth wrote a detailed account of James II's death in two long letters to the abbé de La Trappe (Rancé's successor), dated 11 September and 9 October 1701, published in the *Revue de l'Histoire de Versailles* 29 (1927), 215–25. A much briefer account was published in London in 1701 entitled *The Last Dying Words of the Late King James to his Son and Daughter, and the French King*, reprinted in 1704 as *King James the Second His Last Expressions and Dying Words*.

[31] For details of James II's memoirs, and a description of the two extant copies of 'The Life of James II', see Corp, 'Inventory', 127–9. The text of the latter was published in *The Life of James II*, I, and II, pp.1–616. See also Corp, *Cour des Stuarts*, 141–3.

[32] *The Life of James II*, II, 619.   [33] *Ibid.*, 619.

This advice was repeated in James II's will[34] and is to be found in the account of his last illness and death. Before he died, he insisted to his son that it was better to remain a Catholic in exile than to regain the throne of England at the price of losing his soul. According to the same account, 'the King, with the little strength which he still had, embraced his son . . . saying to him: "Never separate yourself from the Catholic religion. No sacrifice is too great when it is made for God."'[35]

Most of the book is concerned with more worldly advice. James II considered the causes of the Glorious Revolution and of his exile in France, and denied that they were the result of his religious policies. In his opinion they were a punishment from God for the immoral life which he had led, particularly after his conversion to Catholicism. He therefore advised his son against 'the sins of the flesh'.[36] 'Do not wonder if I enlarge so much on this Subject', he said, 'having found by sad experience all what I have sayd on it to be true.'[37] On another occasion he gave an account of what the daily life of a good Christian king should be, a mixture of work and spiritual meditation, with some physical exercise.[38]

James II also gave his son specific advice concerning the Anglican church. In his public Declaration of April 1692 he had promised that 'we will protect and maintain the Church of England as it is now by law establish'd, in all their rights, priviledges and possessions'.[39] In his advice he explained:

No King can be happy without his Subjects be at ease, and the people cannot be secure of enjoying their own without the King be at his ease also, and in a condition to protect them and secure his own right; therfore preserve your prerogative, but disturbe not the Subjects in their property, nor conscience, remember the great precept, Do as you would be done to, for that is the law and the Prophets.[40]

---

[34] See note 29: 'Let him allways bear in mind these words of Our Saviour: what will it availe a man to gain the whole world and lose his own soul? Upon my decease he will have an undoubted Right to the Crown of England. But should he be kept from it by his Religion, if Our Saviour's words be true, he will be a gainer by that loss.'

[35] See note 30, Perth to abbé de La Trappe, 11 September 1701, 216 (my translation). The account in the *The Life of James II* is: 'the King . . . speaking with a force and vehemence . . . conjured him to adhere firmly to the Catholic faith, let what will be ye consequences of it, and be faithful to the service of God' (II, 593). According to the account published in London in 1701, James II urged his son to 'serve him [God] with all your Power and Strength, and never put the Crown of England in competition with your Eternal Salvation'.

[36] *The Life of James II*, II, 625.   [37] *Ibid.*, 629.

[38] *Papers of Devotion*, 79–80; Corp, *Cour des Stuarts*, 131–2.

[39] The Declaration was included in *The Life of James II*, II, 479–88. This citation is from 487.

[40] *Ibid.*, II, 620–1. James returned to the point in his will: 'We as a father advise and require him never to molest his subjects in the enjoyment of their Religion, Rights, Libertys, and Propertys' (see note 29).

James II also advised the Prince of Wales on how to govern the three kingdoms. On the subject of England, he said: 'make it one of your businesses to know the true Constitution of the Government, that you may keep yourself as well as the Parliament within its true bounds'.[41] In a particularly important passage he advised his son:

Be very carefull in the choice of your cheef Ministers, tis of the last concern to you, it being impossible for a Prince to do all himself, they must not only be Men of good sense, and sound judgment, but of great probity and well founded as to Christianity, and that it appear to be their way of living. I . . . never knew but one of the late King my Brother's Ministers, namly the Ld Clifford, that served him through-out faithfully, and without reproche; let them see you have intire trust and confidence in them, but let them not impose upon you, the favors and graces you do, let those upon whom you bestow them, be sensible they owe them wholly to yourself, and not to others, or their owne importunity; Let your eares be open to such as you know to be good men, that you may be truly inform'd of all truths, which others might not be willing you should be informed of.[42]

Finally James II gave his son some very detailed advice on how to choose the officials in the royal household and all the people attached to it, including the secretaries of state and the commissioners of the treasury. 'Whoever is a good Christian', he said, 'must be a good moral man, but the same consequence dos not allways follow morality.'[43] He also insisted that he should employ Catholics and Dissenters as well as Anglicans, and suggested the following arrangement:

Commissioners of the Treasury five, three Church of England one Catholick and one dissenter.

No Admiral nor Commissionary of the Admiralty.

Cabinet Councell – two Secretarys of State, Secretary of War, of Admiralty, first Commissioner of Treasury, and two others. Secretarys of State, one of them Catholick the other Protestant. Secretary War Catholick, Secretary of the Navy Protestant.

Lord Lieutenants to have salarys, good Dep: Lieutenants.

Army, Household, Bed Chamber most Catholicks.

Embassadors and no Envoyes Catholicks and Protestants

As many Catholicks as can be in the Army some Ch. of England and Dissenters.[44]

This last point was of major importance: 'Be never without a considerable body of Catholick troops without which you cannot be safe, then people will thanke you for Liberty of Conscience. Be not persuaded by any to depart from that.'[45]

[41] *Ibid.*, 634.   [42] *Ibid.*, 638.   [43] *Ibid.*, 639.   [44] *Ibid.*, 641–2.   [45] *Ibid.*, 621.

Briefly examined in this way, these documents cannot reveal all the nuances possible in private conversation, but they do give us some idea of the political instruction which James III received from his father.

James III's Preceptor: John Betham

by Geoffrey Scott

As a child, King James II seems to have been denied any systematic education, and it was only in his adult life, by reading widely, that he was able to attempt to compensate for this earlier deficiency. His son James, Prince of Wales, was more fortunate in his childhood education, even though this was given in exile. On fleeing at the Revolution, the royal family discovered in France a country bristling with educational innovations and experiments, and an exiled Catholic community which had successfully blended English pedagogical traditions with current French practice. The importance of John Betham lies in his quite clear determination to expose his charge to the two educational systems he himself favoured, that of the English secular clergy and the Jansenist tradition of Pierre Nicole.

Betham came from Warwickshire gentry stock and had been educated at the English college in Douai before moving to Paris in 1667, where he began studying for a doctorate in theology at the Sorbonne. His arrival in Paris, with Bonaventure Giffard (later bishop) and Edward Paston (later president of the English College, Douai), marked the revival in the French capital of the English secular clergy's house of higher studies, which was put under the patronage of St Gregory the Great. Betham himself generously endowed this new foundation and became its first superior. In 1678 he took his doctor's cap, having completed ten arduous years of study.[46] After the accession of James II in 1685, he was appointed preacher-in-ordinary at the court of St James and Somerset House, and two of his court sermons were later published.[47] These were not particularly polished orations, but they do show Betham's knowledge

[46] 'Register Book of St Gregory's College, Paris', 93–6, 101–9, 111; J. Gillow, *Bibliographical Dictionary of the English Catholics* (London, 1885), I, 204–5; G. Anstruther, *The Seminary Priests* (Great Wakering, 1976), III, 13–14; Hugh Tootell (alias Charles Dodd), *The Church History of England* (Brussels [Wolverhampton], 1742), III, 485.

[47] John Betham, *A Sermon of the Epiphany, Preach'd in the Queen Dowager's Chapel at Somerset House* (London, 1687); *A Sermon Preach'd before the King and Queen in their Majesties Chapel at St James's upon the Annunciation* (London, 1686). In 1687–88 Betham was considered as a possible bishop for Scotland by James II, but the king eventually decided to appoint Lewis Innes instead. The revolution intervened before any appointment could be made (Halloran, *Scots College Paris*, 60–3).

of the Fathers, and in dwelling on man's total dependence on God's grace they give some indication of his theological position: 'All mortifications multiplied beyond the reach of arithmetic', he preached, 'would fall short of making satisfaction for the least capital crime.' Betham seems to have remained in England during the Revolution, and did not return to France until March 1692, when he was summoned to Saint-Germain. That Betham suffered neither banishment nor imprisonment for his priesthood at the time might be explained through his friendship with a number of prominent Anglicans, including William Wake, later archbishop of Canterbury, all of whom were delighted with his appointment as preceptor.[48]

Soon after taking up this appointment, Betham published *A Brief Treatise of Education, with a Particular Respect to the Children of Great Personages, for the use of his Royal Highness, the Prince* (Paris, 1693).[49] This was not an original work, being mostly a careful edition of part of the Jansenist Pierre Nicole's *De l'Education d'un prince*, first published in Paris in 1671. Betham designated it 'The First Part', but the second does not seem to have been published. This direct borrowing from a Jansenist educationalist shows Betham's total sympathy with the movement. Manuals guiding those instructing the children of the great were frequently produced by Jansenist writers. As far back as 1643, the year of his death, Saint-Cyran had published a catechism for the young aristocrats under his charge at Port-Royal. It was the first in a long line of Jansenist tracts which aimed to educate the children from royal and aristocratic circles as the first stage in the improvement of society as a whole. Later Nicole reported that Pascal himself admitted that he was prepared to sacrifice all he had to devote himself to such a project as this.[50] Such Jansenist manuals were used alongside other textbooks written for the young of the French court and nobility by more recognisably orthodox teachers. Bossuet had, for instance, compiled a programme of instruction for the dauphin on his appointment as preceptor in 1670, and his popular *Discourse on Universal History* must have been known to Betham when he was compiling his book. Claude Fleury, another secular priest and royal preceptor, had published a catechism and some philosophical histories during the 1680s designed to inculcate moral lessons to a lax court

---

[48] J.A. Williams, 'Bishop Giffard and Ellis and the Western Vicariate, 1688–1715', *Journal of Ecclesiastical History* 15, no. 2 (October 1964), 221–2.

[49] The two known copies, in the British Library and the Bodleian Library, Oxford, are twenty-two pages long, and form 'The First Part'. The portrait of the prince which serves as a frontispiece derives from the engraving by Van Schuppen, after Largillière, of 1692 (Sharp, *The Engraved Record*, 85–6, nos. 91, 93).

[50] H.C. Barnard, *The Little Schools of Port-Royal* (Cambridge, 1913), 16, 23, 38, 42, 43.

by means of a critical survey of the 'Manners' of the Old Testament Jews and early Christians.

Betham's Jansenist sympathies were undoubtedly due to the influence of his early education at Douai, where strong opposition to the Jesuits had helped to encourage an English Jansenism. Whilst the secular clergy looked forward to the re-establishment of a properly constituted English hierarchy, the Jesuits stood out for the status quo, that is, England remaining as a missionary territory in which the Jesuits continued to enjoy maximum freedom from episcopal control. Betham had entered Douai not long after a group of Douai clergy, led by Thomas White alias Blacklo, had made overtures to Cromwell in the hope he might favour an English Catholic hierarchy with some measure of independence of the pope.[51] As we shall see, there was to be an echo of Blackloist sympathies discernible in Betham, who was to be accused in 1705 of being favourable to Cromwell's rule and opposed to absolute monarchy. Any hopes of a restored hierarchy under James II were, however, dashed at the Revolution.

Betham's presence at the Stuart court in exile demonstrates that the clergy there were not uniformly opposed to reaching some *modus vivendi* with the post-Revolution settlement in England, whilst his apparent Jansenism made him more understanding of Anglicanism. It is important, then, to appreciate that Betham's publication of his educational treatise in 1693 was set against the background of parties within the exiled court who were looking for ways to recover the throne for James II by encouraging him to promise religious toleration. Shortly before he became the royal preceptor, therefore, we find Betham giving his approval to the Declaration of 17 April 1693 which included a guarantee to protect and defend the members of the Church of England in the event of a restoration.[52] The appointment of such a moderate churchman would have reduced the pressure on the king to have the prince brought up an Anglican.

The role of the royal preceptor can best be discovered from Betham's treatise and from the 'Rules for the family of our dearest son, the Prince of Wales', written in 1695 and revised in July 1696.[53]

Betham begins his *Brief Treatise* with an accurate translation of Nicole's *De l'Education d'un prince*, using identical paragraph numbering. Only occasionally does he paraphrase some of the longer sections of the French work and

[51] A.C.F. Beales, *Education under Penalty* (London, 1963), 104.
[52] G.H. Jones, *The Mainstream of Jacobitism* (Cambridge, MA, 1954), 32.
[53] See above, notes 8 and 9.

transpose others. He abbreviates by excising some of Nicole's more ponderous moralising paragraphs. Betham's *Treatise* ends abruptly with paragraph 44, 'On the need to encourage children's curiosity', which is identical to Nicole's Section XIII of the second part of his treatise which makes suggestions about studies. What Betham omits, and what he presumably intended to publish later as a second part of his *Treatise*, was an edition of the subsequent sections of Nicole's work which included a section relating to biblical history and various treatises drawing on earlier themes. Betham's abbreviated *Brief Treatise*, then, closely following Nicole's work, insists that those involved with the Prince's education 'need to make a good choice . . . [of] one who undertakes the breeding of a Young Prince'. It is not enough that this royal tutor 'be not vicious, have some knowledge of polite literature, be skilled in Belles Lettres, and conversant in History, Mathematics, and Knowing the World'. For without an accurate judgement, the tutor will merely fill the Prince's mind 'with all the fooleries of books, & his own too . . . and load his pupil with confused knowledge, & stifle what nature has bestowed on him of right sense or Reason'. In a summary which is clearly leaning on the Jansenist pedagogical tradition, the treatise explains that:

the most essential quality for a tutor . . . is a Quality without a name, and not fixed to any Profession. It is not necessary for a Tutor to teach him [the Prince] all, but to teach him the use of all. He should stand by and be a witness of what is taught him by others. The Quality . . . is not to be supplied from abroad; it cannot be borrowed from others, nor procured by Study; it has its beginnings from Nature.

Thus, tutor and pupil are to be inseparable; there would be no teaching 'at certain hours', no 'set lesson', but the preceptor would teach his charge 'at and every hour – in his Play, in his Visits, in Conversation and Table talk, and as when he makes him read books'. 'Nothing sinks into the mind under the unpleasant shape of a Lesson', rather, 'as this method of instructing is insensible, so also is the Profit gained. It is not perceived by certain gross and exterior signs.'[54] Betham omits Nicole's opinion that intelligence is therefore not to be judged merely by good translations made of the classics.

King James's 'Rules for the Family' deal with the Prince's household. They reflect the emphasis which the Catholic Reformation gave to the need for moral guidance of children within a close-knit Christian household, and they are similar to Betham's treatise in regard to the preceptor's role. Thus, the governor should always be present with the prince, 'unless he is at his book

---

[54] Betham, *Treatise*, 2, 3, 6, 7.

or catechisme with his preceptor', and both officials should act in concert to fix the 'times to be set forth for our son's learning his book and Catechism'. They should control the prince's access to all published and written material, including songs. As in Betham's treatise, the preceptor is given the freedom to take as much time as he wishes over the tuition, which is to begin daily after Mass at 9.00 a.m. On Sundays and holy days, the preceptor should instruct the prince in Catechism and good books rather than in secular works.[55]

Presumably James II was encouraged in his choice of Betham by those in the court circle who favoured Jansenism. Earlier Jansenist teachers, such as Saint-Cyran, had emphasised the importance of close personal ties between teacher and pupil. It was the Port-Royalists' sensitive understanding of human nature which had made them valued as confessors, but this attribute helped also to encourage them to give a strong moral framework to their educational theories. This we find also in the treatise of Betham, who was himself a popular confessor to the court of Saint-Germain. Betham was in full agreement with the Port-Royalists' principal educational aims: the need to preserve the innocence of the child, purified of original sin, through a strict control exercised over its environment by the tutor, and the inculcation of sound judgement in the child by means of a development of the reason. Secular knowledge, therefore, was subordinated to moral education. Betham's treatise and its exemplar, Nicole's *De l'Education d'un prince*, look more favourably on the moral integrity of the preceptor than on his academic knowledge and attainments. Not surprisingly, both works allow plenty of time to the tutor to expatiate on moral lessons for the pupil's education.[56]

If we now turn to the content of the preceptor's instruction of the young prince, we are dependent both on Betham's treatise and on the evidence of the manuscript instructions passed to the prince by his dying father in September 1701.[57] These latter reveal what James II apparently believed his son should have learned as a child. Again, the parallels with contemporary and near-contemporary Jansenist educational doctrine are striking. Betham's edition of Nicole begins by pointing out the grave responsibilities which lie on the shoulders of a prince, the carrying of which would make him 'a great Instrument of men'. 'A Prince', he contemplates, 'is not his own, he is the State's. He is accountable to the People', and he must be taught true judgement

[55] HMC *Stuart* VII, 115–17.

[56] P. Miller, *James* (London, 1971), 32; R. Clark, *Strangers and Sojourners at Port-Royal* (Cambridge, 1932), 126–8; Barnard, *The Little Schools*, 55–6, 72–3, 79.

[57] A. Rankine, *Memoirs of the Chevalier de St. George* (London, 1712), 39–41.

before all else. Betham acknowledges the usefulness of studying history, the sciences, languages, chronology, geography, civil law and 'what is remarkable in the world. All this is good, but it is not the last end of Instruction, but should be used to frame his [the prince's] manners and judgement.' By these means, the soul will 'relish Truths' and be filled 'with Principles for finding out the Truth'.

With the sobriety common in Jansenist spiritual and didactic tracts, the treatise insists that morality 'is the Science in which a Prince should be principally instructed and moulded. One cannot be too soon to know oneself.' Those 'Great Ones' who fritter away their lives in hunting and recreation are frowned upon, and the preceptor is encouraged to direct his young pupil to the Jansenist treatises which form an appendix to Nicole's book: the Discourse of the Necessity of not living by hazard, the Treatise of Grandeur, the Treatise of Christian Civility, and the Three Short Discourses of Pascal on the Condition of the Great, which warn against the dangers of concupiscence. Betham and Nicole are sensible in insisting that the earlier moral training begins, the better, and that it should be given in proportion to the child's age and ability, as the Port-Royalist writers tend to recommend. The treatise encourages that reserve dear to Jansenists by demanding that the prince read 'the Treatise where it is showed how dangerous the Discourses of Men are', since the life of Great Ones, passed 'in almost continuous commerce with men', is fraught with dangers. The treatise promotes the Port-Royalist doctrine that an education in truth would help to re-establish 'lost innocence'; the body, therefore, should be kept in control from an early age to avoid 'Debauchery and Disorder' later. 'A ply and bent given to a Body in youth is often a great hindrance later on.'[58] The dying King James II's instructions to his son contain the same moral earnestness and exhortation as Betham's treatise. They warn of the duties and responsibilities of kingship and exhort the prince to avoid seeking his own pleasure, and to preserve the innocence of childhood.

Betham's debt to Nicole is obvious. Both give prominence to a practical learning through the senses as a way of sharpening the memory and of encouraging 'a commendable curiosity'. They recommend a cross-curricular study of geography through the application of work in history and natural history, suggesting the use of books 'with Cuts of great Towns'. The works of Lipsius are preferred for the study of antiquity because of their illustrations. Travellers' tales about the Indies and China were only useful for showing the folly man sinks to when 'he follows his own fancies and the dark lights of his own

---

[58] Betham, *Treatise*, 1, 4, 8, 9–14, 16.

mind'. Finally, both author and editor included the 'Abridgement of Johnston' of Ulisse Aldrovandi of Bologna's *Natural History* to show unknown beasts and animals. Both believe that even young children can be introduced to the study of anatomy, although Betham diverges from Nicole's conviction that curiosity cannot be a vice in young children to include his own caveat 'but one must have a care of leading them into some curiosities that are dangerous in this particular'.[59]

Unfortunately we have little direct evidence as to Betham's relations with his young charge and with the court as a whole during the first ten years of his preceptorship. It seems, however, that he was not acceptable to all. His appointment brought out into the open the conflict which had smouldered throughout the century between the English secular clergy, among whom Betham was a leading light, and the English regular clergy, whose cause was championed by the Jesuits. Besides the traditional animosity caused by their opposite views on ecclesiastical structures, the secular clergy and Jesuits had diverging views on the nature and practice of education, and both sides were determined to gain access to the Prince of Wales who one day might be king of England.

Besides Betham's massive dependence on Jansenist sources for his treatise, he also represented the English secular clergy's pedagogical traditions as they were maintained at the English College at Douai. As the base for the more academically distinguished clergy from Douai coming to complete the arduous ten-year course leading to a doctorate from the Sorbonne, St Gregory's College in Paris was an obvious pool from which the nearby court of Saint-Germain might draw competent preachers, confessors and teachers. Betham and others from St Gregory's had already established for themselves a reputation as court chaplains in London. Others, like Bonaventure Giffard, a fellow student of Betham's and a co-founder with him of St Gregory's, knew the English university system intimately. Giffard had been intruded president of Magdalen College, Oxford during James II's reign. Betham and Giffard shared Jansenist leanings with another contemporary of theirs at St Gregory's, Edward Paston, who, as president of the English College, Douai in 1688, had to face a student rebellion when he went too far in trying to introduce into the college some of the Jansenist, quasi-monastic austerities he had favoured in Paris. Although the college was a Tridentine seminary based on a Jesuit model, its educational philosophy at least for the more junior students closely resembled the child-centred approach favoured by Nicole and

---

[59] *Ibid.*, 19–22; Barnard, *The Little Schools*, 94.

Betham rather than the more directive and structured training common in Jesuit colleges like Saint-Omer (founded 1592–93).[60]

It has been suggested that St Gregory's, Paris was the centre for a spiritual and devotional revival among the English secular clergy in the late seventeenth century. This was to give the secular clergy a regenerated sense of mission together with a rigorism which Chaunu sees developing into a positive form of Jansenism, or a 'compensatory Augustinianism' as he terms it. This 'Augustinianism' was spread abroad in Protestant countries like England where Catholicism had to be stripped of all non-essentials so as to appeal to Protestants. Such a purified Catholicism appealed to Anglicans in England at the turn of the century in the preaching and teachings of priests like Bonaventure Giffard and John Gother. It seems to have been encouraged at Douai in the reforms of Edward Paston, and it can be discerned at the court of Saint-Germain in the sensible and seemingly balanced attitude to the Christian life taught by John Betham, who was 'suspicious of notions of papal infallibility, indulgences, excessive devotion to saints or use of devotional "aids", like scapulars'.[61]

We must appreciate the loose alliance between English secular clergy and French Jansenists if we are to try to understand some aspects of the religious and devotional life of the exiled Stuart court in the decade following the revolution. The court was soon torn in half between those who supported Jesuit notions of education and spirituality and those who favoured the secular clergy's viewpoint. The king, as has already been shown, was eclectic in his following of schools of spirituality. Ultimately, however, he never seems to have abandoned that Jesuit framework for his piety which he had adopted soon after his conversion. The conflict emerged into the open when both sides competed to win the right to educate the Prince of Wales. After the dominating influence of the Jesuit, Father Petre, in England on James II, the exiled king found himself increasingly attracted to a more rigorous Catholicism exemplified in the secular clergy and its circle. Thus, the king is known to have read Jansenist works, to have visited Port-Royal itself in September 1693, and in September 1695 to have spent five days at St Gregory's, Paris. Furthermore, he was surrounded by courtiers with known Jansenist sympathies, and it seems probable that Betham's fall from favour in 1705 was partly due to the king's death and hence

[60] Clark, *Strangers*, 159, 175; Beales, *Education under Penalty*, 145–6, 161, 172; A.F. Allison, 'The Origins of St Gregory's, Paris', *Recusant History* 21, no. 1 (May 1992), 11–25.

[61] E. Duffy, 'The English Secular Clergy and the Counter Reformation', *Journal of Ecclesiastical History* 34, no. 2 (April 1983), 219, 223–4, 229–30 (with quotes from Chaunu); E. Duffy, ' "A Rubb-up for Old Sores". Jesuits, Jansenists and the English Secular Clergy, 1705–1715', *Journal of Ecclesiastical History* 28, no. 3 (July 1977), 291–317.

the end of his patronage.[62] The queen, who was to be ultimately responsible for Betham's removal from the court, was firmly attached to the Jesuit party once the court had settled in France. Her influence might well lie behind the appointment, for instance, of the Jesuit Michael Constable as the prince's tutor in mathematics and religious instruction.[63]

Nowhere else can this conflict be more clearly discerned than in a pamphlet war in the first decade of the court's life at Saint-Germain, when each side tried to dominate through the use of the press. From the Jesuit press at Saint-Omer, there poured out very many books and pamphlets during these years, usually under false imprints which were aimed at the court.[64] Many of these were translations of French devotional works. Others were new editions, specifically designed by the Jesuits, it seems, to bring members of the court within their orbit. Thus, by way of example, the Jesuit Edward Scarisbrick's devotional work, *The Life of Lady Warner* (Saint-Omer, 1692), was dedicated to the Queen, as was Alfonso Rodriguez' *Practice of Christian Perfection* (Saint-Omer, 1697), which was translated by James II's confessor, the Jesuit Francis Sanders. In 1697, the second part of the Jesuit Thomas Fitzherbert's *A Treatise of Policy and Religion* was newly edited with a fulsome dedication to the Prince of Wales, which acknowledged the ripeness of his capacity and expressed the hope that the book would always be kept in the prince's closet to guide him through his life.

Amongst all these Jesuit works, the one which comes closest to being a parallel to Betham's *Brief Treatise* is *A Catechism for the use of His Royal Highness the Prince of Wales* (Paris, 1692), by C.A. SJ, probably the Jesuit Christopher Anderton.[65] He is presumably the same C.A. who translated *A short instruction for the better understanding and performing of mental prayer* (Paris, 1691), which he dedicated to Sister Ignatia (born Lady Arabella) FitzJames, a Benedictine nun of Pontoise and sister of the Duke of Berwick.[66] Anderton's *Catechism* was in the form of a primer, with very wide margins, presumably to allow the prince to take notes and practise his handwriting, since the alphabet and spelling instructions are included. Calling himself the prince's 'beadsman', Anderton acknowledges that he is subject to his 'Lady Governess' (either the Duchess of Powis or the Countess of Erroll). He extravagantly praises the Prince's accomplishments and natural talents, and believes himself to be the first to teach him 'the principles of learning' and Christian doctrine. This little manual

[62] Clark, *Strangers*, 221, 225, and chapter XVII; 'Register Book of St Gregory's', 113.
[63] Miller, *James*, 48.
[64] T. Clancy, *English Catholic Books, 1641–1700* (Chicago, 1974, 1996), *passim*.
[65] I am grateful to Father Tom Clancy, SJ, for information about this book and its author. There is a copy in the Bodleian Library.
[66] Clancy, *English Catholic Books*, no. 909.0.

exhibits those elements of Jesuit instruction which brought the Order into conflict with Jansenists and their supporters among the English secular clergy. Thus, the *Catechism* proceeds by way of short questions and answers, enlarging, in a typical Jesuit manner, on the importance of Purgatory, the nature of the Real Presence in the Eucharist, and the necessary procedures to make a good confession. (Jansenists criticised the Jesuits' easy recourse to the sacrament of penance.) In order to help the prince's memory, the Commandments and prayers are printed in rhyming verse, whilst other prayers are given in Latin and English in parallel columns. In the Litany, Jesuit saints preponderate. While this was a catechism, and Betham's *Treatise* a rationale of education theory, both works were even further apart in the emphasis they individually gave to the nature of the Christian faith and conduct. Betham's humanism, reflecting Nicole's, contrasts with Anderton's dogmatism.

Although Jesuit catechisms were amongst the first to be published by the Catholic church in the late sixteenth century, English Catholic catechisms in the seventeenth century had often been the work of the English secular clergy, especially those educated at Douai. The secular so-called 'Douai Catechism' had first appeared in 1649, and was followed in 1672 by *An Abstract of the Douay Catechism*, with devotional exercises appended. Betham was, not surprisingly, fully in sympathy with this secular Douai tradition. Thus the early eighteenth-century editions of the *Douay Abstract* are accompanied by an approbation dated February 1703 from John Betham, preceptor to the king of England at Saint-Germain, Thomas Witham at St Gregory's, Paris, and the English Benedictine, Bede Moore, at St Edmund's, Paris. There seems to be little in common between this small *Douay Abstract* and its contemporary, the famous Jansenist catechism, the *Montpellier Catechism* (first edition 1702), although both were primarily written for seminaries. There is also little in common between Anderton's Jesuit catechism for the Prince of Wales and the seculars' *Douay Abstract*. The overall schemes differ; the *Abstract* glosses over the doctrine of Purgatory, but contains a very lengthy and serious-minded preparation for the reception of the sacrament of penance, differences which again adumbrate the distinction between the Jesuit and Jansenist/secular approaches to religious education.[67]

This tension between the secular and Jesuit clergy at Saint-Germain is further highlighted in another book published specifically for the Jacobite

---

[67] P. Pickering, 'Bishop Challoner and Teaching the Faith', *Clergy Review* 65, no. 1 (January 1980), 6–15. My details of the approbations come from the 1715 edition of the *Douay Abstract*, although there had been an earlier edition in 1697.

court in 1700, *The Psalms of David Translated from the Vulgate*, the work of John Caryll, in collaboration with David Nairne.[68] Betham's approbation of this work, in which he is again entitled the royal preceptor, was given at Saint-Germain in March 1700, together with that of John Ingleton, the 'Subpreceptor to His Highness'. This translation was an updated version of the Psalms found in the Douai Bible of 1609, and it is not without significance that seventeenth-century Jansenist scholars had been determined translators of the Scriptures into the vernacular, embroidering the text with moral commentary. They had clashed with the Jesuits for replacing the traditional Latin with the vernacular as the principal teaching medium.[69] A vernacular psalter for devotional use at Saint-Germain in 1700 would also without doubt appeal to Anglicans in the court circle. Both Betham's and Ingleton's approbations emphasise that this psalter was intended for the private devotions of the laity who are directed to it as an epitome of the whole of Scripture and as 'a most superior form of prayer'. The psalms had a universal appeal and the tacit argument of the two approbations is that they should be preferred to more traditionally Catholic forms of piety, such as those favoured by the Jesuits. Ingleton maintained that St Jerome's advice be followed and the psalms be learned by heart, echoing Nicole's insistence that in the moral education of children scriptural texts should be learned by heart so that the word of God was inserted in the memories of the young. Thus, the good teacher, Nicole explains in his chapter on the Manner of Christian Studies, from his *De l'Education d'un prince*, encourages others to learn the Psalms and other texts by heart in order to sanctify the memory of these divine words.[70]

By the time that Betham had approved of the published works described above, his career as the prince's preceptor was already in jeopardy. After James II's death in 1701, Louis XIV assumed responsibility for the continuing education of the new king, while Queen Mary and Madame de Maintenon sought to reduce Betham's influence over him by revealing his Jansenist bias. Although Betham's position of preceptor was renewed in October 1701, grave misgivings had surfaced by the end of 1703, when the queen heard the advice of Maintenon and the bishop of Toul, who both recommended that a third person always be present when the king was with his tutor in order to prevent Jansenist doctrine being taught. Perth, still governor, should have taken up the post of intermediary, but his Jansenist sympathies were well known. As

[68] Clancy, *English Catholic Books*, no. 909.0.
[69] Barnard, *The Little Schools*, 45–6, 97, 112, 118, 124.
[70] P. Nicole, *De l'Education d'un prince* (Paris, 1671), Part II, xliv–xlv; 'De la Manière d'Estudies Chrestiennement', xxi.

no one wished to embarrass the sixty-year-old Betham, the recommendation was not acted upon.[71]

In February 1704 Betham was summoned before Cardinal de Noailles to answer eight charges against him related by the king to his mother. They were sufficiently damning for Betham to feel that he had been betrayed by his pupil. Betham was alleged to have rejoiced at Quesnel's escape, to have stated that 'if the Pope should say 2 and 3 made not 5, I would not believe it', that he could not trust some of the queen's officials, that he had told the king Monsieur Arnauld would be canonised, that he opposed the bishop of Chartres's ordinance on the *cas de conscience*, that he had tried to turn the king against the Jesuits, and, finally, that he was opposed to the use of *lettres de cachet*. In the light of Betham's *Treatise*, part of the fifth charge is worth noting: 'That I had tired the King in making him read the books writ by those of Port-Royal, and in particular, the Essai Moral.'

Betham went on to refute these charges. He disingenuously denied any connection with Port-Royal and insisted he had remained orthodox in his preaching. He did not believe papal infallibility was an article of faith, and as this doctrine was so shocking to Protestants, Stuart support for it might impede a restoration. Protestant anxiety was, furthermore, not calmed by the notion that some members of the royal household supported the notoriously Jesuit practice of equivocation. He had not said that Arnauld would be canonised, but that he was due for a Cardinal's cap. As to employing Nicole's *Essai Moral*, Betham replied that James II had, in the presence of the queen and his confessor, ordered him to make the prince read it. Betham believed the bishop of Chartres's ordinance to have been too violent to help in reconciling the Jansenists. It was the imputation that he had turned the prince against the Jesuits which most offended Betham, for he confessed that he had only mentioned them when prompted by the prince's questions regarding those who were supposed to teach the doctrine of 'loose morality'. Finally, his aversion to *lettres de cachet* came from his preference for the situation in England, where freedom of speech and full legal rights were to be found.

The cardinal promised that his discussion with Betham should remain confidential, but advised him to stay clear of the controversial questions listed. In particular, he should 'lay aside the *Essai Moral*', and instead expose the new king to Jesuit devotional works, which he named. It appears from this time forward that Betham and Ingleton were extremely cautious whenever Jesuits or their books were mentioned in the king's presence. The constant reporting to the queen by her son of all that Betham said does not leave one with a strong

---

[71] Miller, *James*, 72, 75–6; HMC *Stuart* I, 164, 188, 189; Clark, *Strangers*, 226–8.

impression that the sixteen-year-old king was very independently minded, and Betham twice highlights this weakness: 'no child', he confides, 'is more apt to mistake in relating a thing than his Majesty'. In October 1704, the criticisms levelled at Betham reached Louis XIV, who recommended that Betham be discreetly dismissed in a way which would not hurt his feelings. Louis was particularly incensed by Betham's alleged statement that he preferred to live under Cromwell or the Prince of Orange than King Louis XIV.

In November 1704 Cardinal de Noailles recommended Betham to retire quietly and make a gradual withdrawal from Saint-Germain in order to save the queen from embarrassment. When Betham came face to face with the queen, both broke down, and she tried, unsuccessfully, to shift the blame for his dismissal on to Louis. Betham indicated that he felt betrayed and calumniated, but he explained, to the queen's apparent satisfaction, his views of the Jesuit teaching on equivocation. He tried hard to clear his name, since his 'being dismissed' would 'be thought the punishment of some high misdemeanour', but the queen, embarrassed, shunned him and he was forced to use Noailles as an intermediary. At Epiphany, Betham had an audience with the king, whom he blamed for carrying false stories to his mother. James burst into tears of contrition after hearing his tutor's profession of respect, and felt obliged to read Betham's written justification. Betham had compiled this to remove any hint of unorthodoxy. The king, however, continued to remain cool towards him, and Betham had to admit sadly that for some time the king had distanced himself from him. Although the queen tried to be as gracious as possible, and recommended that Betham still continue to act as a royal counsellor, Betham declined and left for Paris on 9 January 1705. He seems, however, to have continued to visit the court occasionally after this date.[72] By the time of his departure, Betham was already heavily involved in other matters which would occupy him until his death in April 1709. These included the campaign to have a secular priest rather than a regular appointed as the next Vicar Apostolic in England and the defence of the English College at Douai against charges of Jansenism.[73]

Despite the circumstances of his departure from Saint-Germain, Betham's tutelage of the prince had a lasting effect and the influence of the Jansenist tradition mediated to the prince through Nicole and Betham remained. It provided the obvious preparation for James's alleged Quietist sympathies, which he derived from Fénelon whom he first met in 1709, the year of Betham's

[72] Westminster Diocesan Archives, Paris Seminary volume, ff. 231–45; *Catholic Gentleman's Magazine* 1, no. 9 (1818), 643–55 for the printed text; Clark, *Strangers*, 226–8; Duffy, ' "Rubb-up" ', 296; HMC *Stuart* I, 188–93; HMC *Stuart* II, 198–204, 520.

[73] 'Register Book of St Gregory's', 119; Clark, *Strangers*, 183–5; B. Hemphill, *The Early Vicars Apostolic of England, 1685–1750* (London, 1953), 35–41; Duffy, ' "Rubb-up" ', 294, 296, 300–7.

death. Fénelon's description of the king in November 1709, pointing out his
moderation, detachment and moral sensibility, is a mirror image of Nicole's
and Betham's ideal prince. Betham's own character may well have been rubbed
off on this disciple of his whom he had educated from the age of three years
until he was fifteen.

When James III met Fénelon in 1709 he was, in effect, still continuing his
education. In March 1706, conscious that he would soon achieve his majority,
he had asked to be allowed to serve incognito as a volunteer in the French
army in Flanders, but Louis XIV had refused.[74] As a result he had embarked
on the planned invasion of Scotland in 1708 without any previous military
experience. After his return to France he renewed his request and this time
Louis agreed.[75] Referring to himself as a Knight of the Order of the Garter,
or *Chevalier de Saint-Georges*, James III then served in the French army of
Flanders during the campaigns of 1708, 1709 and 1710, and was present at
both Oudenarde and Malplaquet.

James's military training was entrusted to Lieutenant-General Richard
Hamilton (his master of the robes), and to his former under-governor Dominic
Sheldon, now also a lieutenant-general (and later appointed vice-chamberlain).
Mary of Modena wrote to the former in 1708: 'Remember your promise to
me not to quit the King one step in a day of action and also to tell him frankly
and positively what is fitt for him to do, for he promised the King of France
and me at parting, that he would upon such occasions, do what you and
Mr Sheldon should advise.'[76] James III soon became a dashing cavalry officer
and showed great courage on the field of battle, having to be restrained from
exposing himself too much to the opposing English army.[77] By the end of 1710

[74] Dangeau, XI, 61, 23 March 1706.

[75] Dangeau, XII, 114, 116, 9, 10, 11 April 1708; Sourches, XI, 59, 11 April 1708.

[76] BL Add. MSS 18966, Mary of Modena to Richard Hamilton, 1 September 1708 (quoted in
R. Clark, *Anthony Hamilton* (London, 1921), 296).

[77] Archives Municipales de Saint-Germain-en-Laye, Mary of Modena to Richard Hamilton, 30
September 1709 (a recently purchased letter which ought to be part of BL Add. MSS 18966):
'I knew no particulars upon which I could relye till I received your tre which is so exact, and so
plain . . . I understand all you say to me, as if I had seen it, and I thank God my heart is now at
ease all manner of ways, finding that the King has don, as I could wish, and I can never thank
you enough, nor the others that were with him, for having kept him from doing mor, for if he
had, he would have been indeed like an aventurier, as Me de Maintenon writt me word at first
he had, which I dont find by yours.' Hamilton had kept the queen waiting much too long for his
letter, so her only news from Malplaquet had come via the French court; hence her letter to him
of 16 August 1710 in BL Add. MSS 18966 (quoted in Clark, *Hamilton*, 297): 'I hope you will not
fail writting to me . . . but you having forgott it once I now put you in mind of it for fear you
should forget it again.'

he had thus added considerable military experience to the thorough general education he had already received from Betham and others at Saint-Germain. In 1711 he extended his practical knowledge of the world by making a tour of the eastern provinces of France. By the time he moved his court away from Saint-Germain in the summer of 1712, in anticipation of the Treaty of Utrecht, James III had become one of the best-educated princes who either did ascend, or might have ascended, the throne of England.

CHAPTER TWELVE

From France to Lorraine, 1712–1715

James's decision to leave Saint-Germain was imposed on him by political necessity, but it was not unwelcome. He was glad to leave a place which had become associated in his mind with failure and personal loss. In February 1712 the new dauphin and dauphine had both died at Versailles of measles. In March their elder son, the duc de Bretagne, had died of the same illness. In April Princess Louise-Marie had died of smallpox. While waiting for his eventual restoration, it is clear that James was not unwilling to live elsewhere.

The tragedy of his sister's death was increased by the circumstances surrounding it. James himself had contracted smallpox at the beginning of April and was not yet out of danger when his sister began to show the same symptoms. Fearing lest worry might hinder his recovery, James was deliberately not told about his sister's condition – not even when he was himself pronounced to be out of danger. No one was particularly worried about the princess, and the court seems to have been completely optimistic that she too would eventually recover. In fact her death came very suddenly on the morning of 18 April. It was not until nine days later that James himself was felt to have recovered. He was then told that his sister had fallen ill and died, and even been buried in Paris, without his knowing anything about it.[1] Given that their apartments were both in the north wing of the château, and that their Bedchambers in the corner pavilions actually faced each other, this revelation must have made the loss of his sister worse than it would otherwise have been. There were by then many other people in the château who were also suffering from smallpox.

---

[1] The sequence of events can be followed in Dangeau and Sourches, 2–27 April 1712. Having felt ill for a few days, James was diagnosed as having smallpox on 2 April. His sister was known to have contracted it by 12 April. James was said to be out of danger on the 14th, and Berwick reported to Louis XIV on the evening of the 17th that the princess was also recovering, only to return the following morning with the news that she was dead. Her body was taken to Paris on the 20th. For confirmation of Berwick's optimism and the princess's sudden death, see BL Add. MSS 31257, ff. 56 and 58, Middleton to Gualterio, 17 and 24 April 1712. For details of the funeral, see Corp, *Cour des Stuarts*, 153; and Pontchartrain to Berwick, 18 and 19 April 1712 (Christian and Odette de Sèze, sale catalogue of *Livres anciens et modernes: autographes, varia* (Périgueux, 1991), item 92). For the account by Dr Lawrence Wood, the physician of the household, see Bodleian Library, Carte MSS 208, f. 372, 'Relation of the princesse's case, Analysed'.

Francis Plowden (comptroller of the household) had died on 20 April, and both Roger Strickland (groom of the Bedchamber) and his brother Francis (page of honour) were seriously ill. Most people had left the château to live in the town and, as John Stafford put it, the court had been transformed into a hospital.[2]

Within a few weeks both the Strickland brothers had recovered and the epidemic had passed, but the loss of the princess (as of the dauphin and dauphine) was irreparable. The Duke of Perth, who had not always approved of the younger generation at court, wrote that 'notre chere Princesse estoit la joe et l'ame de toutes les conversations. C'estoit chez elle que tout ce qui pouvoit divertir et plaire se trouvoit et elle avoit l'art d'obliger grands et petits.'[3] James had been away from Saint-Germain throughout the summer months of 1708–11, but had returned each autumn to enjoy the winter season with his sister and his cousins. He was not sorry to leave in the summer of 1712 and had no particular wish to return.[4]

But it was necessary to find a suitable place to establish his court. As we have seen, Louis XIV had already promised to continue paying the Stuart pension, even though the Tory ministers insisted that James should leave France as a condition of peace. In May (shortly after James's recovery from smallpox) Louis proposed that he should move to Lorraine, conveniently close to England, whence he could negotiate his restoration after the peace treaty had been signed.[5]

The negotiations between Versailles and London moved slowly, but James III did what he could to hasten them. There were two problems to be overcome. The first was to obtain the agreement of the Tory ministers that James should reside in Lorraine, where the duke was perfectly willing to receive him. The second was to obtain a formal safe conduct, guaranteeing that neither Great Britain nor the emperor, nor any of their allies, would interfere with James or his court in any way once they had left the security of France.

At the end of June James selected a small group of servants and ordered them to be ready to leave Saint-Germain 'at a days warning'.[6] On 11 July he took his formal leave of Louis XIV, who was about to go to Fontainebleau.[7]

[2] BL Add. MSS 31258, ff. 77 and 84, Stafford to Gualterio, 24 April and 1 May 1712.

[3] BL Add. MSS 31256, f. 47, Perth to Gualterio, 23 April 1712.

[4] Bibl. Mun. de Versailles, MS 1461/P.67, 420, Mary of Modena to Maintenon, 16 August 1712: 'depuis qu'il a eu le malheur de perdre sa pauvre soeur, ce lieu ici est encore bien plus triste qu'il n'estoit pour lui'.

[5] See above, p. 72.

[6] Bodleian Library, Carte MSS 212, f. 36v, Nairne to Abram, 3 July 1712.

[7] BL Add. MSS 31257, f. 101, Middleton to Gualterio, 10 July 1712.

Then, because the negotiations were taking too long and he was keen to get away, he arranged to borrow the Château du Raincy from the marquis de Livry, the *premier maître d'hotel* (lord steward) at the French court. This château, which had been designed by Louis Le Vau in the 1650s, and had a large garden traditionally attributed to André Le Nôtre,[8] lay to the east of Paris. James moved there on 21 August, having asked his mother to live at Chaillot so they could more easily see each other.[9]

Very little is known about James's residence at Le Raincy, where he remained for two and a half weeks. He was accompanied by both Middleton and Nairne, and must have had a small number of servants from the Bedchamber and the Stables. But the catering arrangements could have been provided by the servants of the marquis de Livry. It took one and a quarter hours to travel to Chaillot, where James dined several times, receiving at least one return visit from the queen.[10] It took even less time to travel to Paris, and on 26 August James went from Le Raincy to attend a performance of *Le Ballet des saisons* by Collasse at the Opéra. He wished to see Lord Bolingbroke,[11] who had just given formal agreement for him to reside at Bar-le-Duc in Lorraine.[12]

Once this had been decided James prepared to leave Le Raincy and move to Châlons-sur-Marne, close to the border between France and Lorraine. He was to live there temporarily until the necessary formal safeconduct had been obtained.[13] Once again the negotiations were long drawn out. Although James travelled to Châlons on 7 September,[14] he was not able to move on to Bar-le-Duc until February 1713, over five months later.

While James was at Châlons he probably stayed in the Hôtel Dubois de Crancé, which belonged to the governor of the town, but that is not certain. It is not even clear which members of his household were there with him. Dangeau's comment that he took with him 'fort peu de gens'[15] is not very helpful. Nor indeed is John Stafford's in early November 1712 that 'sa Cour y est un peu grossie', because of the arrival of various Jacobite officers from the

[8] K. Woodbridge, *Princely Gardens* (London, 1986), 184–5.
[9] Bibl. Mun. de Versailles, MS 1461/P.67, 420, Mary of Modena to Maintenon, 16 August 1712; BL Add. MSS 31257, f. 125, Middleton to Gualterio, 21 August 1712; BL Add. MSS 31258, f. 148, Stafford to Gualterio, 21 August 1712.
[10] Bibl. Mun. de Versailles, MS 1461/P.67, 425, Mary of Modena to Maintenon, 1 September 1712; BL Add. MSS 31258, f. 169, Stafford to Gualterio, 4 September 1712.
[11] Corp, 'Music at Urbino', 352, note 8.   [12] See above, p. 72.
[13] BL Add. MSS 31257, f. 129, Middleton to Gualterio, 4 September 1712.
[14] Dangeau, XIV, 220, 8 September 1712.
[15] *Ibid.* Cf. Saint-Simon, XXIII, 271: he left with 'une petite suite'.

French army in Flanders, including the Earl of Newcastle (gentleman of the Bedchamber) and General Rothe (Lord Middleton's son-in-law).[16] The secretariat included Monnot as well as Middleton and Nairne,[17] and the household servants included General Richard Hamilton (master of the robes),[18] but there is no definite evidence which of the other servants had been selected to be with the king at Châlons. Shortly before James finally left France for Lorraine he received a short visit from the Duke of Berwick.[19]

While James III was waiting at Châlons he decided to adopt again the temporary incognito, as the Knight of St George (*Chevalier de Saint-Georges*), that he had previously had when serving with the French army in 1708–10.[20] This meant that he began to eat his meals with some of his senior officers and servants, and also that he allowed the French noblemen who came to visit him to sit down in his presence. In November he spent several days with the marquis de Sillery in his château south-east of Reims, and insisted on also maintaining there 'la même familiarité' with everyone who came to visit him.[21]

By the beginning of 1713 James III had grown weary of waiting in Châlons and was eager to move on to Bar-le-Duc, where the Duke of Lorraine had promised him the use of the much larger and more convenient château. But no safeconduct had been forthcoming, and an impasse had been reached in the negotiations at Utrecht. The Tory ministers were not prepared to sign the treaty so long as James remained in France; Louis XIV was not prepared to force him to leave until he had a safeconduct. At the end of January Louis tried to overcome the impasse by offering James some French troops to escort him to Bar and to provide a permanent guard until the treaty was signed and a safeconduct forthcoming, but James declined his offer and decided to travel to Bar without any allied guarantees of his safety.[22] Writing to Louis XIV that he would always find in him (James) 'le respect, l'attachement, et si je l'ose dire, la tendresse d'un fils',[23] he left Châlons on 20 February and reached

[16] BL Add. MSS 31258, f. 203, Stafford to Gualterio, 6 November 1712.

[17] BL Add. MSS 31257, f. 133, Middleton to Gualterio, 30 September 1712. Nairne was ill and his letters were being written for him by Monnot.

[18] Dangeau, xiv, 349, 21 February 1713.

[19] BL Add. MSS 31258, f. 273, Stafford to Gualterio, 19 February 1713.

[20] Dangeau, xiv, 225, 16 September 1712; L. Bély, 'L'incognito des princes: l'exemple de Jacques III', *Revue de la Bibliothèque Nationale* 46 (hiver 1992), 40–3.

[21] Bibliothèque de l'Arsenal MS 3864, memoirs of the baron de Breteuil, 136–7; BL Add. MSS 31258, f. 206, Stafford to Gualterio, 13 November 1712.

[22] See above, pp. 73–4.

[23] Bibl. Mun. de Versailles, MS 1461/P.67, 552, James III to Louis XIV, 20 February 1713.

Bar the following day.[24] Once he was there he was at last able to set about properly re-establishing his court.

When James arrived at Bar he was greeted by the Duke of Lorraine and his *grand chamberlain*, who happened to be an Irish Jacobite, Owen O'Rourke. The duke had brought with him four companies of foot guards, amounting to 300 men, who were to remain permanently with the king, and thirty of whom were always to be on duty. But it seems that James's decision to leave France had taken the duke by surprise, and that nothing had been done to prepare the château to accommodate the English court. James and his servants were therefore given temporary accommodation in the town for about a week while the duke returned to Lunéville.[25]

The King himself occupied 'the principal house' in the town, situated in the rue des Tanneurs (now the rue Docteur Nève), and owned by one of the town councillors, a Monsieur Marchal. It was described (at the end of the nineteenth century) as 'a plain square, three-storeyed building (counting the upper range of rooms, which is very low, as a storey) . . . It has eight windows frontage . . . abutting width ways on [a] very narrow passage' called the rue Saint-Antoine. It was clearly not large enough to accommodate more than a few servants, so billets were issued by the town council to provide lodgings for most of the members of the court, as well as stabling for their horses.[26] Presumably the guards already had barracks somewhere in the town.

The château was situated high up on a promontory beside the old town (*la ville haute*), overlooking the rue des Tanneurs in the new town (*la ville basse*) and, beyond it, the river Ornain. When it was ready at the beginning of March, Lord Middleton described the furniture and fittings in the king's apartment as magnificent,[27] and indeed the general position of the building must have reminded the members of the court, if only superficially, of Saint-Germain, also situated high up with an esplanade overlooking the nearby river. Before coming back from Lunéville to check that James was satisfied with his new accommodation, the duke sent fifty horse guards to supplement the 300 foot guards already there, so that James and his

[24] Bodleian Library, Carte MSS 212, f. 50r, Nairne to Berry, 17 February 1713; Dangeau, XIV, 349, 21 February 1713; BL Add. MSS 31257, f. 173, Middleton to Gualterio, 2 March 1713.

[25] BL Add. MSS 31258, f. 278, Stafford to Gualterio, 1 March 1713; BL Add. MSS 31257, f. 173, Middleton to Gualterio, 2 March 1713.

[26] H.W. Wolff, 'The Pretender at Bar-le-Duc', *Blackwood's Magazine* 156, no. 1446 (August 1894), 232–3.

[27] BL Add. MSS 31257, f. 173, Middleton to Gualterio, 2 March 1713.

entourage could be properly attended when hunting or making visits in the area.[28]

James III and his court were based at the Château de Bar for over two and a half years until October 1715, when he left Lorraine to make his way (through France) to Scotland. But the king was frequently absent, making visits to Nancy, to the Prince de Vaudemont at nearby Commercy, and in order to take the waters at the celebrated spa of Plombières. The members of the court therefore had to become accustomed to regular travelling. Moreover, James found the château too cold in the autumn, and preferred to spend the winter months down below in the town. He returned to his former lodgings in the rue des Tanneurs, but also took over the house which adjoined it (on the side away from the little rue Saint-Antoine) and part of the house beyond that as well. According to Henry Wolff, who consulted the records of the town council in the 1890s, James insisted

that a second house ajoining [should] be added, belonging to M. de Romécourt, besides a portion of one belonging to M. Lepaige, with a kitchen specially built, and a *garde-manger*, a new door, and sundry other conveniences, to say nothing of the hiring of further accommodation for his horses, his kennel, his *gens de vénerie*, his guards, some of his suite – all of whom and all of which he [wanted] very near him . . . M. de Romécourt's house [was] a complete match to M. Marchal's, but smaller, bringing up the frontage to thirteen windows.[29]

The size of the king's household at Bar-le-Duc was a little more than half what it had been at Saint-Germain, including about sixty-five people instead of about 120.[30] In selecting those servants who were to remain behind with the queen, the choice naturally fell on the oldest and those least able to travel. But James also took into account the size of the accommodation he was to be offered and the number of rooms in the duke's apartment which he was himself to occupy. In particular, the shortage of additional antechambers meant that, like his father when he had occupied the apartment of Louis XIV, James III mainly reduced the staff of the Chamber. With one exception (referred to below), all the ushers of the Privy, Presence and Guard Chambers were left behind at Saint-Germain.

[28] BL Add. MSS 31258, f. 278, Stafford to Gualterio, 1 March 1713; Westminster Diocesan Archives, Epist. var. IV, f. 8, Ingleton to Mayes, 12 March 1713; Chiddingstone Castle, Bower MSS, James III to Mary of Modena, 8 March 1713.

[29] Wolff, 'The Pretender', 237.

[30] Except where shown, the following account is based on a great many references scattered through the Stuart Papers and the Nairne Papers, too many to be worth citing individually.

The servants of the Bedchamber included the two gentlemen (Lord New-castle and Lord Edward Drummond), five of the nine grooms (David Floyd, Richard Trevanion, Daniel MacDonnell, Charles Booth and Roger Strickland), and two of the four pages (Baltassare Artema and a Mr Styles). There was no closet keeper. The remaining servants were the essential ones: a laundress, a sempstress and two barbers, one of whom (Thomas de Saint-Paul) acted as valet.

The substantially reduced number of Chamber servants was under the su-pervision of Lt General Dominic Sheldon, the vice-chamberlain (appointed in 1711, having previously been under-governor). They included the king's con-fessor (Dr John Ingleton, previously under-preceptor), two chaplains (Father Thomas Lawson and Father Thadée Connell), an almoner (Lewis Innes) and one of the two physicians (Dr Lawrence Wood). There were no musicians and, it seems, no messengers.

The correspondence was handled by only three of the seven secretaries (Lord Middleton, David Nairne and Etienne du Mirail de Monnot). The master of the robes (Lt General Richard Hamilton), who had been at Châlons, returned to Saint-Germain in February 1713,[31] taking with him both the yeoman and the groom, so that the king's clothes were cared for and prepared by the Bedchamber staff.

By contrast, James took to Bar virtually all the servants employed in the household below stairs and in the Stables. The former were placed under Sir William Ellis, partly because the other clerk controller of the Greencloth (Sir John Sparrow) was too elderly to travel, and partly because Ellis was a commissioner of the household. It is difficult to be certain, given the lack of enough detailed documentation, but the only other servants left behind seem to have been those employed in the scullery, the pantry and the woodyard, and the purveyor of the poultry. The king sent most of his silver plate back to Saint-Germain when he arrived at Bar,[32] and the bread, wood and poultry were presumably purchased in the town by the other servants.

The Stables were directed by one of the three equerries (James Delattre, previously responsible only for the great stable) and one of the two purveyors (John Sheridan, previously only the riding purveyor). What this meant was that the servants in charge of the little stables, which contained coaches and the horses for pulling them, were left behind. With the exception of two or

---

[31] Dangeau, xiv, 349, 21 February 1713.
[32] BL Add. MSS 9128, f. 1, anon. to the Duchess of Hanover, 5 April 1714.

three elderly servants, everyone else employed in the Stables was taken to Bar with, it seems, the footmen acting as temporary messengers.[33]

It has generally been believed that the household at Bar was almost entirely Protestant,[34] and that James took with him all the Protestants who had been at Saint-Germain.[35] This is totally wrong, and based on some misleading comments made at the time.[36] In fact the court at Bar was overwhelmingly Catholic.

By 1713 there were only nine protestants employed in the king's household, and of these six had remained at Saint-Germain.[37] There was only one Protestant employed in the queen's household, and he also had remained at Saint-Germain.[38] The only protestants who were employed in the household at Bar were Sir William Ellis, Mr Styles and Thomas Higgons. The latter was a gentleman usher of the Privy Chamber, and the only servant from the Privy, Presence and Guard Chambers to accompany the king to Bar.

The reason for this extraordinary misunderstanding seems to be that when he left France James III was able to persuade the Duke of Lorraine and the bishop of Toul to let him introduce religious toleration for those Protestants who were at his court[39] – in this case for all three of them.[40] As early as June 1712 Nairne had noted that an Anglican clergyman named Thorp, who lived at Saint-Germain, would be allowed to accompany the court to Lorraine,[41] and he presumably travelled to Bar-le-Duc in February 1713. But by then James had decided that it would be more politically effective to invite an influential Tory clergyman to come over from England, to join the court as a salaried

---

[33] HMC *Stuart* I, 329, Mary of Modena to Dicconson, 5 July 1714.

[34] Haile, *Mary of Modena*, 451.   [35] Wolff, 'The Pretender', 233.

[36] Sourches (XIII, 386, 9 May 1712) stated that James would apparently leave all the Catholics at Saint-Germain and take only Protestants with him; the duchesse d'Orléans wrote that 'he has taken only Protestants into his service' (*Letters of Madame*, II, 61, to the Raugravine Louisa, 10 September 1712); the Hanoverian Robethon added that 'he left all the Roman Catholics with the Queen his mother at St. Germain. None but Protestants are about him at Bar, except Lord Middleton' (letter to Galke, March 1713, cited in Haile, '*Old Chevalier*', 137).

[37] Sir John Sparrow (clerk controller of the Greencloth), John Bayly (purveyor of the poultry), Thomas Woolhouse (groom of the Privy Chamber), Peter Moirie (gallery keeper), Gerald Devereux (purveyor of the Stables), Sir Charles Carteret (gentleman usher of the Presence Chamber).

[38] Thomas Heywood (page of the Bedchamber).

[39] HMC *Stuart* IV, 467 Dicconson to Mary of Modena, 26 July 1717.

[40] Ellis was unmarried and Higgons had a Catholic wife, but it should be added that Styles had a wife and children who seem to have been Protestant.

[41] Bodleian Library, Carte MSS 212, f. 33r, Nairne to Abram, 5 June 1712.

member of the household.[42] Thorp was therefore sent back to Saint-Germain and replaced by Charles Leslie, who was given a salary considerably higher than those paid to the Catholic chaplains. When Leslie arrived in August 1713,[43] he quickly realised that James genuinely wanted religious toleration – for himself as well as for everyone else. In a letter that he sent from Bar to London in the autumn of 1713, Leslie wrote of the king that 'I never yet was refused access to him when I desired it, and He of himself often sends for me and gives me special Marks of his Favour . . . He will press no man's conscience, and he may reasonably expect his own should not be pressed.'[44] Leslie's appointment was noted at Versailles where Dangeau (adding to the misunderstanding about the number of Protestants in the household) wrote that 'comme il y a beaucoup d'autres anglicans parmi ses domestiques, il leur a fait venir un ministre anglican qui prêche dans sa maison'.[45] The Anglicans at the court of Bar were, of course, the 'many English' travelling abroad after the return of peace, who went 'from Paris to Bar on the pretext of seeing Champagne'.[46]

Even though there were so few Protestants at Bar it is clear that James III was very careful to respect Anglican feeling. In May 1712 he had told his Jesuit confessor, Father Thomas Eyre, that he would not take him or any other Jesuit when he left France because Jesuits were regarded as 'odieux' by his friends in England.[47] John Ingleton therefore replaced Eyre as the king's confessor. In July 1712 James had asked Cardinal Gualterio to send a petition to the pope asking for permission to exempt his household from having to fast during the following Lent.[48] And in February 1714 he instructed Bishop Philip Ellis, Sir William's Catholic brother, not to visit the court at Bar because he was unpopular in England.[49] Most important, however, was the king's willingness

---

[42] HMC *Stuart* I, 260, Berwick to James III, 28 March 1713.

[43] *Ibid.*, 273, Berwick to James III, 22 August 1713.

[44] The letter was published in London in 1714. Different extracts are reproduced in Haile, '*Old Chevalier*', 460; and A. Shield and A. Lang, *The King over the Water* (London, 1907), 184–5.

[45] Dangeau, xv, 46, 16 December 1713.

[46] BL Add. MSS 9128, 1, anon to the Duchess of Hanover, 5 April 1714.

[47] BL Add. MSS 20310, f. 54, Eyre to Gualterio, 22 May 1712. Dangeau recorded that when James III had smallpox he refused to make his confession to Father Eyre but instead called for the *curé* of the parish church (xiv, 127, 14 April 1712). (The *curé* from 1698 to 1729 was Jean-François de Benoist de Chasel.) James III also insisted that Lewis Innes should 'goe along with him, notwithstanding his infirmities', which (in the opinion of his brother) rendered him 'most unfitt for long voyaging' (Halloran, *Scots College Paris*, 83, T. Innes to W. Stuart, 30 May 1712).

[48] BL Add. MSS 20311, f. 227, draft of a petition by Gualterio to the S. Congregatione del Santo Offitio, 22 July 1712.

[49] BL Add. MSS 31259, f. 12, Nairne to Gualterio, 1 February 1714.

to sacrifice even Lord Middleton in order to appease the Anglican Tories in London.

Middleton had been disliked in England ever since his conversion to Catholicism, and in the autumn of 1713 Lord Oxford insisted that he should be dismissed and replaced as secretary of state by an Anglican, if the negotiations for a peaceful restoration were to be continued. James deeply resented this condition, but gave way at a time when he had decided he would never make an insincere conversion to Anglicanism, and needed to be able to offer something to persuade the Tory ministers of his good faith. In December 1713 Middleton agreed to resign and return to Saint-Germain.

The king, however, was keen to show how much he appreciated Middleton's services. The latter's son, Lord Clermont, had been captured during the expedition to Scotland in 1708 and had not been allowed to return to France until the Treaty of Utrecht. Since June 1713 he had been waiting, unemployed, at Saint-Germain. James III, therefore, compensated Middleton by appointing his son to be a gentleman of the Bedchamber. As he had not intended to make any new appointments until after his restoration this was regarded as a great honour. Clermont's arrival at Bar in January 1714 increased the number of gentlemen to three.[50]

As there were only four Anglicans at Bar (Ellis, Styles, Higgons and Leslie) it was absurd to insist that James should appoint one of them to be his new secretary of state. (Perhaps Oxford believed there were more.) Ellis was fully employed running the household below stairs, Leslie had only recently arrived to be the Anglican chaplain, and Styles was only a page. The choice therefore fell on Thomas Higgons, who was knighted and sworn in as secretary of state on 16 December. It was both unfair and unreasonable, if only because Higgons, living within an anglophone community, was not able to write correct French.[51] The king made the best of the situation, describing Higgons as 'de bonne maison, toujours attaché à mes interets, pour lesquels il a meme esté dans les Prisons de Londres du temps du Roy mon pere, et depuis longtemps dans ma famille', but he restricted Higgons to the negotiations with the Tory ministers, and entrusted all the Roman correspondence

---

[50] Haile, *Mary of Modena*, 441, and '*Old Chevalier*', 142, James III to the Duke of Lorraine, wrongly dated June 1713 in both sources; BL Add. MSS 31255, f. 3, James III to Gualterio, 16 December 1713; BL Add. MSS 31256, f. 70, Perth to Gualterio, 21 December 1713; HMC *Stuart* I, 288, Berwick to James III, 2 January 1714; BL Add. MSS 31259, f. 9, Nairne to Gualterio, 25 January 1714; BL Add. MSS 31257, f. 179, Middleton to Gualterio, 17 March 1714. See also above, p. 127.

[51] HMC *Stuart* I, 291, Berwick to James III, 16 January 1714.

to David Nairne, who was promoted to occupy a new post as secretary of the Closet.[52]

The salaries of the royal household continued to be paid at Bar-le-Duc, as they had been at Saint-Germain, out of the pension given to the Stuarts by Louis XIV. They were never reduced, though Dr Wood, who was the only physician at the court, had his salary more than doubled.[53] There was no gentleman waiters' table at Bar, because most of the people who had had diet at Saint-Germain had remained there. But James decided to eat with his courtiers, and kept two tables in his apartment: the first for the gentlemen of the Bedchamber, the vice-chamberlain, the secretary of state and other important people who happened to be visiting, the second for the other senior servants (such as David Nairne).[54] Those people who would have had diet at Saint-Germain, but who were not invited to eat at either of these tables, were given board wages (called 'personal allowances') to supplement their salaries.[55]

The king also had to compensate servants for making them leave the homes they were renting at Saint-Germain. Those who could not be lodged in the château itself were given lodging money to enable them to pay for their accommodation in the town.[56] Transferring his court to Bar, therefore, involved James in considerable additional expenditure, because in effect he now had to maintain two completely separate households.[57] This did not affect the court at Bar, but it eventually necessitated some retrenchments at Saint-Germain.

When it was first suggested that James should leave France with only some of his servants, leaving the rest at Saint-Germain with those of the queen, Louis XIV had promised to divide the Stuart pension equally between him and his mother.[58] This arrangement, however, was not put into effect until June 1713,[59] and until then the entire pension was received by William Dicconson, who transmitted to Sir William Ellis at Bar whatever money James needed for himself and his court. Dicconson kept the rest at Saint-Germain to pay both

[52] BL Add. MSS 31255, f. 3, James III to Gualterio, 16 December 1713; BL Add. MSS 31259, f. 1, Nairne to Gualterio, 16 December 1713; BL Add. MSS 31254, Mary of Modena to Gualterio, 11 January 1714; Bodleian Library, Carte MSS 212, f. 62, note by Nairne, undated.

[53] SP 8/92 and SP 9/30, the Establishment of the King's Household in 1715 and 1716.

[54] BL Add. MSS 20298, f. 67, Nairne to Gualterio, August 1718.

[55] HMC *Stuart* IV, 31, proposals of Dicconson, April 1716; SP 39/117, a note of 'Travelling Charges per Diem', 12 December 1718; SP 42/18, 'Directions for Sir William Ellis', February 1719.

[56] SP Box 3/90, 'a list of the Kings Servants who have been lodged, or have had lodging monie since His Ma.tie parted from St. Germans'.

[57] BL Add. MSS 31258, f. 247, Stafford to Gualterio, 1 January 1713.

[58] See above, p. 73.   [59] HMC *Stuart* I, 268, Berwick to James III, 26 June 1713.

the servants of the queen and those of the king who had stayed behind, and Ellis was appointed treasurer of the household at Bar-le-Duc.

At first James had some problems of credit, because the French pension had fallen into arrears, and because Louis XIV could only afford to send him away with an advance of two months' money, instead of the three he had promised.[60] But the household at Bar was as well paid as it had been at Saint-Germain. Mary of Modena transferred substantial amounts from her investments in the *luoghi di monte* in Rome,[61] including 29,185 *livres* in January 1713.[62] The duke also helped out by giving James a total of 308,610 *livres* while he was in Lorraine, and an additional 49,344 *livres* was received from the pope in March 1714.[63] So long as there seemed a realistic prospect of a peaceful restoration, the court at Bar had no significant financial problems.

However, the situation was completely altered by the death of Queen Anne in August 1714. The accession of George I meant that a Jacobite restoration could now only take place as a result of military action, which was bound to require a great deal more money. Large sums were sent from England,[64] and the pope sent a further 141,935 *livres*,[65] but James needed to reduce his expenditure and make what savings he could.[66] In October 1714 he substantially reduced his expenditure on the Stables, which was the only department in which this could easily be done. He sent his berline back to Saint-Germain and kept 'only one coach with 2 horses and 6 saddlehorses'. Eight servants were also sent back to Saint-Germain, three of whom were even made redundant.[67]

The Hanoverian succession and the fall of the Tory ministry also made James reconsider some of the decisions which Lord Oxford had imposed on him. In November 1714 he recalled Lord Middleton to be his chief minister, while leaving Higgons with the title of secretary of state.[68] In February 1715 he

---

[60] *Ibid.*, 246, Mary of Modena to Dicconson, 8 September 1712.

[61] The money was transferred by Giovanni Angelo Belloni, her banker in Rome. BL Add MSS 31258 contains plenty of correspondence on the subject: e.g. f. 206, Stafford to Gualterio, 13 November 1712, acknowledging the receipt of 6000 *livres*.

[62] BL Add. MSS 31258, ff. 247 and 265, Stafford to Gualterio, 1 and 29 January 1713.

[63] SP 44/81, account by Dicconson, 29 August 1719.

[64] Bodleian Library, Carte MSS 211, ff. 319 and 323–4, accounts by Dicconson, undated.

[65] SP 44/81, account by Dicconson, 29 August 1719.

[66] Dicconson's 'account of ye Kings expence for ye last six months of last year 1714' is in Bodleian Library, Carte MSS 211, f. 318.

[67] *Letter Book of Sabran*, 176, Wood to Sabran, 11 October 1714; SP 7/111, a list of persons by Dicconson, April 1716.

[68] BL Add. MSS 31259, ff. 85, 90 and 94, Nairne to Gualterio, 2, 10 and 23 November 1714; BL Add. MSS 31257, f. 203, Middleton to Gualterio, undated, but late November 1714.

decided to have a Jesuit confessor, instead of Dr Ingleton.[69] As James had no wish to dismiss his old under-preceptor he attempted to have him appointed Vicar Apostolic in England to create the necessary vacancy.[70] When this failed he tried unsuccessfully to obtain for him a benefice. It is possible that the pope and Cardinal Gualterio both preferred that Ingleton should remain where he was, and that the king should not appoint a Jesuit.[71]

The death of Queen Anne had another important effect on the court of Bar-le-Duc. So long as she had lived, James had been willing to bide his time and negotiate with the Tories to become her successor. He had been willing to adopt an incognito as the Knight of St George, and exclude the crown and other indications of royalty from his portraits. Once George of Hanover had succeeded to the throne, James threw off his incognito and resumed his royal status as King James III. This was soon made public in some new engraved portraits of James which were published in the second half of 1714.

Shortly after his arrival at Bar-le-Duc the previous year, and while Queen Anne was still alive, the king decided to commission a new portrait to be sent to his mother. Mary of Modena had left Saint-Germain to live for an extended period at Chaillot, and the new portrait was intended to decorate her apartment there. Alexis-Simon Belle was in Paris, busy painting the portraits of the Abbé Gaultier, Matthew Prior and the latter's Tory friend, Simon Harcourt, but James discovered that Pierre Gobert, another court portraitist, was already in Lorraine. The commission was therefore given to Gobert, who personally took the finished portrait back to Chaillot in August. Although the queen did not think it a good likeness of her son, she commissioned her own portrait from Gobert to be sent back to Bar-le-Duc.[72]

In 1714 Belle was invited to come to Lorraine and paint several new portraits. One was of Charles Leslie, which was immediately engraved by François Chéreau in Paris and widely circulated in England to demonstrate that there was full religious toleration for Protestants at the court.[73] Another was of David Nairne, to commemorate his appointment as secretary of the Closet.[74]

---

[69] *Letter Book of Sabran*, 274, Powel to Sabran, 24 June 1715.

[70] BL Add. MSS 31255, f. 29, James III to Gualterio, 3 February 1715.

[71] BL Add. MSS 31260, f. 224, Nairne to Gualterio, 25 November 1717.

[72] Corp, *King over the Water*, 49–50; *Stuart Papers*, ed. Madan, 'Mémoires historiques relatifs à SM. la Reine d'Angleterre, continuation', 437 (4 August 1713), 440 (11–12 August 1713), 459–60 (12 September 1713).

[73] The original portrait is at Castle Leslie, County Monaghan, Ireland (kindly drawn to my attention by Richard Sharp). For the engraving, and the various copies of it, see Sharp, *Engraved Record*, 171–2.

[74] See above, p. 197, and Fig. 18.

A third portrait shows Sir Carnaby Haggerston, a Catholic baronet from Northumberland who was then at school in Lorraine.[75] But the most important were three new portraits of the king.[76]

Two of them are similar to his portrait of 1712,[77] but one shows his left side and the other his left profile. The third, which has not survived, showed James, for the first time, wearing the robes, collar and Great George of the Order of the Garter. Shortly after it had been painted the news reached Lorraine that Queen Anne had died and been succeeded by George I. James then ordered Belle to have the new Garter portrait engraved in Paris with two alternative inscriptions: 'Jacobus III. Magnae Britanniae Rex' for the English and Scots, and 'Jacques III. Roy d'Angleterre etc' for the French and other potential foreign supporters. In addition he ordered the engraving of his 1712 portrait to be reissued, and now identified as 'Jacques III. Roy de la Grande Bretagne'.[78]

When James had first heard about the death of Queen Anne, in August 1714, he had immediately left Bar and travelled to Paris, hoping that the French government would help him cross the sea to England. He took with him a small group of servants, whom he left at Meaux while he conferred with Mary of Modena at Chaillot. To his surprise and disappointment Louis XIV refused to break the Treaty of Utrecht by letting him proceed, and asked him to return to Lorraine.[79] He therefore retired to Plombières where, advised by Higgons and Nairne, he issued his famous Protestation, accompanied by an engraved 'Genealogie de la Maison Royalle de la Grande Bretagne'.[80]

The next year was a period of waiting, while the Tory leaders planned a Jacobite rebellion in the west of England, to be supported by an invasion force consisting of the Irish regiments from the French army. It was a tense period

---

[75] National Gallery of Ireland.

[76] Bodleian Library, Carte MSS 211, f. 318, payment to Belle, 11 September 1714, in account by Dicconson; SP 289/124, J. Stafford to James III, 9 February 1748.

[77] See above, p. 195, and Fig. 24.   [78] Corp, *King over the Water*, 50.

[79] BL Add. MSS 31259, ff. 65 and 73, Nairne to Gualterio, 21 August and 19 September 1714; *Letter Book of Sabran*, 157, Wood to Sabran, 26 August 1714. Louis XIV remained fully committed to helping James III, but felt that the best way to do so was to weaken George I by creating an alliance with Charles XII of Sweden against Hanover, and by encouraging a reconciliation between Sweden, the emperor and Prussia. Military help had to be deferred until these aims had been achieved, and in the meantime it was essential to avoid any premature action which might fail and thereby strengthen George I. See E. Schnakenbourg, 'La Politique française dans le Nord à la fin du règne de Louis XIV: la mission du comte de Croissy près du roi Charles XII de Suede. mai – novembre 1715', *Revue de l'Historie Diplomatique* 112 (1998), 251–74, particularly pp. 259–60 and 262.

[80] HMC *Stuart* I, 333; SP 3/101.

for James, who felt that valuable time was being wasted and that he should really get to England before the general election of March 1715. Instead he accepted an invitation to spend a month and a half with the Duke of Lorraine at Nancy. Dr Wood's correspondence from this period probably reflected James's own feelings: 'great sports' at Nancy, he wrote, but 'unseasonable, for his only time for recovering his kingdom is from dissolution to meeting of Parliament'; 'wishes the King rather tossing att sea than at carnavals'.[81]

Nevertheless this visit to Nancy did give James considerable pleasure. He had not attended any operatic performance since August 1712, when he had gone from Le Raincy to see Lord Bolingbroke in Paris, and had not taken any musicians to Bar-le-Duc. Apart from anything he might have heard by talented amateurs like Nairne, or during his visits to Lunéville or Commercy, James had been starved of music for nearly two and a half years. But the Duke of Lorraine had recently built a new opera house at Nancy, designed by Francesco Galli-Bibiena, and had ordered Henry Desmarets (his *Surintendant de la Musique*) to produce a winter season of operas. In January and February 1715 the repertory consisted of revivals of works by Lully, which James already knew and loved, and the first performance of Desmarets' *Diane et Endymion*. James later recalled that he had much preferred the opera at Nancy to the one at Paris.[82]

By the early summer the plans for a Jacobite rebellion and invasion were virtually complete. Lord Bolingbroke fled to France at the end of March, and at the beginning of July Sir Thomas Higgons agreed to make way for him to become secretary of state.[83] Bolingbroke was to remain at Saint-Germain and coordinate the plans, while Middleton and Nairne would be advising the king at Bar-le-Duc. It was decided that James should secretly leave Lorraine in the second half of July and, without either informing Louis XIV or obtaining his permission, should take a ship to join the Duke of Ormonde in the west of England. To provide camouflage for this plan, James arranged that his mother should visit him in Lorraine. While she was there it was assumed that no one would suspect him of planning to leave.

Mary of Modena arrived at Bar-le-Duc at the beginning of July and was lodged in the rue des Tanneurs.[84] A few days later she and her son paid a

---

[81] *Letter Book of Sabran*, 225 and 230, Sabran's notes of letters from Wood, 3 and 19 February 1715.

[82] HMC *Stuart* VI, 150, James III to Duke of Lorraine, 15 March 1718.

[83] HMC *Stuart* VII, 128, Higgons to James III, 8 August 1718; SP 92/92, Higgons to Inverness, 1 April 1726.

[84] Wolff, 'The Pretender', 240. She arrived with four coaches, each drawn by six horses, one 'littière' and 'quelques chaises'.

visit to the prince de Vaudemont at Commercy. Back at Bar the final plans
were laid. James left on 21 July, probably with only two personal servants,
and ordered Nairne to meet him at a secret rendezvous point in Paris at the
beginning of August. No one else at Bar was told of the plan, other than
Middleton and Higgons. Apart from Bolingbroke, only the Duke of Perth was
privy to the secret at Saint-Germain. However, once it was known that James
had safely embarked, the Jacobites at Saint-Germain were to be told that they
could all follow their king to England as soon as they wished.[85]

Shortly after James had reached Paris he was informed that the Whig
ministers in England, fearing a possible rebellion, had begun to arrest the
leading Tories and that the Duke of Ormonde had fled to France. Under these
circumstances he was advised by the Jacobites in England that he should
definitely not attempt to cross over and join them. As he could not remain
in Paris, where his presence would soon be discovered, he therefore had
no choice but to return to Lorraine. When Nairne arrived to keep the rendezvous it was already too late, so he also had to return.[86] A few days later,
now that the plan had failed, Mary of Modena left Bar to return to Saint-
Germain.[87]

The queen might have stayed longer, but the news had reached the court
that Louis XIV was probably dying.[88] Although she reached Saint-Germain
on 29 August[89] she was not in time to see him again.[90] Louis died at Versailles
on 1 September. It was a major blow for the Jacobite cause. Louis had respected
the Treaty of Utrecht, but had remained friendly and supportive. Power now
passed to the duc d'Orléans, who became Regent for Louis XV, the surviving
child of the late dauphin and dauphine (duc and duchesse de Bourgogne).
As Orléans was the only member of the French royal family who disliked
the Stuarts, this meant that respect for the Treaty of Utrecht would now
be accompanied by an actively pro-Hanoverian policy. One of the king's
chaplains, who had recently returned from Bar to Saint-Germain, wrote a few

[85] Bodleian Library, Carte MSS 211, f. 329, James III's instructions for Nairne, 21 July 1715; BL
Add. MSS 31259, f. 171, Nairne to Gualterio, 21 July 1715.
[86] BL Add. MSS 31259, ff. 171 and 173, Nairne to Gualterio, 28 July (postscript) and 3 August 1715;
BL Add. MSS 31256, f. 157, Perth to Gualterio, 11 August 1715; BL Add. MSS 31259, f. 175,
Nairne to Gualterio, 16 August 1715; Bodleian Library, Carte MSS 211, f. 330, Nairne to Innes,
middle of August 1715.
[87] BL Add. MSS 31259, f. 177, Nairne to Gualterio, 23 August 1715.
[88] Bibl. Mun. de Versailles, MS 1461/P.67, 699, Mary of Modena to Maintenon, 27 August 1715.
[89] HMC Stuart I, 408, Bolingbroke to James III, 30 August 1715.
[90] Ibid., 409, James III to Bolingbroke, 3 September 1715.

weeks later that 'there had been a coldness, time of the late King, betwixt her [Mary of Modena] and Orleans'.[91]

In the short term, however, the death of Louis XIV made James even more keen to make a third attempt to leave Lorraine and cross the sea to Great Britain.[92] This time he not only would pass secretly through France, without informing the French government, but would not be deterred from embarking by any pessimistic reports coming from his kingdoms. The Earl of Mar had started a Jacobite rising in Scotland on 17 September (6 September OS) and James determined that nothing would this time stop him from joining his supporters.

In October James prepared his plans to make a second secret departure from Lorraine. He was well aware that Hanoverian spies had been sent to keep an eye on him, and had already assured Bolingbroke that all they could learn was '*basse cour* talk' because, except for Middleton, Higgons, Nairne 'and myself, nobody cann tell them any secrets'.[93] Nevertheless, he was not taking chances. In September he ordered David Floyd, whose father was one of the most senior grooms of the Bedchamber, to leave the court because he seemed to have 'Whiggish principles'.[94]

The story of James's departure from Lorraine, and of his various adventures in France before he was able to sail for Scotland, has been told by his biographers and does not need to be repeated here in any detail. The impact of his departure on the Stuart court in exile, however, has been overlooked.

Although James confided in no one but his secretaries, three other people had to be brought into the secret at the last moment. James decided to make his escape while staying with the prince de Vaudemont at Commercy. And he decided to travel with two of his servants. They were Baltassare Artema (page of the Bedchamber) and Thomas de Saint-Paul (barber and valet), chosen not only because of their loyalty but also because they were not British. An Italian and a Frenchman would be less conspicuous while James was travelling incognito through France, and would not be vulnerable to a charge of treason if their ship happened to be captured.

---

[91] *Letter Book of Sabran*, 307, Lawson to Sabran, 23 September 1715.

[92] For James III's keenness to leave even before the death of Louis XIV, see Bodleian Library, Carte MSS 211, f. 330, Nairne to Innes, *c.* 16–20 August 1715.

[93] HMC *Stuart* 1, 385, James III to Bolingbroke, 6 August 1715. This letter was actually written when Mary of Modena was at Bar and Nairne was in Paris, and therefore referred to the queen rather than Nairne.

[94] *Ibid.*, 424, James III to Bolingbroke, 23 September 1715. For an earlier incident concerning bad behaviour by David Floyd, see above, pp. 129–30.

Before he left Commercy James signed a patent promoting the Earl of Mar to be a duke[95] and gave detailed instructions to David Nairne for the household.[96] Those who were at Commercy were to remain there until the end of the week, and Nairne was to send letters to Paris as if the king were still with them. They were then to return to Bar-le-Duc, where everyone was to remain except for seven people who were allowed to rejoin the court at Saint-Germain. Apart from Nairne himself, this group included Lord Middleton, Higgons, Roger and Francis Strickland, Dr Ingleton and Father Thadée Connel, accompanied by one footman and the necessary coachman, postillions and grooms from the Stables. The gentlemen and most of the grooms of the Bedchamber, the vice-chamberlain, the commissioner of the household, the equerry of the Stables and all the other lesser servants were to remain at Bar to await developments.

James, meanwhile, planned to go straight to Paris, to see his mother and the duc de Lauzun, and then travel as quickly as possible to the coast. But he did not move quickly enough. The news of his disappearance reached Lord Stair, the British ambassador in Paris, who employed assassins to stop him reaching the coast. James was turned back from Nantes, and headed instead for Normandy, where he was very nearly captured and killed at Nonancourt. He finally reached Saint-Malo, where he found the Duke of Ormonde and Lord Tynemouth (the eldest son of the Duke of Berwick), but the weather was too bad to let him sail. In desperation, and after waiting for several weeks, he rode across land with Tynemouth, Artema and Saint-Paul to Dunkirk, where he found a ship. He eventually set sail on 27 December, over two months after he had left Commercy. He embarked with Artema and Saint-Paul, and a young highlander called Allan Cameron whom he had met at Dunkirk. While he was there he had received another substantial sum of money from the queen,[97] and a further 300,000 *livres* in gold and silver from his childhood friend, Philip V of Spain.[98] Tynemouth was to sail with the Spanish money in another ship, accompanied by his uncle, Francis Bulkeley.

For much of this time the court of Saint-Germain had no news of James's whereabouts. The group of seven had left Bar on 2 November and reached

---

[95] Ruvigny, *Jacobite Peerage*, 113.

[96] Bodleian Library, Carte MSS 211, f. 332, 'Memorandum of the Orders and Commissions with which the King chargd Nairn, before he parted', with Nairne's marginal comments explaining how he had carried out the instructions.

[97] BL Add. MSS 20311, f. 313 for correspondence concerning the sale of fifty-seven of Mary of Modena's *luoghi di monte*, 15–23 November 1715.

[98] SP 44/81, account by Dicconson, 29 August 1719. A few weeks later Philip V gave him a further 171,750 *livres* in bills of exchange and silver.

Saint-Germain on the 8th, expecting to hear that the king had already sailed.[99] Instead they were told that he had disappeared. It was not for another two weeks that the news arrived that he had safely reached Saint-Malo.[100]

James had given the queen a list of all the officers and household servants who should be ordered to follow him, but there were strict instructions that no one should leave Saint-Germain until news arrived that he had both embarked and landed safely in Scotland. The news that he had sailed was received on 1 January, but it was not until the 10th that it was known that he had safely arrived at Peterhead on the 2nd. Throughout this period of over two months (8 November to 10 January) the people on the list had to remain ready to leave at a single day's notice.[101] In the event, Middleton, Higgons, Nairne and the other officers and servants set out from Saint-Germain on 13 January.[102] They included Roger Strickland, and also Lord Clermont, Lord Edward Drummond, Charles Booth and Dr Lawrence Wood, who must have left Bar-le-Duc during the extended period of waiting. The names of the others are unknown.[103] Lord Bolingbroke, on the other hand, did not go, and remained at Saint-Germain with the queen.

As soon as they were gone, Mary of Modena ordered Norbert Roettiers to prepare new sets of coinage for Scotland and England. He was to use the portraits he had already engraved, beginning with the one on the crown piece which he had produced in 1708. There were to be two series of four punches, one for Scotland inscribed James VIII, and one for England inscribed James III. The coins (guineas, crowns, shillings and sixpences) would then be minted from the Spanish gold and silver sent by Philip V.[104]

It is not known when and where these household servants landed in Scotland. Before their arrival James III was proclaimed king at Fetteresso, a house belonging to the Duke of Perth's daughter, the Dowager Countess Marischal. With no one to attend him, James appointed her son, the Earl Marischal, to

[99] BL Add. MSS 31259, ff. 199 and 201, Nairne to Gualterio, 1 and 17 November 1715; Dangeau, xv, 230, 8 November 1715. They travelled slowly because they brought with them all the court's archives.

[100] BL Add. MSS 31259, f. 201, Nairne to Gualterio, 17 November 1715.

[101] BL Add. MSS 31259, f. 205, Nairne to Gualterio, 29 December 1715; BL Add. MSS 38851, f. 65, Nairne to Vaudemont, 29 December 1715; Dangeau, xv, 287, 1 January 1716; BL Add. MSS 31256, f. 182, Perth to Gualterio, 2? January 1716; BL Add. MSS 20298, f. 2, Nairne to Gualterio, 5 January 1716; Bibl. Mun. de Versailles, MS 1461/P.68, 165, Mary of Modena to Maintenon, 10 January 1716; BL Add. MSS 38851, f. 68, Nairne to Vaudemont, 10 January 1716.

[102] BL Add. MSS 31259, f. 207, Nairne to Gualterio, 13 January 1716.

[103] SP 9/30, 'Sallaries for His Majesty's Servants', July 1716 implies that they were accompanied by three footmen, one chairman and five grooms.

[104] HMC Stuart I, 502, G. Hamilton to James III, 13 January 1716.

be a fourth gentleman of the Bedchamber.[105] After leaving Fetteresso, James stayed at Brechin with the Earl of Panmure, and then visited Lord Middleton's nephew, the Earl of Strathmore, at Glamis. It was probably while he was at Perth that his household servants finally rejoined him. If so, they were only just in time. On 11 February (31 January OS) the Jacobite army was forced to retreat from Perth to Montrose where, on the 15th (4th OS), James embarked for France. Before leaving he issued his well-known Declaration to the people of Scotland, which he dictated to David Nairne.[106] The ship which carried James back to France also carried Middleton and Nairne, Roger Strickland, the Duke of Mar, and presumably Artema and Saint-Paul, but Sir Thomas Higgons, Lord Clermont, Lord Edward Drummond and Dr Wood were all left behind.[107]

After the departure of the household servants on 13 January the first news from Scotland to reach Saint-Germain came on 5 February when General George Hamilton arrived with a message from James III to the Regent, asking for urgent help to be sent. The situation seemed serious, but not desperate, and Hamilton was promised that Roettiers would soon finish the punches for the new coins.[108] The court then endured another period of suspense. It was finally broken on 25 February when Roger Strickland arrived with the disastrous news that James, Middleton and Nairne, accompanied by Mar, had had to leave Scotland and had landed at Boulogne-sur-Mer.[109]

---

[105] BL Add. MSS 31256, f. 186, Perth to Gualterio, 9 February 1716.

[106] Drambuie Collection, reproduced as an illustration in F. Maxwell-Stuart, *Lady Nithsdale and the Jacobites* (Traquair, 1995), 70.

[107] BL Add. MSS 31256, f. 188, Perth to Gualterio, 1 March 1716; Bibl. Mun. d'Avignon, journal of Dr Brun entitled 'Mémoirs du temps', July 1716, printed in G. Dickson (ed.), *Des Ecossais à Avignon* (Paris, 1993), 267; HMC *Stuart* VII, 129, Higgons to Mar, 8 August 1718. The ship carrying the Spanish gold had meanwhile run aground off Dundee, and both Tynemouth and Bulkeley had been taken prisoner.

[108] Dangeau, xv, 316, 6 February 1716; HMC *Stuart* I, 502, G. Hamilton to James III, 13 February 1716.

[109] HMC *Stuart*, I, 510 and 536, James III to Mar, 23 and 26 February 1716.

CHAPTER THIRTEEN

From Lorraine to the Papal States, 1716–1718

James III's personal involvement in the Jacobite rising of 1715–16 had serious repercussions for the Stuart court in exile. If the rising had succeeded, and James had recovered his thrones, then Mary of Modena might have left the château-vieux and returned in triumph to London, bringing with her all the household servants from both Saint-Germain and Bar-le-Duc. Its failure, on the other hand, condemned the court to an indefinitely extended period of exile, under increasingly difficult circumstances. Most of the household servants were obliged to remain without the king at Saint-Germain, where it became clear that the court could only continue for as long as the queen remained alive. Meanwhile those servants who followed the king, their numbers already reduced by the move to Bar-le-Duc, watched his court change beyond recognition. This process began during 1716 and was completed by the time that the queen died in the spring of 1718. When James finally found a new permanent home in Rome, in the autumn of 1719, the court he established there was completely transformed.

When James landed at Boulogne-sur-Mer on 23 February 1716 he was in no hurry to reach Saint-Germain, partly because the Regent would not let him stay there, and partly because arrangements needed to be made to provide him with accommodation elsewhere. While the Duke of Mar, therefore, travelled directly to Paris, James and his servants moved more slowly, finally arriving at the château on 26 February – his first visit for three and a half years. He only remained there for three days, going each evening to sleep a few miles away at Malmaison,[1] and taking with him a small staff of servants from his Bedchamber.[2]

---

[1] HMC *Stuart* I, 536, James III to Mar, 27 February 1716; HMC *Stuart* II 2, Bolingbroke to James III, 3 March 1716; Dangeau, xv, 327, 26 February 1716; *Letters of Madame*, II, 109, to Raugravine Louisa, 28 February 1716. Malmaison was a small *gentilhommière* belonging to Jacques-Honoré Barentin (*président au Grand Conseil*), situated near the Château de Rueil, midway between Saint-Germain and Paris.

[2] For example, Elizabeth O'Neal, the wife of one of the King's pages of the Bedchamber, went with her husband to Malmaison and cooked the King's meals, as she recalled in her letter to him of 14 July 1737 (SP 199/61).

James never saw either Saint-Germain or his mother again after 29 February 1716. For eight days he hid in a house in the Bois de Boulogne, where he, Mar and Ormonde discussed future plans and met the Spanish ambassador.[3] It was during this period that he dismissed Lord Bolingbroke as his secretary of state, having discovered the latter's inexcusable indiscretion in revealing secrets to a mistress whom he shared with the pro-Hanoverian Abbé Dubois. James then returned to Lorraine, where he hoped that he might be able to live once again. When he joined the prince de Vaudemont at Commercy on 9 March he was accompanied by only three people, Roger Strickland, Styles (who had replaced Artema) and Saint-Paul, supported by three footmen and five grooms.[4] Middleton had decided to remain with the queen, who needed his advice now that Bolingbroke had been dismissed, so the king ordered Nairne to join him at Commercy on the 12th.[5]

On the day following James's arrival, the Duke of Lorraine came to inform him that he had received an ultimatum from the Regent ordering him not to allow James to settle in his duchy.[6] On the 12th, therefore, James left and returned to an unknown place near Châlons-sur-Marne, possibly the Château de Sillery, where he and his four servants remained for twelve days. While he was there James was joined by Mar,[7] whom he appointed to be both a gentleman of the Bedchamber and his new secretary of state. Such a double appointment was unprecedented, and showed that the practices of the court of Saint-Germain could no longer be maintained within the minute entourage that he now had.

While he was near Châlons James was forced to accept that the only place he could now go to was Avignon, the chief town in the Comtat Venaissin, the papal enclave in the south of France. With great reluctance he and Mar set out on 24 March, accompanied by Nairne and Roger Strickland and the ten other servants.[8] They reached Avignon on 2 April.[9]

---

[3] Saint-Simon, xxx, 41.

[4] Andrew Symes, John Noel and Jacques Catillon (footmen); Patrick Maguirk, Francis Ridge, Mark Manning, John Owens and Roger Ryan (grooms). This can be deduced from SP 9/30, 'Sallaries for His Majesty's Servants', July 1716; and SP 7/111, a list of 'persons proposed to be sent down' to Avignon by Dicconson, April 1716.

[5] BL Add. MSS 38851, f. 71, Nairne to Vaudemont, 8 March 1716.

[6] Dangeau, xv, 337 and 344, 13 and 16 March 1716.

[7] HMC *Stuart* II, 19, Mar to James III, 17 March 1716.

[8] BL Add. MSS 31259, f. 209, Nairne to Gualterio, 23 March 1716. James III's letter of 21 March to the Duke of Lorraine makes it clear that he must have stayed somewhere else for the first three days, because he states that by 23 March he would have been in his present hiding place for only eight days (Haile, *Mary of Modena*, 478).

[9] BL Add. MSS 31259, f. 211, Nairne to Gualterio, 4 April 1716.

Within a very short time James was joined there by the Duke of Ormonde and by a large number of new Scottish exiles, including two marquesses, five earls, two viscounts and many younger sons and brothers of Scottish peers. When the Duke of Perth died at Saint-Germain in May 1716, his eldest son, who was also at Avignon, inherited his father's peerage and increased the number of dukes to three. The 2nd Duke of Melfort, whose wife had inherited the Lussan estates across the Rhône from Avignon, soon brought the total to four. In the middle of May Nairne informed Cardinal Gualterio that the king's court at Avignon was larger than it had ever been at Saint-Germain.[10]

Nairne was exaggerating, but there *was* a very large number of Jacobite exiles with the king.[11] In June it was estimated that there were well over 1500 and that they were continuing to arrive every day.[12] This, however, did not mean that James III was able to re-establish his court. Quite the contrary. The new exiles had arrived without any financial means, so James had to support them all.[13] This meant that he could not afford to maintain the appearance of a royal household as he had done at Bar-le-Duc.

The king and the Duke of Ormonde occupied the Hôtel de Serre, near the parish church of Saint-Didier. It was permanently protected by a detachment of Swiss Guards. The Duke of Mar and all the other exiles had to find their own lodgings in the town.[14] When William Dicconson sent a list of 'the Persons proposed to be sent Down' from Saint-Germain to Avignon, James accepted most of them, but not all.[15] The royal household which was established at Avignon was no more than a skeleton, though nearly all its members had previously served the king at Saint-Germain.

In his Bedchamber James was served by three gentlemen (Newcastle, Marischal and Mar), two grooms (Richard Trevanion and Roger Strickland), one page (Styles), a newly recruited French valet (Bonbled) and his valet-cum-barber (Saint-Paul). During July the gentlemen were joined by Lord Edward Drummond and Lord Clermont, and the grooms by Charles Booth, all of whom had escaped from Scotland.[16] The humble but necessary posts of

[10] BL Add. MSS 31259, f. 225, Nairne to Gualterio, 12 May 1716.
[11] Bibl. Mun. d'Avignon, MS 3188, journal of Dr Brun, ff. 213–14, 'Liste des Anglois qui se trouvent presentement a Avignon, juillet 1716'; Bibl. Mun. d'Avignon, MS 2827, 611–12, 'Liste des Anglois de la suite de Jacques III Roy d'Angleterre, arrivé a Avignon en 1716, le 2 avril', c. October 1716. See also HMC *Stuart* IV, 56; and National Library of Scotland, MS 2960, f. 161.
[12] BL Add. MSS 20311, f. 369, anon. (at Lyons) to Gualterio, 16 June 1716.
[13] BL Add. MSS 31259, f. 215, Nairne to Gualterio, 13 April 1716.
[14] SCA, BL 2/210/7, Nairne to T. Innes, 6 September 1716.
[15] SP 7/111, a list attached to some proposals by Dicconson of April 1716 (and not reproduced in HMC *Stuart* IV, 31); SP 9/30, 'Sallaries for His Majesty's Servants', June 1716.
[16] BL Add. MSS 38851, f. 88, Nairne to Vaudemont, 23 July 1716; *Ecossais à Avignon*, ed. G. Dickson (Paris, 1993), 265–8, journal of Brun, 1, 2 and 24 July 1716.

laundress and sempstress seem to have been given to locally employed women. The king's clothes, however, were entrusted to the groom of the robes (James Rodes) who went to Avignon but had not been present at Bar.

The only member of the Chamber to join the court was the vice-chamberlain, Dominic Sheldon. There was no confessor, no almoner and there were no chaplains. It was the first time that the Stuart court in exile had not included a single Catholic priest. There was not even a chapel, and James attended Mass every morning in the parish church nearby.[17] The king had left Ingleton behind and used one of the local priests, Father Viganegne, as his confessor.[18] To emphasise the fact that he had not brought any of his own priests with him, James invited Charles Leslie to rejoin the court, while another Protestant clergyman (Ezekiel Hamilton) arrived among the new Scottish exiles.[19]

The king would have brought with him his physician, Lawrence Wood, but the latter had been captured and imprisoned in Edinburgh.[20] He therefore appointed Dr John Blair, one of the new exiles, to be his second physician within a few days of arriving.[21] It was not until July that Wood was released from prison, and not until 28 September that he reached Avignon.[22] The day after his arrival he examined the king, diagnosed advanced haemorrhoids and insisted that James should be operated on by a surgeon from Paris.[23] Martin Guerin, the nephew of Louis XV's personal surgeon, was then sent down to Avignon and successfully performed the operation during the second half of October.[24] The king rewarded Guerin by appointing him to be his Chirurgeon Extraordinary,[25] but this was only an honorary appointment.[26] He also gave a knighthood to Dr Wood.[27]

The household below stairs contained no more than five servants, super-vised by Sir William Ellis. It consisted of the clerk of the kitchen (Jeremiah

[17] *Ecossais à Avignon*, ed. Dickson, 250, journal of Brun, 8 April 1716.

[18] B. Bevan, *James III* (London, 1967), 93.

[19] BL Add. MSS 31259, f. 231, Nairne to Gualterio, 26 May 1716.

[20] *Ecossais à Avignon*, ed. Dickson, 267, journal of Brun, 17 July 1716.

[21] Ruvigny, *Jacobite Peerage*, 224.

[22] *Ecossais à Avignon*, ed. Dickson, 274 and 276, newspaper articles inserted in the journal of Brun, July and September 1716.

[23] *Ibid.*, 276, journal of Brun, 29 September 1716.   [24] Dangeau, xv, 474, 16 October 1716.

[25] Ruvigny, *Jacobite Peerage*, 224. He also appointed one of the Scots who helped Guerin, along with Wood and Blair, to be his physician extraordinary.

[26] *Ibid.* Guerin was made both a hereditary Knight of Latran and a Count Palatine, and embarked on a brilliant career as a military surgeon (SP 224/164, Maclean to Edgar, 4 July 1740). James showed his appreciation by giving Guerin's son a similar honorary appointment in 1740 (SP 225/42, Edgar to Guerin, 21 July 1740).

[27] SP 139/76, James III to Macdonnell, 20 September 1730.

Broomer), one cook and kitchen boy (John Martinash and James Miner), and the yeoman of the wine cellar and his assistant (Charles Macarty and Barnaby Hute). None of the other sub-departments of the household was introduced at Avignon, though the cook had previously been yeoman of the larder. The Stables, finally, were similarly small. The staff consisted of two equerries (James Delattre and Mar's brother-in-law, John Hay), one chairman (Henry Kerby), and the three footmen and five grooms who had accompanied the king on his journey.

The number of Jacobites at Avignon was certainly very large, but the size of the royal household had been reduced to no more than thirty-three people, of whom twenty-seven had previously served at Saint-Germain. At Bar the household had been overwhelmingly English, with a few French, Irish and Scots, and one Italian. At Avignon the balance had changed. The household remained mainly English, but there were six Scots (two of whom were Anglicised), five French and four Irish. It must have been noticeable that the Jacobites at Avignon were nearly all Scottish, but that the king's household was still mainly English.

These figures, however, do not include the members of the secretariat — apart from Mar, who had two posts. Nairne continued to handle all the Roman correspondence, but Mar was meant to deal with everything else, and had two under-secretaries, John Patterson and Robert Creagh, to help him. The former was from Scotland, but the latter was an Irishman who had lived for many years at Saint-Germain and been recommended by Nairne — perhaps because neither Mar nor Patterson could write French.[28] A difficulty arose in June 1716 when Sir Thomas Higgons arrived at Avignon, after leaving Scotland and having been obliged to take 'a great tour . . . through Poland and Germany to escape out of the hands of my enemies'.[29] Higgons had continued to act as secretary of state after the appointment of Bolingbroke because the latter had never gone to Lorraine, but with Mar present in Avignon that was no longer necessary, and he had no obvious role. Higgons accepted the new situation with good grace, and went away to take the waters at Bourbon, before returning to live at Saint-Germain.[30]

Just as most of the king's servants at Avignon were English, so too were they nearly all Catholic. There had been four Protestants in the royal household at Bar-le-Duc (Ellis, Styles, Higgons and Leslie). At Avignon there were

28 HMC *Stuart* II, 19, Mar to James III, 17 March 1716.
29 HMC *Stuart* VII, 129, Higgons to Mar, 8 August 1718.
30 *Ibid.*, 398, Higgons to Mar, 17 October 1718; SP 41/38, Higgons to Mar, 9 January 1719.

still only six (Ellis, Styles, Mar, Leslie, Blair and Hay), whereas most of the new exiles were Protestant. Although he was now living within papal territory, James insisted on maintaining full religious toleration within his court. Anglican services were held in the apartment of the Duke of Ormonde, with the doors closed in order to avoid any provocation.[31] Some of the local people resented this, and of course some of the exiled Protestants behaved badly,[32] but Charles Leslie, at least in the opinion of Nairne, was 'un vieux bonhomme fort moderé'.[33]

When James arrived in Avignon he was given 123,100 *livres* by the pope,[34] but he had no regular source of income other than the Stuart pension from the French crown, which was now all being paid once again directly to the queen at Saint-Germain. With the help of Dicconson and Ellis, the king then regulated the finances of the court. The Duke of Ormonde had his own money and servants, and was paid nothing, though he had his accommodation in the Hôtel de Serre. The newly arrived exiles were given monthly allowances: the surviving lists contain 370 names, with pensions ranging from 200 *livres* for the peers down to only 15 *livres* for the least important people, amounting to a total of 11,422 *livres*.[35] The salaries of the members of the household were substantially reduced, but they were compensated by being able to eat all their meals at the king's expense. There were two tables in the king's apartment, as there had been at Bar-le-Duc. The king ate with the secretary of state, the gentlemen and grooms of the Bedchamber, the vice-chamberlain and the most important of the new exiles, such as Lords Nithsdale and Panmure and the 2nd Duke of Perth. All the other more senior members of the household, including David Nairne, ate at the second table, and the clerk of the kitchen was instructed to give 'the remainder of the meat which comes off the King's table' to the under-servants in the household below stairs and the Stables. Because everyone had diet, board wages were abolished. Lodging money, however, continued to be paid to the lesser servants not accommodated in the Hôtel de Serre whose families still lived at Saint-Germain. This arrangement, as Dicconson said, allowed the members of the household at Avignon to

[31] BL Add. MSS 31259, f. 231, Nairne to Gualterio, 26 May 1716.

[32] BL Add. MSS 20311, f. 369, anon. to Gualterio, 16 June 1716: 'leur conduite en general alegard de la religion nedifie pas'.

[33] BL Add. MSS 31259, f. 237, Nairne to Gualterio, 10 June 1716.

[34] SP 44/81, account by Dicconson, 29 August 1719.

[35] In chronological order, 1716–17: SP 40/149; SP 281/163; SP Box 3/83; SP 40/150. The new exiles were not all given pensions: 'The King's rule . . . was to give pensions only to such as could not live in Britain without hazard of their lives, but not to those whose condition was the same as before the troubles' (HMC *Stuart* IV, 202, Dicconson to Mar, 20 April 1717).

'live as easily as those that remain here', at Saint-Germain.[36] The money to finance the court in Avignon was transmitted to Ellis by Dicconson, who had responsibility for all the Stuart finances, receiving not only the French pension, but also some additional money sent secretly by various Jacobites in England during 1716.[37]

As usual there was a problem of attempted espionage and various rumours, deliberately circulated by the Whig ministry in London to undermine Jacobite confidence, that the Stuart court could not be relied on to keep its secrets. Lord Stair, the ambassador in Paris, sent spies and even an assassin to Avignon, but as the only people who knew the king's secrets were Mar, Nairne, Patterson and Creagh there was nothing apart from '*basse cour*' talk which they could discover.[38] It was only when Mar began to betray James III in 1717 that the repeated rumours finally began to have some truth.[39]

Meanwhile the court at Avignon needed to be entertained. Although he had not brought any musicians with him, it is clear from his account book that James III employed local musicians to perform at the Hôtel de Serre on several occasions.[40] There was no opera in the city, but music could also be heard in the cathedral and the churches, and some of it seems to have been quite well performed.[41] The court was also entertained by the local nobles and in particular by Alaman Salviati, the vice-legate. On 4 February 1717, as a mark of respect before James left, Salviati gave a 'grande fête' in his honour, to which the king went, accompanied by Ormonde, Mar, Perth, Panmure, his gentlemen of the Bedchamber and more than a hundred of his courtiers.[42] On this occasion James created the Spanish Count of Castelblanco, married to the 2nd Duke of Melfort's sister, Duke of St Andrews.[43]

[36] HMC *Stuart* IV, 31, proposals by Dicconson, April 1716; BL Add. MSS 20298, f. 67, Nairne to Gualterio, August 1718; SP Box/90, 'a List of the King's Servants who have been lodged, or have had lodging monie since His Ma.tie parted from St. Germans' by Ellis, undated but probably 1719–20. The top salaries were reduced as follows: secretary of state 300 *livres*, down from 471; gentleman of the Bedchamber 200 down from 353; vice-chamberlain 200 down from 314; groom of the Bedchamber 150 down from 204.

[37] SP 44/81, account by Dicconson, 28 August 1719, gives the details.

[38] Haile, *Mary of Modena*, 493, Stair to Methuen, 12 February 1716. One of Stair's spies, named Macdonald, arrived in Avignon in April, was quickly identified and was sentenced to death by the vice-legate. At the last moment he was reprieved and expelled from the papal territory (Bodleian Library, Rawlinson MSS D.360, f. 39, Macdonald's Narrative, October 1716).

[39] See E. Gregg, 'The Jacobite Career of John, Earl of Mar', in E. Cruickshanks (ed.), *Ideology and Conspiracy: Aspects of Jacobitism, 1689–1759* (Edinburgh, 1982), 179–200.

[40] Corp, 'Music at Urbino', 353.

[41] *Ecossais à Avignon*, ed. Dickson, 250, journal of Brun, 8 and 9 April 1716.

[42] *Ibid.*, 281, journal of Brun, 4 February 1717.   [43] Ruvigny, *Jacobite Peerage*, 161.

This creation was one of the eleven new peerages given by James III between September 1716 and February 1717, an important break with the more restrained policy established at Saint-Germain. Seven were Scottish baronies, but there were two other new dukedoms. In December the Marquess of Wharton was created Duke of Northumberland, and on 1 February the Marquis of Tullibardine was created Duke of Rannoch. The remaining title was given to General Arthur Dillon, also on 1 February, because he had travelled from Paris to escort James to the frontier with Savoy. He was created Viscount Dillon.[44]

In addition to these peerages James had created in April 1716 one Knight of the Garter and two Knights of the Thistle. They were, respectively, the Duke of Mar, and the Duke of Ormonde and Earl of Panmure.[45] As Mar already had the Thistle (from Queen Anne) and Ormonde already had the Garter (from James II), James decided that the two orders should be made compatible, so that they could be worn at the same time. This was another break with the traditions of the court of Saint-Germain, where both James II and James III had insisted that the Thistle should never be worn with the Garter. Modelling his new regulations on those established by Louis XIV in 1700 for the *Saint-Esprit* and the *Toison d'Or*, James ordered that the St Andrew medal of the Thistle should now be suspended from a green ribbon worn around the neck, to be clearly visible below the blue sash of the Order of the Garter, which would continue to be worn from the left shoulder to the right hip.[46]

This new arrangement was intended as a compliment to the Scots, and was to be shown in all the future Stuart portraits. No new ones, however, were painted in Avignon, so the Scots College in Paris was instructed to celebrate the decision by commissioning a new engraving of the full-length portrait by Belle of 1703, which was in its possession. The composition was altered to include the face-mask from Belle's later portrait of 1712. However, the prints were all seized by the French government before they could be distributed, and only one copy is known to have survived.[47]

In October 1716 the anti-Jacobite policy of the duc d'Orléans culminated in his agreeing to the request of the British government that James III should

---

[44] *Ibid.*, 40; *Ecossais à Avignon*, ed. Dickson, 281 and 283, journal of Brun, 23 January and 14 February 1717.

[45] Corp, 'Clandestine Support', 14, 17, 23.   [46] Corp, 'La Tour's Portrait', 322–4.

[47] Corp, *King over the Water*, 55; SCA, BL 2/210/4 and 5, Nairne to T. Innes, 2 and 14 July 1716: 'Mr de Villers desires some copies of the French print . . . I wish your brother would . . . send him a dozen of copies . . . and if he desires more to disperse, [and] you can spare them . . . none can disperse them better'; 'I hope you'l get the Prints out of the Douane. That would be hard if they should stop them.'

be forced to leave Avignon and transfer his court to the Papal States in Italy. It was understood that he could not leave until he had recovered from his operation and was well enough to travel but, to exert maximum pressure, the Regent cut off the Stuart pension, stating that payments would not be resumed until he had gone.[48] James had no choice but to agree, and instructed his servants to be ready to leave at the beginning of February. The *équipages* were to travel by sea from Marseilles, while James and his courtiers had to cross the Mont-Cenis pass in the depth of winter.[49]

There was no obligation for those Jacobites who were not members of the household to follow the king, but as the most important among them had been proscribed by the Regent[50] they had little real alternative. James left on 6 February with a group of about sixty people, including Ormonde, Mar, Nairne, Sheldon, Booth, Delattre and Hay. The other gentlemen of the Bedchamber, accompanied by the rest of the household servants and the new Scottish exiles, followed during the next few days.[51] To reduce the inevitable problem of finding sufficient accommodation, James kept his party as small as possible, leaving the others to find their own lodgings as they followed.[52]

As a temporary residence for the Stuart court, James had been offered a palace in Pesaro belonging to Cardinal Giovanni Antonio Davia, whose sister-in-law (Lady Almond) had been a lady of the Bedchamber to Mary of Modena. Instructions were therefore sent ahead to the various cities in northern Italy where James would have to stay, specifying the accommodation that he and his courtiers would need during the six-week journey to get there. Each house to be rented was to have at least three apartments, one each for the king, Ormonde and Mar, a single room for Sheldon, and a kitchen. In addition to the antechamber and Bedchamber, the King's own apartment was to contain a closet for David Nairne, a secret staircase and one or two rooms for the valets. The apartment of the Duke of Mar was to be as close as possible to that of the king, and should also have a closet, where Mar and his clerks (John Patterson and Robert Creagh) could work. The kitchen was to contain some additional rooms 'for various uses, such as a room to make jams and a pantry, a store for bottles and some places to sleep, if possible, for the people who handle these jobs'. There had to be a 'stable for 30 horses' and a 'depot for

[48] Haile, *Mary of Modena*, 488, 494–5.

[49] *Ecossais à Avignon*, ed. Dickson, 81, journal of Brun, 2 February 1717.

[50] Saint-Simon, XXXI, 43–4.

[51] *Ecossais à Avignon*, ed. Dickson, 281–2, journal of Brun, 4 and 6 February 1717; Dangeau, XVII, 21, 10 February 1717.

[52] HMC *Stuart* IV, 90, Mar to Kinnaird, 1 March 1717.

a carriage', but everyone else could, if necessary, be lodged elsewhere 'out of the Royal Palace in another part of the city'.[53] It had been similar at Avignon, but these instructions emphasise the extent to which James III's court had changed since it had left Saint-Germain.

As if to underline the contrast, these instructions were already out of date by the time James reached the Italian cities where he was to stay. The Duke of Mar deserted him near Chambéry, pretending that he had negotiations to pursue in Paris, but in reality intending to purchase a pardon from George I by betraying his secrets to the British ambassador.[54] James was left without a secretary of state and, temporarily, without a gentleman of the Bedchamber. Lord Clermont had to be instructed to catch up with the king's party, in order to wait on him in his Bedchamber, but James had no choice but to conduct his own correspondence.[55] The apartment reserved for Mar in the Palazzo Davia remained unoccupied, as also did that of the Duke of Ormonde when he left in May to negotiate an alliance with Russia.[56]

While James was at Pesaro from 20 March to 22 May 1717 he contin-ued the catering and other financial arrangements for the court which had been established at Avignon,[57] but he formally terminated one of the distin-guishing features of his court at Saint-Germain. He abolished waiting in the Bedchamber by both the gentlemen and grooms, contenting himself with being served by his valets only.[58] Waiting in the Chamber had already been phased out at Bar-le-Duc because of the shortage of space in the king's apart-ment. The gentlemen and grooms of the Privy, Presence and Guard Chambers had therefore been left behind at Saint-Germain in 1712. But this new de-cision had more far-reaching consequences because the relevant household officials had already followed the king to Pesaro. (They included Lord Edward

---

[53] The copy of the instructions sent to Bologna has survived, and is translated and quoted in full in M. Ascari, 'James III in Bologna: An Illustrated Story', *Royal Stuart Paper* LIX (London, 2001), 28–9, where it is incorrectly dated 1726. See also H.C. Stewart, 'The Exiled Stewarts [*sic*] in Italy, 1717–1807', *The Scottish Historical Society Miscellany* VII (Edinburgh, 1941), 71.

[54] Gregg, 'Jacobite Career of Mar', 184.

[55] Clermont had already joined the king by the time he reached Bologna (H.C. Stewart, 'The Exiled Stewarts', 70–1, chronicle of Francesco Ghiselli, 13 March 1717).

[56] BL Add. MSS 31260, f. 67, Nairne to Gualterio, 9 May 1717.

[57] BL Add. MSS 20298, f. 35, Nairne to Gualterio, 7 July 1718.

[58] HMC *Stuart* VI, 151, James III to Lady Nithsdale, 16 March, 1718: 'the number of persons of quality and merit now banished on my account and the uncertainty of my abode and all that relates to me . . . have made me long since abolish fixed waiting'; HMC *Stuart* VII, 353, Mar to E. Drummond, 3 October 1718: 'a resolution he [James III] has for some time taken [not] to give anybody the name of a place during his being in his present circumstances; and you know he allows not even those of his own family, who have places, to attend him in those qualities'.

Drummond, Lord Clermont, Charles Booth and Roger Strickland, as well as Dominic Sheldon.[59]) It not only left them without any employment, but also eroded the distinction which had been maintained at Avignon between the old servants from Saint-Germain who were employed and had salaries and the new exiles from Scotland who were unemployed and had pensions. (The gentlemen of the Bedchamber, the vice-chamberlain and the Scottish peers all received 200 *livres* each month; the grooms of the Bedchamber and the Scottish lieutenant-generals all received 150 *livres*.) The skeleton staffs below stairs and in the Stables continued to be employed, but the other two departments of the household effectively ceased to exist.

The final transformation of the king's court took place during 1717 and 1718, and involved considerable bitterness. The new Scottish exiles, who were Protestant, actively intrigued against the English and Anglicised servants from Saint-Germain, who were Catholic.[60] When they succeeded in obtaining the support of James III, whom they completely alienated from his Saint-Germain background, the old servants saw no point in remaining.

The process began in the summer of 1717 when James III visited Rome to meet Pope Clement XI and to discuss his future residence in the Palazzo Ducale at Urbino. Apart from some '3 ou 4 valets de chambre et autres domestiques', James was accompanied by only three people. They were David Nairne (his secretary of the Closet), John Hay (one of his two equerries, and brother-in-law of the Duke of Mar) and Charles Booth. The latter had been a groom of the Bedchamber since about 1700, had accompanied James on his various military campaigns, and had for long been one of his favourite servants. After the abolition of waiting in the Bedchamber at Pesaro, when he might have been left with nothing to do (like the gentlemen and the other groom), Booth had been given responsibility for managing what was left of the royal household: the servants below stairs, 'the Table' and the Stables. He was therefore hierarchically senior to Hay and to the other equerry (Delattre).

While they were in Rome the king became increasingly friendly with Hay, who was only three years younger than him, rather than with Booth, who was twenty-one years older. It was perhaps natural that the younger men should get on better together, but it provoked a growing sense of dissatisfaction and then resentment in the mind of Booth. It is clear from several letters that the

---

[59] Lord Newcastle and Richard Trevanion did not go to Italy. Nor did Charles Leslie.

[60] For an illustration of the attitude of the new exiles, see HMC *Stuart* v, 204, Southesk to Patterson, 13 November 1717: 'they now give themselves their great St Germains airs and esteem themselves the only sufferers for the King, while they have been growing rich by him these nine and twenty years'.

latter was the only member of the party who did not enjoy the visit,[61] and it was immediately afterwards, when the court was first established in the large and capacious palace at Urbino, that matters came to a head.

According to James III's own account, he decided that Hay should be placed in charge of the servants below stairs and 'the Table', leaving Booth in charge of the Stables only. He said he regarded this as merely swapping offices, so that Booth would become his equerry and 'quitt ye empty title of groom'. The latter, however, understandably regarded it as a demotion and therefore refused to accept the new arrangement, saying that he would rather be used like the other officers of the former Bedchamber, 'who wait not at all'. Booth went further and said he would like to return temporarily to France, which he did. As the king could not find a suitable replacement for him, he had to leave Hay where he was and continue the existing arrangement, giving responsibility for the household below stairs, 'the Table' and the Stables to Lord Clermont. But he was very angry and commented: 'As for the choice of Ld Clermont I believe it cant be disaproved nor had I indeed any choice here, for he is ye only untainted from St Germains principles. I mean of St Germain's people, for out of them there was a necessity of chusing at this time.'[62] Leaving aside his valet and yeoman of the robes, and the seven or eight lesser servants below stairs and in the Stables, this could only have referred to Lord Edward Drummond and Roger Strickland from the Bedchamber, Dominic Sheldon the vice-chamberlain, Dr Lawrence Wood the physician, Sir William Ellis the treasurer and perhaps David Nairne.[63]

This, however, was not the end of the matter, because the king soon wanted to replace Clermont as well. In November 1717 he confided to Cardinal

---

[61] HMC *Stuart* IV, 317, James III to Mar, 5 June 1717; *ibid.*, IV, 337, Nairne to Patterson, 11 June, 1717; *ibid.*, VI, 291, Nairne to Mar, 10 April 1718. The travelling arrangements are also revealing. Sending Nairne by another route, James travelled to Rome with both Booth and Hay in his coach. On the return journey the king was accompanied by Hay, while Booth travelled in a second coach with Nairne (HMC *Stuart* IV, 252, James III to Mar, 19 May 1717; Bodleian Library, Carte MSS 208, 'Journal du Sejour de S.M.B. à Rome', 4 July 1717).

[62] BL Add. MSS 38851, f. 109, James III to Dillon, 30 July 1717; HMC *Stuart* V, 14, Innes to Mar, 5 September 1717. See also HMC *Stuart* IV, 445, James III to Mar, 13 July 1717: 'He [Hay] hath my favour and he knows it, and nobody shall be able to take it from him . . . for 'tis a pleasure to be attended by such a one.'

[63] BL Add. MSS 31260, f. 101, Nairne to Gualterio, 5 August 1717, gives no hint of this disagreement: 'Le Roy . . . a chargé Milord Clermont du soin de toutes les affaires de sa maison, de sa table et de ses Ecuries en l'absence de Mr Booth, qui ne doit servir a son retour qu'au desous de Milord qui continuera toujours a donner les ordres en chef, et Mr Booth ordonnera en detail avec subordination a Milord comme a son officier superieur.' For Mar's comments, see HMC *Stuart* V, 2, Mar to Dillon, 2 September 1717.

Gualterio that 'la santé et la discretion peu certaines du premier [Clermont], et . . . la personne rustique de l'autre [Booth] me faisoient de la peine'.[64] When the Duke of Mar returned to the court at the end of that month, having failed to obtain a pardon from George I, James was already predisposed against his old servants. Mar rapidly established a complete ascendancy over his mind. James wrote to Ormonde in March 1718 that 'I must confess to you that, though I never much admired St Germain's proceedings, I am now quite surprised of them, and that, bar Queen Mary, I do not desire to have any more to do with them . . . I am not at all fond of the ways of those I have so long lived with.'[65] Totally unaware that Mar was a traitor, James wrote that in him and some of the new Scottish exiles he had discovered 'une probité inconnüe parmi la plupart de nos St Germanois'.[66]

It did not take Mar long to persuade James that Hay should be placed in charge of his entire household. The precise date when this happened is not clear, but as Hay was given the 'empty title' of groom of the Bedchamber on 13 January 1718,[67] it was probably then. Nairne commented a few months later that Mar was now the king's 'oracle' and that Hay 'qui est un jeune homme d'un merite et d'une capacité assés mediocre a tout pouvoir dans sa maison'. He continued: 'Milord Clerm.t et le pauvre Mr Booth ont été ecarté pour faire place a luy qui certainement n'a ni l'experience ni l'esprit solide de l'un ni l'autre, mais ce n'est pas toujours le vray merite qui est la regle de ses inclinations.'[68]

By the time Nairne wrote this letter, Hay and Mar had succeeded in driving away from the court nearly all the old Saint-Germain servants. Lord Edward Drummond left Urbino to spend the winter of 1717–18 in Rome.[69] He and his brother-in-law Lord Clermont then returned to Saint-Germain in the early

---

[64] BL Add. MSS 31255, f. 72, James III to Gualterio, 25 November 1717.

[65] HMC *Stuart* VI, 102, James III to Ormonde, 7 March 1718. This attitude may be compared with the description in Dr Brun's journal of the reception of Lord Edward Drummond by James III at Avignon on 2 July 1716: 'le Roy . . . l'a embrassé et baisé fort tendrement plusieurs fois et le Milord l'a baisé et embrassé de même devant tout le monde' (*Ecossais à Avignon*, ed. Dickson, 266). For the musical dimension of James's complete rejection of his Saint-Germain background, see Corp, 'Music at Urbino'.

[66] HMC *Stuart* V, 513, James III to Gaillard, 28 February 1718. See also *ibid.*, 373, James III to Dillon, 7 January 1718.

[67] Ruvigny, *Jacobite Peerage*, 224.

[68] BL Add. MSS 20298, f. 41, Nairne to Gualterio, 30 July 1718.

[69] BL Add. MSS 31260, f. 222, Nairne to Gualterio, 23 November 1717; BL Add. MSS 31261, f. 60, Nairne to Gualterio, 10 March 1718.

summer of 1718.[70] Roger Strickland and Dr Lawrence Wood left in October 1717;[71] Dominic Sheldon left in March 1718.[72] Charles Booth came back to Urbino in November 1717, but left again in May 1718.[73] The only servants of any importance who remained were Sir William Ellis, by then indispensable as treasurer, Delattre the equerry, and David Nairne. The latter confided to Cardinal Gualterio that 'je ne scais pas comment je n'ay pas deja eu le sort des autres. Mais je conte que mon tour viendra.'[74] Mar justified this purge of the old servants by accusing them of 'Whiggism'![75]

The departure of the old servants, the abolition of the Chamber and the Bedchamber, and the elimination of any distinction between those courtiers with and those without 'empty titles' effectively transformed the court of James III so that it was no longer the same establishment that it had been in France and Lorraine. The royal household, now controlled by Hay, contained no more than fifteen people. Nearly everyone with the king was now Scottish, or French or Italian, but not English.[76] And virtually everyone of any importance was Protestant. There continued to be religious toleration at the Stuart court, but now James III was himself part of the small minority of Catholics. He showed his respect for Protestant feeling by appointing a Carmelite friar

---

[70] BL Add. MSS 31261, f. 101, Nairne to Gualterio, 27 April 1718; HMC Stuart VII, 5, Clermont to Mar, 3 July 1718.

[71] BL Add. MSS 31260, ff. 178 and 180, Nairne to Gualterio, 7 and 10 October 1717. Dr Wood was replaced as physician by Dr Maghie, who was Scottish (HMC *Stuart* V, 427, account by Dicconson, 31 January 1718).

[72] BL Add. MSS 31261, f. 66, Nairne to Gualterio, 17 March 1718.

[73] SCA, BL 2/217/2, Nairne to T. Innes, 6 November 1717; SCA, BL 2/222/11, Nairne to T. Innes, 5 May 1718.

[74] BL Add. MSS 20298, f. 41 Nairne to Gualterio, 30 July 1718. See also SCA, BL 2/222/11, Nairne to T. Innes, 5 May 1718: 'I am perhaps a little usefull, and for that reason more than inclination I continue still to be trusted and imployd, but I shall not be surprised if my turn comes as well as others.' For Nairne's strained relations with Mar, which had originally deteriorated in Avignon, see SCA, BL 2/210/7, Nairne to T. Innes, 6 September 1716; and BL Add. MSS 20298, ff. 35, 41 and 47, Nairne to Gualterio, 7 and 30 July and 7 August 1718.

[75] HMC *Stuart* VII, 388, Mar to Patterson, 15 October 1718: 'There are indeed some of those who have long been of the King's family, who have left him some time ago, so very few of them are now with him . . . but they are only those of St Germains who have contrived it so that the King could no longer endure their ways, since he had others to make choice of . . . He did though all he could to make their services tolerable, but found it was in vain and that the spirit of Whiggism, which they have wonderfully got, is not easily to be cured.'

[76] Mar brushed aside complaints from the Jacobites in England by stating that 'the King wishes he had more of England's own relations to employ . . . but, till he has, he is necessitated to make use of those he has with him, though he gives none of them the name of any place or employment' (HMC *Stuart* VII, 388, Mar to Patterson, 15 October 1718).

(named Peter Brown), rather than a Jesuit, to be his new confessor. An Italian in Urbino noticed that when the king went each day to hear Mass in the cathedral beside the Palazzo Ducale, he had to be accompanied by the local nobles, followed by a small number of his own Catholic gentlemen, 'whilst those who were not Catholic remained behind in the *Sala del Magnifico*'.[77]

When the Stuart court had first been established in France both the servants and the organisation had been brought directly from Whitehall to Saint-Germain. This continuity had been preserved not only in France until 1712, but even in Lorraine until 1715. It was finally lost in Pesaro and Urbino in 1717–18. When James III was later able to re-establish a permanent court in Rome, following his marriage in the second half of September 1719, a new organisation was established, new servants were recruited, and new traditions had to be created. The Stuart court in the Palazzo Muti was maintained with considerable splendour, but it was fundamentally different to the court in which James III had grown up at Saint-Germain.

---

[77] H.C. Stewart, 'The Exiled Stewarts', 84, diary of Giovanni Gueroli Pucci. When asking for a papal dispensation to allow members of the court to eat meat during Lent, Nairne stated that there were now very few members of the court who would observe Lent anyway (BL Add. MSS 31261, ff. 8 and 25, to Gualterio, 7 and 27 January 1718).

CHAPTER FOURTEEN

The court of Queen Mary at Saint-Germain, 1712–1718

The death of Princess Louise-Marie in April 1712, followed by the permanent absence of James III, had a devastating effect on the Stuart court at Saint-Germain. The servants of the princess were given pensions, but remained unemployed at the court. The many servants of the king who did not follow him to Bar-le-Duc (or to Avignon and the Papal States) retained their salaries, but had no one to serve. The court inevitably lost its sense of purpose.

Several additional factors contributed to the decline of the court during its last six years. Mary of Modena began to spend long periods at the Couvent de la Visitation at Chaillot, thus leaving even her own household with no one to serve. The Treaty of Utrecht filled the town of Saint-Germain with thousands of demobilised Irish soldiers, whose families were reduced to poverty and starvation. The late payment of the Stuart pension, particularly after the death of Louis XIV, meant that even the household servants began to experience growing financial difficulties, often having to live on credit. The succession of George I and the defeat of the Jacobite rising of 1715–16 destroyed all hope of an immediate restoration, thus making credit more difficult to obtain. And the arrival in 1716 of large numbers of new exiles from Scotland compounded the financial problems, creating a new friction between the rival claims of the different national groups. The last years of the Stuart court at Saint-Germain witnessed its rapid decline and decay.

In the long term these final years were to have a decisive influence on people's perceptions of the court. Even at the time they probably cast a shadow over the previous two decades, when the Stuarts had maintained a large and magnificent establishment, culturally rich, politically important, and enjoying regular social contact with the court of France. But the memory of those earlier years ultimately depended on the survival of the Stuart archives. The documentary evidence for the period of prosperity was mainly destroyed in Paris at the end of the eighteenth century.[1] By contrast, the voluminous correspondence sent to Avignon and Italy describing the growing difficulties at Saint-Germain after 1716 was carefully preserved with the Stuart Papers

---

[1] Corp, 'Inventory'.

in Rome. It is this, more than anything else, which has produced so much misunderstanding about the exiled court in France.

Mary of Modena rented an apartment at Chaillot for 3000 *livres* a year,[2] and moved there in August 1712 when James III went to Le Raincy. She was still there at the end of October, and showed no signs of going back to Saint-Germain. Both Madame de Maintenon and the Duke of Berwick urged her to return to the court, alleging that it would be better for her health, but in reality, as Berwick put it in a letter to James III, because it would be 'better for your Majesty's interest and for the comfort of your subjects' at Saint-Germain.[3] It was not until early December, after an absence of nearly four months, that she finally gave way and resumed her public duties.[4]

Her return injected new life into the court, and in January 1713 Louis XIV visited her there, possibly for the last time.[5] John Stafford, no doubt with considerable relief, noted that she 'reçoit presque tous les jours quelques visites de Marly depuis que la Cour de France y est',[6] and in the following months the queen made return visits to both Marly and Versailles.[7]

In May, however, she went back to Chaillot, leaving the court at Saint-Germain once again without a royal presence. This time she seems to have been away until the beginning of November, making only a short visit to Marly in August.[8] She was in very poor health, was able to live more cheaply at Chaillot, and was understandably keen to escape from all the poor Jacobites at Saint-Germain, but the court inevitably suffered as a result.

In the following years Mary of Modena continued to spend the summer months away from the court. In 1714 and 1716 she went to Chaillot,[9] and in

---

[2] SP 46/75, Dicconson to Nairne, 22 April 1720. She paid nothing for the apartment until 1703. Dicconson stated that she then paid for the six years from 1703 to 1709, and every year from 1712 until her death. He had no record of any payments from 1709 to 1712.

[3] HMC *Stuart* I, 249, Berwick to James III, 30 October 1712.

[4] BL Add. MSS 31258, f. 230, Stafford to Gualterio, 11 December 1712: 'après avoir fait ses devotions le matin a la petite Chapelle, elle descendit a la grande, y entendit Vespres et Complies, le Predication du Pere Gaillard Jesuite, et les prieres du soir tout de suitte. Hier S.M.té a entendu le Messe a la Chapelle dans sa Tribune . . . Elle a disné en publique, a repris le train de ses fonctions ordinaires.'

[5] Dangeau, XIV, 328, 22 January 1713. It was his last recorded visit.

[6] BL Add. MSS 31258, f. 260, Stafford to Gualterio, 11 January 1713.

[7] Dangeau, XIV, 349 and 389, 21 February and 21 April 1713.

[8] HMC *Stuart* I, 268 and 279, Berwick to James III, 26 June and 17 October 1713; *Stuart Papers*, ed. Madan, 407, 437, 440, 459, 462–3, 469; Dangeau, XIV, 469, 26 August 1713.

[9] *Letter Book of Sabran*, 171, Stafford to Sabran, 1 October 1714; HMC *Stuart* III, 178 and 200, Mary of Modena to Mar, 5 and 11 November 1716.

1715 she visited James III in Lorraine.[10] Because she was away, fewer French courtiers visited Saint-Germain, and when Louis XIV died in September 1715 she seems to have maintained contact with no one other than Madame de Maintenon, the dowager duchesse d'Orléans and the duc de Villeroi.[11] Maintenon may perhaps have visited Saint-Germain from time to time,[12] but this is unlikely to have been often because she had retired to live in the school she had founded at Saint-Cyr. Moreover, whenever Mary of Modena was in residence at Saint-Germain it was she who made the journey between the two places, going to dine at Saint-Cyr once a week.[13] Saint-Germain was therefore dead as a social centre attracting important French courtiers, even before the Regent's alliance with George I made links with the Jacobite court a political and social disadvantage. The Regent himself visited the queen there in May 1717,[14] and the duc de Lorraine came shortly before her death, in March 1718.[15] When Czar Peter the Great decided to see her in June 1717, returning to Paris after visiting Versailles and observing Madame de Maintenon at Saint-Cyr, she was staying at Chaillot.[16]

The Treaty of Utrecht, which stipulated that James III should leave France, also stated that Mary of Modena should receive the jointure guaranteed to her by Parliament as part of her marriage settlement.[17] As a result large numbers of poor Jacobite exiles, including Irish soldiers demobilised with the return of peace, converged on Saint-Germain expecting to receive charity.[18] It was impossible to provide for them all, and by July 1713 Father Giustiniani, the queen's almoner, reported at Chaillot that 'il y avoit des pauvres gens qui passoient jusqu'à 80 heures sans prendre nulle nouriture'.[19] The Irish in the town were soon dying of starvation,[20] so the queen borrowed money on the security of her jointure in an attempt to feed them. When it became clear, after

---

[10] See above, pp. 294–5.

[11] Bibl. Mun. de Versailles, MS 1461/P.68, 245, Mary of Modena to Maintenon, 13 November 1716.

[12] Her last recorded visit was on 10 February 1714 (Dangeau, xv, 80).

[13] Saint-Simon, xxxvi, 182–3 gives the details.

[14] HMC *Stuart* v, 12, Innes to Mar, 5 September 1717.

[15] Saint-Simon, xxxiii, 64. This was during his incognito visit to Paris (*ibid.*, 80).

[16] Saint-Simon, xxxi, 382.

[17] HMC *Stuart* ii, 525, Mary of Modena to Dicconson, 23 June 1713.

[18] Mary of Modena commented at Chaillot that Saint-Germain was 'toute pleine d'Irlandois, qui sont la pauvreté même. Il a passé 20,000 hommes en France et de cela il ne reste pas 6000 hommes effectifs. Le reste a péri dans les armées, mais leurs enfans et leurs femmes sont demeurez à notre charge.' She added that 'dès que le bruit s'est répandu que je devois toucher mon douaire' they had all begun to come to Saint-Germain (*Stuart Papers*, ed. Madan, 440).

[19] *Stuart Papers*, ed. Madan, 463, 'Memoirs historiques', 26 July 1713.   [20] *Ibid.*, 444, 447.

the accession of George I, that she would never receive any part of it, the Irish had to go elsewhere, but she was left with considerable debts.[21] Nevertheless she continued to support them as well as she could.[22]

In August 1713, while Mary of Modena was staying at Chaillot, she was informed that the Château de Saint-Germain was 'presque désert'. She is reported to have replied that 'il est vrai que ce qu'il y a de meilleur a passé depuis peu en Angleterre'.[23] No evidence, however, has survived to support this alleged comment. When Lady Sophia Bulkeley tried to obtain a pass to go to England in June 1713, in order to recover her jointure, she was refused the necessary papers.[24] The only household servant who seems to have succeeded in returning is Thomas Neville, one of the grooms of the Bedchamber (who had also at one time been entrusted with James III's privy purse). By 1717, when he was still receiving his salary, he was living on his estate in Leicestershire, 'marryed to My Lady Winter, by whom we believe he has the benefit of a good Joynture'.[25] The fact is that virtually all the servants of both James III and Queen Mary herself remained at Saint-Germain until her death in 1718, regardless of rank, even though many of them had nothing to do.

Apart from a small reduction caused by deaths[26] and the discharging of some of the lesser servants below stairs and in the stables, the household of James III remained the same. New servants were obviously not needed. The household of the queen, on the other hand, was marginally increased.[27] Mary of Modena employed more servants in her Bedchamber. She also for the

---

[21] *Letter Book of Sabran*, 163, Mrs Griffith (the queen's sempstress and starcher, wrongly called Griffin) to Sabran, 19 September 1714.

[22] Corp, 'Inventory', 141. Giving the money was the responsibility of John Kearney, assisted by two clerks.

[23] *Stuart Papers*, ed. Madan, 440.

[24] HMC *Stuart* VII, 605, Sophia Bulkeley to Mar, 5 December 1718. For her previous attempts to obtain money, see Bodleian Library, Rawlinson MSS D.21, f. 7, Sandars to Meredith, 3 February 1700; f. 27, Sophia Bulkeley to Meredith, 5 October 1703; f. 31, Sandars to Meredith, 28 November 1705.

[25] SP Box 3/1/89, list of the king's and queen's servants and pensioners, July 1717; Estcourt and Payne, *The English Catholic Nonjurors of 1715*, 72. His estate was at Holt. He had married Frances (née Napper), the widow of Sir Charles Wintour of Lydney, Gloucestershire. In 1714 Charles Skelton and his wife Lady Barbara (née Lennard) visited England, but they were not household servants (*Letter Book of Sabran*, 166, Giustiniani to Sabran, 25 September 1714).

[26] Very few of the king's servants died during these years. Dudley Bagnoll, a groom of the Bedchamber, left Saint-Germain in 1716 to accompany his kinsman the Duke of Ormonde to Avignon and elsewhere (Bibl. Mun. d'Avignon, MS 3188, ff. 213–14, 'Liste des Anglois qui se trouvent presentement a Avignon, juillet 1716').

[27] SP Box 3/1/89 and 80 give the queen's household in 1717 and 1718 respectively.

first time employed a lord chamberlain and a master of the horse. Whenever she was at Saint-Germain the queen was surrounded by the same large and impressive household that she had always had.

In 1712 her Bedchamber servants included five ladies and five women. The former were the Duchess of Perth, the Countess of Middleton, Viscountess Clare, Lady Charlotte Talbot and Lady Sophia Bulkeley. The latter were Bridget Strickland (widow of Robert), Veronica Molza (wife of Count Carlo), Winifred Strickland (widow of Sir Thomas), Mary Plowden (widow of Francis) and Theresa Stafford (wife of John). By 1717 she had increased the number of Bedchamber women by appointing Henrietta Bulkeley (a daughter of Lady Sophia, and sister of both Lady Clare and the Duchess of Berwick). She continued to employ six pages and the various other more junior members of the Bedchamber staff.

When Lord Caryll had died in 1711 his political duties had been taken over by Lord Middleton, but his work as private secretary to Mary of Modena had been entrusted to her vice-chamberlain, John Stafford. The latter continued to hold both posts until his death in November 1714, after which the position of private secretary was given to one of the clerks in the secretariat, Nicholas Dempster. It was at this point that the queen revived the post of lord chamberlain for the Duke of Perth. The latter explained that 'la Reine a eü [la bonté] de me mestre a la teste de sa Maison en me faisan son Chambellant, un employ qu'on n'a pas a la Cour de France car par la j'exerce l'office de son Chevallier d'honneur et encor commande a tous les Domestiques, Gentilhomes et autres hormis ceux qui regard l'Escurie . . . C'est l'employ qui estoit immediatement au dessus de celuy qu'avoit feu Mons.r Stafford.'[28]

Shortly before Stafford's death the queen's confessor, Father Bartolomeo Ruga, decided to retire. He was eighty years old and had held the post since 1701. Mary of Modena wanted to replace him with another Italian Jesuit and selected Father Gian-Battista Giustiniani.[29] The latter, however, preferred to take up an appointment in Genoa and declined the post, so the queen was obliged to appoint a French Jesuit instead.[30] This was Father Honoré Gaillard, a well-known preacher who had already addressed the Jacobite court in the

[28] BL Add. MSS 31256, f. 95, Perth to Gualterio, 9 December 1714.
[29] He had either replaced or effectively superseded Giacomo and Peregrino Ronchi, respectively senior and junior almoner.
[30] *Letter Book of Sabran*, 162–3, Giustiniani to Sabran and reply, 12 and 19 September 1714; 170, Beeston to Sabran, 29 September 1714.

Chapelle Royale at Saint-Germain on at least one occasion.[31] According to a Jesuit source, the queen said 'she was abandoned by the Jesuits; could not confess in English, nor without difficulty in French' but that, because 'she could not make a new confidence and had often spoken to F. Gaillard', she would therefore accept him.[32]

Giustiniani's decision to return to Italy meant that he also had to be replaced, and it was at this moment, in November 1714, that the Duke of Perth was appointed lord chamberlain. At first the queen said that she did not mind who was chosen,[33] but when Perth argued that Giustiniani's successor should not be another Jesuit he was opposed by Father Gaillard. The appointment was delayed for several weeks, as both sides tried to influence the queen. Perth was supported by Lewis Innes,[34] who had been given the title of lord almoner since March 1714, and was thus Giustiniani's senior,[35] but the queen eventually overruled him and decided that she would after all appoint a Jesuit. The man selected was Father Thomas Lawson, one of the chaplains at Bar-le-Duc, who returned to take up his new post in March 1715.[36] His appointment had the advantage of removing a Jesuit from the Stuart court in Lorraine, but Mary of Modena might also have distrusted Perth's judgement. As he grew older he was becoming increasingly Anglophobe[37] and continuing his intrigues against Lord Middleton.[38]

The Château de Saint-Germain might not have attracted the French courtiers, but it was still a magnet for thousands of visitors, including many English after the return of peace, and many Scots after the failure of the Jacobite rising. The gentlemen ushers in the queen's apartment were therefore

---

[31] BL Add. MSS 31258, f. 230, Stafford to Gualterio, 11 December 1712. For his many sermons at the French court, see F. Bluche, *Louis XIV* (Paris, 1984), 961–2. He continued to preach at Versailles after becoming Mary of Modena's confessor, and Bluche has described him as the most important of all the preachers at the French court (*ibid.*, 566).

[32] *Letter Book of Sabran*, 174, Darell to Sabran, 9 October 1714.

[33] *Ibid.*, 183, Darell to Sabran, 24 October 1714.

[34] Ibid., 188, Darell to Sabran, 12? November 1714.

[35] Having been a junior almoner to the queen and then the king, Innes had been at Bar-le-Duc until the end of 1713 and again during the summer and autumn of 1714 (Ruvigny, *Jacobite Peerage* 224; BL Add. MSS 31256, f. 90, Perth to Gualterio, 9 September 1714; *Letter Book of Sabran*, 183 and 199, Darell to Sabran, 24 October, and Wood to Sabran, received 30 November 1714; SP Box 3/1/89, list of the king's and queen's servants and pensioners, July 1717; SP 207/59, T. Innes to James III, 2 June 1738).

[36] *Letter Book of Sabran*, 199, Giustiniani, 1 December 1714; 215, the Father Provincial, 27 December 1714; 235, Darell, 8 March; 243, Giustiniani, 25 March 1715 (all to Sabran).

[37] See BL Add. MSS 31256, f. 92, Perth to Gualterio, 22 October 1714, in which he described the English as 'nos plus cruels ennemis'.

[38] BL Add. MSS 31256, ff. 45 and 90, Perth to Gualterio, 29 February 1712 and 9 September 1714.

kept very busy whenever she was in residence. Of these the most important were the three who served in the Privy Chamber. They included William
Crane (a grandson of Lord Widdrington), Count Carlo Molza (who temporarily returned with his wife Veronica to Modena in 1717),[39] and John Caryll (a
nephew of Lord Caryll).[40]

The small group of servants working for the queen below stairs continued
to be supervised by the clerk of the Greencloth (Christopher Chilton) and the
remaining commissioner of the household (William Dicconson), while those
of the stables were directed by the two equerries (John Nugent and Bernard
Howard). When, however, Lord Middleton resigned as secretary of state and
returned to Saint-Germain in December 1713, Mary showed her high regard
for him by appointing him to be her master of the horse.[41] The position
probably enhanced the prestige of her household. At the end of November,
after the fall of the Tory ministry in London, Middleton left to advise James
III at Bar-le-Duc, but he returned permanently to Saint-Germain in January
1716. When the Duke of Perth died in April of that year, the queen transferred
Middleton to succeed him as lord chamberlain, and appointed the 2nd Duke
of Perth, who arrived from Avignon, to be her new master of the horse.[42]

During these years the queen's finances and the payment of all salaries
and pensions continued to be managed by her treasurer, William Dicconson,
and his clerk, Thomas Banckes. The queen herself was obliged to make considerable retrenchments, mainly to pay for the poor Irish,[43] but the salaries
and pensions that she paid each month were never reduced, and the Jacobite
servants and courtiers (as distinct from the poor Irish in the town) initially
maintained their comfortable standard of living. However, the payment of the
monthly sum of 50,000 *livres* from the French crown, on which those salaries
and pensions depended, remained permanently in arrears, and by the winter
of 1714–15 many members of the court began to experience serious problems
of credit. In February 1715 Lady Strickland wrote that the queen's servants
were 'poor enough, yet not without hopes of better times',[44] but by August the
situation had deteriorated. Dicconson wrote to Mary of Modena in Lorraine

[39] SP Box 3/1/89, list of the king's and queen's servants and pensioners, July 1717.

[40] He is referred to as 'Caryll the Usher' in Howard Erskine-Hill, *The Social Milieu of Alexander Pope*
(London, 1975), chapter 3, particularly 76–7.

[41] BL Add. MSS 31255, f. 3, James III to Gualterio, 16 December 1713; BL Add. MSS 31256, f. 70,
Perth to Gualterio, 21 December 1713; BL Add. MSS 31254, f. 28, Mary of Modena to Gualterio,
11 January 1714.

[42] HMC *Stuart* II, 218, Mar to Maule, 10 June 1716.

[43] HMC *Stuart* I, 276, Mary of Modena to Dicconson, 13 September 1713.

[44] *Letter Book of Sabran*, 243, Lady Strickland to Sabran, 28 February 1715.

describing 'St Germains' miserys', adding that there seemed no prospect of the arrears of the Stuart pension being paid in the forseeable future.[45] When Louis XIV died in September 1715 the queen had received nothing for four months, and Father Lawson wrote of the 'strange poverty att St Germains'. Commenting that he himself lived 'upon borrowing', he observed that 'many sell all to get bread'.[46] It was at this moment that the queen had to devote all her resources to helping finance James III's expedition to join the Jacobite rising in Scotland.[47]

The end of 1715 was a period of terrible suspense at Saint-Germain, while the courtiers awaited the outcome of the military operations. Lord Bolingbroke was in attendance on the queen as secretary of state, and the king was known to have landed at Peterhead, so there seemed a serious hope of a successful restoration and an end to 'St Germains' miserys'. The failure of the rising not only destroyed these hopes, but also had disastrous financial consequences. The Regent became less inclined to pay the arrears of the Stuart pension, so obtaining credit became more difficult. The position of the servants and courtiers thus considerably deteriorated. That was bad enough, but it was followed by the arrival of hundreds of new exiles from Scotland, virtually all of whom were penniless and looking to the queen for charity.

The documentary evidence for the last years of the Stuart court in France cannot be properly understood unless a clear distinction is made between the old servants and pensioners who were already being maintained before 1716, and the new Scottish pensioners who arrived after the failure of the rising. The position of the former was already very difficult, but it was not immediately made worse by the presence of the latter, because their salaries and pensions were guaranteed – whenever the Stuart pension was actually paid. It was the queen and James III who had to find extra money to provide for the new arrivals.

Since the 1690s the allocation of their French pension had been fixed by the Stuarts. They kept approximately 35.5 per cent for themselves, and spent approximately 64.5 per cent on salaries and pensions. By 1716, having some- what reduced the household of the king, these figures had slightly changed to 36.5 per cent and 63.5 per cent respectively.[48] It was from the Stuarts' own

[45] HMC *Stuart* I, 384, Mary of Modena to Dicconson, 5? August 1714.

[46] *Letter Book of Sabran*, 307, Lawson to Sabran, 23 September 1715. Also 302, Mrs Griffith to Sabran, received 16 September 1715; 312, Darell to Sabran, 2 October 1715.

[47] See above, pp. 297–8.

[48] The surviving lists of salaries and pensions for 1693, 1696, 1703, 1709, 1715 and 1716 are shown in Corp, 'Inventory', 134.

share that money for the new Scottish pensioners had to be found. The Duke of Mar wanted all the servants, the old pensioners and the new pensioners to be placed together, with no priority given to the former groups. This might have helped the queen, but it would have been a calamity for her court and she refused to agree.[49] By discharging some of the more able-bodied under-servants, by retrenching some pensions paid to people who had obtained additional ones from the court of France,[50] and by taking advantage of the natural losses resulting from deaths, she and Dicconson were able to reduce the proportion spent on the old servants and pensioners to 61 per cent by 1717. The salaries of the household servants at Saint-Germain were never reduced, and all the money to maintain the new Scottish exiles came from the queen. It was a considerable achievement, which was watched with gratitude by the original exiles and with admiration by the French courtiers.[51]

The standard of living of individual Jacobites clearly varied a great deal, depending on their private circumstances, including their ability to obtain money from Great Britain and their investments in the *rentes* on the Hôtel de Ville. But everyone suffered a decline. The surviving portraits of the Jacobite courtiers give some indication of this lack of disposable income. Belle painted Anthony Hamilton in 1713 and the Duke of Perth in 1714, but no more portraits are known to have been produced after these.[52] Mary of Modena's last commissions were two large allegorical paintings by Gobert for the tribune of the chapel at Chaillot. One showed Mary herself as St Helen, holding the wooden cross of St Edward and presenting it to her son. The other was a posthumous double portrait, described as the apotheosis of James II and Princess Louise-Marie.[53] She ordered them in 1713, but had still not paid for them when she died in 1718.[54] Confronted with the new demands for charity from the Scottish exiles in 1716, she stopped spending money on pictures.

---

[49] HMC *Stuart* IV, 512, Dicconson to Wivell, 13 August 1717.

[50] For example, Sir Adam Blair had his pension reduced by 400 *livres*, from 1650 *livres* to 1250 *livres per annum*, when he obtained a French pension of that amount in 1714 (HMC *Stuart* VII, 670, Blair to Mar, 26 December 1718, enclosing Dicconson to Ellis, undated).

[51] See the comments after her death by Dangeau (XVII, 304, 7 May 1718), Saint-Simon (XXXIII, 152), Villeroi (Bibl. Mun. de Versailles, MS 1461/P.68, 370, to Madame de Maintenon, 11 May 1718), and the dowager duchesse d'Orléans (*Letters of Madame*, II, 175, to Raugravine Louisa?, 19 September 1718).

[52] Of the new Scottish exiles he painted Maurice Murray of Abercairny, Lord Forbes of Pitsligo and Arthur Elphinstone (later 6th Lord Balmerino) (Corp, *King over the Water*, 103).

[53] Corp, *King over the Water*, 51–2.

[54] SP Box 3/1/88, James III to Dicconson, undated (August 1718).

When he arrived in Avignon Sir William Ellis calculated how much of the French pension which the Stuarts then kept for themselves (36.5 per cent) should be sent to him by Dicconson each month. The figure was approximately 20 per cent or 10,000 *livres*, later increased to 24 per cent or 12,000 *livres*.[55] This figure left the queen with only 12.5 per cent, and would have obliged her to borrow money in France and from Jacobites in England. But shortly afterwards James III was given 123,000 *livres* by the pope, who began to pay him a regular pension in November 1716. As a result, his share of the French pension could be diverted to pay for the new exiles.[56] In 1716 Mary of Modena spent 63.5 per cent of her pension on the old servants and pensioners, and 21.4 per cent on the new pensioners, retaining 15 per cent for herself.[57] The following year, when the lists had been reduced, the old servants and pensioners received 61 per cent and the new pensioners 19.5 per cent, the queen retained 15 per cent, and the remaining 4.5 per cent was set aside for extraordinary charitable expenses to support those Jacobite exiles not awarded regular allowances.[58] The salaries and pensions were often paid late, because the French pension itself remained permanently in arrears and money had to be borrowed to make even partial payments.[59] Dicconson wrote in August 1717 that 'the Queen thinks she does wonders, if she can continue to pay the King's servants and her own their respective appointments at a time that near 500 new pensioners are come upon her without any fund to maintain them'.[60]

Given the critical state of the queen's finances, and the difficulties experienced by all the exiles because of the arrears in the French pension, the Regent's threat to stop it completely was bound to force James III to leave Avignon. But he was not able to travel until he had recovered his health, so

[55] SP 40/117, rough calculations by Ellis, undated (April 1716); HMC *Stuart* v, 594, account by Dicconson, 6 October 1717. When he reached Avignon in April 1716 James III only had 4269 *livres* (SP Misc. 32, account book started at Châlons-sur-Marne on 23 March 1716).

[56] HMC *Stuart* v, 594 and 428, accounts by Dicconson, 6 October 1717 ('If the King should call again for his 12,000 a month, then there will be no possibility of paying either the new pensions or the extraordinaries') and 31 January 1718.

[57] SP 9/30, list of the servants of the king, June 1716. The 15 per cent amounted to 7500 *livres* each month, of which 6000 were spent on the 'Queen's Table, Stables, Clothes, wax lights, guards and other standing expenses' and 1500 on 'buying horses, coaches and other unavoidable expenses'.

[58] HMC *Stuart* v, 593, account by Dicconson, 6 October 1717.

[59] Chiddingstone Castle, Bower MSS, Mary of Modena to Mar, 17 December 1716 ('the pension of which wee have had but one payment these 3 months and wee are still 6 months behynd'); HMC *Stuart* III, 456, Abercromby to Mar, 18 January 1717.

[60] HMC *Stuart* IV, 512, Dicconson to Wivell, 13 August 1717. The main list of new pensioners contained 370 names, at a cost of 11,422 *livres* each month (see above, p. 305).

the number of months by which the pension was in arrears was inevitably increased. In September 1717, shortly after James III had established his court at Urbino, Lewis Innes wrote that 'Dicconson is reduced to borrowing to pay the ordinary, the Queen's allowance being farther behind than ever, the month of February not being yet paid, nor any word of it.'[61] In October Dicconson himself wrote that 'we at St Germains are 9 months in arrear'.[62]

The continued payment of the new pensions and charitable 'extraordinaries' was only possible so long as James III himself could survive at Urbino without having to call for any of the French pension. In a 'memoir on money matters' dated October 1717 he reviewed the various options for making retrenchments when he was next obliged to do so, but concluded that for the time being he could keep going without additional money until February 1719:

I have wherewithal to keep myself till that time without calling for any money from the Queen. By Mr. Dicconson's account the French pension will supply the present lists and 6,000 *livres* a month. I know that overplus is not to be imagined sufficient to supply the most ordinary extraordinaries, but then I apply to that use the 150,000 *livres* we are to have next February [1718] . . . I shall not expect a shilling of that whole sum, which may be laid by not only for extraordinary occasions, but to be employed in paying the pensions of such, who cannot subsist whole months without money, when our ordinary pension is not paid. I think . . . we can hold out as we are till the time above mentioned.[63]

It was thus the king's new papal pension which enabled the Stuarts to keep their Scottish subjects from starving after the failure of the 'Fifteen'.

This was ironic, because most of the new exiles were Protestant. The presence of large numbers of them at Saint-Germain inevitably resulted in friction with the local ecclesiastical authorities. The death of Louis XIV had not significantly changed French policy, and it was made clear that no Protestant services would be tolerated there except within the château itself.[64] To minimise the problem, they were ordered to keep away from the Paris area and live at Saint-Omer and Dunkirk.[65]

[61] HMC *Stuart* v, 12, Innes to Mar, 5 September 1717.
[62] HMC *Stuart* v, 594, account by Dicconson, 6 October 1717.
[63] *Ibid.*, 601, memoir by James III, October 1717.
[64] HMC *Stuart* IV, 466 and 479, Dicconson to Mary of Modena, 26 and 29 July 1717.
[65] HMC *Stuart* III, 2, H. Patterson to J. Patterson, 1 October 1716. Many had gone to Avignon, but they had not all stayed there. Those who were still there when James went to Italy in 1717 were ordered to disperse themselves to Toulouse and Bordeaux (*ibid.*, 502–3, Mar to Gordon and to Dicconson, 2 February 1717).

The new exiles resented this treatment, particularly as there was toleration for those of them at Avignon, Pesaro and Urbino. They also felt that they should be given priority over the old servants and pensioners because they had risked their lives in the recent rebellion. One of them informed John Hay in April 1718 that 'there is a great outcry amongst our people at St. Omer and Dunkirk against Mr. Dicconson. In the first place they have not received a farthing there these three months, and, when they do, it is always told them that it will in all probability be the last they are to expect.'[66] This contributed to the hostility felt by Mar, Hay and their Scottish friends at Urbino towards the old servants from and at Saint-Germain.

At the end of February 1718 Mar persuaded James that Lewis Innes, who as lord almoner was one of the queen's closest advisors at Saint-Germain, should be dismissed. Mar alleged that Innes had altered the sense of a proclamation that the king had issued to the Anglican church, but in reality he resented the fact that anyone at Saint-Germain, particularly a Catholic priest, should continue to have any political influence. Seemingly unaware of the extent to which he was both dominated and misled by Mar, James wrote that 'I will be master in my own business, and . . . I must and will show that I cannot be imposed by tricks and that honest men alone can thrive with me.'[67] Mary of Modena was deeply upset to receive a categorical command from her son to dismiss Innes, particularly as she regarded it as completely unjust, but she had little option but to obey.[68] A few weeks later, at the beginning of May, she died.

The dismissal of Lewis Innes, who had been principal of the *Collège des Ecossais* in Paris before 1689, and who had acted as secretary of state for Scotland to James II while Lord Melfort was in Rome (1689–91), really marked the end of the Stuart court at Saint-Germain. The death of the queen merely confirmed that the court no longer had any influence over the formulation of Jacobite policy. It also coincided with the purge of the old Saint-Germain servants from the court at Urbino. When Roger Strickland, Lord Edward Drummond, Lord Clermont, Dominic Sheldon and Charles Booth

---

[66] HMC *Stuart* VI, 314, Freebairn to Hay, 15 April 1718. Also *ibid.*, 216, Freebairn to Hay, 29 March 1718: 'everybody is calling out against the Court of St Germains for some one thing or another'.

[67] *ibid.*, 102, James III to Ormonde, 7 March 1718.

[68] HMC *Stuart* V, xxi; *ibid.*, James III to Gaillard, 28 February 1718; HMC *Stuart* VI, 306, Mar to James III, 13 April 1718; *ibid.*, 419, Gaillard to James III, 9 May 1718; *ibid.*, 560, Innes to James III, 21 June 1718. See also SCA, BL. 2/222/11, Nairne to T. Innes, 5 May 1718: 'I cannot yet overcome the impression which the sudden resolution taken about your brother has made upon me, it sticks with me still, and many things I have remarkd of late and do remark dayly make me wish heartily I had my quietus . . . I was silent out of respect yet I was far from approving . . . this . . . is only for your brother and yourself.'

returned to France the Château de Saint-Germain was still the centre of an important Jacobite community, but it was no longer the seat of a royal court.

That community, however, still needed to be financed. At the time of her death the queen was giving salaries and pensions to nearly 800 people,[69] and her own pension from the court of France was nine months in arrears.[70] The dowager duchesse d'Orléans explained that, in addition to paying the salaries of her own servants, 'the Queen of England . . . supported her son as well as his household, she gave pensions to most of her ladies and succoured entire families of English [sic]. She deprived herself of necessities in order to help the poor in the hospitals.'[71] All of these people faced poverty and starvation unless arrangements could be made to provide them with some permanent subsistence.[72]

There were four separate problems confronting William Dicconson who, as the late queen's treasurer, remained responsible for all payments. The first was to obtain the arrears of the French pension, to pay all the salaries and pensions up to May 1718 and to pay off all the queen's (and king's) debts in France.[73] The second was to decide what to do with any money left over. The third was to obtain new pensions from the French government for as many people as possible. And the fourth was to arrange alternative subsistence for all those unable to obtain a French pension. Dicconson devoted himself to all four of these during the rest of 1718 and throughout 1719, in the meantime using what little money he had to ensure that no one was allowed to starve.[74]

[69] SP 213/172 and SP 214/142, Dicconson to Ellis, 22 February and 22 March 1739.

[70] HMC *Stuart* VII, 159, Dicconson to James III, 15 August 1718. (The arrears amounted to 452,181*l.* 16*s.* 6*d.*). Dangeau was misinformed when he noted in his journal that it was 'six ou sept mois' in arrears (XVII, 304, 7 May 1718). According to Lady Sophia Bulkeley, most individual pensions in France were 'about five *years*' in arrears (HMC *Stuart* VII, 193, to Mar, 22 August 1718, my emphasis).

[71] *Letters of Madame*, II, 175, to the Raugravine Louisa?, 19 September 1718.

[72] When the queen died she charged Father Gaillard 'd'aller faire une solicitation pour le payment prompt des arrerages dûs de sa pension, à fin qu'on puisse satisfaire aux salaires de ses domestiques' (HMC *Stuart* VI, 420, Gaillard to James III, 9 May 1718). See also HMC *Stuart* VII, 211, Roger Strickland to Patterson, 28 August 1718: 'Since the queen's death this place is become the den of all that you can imagine most dismal in nature. A detail of what passes here would be too melancholy a subject.'

[73] The queen had paid all her debts in England before she died. See SP 192/134, Dicconson to Edgar, 25 December 1735: 'I had remitted by her Majesty's order into England . . . a considerable summ about 16 or 17 hundred pounds (as I remember) to pay several debts there, to tradesmen etc which was owing by ye Queen at ye Revolution, which the government there had refused to pay.' This was done 'some time before her death'. The bills actually totalled £4039 9*s.* 6*d.* and were all paid in 1716–17. The details are given in Bodleian Library, Rawlinson MSS. c.987, 145.

[74] HMC *Stuart* VII, 234, Mar to Mary Skelton, 2 September 1718.

The most urgent task was to obtain the arrears of the French pension, because the longer payment was delayed, the more the interest on the outstanding debts, and the charity payments he had to make, would erode the amount of money eventually left over.[75] One month was received in August 1718, but the remaining eight were not forthcoming until June 1719. The fact that the money was paid at all was largely due to the intervention of John Law, a Scotsman of Jacobite sympathies, whose *Banque Générale* became the *Banque Royale* in December 1718 and who created the *Compagnie des Indes* in March 1719.[76]

The receipt of the first month in August 1718 showed clearly that priority was now being given to the new pensioners over the servants and the old pensioners. The king decided that the money should be divided equally between the two groups.[77] Given that about 61 per cent was intended for the old servants and pensioners, and only 19.5 per cent for the new pensioners,[78] this meant that the latter received their arrears very much more quickly. The son of one of the old servants observed in November 1718 that the new pensioners had by then received all that was owed to them up to May 1718, whereas few of the old servants had been paid beyond August 1717.[79]

Once the arrears of the French pension had been received Dicconson was able to pay all the salaries and pensions up to May 1718, and to clear all the royal debts, including the legacies which the queen had specified in her will were to be paid before a restoration.[80] He then had to decide what to do with

[75] *Ibid.*, 159, 358 and 472, Dicconson to James III, 15 August, 3 October and 31 October 1718; 484, James III to Dicconson, 2 November 1718; SP 44/42, Dicconson to Murray, 12 August 1719.

[76] HMC *Stuart* VII, 8, 159, and 646, Dicconson to Mar, 4 July 1718, to James III, 15 August 1718, to James III, 19 December 1718; 128, Higgons to James III, 8 August 1718; 484, James III to Dicconson, 2 November 1718; SP 43/109 and 140, Dicconson to James III, 12 and 29 June 1719; SP 44/42, Dicconson to Murray, 12 August 1719; SP 45/3, James III to Law, 24 September 1719. In January 1718, when still director of the *Banque Générale*, Law had already made the Queen a loan of 50,000 *livres*, or one month's pension (HMC *Stuart* V, 353, G. Hamilton to Mar, 3 January 1718).

[77] HMC *Stuart* VII, 253, James III to Dicconson, 7 September 1718; 285, Mar to Panmure, 15 September 1718; 332, Dicconson to Gordon, 27 September 1718; 358 and 472, Dicconson to James III, 3 and 31 October 1718.

[78] See above, p. 324.

[79] HMC *Stuart* VII, 577, C. Chilton to Mar, 28 November 1718. Lady Sophia Bulkeley and Richard Trevanion, for example, were both receiving only 100 *livres* each month (*ibid.*, 287, Mar to Sophia Bulkeley, 15 September 1718; SP Box 3/1/88, James III to Dicconson, undated (August 1718)).

[80] Full details of the payments of the queen's debts and legacies are given in SP 192/134, 135, Dicconson to Edgar, 25 December 1735: 'I know no debts of ye late Queen Mothers which were not acquited either before HM's death or immediately after.'

the surplus. There were three main alternatives: to distribute the money among the old servants only; to give it to both the servants and all the pensioners, old and new; or to distribute nothing at all and keep the money to be used as charity to stop people starving.[81] When consulted, James ordered him to adopt the third alternative, without making any distinction between the people on the various lists, arguing that the obligation of a king to his subjects should take priority over those of a master to his servants.[82] The only qualification to this was that nothing should be given to anyone who already had a French pension or to any of the under-servants who were able to find alternative employment.[83]

The thirteen months after the death of Mary of Modena, during which the household servants waited for their salaries to be paid, were obviously extremely difficult, but what concerned them above all was whether or not they would continue to receive any money in the longer term. Before the thirteen months had finished several had decided to leave Saint-Germain, either in an attempt to get money in Great Britain or to live more cheaply elsewhere. Among the more important servants, the Duchess of Perth went to Scotland to try to obtain her jointure,[84] Lady Strickland retired to the convent of English Poor Clares at Rouen,[85] Bridget Strickland went to join the English Benedictines at Dunkirk,[86] and Count Carlo and Countess Veronica Molza returned to live in Modena.[87] The latter's daughter Margaret, who was married to John Nugent, wrote to David Nairne in October 1718 that 'our Chateau has the air of a real desert, for it grows emptier every day'.[88] It was after they had left that a list of people to receive French pensions was finally settled.

One list had been drawn up in May 1718, immediately after the death of Mary of Modena, when the Regent had asked the duc de Noailles to give him the details of all the pensions which she had been paying.[89] This, it was hoped, would result in a decision by the French government to continue

---

[81] SP 43/109 and 140, Dicconson to James III, 12 and 29 June 1719.

[82] SP 44/13, 77, 45/4, James III to Dicconson, 9 July, 29 August, 24 September 1719; SP 44/42, Dicconson to Murray, 12 August 1719. For the bitterness of the old servants at this decision, see SP 44/27, Higgons to James III, 1 August 1719.

[83] SP 44/77, James III to Dicconson, 29 August 1719.

[84] HMC Stuart VII, 35, Mar to Dowager Duchess of Perth, 14 July 1718; SP Box 3/1/87, money owed by members of the household to the king and the queen, 1709–19.

[85] HMC Stuart VI, 546, Lady Strickland to James III, 18 June 1718.

[86] HMC Stuart VII, 491, Bridget Strickland to Mar, 2 November 1718.

[87] SP Box 3/1/89, list of the king's and queen's servants and pensioners, July 1717.

[88] HMC Stuart VII, 396, Margaret Nugent to Nairne, 16 October 1718.

[89] Dangeau, XVII, 306, 9 May 1718; HMC Stuart VI, 434, F. Oglethorpe to Mar, 15 May 1718; ibid., 487, James III to Noailles, 28 May 1718.

paying all the exiled Jacobites the allowances they had been receiving, and James III had written to the Regent asking him to do this.[90] The dowager duchesse d'Orléans had even been told at the end of May that 'my son, out of compassion for her [the Queen's] poor servants, will allow many of them to retain their pensions'.[91] Nothing, however, had happened for several months, and it is not clear what was done with the list drawn up by Noailles.

In September 1718 the Regent asked Dicconson to let him have two new lists. He wanted one which included all the queen's servants separated into 'three classes, viz., the chief persons, those of an inferior rank and the lowest of all', and a second list of 'the King's servants that are paid at St Germains' (rather than Urbino). As the arrears of the pension had still not been paid at that time, it was feared that the Regent would use the lists to avoid paying the full amount due.[92] These fears turned out to be unfounded,[93] but Dicconson's two lists, like the one drawn up earlier by Noailles, do not seem to have been used. Finally, in November 1718, the Duke of Berwick intervened. Drawing up his own list, he persuaded the Regent to pay pensions to several but not all of the 'chief persons' who had served the queen. Neither the servants of 'an inferior rank' nor 'the lowest of all' were included. More important, his list did not include any of the servants of the king either.

Berwick's motives are not clear. By 1718 his relations with his half-brother James III were very strained, because he had refused to take part in the recent Scottish rising.[94] Perhaps the Regent was only prepared to accept a very limited list, but the omissions were attributed by the Jacobites to Berwick himself and they created great resentment towards him.[95] Neither Saint-Germain nor Urbino was satisfied with what he obtained.[96]

Berwick's list was restricted to the ladies of the Bedchamber, the Bedchamber women of the queen, the former Bedchamber women of the princess, and

[90] HMC *Stuart* VI, 488, James III to duc d'Orléans, 28 May 1718. He also asked the duc de Lorraine to intervene with the Regent on his behalf (*ibid.*, 495, James III to duc de Lorraine, 30 May 1718). Both the duc de Lauzun and Father Gaillard also 'asked the Regent for the continuation of the Queen's pension for St Germains' (*ibid.*, 490, F. Oglethorpe to Mar, 30 May 1718).

[91] *Letters of Madame*, II, 170, to the Raugravine Louisa, 29 May 1718.

[92] HMC *Stuart* VII, 271, Dicconson to James III, 12 September 1718.

[93] *Ibid.*, 537, Dicconson to Mar, 14 November 1718.

[94] HMC *Stuart* I, 451, Berwick to James III, 3 November 1715.

[95] Berwick himself had an annual income of 35,000 *livres* during the Regency (SP 171/158, Duchess of Berwick to James III, 20 July 1734).

[96] E.g. HMC *Stuart* VII, 577, C. Chilton to Mar, 28 November 1718; 622, James III to Dicconson, 12 December 1718; 629, Mar to Gordon, 13 December 1718; 636, Mar to Maule, 16 December 1718; SP 57/126, Higgons to James III, 2 February 1722; SP 57/151, Booth to James III, 9 February 1722; SP 61/54, Dowager Duchess of Perth to James III, 27 July 1722.

four of the queen's gentlemen, who were to receive annual pensions amounting to approximately three quarters of their previous salaries. Berwick, however, specifically excluded everyone who had left Saint-Germain (as well as those who already had pensions from the French crown). Thus pensions were given to the Countess of Middleton, Lady Charlotte Talbot and Lady Sophia Bulkeley (his mother-in-law), but not to the Duchess of Perth and Viscountess Clare; to Mrs Plowden and Mrs Stafford, but not to Mrs Strickland, Countess Molza and Lady Strickland. The four gentlemen included in the list were the lord chamberlain (Lord Middleton), the treasurer (Dicconson) and two of the gentlemen ushers of the Privy Chamber (William Crane and John Caryll), all of whom had attended the queen's funeral. But neither the three others who had attended her funeral – the equerry (John Nugent), the almoner (Dr John Ingleton) and the third gentleman usher of the Privy Chamber (Count Carlo Molza)[97] – nor the master of the horse (the 2nd Duke of Perth), who was away, received anything.[98] The many other servants of the queen for whom no pensions were provided included her secretary (Nicholas Dempster), the other gentlemen ushers (Guy Forster, Joseph Persico, Edmund Barry and Matteo Maria Turrini), the pages of the Bedchamber (Dominique Dufour, Arthur Lavery and George Peirson), the groom of the Great Chamber (Lawrence Bowsey), the master cook (Philippe Lesserteur), the master of the music (Innocenzo Fede), and her priests, of whom the most important – but only until March 1718 – had been Lewis Innes.[99]

At the end of December James III wrote to Father Gaillard, asking him to speak to the Regent to have more of the queen's servants included on Berwick's list. 'When I say servants', he wrote, 'I do not mean the inferior ones, who are strong enough to gain their own livelihood, but the gentlemen and a few others, who from age or infirmity can not work for their maintenance.' His

---

[97] According to Saint-Simon, the queen's funeral was attended by these four, but also Count Carlo Molza, John Nugent, Dr John Ingleton and Father Gaillard (XXXIII, 337–42).

[98] HMC *Stuart* VII, 553, Dicconson to James III, 21 November 1718; 555, Booth to Mar, 21 November 1718; 605, Sophia Bulkeley to Mar, 5 December 1718. The comparison of the new pensions and former salaries was as follows: ladies of the Bedchamber 3000–3770; queen's Bedchamber women 2000–2200; former Bedchamber women of the princess 1000–1430; lord chamberlain 3000–5659; treasurer 2000–3112; gentlemen ushers of the Privy Chamber 1000–1132. Of the Bedchamber women to the princess, an exception was made of Lady Lee, whose husband was a lieutenant-general with a military salary.

[99] Most of these people are included in the 'liste des officiers de la Reine qui, par suite de son décès, demeurent sans emploi', 1718 (Arch. Dépt. des Yvelines, B.537 Saint-Germain). When Turrini died in February 1719 he owed 136 *livres* 11s. to a *boulanger* at Saint-Germain named Vincent Ratteau. The latter's 'memoire du pain fourny a Monsieur de Turaine gentilhomme de la Reine d'Angleterre' is also in Arch. Dépt. des Yvelines, B.537 Saint-Germain.

letter significantly included Innes: 'the Regent has kindly granted pensions to some of the Queen's servants', but his 'favours have been so limited and so unequal in their distribution as for instance the Duke of Perth, the Duchess his stepmother, the two Ladies Strickland [*sic*], the Countess Molza and Mr Innes, the last four certainly surpassing, without wronging the others, both for length and faithfulness of service all those I have noticed in a list sent to me'.[100] As a result of Gaillard's intervention the list was expanded to include the equerry (John Nugent)[101] and various people who had been receiving pensions, though the latter group had their allowances substantially reduced.[102] None of the ladies and women who had been absent from Saint-Germain at the end of 1718, however, was included in the expanded list.[103]

By the end of 1719 the arrears of the Stuart pension had all been paid, and some of the queen's servants had begun to receive their new French pensions, but the position of the king's servants, his old pensioners, and the new pensioners from Scotland was desperate. When Lord Middleton died in August 1719 his pension was immediately cancelled and not continued for Lord Clermont.[104] The latter, like Lord Edward Drummond, had independent sources of income, but many of the older servants did not, and they were totally dependent on Dicconson's charity fund. By the end of 1719 several had died, many had left,[105] and a few had been invited to join the new household in the Palazzo Muti in Rome. Those who could had found alternative employment, but there were many who remained to be looked after by Dicconson. John Law then made a second generous gesture towards his fellow Jacobites. In January 1720 he was appointed *Contrôleur-Général des Finances* and immediately arranged to pay a single 'gratification' to all the servants who were still at Saint-Germain. A few days after taking office he gave Dicconson 124,050 *livres* (the

---

[100] HMC *Stuart* VII, 667, James III to Gaillard, 28 December 1718. Regarding his own servants, James added: 'I will say nothing here of my own wants, nor of those of the persons depending on me, for I believe it is not the time for mentioning them.'

[101] SP 152/91, Nugent to James III, 23 March 1732. He received a pension of 1000 *livres*; his salary had been 1412 *livres*. The other equerry, Bernard Howard, already had a French pension of 1200 *livres* (SP Box 3/1/89, list of the king's and queen's servants and pensioners, July 1717).

[102] Lady Nagle had had a pension of 3316 *livres* from the queen. Her new French pension was only 800 *livres* (SP 41/49, Lady Nagle to James III, received January 1719).

[103] See SP 61/54, Dowager Duchess of Perth to James III, 27 July 1722. Payment of all these new pensions started in August 1719 (SP 44/32, Ingleton to Nairne, 7 August 1719).

[104] SP 145/53, Dicconson to Ellis, 13 May 1731.

[105] For example, Roger Strickland had gone to England to claim the estate of his uncle, Admiral Sir Roger Strickland, who had died in August 1717 (HMC *Stuart* VII, 604, Mar to Roger Strickland, 5 December 1718).

equivalent of approximately two and a half months of the old Stuart pension)
to be divided, according to their ranks and previous allowances, between the
servants of the king, those of the queen who had been excluded from Berwick's
list of French pensions, and both the old and the new pensioners. Each person
was given the equivalent of several months' allowance, depending in part on
their personal circumstances.[106] This money would not last indefinitely, but it
was hoped that more might be forthcoming at a later date.

The Jacobites were very lucky to get their gratifications so quickly, because
in May 1720 Law's financial 'system' collapsed – ruining several of them in
the process.[107] Law was forced to resign as *Contrôleur-Général*, and by the
end of the year he had left the country, bringing to an end all immediate
hope of further money from the French government. Dicconson therefore
used the money he still had left over from the arrears of the French pension
to establish what he called the 'Bread Money List'.[108] Those on this list were
given enough food or money to keep themselves alive. When the original fund
was finally used up, James III began to remit small amounts from Rome so that
Dicconson could continue paying the 'Bread Money' indefinitely.[109] Many of
the old servants and pensioners ended their days in this relative poverty.

The Bread Money was regarded as a substitute for a pension rather than as
charity,[110] but it was not intended to be given to the more important servants.
James III was reluctant to commit himself to giving permanent pensions to
people in France, but his marriage to Maria Clementina Sobieska in September
1719 brought him a large dowry, enabling him to make some provision for
the more important servants who still had nothing. He gave a pension to

---

[106] SP 45/111, 121, James III to Dicconson, 11 December 1719, 1 January 1720; SP 45/124, 138, 151,
Dicconson to James III, 1, 15, 22 January 1720; SP 46/9, James III to Dicconson, 5 February
1720. Dicconson's copy of the list of gratifications is SP 281/166 (misfiled); the copy sent to
Rome is SP Box 3/1/80.

[107] One Jacobite who lost heavily was Lord Edward Drummond (SP 61/54, Dowager Duchess of
Perth to James III, 27 February 1722). The most spectacular loss was suffered by Lady Mary
Herbert, daughter of the 2nd Duke of Powis, whose 'equity stake amounted to some 6.5 million
livres' before the crash (M. Murphy, 'A House Divided: the Fall of the Herberts of Powis,
1688–1775', *Recusant History* 26, no.1 (May 2002), 91).

[108] SP 46/112, Dicconson to James III, 6 May 1720: 'for the present I have about 15 or 1600 *livres*
of charity in my hands which I will imploy for the present relief of ye most necessitous'.

[109] SP 50/6 and 84, 10 November and 9 December 1720; SP 50/119, Dicconson to James III, 22
December 1720; SP 60/6, Dicconson to James III, 8 June 1722; SP 60/110, James III to
Dicconson, 3 July 1722; SP 61/53, Dicconson to James III, 27 July 1722; 86/63, Mary Connell
to Inverness, 16 October 1725.

[110] SP 102/87/3, Ellis to Dicconson, 26 February 1727.

Charles Booth and to one of the new Scottish exiles (Lord Maclean),[111] and began to make occasional payments to various other people, such as Bridget Strickland, George Rattray (a former groom of the Bedchamber) and Sir Thomas Higgons.[112] By 1731 he was giving pensions to twenty-three people in France, at an annual cost of 20,987 *livres*.[113]

One way or another, all of the king's servants at Saint-Germain who did not receive Bread Money were eventually provided with some subsistence – from the French crown, by joining the French army or (like Bridget Strickland and George Rattray) by obtaining a pension from James himself. One of the last to receive anything was Sir Thomas Higgons. As a former secretary of state he felt that he deserved special treatment, but his previous employment counted against him both in Paris and in London. At the beginning of 1722 he spoke to Cardinal Dubois, the French chief minister, whom he used to know well, but obtained nothing. He even approached Lord Carteret, one of the Whig secretaries of state, who was married to his first cousin Grace (née Granville), in the hope that Cartaret might write to Dubois on his behalf.[114] But, as he informed James III, he 'received so impertinent an answer which mortifys to think I should be obliged to ask favours of yr enemys whom I mortally hate and despise'. In explaining this to the king he added: 'Your Majesty's servants which have nothing to subsist them are a very few in number, and I am ashured if we had any body of note and consideration to countenance us, the Regent would releif us.'[115]

A few months later the marquise de Mézières (born Eleanor Oglethorpe) persuaded Cardinal Dubois to expand the list originally produced by Berwick. The people who had deliberately been excluded were not now to be considered, but James III was asked to send a list of the more important servants of both himself and the queen who had been overlooked in 1718 and who were

---

[111] The former received 1200 *livres per annum*, which was regarded as compensation for the captain's pay which he had given up when he left the French army to become a groom of the Bedchamber (SP Misc. 33; H. Tayler, *The Jacobite Court at Rome in 1719* (Edinburgh, 1938), 130, Inverness to Dunbar, 10 February 1725; SP 148/112, Dicconson to Ellis, 9 September 1731).

[112] There were many such payments. See, e.g., SP Misc. 33; SP 102/87/16, Ellis to Waters, 13 May 1727.

[113] SP Box 3/1/85, list of pensions paid in France, undated (1731). By 1733 the cost had risen to 21,462 *livres* (SP 167/47, 'Estat des Pensions du Roy payées par Mr Waters à Paris'). Rattray had received his pension by 1727 (SP 110/136, accounts of Ellis for 1727; SP 111/114, Ellis to James III, October 1727).

[114] Lord Carteret had apparently obtained a captain's commission in the French army for the son of Sir Charles Carteret, who had been a gentleman usher of the king's Presence Chamber at Saint-Germain, and whose wife had been a Bedchamber woman to Princess Louise-Marie.

[115] SP 57/126, Higgons to James III, 2 February 1722.

still at Saint-Germain.[116] The new pensioners included all the priests, except Lewis Innes,[117] but not Sir Thomas Higgons. At the end of 1722 he reminded the king that 'I am now allmost the only one of yr servants that has nothing to subsist him, the two Nagles are made captains, Yr Majesty allows Booth a pension, and everyone has some way or other to procure them bread. I have no resource.'[118]

Higgons was finally awarded a pension of 3000 *livres* a year from the French crown in May 1724, five months after the death of the Regent.[119] Like all the French pensions it was paid irregularly and in arrears, and James III continued to have to send him additional money from Rome.[120] But the possession of a pension at least enabled Higgons, like the other servants who remained at Saint-Germain, to obtain credit. It had taken exactly six years, but by May 1724 the finances of the old court of Queen Mary had finally been settled.

[116] SP 62/36, Mézières to James III, 14 September 1722; SP 62/106, James III to Mézières, 20 October 1722.

[117] SP 44/32, Ingleton to Nairne, 7 August 1719; SP 84/150, Innes to James III, 29 July 1725. The priests received 800 *livres* each. Innes claimed that he was left out because he had offended Berwick by urging him too strongly to obey the king's command to go to Scotland in 1715–16 (SP 121/63 and 128/27, Innes to James III, 12 October 1728 and 16 May 1729).

[118] SP 64/29, Higgons to James III, 20 December 1722. The two Nagles were James (gentleman usher of the Privy Chamber) and David (gentleman usher of the Presence Chamber), sons of Sir Richard Nagle (secretary of state and war).

[119] SP 81/139, Higgons to Inverness, 24 April 1725; SP 162/90, Dicconson to Edgar, 14 June 1733.

[120] SP 74/93 and 77/157, Inverness to Higgons, 23 May 1724 and 7 November 1724; SP 92/92, Higgons to Inverness, 1 April 1726; SP 115/120, Higgons to James III, 26 April 1728; SP 102/87/173, Ellis to Waters, 6 July 1728.

CHAPTER FIFTEEN

The Jacobite community at Saint-Germain after 1718

In the years which immediately followed the death of Mary of Modena in May 1718 the Jacobite community at Saint-Germain was transformed. Before 1718 there had been a clear distinction between those who received regular salaries and pensions from the Stuarts and those outside the court who did not. The former had a comfortable standard of living, whereas many of the latter were very poor. After 1718 the distinction was between the minority who managed to obtain subsistence[1] and who thus continued to live in relative comfort, and the great majority (which now included many old servants and pensioners) who lived in relative poverty. The former mainly lived in the château, where they enjoyed grace and favour accommodation. The latter lived mainly in the town, where they had to devote part of their limited resources to paying rent. The major financial problems experienced by that group have obscured the fact that an important Jacobite community continued to occupy the Château de Saint-Germain for much of the rest of the eighteenth century.

For at least twenty years following the death of the queen the château continued to be occupied exclusively by Jacobites.[2] The apartments there had originally been allocated by the Stuarts themselves,[3] but after the death of the queen this responsibility was entrusted to the duc de Noailles.[4] The latter made a point of giving any apartments which happened to become vacant to other Jacobites. Although several of the old servants died during the 1720s and 1730s, their lodgings were often inherited by their widows or children. Whenever that was not the case Noailles consulted the Jacobite

---

[1] Neither Lord Edward Drummond nor Lord Clermont obtained a pension from James III or the French crown. The former had an income from the Perth estates in Scotland (*House of Lords Sessional Papers, 1852–53*, XXVI, Evidence before Lords Committees for Privileges and before the House, 1846–48, 105). The latter had inherited the estates of his step-grandmother in 1706, and had his father's English outlawry reversed in February 1727 (Jones, *Middleton*, 257–8).

[2] The only French people were the *concierge* (Jacques-Louis Soulaigre), the *procureur* (François Duchateau), the chaplain (abbé de Brie), his two *clercs* (abbé Lecaudé and abbé Roland), a boy in charge of the *garde meuble* (Sr Fortin) and the porter.

[3] E.g. HMC *Stuart* I, 313, Mary of Modena to Dicconson, 4 April 1714.

[4] SP 190/123, Noailles to Chilton, 19 October 1736; SP 190/130, Chilton to Sheridan, 21 October 1736.

community, even James III himself,[5] and gave the vacancies to retired officers from the Irish regiments in the French army. This meant that the Stuart court at Saint-Germain remained relatively unchanged for a surprisingly long time. The apartments previously occupied by James III (*du Dauphin et de la Dauphine*), Mary of Modena (*de la Reine*) and Princess Louise-Marie (*du Roi*) remained empty, as they had after 1712 whenever the queen had gone to Chaillot, but most of the others continued to be occupied by the same people. When Lady Pomfret visited the château in 1738 she noted, not only that 'the apartments are noble, and the conveniences for the servants very great', but that 'there are still some remains of that abdicated court . . . [including Lady Middleton] in perfect health and senses'.[6]

There are two documents which list all the people living in the château in 1738 when Lady Pomfret made her visit.[7] They not only give us precise details of all the apartments and their occupants, but emphasise how little had changed since 1718. The servants of the king still living there included two gentlemen of the Bedchamber (Lord Edward Drummond and Lord Clermont, now 3rd Lord Middleton), two grooms of the Bedchamber (Charles Booth and George Rattray), the widows of two other grooms (Daniel MacDonnell and Thomas Sackville), the son of yet another (David Floyd) and the widow of a page (Charles O'Neal). There were two gentlemen ushers of the king's Privy Chamber (James Nagle and Richard Bourke), the widow of another (Edmond or Patrick Fitzgerald), the daughters of a gentleman of the king's Presence Chamber (Sir Charles Carteret), the daughter of the king's physician (Dr Maghie), and even the widow of the comptroller of the household (Bevil

---

[5] SP 223/116 and 227/31, Dicconson to Edgar, 12 June and 9 October 1740.

[6] *Correspondence between Frances, Countess of Hartford (afterwards Duchess of Somerset) and Henrietta Louisa, Countess of Pomfret*, 1 (London, 1805), 10, Pomfret to Hartford, 29 October 1738: 'within [the château] is a court, that coaches [to the rank of a duke] have the privilege of entering. And the whole castle is encompassed by a large dry ditch, over which are drawbridges . . . since the death of [James II's] widow the royal apartments have been unfurnished.' (I owe this reference to Dr John Rogister.)

[7] Arch. Dépt. des Yvelines, A.369/3, 'Le nom des habitants, étage par étage, le nombre de pièces qu'ils occupent, cheminées comprises, ainsi que les entre-sols au Château-Vieux de Saint-Germain', undated [1737]; A.369/2, 'Etat des Appartements du Vieux Château Royal de St. Germain en Laye', 1738. These lists seem to have been drawn up because major repairs were carried out in 1737 in the empty royal apartments, the theatre and the apartments occupied by the French people mentioned in note 2 (AN O/1/1716, 'Reparations Indispensables et nécessaires de faire' in the apartments of the king and the queen, and 'etat des Reparations. . . . dans les Chateaux de St Germain en Laye', both 1737). Those parts of the château continued to be maintained by the French crown (AN O/1/1717, 'les détails des objets qui ont étés supprimés depuis 1737', 26 September 1784).

Skelton) who had died in 1696. The secretariat was represented by the widow of Sir Thomas Higgons.

The queen's servants included two ladies of the Bedchamber (Lady Middleton and Lady Clare), the son of another (Lady Charlotte Talbot) and three Bedchamber women (Mary Plowden, Theresa Stafford and Henrietta Bulkeley). There was her treasurer (William Dicconson), her almoner (Dr John Ingleton) and her equerry (John Nugent). There was also one of the Bedchamber women to the princess (Lady Murray) and the daughters of another (Lady Carteret, married to Sir Charles Carteret already mentioned).

The other occupants included the wife of the 2nd Duke of Melfort (previously married to James II's illegitimate son the Duke of Albemarle), the dowager Duchess of Berwick, the 6th Viscount Clare (son of Lady Clare) and his sister Laura (widow of the comte de Breteuil), the 2nd Earl Dillon, the dowager Countess Dillon (née Sheldon), the dowager Countess of Falkland (née Dillon), Lord Castleconell, Lord Maclean and James III's official representative in Paris, Daniel Obryen (later Lord Lismore). The few remaining occupants were the more recent arrivals connected with the Jacobite regiments.

The best apartment of all was the one occupied by Lady Middleton on the second floor, originally intended for the *Enfants de France*, and where James III and his sister had been brought up. The next best were the ones on the floor below, particularly in the east and west wings. The Duchess of Melfort lived in the former, originally created by Louis XIV for Madame de Montespan, below the empty apartment of the queen. A detailed inventory has survived, showing all the duchess's furniture, and listing her large collection of paintings.[8] Opposite in the west wing, Lord Edward Drummond and his wife Elizabeth (daughter of Lord Middleton) occupied an enormous apartment, which was actually four separate apartments combined. It had originally served the Duke and Duchess of Perth as well as Drummond and his wife, and extended the entire length of the west wing below the theatre.

The apartments in the north wing, overlooking Le Nôtre's *grand parterre* with its three *bassins*, were occupied by the Duchess of Berwick, her sisters (Lady

---

[8] The inventory is dated 7 August 1741 and was published in *House of Lords Sessional Papers, 1852–53*, 275–82 (see note 1). After listing and valuing all the paintings in detail, it adds that 'trois tableaux peints sur toile dans leurs bordures de bois doré', representing the Dowager Duchess of Melfort (widow of the 1st Duke), the Duchess of Melfort (wife of the 2nd Duke) and 'mademoiselle de Condé', and 'huit portraits de famille peints sur toile dans leurs bordures de bois doré et sculptés n'ont été prisés mais seulement tirés pour mémoire'. (I am very grateful to Peter Drummond-Murray for drawing my attention to this volume and for generously lending me his own copy.)

Clare and Henrietta Bulkeley) and Mary Plowden. The apartment of William Dicconson was in the south wing, commanding a view over the main entrance. It was there that he had previously paid people's salaries and pensions, and where he now administered the Bread Money and various charities for the poor Jacobites in the town.[9]

Given such an impressive location and these occupants (not to mention those other servants, such as Lady Sophia Bulkeley, who died there during the intervening years), it is hardly surprising that many Jacobites chose to live in the town of Saint-Germain rather than Paris or Versailles. They included most of the twenty officers on the Colonels List, who received pensions from the French government but who were nominated by James III.[10] This was an important financial benefit for James because the people on the list did not necessarily have to be military officers to obtain the pension. Thus the king added to the list in 1730 the well-known Freemason Andrew Ramsay, who had been a member of his court in Rome during 1724 and was by then serving the Bouillon family.[11] In 1731, however, the French government decided that James should only be allowed to nominate a new person to the list on condition that the person to be taken off was still alive.[12] As the French knew perfectly well that the king would not deprive anyone of his subsistence, this meant that the number of people on the Colonels List would inevitably decline, and by 1737 there were only thirteen left.[13]

In addition to these people living in the town, the Jacobite community also attracted many visitors. When Andrew Ramsay had gone there in 1727, for example, he had discovered that the Duke of Mar and Lord Lansdowne were both there, and that the Duke of Berwick had been there a few days before.[14] A particularly important gathering took place several years later when James III donated to the parish church of Saint-Germain the relics of St Clement (Pope Clement I) which had been given him by Pope Clement XII. A very large crowd assembled to attend the ceremony to mark their arrival, and Dicconson

---

[9] The Bread Money List originally cost 550 *livres* a month (SP 102/87/3, Ellis to Dicconson, 26 February 1727), but when people died they were not replaced, so it gradually reduced. By 1738 it cost 445*l*. 6*s*. 8*d*. (SP 212/47, Dicconson to Edgar, 28 December 1738). It still cost 404 *livres* in 1747 (SP 288/155, Flyn to Edgar, 29 December 1747).

[10] The ten colonels received 530 *livres* 10*s*. each and the lieutenant-colonels received 442 *livres* 4*s*. each per annum (SP 54/117, the Colonels List, 13 July 1721; SP 132/19, Dicconson to Obryen, 12 November 1729).

[11] SP 132/101, the Colonels List, December 1729; SP 146/71, the Colonels List, 20 June 1731.

[12] SP 144/151, Dicconson to Ellis, 29 April 1731.

[13] SP 191/173, Dicconson to Edgar, 25 November 1736.

[14] SP 102/34, Ramsay to Inverness, 26 January 1727.

noted that 'I never saw the Church so adorned with Tapestry and Lustres, nor illuminated with cierges in my life.'[15]

The most notable visitor during these years was the 3rd Duke of Beaufort, who took into his household one of the former pages of the queen's Bedchamber, Dominique Dufour, and employed him as his wine merchant.[16] When he began his grand tour in the winter of 1725–26 he visited Saint-Germain *en route* and organised a large ball in the château. According to Dufour's 'memoire de l'argent que j'ay recue a diferante fois pour la dépense du bal de St Germain', the cost of this ball was over 5325 *livres.*[17] It took place in January 1726, but Beaufort was still there in March, before setting off for Italy.[18]

During the same year a lodge of Freemasons was founded in Paris containing twenty-three people, of whom at least sixteen were Jacobites, most of them living in the Château de Saint-Germain. They met in premises occupied by Barnaby Hute,[19] who had been assistant in the wine cellar at Saint-Germain, Bar-le-Duc and Avignon, but who had returned to live in Paris rather than following the king to Italy. It is possible (even probable) that Freemasonry had been introduced to the Stuart court at Saint-Germain in the early 1690s,[20] but

---

[15] SP 155/55, Dicconson to James III, 30 November 1732. See also SP 158/123, certificate of the *marguilliers*, January 1733. For the anger of the French court at such a large Jacobite ceremony, see SP 163/155, Dicconson to Edgar, 2 August 1733. The relics were exposed annually on St James's Day (SP 259/143, Conygham to James III, 15 June 1743).

[16] Dufour's father had accompanied Mary of Modena on her flight to France in 1688 (see above, p. 104, note 1). Dufour travelled from London to Burgundy every year to buy wine for the duke and for himself, having a cellar at Saint-Germain (rue du Vieille Abreuvoir, beside the château) as well as in London (SP 149/149, Dicconson to Ellis, 28/10/31). He died at Saint-Germain in 1734 (SP 174/30, Dicconson to Edgar, 10/10/34). For Dufour's employment by the Duke of Beaufort, see Badminton archives, Fm 1/4/2 and 3, 'accounts of Mr Dufour with the Duke of Beaufort', 1725–33, and Fm 1/4/13, the Duke's account with Hoare's Bank, 1729–33, very kindly communicated to me by Lucy Abel Smith and Margaret Richards, and published with permission from His Grace the Duke of Beaufort.

[17] Badminton archives, Fm 1/4/2, 130.

[18] *Ibid.*, 147, 159 and 169. When Beaufort reached Rome he went to see Sir William Ellis (SP 98/82, Ellis to Inverness, 23 October 1726). He also took into his employment Théophile Lesserteur, whose father had been Mary of Modena's master cook, whose mother had been James III's sempstress, and who had himself been working in the Stuart court in Rome (SP 112/28, James III to Ellis, 9 November 1727; SP 150/89, Dicconson to Ellis, 9 December 1731; and the Badminton archives already cited).

[19] Corp, 'Clandestine Support', 10–12 and 20–1; Corp, 'Jacques II lance maçonnerie', 18–22. Except where shown, the information on Freemasonry is taken from A. Kervella, *La Maçonnerie écossaise dans la France de l'Ancien Régime* (Monaco, 1999) and *La Passion écossaise* (Paris, 2002). The latter work contains the most detailed and authoritative examination of the twenty-three people in this lodge (pp. 165–88).

[20] Kervalla has suggested in *La Passion écossaise* (p. 118) that the following four household servants at Saint-Germain, who invested together in the lead mines between Le Huelgoat and Châtelaudren

by the 1720s it was definitely well established there. Its further development in France was to have an important impact on the Jacobite community in the château.

After 1715 the Hanoverians deliberately set about infiltrating and then taking over the masonic lodges of England and France, which had originally been closely associated with the royal House of Stuart. Having succeeded in London by 1723, they then turned their attention to Paris, hoping to secure the support and cooperation of the anti-Jacobite faction at the French court. The Jacobites responded by grouping together their various lodges in 1728 to form the *Grande Loge de France*, of which the first Grand Master was the Duke of Wharton, succeeded in 1731 by the 5th Earl of Derwentwater.[21] The pro-Hanoverians then founded various new lodges of their own in France during the early 1730s, and attempted to gain control of the *Grande Loge*.

The difference between the two sides not only was political and dynastic, but involved different attitudes towards the place of religion within Freemasonry. Whereas the Jacobite lodges in France were specifically Catholic, the Hanoverian ones taking their orders from the Grand Lodge of England were prepared also to admit Protestants and even non-believers.

In December 1735 Lord Maclean, who lived in the Château de Saint-Germain, replaced Lord Derwentwater as Grand Master, but the latter was re-elected the following December for a second term. It was then, during 1737, that the struggle between the two opposing groups became particularly intense. In these circumstances Sir Andrew Ramsay, who had recently married a daughter of Sir David Nairne and been made a baronet by James III,[22] attempted to win the support of Cardinal Fleury for the Jacobites.

Ramsay was the Grand Orator of the *Grande Loge de France*. In March 1737 he wrote to Fleury and asked him to 'soutenir la société des free-masons dans les grandes vues qu'ils se proposent',[23] and suggested that he might even

---

in Brittany in 1704, may already have been Freemasons: James Porter (vice-chamberlain), Henry Parry (clerk of the kitchen), Thomas Neville and Charles Booth (both grooms of the Bedchamber).

[21] Charles Radcliffe had succeeded to the title on the death of his nephew earlier that year. His two elder brothers, James and Francis, had lived at Saint-Germain between 1702 and 1705 as companions to James III. James, the 3rd Earl, had been executed in 1716 (R. Arnold, *Northern Lights: The Story of Lord Derwentwater* (London, 1959), 45, 47).

[22] SP 179/185, Nairne to James III, received 6 June 1735. Nairne, who had been knighted in 1719, had remained in the secretariat of the Stuart court in Italy until 1729, and had returned to Paris at the end of 1733. After 1735 he lived with his daughter and son-in-law.

[23] P. Chevallier, *Histoire de la Franc-Maçonnerie française*, I (Paris, 1974), 18, Ramsay to Fleury, 16? (received 20) March 1737. (For the dating of this letter, see Kervella, *Maçonnerie écossaise*, 155).

nominate 'des gens sages et choisis par V.E. . . . à la tête de ces assemblées'.[24] 'Mylord Comte de Derwentwater', he added a few days later, 'voulut ramener icy tout à son origine, et restituer tout sur l'ancien pied. Les ambassadeurs de Hollande et de George duc de Hanovre [i.e. George II] en prirent ombrage et blasphèment contre ce qu'ils ignoraient, s'imaginant que les Freemaçons catholiques, roylistes et jacobites, ressemblaient aux freemaçons hérétiques apostats et républicains.'[25] Fleury, however, supported the Hanoverians, as he did in his foreign policy. In August 1737 he ordered the police to raid the *Grande Loge*, and in June 1738 he used his influence to have Lord Derwentwater replaced as Grand Master by the pro-Hanoverian duc d'Antin.

Defeated in Paris as well as in London the Jacobites decided to preserve their traditions by creating a totally separate system of Freemasonry. In April 1738 James III persuaded Pope Clement XII to issue a Bull (*In eminenti apostolatus specula*) denouncing the Hanoverian system, which admitted Protestants and non-believers.[26] Later the same year Ramsay withdrew to Saint-Germain to create a new Catholic Jacobite lodge. To protect it from anti-Jacobite infiltration he introduced thirty-three exclusive new higher grades, known as the *Rite Ecossais Ancien et Accepté*. In 1741 the Earl of Derwentwater also went to live in Saint-Germain,[27] thereby considerably strengthening the group of Jacobite Freemasons living there.[28]

This development drew the attention of the French authorities to the community in the Château de Saint-Germain, and made some people question the wisdom of letting the Jacobites maintain their exclusive occupation of the apartments there. It also coincided with another development which was designed to alienate the French government. The Jacobites in the château were accused of Jansenism.

In itself this was nothing new: Dr Betham had already been accused of Jansenism at the beginning of the century.[29] But Lord Edward Drummond

---

[24] *Ibid.*, Ramsay to Fleury, 22 March 1737.

[25] P. Chevallier, *Les Ducs sous L'Acacia, 1725–43* (Geneva, 1964), 216. Ramsay to Caumont, 1 April 1737. The British ambassador was Lord Waldegrave, whose father (married to a sister of the Duke of Berwick) had been comptroller of the household at Saint-Germain from 1689 to 1690.

[26] J.A. Ferrer Benimeli, *Los Archivos secretos Vaticanos y la Masonería* (Caracas, 1976), 193–8, Cardinal Corsini to the Grand Duke of Tuscany, April 1739. (I am very grateful to Jane Clark for giving me this reference.)

[27] Arnold, *Northern Lights*, 194.

[28] When Ramsay died at Saint-Germain in May 1743 the parish register recording his death was signed by the 10th Earl of Eglinton and Lord Derwentwater. It is reproduced in Corp, *Cour des Stuarts*, 216.

[29] See above, pp. 275–7; and Clark, *Strangers and Sojourners*, 241–55.

had been converted by the celebrated miracles at the tomb of Deacon Pâris at Saint-Médard in 1727, and during the 1730s had become closely involved with the *convulsionnaires*. In 1737, when he was nearly arrested,[30] the nuncio wrote to Rome that Lewis Innes had perverted the Scots who lived at Saint-Germain, particularly Lord Middleton and Lord Edward Drummond, 'who was so openly declared in favour of Jansenism that he had refused to be present at a mission held a few months before by the Jesuit fathers at Saint-Germain and during this time withdrew to Paris to the Scots College'.[31] Two years later he *was* arrested, at a country house belonging to Monsieur d'Angervillers, and sent to the Bastille. After his wife had intervened, he was set free but ordered to return to Saint-Germain and stop attending Jansenist assemblies. In 1741, the year that Lord Derwentwater went to live at Saint-Germain, he asked permission to go to Paris, but was refused.[32]

This combination of Jansenism and Jacobite Freemasonry might have proved disastrous for the community living in the château. The duc de Noailles remained sympathetic, but he nevertheless gave one vacant apartment to a Frenchman,[33] and decided that another should be used to store James III's books and papers rather than given to another Jacobite.[34] Then, in 1743, he significantly broke the Jacobite monopoly by giving the most important apartment in the château to a French nobleman. The *Appartement du Roi*, used by James II, and vacant since the death of Princess Louise-Marie, was given to the marquis de Tessé, whose grandson was married to a grand-daughter of Noailles himself.[35] At around the same time some of the most prestigious Jacobites in the château died. They included Charles Booth in October 1740, the Duchess of Melfort in May 1741, William Dicconson in November 1742 and Lady Middleton in March 1743.[36] Booth and Dicconson left elderly widows. The Melfort apartment on the first floor was inherited by Lord Forth (later 3rd Duke of Melfort), and the Middleton apartment on the second floor was inherited by the 3rd Earl. But the latter therefore vacated the one he had previously occupied on the floor above.

---

[30] Clark, *Strangers and Sojourners*, 248.   [31] *Ibid.*, 236.

[32] *Ibid.*, 248–50.   [33] SP 245/173, Mary Skelton to Edgar, 25 November 1742.

[34] SP 247/70, Flyn to Edgar, 3 February 1743.

[35] AN O/1/1717, 'Les détails des objets qui ont étés supprimés depuis 1737', 26 September 1784. It is difficult to know how to interpret this. The father of Tessé's daughter-in-law was the duc de Charost, who once addressed a letter to Andrew Ramsay as 'Cher Frère' (SP 63/38, Charost to Ramsay, 21 November 1722). Ramsay pretended that 'il m'appelle frere parceque feu Mr l'archeveque de Cambray était notre pere commun' (SP 63/59, Ramsay to Inverness, 23 November 1722).

[36] Lart, *Parochial Registers*, i, notes on 154–61.

The Jacobite community at Saint-Germain was temporarily reprieved by the death of Cardinal Fleury in 1743, followed by the outbreak of war between France and England and the arrival of the Prince of Wales from Rome. In January 1745 'allmost all ye Gentlemen of this town' visited the prince in Paris,[37] and many of the Irish and Scottish officers in the French army began to spend their winters at Saint-Germain.[38] During this short period of renewed Franco-Jacobite alliance, the duc de Noailles even gave the Middleton apartment to the Derwentwater family. The Earl of Derwentwater had left Saint-Germain to join the prince in Scotland, but had been captured *en route*. In November 1746, while he was in London awaiting sentence, Lord Middleton died at Saint-Germain leaving no heir. Noailles promptly reallocated the apartment to Lady Derwentwater, who discovered a few weeks later that her husband had been executed.

But by then the Jacobites had been defeated in England and Scotland, and there was renewed pressure on Noailles to stop giving the apartments to them. Even in January 1746 he had given a third apartment to a Frenchman.[39] In March 1748, when it seemed that Dicconson's widow was likely to die, it was feared that her apartment on the first floor would probably be given to 'a certain French gentleman of credit' who had asked for it.[40] The abbé David Flyn, who had taken over Dicconson's financial responsibilities, then visited the Prince of Wales in Paris and 'lay'd before him our grievance concerning the lodgings of this castle, in which he seem'd to take great share'. The prince ordered Flyn 'to draw up a formal mémoire of the affaire' which he could convey to the duc de Noailles.[41] In the event Mrs Dicconson recovered and lived for another three and a half years. But long before then England had made peace at Aix-la-Chapelle, the prince had been expelled from France and another important apartment had been allocated to a French person.

It was Lord Edward Drummond who occasioned the latter development. In 1747 he and his wife had left Saint-Germain to live in Paris but had

[37] SP 262/44, Flyn to Edgar, 29 January 1745. The prince paid a return visit in June 1747, but did not actually visit the Château de Saint-Germain. 'The Prince came . . . to pass some days in the princesse de Conti's house at Luciene [*sic* Louveciennes] near Marli about a small league from this town, and invited my Lady Derwentwater and familly to see ye waterworks', i.e. the 'Machine de Marly' on the Seine, immediately below the princesse de Conti's house (SP 284/189, Flyn to Edgar, 25 June 1747). 'I came back last night from a cuntry house of Princess de Contise . . . where I had been to geat a sight of ye Castle of St Germans and ye *anvirons* which are really very pritty' (SP 284/201, Prince Charles to James III, 26 June 1747).
[38] SP 290/75, Flyn to Edgar, 31 March 1748.
[39] AN O/1/1710, Lassurance to Tournehem, 29 January 1746.
[40] SP 289/191, Flyn to Edgar, 3 March 1748.   [41] SP 290/19, Flyn to Edgar, 10 March 1748.

been ordered by the police to return. In 1748, however, they seem to have obtained permission to leave the château and settle permanently in Paris, where they acquired a new home in the rue Popincourt (Faubourg Saint-Antoine). Although he used his *hôtel* to hold assemblies of *convulsionnaires*, he seems now to have been regarded as merely very pious. He rarely went out, was said to have become very keen on his garden (something he had never had at Saint-Germain), and was left undisturbed.[42] His enormous apartment on the first floor of the west wing of the château was meanwhile reallocated to the Melfort family, which had acquired considerable influence at the French court. This, however, meant that the superb Melfort apartment in the opposite wing of the château became vacant, and it was given by Noailles to a French lady named Madame de Saulsoy.[43]

It was now thirty years since the death of Mary of Modena, and the château de Saint-Germain was still overwhelmingly Jacobite.[44] In 1752, when the Earl of Tyrconnell died in Berlin, where he had been French ambassador, his body was brought back and buried in the parish church, immediately outside his apartment in the north-west pavilion of the château.[45] But the changes now began to come more rapidly and concerned the royal apartments. In 1750 the three *bassins* on the *grand parterre* of Le Nôtre had been filled in and suppressed,[46] thus ruining the prospect from the apartments of the king

---

[42] Clark, *Strangers and Sojourners*, 250–1. Their Jansenism, however, was not forgotten. When Lord Edward's wife Elizabeth (née Middleton) fell ill in 1754 the local *curé* refused to administer the last rites because she would not say to whom she had made her confession. Lord Edward and Lieutenant-General Rothe (married to Lord Middleton's other daughter) complained to the *Premier Président* of the *Parlement de Paris*, who ordered the *curé* to do as he was asked. When he still refused he was sentenced to be banished in perpetuity from France. The archbishop of Paris supported the *curé*, and interdicted another priest who had meanwhile given the last rites. Lady Edward recovered and lived until August 1774, but a similar incident took place when Lord Edward himself, by then 6th Duke of Perth, died in February 1760. The priest who administered the last sacraments was also interdicted by the archbishop. He was only buried in the local churchyard after his wife, his sister-in-law and Lieutenant-General Rothe had again petitioned the *Parlement*, after which his widow moved to another parish (*ibid.*, 252–3; BN MSS Fd. Fr., *Dossiers Bleus* 243/29778 – Drummond, 4 and 61; *House of Lords Sessional Papers*, 261 and 288).

[43] AN O/1/1712, Montmorency-Laval to Marigny, 3 March 1765 and 25 February 1766. I have not been able to identify Madame de Saulsoy. When she died in 1770 her apartment was again given to a Jacobite, the comtesse Redmond de Nugent (AN O/1/1713, Redmond de Nugent to Marigny, 7 July 1770, and Redmond to Marigny, 13 July 1770).

[44] In 1747 John Gordon of Glenbucket asked to be given an apartment because the town was full of French people whom he could not understand, whereas in the château he would be surrounded by people who spoke his own language (SP 288/81, Flyn to Edgar, 26 November 1747).

[45] He died in Berlin in March and was buried in the parish church in August (Lart, *Parochial Registers*, II, 164).

[46] R. Berthon, *Saint-Germain-en-Laye* (Pontoise, 1966), 118.

and the dauphin. The former had been empty again since the death of the marquis de Tessé in 1746, and when Dézallier d'Argenville published his *Voyage Pittoresque des Environs de Paris* in 1755 he noted, somewhat misleadingly, that it was 'démeublé, et n'offre rien de remarquable depuis que Sa Majesté ne fait plus de séjour à Saint-Germain'.[47] The duc de Noailles now decided that the time had come for all the royal apartments to be occupied. In 1753 the apartment of the queen was given to the comtesse de Montmorency-Laval,[48] and in 1754 (with some irony) that of the king, where James II had spent his final years, was given to the princesse de Talmont, the former mistress of his grandson Prince Charles.[49] At around the same time the apartment of the dauphin (which included that of the dauphine) was given to the comte de Périgord,[50] while Lieutenant-General Francis Bulkeley ceded the apartment he had inherited from his sister (the Duchess of Berwick) to the princesse d'Armagnac.[51]

The most significant change, and one which provoked considerable ill-feeling, involved the eviction of the Derwentwater family by the French novelist Claude Crébillon (known as Crébillon *fils*). Since 1748 he had been married to Henrietta Stafford, the daughter of John Stafford and Theresa (née Strickland). The couple were short of money and had been economising by living for some years in a small Jacobite community at Sens, but they were keen to return to the Paris area. In 1754, hearing that Lady Derwentwater and her two daughters intended to pay an extended visit to England, Henrietta Crébillon arranged to borrow their large apartment on the second floor of the château, promising to vacate it whenever they should return. She also obtained the eventual *survivance* when the apartment was no longer needed by the Derwentwater family.[52]

During 1755 news arrived that Lady Derwentwater had died in England and that her daughters wished to return to their apartment. Crébillon, however, refused to vacate it, pretending that he and his wife had been given the

---

[47] *Voyage Pittoresque*, 174–80.

[48] AN o/1/1710, Montmorency-Laval to Lassurance, 26 July 1753. She was born Maria-Luisa Barberini, and had married in 1747 Joseph-Auguste, second son of the comte de Laval.

[49] AN o/1/1710, Talmont to Vandière, May 1754. She was born Marie-Anne-Louise Jablonowska, and had married the prince de Talmont in 1730.

[50] AN o/1/1713, Galant to Marigny, 27 February 1768. He was Gabriel-Marie de Talleyrand.

[51] AN o/1/1710, Armagnac to Vandière, 6 August 1753. The princesse d'Armagnac was Françoise-Adélaïde (eldest daughter of Adrien-Maurice, duc de Noailles), widow of Charles de Lorraine, comte (but called prince) d'Armagnac.

[52] Except where shown, all details concerning Crébillon are taken from Corp, 'Crébillon', 23–42.

survivance on the death of Lady Derwentwater herself.[53] It seems that the duc de Noailles was persuaded to support Crébillon, because in September 1755 Flyn reported to James III that Lady Derwentwater's 'lodging in this house' had been 'granted to a frenchman'.[54] Whether or not Henrietta agreed with her husband in doing this is unclear, because she herself died shortly afterwards in November 1755.[55]

Crébillon continued to live by himself in the Derwentwater apartment, on extremely bad terms with his mother-in-law (with whom he had a major financial disagreement), for the rest of 1755 and during 1756. He then negotiated an elaborate series of exchanges with some of the other occupants. In October 1756 an unmarried Jacobite (Jane Sarsfield), who had a small apartment on the first floor of the south pavilion, died. Her sister (Bridget), who had shared it with her before her marriage to the comte de Chambors,[56] had the *survivance* to the apartment, but felt it was too small for a married couple. Crébillon therefore suggested to Chambors that he should go directly to Louis XV and obtain his permission to exchange apartments. By the time this had been achieved in January 1757, Crébillon had already negotiated another exchange, this time with Elizabeth Carteret, who lived in a larger apartment on the third floor. In this way, more of the best apartments had passed out of Jacobite hands and King Louis XV had been invited to take a direct interest in their allocation.

These events coincided with the outbreak of the Seven Years War. In earlier years an Anglo-French war would have brought renewed hope to the Jacobites, but times had changed. It was nearly forty years since the death of Mary of Modena, and the new generation in France regarded the Jacobite cause with growing indifference. The younger Jacobites had themselves integrated into

[53] SP 357/140, Flyn to Edgar, 18 August 1755, reported the death of Lady Derwentwater and the absence of her daughters: 'I fear their Lodging in this Castle will be given to some other on acc.t of their absence.'

[54] SP 358/88, Flyn to Edgar, 21 September 1755.

[55] The detailed thirty-three-page inventory of all the contents of the apartment, whether belonging to Lady Derwentwater or to the Crébillons, and dated 20 November 1755, is in Arch. Dépt. des Yvelines, prévôté de Saint-Germain. (I am grateful to Jean Sgard for giving me this reference, and a transcription of the complete inventory.)

[56] Jane and Bridget Sarsfield were the daughters of Ignatius Sarsfield, 'a Major of Foot who after distinguishing himself by his services in Ireland, followed the late King [James II] to France, and died in Savoy . . . and was descended in a direct line from the branch of the Viscounts Sarsfield of Kilmallock' (Ruvigny, *Jacobite Peerage*, 206). Joseph-Jean-Baptiste de la Boissière-Chambors was created comte de Chambors after the death of his son, the marquis de Chambors, on 21 August 1755.

local society, often marrying French people, but maintaining contact with their families in Great Britain and freely travelling between the two countries. The community in the Château de Saint-Germain was thus increasingly regarded by many French as a group of enemy aliens. Mary Plowden wrote to James III at the beginning of 1757 that 'our present situation in France is terrible, as your Majesty may immagine. God send us peace, and a little quiet.'[57]

It was a sign of the times that there should be friction within the château itself between the elderly Lady Castleconnel and one of the new French residents, the comte d'Artagnan.[58] It was also significant that the difference between Jacobite and anti-Jacobite Freemasonry should be terminated during these years. In December 1743 the *Grande Loge de France* had attempted to prevent the so-called *Maîtres Ecossais* from adopting the exclusive thirty-three higher grades of the *Rite Ecossais Ancien et Accepté*. Now, in 1755, by which time the *Grande Loge* was no longer pro-Hanoverian, it accepted these grades and affirmed its adherence to Catholicism. Ramsay, Derwentwater and Maclean were all dead, and the *Rite Ecossais* was now adopted as French rather than Jacobite.[59]

What Lady Pomfret had once called the 'remains' of the Stuart court at Saint-Germain effectively disappeared during the 1760s. In 1766 both James III and the old duc de Noailles died. During the same year the parish church of Saint-Germain, containing the monuments to James II, Mary of Modena and Princess Louise-Marie, and over 150 Jacobite tombs, was destroyed to allow a larger church to be built in its place. At around the same time the cemetery in the town, where thousands of the Jacobites had been buried, was also destroyed to make way for a new market place.[60] Vacant apartments were now regularly given to French people, and the number of Jacobites living in the château rapidly declined. Mary Plowden died in 1765; Theresa O'Donnell, the widow of John Stafford, and the last of the servants of the Stuart court to inhabit the château, finally died in 1778.[61] Those Jacobites who remained were only the children and grandchildren of the original occupants, increasingly bearing the names of the French men whom they had married.[62]

[57] SP 369/20, Mary Plowden to James III, February 1757.

[58] AN O/1/1711, Lady Castleconnel to Marigny, 23 June 1757, and Artagnan to Marigny, 15 July 1757. He was Paul de Montesquiou.

[59] *Dictionnaire de la Franc-Maçonnerie*, ed. D. Ligou (Paris, 1987), 399, 1026.

[60] Berthon, *Saint-Germain-en-Laye*, 115–16; Corp, *Cour des Stuarts*, 214.

[61] Her will, dated 27 July 1771, is with the Blount MSS at Mapledurham. (I am grateful to Dr Richard Williams for this reference and for kindly sending me a copy.)

[62] In 1771 they still included the daughters of Lord Dillon, whose brother Arthur was bishop of Evreux (1753–58), archbishop of Toulouse (1758–62) and archbishop of Narbonne (1762–93).

Even the French occupants of the royal apartments came and went as the years went by. In 1776 Louis XVI gave the adjacent château-neuf to his younger brother the comte d'Artois. It was then suggested that the château-vieux should be vacated. The following report was sent to Prince Charles in Florence by the Abbé Flyn's nephew, Esmé:

I am obliged to lay before your Majesty what has been lately agitat'd amongst the Ministers here in order for to save much expences . . . that for the future the king's life guards should occupy the old castel here, and those who actually live in it should retire. Upon this rumour the few remains of your Majesty's subjects made their representations to Mr de Noaille preying that he wd represent the King how disagreable it wd be for people of their age and of their narrow circumstances for to quitt their habitation upon wch Mr de Noaille spoke much in our favour.[63]

No doubt the occupants of the royal apartments, Monsieur Rollin d'Essars, the *Grand Maître honoraire des Eaux et Forêts de France* (*Appartement de la Reine*), the marquis de Colbert (*Appartement du Dauphin*) and Monsieur de Salaignac (*Appartement des Enfants de France*)[64] added their support to prevent the château being given to the king's *gardes du corps*. In any event, the idea of evicting the occupants was dropped, and not revived until the French Revolution. By then the only Jacobites left in the château were the Melfort family, Frances Nagle (daughter of James Nagle, gentleman usher of the Privy Chamber), the comtesse de La Noue (née Carteret), Dr Esmé Flyn, the comtesse de Casteja (née Carroll), an Irish captain named Hennessy, and the comte de Lally-Tollendal.[65] Of these, only the first three had any direct connection with the old Stuart court, and only the Melforts had any political importance.

The history of the Melfort family is complicated because the first duke, who had been secretary of state and then gentleman of the Bedchamber to James II, had nineteen children by his two wives.[66] Only three of them are of relevance here: Lady Mary Drummond, who was born at Saint-Germain in

One was unmarried, the other was the baronne de Blaisel (AN o/1/3433, 'inventaire des meubles du Château de St Germain-en-Laye', 1771).

[63] SP 486/41, E. Flyn to Prince Charles, 12 August 1776.

[64] AN o/1/1713, Rollin d'Essars to Angivillers, 4 November 1774; AN o/1/1714, Galant to Angivillers, 27 December 1776. Alexandre-Antoine Colbert was the second son of the marquis de Chabanois, who was a nephew of the marquis de Villacerf.

[65] Arch. Dépt. des Yvelines, 2/Q/47, 'Proces Verbal de la Vérification des appartements vacants dans le vieux Chateau [de Saint-Germain]', 15 June 1793.

[66] For Melfort himself, see the article by the present author in the *Oxford Dictionary of National Biography* (forthcoming); and Corp, 'Melfort'. For his family in France, see Bourgeois, *Entre Deux Révolutions . . . Les Audibert de Lussan et les Drummond de Melfort* (Paris, 1912).

1692; Lord Andrew Drummond, who was born while Melfort was ambassador in Rome (1691); and John, Marquis of Forth and later 2nd Duke of Melfort, born in Scotland in 1682.

Lady Mary married the Spanish Count of Castelblanco (created Duke of St Andrews at Avignon in 1717) and thus gave the family excellent connections at the court of Madrid. One of her grand-daughters married the Duke of Liria, grandson of the Duke of Berwick. Another married, in 1776, the brother of King Charles III of Spain (son of James III's childhood friend Philip V).[67]

Lord Andrew became a colonel in the French army and married an heiress with estates in Poitou. His son Louis-Hector, known as comte Drummond de Melfort, had a very distinguished career in the French army and published, in 1776, the celebrated *Traité sur la Cavalerie*. In 1780 he was promoted to be lieutenant-general and purchased the Château d'Yvoy-le Pré (near Aubigny and Sancerre), where he died in 1788. His son Louis-Pierre, comte Drummond de Melfort, re-established links with the British aristocracy, marrying (in June 1789) a daughter of the 6th Earl of Barrymore, and then (in April 1795) a daughter of the 4th Marquis of Seaforth.[68]

John, 2nd Duke of Melfort married Marie-Gabrielle d'Audibert, widowed Duchess of Albemarle, who had large estates at Lussan, to the west of Avignon. When not on their estates, the couple lived in Paris, but their relations deteriorated, and by the mid-1720s the duchess had left her husband to live with her children in the apartment on the first floor of the Château de Saint-Germain, immediately below that of the queen in the east wing. When she died there in 1741 she left both her estates and her apartment to her eldest son James, Lord Forth, who became the 3rd Duke in 1754.[69]

The latter was brought up at Saint-Germain with his younger brother Lord Louis, and after the death of their mother they continued to share her apartment. Lord Louis never married, but in 1747 the 3rd Duke married a French lady named Marie de Béranger. As the two brothers did not wish to be separated, their apartment was now felt to be too small. However the following year Lord Edward Drummond decided to move to Paris, thereby vacating his much larger apartment on the other side of the courtyard, below

---

[67] Her daughter Margarita married the Marquis of Vallabriga. Her grand-daughter married the Infante Luis, who had previously been cardinal archbishop of Toledo.

[68] There are family papers in AN T/781 and T/935/16, seized after Louis-Pierre, comte Drummond de Melfort left the country during the French Revolution. I am also most grateful to Peter Drummond-Murray for generously giving me copies of private family papers recording the marriages of Pierre-Louis and the births of his children by his second wife in 1790, 1791 and 1792.

[69] *House of Lords Sessional Papers*, 121, 152, 263, 275; SP 234/123, Dicconson to Edgar, 9 July 1741.

the theatre in the west wing. The 3rd Duke of Melfort, his wife and his brother were therefore able to move across to occupy the apartment of their cousin.[70]

The Melforts remained in their new apartment until the French Revolution. The 3rd Duke died there in 1766, leaving his widow to bring up their children. By then the Jacobite community in the château was becoming ever smaller and more vulnerable, but the widowed duchess was protected by her brother-in-law, who had become an important officer in the French army.[71] Having commanded the *Régiment Royal Ecossais* at the battle of Culloden, he had been steadily promoted and had particularly distinguished himself during the Seven Years War. Promoted *maréchal de camp* in 1761, he was made *Commandeur de l'Ordre de Saint-Louis* in 1775, one year before the suggestion that all the occupants of the château should be evicted from their apartments. According to his sister-in-law, with whom he lived, Louis XV had even had the Melfort apartment specially decorated as a mark of his high regard.[72] Lord Louis was promoted lieutenant-general in 1780 (the same year as his first cousin Louis-Hector, comte Drummond de Melfort), given the *Grand Croix de Saint-Louis* in 1787, and died in Paris in 1792. It was probably through his influence that the duchess was given an annual pension of 3000 *livres* (the same amount granted to Mary of Modena's ladies of the Bedchamber), and her daughter an annual pension of 837 *livres* 10s.[73]

During the 1780s the three surviving sons of the 3rd Duke (James, the 4th Duke; Lord Edward; and Lord Maurice) re-established friendly relations with their cousins in Scotland.[74] When, therefore, the French Revolution broke out they were in a position to emigrate either to Spain or to Great Britain. The 4th Duke went to Spain in 1790. Lord Edward, who had become a priest, went to England and then to Rome. Because they were émigrés all the Melfort estates in the south of France were confiscated and sold.[75] Meanwhile the dowager duchess and Lord Maurice continued to live in the château.

The fact that they remained there provides us with one last glimpse of the old Stuart court before it was finally destroyed for ever. In 1793 all the

---

[70] AN O/1/1710, memoranda by Lady Henrietta Drummond, 12 February 1750 and June 1751.

[71] AN O/3/1878/VIII, certificate from the *Ministère de la Guerre* giving the military record of Lord Louis Drummond, 19 August 1814.

[72] AN O/3/1878/VIII, Duchess of Melfort to Louis XVIII, 7 August 1815: 'Le frere de son mari, très connu du Roi qui habitoit avec elle le chateau de St Germain étoit Lord Louis Drummond . . . Ce Général fut distingué de Sa Majesté Louis quinze que se fit un plaisir de lui faire embellir son logement au chateau de St Germain.' See AN O/1/1713, Louis Drummond to Marigny, 4 September 1768, discussing the transfer of parquets from the royal apartments to his.

[73] *House of Lords Sessional Papers*, 157–8; Corp, *Cour des Stuarts*, 217.

[74] Bourgeois, *Entre Deux Révolutions*, 78–90.

[75] *Ibid.*, 86; AN O/3/1878/VIII, Duchess of Melfort to Louis XVIII, 7 August 1815.

occupants of the château were evicted, so that the first floor could be turned into a political prison.[76] The only people to remain were the dowager duchess and Lord Maurice, who became prisoners in their own apartment. The following year the prison was closed and the Melforts left Saint-Germain to live in Normandy, where Lord Maurice was married. In 1795 Talleyrand, who was a friend, wrote to say that it was 'now quite safe for him to return to his former domicile in the Château de St Germain', so he, his new wife and his mother came back, and remained there for several years.[77] Their daughter, who was born in the room immediately above the west entrance from the old *cour des cuisines*, has left the last description we have of one of the apartments:

I was the last of my family whose birth took place in the Château de St Germain. The room in which I was born . . . [in November 1796] was very large, with an immense window opening on a balcony . . . There were . . . objects within and without the Château which have left an indelible impression on my memory, for at St Germain the earlier years of my childhood were passed. The apartments occupied . . . by my family . . . consisted of about fifteen or sixteen rooms, and formed the *entresol*. They were large, and well furnished, each room opening into a corridor which ran round the entire Château. The furniture, covered with damask, was ornamented in the Louis XIV style. The coverlet of my grandmother's bed was, I remember, of splendid red brocade, embroidered most richly in gold with the Royal Arms of England; for it had served as the covering of the horse on which Prince Charles Edward rode at the Battle of Culloden . . . The family pictures in the drawing-room were numerous, and there was also a painting of the Blind Homer dictating his poems to a boy. In the bedroom where I was born, there was a mirror over the fireplace, surmounted by a beautiful Correggio, a Sleeping Child, so exquisitely painted.[78]

By this time the château as a whole was in a terrible state of repair,[79] and in 1803 the Melforts decided to visit Scotland, where the Bourbon court in

---

[76] *Saint-Germain-en-Laye à la fin du XVIIIe siècle*, exhibition catalogue (Saint-Germain-en-Laye, 1989), 9.

[77] Lady Clementina Davies, *Recollections of Society in France and England* (London, 1872), I, 43, 46. Esmé Flyn also recoved his apartment (Archives de la Guerre, x/e/400, Petition by Flyn, 1798).

[78] *Ibid.*, 47–8. The painting showing Homer is one of the twenty-one pictures (and also eleven portraits) listed in the inventory of 1741 (see note 8), where it is simply described as 'représantant le poëte Homère'.

[79] The gradual deterioration of the château is well documented in AN o/1/1710–1717. The 'inconvénients généraux et propres au Château de Saint-Germain' by 1793 are quoted in Corp, *Cour des Stuarts*, 213. The most important was: 'Le Défaut de Latrines, est un inconvenient qui pèze bien désagréablement sur les habitations au Desous les unes les autres. Cela se sent.' The 'Rapport fait au Ministre' on the condition of the château in 1801 is in Archives de la Guerre, x/e/400.

exile was established at Holyrood House, during the peace of Amiens. The resumption of hostilities meant that they could not return until 1814, and while they were away the building was transformed into an *Ecole Spéciale de Cavalerie*,[80] where Louis-Hector Drummond de Melfort's *Traité* was no doubt studied. The Emperor Napoleon visited the school in 1812, shortly before setting out for Moscow, and was so shocked by its condition that he ordered the building to be thoroughly renovated.[81] This meant that when Louis XVIII was restored in 1814 the building was in good enough condition to be taken over by the king's *gardes du corps* – thus finally implementing the proposal first put forward in 1776. The Melforts returned as soon as they could in August 1814, and immediately wrote from Dunkirk to petition the king for the return of their apartment, but they were already too late.[82] They petitioned again unsuccessfully in August 1815,[83] after the battle of Waterloo, and were eventually given an apartment at Versailles, where the duchess died in 1819.[84] It was under these circumstances that the Jacobite community at Saint-Germain finally came to an end.[85]

[80] Archives de la Guerre, x/e/400, *Ministre Directeur de l'Administration de la Guerre* to the *Ministre de la Guerre*, 18 April 1809.

[81] *Le Journal de Saint-Germain* 367 (21 April 2000), 23 reproduces part of a recently discovered letter by Napoleon describing his visit, including the following: 'des latrines empoisonnent toute la maison'. The repairs are shown in Archives de la Guerre, x/e/400, 'Etat des lieux du Château de Saint Germain en Laye', 12 June 1812; and AN o/2/326/II, 'Dépenses extraordinaires: Saint-Germain-en-Laye, 1813: Changement et constructions pour supprimer l'odeur des latrines.'

[82] Archives de la Guerre, x/e/400, Duchess of Melfort to *Ministre de l'Intérieur*, 10 August 1814; Bévière to *Ministre de l'Intérieur*, 16 August 1814; Bévière to *Ministre de la Guerre*, 2 September 1814; AN o/3/1878/VIII, *Ministre de la Maison du Roi* to Bévière, 30 September 1814.

[83] AN o/3/1878/VIII, Maurice Drummond to Pradel, 7 August 1815; and Duchess of Melfort to Louis XVIII, 7 August 1815.

[84] Bourgeois, *Entre Deux Révolutions*, 88.

[85] A few years later the head of the Nugent family in France asked to be made a *Gentilhomme honoraire de la Chambre du Roi* (AN o/3/362/379, Nugent to the *Grand Chambellan*, 11 April 1824, 30 April 1825 and 16 January 1830).

Epilogue

The Château-Vieux de Saint-Germain was occupied by the king's *gardes du corps* for over twenty years. Then, in 1836, it was converted into a military prison. One result of this transformation was that the apartments within the château were all destroyed. Another, and more important, was that the collective memory of the changes to the royal apartments during the eighteenth century was lost. Of the many biographies of James II, Mary of Modena and James III there is not one which contains any useful information about the apartments in which they lived. Moreover, most of these biographies repeat some incorrect comments about the château which were published during the 1840s. This study of the Stuart court in exile would not be complete without a final discussion of this confusion and how it came about.

It must be remembered that the royal apartments on the second floor had been occupied by various French people, and considerably altered, since the middle of the eighteenth century. As a result they could not be freely visited. In 1785 the chaplain sent a request to Versailles asking to be given some portraits of the French royal family so that he could hang them in his *salon*. He explained that he needed them because of the large number of 'Princes, les grands, [et] les plus illustres etrangers qui viennent visiter St. Germain'.[1] The reason why people went there was to see the chapel, not the royal apartments. Indeed, when a new guidebook to the *environs de Paris* was published in 1786, giving a detailed description of the *Chapelle Royale*, the royal apartments were not even mentioned.[2]

During the French Revolution the paintings in the chapel were all removed and taken to Paris.[3] By contrast a report of 1793 observed, in connection with the *appartement du roi*, once occupied by James II, that 'on a fait une espèce de

---

[1] AN 0/1/1715, Brouains to Angivillers, 30 July 1785. In this letter the chaplain stated that the two large paintings *Le Triomphe de David* and *Le Triomphe de Judith* were in such bad condition that they would soon be beyond restoration. Seven days earlier Brouains suggested to Angivillers that the painting by Poussin should be removed (same reference).

[2] J.A. Dulaure, *Nouvelle Description des environs de Paris* (Paris, 1786), 1, 228–34.

[3] *Louis XIV à Saint-Germain*, 47.

Muséum de cet appartment'.[4] As the rooms had all lost their furniture, mirrors and tapestries,[5] it is hard to know what this museum might have contained. By that date it is extremely unlikely that portraits of the French royal family would have been displayed there, so the museum might perhaps have contained the many Stuart portraits which had remained in the château, some of which were still there at the beginning of the nineteenth century.[6] If so they would have been hung on walls redecorated for the princesse de Talmont.

When the château was converted into a military prison the apartments of the courtiers were divided up into 542 small cells. Those of the royal family, and the theatre, were used to create additional rooms, some for the prison governor and his staff, others to be used as communal rooms for the prisoners.[7] The antechamber in the *Appartement du Roi*, for example, was converted into 'a tailer's atelier' where 'the military needle-men [were] seated . . . at their penal tasks'. This was the condition of the château when Agnes Strickland visited it in the 1840s, while researching her biography of Mary of Modena.[8] Unaware that the royal apartments had been redecorated during the second half of the eighteenth century, Strickland recorded that 'a portion of the private suite of the king and queen's apartment remains unaltered', by which she meant the rooms in the north-east pavilion which formed part of the *Appartement du Roi* but not that of *la Reine*. As an example, she referred to 'King James's morning room or cabinet, with its dark green and gold panneling and richly carved cornice'.[9] In the absence of any other information, this comment was seized upon by future biographers, and the painted *boiseries* of the princesse de Talmont have since been referred to on many occasions as the decoration chosen by James II.[10] In addition, there is an engraving of the early 1830s, en-titled *La Chambre de Jacques II*, which shows a small group of people standing in

---

[4] Arch. Dépt. des Yvelines, 2/Q/47, 'Proces Verbal de la Vérification des appartements vacants dans le vieux Chateau [de Saint-Germain]', 15 June 1793.

[5] According to the 'inventaire des meubles du Château de St Germain-en-Laye' of 1771, the only apartments furnished from the *Garde Meuble du Roi* were those of the princesse de Talmont, the Chaplain, the Dillon sisters and Theresa O'Donnell (previously Mrs John Stafford). The princesse lived in the *Appartement du Roi*, but when she died in 1773 the furnishings on loan from the *Garde Meuble* were all withdrawn (AN 0/1/3433, inventory, with an additional *envoi* dated 29 December 1773).

[6] A. Strickland, *Lives of the Queens of England*, IX (London, 1846), 313; and x (London, 1847), 236. According to Strickland, the family portrait by Largillière, which no longer exists (Corp, *King over the Water*, 35), was discovered 'in a great state of dilapidation, among some rubbish in an out-house, near the chateau'.

[7] Berthon, *Saint-Germain-en-Laye*, 155–56.   [8] Strickland, *Lives*, IX, 333.   [9] *Ibid.*

[10] For example, C. Oman, *Mary of Modena* (London, 1962), 157; M. Ashley, *James II* (London, 1977), 287.

an unfurnished room. Given the position of the doors, windows and fireplace, this room could not possibly have been James II's Bedchamber. Moreover, its low ceiling suggests that the princesse de Talmont had introduced an *entresol* above her apartment when completely redesigning and redecorating its rooms.[11]

In her attempt to obtain more information about the appearance of the Stuart court, Strickland consulted a great granddaughter of Mary Plowden, who had been born in 1770 and was by then a 'time-honoured lady' in her seventies. This was Lady Bedingfield (née Charlotte Jerningham), who told her a story she had heard about her own grandmother Mary (the daughter of Mary Plowden), born at Saint-Germain in 1704.[12] The story related how

Mrs Plowden's infant family lived with her in the palace of St. Germains, and she sometimes found it necessary, by way of punishment, to shut up her little daughter, Mary, a pretty spoiled child of four years old, in the lobby leading from her own apartment to the queen's backstairs, but the young lady always obtained her release by climbing to the little window that looked down into the king's closet, and tapping at the glass until she had attracted his attention.

As James II 'was very fond of children', he would then send a servant to bring her to him, 'and when Mrs Plowden next entered the royal presence with the queen, she was sure to find her little captive closeted with his majesty, sitting at his feet, or sometimes on his knee'.[13] It is a charming story, and has been repeated on numerous occasions to illustrate the personality of the exiled King.[14] In fact the architecture of the château makes the story impossible, while James II had anyway died in 1701, three years before the child was born.

Another story concerned the apartment of the queen, occupied by various French people since 1753. The 'oldest inhabitants of the town of St. Germains' apparently informed Agnes Strickland that until the Revolution 'the Chamber, in which Mary Beatrice of Modena died, was scrupulously kept in the same state in which it was wont to be during her life. Her toilette-table, with its

---

[11] Corp, *Cour des Stuarts*, 226 reproduces the engraving and briefly explains why the room shown in it could not possibly be the king's Bedchamber. The plan of the second floor from 1836 to 1855 is shown as Plate 1 in P. Selmersheim (ed.), *Monographie de la restauration du Château de Saint-Germain-en-Laye d'après les projets et les détails d'exécution tracés par feu Eugène Millet* (Paris, 1892).

[12] Lart, *Parochial Register*, II, 114. Mary Plowden's daughter Mary married Sir George Jerningham, 5th Bart. Their son, Sir William Jerningham, 6th Bart was the father of Charlotte, Lady Bedingfield.

[13] Strickland, *Lives*, IX, 334.　　[14] For example, Oman, *Mary of Modena*, 157.

costly plate and ornaments, the gift of Louis XIV, was set out daily, as if for her use, with the four wax candles in the gilt candlesticks ready to light, just as if her return had been expected.' Strickland asked Lady Bedingfield for confirmation of this story and received the following reply: 'I was a very young girl when I saw the Castle of St. Germains . . . The state rooms were kept up, and I remember being struck with the splendour of the silver ornaments on the toilet of the queen.'[15] This story, like the others, has received wide circulation, but it is similarly inaccurate. In fact the silver toilette of Mary of Modena was sent to Urbino in 1718 and given by James III to Queen Maria Clementina the following year.[16] Lady Bedingfield was not able to visit Saint-Germain before 1784,[17] by which time the queen's apartment was occupied by Monsieur Rollin d'Essars.

These stories were published in Agnes Strickland's account of the last years of Mary of Modena, which attracted considerable attention. Shortly afterwards Queen Victoria expressed an interest to see the rooms once occupied by James II, during her state visit to France in 1855. Hastily closing the military prison, Napoleon III agreed to show them to her, believing, as she did, that they were still basically unchanged.[18] The rooms were then opened to tourists, while Napoleon III decided what to do with the château as a whole.

In 1862 it was decided that the château should be transformed into a new *Musée des Antiquités Nationales*. The original rooms were situated in the *Appartement du Dauphin* and opened in 1867,[19] thereby completely obliterating all trace of the apartment once occupied by James III. A second and quite separate decision was taken to destroy the pavilions in the five corners of the château, which had been the building's distinguishing feature throughout the Stuart and Jacobite period. The first pavilion to be destroyed was the one in the north-west, which disappeared in 1862.[20] Two years later it was decided to destroy the one in the north-east, containing the rooms which tourists

---

[15] Strickland, *Lives*, x, 235–6.

[16] SP 36/141, 'a particular of what is in the five Caisses sent from St. Germans' on 26 September 1718; SP 98/84, 'an accompt of what was in the five cases sent from Paris on 26 September 1718 as by an Inventory sent by Mr Dicconson', annotated in 1726 by Ellis.

[17] She was brought up at Cossey in Norfolk 'until the age of fourteen, when she was sent to the Ursulines in the rue St. Jacques, Paris' (M. Mason, 'Nuns and Vocations of the Unpublished Jerningham Letters', *Recusant History* 21, no. 4 (October 1993), 504).

[18] Corp, *Cour des Stuarts*, 225–7.   [19] Lacour-Gayet, *Le Château de Saint-Germain-en-Laye*, 206.

[20] Two photographs by Charles Marville showing it being destroyed were published in Corp, 'Maison du Roi', 8–9. Two other photographs, of the west façade and of the south-east pavilion viewed from the south pavilion, taken by Lesecq in 1855, are preserved as Plate II in Selmersheim, *Monographie*. According to Selmersheim, the interiors of the five pavilions 'restèrent inachevés, sauf, cependant, ceux des pavillons Nord-Ouest et Nord-Est qui possédaient

were visiting in the belief that they had been occupied by James II. When the marquise Campana di Cavelli heard of this she hastened to see them in July 1864 before they disappeared for ever. The comment which she published a few years later, by which time it was no longer possible to compare the rooms with any documentary evidence, confirmed the impression given by Strickland and added to the confusion: 'on montrait naguère au visiteur, avant les dernières transformations de Saint-Germain, les appartements de Jacques II et des Jacobites les plus illustres qui avaient suivi ce roi dans l'exil'.[21]

The restoration of the château continued until 1907, by which time its external appearance had been totally changed. The main entrance in the south wing was suppressed in 1875; the last of the five pavilions was destroyed in 1900.[22] Instead of restoring the château to what it had originally been when built by François I and Henri II, the architects followed their own inclinations and made very far-reaching changes both to the shape of the building and to its decoration. As a result the château which one can see today does not even resemble the one occupied by Louis XIV, still less the one to which the Stuarts came in 1689 and in which the Jacobite community continued to live during most of the eighteenth century.[23] Just as the Stuart court in France has been consistently misrepresented and misunderstood by historians since the end of the eighteenth century, so the building in which it was situated continues to deny the visitor any accurate idea of its physical appearance.

des lambris et des plafonds en menuiserie d'un bon caractère qu'on pût remplacer et agencer dans le bâtiment Sud pour les salles affectées à l'administration . . . Les autres annexes ne présentaient, à l'intérieur, aucun arrangement et aucun revêtement' (no pagination). This became the official justification for the destruction of these important pavilions. See Lacour-Gayet, *Le Château de Saint-Germain-en-Laye*, 119–22: 'Quand on décida, sous le règne de Napoléon III, d'abattre les cinq pavillons de Mansart . . . on constata que ces constructions n'avaient jamais été complètement achevées. Des étages entiers manquaient d'escaliers; des échelles de bois y suppléaient.'

[21] Corp, *Cour des Stuarts*, 229; Campana di Cavelli, *Les Derniers Stuarts*, I, 1 and 3.

[22] Lacour-Gayet, *Le Château de Saint-Germain-en-Laye*, 122, 204.

[23] The main architect responsible for the destruction was Eugène Millet. For a comparison between the château as it is today and how it was in the sixteenth century, see *ibid.*, 204–5. The visitor should also beware of the parish church opposite. A plaque on the wall outside, recently placed there with the agreement of the *mairie*, announces in English that 'Here lies King James VII of Scotland II of England' (*sic*). James II's body was actually entrusted to the English Benedictine monks in Paris and destroyed in 1793, and therefore does not lie anywhere (Corp, 'The Remains of James II', in 'Last Years of James II', 25). Within the church there is a shrine to the memory of James II. It is to be seen in a side chapel in that part of the church which lies outside the area originally occupied by the much smaller parish church in which James II worshipped (see the superimposed plans in P. Torry, *Une Paroisse royale, Saint-Germain-en-Laye* (Mayenne, 1927), 249).

Appendix: The senior household servants

(This list excludes people in England and others with honorary appointments. Some posts remained vacant for extended periods.)

James II

Chamber

Gentleman of the Bedchamber
    Earl of Dumbarton, 1689–92
    Earl of Abercorn, 1689–91
    Richard Hamilton, 1692–96
    Earl of Clancarty, 1694–1701 (left the court in 1697)
    Earl of Newcastle, 1698–1701
    Duke of Melfort, 1698–1701
Groom of the Bedchamber
    David Floyd, 1689–1701
    Richard Biddulph, 1689–1701
    Francis Stafford, 1689–1700
    Sir Randall MacDonnell, 1689–1701
    Richard Trevanion, 1689–1701
    Henry Slingsby, 1694–1701
    Dudley Bagnoll, 1698–1701
Master of the robes
    Richard Hamilton, 1696–1701
Lord chamberlain
    Duke of Powis, 1689–96
Vice-chamberlain
    James Porter, 1689–1701
Confessor
    John Warner, 1689–92
    Francis Sanders, 1692–1701

Secretariat

Secretary of state
    Earl of Melfort, 1689–94
    Henry Browne, 1689–91
    Earl of Middleton, 1693–1701
    John Caryll, 1694–1701
Secretary of state and war for Ireland
    Sir Richard Nagle, 1691–99
Under-secretary
    David Nairne, 1689–1701
    John Kearney, 1691–1701
    David Lindsay, 1694–1701

Household below stairs

Comptroller of the household
    Lord Waldegrave, 1689–90
    Bevil Skelton, 1690–96
    John Stafford, 1696–1700
    Francis Plowden, 1700–1
Clerk controller of the Greencloth
    Sir John Sparrow, 1689–1701
    Henry Conquest, 1689–1701
Commissioner of the household
    Duke of Powis, 1689–96
    Robert Strickland, 1689–1700
    Bevil Skelton, 1689–96
    Henry Conquest, 1694–1701
    John Stafford, 1696–1700
    Sir Richard Nagle, 1698–99
    Sir William Ellis, 1698–1701
    Thomas Sheridan, 1699–1701
    Sir Richard Bulstrode, 1700–1
    Francis Plowden, 1700–1

Stables

Equerry
    Ralph Sheldon, 1689–1701
    Arthur Magennis, 1689–98
    Richard Biddulph jun., 1698–1701

Riding purveyor
    John Lewin, 1689–1701

James III

Governor
    Duke of Perth, 1701–6
Under-governor
    William Dicconson, 1701–6
    Dominic Sheldon, 1701–6

Bedchamber (re-established in 1703)

Gentleman of the Bedchamber
    Earl of Newcastle, 1703–18
    Duke of Perth, 1703–9
    Lord Edward Drummond, 1709–18
    Lord Clermont, 1713–18
    Earl Marischal, 1716–18
    Duke of Mar, 1716–18
Groom of the Bedchamber
    Thomas Neville, 1701–*c.*1713
    George Rattray, 1701–18
    Charles Leyburne, 1701–18
    Sir John Gifford, 1700–7
    Thomas Sackville, 1701–18
    David Floyd, 1701–18
    Richard Biddulph, 1701–4
    Sir Randall MacDonnell, 1701–11
    Richard Trevanion, 1701–18
    Dudley Bagnoll, 1701–16
    Charles Booth, 1701–18
    Count Antonio Davia, 1702–3
    Richard Baggot, 1702–16
    Daniel MacDonnell, 1701–17
    Roger Strickland, 1706–18
    Bernard Howard, 1713–18
    John Hay, 1718–
Master of the robes
    Richard Hamilton, 1701–16

Chamber

Vice-chamberlain
    James Porter, 1701–11
    Dominic Sheldon, 1711–18
Gentleman usher of the Privy Chamber
    John Baggot, 1701–16
    James Nagle, 1701–18
    Thomas Higgons, 1701–13
    James Simms 1701–18
    Lawrence Du Puy, 1701–18
    Richard Waldegrave, 1702–3
    Richard Bourke, 1708–18
    James Murray, 1706–10?
    Edmond Fitzgerald, 1710–18
Gentleman usher of the black rod
    Sir Charles Carteret 1701–18
Confessor
    Francis Sanders, 1701–10
    Thomas Eyre, 1710–12
    John Ingleton, 1712–15

Secretariat

Secretary of state
    Earl of Middleton, 1701–13
    Lord Caryll, 1701–11
Secretary of the Closet
    David Nairne, 1713–18
Under-secretary
    David Nairne, 1701–13
    David Lindsay, 1701–3
    John Kearney, 1701–18

Household below stairs

Comptroller of the household
    Francis Plowden, 1701–12
Clerk controller of the Greencloth
    Sir John Sparrow, 1701–18
    Henry Conquest, 1701–8
    Sir William Ellis, 1702–

Commissioner of the household
    Henry Conquest, 1701–8
    Sir William Ellis, 1701–
    Thomas Sheridan, 1701–12
    Sir Richard Bulstrode, 1701–11
    Francis Plowden, 1701–12
    William Dicconson, 1708–18
Treasurer
    Sir William Ellis, 1713–

Stables

Equerry
    Ralph Sheldon, 1701–18
    Richard Biddulph jun., 1701–7
    James Delattre, 1704–
    Randall MacDonnell, 1711–17
    John Hay, 1716–18
Riding purveyor
    John Lewin, 1701–6
    John Sheridan, 1707–

The queen

Bedchamber

Lady of the Bedchamber
    Duchess of Tyrconnell, 1690–1718 (left the court in 1702)
    Countess of Almond, 1689–1703
    Lady Sophia Bulkeley, 1689–1718
    Countess, later Duchess of Perth, 1700–18
    Lady Charlotte Talbot, 1702–18
    Viscountess Clare, 1706–18
    Countess of Middleton, 1712–18
Bedchamber woman
    Pellegrina Turrini, 1689–1709
    Isabella, Lady Waldegrave, 1689–1706
    Bridget Strickland, 1689–1718
    Contessa Veronica Molza, 1689–1718
    Winifred, Lady Strickland, 1700–18
    Mary Biddulph, 1701–2

Mary Plowden, 1702–18
Theresa Stafford, 1708–18
Henrietta Bulkeley, c.1712–18
Master of the robes
Francesco Riva, 1689–1703

Chamber

Lord chamberlain
Duke of Perth, 1714–16
Earl of Middleton, 1716–18
Vice-chamberlain
Robert Strickland, 1689–1700
John Stafford, 1700–14
Treasurer and receiver-general
Robert Strickland, 1700–9
William Dicconson, 1709–18
Secretary
John, later Lord Caryll, 1689–1711
John Stafford, 1711–14
Nicholas Dempster, 1714–18
Gentleman usher of the Privy Chamber
Thomas Neville, 1689–95
William Crane, 1689–1718
George Benyon, 1689–1700?
Count Carlo Molza, 1700–18
John Caryll, 1701–18
Captain Hatcher, 1701–after 1703
Confessor
Marco Antonio Galli, 1689–1701
Bartolomeo Ruga, 1701–13
Honoré Gaillard, 1713–18

Household below stairs

Clerk of the Greencloth
Henry Conquest, 1689–1708
Christopher Chilton, by 1693–1718
Paymaster
Henry Conquest, 1708–9

Stables

Master of the horse
    Earl of Middleton, 1713–16
    2nd Duke of Perth, 1716–18
Equerry
    Charles Leyburne, 1689–98
    Arthur Magennis, 1698–1709
    Bernard Howard, 1702–13
    John Nugent, 1707–18

The Prince of Wales

Governess and governor
    Duchess of Powis, 1689–91
    Countess of Erroll, 1691–93
    Lady Strickland, 1694–95 (acting)
    Earl, later Duke of Perth, 1696–1701
Under-governess and under-governor
    Lady Strickland, 1689–92
    Mary Stafford, 1692–94
    Francis Plowden, 1695–1700
    Edmund Perkins, 1695–97
    William Dicconson, 1700–1
    Dominic Sheldon, 1700–1
Groom of the Bedchamber
    Thomas Neville, 1695–1701
    Thomas Belasyse, 1695–98?
    Walter Strickland, 1695–1701 (left the court in 1699)
    George Rattray, 1698?–1701
    Charles Leyburne, 1698–1701
    Sir John Gifford, 1700–1
    Thomas Sackville, 1700–1

The Princess

Governess
    Mary Stafford, 1694–1700
    Countess of Middleton, 1700–10
Lady of the Bedchamber
    Countess of Middleton, 1710–12

Bedchamber women
    Elizabeth Simms, 1700–10
    Mary Biddulph, 1700–2
    Mary Plowden, 1700–2
    Rose, Lady Lee, 1700–11 or 12
    Bridget Nugent, 1700–11 or 12
    Anne Nugent, 1702–11 or 12
    Mary, Lady Carteret, 1711–12
    Anne, Lady Murray, 1711–12

Select bibliography

PRIMARY SOURCES

The archives of the Stuart court at Saint-Germain and Bar-le-Duc, which included many important papers brought from England in 1688–89, were nearly all destroyed in Paris during the French Revolution. Several lists of them, however, were compiled between 1715 and 1738, and these have survived. They were collated by the present author to produce a comprehensive inventory of the court archives, published with an introductory article in the journal *Archives* in 1998 (23, no. 99, 118–46). That inventory identifies and locates all the documents which still exist (as well as those which do not), and should be referred to by anyone wishing to pursue the subject in further detail. What follows here is only a summary list of the most important archival sources used in the preparation of this book. All other archival references are given in the footnotes.

Manuscript sources in Great Britain

1. The Stuart Papers, Royal Archives, Windsor Castle. These are mainly the archives of the court of James III after 1716, and the private and household papers of his two sons, Prince Charles and Prince Henry, Cardinal Duke of York. However, they include various documents of 1689–1715 which were sent from Paris to Rome, mainly during the 1730s. Nearly all of them, covering the period up to the end of 1718 (SP 1–40), were published in seven volumes by the Historical Manuscripts Commission (see below). Several which were only calendared and not printed in full have been used here. Some letters of 1716–17, which had already been removed from the Stuart Papers are (with other Jacobite correspondence) in British Library Add. MSS 38851 and among the unsorted Bower MSS at Chiddingstone Castle. The unpublished Stuart Papers from 1719 onwards (SP 41–541, SP Box 1–11, SP Misc. 6–100) also contain valuable retrospective information about the earlier period.

2. The Nairne Papers, Bodleian Library, Oxford. These are part of the official archives of Sir David Nairne, assembled during his many years as a member of the political secretariat at Saint-Germain-en-Laye, Bar-le-Duc, Avignon and Urbino. They were deposited after his death with the rest of the court archives in the *Collège des Ecossais* in Paris. Eleven volumes (out of approximately fifteen) survived the general destruction during the French Revolution because they had previously been stolen

and presented to the Bodleian Library. They have frequently been used by political historians and their references are Carte MSS 180, 181, 208–12, 238, 256–8.

3. The Gualterio Papers, British Library, London. Cardinal Filippo Antonio Gualterio was the papal nuncio in France from 1700 to 1706 and subsequently became Cardinal Protector of England. His papers contain many letters from the Stuarts and their courtiers, as well as the drafts of his replies, and thus partly compensate for the loss of the court's own archives. The main references are Add. MSS 20292–313 and 31244–67.

4. The Journal of David Nairne, 1655–1708, National Library of Scotland, Edinburgh. This private journal was kept by Nairne from 1689 to 1691, during part of 1692, and from 1693 onwards. (The entries covering 1655–89 were written after 1696 when Nairne had access to the 'Memoirs of James II'.) It is the most important single source for the Stuart court at Saint-Germain-en-Laye. The reference is MS 14266. (A second volume, which Nairne started in 1708, has not survived.)

5. The Blairs Letters, Scottish Catholic Archives, Edinburgh. This collection contains letters (including many written by Nairne) sent to the Scots College in Rome from the court at Saint-Germain and to the Scots College in Paris from the court at Avignon and Urbino. The relevant references are BL 1 and 2.

6. The Caryll Papers, British Library, London. Within this large collection of family papers there are two volumes which refer to the exiled court. The references are Add. MSS 28224 and 28250.

7. The Perth Papers, British Library, London. These are nineteenth-century copies of a small selection of the papers of the first two Dukes of Perth, many of which have been published (see below). The reference is Add. MSS 19254.

8. The Meredith Papers, Bodleian Library, Oxford. Edward Meredith was a Jesuit in Rome who corresponded with the court at Saint-Germain. The reference is Rawlinson MSS D.21.

9. 'The Life of James II' by Benet Weldon, British Library, London. Weldon was a Benedictine monk living in Paris while the Stuart court was at Saint-Germain. The reference is Add. MSS 10118.

Manuscript sources in France

1. The papers of the Secretariat of the *Maison du Roi*. Although seriously incomplete, these papers include the *Journal du Garde Meuble*, several boxes of documents concerning the management of the châteaux and gardens at Saint-Germain, and detailed plans of all the apartments in the château-vieux. The most important references are:

Archives Nationales, Paris: O/1/608, 920, 1710–22, 3306–8, 3433
Bibliothèque Nationale, Paris: Est. Va. 78c and 448e
Archives Départementales des Yvelines, Versailles: A.369

These papers also include the *Comptes des Bâtiments du Roi* and the *Inventaire Général*, both of which have been published (see below).

2. The papers of the *prévôté* of Saint-Germain, Archives Départementales des Yvelines, Versailles. The most important references are B.350, B.537 and 2/Q/47.

3. The registers of the parish church of Saint-Germain-en-Laye, Archives Municipales de la Ville de Saint-Germain-en-Laye. The entries concerning the Jacobites have been published, but with many mistakes (see below).

4. The papers of Madame de Maintenon, Bibliothèque Municipale de Versailles. These are copies, made in about 1740, of letters received by Madame de Maintenon from 1673 until her death. They include many written by Mary of Modena after 1692. The reference is MS 1461/P.64–8.

5. The *Journal des Cérémonies* of the seigneur de Bonneuil, Bibliothèque Nationale, Paris, MS Fd. Fr. 16633.

6. The *Journal des Cérémonies* of the marquis de Sainctot, Bibliothèque Nationale, Paris, Fd. Fr. 6679; and Bibliothèque Mazarine, Paris, MS 42.

7. The *Mémoires* of the baron de Breteuil, Bibliothèque de l'Arsenal, Paris, MS 3862–4, extracts from which have been published (see below). Breteuil, like Bonneuil and Sainctot, was *introducteur des ambassadeurs* at the French court.

8. The papers of William Bromfield, Bibliothèque de l'Arsenal, Paris, MS 10533. Bromfield was a Quaker who was sometimes at Saint-Germain and who corresponded with his friends at the court.

9. The papers of the Benedictine nuns at Pontoise, Archives Départementales du Val d'Oise, Cergy-Pontoise: 68/H/3–5, 8, 10.

Musical manuscripts

Great Britain
>   British Library, London: Add. MSS 31476, 31480, 31502
>   Bodleian Library, Oxford: Mus. Sch. E.400–3

France
>   Bibliothèque Nationale, Paris: F.1674, 1679, 1680, 1681, 1698, 1713; H.659/1–7; vm^6.1; vm^7.52, 53, 54, 4822, 137317, 137323; vmf 43; Rés. 1261; Rés. vm^2.62, 68; Rés. vmf. 43
>   Bibliothèque Inguimbertine, Carpentras: MS 1038
>   Bibliothèque Municipale de Lyon: MS 129949
>   Bibliothèque Municipale de Versailles: MS Mus. 4, 27, 58, 59, 93, 161, 323; MSD 12

Belgium
>   Bibliothèque Royale, Brussels: II.3847

United States of America
>   University of California at Berkeley MS 118
>   University of Chicago MS 959

Printed sources from British manuscripts

1. Stuart Papers

Historical Manuscripts Commission, *Calendar of the Stuart Papers belonging to His Majesty the King preserved at Windsor Castle*, 7 vols. covering the period up to December 1718 (London, 1902–23).

Melville Henry Massue, marquis de Ruvigny et de Raineval, *The Jacobite Peerage* (Edinburgh, 1904). This is based on SP Misc. 18 and 19.

2. Letters and other private papers

Letters from James, Earl of Perth to his Sister the Countess of Erroll, ed. W. Jerdan (London, 1845). They cover the years 1688–96.

'The Remains of Denis Granville', *Journal of the Surtees Society* 47 (1865); 37 Miscellanea (1861). The correspondence of Granville, 1700–3.

N. Hooke, *Correspondence, 1703–7*, ed. W.D. Macray, 2 vols. (London, 1870).

The Letter Book of Lewis Sabran, 1713–15, ed. G. Holt (London, 1971).

3. Government Papers

Calendar of State Papers, Domestic Series: James II, 1687–89 (London, 1972); *William and Mary, 1689–90* (London, 1895), *1690–91* (London, 1898); *William III, 1698* (London, 1933), *1700–02* (London, 1937); *Anne, 1703–04* (London, 1924).

Historical Manuscripts Commission, *Calendar of the Papers Belonging to the Marquess of Bath*, III (London, 1908). This contains the diplomatic correspondence of Matthew Prior at the English Embassy in Paris, 1698–1700.

C. Cole, *Memoirs of Affairs of State* (London, 1733). This contains the diplomatic correspondence of the Earl of Manchester at the English Embassy in Paris, 1699–1701.

Printed sources from French manuscripts

1. Memoirs and journals

Philippe de Courcillon, marquis de Dangeau, *Journal*, ed. E. Soulié and L. Dussieux, 19 vols. (Paris, 1854–60).

Louis-François du Bouchet, marquis de Sourches, *Mémoires*, ed. comte de Cornac, 13 vols. (Paris, 1882–93).

Louis de Rouvroy, duc de Saint-Simon, *Mémoires*, ed. A. de Boislisle, 41 vols. (Paris, 1879–1930).

Jean-Baptiste Colbert, marquis de Torcy, *Journal inédit pendant les années 1709, 1710 et 1711*, ed. F. Masson (Paris, 1884).

Louis Nicolas Le Tonnellier, baron de Breteuil, *Mémoires*, ed. E. Lever (Paris, 1992).

Dr Brun, 'Mémoirs du Temps', in *Des Ecossais à Avignon*, ed. G. Dickson (Paris, 1993).

2. Letters and other private papers

Anthony Hamilton, *Œuvres*, ed. J.B.J. Champagnac, 2 vols. (Paris, 1829). This includes letters written by Hamilton from 1702 to 1716.

Stuart Papers relating chiefly to Mary of Modena and the Exiled Court of King James II, ed. F. Madan, 2 vols. (London, 1889). These are from the archives of the convent of Visitation nuns at Chaillot.

The Letters of Madame: The Correspondence of Elizabeth-Charlotte of Bavaria, Princess Palatine, Duchess of Orléans, ed. G.S. Stevenson, 2 vols. (London, 1924). This selection, translated into English, contains all the important references to the Stuarts.

3. Government Papers

Archives de la Bastille, ed. F. Ravaisson, IX (Paris, 1877).

Inventaire général du mobilier de la couronne sous Louis XIV, ed. Jules Guiffrey, 2 vols. (Paris, 1885–86).

Comptes des bâtiments du roi sous le règne de Louis XIV, ed. Jules Guiffrey, vols. III–V (Paris, 1891, 1894, 1901).

C.E. Lart, *The Parochial Registers of Saint-Germain-en-Laye: Jacobite Extracts*, 2 vols. (London, 1910, 1912).

Printed sources from Italian manuscripts

M. Haile, *Queen Mary of Modena: Her Life and Letters* (London, 1905).

Emily, Marquise Campana di Cavelli, *Les Derniers Stuarts à Saint-Germain-en-Laye*, II (Paris, 1971).

FURTHER READING

Barclay, A., 'The Impact of James II on the Departments of the Royal Household', unpublished PhD thesis, University of Cambridge, 1993.

Cruickshanks, E. (ed.), *Ideology and Conspiracy: Aspects of Jacobitism, 1689–1759* (Edinburgh, 1982).

Cruickshanks, E. and Black, J. (eds.), *The Jacobite Challenge* (Edinburgh, 1988).

Gibson, J., *Playing the Scottish Card: The Franco-Jacobite Invasion of 1708* (Edinburgh, 1989).

Gregg, E., *Jacobitism* (London, 1988).

'Monarchs without a Crown', in R. Oresko, G.C. Gibbs and H.M. Scott (eds.), *Royal and Republican Sovereignty in Early Modern Europe* (Cambridge, 1997), 382–422.

Haile, M., *James Francis Edward, the 'Old Chevalier'* (London, 1907).

Holt, G., 'Some Chaplains at the Stuart Court, Saint-Germain-en-Laye', *Recusant History* 25, no. 1 (May 2000), 43–51.

Jones, G.H., *The Mainstream of Jacobitism* (Cambridge, MA, 1954).

Charles Middleton: The Life and Times of a Restoration Politician (Chicago, 1967).

McLynn, F., *The Jacobites* (London, 1985).

Middleton, D., *The Life of Charles, Second Earl of Middleton* (London, 1957).

Petrie, Sir Charles, *The Jacobite Movement, 1688–1807*, 2 vols. (London, 1948, 1950).

Rouffiac, N., 'Les Jacobites à Paris et Saint-Germain-en-Laye, 1688–1715', unpublished thesis, Ecole Nationale des Chartes, Paris, 1991.

Rowlands, G., 'An Army in Exile: Louis XIV and the Irish Forces of James II in France, 1691–1698', *Royal Stuart Paper* LX (London, 2001).

Sharp, R., *The Engraved Record of the Jacobite Movement* (Aldershot, 1996).

Shield, A. and Lang, A., *The King over the Water* (London, 1907).

Szechi, D., *Jacobitism and Tory Politics, 1710–1714* (Edinburgh, 1984).

   The Jacobites: Britain and Europe, 1688–1788 (Manchester, 1994).

Wolff, H.W., 'The Pretender at Bar le Duc', *Blackwood's Magazine* 156 (August 1894), 226–46.

Woolf, N., *The Medallic Record of the Jacobite Movement* (London, 1988).

Index